The Handbook of Systemic Family Therapy

The Handbook of Systemic Family Therapy

Volume 3

Systemic Family Therapy with Couples

Editor-in-Chief

Karen S. Wampler
Michigan State University
East Lansing, MI, USA

Volume Editor

Adrian J. Blow
Michigan State University
East Lansing, MI, USA

WILEY Blackwell

This edition first published 2020
© 2020 John Wiley & Sons Ltd

The right of Karen S. Wampler to be identified as the author of the editorial material in this work has been asserted in accordance with law.

Registered Office(s)
John Wiley & Sons, Inc., 111 River Street, Hoboken, NJ 07030, USA
John Wiley & Sons Ltd, The Atrium, Southern Gate, Chichester, West Sussex, PO19 8SQ, UK

Editorial Office
111 River Street, Hoboken, NJ 07030, USA

For details of our global editorial offices, customer services, and more information about Wiley products visit us at www.wiley.com.

Wiley also publishes its books in a variety of electronic formats and by print-on-demand. Some content that appears in standard print versions of this book may not be available in other formats.

Library of Congress Cataloging-in-Publication Data

Names: Wampler, Karen S., editor.
Title: The handbook of systemic family therapy / editor-in-chief, Karen S.
　Wampler.
Description: Hoboken, NJ : Wiley, [2020] | Includes index.
Identifiers: LCCN 2019044963 (print) | LCCN 2019044964 (ebook) | ISBN
　9781119438557 (cloth) | ISBN 9781119645702 (adobe pdf) | ISBN
　9781119645757 (epub)
Subjects: LCSH: Family psychotherapy.
Classification: LCC RC488.5.H3346 2020 (print) | LCC RC488.5 (ebook) |
　DDC 616.89/156–dc23
LC record available at https://lccn.loc.gov/2019044963
LC ebook record available at https://lccn.loc.gov/2019044964

Cover image: © Lava 4 images/Shutterstock
Cover design by Wiley

Set in 10/12pt Galliard by SPi Global, Pondicherry, India

Printed and bound by CPI Group (UK) Ltd, Croydon, CR0 4YY.

10　9　8　7　6　5　4　3　2　1

In memory of Douglas J. Sprenkle
Educator, scholar, colleague, mentor, and friend.

Karen Smith Wampler, PhD, passed away unexpectedly, just weeks before *The Handbook of Systemic Family Therapy* went to press. The handbook is dedicated to her lasting memory.

Karen served as Editor-in-Chief for all four volumes of *The Handbook of Systemic Family Therapy*. From the beginning, she had a vision of what our field needed to know to move into the future. Her work was finished in late November 2019, just in time for her next adventure in New Zealand and Australia. She was wise in her selection of Co-Editors for each volume: Rick Miller and Ryan Seedall (Volume 1), Lenore McWey (Volume 2), Adrian Blow (Volume 3), and Mudita Rastogi and Reenee Singh (Volume 4). She was grateful for the chance to work with each of these scholars and with her Assistant Editor, Leah W. Maderal. She was delighted and humbled to see "the book" grow to 106 chapters and 292 authors and co-authors. It cheered her heart—there was so much to know and so much to learn about systemic family therapy. She saw this work as her magnum opus, and it is.

Karen had a career as researcher and teacher, mentor, dissertation and thesis advisor, program director, and department chair that spanned 33 years. Her impact on the field of systemic family therapy lives on in these volumes, in her many research publications and chapters, in students she loved and trained, in colleagues who benefited from her wisdom, enthusiasm, and support, and in the many individuals and groups she touched with her kindness, generosity, intelligence, humor, and goodwill.

To paraphrase Shakespeare: "*We shall not look upon her like again.*"

Contents

About the Editors
The Handbook of Systemic Family Therapy

Editor-in-Chief

Dr. Karen S. Wampler, PhD, retired as Professor with Tenure and Chair of the Department of Human Development and Family Studies at Michigan State University. Professor Emerita at Texas Tech University, she served as Department Chair, MFT Program Director, and the C. R. and Virginia Hutcheson Professor. During her 10 years at the University of Georgia, Dr. Wampler developed the MFT doctoral program as well as the Interdisciplinary MFT Certificate Program, a collaboration with MFT, Social Work, and Counseling. She is past editor of the *Journal of Marital and Family Therapy*. Her primary research interests are the application of attachment theory to couple interaction, family therapy process research, and observational measures of couple and family relationships. She has authored over 50 refereed journal articles and 10 book chapters and has been funded by NIMH. A licensed marriage and family therapist, she is a Fellow of AAMFT, past member of the Commission on Accreditation for Marriage and Family Therapy Education, and recipient of the Outstanding Contribution to Marriage and Family Therapy Award. The Family Therapy Section of NCFR has recognized her with the Distinguished Service to Family Therapy and Kathleen Briggs Mentor awards.

Associate Editors

Volume 1: Richard B Miller and Ryan B. Seedall

Richard B Miller, PhD, is Chair of the Sociology Department, a former Director of the School of Family Life, and a former Associate Dean in the College of Family, Home, and Social Science at Brigham Young University (BYU). He is also a professor in the Marriage and Family Therapy Program at BYU. Prior to teaching at BYU, he taught at Kansas State University for 11 years, where he served as Director of the Marriage and Family Therapy Program. He is passionate about facilitating and enhancing clinical research in the field, and he has worked to introduce more advanced statistical methods in SFT doctoral programs and among SFT researchers, in general.

His personal program of research focuses on therapist effects and therapist behaviors in couple therapy. He is also involved in working toward the development of the practice of couple and family therapy in China. He has published over 100 journal articles and book chapters, and, along with Lee Johnson, he edited the book *Advanced Methods in Marriage and Family Therapy Research*. An MFT professor for over 30 years, he loves mentoring and collaborating with graduate students.

Ryan B. Seedall, PhD, is Associate Professor in the Marriage and Family Therapy Program at Utah State University, having received his SFT training from Brigham Young University (MS) and Michigan State University (PhD). He completed post-doctoral training with Dr. James Anthony in the NIDA-funded Drug Dependence Epidemiology Fellowship Program. His primary program of research focuses on understanding and improving relationship and change processes within the couple relationship and in couple therapy. He aims to improve couple and family relationships through research on couple interaction and support processes, especially within the context of chronic illness. He is also interested in protective family dynamics and prevention efforts, including ways to reduce mental health disparities. Lastly, he is interested in identifying specific interventions that are useful when working with couples (e.g., enactments) and also client-related factors that are strongly associated with process and outcome in therapy (e.g., attachment and social support). Dr. Seedall has published over 30 peer-reviewed journal articles and seven book chapters. He lives in Hyde Park, Utah, with his wife (Ruth) and four children (Spencer, Madelyn, Eliza, and Benjamin).

Volume 2: Lenore M. McWey

Lenore M. McWey, PhD, is a Professor and the Director of the Marriage and Family Therapy Program at Florida State University. She is a Licensed Marriage and Family Therapist and American Association for Marriage and Family Therapy Approved Supervisor. She has received federal funding from the National Institutes of Health (NIH) to support her research on children and families involved with the child welfare system, and the results of her work have been published widely in high-impact, peer-reviewed journals. She currently serves as a scientific reviewer for the Health, Behavior, and Context Subcommittee of the Eunice Kennedy Shriver National Institute of Child Health and Human Development of NIH. Dr. McWey has been the recipient of the Florida State University Distinguished Teacher of the Year and the Outstanding Graduate Faculty Mentor awards.

Volume 3: Adrian J. Blow

Adrian J. Blow, PhD, works as a couple and family therapy intervention researcher and educator at Michigan State University (MSU). Dr. Blow is a Professor and Department Chair in the Human Development and Family Studies Department and faculty member of the Couple and Family Therapy Program. He obtained his PhD from Purdue University in 1999 where the late Doug Sprenkle served as his primary mentor. After Purdue, he joined the faculty at Saint Louis University where he worked for 6 years. He subsequently joined MSU in 2005. His research is focused on families and trauma, on military families, and on change processes in interventions pertaining to systemic family therapy. He has acquired over two million dollars in research grants as principal investigator and published numerous peer-reviewed publications (60) and book chapters (12). He has mentored many students and in 2017 was awarded the American Association for Marriage and Family Therapy (AAMFT) Training Award, which recognizes excellence in family therapy education. He has served the field of systemic family therapy in a number of capacities and was the AAMFT Board Secretary from 2012 to 2014 and Board Treasurer from 2016 to 2019. He is married to Dr. Tina Timm, Associate Professor in the MSU School of Social work. He has six children.

Volume 4: Mudita Rastogi and Reenee Singh

Mudita Rastogi, **PhD**, practices at Aspire Consulting and Therapy as a Licensed Marriage and Family Therapist, coach, and educational trainer. Dr. Rastogi obtained her PhD in Marriage and Family Therapy from Texas Tech University, her master's degree in psychology from University of Bombay, and her BA (Honors) in Psychology from University of Delhi. Prior roles include serving as Professor at the Illinois School of Professional Psychology, Program Director for the SAMHSA-funded Minority Fellowship Program at the American Association for Marriage and Family Therapy, Associate Editor for the *Journal of Marital and Family Therapy*, editor of the books *Multicultural Couple Therapy* and *Voices of Color*, and Associate Editor for the *Encyclopedia of Couple and Family Therapy*. Dr. Rastogi's publications focus on culture, gender, and global issues within the context of family and couple therapy. Dr. Rastogi is a Clinical Fellow and AAMFT Approved Supervisor having practiced in both India and the United States. She is a founding member of the Indian Association for Family Therapy. Dr. Rastogi's clinical and training interests include systemic family therapy, diversity and inclusion, global mental health, parenting, child-free couples, gender, and trauma. Additionally, she maintains an interest in partnering with grass-roots, not-for-profit organizations.

Reenee Singh, **DSysPsych**, is the Chief Executive of the Association for Family Therapy and Systemic Practice in the United Kingdom. She is the Founding Director of the London Intercultural Couples Centre at The Child and Family Practice in London, where she practices as a Consultant Family and Systemic Psychotherapist. She is the past editor of the *Journal of Family Therapy*, co-director of the Family Therapy and Systemic Research Centre at the Tavistock and Portman NHS Foundation Trust, and visiting professor at the University of Bergamo. Dr. Singh is the author of two books and numerous academic articles on issues of "race," culture, and qualitative research. Dr. Singh has lived and worked in Singapore, India, and the United Kingdom. She has taught all over the world and presents her work at national and international conferences.

List of Contributors

Hana H. Abu-Hassan, MD, Department of Family and Community Medicine, School of Medicine, University of Jordan, Amman, Jordan and Department of Family Medicine and Public Health, University of California, San Diego, La Jolla, CA, USA

Sheila M. Addison, PhD, LMFT, Margin to Center Consulting, Oakland, CA, USA

Volkmar Aderhold, MD, Institute of Social Psychiatry, Ernst Moritz Arndt University, Greifswald, Germany

Renu K. Aldrich, PhD, LMFT, Arlington, VA, USA

Rhea V. Almeida, PhD, Institute for Family Services, Somerset, NJ, USA

Jenny Altschuler, PhD, Affiliate, Tavistock Clinic, London, UK

Shayne R. Anderson, PhD, LMFT, School of Family Life, Brigham Young University, Provo, UT, USA

Louise Anthias, DProf, Bath, Somerset, UK

Christina M. Balderrama-Durbin, PhD, Department of Psychology, Binghamton University – State University of New York (SUNY), Binghamton, NY, USA

Alyssa Banford Witting, PhD, LMFT, School of Family Life, Brigham Young University, Provo, UT, USA

Eran Bar-Kalifa, PhD, Department of Psychology, Ben-Gurion University of the Negev, Beer-Sheva, Israel

Suzanne Bartle-Haring, PhD, Human Development and Family Science, The Ohio State University, Columbus, OH, USA

Brian R. W. Baucom, PhD, Department of Psychology, University of Utah, Salt Lake City, UT, USA

Julian Baudinet, PsyD, The Maudsley Centre for Child and Adolescent Eating Disorders, South London and Maudsley NHS Foundation Trust, London, UK

Erin R. Bauer, MS, Human Development and Family Science, University of Central Missouri, Warrensburg, MO, USA

Saliha Bava, PhD, LMFT, Marriage and Family Therapy Program, Mercy College, Dobbs Ferry, NY, USA

Andrew S. Benesh, PhD, LMFT, Psychiatry and Behavioral Sciences, Mercer University, Macon, GA, USA

Kristen E. Benson, PhD, LMFT, Human Development and Psychological Counseling, Appalachian State University, Boone, NC, USA

Jerica M. Berge, PhD, MPH, LMFT, Department of Family Medicine and Community Health, University of Minnesota Medical School, Minneapolis, MN, USA

J. Maria Bermudez, PhD, LMFT, Marriage and Family Therapy, Human Development and Family Science, University of Georgia, Athens, GA, USA

Hydeen K. Beverly, MSW, Steve Hicks School of Social Work, The University of Texas at Austin, Austin, TX, USA

Dharam Bhugun, PhD, MSW, MM, Southern Cross University, Gold Coast Campus, Bilinga, Queensland, Australia

Richard J. Bischoff, PhD, Child, Youth, and Family Studies, University of Nebraska-Lincoln, Lincoln, NE, USA

Esther Blessitt, MSc, The Maudsley Centre for Child and Adolescent Eating Disorders, South London and Maudsley NHS Foundation Trust, London, UK

Adrian J. Blow, PhD, LMFT, Human Development and Family Studies, Michigan State University, East Lansing, MI, USA

Guy Bodenmann, PhD, Department of Psychology, University of Zurich, Zurich, Switzerland

Danielle L. Boisvert, MA, Department of Family and Community Medicine, Saint Louis University, Saint Louis, MO, USA

Ulrike Borst, PhD, Ausbildungsinstitut für systemische Therapie, Zurich, Switzerland

Pauline Boss, PhD, LMFT, Department of Family Social Science, University of Minnesota, St. Paul, MN, USA

Angela B. Bradford, PhD, LMFT, Marriage and Family Therapy Program, School of Family Life, Brigham Young University, Provo, UT, USA

Spencer D. Bradshaw, PhD, Community, Family, and Addiction Sciences, Texas Tech University, Lubbock, TX, USA

Brittany R. Brakenhoff, PhD, Human Development and Family Science, The Ohio State University, Columbus, OH, USA

Andrew S. Brimhall, PhD, LMFT, Human Development and Family Science, East Carolina University, Greenville, NC, USA

Benjamin E. Caldwell, PsyD, Educational Psychology and Counseling, California State University Northridge, Northridge, CA, USA

Ryan G. Carlson, PhD, LMHC, Counselor Education, Department of Educational Studies, University of South Carolina, Columbia, SC, USA

Alan Carr, PhD, School of Psychology, University College Dublin, Dublin, Ireland

Marj Castronova, PhD, LMFT, MEND, Behavioral Health Center, Loma Linda University Health, Redlands, CA, USA

Laurie L. Charlés, PhD, LMFT, MGH Institute of Health Professions, Boston, MA, USA

Ronald J. Chenail, PhD, Department of Family Therapy, Nova Southeastern University, Fort Lauderdale, FL, USA

Jessica ChenFeng, PhD, LMFT, Department of Physician Vitality, School of Medicine, Loma Linda University Health, Loma Linda, CA, USA

Amy M. Claridge, PhD, LMFT, Department of Family and Consumer Sciences, Central Washington University, Ellensburg, WA, USA

Kate F. Cobb, MA, LMFT, Couple and Family Therapy, University of Iowa, Iowa City, IA, USA

Katelyn O. Coburn, MS, School of Family Studies and Human Services, Kansas State University, Manhattan, KS, USA

Carolyn Pape Cowan, PhD, Department of Psychology, Institute of Human Development, University of California, Berkeley, Berkeley, CA, USA

Philip A. Cowan, PhD, Department of Psychology, Institute of Human Development, University of California, Berkeley, Berkeley, CA, USA

Sarah A. Crabtree, PhD, LMFT, The Albert & Jessie Danielsen Institute, Boston University, Boston, MA, USA

Lauren Cubellis, MA, MPH, Department of Anthropology, Affiliate Tavistock Clinic, St. Louis, MO, USA

Carla M. Dahl, PhD, Congregational and Community Care, Luther Seminary, St. Paul, MN, USA

Andrew P. Daire, PhD, Department of Counseling and Special Education, School of Education, Virginia Commonwealth University, Richmond, VA, USA

Gwyn Daniel, MA, MSW, Visiting Lecturer, Tavistock Clinic, London, UK

Carissa D'Aniello, PhD, Couple, Marriage and Family Therapy Program, Texas Tech University, Lubbock, TX, USA

Frank M. Dattilio, PhD, Department of Psychiatry, University of Pennsylvania Perelman School of Medicine, Philadelphia, PA, USA

Rachel Dekel, PhD, School of Social Work, Bar Ilan University, Ramat Gan, Israel

Tamara Del Vecchio, PhD, Department of Psychology, St. John's University, Queens, NY, USA

Melissa M. Denlinger, MS, Human Development and Family Studies, Iowa State University, Ames, IA, USA

Janet M. Derrick, PhD, Four Winds Wellness and Education Centre, Kamloops, British Columbia, Canada

Guy Diamond, PhD, Center for Family Intervention Science, Drexel University, Philadlephia, PA, USA

Brian Distelberg, PhD, School of Behavioral Health, Behavioral Medicine Center, Loma Linda University, Loma Linda, CA, USA

William J. Doherty, PhD, Department of Family Social Science, University of Minnesota, St. Paul, MN, USA

Megan L. Dolbin-MacNab, PhD, LMFT, Department of Human Development and Family Science, Virginia Tech, Blacksburg, VA, USA

James Michael Duncan, PhD, School of Human Environmental Science, University of Arkansas, Fayetteville, AR, USA

Jared A. Durtschi, PhD, School of Family Studies and Human Services, Kansas State University, Manhattan, KS, USA

Lekie Dwanyen, MS, Department of Family Social Science, University of Minnesota, St. Paul, MN, USA

Lindsay L. Edwards, PhD, Division of Counseling and Family Therapy, Regis University, Thornton, CO, USA

Todd M. Edwards, PhD, LMFT, Marital and Family Therapy Program, University of San Diego, San Diego, CA, USA

Ivan Eisler, PhD, The Maudsley Centre for Child and Adolescent Eating Disorders, South London and Maudsley NHS Foundation Trust, London, UK

Norman B. Epstein, PhD, LMFT, Department of Family Science, School of Public Health, University of Maryland, College Park, MD, USA

Ana Rocío Escobar-Chew, PhD, LMFT, Psychology Department, Universidad Rafael Landívar, Guatemala, Guatemala

Laura M. Evans, PhD, Department of Human Development and Family Studies, The Pennsylvania State University, Brandywine Campus, Media, PA, USA

Mairi Evans, MA, Post Graduate Research School, Bedfordhsire University, Bedfordshire, UK

Adam M. Farero, MS, Human Development and Family Studies, Michigan State University, East Lansing, MI, USA

Daniel S. Felix, PhD, LMFT, Sioux Falls Family Medicine Residency, University of South Dakota, School of Medicine, Sioux Falls, SD, USA

Stephen T. Fife, PhD, LMFT, Community, Family, and Addiction Sciences, Texas Tech University, Lubbock, TX, USA

Heather M. Foran, PhD, Institute of Psychology, Alpen-Adria-University Klagenfurt, Klagenfurt, Austria

Liz Forbat, PhD, Faculty of Social Science, University of Stirling, Stirling, UK

Iris Fraude, BSc, Institute of Psychology, Alpen-Adria-University Klagenfurt, Klagenfurt, Austria

Christine A. Fruhauf, PhD, Human Development and Family Studies, Colorado State University, Fort Collins, CO, USA

Joaquín Gaete-Silva, PhD, Calgary Family Therapy Centre, Calgary, Alberta, Canada

Kami L. Gallus, PhD, LMFT, Human Development and Family Science, Oklahoma State University, Stillwater, OK, USA

Casey Gamboni, PhD, LMFT, The Family Institute at Northwestern University, Evanston, IL, USA

Reham F. Gassas, PhD, Department of Mental Health, King Abdulaziz Medical City, Riyadh, Kingdom of Saudi Arabia

Abigail H. Gewirtz, PhD, Department of Family Social Science, Institute of Child Development, University of Minnesota, Minneapolis, MN, USA

Jennifer E. Goerke, MA, School of Counseling, The University of Akron, Akron, OH, USA

Eric T. Goodcase, MS, LMFT, School of Family Studies and Human Services, Kansas State University, Manhattan, KS, USA

Arthur L. Greil, PhD, Division of Social Sciences, Alfred University, Alfred, NY, USA

Cadmona A. Hall, PhD, LMFT, Department of Couple and Family Therapy, Adler University, Chicago, IL, USA

Eugene L. Hall, PhD, LMFT, Department of Family Social Science, University of Minnesota, Saint Paul, MN, USA

Nathan R. Hardy, PhD, LMFT, Human Development and Family Science, Oklahoma State University, Stillwater, OK, USA

Terry D. Hargrave, PhD, LMFT, Department of Marriage and Family Therapy, Fuller Theological Seminary, Pasadena, CA, USA

Steven M. Harris, PhD, LMFT, Department of Family Social Science, University of Minnesota, Twin Cities, MN, USA

DeAnna Harris-McKoy, PhD, LMFT, Department of Counseling and Psychology, Texas A&M University – Central Texas, Killeen, TX, USA

Jaimee L. Hartenstein, PhD, School of Human Services, University of Central Missouri, Warrensburg, MO, USA

Rebecca Harvey, PhD, Marriage and Family Therapy Program, Southern Connecticut State University, New Haven, CT, USA

Stephen N. Haynes, PhD, Psychology, University of Hawai'i at Mānoa, Honolulu, HI, USA

Arlene Healey, MSc, DipSW, TMR Health Professionals, Belfast, UK

Lorna L. Hecker, PhD, LMFT, Private Practice, Fort Collins, CO, and Marriage and Family Therapy Program, Department of Behavioral Sciences, Purdue University Northwest, Hammond, IN, USA

Katie M. Heiden-Rootes, PhD, LMFT, Medical Family Therapy Program, Department of Family and Community Medicine, Saint Louis University, St. Louis, MO, USA

Sarah L. Helps, DClinPsy, Children, Young People and Family Directorate and Directorate of Education and Training, Tavistock and Portman NHS Foundation Trust, London, UK

Katherine Hertlein, PhD, LMFT, Department of Psychiatry and Behavioral Health, University of Nevada, Las Vegas, Las Vegas, NV, USA

Richard E. Heyman, PhD, Family Translational Research Group, New York University, New York, NY, USA

Christopher J. Hipp, EdS, LPC, Department of Educational Studies, University of South Carolina, Columbia, SC, USA

Jennifer Hodgson, PhD, LMFT, Human Development and Family Science, East Carolina University, Greenville, NC, USA

Kendal Holtrop, PhD, LMFT, Human Development and Family Studies, Michigan State University, East Lansing, MI, USA

Niyousha Hosseinichimeh, PhD, Department of Industrial and Systems Engineering, Virginia Tech, Blacksburg, VA, USA

Benjamin J. Houltberg, PhD, LMFT, Performance Science Institute, Marshall School of Business, University of Southern California, Los Angeles, CA, USA

Patricia Huerta, MS, LMFT, Human Development and Family Studies, Michigan State University, East Lansing, MI, USA

Scott C Huff, PhD, LMFT, School of Human Services, University of Central Missouri, Warrensburg, MO, USA

Ditte Roth Hulgaard, MD, PhD, Child and Adolescent Psychiatry, University of Southern Denmark, Odense, Denmark

Quintin A. Hunt, MS, Counselor Education, University of Wisconsin-Superior, Superior, WI, USA

Sydni A. J. Huxman, School of Family Studies and Human Services, Kansas State University, Manhattan, KS, USA

Dragana Ilic, PhD, LMFT, Department of Family Therapy, Nova Southestern University, Fort Lauderdale, FL, USA

Jeffrey B. Jackson, PhD, LMFT, Human Development and Family Science, Virginia Tech, Falls Church, VA, USA

Matthew E. Jaurequi, MA, Family and Child Sciences, Florida State University, Tallahassee, FL, USA

Lee N. Johnson, PhD, Marriage and Family Therapy Program, School of Family Life, Brigham Young University, Provo, UT, USA

Adam C. Jones, PhD, LMFTA, Family Therapy Program, Department of Human Development, Family Studies, and Counseling, Texas Woman's University, Denton, TX, USA

Tessa Jones, LMSW, Silver School of Social Work, New York University, New York, NY, USA

Eli A. Karam, PhD, LMFT, Couple and Family Therapy Program, Kent School of Social Work, University of Louisville, Louisville, KY, USA

Heather Katafiasz, PhD, School of Counseling, The University of Akron, Akron, OH, USA

Kyle D. Killian, PhD, LMFT, Marriage and Family Therapy Program, School of Counseling and Human Services, Capella University, Minneapolis, MN, USA

Thomas G. Kimball, PhD, LMFT, Center for Collegiate Recovery Communities, Texas Tech University, Lubbock, TX, USA

Keith Klostermann, PhD, LMFT, LMHC, Department of Counseling and Psychology, Medaille College, Buffalo, NY, USA

Carmen Knudson-Martin, PhD, LMFT, Counseling Psychology, Graduate School of Education and Counseling, Lewis and Clark College, Portland, OR, USA

E. Stephanie Krauthamer Ewing, PhD, MPH, Counseling and Family Therapy, School of Nursing and Health Professions, Drexel University, Philadelphia, PA, USA

Christian Kubb, MSc, Institute of Psychology, Alpen-Adria-University Klagenfurt, Klagenfurt, Austria

E. Megan Lachmar, PhD, LMFT, Marriage and Family Therapy, Human Development and Family Studies, Utah State University, Logan, UT, USA

Jennifer J. Lambert-Shute, PhD, LMFT, Department of Human Services, Valdosta State University, Valdosta, GA, USA

Angela L. Lamson, PhD, LMFT, Human Development and Family Science, East Carolina University, Greenville, NC, USA

Ashley L. Landers, PhD, LMFT, Human Development and Family Science, Virginia Tech, Falls Church, VA, USA

Nicole R. Larkin, MS, CADC, Marriage and Family Therapy, Human Development and Family Science, University of Central Missouri, Warrensburg, MO, USA

Feea R. Leifker, PhD, MPH, Department of Psychology, University of Utah, Salt Lake City, UT, USA

Paul Levatino, MFT, LMFT, Marriage and Family Therapy Program, Southern Connecticut State University, New Haven, CT, USA

Deanna Linville, PhD, LMFT, Couples and Family Therapy Program, University of Oregon, Eugene, OR, USA

Griselda Lloyd, PhD, LMFT, Edith Neumann School of Health and Human Services, Touro University Worldwide, Los Alamitos, CA, USA

Elsie Lobo, PhD, LMFT, Counseling and Family Sciences, Loma Linda University, Loma Linda, CA, USA

Sofia Lopez Bilbao, BA, Counselling Psychology, Werklund School of Education, University of Calgary, Calgary, Alberta, Canada

Gabriela López-Zerón, PhD, Human Development and Family Studies, Michigan State University, East Lansing, MI, USA

David C. Low, MA, MS, LMFT, Family Therapy Training Institute, Family Institute of Aurora Family Service, Milwaukee, WI, USA

Mallory Lucier-Greer, PhD, LMFT, Human Development and Family Studies, Auburn University, Auburn, AL, USA

Kevin P. Lyness, PhD, Department of Applied Psychology, Antioch University, New England, Keene, NH, USA

Mohammad Marie, PhD, School of Medicine and Health Science, Al-Najah National University, Nablus, Palestine

Melinda Stafford Markham, PhD, School of Family Studies and Human Services, Kansas State University, Manhattan, KS, USA

Heather McCauley, ScD, School of Social Work, Michigan State University, East Lansing, MI, USA

Teresa McDowell, EdD, LMFT, Counseling Psychology, Graduate School of Education and Counseling, Lewis and Clark College, Portland, OR, USA

Christi R. McGeorge, PhD, Human Development and Family Science, North Dakota State University, Fargo, ND, USA

Shardé McNeil Smith, PhD, Human Development and Family Studies, University of Illinois at Urbana-Champaign, Urbana, IL, USA

Douglas P. McPhee, MS, Community, Family, and Addiction Sciences, Texas Tech University, Lubbock, TX, USA

Lenore M. McWey, PhD, LMFT, Marriage and Family Therapy Program, Department of Family and Child Sciences, Florida State University, Tallahassee, FL, USA

Lisa V. Merchant, PhD, LMFT, Department of Marriage and Family Studies, Abilene Christian University, Abilene, TX, USA

Carol Pfeiffer Messmore, PhD, LMFT, Marriage and Family Therapy Program, School of Counseling and Human Services, Capella University, Minneapolis, MN, USA

Debra L. Miller, MSW, Human Development and Family Studies, Michigan State University, East Lansing, MI, USA

Richard B Miller, PhD, Department of Sociology, Brigham Young University, Provo, UT, USA

Erica A. Mitchell, PhD, Department of Psychology, University of Tennessee, Knoxville, TN, USA

Danielle M. Mitnick, PhD, Family Translational Research Group, New York University, New York, NY, USA

Mona Mittal, PhD, LMFT, Department of Family Science, School of Public Health, University of Maryland, College Park, MD, USA

Megan J. Murphy, PhD, LMFT, Marriage and Family Therapy Program, Department of Behavioral Sciences, Purdue University Northwest, Hammond, IN, USA

Briana S. Nelson Goff, PhD, School of Family Studies and Human Services, Kansas State University, Manhattan, KS, USA

Hoa N. Nguyen, PhD, Department of Human Services, Valdosta State University, Valdosta, GA, USA

Matthias Ochs, PhD, Department of Social Work, Fulda University of Applied Sciences, Fulda, Germany

Timothy J. O'Farrell, PhD, VA Boston Healthcare System, Harvard Medical School, Boston, MA, USA

Paul O. Orieny, PhD, LMFT, Center for Victims of Torture, St. Paul, MN, USA

Christine Anne Palmer, Aboriginal Elder, Canberra, Australian Capital Territory, Australia

Rubén Parra-Cardona, PhD, Steve Hicks School of Social Work, The University of Texas at Austin, Austin, TX, USA

Jo Ellen Patterson, PhD, Marital and Family Therapy Program, University of San Diego, San Diego, CA, USA

Rikki Patton, PhD, School of Counseling, The University of Akron, Akron, OH, USA

Brennan Peterson, PhD, LMFT, Department of Marriage and Family Therapy, Crean College of Health and Behavioral Sciences, Chapman University, Orange, CA, USA

J. Douglas Pettinelli, PhD, Medical Family Therapy Program, Department of Family and Community Medicine, Saint Louis University, Saint Louis, MO, USA

Morgan E. PettyJohn, MS, Human Development and Family Studies, Michigan State University, East Lansing, MI, USA

Bernhild Pfautsch, Diplom-Psychologist (FH), Department of Social Work, Fulda University of Applied Sciences, Fulda, Germany

Fred P. Piercy, PhD, Human Development and Family Science, Virginia Tech, Blacksburg, VA, USA

Nicole Piland, PhD, LMFT, Community, Family, and Addiction Sciences, Texas Tech University, Lubbock, TX, USA

Shyneice C. Porter, MS, LMFT, Department of Family Science, School of Public Health, University of Maryland, College Park, MD, USA

Shruti Singh Poulsen, PhD, Denver, CO, USA

Keeley Jean Pratt, PhD, LMFT, Human Development and Family Science, The Ohio State University, Columbus, OH, USA

Jacob B. Priest, PhD, LMFT, Couple and Family Therapy Program, Psychological and Quantitative Foundations, University of Iowa, Iowa City, IA, USA

Hayley A. Rahl-Brigman, BS, Institute of Child Development, University of Minnesota, Minneapolis, MN, USA

Julie L Ramisch, PhD, LMFT, Coastal Center for Collaborative Health, Lincoln City, OR, USA

Ashley K. Randall, PhD, Counseling and Counseling Psychology, Arizona State University, Tempe, AZ, USA

Mudita Rastogi, PhD, LMFT, Aspire Consulting and Therapy, Arlington Heights, IL, USA

Kayla Reed-Fitzke, PhD, LMFT, Couple and Family Therapy Program, Psychological and Quantitative Foundations, University of Iowa, Iowa City, IA, USA

Michael D. Reiter, PhD, Department of Family Therapy, Nova Southeastern University, Fort Lauderdale, FL, USA

Kimberly A. Rhoades, PhD, Family Translational Research Group, New York University, New York, NY, USA

Jennifer L. Rick, MS, LMFT, JLR Therapy, Herndon, VA, USA

W. David Robinson, PhD, LMFT, Human Development and Family Studies, Utah State University, Logan, UT, USA

John S. Rolland, MD, MPH, Psychiatry and Behavioral Sciences, Northwestern University Feinberg School of Medicine, Chicago, IL, USA

Lauren M. Ruhlmann, PhD, LMFT, Human Development and Family Studies, Auburn University, Auburn, AL, USA

Nicole Sabatini Gutierrez, PsyD, LMFT, Couple and Family Therapy Program, California School of Professional Psychology, Alliant International University, Irvine, CA, USA

Allen K. Sabey, PhD, LMFT, The Family Institute, Northwestern University, Evanston, IL, USA

Inés Sametband, PhD, Department of Psychology, Mount Royal University, Calgary, Alberta, Canada

Jonathan G. Sandberg, PhD, School of Family Life, Brigham Young University, Provo, UT, USA

Shaifali Sandhya, PhD, CARE Family Consultation, Chicago, IL, USA

Jochen Schweitzer, PhD, Institute of Medical Psychology, University of Heidelberg Hospital and Helm Stierlin Institute for Systemic Training, Heidelberg, Germany

Ryan B. Seedall, PhD, Human Development and Family Studies, Utah State University, Logan, UT, USA

Desiree M. Seponski, PhD, LMFT, Marriage and Family Therapy, Human Development and Family Science, University of Georgia, Athens, GA, USA

Erin M. Sesemann, PhD, LMFT, Human Development and Family Science, East Carolina University, Greenville, NC, USA

Michal Shamai, PhD, School of Social Work, University of Haifa, Haifa, Israel

Tazuko Shibusawa, PhD, LCSW, Silver School of Social Work, New York University, New York, NY, USA

Karina M. Shreffler, PhD, Human Development and Family Science, Oklahoma State University, Stillwater, OK, USA

Sterling T. Shumway, PhD, LMFT, Community, Family, and Addiction Sciences, Texas Tech University, Lubbock, TX, USA

Charles Sim, SJ, PhD, S.R. Nathan School of Human Development, Singapore University of Social Sciences, Republic of Singapore

Timothy Sim, PhD, Department of Applied Social Sciences, The Hong Kong Polytechnic University, Kowloon, Hung Hom, Hong Kong, China

Mima Simic, MD, The Maudsley Centre for Child and Adolescent Eating Disorders, South London and Maudsley NHS Foundation Trust, London, UK

Gail Simon, DProf, Institute of Applied Social Research, University of Bedfordshire, Luton, UK

Jonathan B. Singer, PhD, LCSW, Social Work, Loyola University Chicago, Chicago, IL, USA

Reenee Singh, DSysPsych, Association for Family Therapy and Systemic Practice and The Child and Family Practice, London, UK

Izidora Skračić, MA, Department of Family Science, School of Public Health, University of Maryland, College Park, MD, USA

Amy M. Smith Slep, PhD, Family Translational Research Group, New York University, New York, NY, USA

Natasha Slesnick, PhD, Human Development and Family Science, The Ohio State University, Columbus, OH, USA

Douglas B. Smith, PhD, LMFT, Community, Family, and Addiction Sciences, Texas Tech University, Lubbock, TX, USA

Douglas K. Snyder, PhD, LMFT, Department of Psychological and Brain Sciences, Texas A&M University, College Station, TX, USA

Kristy L. Soloski, PhD, LMFTA, LCDC, Community, Family, and Addiction Sciences, Texas Tech University, Lubbock, TX, USA

Jenny Speice, PhD, LMFT, Family Therapy Training Program, Institute for the Family, Department of Psychiatry, University of Rochester School of Medicine, Rochester, NY, USA

Chelsea M. Spencer, PhD, LMFT, School of Family Studies and Human Services, Kansas State University, Manhattan, KS, USA

Paul R. Springer, PhD, LMFT, Child, Youth, and Family Studies, University of Nebraska-Lincoln, Lincoln, NE, USA

Sandra M. Stith, PhD, LMFT, School of Family Studies and Human Services, Kansas State University, Manhattan, KS, USA

Linda Stone Fish, PhD, MSW, Department of Marriage and Family Therapy, Syracuse University, Syracuse, NY, USA

Peter Stratton, PhD, Leeds Family Therapy and Research Centre, University of Leeds, Leeds, UK

Tom Strong, RPsych, Educational Studies, Counselling Psychology Program, Werklund School of Education, University of Calgary, Calgary, Alberta, Canada

Nathan C. Taylor, MS, School of Applied Human Sciences, University of Northern Iowa, Cedar Falls, IA, USA

Karlin J. Tichenor, PhD, LMFT, Karlin J & Associates, LLC, Indianapolis, IN, USA

Tina M. Timm, PhD, LMSW, LMFT, School of Social Work, Michigan State University, East Lansing, MI, USA

Glade L. Topham, PhD, LCMFT, School of Family Studies and Human Services, Kansas State University, Manhattan, KS, USA

Maru Torres-Gregory, PhD, JD, LMFT, Marriage and Family Therapy Program, The Family Institute, Northwestern University, Evanston, IL, USA

Chi-Fang Tseng, MS, Human Development and Family Studies, Michigan State University, East Lansing, MI, USA

Shu-Tsen Tseng, PhD, Prudence Skynner Family and Couple Therapy Clinic, Springfield Hospital, London, UK

Carolyn Y. Tubbs, PhD, Marriage and Family Therapy, Department of Counseling and Human Services, St. Mary's University, San Antonio, TX, USA

Ileana Ungureanu, MD, PhD, LMFT, Marriage, Couple and Family Counseling, Division of Psychology and Counseling, Governors State University, University Park, IL, USA

Francisco Urbistondo Cano, DCounsPsy, Community Learning Disability Team, NHS Bolton Foundation Trust, Bolton, UK

Damir S. Utržan, PhD, LMFT, Division of Mental Health and Substance Abuse Treatment Services, Minnesota Department of Human Services, St. Paul, MN, USA

Susanna Vakili, MA, LMFT, Private Practice, San Diego and San Juan Capistrano, CA, USA

Catherine A. Van Fossen, MS, Human Development and Family Science, The Ohio State University, Columbus, OH, USA

Amber Vennum, PhD, LMFT, School of Family Studies and Human Services, Kansas State University, Manhattan, KS, USA

Ingrid Vlam, PhD, MBA, Research Graduate School, Bedfordshire University, Bedfordshire, UK

Ashley A. Walsdorf, MS, Marriage and Family Therapy, Human Development and Family Science, University of Georgia, Athens, GA, USA

Marianne Z. Wamboldt, MD, Department of Psychiatry, Helen and Arthur E. Johnson Depression Center, University of Colorado School of Medicine, Aurora, CO, USA

Karen S. Wampler, PhD, LMFT, Human Development and Family Studies, Michigan State University, East Lansing, MI, USA

Richard S. Wampler, PhD, MSW, LMFT, Human Development and Family Studies, Michigan State University, East Lansing, MI, USA

Michael R. Whitehead, PhD, LMFT, Aspen Grove Family Therapy, Twin Falls, ID, USA

Jason B. Whiting, PhD, LMFT, Marriage and Family Therapy Program, School of Family Life, Brigham Young University, Provo, UT, USA

Elizabeth Wieling, PhD, Human Development and Family Science, University of Georgia, Athens, GA, USA

Lee M. Williams, PhD, Marital and Family Therapy Program, University of San Diego, San Diego, CA, USA

Dara Winley, MA, Couple and Family Therapy, Drexel University, Philadelphia, PA, USA

Mathew C. Withers, PhD, LMFT, Psychology, California State University, Chico, Chico, CA, USA

Andrea K. Wittenborn, PhD, LMFT, Human Development and Family Studies, Michigan State University, East Lansing, MI, USA

Armeda Stevenson Wojciak, PhD, Couple and Family Therapy Program, Psychological and Quantitative Foundations, University of Iowa, Iowa City, IA, USA

Sarah B. Woods, PhD, LMFT, Department of Family and Community Medicine, University of Texas Southwestern Medical Center, Dallas, TX, USA

Corey E. Yeager, PhD, Department of Family Social Science, University of Minnesota, St. Paul, MN, USA

Cigdem Yumbul, PhD, Bude Psychotherapy Center, Istanbul, Turkey

Toni Schindler Zimmerman, PhD, LMFT, Marriage and Family Therapy Program, Department of Human Development and Family Studies, Colorado State University, Fort Collins, CO, USA

Max Zubatsky, PhD, LMFT, Department of Family and Community Medicine, Saint Louis University, St. Louis, MO, USA

Preface

The first volume of Gurman and Kniskern's *Handbook of Family Therapy* was published in 1981, two years after I finished graduate school. I read it from cover to cover and used favorite chapters over and over again in my courses. The second volume published in 1991 was equally treasured. Even though 10 years separated the two, it was published as Volume 2 instead of as a revision because, as Gurman and Kniskern explained in the preface, so much new information had emerged that both volumes were needed.

Four volumes were needed in this handbook to capture the breadth and depth of systemic family therapy theory, research, and practice. Material is organized to maximize accessibility by creating volumes on the profession, the parent–child relationship, the couple relationship, and the family across the lifespan. Each volume stands on its own as well as acts as a complement to the others. The three problem-oriented volumes are organized to reflect typical reasons clients initially seek treatment: concern about relationships, worry about a problem or disorder with a family member, or challenging contexts impacting the family. Taken together, the four volumes of *The Handbook of Systemic Family Therapy* offer a comprehensive and accessible resource for clinicians, educators, researchers, and policymakers.

As much as possible, the editorial team wanted to reflect how systemic family therapists actually think about and do their work. For example, instead of providing separate chapters on each evidence-based treatment model, those models are integrated into the material on relevant treatment topics. The pervasive impacts of culture, diversity, and inequitable treatment are major themes, and several chapters are devoted to these important topics. The work includes a global perspective on systemic family therapy. Instead of promoting a specific approach, we asked the authors to describe what is known about intervention and prevention for each topic and the next steps needed to determine best practice. We wanted each chapter to stimulate improved practice as well as to serve as a springboard for further research.

From the beginning, we used a collaborative process to decide on both the structure and the content of the book. The crucial first step in this process was a two-day "think tank" meeting at the American Association for Marriage and Family Therapy (AAMFT) offices in April 2016 with me, Adrian Blow, Pauline Boss, Rick Miller, Mudita Rastogi, Liz Wieling, and Tracy Todd in which we began to sketch a vision for the handbook. The next step was securing editors for each of the four volumes and, to my eternal gratitude, six well-established and highly esteemed scholars agreed to take on these roles: Rick Miller and Ryan Seedall for Volume 1 on the profession, Lenore McWey for Volume 2 on children and adolescents, Adrian Blow for Volume 3 on couples, and Mudita Rastogi and Reenee Singh for Volume 4 on global health. The group worked together over many months to settle on a table of contents and to write a formal proposal to John Wiley & Sons Publishing. All seven of us worked on all four volumes. As systems thinkers, we needed to always look at the project as a whole and never simply as a set of separate volumes.

Close collaboration among the editors continued as we worked to identify, contact, and secure authors for each chapter. We deliberately sought authors who were both scholars and clinicians and could speak to the diverse perspectives inherent in work with families as well as the breadth of the field of systemic family therapy. We worked together to avoid overlap across chapters, identify missing content, and maintain the integrity of each volume. Authors submitted outlines for their chapters that were read by all seven of us. Feedback for each chapter summarized by the primary editor(s) provided an opportunity for further collaboration with the lead author. This approach continued through the manuscript submission, revision, and finalization phases with at least two, and usually three, editors reviewing each chapter.

This project would not have happened without the efforts of Tracy Todd, Chief Executive Officer of the AAMFT. As part of an AAMFT initiative to develop essential resources for "those practicing systemic and relational therapies throughout the world," he worked with Darren Reed at Wiley to formulate a market rationale for a multivolume handbook for the field of systemic family therapy. Tracy and AAMFT continued to support the project with funding for part-time staff and expenses for editorial meetings. While providing invaluable support, Tracy and the AAMFT Board have not been involved in determining the content of the handbook, which has been completely the responsibility of the editors.

It is impossible to adequately thank the editors and the authors for their efforts—all of it as volunteers—to make this project possible. It is a humbling experience to ask so much and see such dedication of so many people to complete this task. The sheer size and complexity of this project would not have been manageable without our Assistant Editor, Leah Maderal. She kept the entire project organized and moving forward, tracking every version of every manuscript as each was submitted and edited. She obtained and updated contributor information and developed systems for safe sharing and storage of all material. In addition, Leah developed and maintained the project website, checked copyright permissions, and worked to get artwork and other special elements in the correct format for Wiley. Renu Aldrich served as Assistant Editor in the early months of the project. Sarah Bidigare played an essential role as Editorial Assistant, double- and triple-checking each manuscript for formatting and adherence to APA Style. Recognizing the importance of this project for systemic family research and the future of the field, Rick Miller obtained funds from Brigham Young University to help support opportunities for editors and authors to interact face-to-face.

I want to take a moment to acknowledge the mentoring and support given to me by the late Doug Sprenkle. Doug and I both started at Purdue in 1975, Doug as a new faculty member and I as a first-year doctoral student. He was a model teacher, supervisor, and mentor of graduate students. He was also a role model for me as editor of the *Journal of Marital and Family Therapy* and in his commitment to developing scholarly resources for the field. Doug was very supportive of the development of the handbook. I deeply regret that he died before seeing it in print.

It has meant everything to me to work with colleagues who have been passionate, committed, and engaged in bringing this project to fruition. Thank you, Adrian, Lenore, Mudita, Reenee, Rick, and Ryan. Throughout this project, I also depended on the wisdom and encouragement of friends and colleagues. I particularly want to thank Pauline Boss, Ruben Parra-Cardona, Liz Wieling, Mudita Rastogi, Jo Ellen Patterson, and Andrea Wittenborn. I am grateful to my children, Nathan and Leah, their spouses, extended family, and friends for their patience and forbearance throughout these last 3 years. Most of all, I thank my husband, Richard Wampler, who has lived through all of the trials and triumphs of this project with me. From explaining genetics and writing two chapters to checking references and looking up doi's for two authors in challenging situations, Richard has played a major role in ensuring the timely completion and uniform quality of the handbook and my survival doing it. Finally, I want to remember the support of my dear friend Carol Parr, who never failed to ask about "the book" during her long and final illness.

I did not hesitate to say "yes" when Tracy contacted me about this project. I knew without a doubt that the field of systemic family therapy had developed to new levels of depth, breadth, impact, and sophistication in practice, theory, and research that were simply not reflected in available comprehensive scholarly resources. Those we contacted to participate in the project had the same reaction—a resource like we envisioned for the handbook was needed for our field and needed quickly. Our hope is that you will find the content as important, compelling, and useful as we have.

Karen S. Wampler

Editor-in-Chief, *The Handbook of Systemic Family Therapy*

References

Gurman, A. S., & Kniskern, D. P. (Eds.) (1981). *Handbook of family therapy* (Vol. 1). New York: Brunner/Mazel.

Gurman, A. S., & Kniskern, D. P. (Eds.) (1991). *Handbook of family therapy* (Vol. 2). New York: Brunner/Mazel.

Volume 3 Preface
Systemic Family Therapy with Couples

It has been a career highlight for me to serve as the Associate Editor of Volume 3, *Systemic Family Therapy with Couples*, (Couples) of *The Handbook of Systemic Family Therapy*. During this process, I became more convinced than ever about the power of intimate relationships in our lives and their ability to bring us overwhelming joy at the highest points, but also some of our saddest moments when they do not go well, or when they end, either through dissolution or death. In editing this volume, six main points stood out that I believe are priority considerations highlighted by the authors.

Conceptualization of problems

Conceptualization is a defining part of systemic family therapy (SFT; see Sprenkle & Blow, 2004; Wampler, K. S., Blow, McWey, Miller, & Wampler, R. S., 2019, for more discussion on this topic). Obtaining a thorough conceptual map of the client(s) is essential to effective practice with couples. From a clinical standpoint, it is critical that therapists consider the role of intimate relationships in presenting problems, even when the presenting client is an individual, and that this conceptualization is used to inform interventions throughout therapy. Optimal conceptualization begins with culturally sensitive assessment at the time of the first session, and it is ongoing throughout treatment.

Effectively treating common relationship problems

Many chapters in this volume represent the predominant reasons why couples seek help, and these difficulties are ideally treated through a dyadic therapy approach. Problems can arise because of typical or common difficulties in the relationship, contextual changes, or life events that affect relationship functioning, or because of injuries done to the relationship by the behaviors of one partner. Effective couple therapists are well equipped to assess and treat these problems through relationship therapy.

Stress is a growing problem for couples as they negotiate the challenges of their day-to-day lives. These stresses may involve health concerns, work demands, or parenting children. Some couples experience more stress because of changes in their life circumstances or family structures, such as aging couples or when individuals remarry or blend a family. These changes inevitably influence optimal couple functioning and couples need strategies on how to deal with these life circumstances. Other couples are forced to deal with difficulties due to unfortunate life events such as infertility or loss of a loved one, and they ideally do grief and loss work, both as individuals and as a couple, to work through these difficult life events. Finally, there are couples who come to treatment because one individual in the relationship has engaged in behaviors that damage the relationship. Infidelity is an example of this type of relational injury, and treatment of this often difficult (although common) presenting problem has been complicated by the changes in technology and its role in infidelity. Another relationship injury that occurs far too often is intimate partner violence (IPV). IPV is toxic in any relationship and SFTs increasingly need to be adept at assessing and treating this problem.

Other chapters in this volume focus on additional types of relational difficulties. Many adults are unpartnered or struggle in relationships. For these individuals who are unable to find someone suitable or who experience multiple failed relationships, a growing body of literature suggests that this is a significant risk factor for both physical and mental health difficulties. Loneliness is a rapidly growing topic of interest in the literature (and media) as more research reveals the deleterious effects of loneliness on people's lives. Clinical approaches need to help these individuals work through ambiguous loss and challenges to self-efficacy that may arise from difficulties in relationships. Others may be partnered but have relationships that are teetering on the brink of failure. Traditional couple therapy approaches may not be a good fit for these cases, especially as couples explore relationship ambivalences or the best ways to end a relationship. Effectively working with these couples/individuals and helping them achieve amicable resolutions has important implications for the long-term well-being of these individuals and their children.

The circularity of individual problems and the relationship

A third category of importance is when individual mental health problems affect relationship functioning and when relationship difficulties in turn exacerbate these individual problems. For example, problems such as alcohol/substance use disorders, affective and anxiety disorders, and posttraumatic stress often become problematic issues in relationships. Given the high prevalence of these disorders and their large health implications for society, they represent key areas for couple therapy intervention and research.

Prevention

Many difficulties that couples face can be prevented before they start or can be "nipped in the bud" before they grow too large. Couple distress can be prevented through education, enrichment, and premarital counseling, programs that have grown over the last decades and provide promising support for a wide range of couples including low-income couples, marginalized groups, those no longer in a relationship, and those living in countries around the world. The increased accessibility, fit, and reach of these interventions holds significant promise for the deterrence of couple problems.

Cultural factors

If SFT for couples is to expand its reach and effectiveness globally, it is essential that intervention approaches fit well across diverse contexts and are culturally relevant. Unique cultural presentations in couple therapy include LGBT couples, intercultural couples, and underserved populations. These couple interventions need to be appropriate, culturally sensitive, and accessible and are ideally delivered by treatment providers who are attuned to these issues.

Research and policy

Finally, we need to consider the future of our field. Even though couple therapies are effective for a wide range of disorders and presenting problems including relationship distress, mental health, and physical health difficulties, there is so much more that we need to know. For example, we still have limited understanding of for whom couple therapy works best and possible modifications to treatments needed to help a wider range of couples across contexts. We also need to dig deeper into our understanding of *how* couple therapy works, including mechanisms of change across these therapies, and considerations in tailoring couple therapy approaches to both individual and couple relationship characteristics. These are high priorities for future research and theory development.

Professional development issues for therapists are important considerations as well. How clinicians are best trained and credentialed and whether these are the best ways to ensure effective therapy needs more attention. Additional research studies on couple therapy and couple therapy outcomes are needed, and careful consideration should be given to how outcomes are measured and conceptualized in these studies. Finally, our field needs to do more to integrate interventions for couples in the healthcare arena. Much more strategic work is needed to convince policymakers of the power of intimate relationships and of the effectiveness of therapy involving couples. Our field needs to be better in organizing, prioritizing, and realizing these important policy change initiatives.

In closing, I want to thank Karen Wampler, Editor-in-Chief, for her vision, leadership, and support in the handbook production. I also want to thank each of my fellow associate editors, Rick, Ryan, Lenore, Mudita, and Reenee, for their encouragement and cheerleading in the process of putting this volume together. The support of my students and colleagues at Michigan State University has been invaluable. Finally, I wish to thank my family. First, my endlessly supportive spouse and companion Tina for her wisdom and encouragement. Second, each of my six children—Caleb (Maggie), Jordan, Savannah, Sophia, Jonah, and Oliver—for all helping me keep my priorities in perspective.

Adrian J. Blow
Associate Editor

References

Sprenkle, D., & Blow, A. (2004). Common factors and our sacred models. *Journal of Marital and Family Therapy*, 30, 113–129.

Wampler, K. S., Blow, A. J., McWey, L. M., Miller, R. B., & Wampler, R. S. (2019). The profession of couple, marital, and family therapy (CMFT): Defining ourselves and moving forward. *Journal of Marital and Family Therapy*, 45(1), 5–18. doi:10.1111/jmft.12294

Foreword

This four-volume handbook captures the breadth, depth, and creative applications of systemic family therapy today. The editors and chapter authors capture our profession's understanding of the healing potential of couple and family systems and take that basic understanding in many important directions. Clearly, we have come a long way.

Over my 44 years in the profession, I have described systemic family therapy in progressively different ways. In the beginning, it was a young, emerging profession based on systems theory, then an adolescent finding its place in the world. I explained to doctoral recruits, for a time, that it was the fastest-growing mental health profession. I explained that while more than half of the presenting problems of clients in a typical mental health clinic had systemic features, most therapists have had little or no training in family therapy. I remember devouring various editions of Gurman and Kniskern's *Handbook of Family Therapy* and books by Haley, Minuchin, Satir, McGoldrick, Whitaker, deShazer, Johnson, and others the way I read some novels – without coming up for air. I remember for a long time buying into the battle of the name brands, as Lynn Hoffman called our preoccupation with famous model developers and their models. I also quoted Doug Sprenkle (to whom this four-volume handbook is dedicated) regarding the importance of "the synergetic interplay of theory, research, and practice," each domain enriching the others.

Doug died recently, but as more than one of his former students explained, he humanized the field, and I see his keen, big-picture mind and therapist's heart in the chapters of this handbook. He would have been pleased that the authors of this handbook address systems in the margins, internationally, across individual, couple, and family presenting problems, in health care, and in a research-informed manner. He would have been pleased that in such a diverse field, we still see commonalities in the power of family systems to heal and are giving greater attention to common factors that contribute to that change and to systemic family therapy research that keeps us honest and grounded in empirical data.

I agree with you, Doug. This handbook marks the fact that systemic family therapy is indeed a profession that has taken its rightful place among our sister professions, who are also embracing the power of systemic interventions. This handbook includes systems interventions that address important issues and problems—child maltreatment, global public health, domestic violence, depression, racial and gender issues, sociocultural attunement, policy and advocacy, adolescent substance use, youth suicide, grief and loss, and so much more. The profession and the practice of systemic family therapy are both given attention, as is multidisciplinarity. So is, as Doug might say, the synergism of theory, research, practice, and policy. The editors' coherent organization includes overarching foundations, practice models of relational treatment for children, adolescents, couples, and families, and research foundations, with a global perspective and attention to cultural diversity throughout. In short, the handbook is broad enough to reflect the health and usefulness of systems interventions that meet the very real needs of people today. I also see room to grow, improve, and address a world yearning for a caring, vibrant, evidence-based discipline that employs the best in ourselves and can positively transform the intimate and varied systems around us.

Fred P. Piercy, PhD, is Professor Emeritus of family therapy at Virginia Tech, Blacksburg, Virginia, and former editor of the *Journal of Marital and Family Therapy*.

Fred P. Piercy

Part I
Overview

1

Current Status and Challenges in Systemic Family Therapy with Couples

Douglas K. Snyder and Christina M. Balderrama-Durbin

Couple therapy continues to gain in stature as a vital component of mental health services. The largest international study of psychotherapists found that 70% of psychotherapists treat couples (Orlinksky & Ronnestad, 2005). A survey of expert psychotherapists' predictions about future practices in psychotherapy showed couple therapy to be the format likely to achieve the most growth in the next decade (Norcross, Pfund, & Prochaska, 2013). Three factors likely contribute to this trend: (a) the prevalence of couple distress in both community and clinic samples, (b) the impact of couple distress on both the emotional and physical well-being of adult partners and their offspring, and (c) increased evidence for the effectiveness of couple-based interventions, not only in treating couple distress and related relationship problems but also as a primary or adjunct treatment for a variety of individual emotional, behavioral, or physical health disorders (e.g., Fischer, Baucom, & Cohen, 2016; Snyder & Whisman, 2003).

Couple therapy has evolved through several distinct phases (Gurman & Snyder, 2011), tracing its origins to the founding of the Marriage Consultation Center in New York City in 1929 and asserting a national identity with the establishment of the American Association of Marriage Counselors in 1942—subsequently renamed the American Association for Marriage and Family Therapy in 1978. Early marriage counselors provided advice and information, largely from an atheoretical and educational perspective; the predominant format for marriage counseling was with individuals, with emergence of the conjoint format (i.e., both partners meeting simultaneously with the same therapist) rising slowly from only 5% in the 1940s to a meager 15% by 1960. Today, conjoint couple therapy is the presumptive format for treating partner relationship distress. Interventions across diverse theoretical orientations share a common emphasis on the interaction between partners' respective behaviors, thoughts, and feelings—as well as their place in the broader context of extended family, community, and culture—thereby implicitly adopting a systemic perspective.

The Handbook of Systemic Family Therapy: Volume 3, First Edition.
Edited by Karen S. Wampler and Adrian J. Blow.
© 2020 John Wiley & Sons Ltd. Published 2020 by John Wiley & Sons Ltd.

In this chapter we first consider the importance of couple therapy in promoting couple and family well-being—noting both the prevalence of couple distress and its impact on individuals' emotional and physical health. We describe findings regarding the effectiveness of couple-based interventions for treating general relationship distress as well as coexisting emotional, behavioral, and physical health problems. We also consider evidence regarding potential moderators and mediators of treatment effectiveness and the implications of these findings for integrative approaches and tailoring interventions to partner and relationship characteristics. Finally, we propose enduring challenges for the field of couple therapy—including training of couple therapists, conducting clinically relevant research, and disseminating findings in an impactful manner.

The Prevalence and Impact of Couple Distress

Couple distress is prevalent in both community epidemiological studies and research involving individual treatment samples. In the United States, the most salient indicator of couple distress remains a divorce rate of approximately 40–50% among married couples (Kreider & Ellis, 2011), with about half of these occurring within the first 7 years of marriage. Independent of divorce, many, if not most, marriages experience periods of significant turmoil that place partners at risk for dissatisfaction, dissolution, or symptom development (e.g., depression or anxiety); roughly one-third of married persons report experiencing clinically relevant levels of relationship distress (Whisman, Beach, & Snyder, 2008). Data on the effects of stigma, prejudice, and multiple stressors experienced by various socioeconomically disadvantaged groups (Raley, Sweeney, & Wondra, 2015) as well as lesbian, gay, and bisexual couples (Meyer, 2003) suggest that these groups may experience additional challenges.

Global perspectives on the prevalence of couple distress—when operationalized by rates of divorce—vary in part as a function of first age and rates of marriage, as well as remarriage. More than 85% of people marry by age 50 across almost all countries, cultures, and religions (United Nations, Department of Economic and Social Affairs, Population Division, 2015). Although rates of marriage have declined in many developed countries since the 1970s, among those who choose not to marry the vast majority of people enter "marriage-like" cohabiting couple relationships (Organization of Economic Cooperation and Development [OECD] Social Policy Division, 2011). Across almost all nation states of the OECD, divorce rates have increased from the mid- to late 1970s to the period 2000–2005. However, these divorce rates understate rates of relationship dissolution because in most Western countries couple cohabitation is now a common form of committed partnership. Cohabiting couples are more likely to experience relationship distress and separate than married couples (Hayes, Weston, Lixia, & Gray, 2010) and are 25–35% more likely to divorce following marriage (Stanley, Rhoades, Amato, Markman, & Johnson, 2010).

Importantly, the common focus on divorce or other indicators of couple distress also fails to recognize other issues that couples often present as a focus of concern, including those that detract from optimal individual or relationship well-being. These include deficits in feelings of security and closeness, shared values, trust, joy, love, physical intimacy, and similar positive emotions that individuals typically value in their intimate relationships. Not all such deficits necessarily culminate in "clinically significant" impaired functioning or emotional and behavioral symptoms as traditionally conceived; yet, frequently, these deficits are experienced as insidious and may culminate in partners' disillusion or their dissolution of the relationship.

In a previous US national survey, the most frequently cited causes of acute emotional distress in individuals were couple relationship problems, including divorce, separation, and other relationship strains (Swindle, Heller, Pescosolido, & Kikuzawa, 2000). Couple distress covaries with overall life dissatisfaction even more strongly than distress in other domains, such as health, work, or children (Fleeson, 2004). Other studies have indicated that persons in distressed couple relationships are overrepresented among individuals seeking mental health services, regardless of whether or not they report couple distress as their primary complaint (Lin, Goering, Offord, Campbell, & Boyle, 1996). In a study of 800 employee assistance program clients, 65% rated family problems as "considerable" or "extreme" (Shumway, Wampler, Dersch, & Arredondo, 2004).

Findings from various US national surveys have indicated that compared with happily married persons, maritally distressed partners are significantly more likely to have a mood disorder, anxiety disorder, or substance use disorder (McShall & Johnson, 2015; Whisman, 1999, 2007). Additional findings from an epidemiological survey in Ontario, Canada, showed that even when controlling for distress in relationships with relatives and close friends, couple distress was significantly correlated with major depression, generalized anxiety disorder, social and specific phobia, panic disorder, and alcohol dependence or abuse (Whisman, Sheldon, & Goering, 2000). Moreover, couple distress—particularly negative communication—has direct adverse effects on cardiovascular, endocrine, immune, neurosensory, and other physiological systems that, in turn, contribute to physical health problems (Robles, Slatcher, Trombello, & McGinn, 2014). The partners in distressed relationships do not live as long and report more health problems (Waite & Gallagher, 2000) and use health services substantially more (about 25% higher costs per person) compared with persons in satisfying relationships (Prigerson, Maciejewski, & Rosenheck, 2000).

Nor are the effects of couple distress confined to the adult partners. Meta-analytic studies show a reliable association between couple relationship distress and negative parent–child interactions (Krishnakumar & Buehler, 2000). Parents in distressed couple relationships are less likely to use positive parenting practices such as acceptance, support, and consistent and appropriate discipline—and instead are more likely to use harsh, inconsistent, and abusive parenting than parents in satisfied relationships. Couple distress has been related to a wide range of deleterious effects on children, including depression, anxiety, withdrawal, poor social competence, health problems, poor academic performance, and a variety of other concerns (Bernet, Wamboldt, & Narrow, 2016; Cummings & Davies, 2010; Hetherington, Bridges, & Insabella, 1998; Vaez, Indran, Abdollahi, Juhari, & Mansor, 2015).

In brief, couple distress has a markedly high prevalence, is among the most frequent primary or secondary concerns reported by individuals seeking assistance from mental health professionals, and has a strong linkage to emotional, behavioral, and health problems in the adult partners and their offspring.

The Effectiveness of Couple Therapy for Relationship Distress

Previous reviews affirm that various versions of couple therapy produce moderate, statistically significant, and often clinically significant effects in reducing relationship distress (Lebow, Chambers, Christensen, & Johnson, 2012; Shadish & Baldwin, 2003; Snyder, Castellani, & Whisman, 2006; Snyder & Halford, 2012). The average person receiving couple therapy is better off at termination than 70–80% of individuals not receiving treatment—an improvement rate that rivals or exceeds the most effective psychosocial and pharmacological interventions for individual mental health disorders (Shadish & Baldwin, 2003). Evidence from two or more randomized clinical trials (RCTs) supports each of four different approaches to couple therapy for relationship distress. Three of these approaches derive broadly from a behavioral tradition–namely, traditional behavioral couple therapy (TBCT) (Jacobson & Margolin, 1979), cognitive-behavioral couple therapy (CBCT) (Epstein & Baucom, 2002), and integrative behavioral couple therapy (IBCT) (Jacobson & Christensen, 1996); the fourth—emotionally focused therapy (EFT) (Johnson, 2004)—initially evolved from a synthesis of experiential and systemic approaches to therapy, but currently emphasizes its theoretical roots in attachment theory. In addition to these four approaches, two additional approaches to couple therapy have each garnered evidence of efficacy from a single RCT each—insight-oriented couple therapy (Snyder, Wills, & Grady-Fletcher, 1991a) and an integrated systemic couple therapy (Goldman & Greenberg, 1992). Shadish and Baldwin (2003) found little evidence of differential effectiveness across different theoretical orientations to couple therapy, particularly once other covariates (e.g., reactivity of measures) were controlled.

Separate from therapies for general couple distress, a variety of empirically supported treatments have been developed for specific relationship problems including infidelity (Baucom, Snyder, & Gordon, 2009), sexual difficulties (McCarthy & Thestrup, 2008), and intimate partner violence (Epstein, Werlinich, & LaTaillade, 2015).

Tempering enthusiasm based on initial outcome data from RCTs of various approaches to couple therapy are more nuanced findings based on treatment effects for each partner separately, as well as follow-up assessments at 6 months or longer. In only 50% of treated couples do *both* partners show significant improvement in relationship satisfaction; moreover, in only 40% of treated couples does relationship satisfaction at termination approach the average level of satisfaction among community (nontherapy) couples (Lebow et al., 2012). Finally, long-term follow-up studies of couple therapy (4–5 years posttreatment) reveal that a substantial percentage of couples who initially showed improvement subsequently experience significant deterioration or become divorced (Snyder et al., 2006).

Table 1.1 contrasts initial treatment outcomes with 4–5-year posttreatment outcomes from two RCTs (each of which compared two approaches to couple therapy), as well as initial outcomes from a third RCT and 4-year outcomes from a noncontrolled study of generic (unspecified) couple therapy.

Perhaps not surprisingly, among initial outcomes across the three RCTs, somewhat poorer results were obtained for trials of TBCT, which did not incorporate more recent interventions examining cognitive components of couple processes nor those promoting emotional acceptance; TBCT also showed poorer outcomes, compared with alternative approaches, at 4–5 years posttreatment. The lowest rate of deterioration at 4 years following treatment was obtained for the insight-oriented approach developed by Snyder and

Table 1.1   Initial versus 4–5-year outcomes for couple treatment of relationship distress.

Treatment modality	Initial outcome: happily married	4–5 years post: distressed, divorced, or deteriorated
Traditional behavioral couple therapy[a]	66%	50% DM/DIV
Traditional behavioral couple therapy[b]	61%	39% DET/DIV
Integrative behavioral couple therapy[b]	70%	36% DET/DIV
Emotionally focused couple therapy[c]	73%	n/a
Insight-oriented couple therapy[a]	73%	20% DM/DIV
Generic couple therapy[d]	n/a	44% DIV

Note. DM = distressed married, DET = deteriorated, DIV = divorced, n/a = not available.
[a] Snyder et al. (1991a)
[b] Christensen, Atkins, Baucom, and Yi (2010)
[c] Johnson, Hunsley, Greenberg, and Schindler (1999)
[d] Cookerly (1980)

Wills (1989). They interpreted these findings as suggesting that insight-oriented techniques challenge latent affective components of relationship distress not adequately addressed by either traditional or newer cognitive-behavioral interventions; they further proposed that spouses' destructive attributions regarding their partner's role in marital conflicts are modified to a greater degree and in a more enduring manner once individuals come to understand and resolve emotional conflicts they bring to the marriage from their own family and relationship histories (Snyder, Wills, & Grady-Fletcher, 1991b).

Separate from approaches to couple therapy examined directly in RCTs, there are numerous other schools and theoretical approaches to couple therapy (Gurman, Lebow, & Snyder, 2015). Gurman (2015) divided these into two broad categories: those originating early in the history of the broader field of family therapy (e.g., structural, strategic, object relations, and Bowenian approaches) and those developed in the last few decades (e.g., narrative, solution-focused, and Gottman method approaches). Moreover, the field of couple therapy has witnessed various approaches to systematic integration across theoretically diverse orientations (e.g., integrative problem centered, functional analytic, and pluralistic)—consistent with Shadish and Baldwin's (2003) suggestion that clinicians should consider "meta-analytically supported" and eclectic approaches as viable options for treating couple distress. We return to the topic of tailoring treatment using integrative approaches later in this chapter.

The Effectiveness of Couple-Based Interventions for Mental and Physical Health Disorders

Given expanding evidence regarding the comorbidity of couple distress with a broad spectrum of mental and physical health disorders, the last two decades have witnessed a proliferation of couple-based interventions for coexisting emotional, behavioral, and physical health concerns (Snyder & Whisman, 2003), as well as mental and physical disorders that may occur independent of couple distress. Indeed, the existing research suggests that persons in distressed intimate relationships are not only more likely to have a mental or physical health problem, they are also less likely to respond to individual treatment for such a problem and have higher rates of subsequent relapse (Snyder & Whisman, 2004). Couple-based approaches for intervening with individual emotional or physical health problems can be conceptualized as following one of three basic strategies (Baucom, Shoham, Mueser, Daiuto, & Stickle, 1998). The first strategy uses general couple therapy to reduce overall relationship distress based on the premise that marital conflict serves as a broad stressor that contributes to the development, exacerbation, or maintenance of specific individual or relationship problems. The second strategy involves developing disorder-specific couple interventions that focus on particular partner interactions presumed to directly influence either the co-occurring problems or their treatment; for example, couple-based treatment for substance abuse includes targeting specific partner behaviors that inadvertently reinforce substance use patterns in their spouse or undermine efforts toward sobriety. The third couple-based strategy involves partner-assisted interventions in which one partner serves as a "surrogate therapist" or coach in assisting the other partner with individual problems; for example, in partner-assisted treatment of agoraphobia, the partner encourages their symptomatic spouse to complete homework assignments involving exposure to feared situations and engaging in alternatives to previous avoidance responses.

Although not exclusively so, the vast majority of couple-based interventions for mental and physical health disorders—especially those subjected to empirical study—have evolved primarily from the cognitive-behavioral tradition. Extended descriptions of these treatments exist elsewhere, and we draw extensively here on the excellent review by Fischer et al. (2016).

Couple-based interventions for psychopathology

Given their high comorbidity with couple distress, it is not surprising that extensive efforts have been directed toward developing couple-based interventions for depression, substance abuse, anxiety, and trauma-related disorders. Abundant evidence suggests that relationship distress and depression influence one another in a recursive and reciprocal fashion, and couple distress at the end of individual treatments for depression predicts future relapses (Whisman & Beach, 2015). Couple therapy for depression emphasizes eliminating major stressors in and outside the relationship, reestablishing positive couple activities, and promoting more effective communication strategies. Behaviorally oriented couple therapies have generally been found to be at least as effective as individual treatments for depression, but more effective in also treating concurrent relationship distress (Whisman & Beach, 2015).

Similar to findings for depression, there is considerable evidence regarding the comorbidity of couple distress and alcohol abuse (McCrady & Epstein, 2009). Couple-based interventions for alcohol abuse (and related treatments for other substance abuse disorders) target couple interactions to promote abstinence and sobriety by decreasing negative communication patterns (particularly around alcohol use behaviors) and increasing positive interactions between partners more generally (McCrady & Epstein, 2009). Behaviorally oriented couple therapy for alcohol and substance use disorders has consistently been at least as effective—and often more effective—as individual treatments, both in terms of substance-related outcomes and relationship well-being.

Couple-based interventions have also been developed for a variety of anxiety and trauma-related disorders including posttraumatic stress disorder (PTSD), agoraphobia, and obsessive–compulsive disorder (Baucom, Stanton, & Epstein, 2003; Johnson, 2005; Monson & Fredman, 2012). Although the specific components of interventions across these disorders vary, common elements include (a) having the asymptomatic partner encourage exposure to feared situations—typically by engaging in "exposure outings" together—and (b) having the asymptomatic partner suspend accommodation responses to the anxious partner that inadvertently reinforce or strengthen that partner's avoidance behaviors. Clinical trials of these treatments generally affirm favorable outcomes in terms of symptom reduction and improved relationship satisfaction, although RCTs comparing couple-based interventions with respective individual treatments are mostly lacking.

Couple-based interventions for physical health problems

Couple-based interventions for medical problems comprise the most recent and expanding area of couple therapy. The interventions vary widely—driven in part by the unique features of the physical condition—but share elements of treatments for general relationship distress (e.g., increasing emotional expressiveness and responsiveness), as well as couple treatments for psychopathology (e.g., promoting patient engagement in important but avoided activities; reducing accommodation and inadvertent reinforcement of countertherapeutic cognitions and behaviors).

Considerable research has garnered support for interventions for couples in whom one partner has cancer (Baucom, Porter, Kirby, & Hudepohl, 2012). Given the high distress that a cancer diagnosis typically creates for both patients and their partners, interventions emphasize coping skills (including partner support for symptom management) and enhanced social support (improved communication targeting both logistic challenges of the disease and emotional exchanges). Although much of the work on couple-based interventions in this area has focused on women with breast cancer, similar interventions have been developed for men with prostate cancer and patients with gastrointestinal cancer (Martire, Schulz, Helgeson, Small, & Saghafi, 2010).

Other medical conditions for which couple-based interventions have obtained preliminary support include arthritis and chronic pain, cardiovascular disease, anorexia nervosa, and type 2 diabetes (Baucom et al., 2012). Across conditions, interventions emphasize partner support and encouragement for the patient's engagement in the medical treatment protocol, improved communication, reduction of caregiver burden (in part by increasing emotional awareness of caregiver strain as well as reduction in misdirected accommodation behaviors), and increased attention to the disorder's adverse impact on the couple relationship. A broad spectrum of additional couple-based approaches have been proposed and clinical guidelines developed for other physical disorders, but these have not yet been subjected to controlled clinical trials—targeting, for example, couples for whom one partner evidences significant age-related cognitive decline (e.g., Alzheimer's disease; Qualls, 2003) or couples struggling with bereavement or complicated grief (Wills, 2003).

Moderators and Mediators of Treatment Effectiveness

Predicting outcomes to couple therapy for relationship distress

For whom does couple therapy work? Given the variability in individuals' responses to couple therapy, investigators have been interested in predicting outcomes to treatment. In evaluating predictors of treatment outcome, investigators have made a distinction between *prognostic indicators*, which predict response to a particular treatment (or response across treatments, irrespective of specific approach), and *prescriptive indicators*, which predict response to one versus another treatment.

Over the past several decades, a substantial body of research has identified general prognostic indicators of response to couple therapy including demographic, relationship, and individual characteristics (Snyder et al., 2006). Although findings regarding prognostic indicators of couple treatment response are mixed and the predictive utility of any single predictor appears modest, incremental prediction from multiple indicators pooled across predictor domains can be substantial. Several studies have found that younger couples respond more favorably to TBCT compared with older couples; one study (Crowe, 1978) found that less educated couples had a better response to TBCT than those with higher education. A prediction study collapsing across behavioral and insight-oriented treatment conditions (Snyder, Mangrum, & Wills, 1993) found that initial status of being unemployed or employed in a position of unskilled labor predicted poorer treatment outcome 4 years after termination. In a controlled trial of IBCT versus TBCT, couples who were married longer showed greater treatment gains, regardless of condition (Atkins et al., 2005).

Results from various studies indicate that couples having the greatest difficulties in their relationship are less likely to benefit from treatment; lack of commitment and steps toward divorce have been associated with poor treatment outcome to TBCT (Snyder et al., 2006). Snyder et al. (1993) found that poorer couple therapy outcomes were predicted by lower relationship quality, greater negative relationship affect and disengagement, and greater desired change in the relationship. In a study of EFT, Johnson and Talitman (1997) found that the best predictor of outcome was the wife's belief that her partner still cared for her. Greater interpersonal sensitivity and emotional expressiveness—as represented by measures of "femininity"—have also been found to predict better outcomes at termination and at long-term follow-up (Snyder et al., 1993).

In contrast to studies regarding general prognostic indicators of responses to couple therapy, research identifying prescriptive indicators of couple treatment response has been rare. An early study by O'Leary and Turkewitz (1981) suggested that younger couples responded better to behavioral interventions emphasizing behavior exchange skills, whereas older couples showed more favorable response to general communication skills training. More recent research comparing IBCT with TBCT suggests that severely distressed couples may respond more favorably to TBCT than to IBCT during the initial stages of treatment, although both treatments produce equivalent gains at outcome and findings suggest that IBCT produces more enduring gains at extended follow-up (Christensen et al., 2010).

Mechanisms of couple therapy for relationship distress

How does couple therapy work? Each of the empirically supported approaches to couple therapy posits particular mechanisms of change. These approaches can usefully be conceptualized as varying along a continuum anchored by a focus on behavior change (behavior exchange and skills-building interventions) on one end to interventions emphasizing intrapersonal dynamics and vulnerabilities on the other end. Specifically, a key focus of TBCT is on increasing specific positive behaviors and decreasing negative behaviors. CBCT adds a focus on changing cognitions such as negative attributions and expectancies. IBCT adds a focus on promoting tolerance and acceptance, with acceptance referring to a positive change in the way someone experiences what was previously viewed as a negative behavior by the partner. EFT focuses on decreasing hostile emotions and increasing expression of emotional vulnerability and attachment needs. Like EFT, insight-oriented couple therapy focuses on the individual vulnerabilities partners bring to the couple relationship and on providing insight into how developmental experiences shape such vulnerabilities and influence the couple relationship.

Snyder and Halford (2012) reviewed the evidence on mediators of couple therapy and drew four important conclusions. First, evidence-based couple therapies indeed modify their hypothesized mediators of therapeutic change. For example, TBCT does produce increases in positive behavior exchange and enhanced communication in distressed couples (e.g., Halford, Sanders, & Behrens, 1993). Similarly, IBCT produces increases in acceptance (Doss, Thum, Sevier, Atkins, & Christensen, 2005), and EFT makes the predicted shifts from hostile to affiliative in-session behaviors and increased disclosure of attachment needs (Makinen & Johnson, 2006).

Second, although evidence-based couple therapies do impact the relevant hypothesized mediators of change, there is not a simple relation between the type of therapy provided and the change in mediators. For example, TBCT with and without cognitive change strategies produces similar reductions in negative cognition and affect (Halford et al., 1993). TBCT also enhances couple acceptance, although not to the same extent as IBCT (Doss et al., 2005). Conversely, IBCT produces changes in the frequency of reported behavior, even though the focus is more on promoting acceptance of behaviors rather than on behavior change per se (Doss et al., 2005). The labels used to describe types of couple therapy might be potentially misleading by implying that specific interventions produce specific effects through specific mediating processes.

Third, there is not a straightforward relation between observed changes in hypothesized mediators and changes in couple relationship distress. Research has found little evidence of an association between changes in couple communication after TBCT and changes in relationship distress (Halford et al., 1993). Similarly, changes in cognitions do not predict couples' gains in satisfaction following CBCT. In the case of EFT, reductions in hostile to more affiliative expressions of emotion reliably predict subsequent in-session disclosure of vulnerability and attachment needs (Greenberg, Ford, Alden, & Johnson, 1993); however, the association of these in-session changes to improvement in couple relationship satisfaction after therapy has not been directly tested.

Finally, the mediators of couple therapy change might vary across the course of therapy. For example, in their study comparing TBCT and IBCT, Doss et al. (2005) reported that change in specific targeted behaviors was a powerful predictor of relationship satisfaction change in the early therapy sessions, whereas emotional acceptance was more strongly related to changes in relationship satisfaction in the sessions in the second half of therapy. Such findings point to the importance of selecting and sequencing specific interventions to optimize therapeutic impact.

Tailoring Couple Therapy to Individual and Relationship Characteristics: An Alternative Approach

The lack of differential effectiveness across couple treatment approaches, combined with suboptimal rates of improvement and deterioration after two or more years, has fostered two alternative lines of attack to treating couple distress: (a) distillation and emphasis on common factors or universal processes hypothesized to contribute to beneficial effects across "singular" or "pure" treatment approaches and (b) integrative models incorporating multiple components of diverse treatment approaches.

Distillation: The common factors approach

The common factors approach argues that shared mechanisms of change cutting across the diverse couple therapies account for the absence of significant differences in their overall effectiveness. Sprenkle and colleagues (Sprenkle & Blow, 2004; Sprenkle, Davis, & Lebow, 2009) have cited five types or classes of common factors characterizing psychotherapy in general and four specific to couple or family therapy. Common factors viewed as generic to psychotherapy include (a) client characteristics (e.g., learning style, perseverance, and compliance with instructions or assignments), (b) therapist characteristics (e.g., abilities to foster a therapeutic alliance and to match activity level to clients' expectations or preferences), (c) dimensions of the therapeutic relationship (e.g., emotional connectedness and congruence between the therapist's and client's specific expectations or goals), (d) expectancy or placebo effects, and (e) nonspecific interventions promoting emotional experiencing, cognitive mastery, and behavioral regulation. Those common factors viewed as specific to couple or family therapies include (a) conceptualizing difficulties in relational terms, (b) disrupting dysfunctional relational patterns, (c) inclusion of multiple members of the extended family system in direct treatment, and (d) fostering an expanded therapeutic alliance across partners or multiple members of the family as a whole.

Christensen (2010) advocated a unified protocol for couple therapy based on an alternative formulation of five central principles of therapeutic interaction, based on evidence-based couple therapies. These principles include (a) altering the couple's view of the presenting problem to be more objective, contextualized, and dyadic; (b) decreasing emotion-driven, dysfunctional behavior; (c) eliciting emotion-based, avoided, private behavior; (d) increasing constructive communication patterns; and (e) promoting strengths and reinforcing gains. Implementing this unified protocol successfully requires a coherent case conceptualization through functional analysis of the couple's interactional pattern.

In their expanded treatise on common factors, Sprenkle et al. (2009) distinguished among contrasting views of common factors—that is, viewing these as important but not exclusive mechanisms contributing to the effectiveness of various therapeutic approaches versus a more radical view of common factors as entirely responsible for treatment effects and specific treatment approaches as irrelevant to outcome. Davis and Piercy (2007) proposed that consideration of common factors should supplement, not supplant, providers' thorough grasp of diverse models underlying couple therapy. As an alternative to common *factors* in couple therapy, Sexton, Ridley, and Kleiner (2004) proposed common *mechanisms* of change to include (a) redefinition of the presenting problem, (b) impasse resolution, (c) therapeutic alliance, (d) reduction of within-session negativity, (e) improved interactional and behavioral competency, and (f) treatment adherence to the specific model being practiced. To date, however, there has been little research documenting specific treatment effects attributable to proposed common factors, common mechanisms, or central principles—nor systematic efforts in designing couple treatment approaches intended to maximize their therapeutic impact.

Among client characteristics potentially contributing to similar outcomes across treatment approaches, there has been increasing emphasis on the role of emotion regulation in health and dysfunction (Snyder, Simpson, & Hughes, 2006). Deficits in emotion regulation may lead to either the overcontrol or undercontrol of affect, with the latter typically receiving the greater attention in the clinical literature. One widely recognized model of emotion regulation (Gross, 2001) distinguishes between antecedent-focused emotion regulation strategies (e.g., situation selection and modification, attentional deployment, and stimulus interpretation) and response-focused strategies promoting either increases or reductions in experiential, physiological, and behavioral emotion response tendencies. A common factors perspective suggests that diverse couple-based treatments may yield similar outcomes to the extent that different specific techniques within each approach therapeutically impact relevant emotion regulation processes.

An alternative to distillation: Integrative approaches to couple therapy

Couple therapists confront a tremendous diversity of presenting issues, marital and family structures, individual dynamics and psychopathology, and psychosocial stressors characterizing couples in distress. Because the functional sources of couples' distress vary so dramatically, the critical mediators or mechanisms of change should also be expected to vary—as should the therapeutic strategies intended to facilitate positive change. Even within the more restricted domain of individual interventions, growing recognition of unique strengths and limitations of competing theoretical approaches has fueled a burgeoning movement toward psychotherapy integration (Norcross, 2005). For example, advocates of various integrative models of psychotherapy have emphasized the strengths of psychodynamic approaches for identifying enduring problematic interpersonal themes, the benefits of experiential techniques for promoting emotional awareness, gains from cognitive interventions targeting dysfunctional beliefs and attributional processes, and advantages of behavioral strategies for promoting new patterns of behavior (Bongar & Beutler, 1995).

Integrative approaches strive to reduce the risk of haphazard, disjointed, or contradictory interventions resulting from an eclectic borrowing of diverse principles or techniques without regard for their potential inconsistency or adverse interaction. That is, integrative approaches emphasize the importance of theories and principles that guide the selection of specific interventions with a given client at a given moment. There are numerous approaches to integration that vary in their emphasis on technique versus theory and their goal of assimilating existing techniques or theoretical constructs into an existing predominant theoretical or conceptual frame-work versus generating a new incorporative theoretical approach (Nielsen, 2017). Previously, we have contrasted three of these approaches to integration—assimila-tive, transtheoretical, and pluralistic (Snyder & Balderrama-Durbin, 2012). We focus here on the pluralistic approach proposed by Snyder (Snyder, 1999; Snyder & Mitchell, 2008).

Pluralism recognizes the validity of multiple systems of epistemology, theory, and practice and draws on these as intact units (as distinct from eclecticism), although not necessarily concurrently or from a transtheoretical perspective. Pluralism is simi-lar to constructs of "empirical pragmatism," "systematic treatment selection," and "prescriptive eclecticism" characterized "… by drawing on effective methods from across theoretical camps (eclecticism), by matching those methods to particular cases on the basis of psychological science and clinical wisdom (prescriptionism), and by adhering to an explicit and orderly model of treatment selection …" (Norcross & Beutler, 2000, p. 248). Because a pluralistic approach is less con-strained than theoretically integrative approaches forced to reconcile competing constructs, it potentially offers greater opportunity to accommodate diverse theo-retical perspectives.

Snyder (1999) advocated a pluralistic approach to couple therapy conceptualizing therapeutic tasks as progressing sequentially along a hierarchy comprising six levels of intervention from the most fundamental interventions promoting a collaborative alli-ance to more challenging interventions addressing developmental sources of relation-ship distress. Because couple therapy often proceeds in nonlinear fashion, the model requires flexibility of returning to earlier therapeutic tasks as dictated by individual or relationship difficulties.

As articulated in Table 1.2, the most fundamental step in couple therapy involves developing a collaborative alliance between partners and between each partner and the therapist by establishing an atmosphere of therapist competence as well as ther-apeutic safety around issues of confidentiality and verbal or physical aggression. Subsequent interventions may need to target disabling relationship crises such as substance use, psychopathology, illness or death of a family member, or similar concerns that, until resolved, preclude development of new relationship skills and progress toward emotional intimacy. Because some couples initially present with overwhelming negativity, the therapist may need to instigate behavior change directly before assisting the couple to develop behavior exchange and communica-tion skills of their own. Along with promoting general relationship skills, the cou-ple therapist may need to assist partners in acquiring a prerequisite knowledge base and competence in specific domains such as sexuality, parenting, finances, or time management.

A common impediment to behavior change involves misconceptions and other interpretive errors that individuals may have regarding their own and their partner's behavior; interventions targeting partners' relationship beliefs, expectancies, and attributions aim to eliminate or restructure cognitive processes interfering with behav-ior change efforts. However, not all psychological processes relevant to couples' inter-actions lend themselves to traditional cognitive interventions. Of particular importance

Table 1.2 Intervention levels and sample indicators for a hierarchical pluralistic approach.

Level	Description	Sample indicators
6	Examine development sources of relationship distress	Promoting understanding of enduring maladaptive relationship patterns Promoting empathic joining and reduced reactivity to covert sources of each partner's interpersonal anxieties
5	Challenge cognitive components of relationship distress	Addressing issues of selective attention, attribution biases, and expectancies
4	Promote relevant relationship skills	Promoting communication skills: decision making; emotional expression and responsiveness Developing requisite skills in specific domains such as sexuality, parenting, and finances
3	Strengthen the couple dyad	Promoting healthy boundaries relative to children, extended family, work, and community Facilitating positive behavior exchanges, negotiating individual and collaborative agreements
2	Contain disabling crises	Preventing aggression against self and others Containing external stressors and facilitating intermediate solutions Addressing major psychopathology Mobilizing appropriate external resources
1	Establish collaborative alliance	Establishing trust in therapist's competence and fairness Clarifying ground rules regarding confidentiality and structure of sessions Setting limits on negative exchanges in sessions

Note. Snyder and Balderrama-Durbin (2012, p. 16). Reproduced with Elsevier.

are partners' developmental relationship experiences, resulting in enduring interpersonal vulnerabilities and related defensive strategies interfering with emotional intimacy, many of which operate beyond partners' conscious awareness. Hence, when couple distress persists despite system-restructuring, skills-building, and cognitive interventions, then interpretation of maladaptive relationship patterns evolving from developmental processes comprises an essential treatment component (Snyder & Mitchell, 2008).

This pluralistic approach not only presumes that couples will vary in the extent to which they require interventions at any level of the treatment hierarchy but also presumes that higher-order interventions (e.g., cognitive or insight-oriented techniques targeting intrapersonal processes) would ordinarily not be implemented unless lower-order interventions (e.g., crisis intervention, relationship strengthening, or skills-building techniques targeting interpersonal processes) had already proven insufficient. This model also posits that higher-order interventions, even if necessary, would not be pursued until a foundation of increased positivity and reduced negativity had already been firmly established. Indeed, this general sequence is consistent with findings from

Christensen and colleagues' (Doss et al., 2005) comparisons of traditional and integrative behavior couple therapy demonstrating that changes in targeted behaviors were a powerful mechanism of change early in therapy, whereas interventions targeting emotional acceptance were more strongly related to changes in relationship satisfaction later in therapy (Doss et al., 2005).

Treatment implications of integrative approaches to couple therapy

Tailoring therapeutic interventions to characteristics of individual partners, their relationship, and extended psychosocial system differs from a priori treatment matching paradigms in which clients are assigned to predesigned treatment modalities based on initial assessment findings. Instead, in an informed pluralistic approach, "matching" proceeds on a continuous basis throughout therapy, based not only on client and extended relationship characteristics but also on emergent features of the therapeutic process—including fluctuations in the therapeutic alliance, unanticipated disruptions by external stressors, or interactions of evolving skill sets with enduring belief systems or covert interpersonal anxieties. For example, at any given time in the couple therapy, the collaborative alliance between partners and therapist may be strained by misunderstanding of the partners' or therapist's roles—requiring clarification to restore trust in the therapist's fairness and commitment to "the relationship as the client." While teaching specific relationship skills to transfer responsibility for ongoing relationship interventions over to partners, unanticipated or emergent crises may require reversion to an earlier level of intervention to facilitate intermediate solutions or mobilize external resources. Although the predominant mode or level of intervention for a given session or phase of treatment may be planned ahead of time based on an overall case formulation, specific interventions within session are matched to both therapist and client characteristics *in the moment*. Doing so effectively requires keen attention to aspects of the therapeutic process, continuous awareness of both overt and covert aspects of partners' ongoing responses, and familiarity with a broad range of specific interventions and the theoretical underpinnings that guide their selection and implementation.

From this perspective, systematic monitoring and feedback of couple therapy progress could enhance therapy outcome by optimizing continual tailoring of interventions across, if not within, sessions (Anker, Duncan, & Sparks, 2009; Halford et al., 2012). For example, recognizing couples' heightened reactivity during initial phases of exploring developmental origins of maladaptive relationship patterns or reversion to increased frequency of disruptive negative exchanges between sessions after prior mastery of communication skills may dictate renegotiation of positive behavior exchanges and either individual or collaborative agreements by the therapist.

Enduring Challenges for the Field of Couple Therapy

We conclude by proposing a selective but ambitious agenda for the field of couple therapy in the coming decades. Enduring challenges include those related to clinical training and practice, the conduct of clinically impactful research, and the dissemination of effective interventions across expanding and increasingly diverse groups.

Challenges for clinical training and practice

Challenge 1: Effective treatment of individuals and couples requires comprehensive assessment of intrapersonal and interpersonal functioning throughout affective, behavioral, and cognitive domains across multiple levels of the family and socio-ecological system. Couples presenting with primary complaints of relationship difficulties often fail to recognize, understand, or acknowledge the role of individual problems in their interpersonal distress. Similarly, individuals seeking treatment for their own emotional or physical health problems may neglect or minimize the interaction of these concerns with interpersonal functioning in their intimate or broader social relationships. Hence, practitioners need to assess systematically their clients' emotional, behavioral, and health functioning and the functioning of their intimate partners across a broad spectrum of individual and system domains (Balderrama-Durbin, Snyder, Heyman, & Haynes, 2020, vol. 3). Training programs need to ensure that aspiring couple and family therapists achieve at least a minimum level of proficiency in assessing and recognizing recursive interactions between individual and relationship functioning—and that they be schooled in psychopathology and principles of individual assessment and treatment, including familiarity with biological interventions for relationship difficulties rooted at least in part in physical or mental illness of one or both partners.

Challenge 2: Differences in urgency of individual and relationship issues and their progression during therapy require an organizational conceptual framework for selecting, sequencing, and pacing interventions; effective treatment may require therapists to conceptualize and practice in an integrative manner across diverse theoretical orientations. For assessment to influence treatment, individual differences in intrapersonal and interpersonal functioning need to be linked to alternative models and modalities of intervention. For some couples, the clinical challenge will not be which specific treatment to select but, rather, how to adapt existing treatments to individual characteristics of partners and their broader context. Training programs need to focus explicitly on instructing developing therapists in the principles and strategies of integrative practice—ensuring a technical understanding of specific therapeutic techniques, the theoretical context in which these evolved, and their demonstrated efficacy for particular problems in specific populations (e.g., Gurman et al., 2015; Norcross, 2005). Well-trained clinicians require explicit and internally consistent theories of integrative practice. At a minimum, such theories need to specify relevant domains of experience, parameters of functional and dysfunctional behavior, intermediate and long-term treatment objectives, and multiple processes of change at both the intrapersonal and interpersonal or systemic levels.

Challenges for clinical research

Challenge 3: Studies of treatment outcome need to be complemented by research on treatment processes, particularly as these relate to couples confronting multiple challenges across individual, interpersonal, and broader systemic domains. Research on couple therapy process should begin with efforts to articulate both common factors in couple-based interventions and specific components that distinguish one approach from another. To the extent that diverse treatment approaches share common attributes, this may facilitate shifting from one therapeutic modality to another to capture unique techniques and benefits specific to that approach. Because some techniques may require a set of interventions linked together in a specific constellation or sequence to be effective, research on articulating therapeutic components should identify the smallest unit of intervention that can be transported across approaches while retaining its efficacy.

Research on variations in treatment process across individual and relationship factors should be integrated with studies of how specific intervention components and their variations are linked to within- and between-session responses of each of the participants. That is, process research interfaces with outcome research by emphasizing more immediate, proximal effects of therapist interventions on partners' behavior and partners' effects on the therapist and each other. Research on such therapeutic event-related processes also needs to attend to changes in these linkages across the course of treatment. For example, the effects of interpreting developmental components of interpersonal distress may be very different if conducted early in therapy than later in treatment once collaborative alliances and constructive communication skills are more firmly established. Exemplars of such process-oriented research include growth curve analyses of change in the RCT of IBCT (Doss et al., 2005) and task analyses of critical change events in EFT (Meneses & Greenberg, 2011).

Challenge 4: Both basic and applied research needs to examine cultural variations in couple relationship structures, partner expectations and roles, and patterns of emotional and behavior exchange—not only between partners but also between the couple and other members of the family and broader community—and the implications of these variations for the development and dissemination of effective couple-based interventions. The nature of couple relationships varies tremendously across culture—and assumptions rooted primarily in research based on Western European or North American populations may have limited generalizability to other groups. Both explicit and implicit definitions of marriage vary across cultures and within a culture at any given time. Individuals may "marry" (or partner) for any number of reasons—including legal, social, emotional, sexual, religious, financial, procreational, or other purposes. Culture defines which partner structures are sanctioned (e.g., heterosexual, gay/lesbian, polygamous), respective partner rights and responsibilities, expectations regarding children and family structure, involvement with the extended family, injunctions against divorce, views toward privacy, access to mental health or related services, and so forth (Halford & van de Vijver, in press). Until such cultural differences are more fully recognized, and their implications for the content and delivery of couple-based interventions fully explicated, the field of couple therapy will fail to achieve global relevance and impact.

Challenges for effective delivery and dissemination

Challenge 5: Effective delivery of couple-based interventions requires that clinicians be sensitive to cultural differences and competent to adapt interventions tailored to these differences. In asserting this maxim, we clarify two points. First, we view "culture" broadly—defined not only by national, ethnic, or religious variations—but more generally to include such constructs as the cultures of poverty or affluence, the military or corporate cultures, the cultures of aging and sexual orientation, and so on. Second, we distinguish between cultural "sensitivity" versus "competence."

All clinicians should strive toward cultural sensitivity—recognizing the limits of their own experiences and biases and honoring individual and relational differences in cognitions and behaviors unfamiliar to them but well within the range of adaptive or healthy functioning—and actively expand their knowledge and clinical skill sets when engaging with clients outside their own limited background. Whereas sensitivity should be a goal attainable by all, universal competence is not. Although clinicians should strive to expand their competence to deliver effective interventions with diverse clients, it is not reasonable to expect or even to strive for cultural competence with all clients. Cultural sensitivity is essential but not sufficient for cultural competence. Indeed, essential components of cultural competence include recognizing the boundaries of one's own efficacy with different subgroups, acquiring additional resources (potentially including referral to an alternative provider) as warranted, informing clients of one's own limitations, and explicitly inviting them to facilitate greater understanding of cultural differences relevant to co-creating effective interventions.

Challenge 6: Effective dissemination of couple-based interventions requires expanding the range of potential providers, developing intermediate levels of intervention, and incorporating new technologies for delivery. Increasing the range of potential providers of couple therapy and related interventions can be achieved in several ways. One involves systematic efforts to train providers from outside the mental health professions, similar to the earliest years of the field when marriage counseling was provided by clergy, family life educators, and physicians. For example, Snyder and colleagues (Snyder, Gasbarrini, Doss, & Scheider, 2011) described positive outcomes from 1- and 2-day trainings of US Army family chaplains in a structured intervention for military couples struggling with issues of sexual infidelity—incorporating a detailed treatment manual, didactic presentation, and video-recorded exemplars of clinical interventions. An alternative method for extending the range of providers of couple therapy involves systematic training of mental health professionals delivering primarily individual therapies in evidence-based couple interventions for specific disorders. For example, Baucom and colleagues (2017) described strategies and positive outcomes for a national program to disseminate CBCT for depression to individual therapists throughout Great Britain, supported by that country's National Institute for Health and Care Excellence.

A second means for enhancing dissemination involves developing intermediate-level interventions emphasizing secondary prevention to couples exhibiting early indicators of relationship distress or otherwise identified as being at risk for developing distress. For example, Snyder and colleagues (2016) described the development and initial dissemination of a multitiered "stepped" approach for promoting relationship resiliency in US Air Force couples. At the lowest level of intervention, awareness of intimate relationship challenges for active military was promoted by informing personnel at multiple existing base service and support units (e.g., Airman and Family Readiness centers, primary and mental healthcare facilities, offices of chaplains and family life consultants) of common challenges facing military couples and providing trifold educational "action sheets" for prominent display and dissemination to potential consumers. At intermediate levels of intervention, the program encouraged brief "conversations" with frontline supervisors or other individuals within the military unit who had already been identified as "natural helpers" and trained specifically to disseminate basic relationship skills at a low intensity. Finally, at higher levels of prevention, family life consultants or clinical staff offered brief seminars or workshops for couples on selected topics (e.g., coping with deployment) that encouraged partner interactions and explicit action strategies. Alternatively, an intermediate-level couple intervention may be delivered within the framework of a typical medical appointment using a program such as the Marriage Checkup developed by Córdova and colleagues (2017).

Finally, effective dissemination of couple-based interventions may increasingly rely on current and emerging technologies such as web-based and smartphone applications. For example, Doss and colleagues (2016) reported outcomes from an RCT of an 8-hour online program for enhancing couple relationships. In a nationally representative sample of couples, the program was effective in significantly improving both relationship functioning (increased satisfaction and confidence and decreased negativity) and individual functioning (decreases in depression and anxiety and increases in perceived health, work functioning, and quality of life).

Conclusion

As we move toward the first-quarter mark of the twenty-first century, we can expect the demand for couple therapy and related couple-based interventions to continue to grow across diverse disorders, populations, and settings. The field will best respond to these expanding needs by training both current clinicians and the next generation of couple therapists to recognize individual differences in couple processes within a broad cultural context, to select and sequence specific interventions tailored to unique characteristics of partners and their relationships, and to pursue new opportunities for disseminating both prevention and intervention protocols to underserved groups.

References

Anker, M. G., Duncan, B. L., & Sparks, J. A. (2009). Using client feedback to improve couple therapy outcomes: A randomized clinical trial in a naturalistic setting. *Journal of Consulting and Clinical Psychology, 77*, 693–704. doi:10.1037/a0016062

Atkins, D. C., Berns, S. B., George, W. H., Doss, B. D., Gattis, K., & Christensen, A. (2005). Prediction of response to treatment in a randomized clinical trial of marital therapy. *Journal of Consulting and Clinical Psychology, 73*, 893–903. doi:10.1037/0022-006X.73.5.893

Balderrama-Durbin, C. M., Snyder, D. K., Heyman, R. E., & Haynes, S. N. (2020). Systemic and culturally-sensitive assessment of couple distress. In K. S. Wampler & A. J. Blow (Eds.), *The handbook of systemic family therapy: Systemic family therapy with couples (3)*. Hoboken, NJ: Wiley.

Baucom, D. H., Fischer, M. S., Worrell, M., Corrie, S., Belus, J. M., Molyva, E., & Boeding, S. E. (2017). Couple-based intervention for depression: An effectiveness study in the National Health Service in England. *Family Process, 57*, 275–292. doi:10.1111/famp.12332

Baucom, D. H., Porter, L. S., Kirby, J. S., & Hudepohl, J. (2012). Couple-based interventions for medical problems. *Behavior Therapy, 43*, 61–76. doi:10.1016/j.beth.2011.01.008

Baucom, D. H., Shoham, V., Mueser, K. T., Daiuto, A. D., & Stickle, T. R. (1998). Empirically supported couple and family interventions for marital distress and adult mental health problems. *Journal of Consulting and Clinical Psychology, 66*, 53–88. doi:10.1037/0022-006X.66.1.53

Baucom, D. H., Snyder, D. K., & Gordon, K. C. (2009). *Helping couples get past the affair: A clinician's guide.* New York, NY: Guilford.

Baucom, D. H., Stanton, S., & Epstein, N. B. (2003). Anxiety disorders. In D. K. Snyder & M. A. Whisman (Eds.), *Treating difficult couples: Helping clients with coexisting mental and relationship disorders* (pp. 57–87). New York, NY: Guilford.

Bernet, W., Wamboldt, M. Z., & Narrow, W. E. (2016). Child affected by parental relationship distress. *Journal of the American Academy of Child and Adolescent Psychiatry, 55,* 571–579. doi:10.1016/j.jaac.2016.04.018

Bongar, B., & Beutler, L. E. (1995). *Comprehensive textbook of psychotherapy: Theory and practice.* New York, NY: Oxford University Press.

Christensen, A. (2010). A unified protocol for couple therapy. In K. Hahlweg, M. Grawe-Gerber, & D. H. Baucom (Eds.), *Enhancing couples: The shape of couple therapy to come* (pp. 33–46). Göttingen, Germany: Hogrefe Publishing.

Christensen, A., Atkins, D. C., Baucom, B., & Yi, J. (2010). Marital status and satisfaction five years following a randomized clinical trial comparing traditional versus integrative behavioral couple therapy. *Journal of Consulting and Clinical Psychology, 78,* 225–235. doi:10.1037/a0018132

Cookerly, J. R. (1980). Does marital therapy do any lasting good? *Journal of Marital and Family Therapy, 6,* 393–397. doi:10.1111/j.1752-0606.1980.tb01331.x

Córdova, J., Cigrang, J., Gray, T., Najera, E., Havrilenko, M., Pinkley, C., … Redd, K. (2017). Addressing relationship health needs in primary care: Adapting the marriage checkup for use in medical settings with military couples. *Journal of Clinical Psychology in Medical Settings, 24,* 259–269. doi:10.1007/s10880-017-9517-8

Crowe, M. J. (1978). Conjoint marital therapy: A controlled outcome study. *Psychological Medicine, 8,* 623–636. doi:10.1017/S0033291700018833

Cummings, E. M., & Davies, P. T. (2010). *Marital conflict and children: An emotional security perspective.* New York, NY: Guilford.

Davis, S. D., & Piercy, F. P. (2007). What clients of couple therapy model developers and their former students say about change. Part II: Model-independent common factors and an integrative framework. *Journal of Marital and Family Therapy, 33,* 344–363. doi:10.1111/j.1752-0606.2007.00031.x

Doss, B. D., Cicila, L. N., Georgia, E. J., Roddy, M. K., Nowlan, K. M., Benson, L. A., & Christensen, A. (2016). A randomized controlled trial of the web-based Our Relationship program: Effects on relationship and individual functioning. *Journal of Consulting and Clinical Psychology, 84,* 285–296. doi:10.1037/ccp0000063

Doss, B. D., Thum, Y. M., Sevier, M., Atkins, D. C., & Christensen, A. (2005). Improving relationships: Mechanisms of change in couple therapy. *Journal of Consulting and Clinical Psychology, 73,* 624–633. doi:10.1037/0022-006X.73.4.624

Epstein, N., & Baucom, D. H. (2002). *Enhanced cognitive-behavioral therapy for couples: A contextual approach.* Washington, DC: American Psychological Association.

Epstein, N. B., Werlinich, C. A., & LaTaillade, J. J. (2015). Couple therapy for partner aggression. In A. S. Gurman, J. L. Lebow, & D. K. Snyder (Eds.), *Clinical handbook of couple therapy* (5th ed., pp. 389–411). New York, NY: Guilford.

Fischer, M. S., Baucom, D. H., & Cohen, M. J. (2016). Cognitive-behavioral couple therapies: Review of the evidence for the treatment of relationship distress, psychopathology, and chronic health conditions. *Family Process, 55,* 423–442. doi:10.1111/famp.12227

Fleeson, W. (2004). The quality of American life at the end of the century. In O. G. Brim, C. D. Ryff, & R. C. Kessler (Eds.), *How healthy are we: A national study of well-being at midlife* (pp. 252–272). Chicago, IL: University of Chicago Press.

Goldman, A., & Greenberg, L. (1992). Comparison of integrated systemic and emotionally focused approaches to couples therapy. *Journal of Consulting and Clinical Psychology, 60,* 962–969. doi:10.1037/0022-006X.60.6.962

Greenberg, L. S., Ford, C. L., Alden, L. S., & Johnson, S. M. (1993). In-session change in emotionally focused therapy. *Journal of Consulting and Clinical Psychology, 61*, 78–84. doi:10.1037/0022-006X.61.1.78

Gross, J. J. (2001). Emotion regulation in adulthood: Timing is everything. *Current Directions in Psychological Science, 10*, 214–219. doi:10.1111/1467-8721.00152

Gurman, A. S. (2015). The theory and practice of couple therapy: History, contemporary models, and a framework for comparative analysis. In A. S. Gurman, J. L. Lebow, & D. K. Snyder (Eds.), *Clinical handbook of couple therapy* (pp. 1–18). New York, NY: Guilford.

Gurman, A. S., Lebow, J. L., & Snyder, D. K. (2015). *Clinical handbook of couple therapy* (5th ed.). New York, NY: Guilford.

Gurman, A. S., & Snyder, D. K. (2011). Couple therapy. In J. C. Norcross, G. R. VandenBos, & D. K. Freedheim (Eds.), *History of psychotherapy: Continuity and change* (2nd ed., pp. 485–496). Washington, DC: American Psychological Association.

Halford, W. K., Hayes, S., Christensen, A., Lambert, M., Baucom, D. H., & Atkins, D. (2012). Toward making progress feedback an effective common factor in couple therapy. *Behavior Therapy, 43*, 49–60. doi:10.1016/j.beth.2011.03.005

Halford, W. K., Sanders, M. R., & Behrens, B. C. (1993). A comparison of the generalization of behavioral marital therapy and enhanced behavioral marital therapy. *Journal of Consulting and Clinical Psychology, 61*, 51–60. doi:10.1037/0022-006X.61.1.51

Halford, W. K., & van de Vijver, F. J. R. (Eds.) (in press). *Cross-cultural family research and practice*. New York, NY: Elsevier.

Hayes, A., Weston, R., Lixia, Q., & Gray, M. (2010). *Families then and now 1980–2010*. Melbourne, Australia: Australian Institute of Family Studies.

Hetherington, E. M., Bridges, M., & Insabella, G. M. (1998). What matters? What does not? Five perspectives on the association between marital transitions and children's adjustment. *American Psychologist, 53*, 167–184. doi:10.1037/0003-066X.53.2.167

Jacobson, N. S., & Christensen, A. (1996). *Integrative couple therapy: Promoting acceptance and change*. New York, NY: Norton.

Jacobson, N. S., & Margolin, G. (1979). *Marital therapy: Strategies based on social learning and behavior exchange principles*. New York, NY: Brunner/Mazel.

Johnson, S. M. (2004). *The practice of emotionally focused couple therapy* (2nd ed.). New York, NY: Brunner-Routledge.

Johnson, S. M. (2005). *Emotionally focused couple therapy with trauma survivors: Strengthening attachment bonds*. New York, NY: Guilford.

Johnson, S. M., Hunsley, J., Greenberg, L., & Schindler, D. (1999). Emotionally focused couples therapy: Status and challenges. *Clinical Psychology: Science and Practice, 6*, 67–79. doi:10.1093/clipsy/6.1.67

Johnson, S. M., & Talitman, E. (1997). Predictors of success in emotionally focused marital therapy. *Journal of Marital and Family Therapy, 23*, 135–152. doi:10.1111/j.1752-0606.1997.tb00239.x

Kreider, R. M., & Ellis, R. (2011). *Number, timing, and duration of marriages and divorces: 2009* (Current population reports no. P70–125). Washington, DC: US Census Bureau.

Krishnakumar, A., & Buehler, C. (2000). Interparental conflict and parenting behaviors: A meta-analytic review. *Family Relations, 49*, 25–44. doi:10.1111/j.1741-3729.2000.00025.x

Lebow, J. L., Chambers, A. L., Christensen, A., & Johnson, S. M. (2012). Research on the treatment of couple distress. *Journal of Marital and Family Therapy, 38*, 145–168. doi:10.1111/j.1752-0606.2011.00249.x

Lin, E., Goering, P., Offord, D. R., Campbell, D., & Boyle, M. H. (1996). The use of mental health services in Ontario: Epidemiologic findings. *Canadian Journal of Psychiatry, 41*, 572–577. doi:10.1177/070674379604100905

Makinen, J. A., & Johnson, S. M. (2006). Resolving attachment injuries in couples using emotionally focused therapy: Steps toward forgiveness and reconciliation. *Journal of Consulting and Clinical Psychology, 74*, 1055–1064. doi:10.1037/0022-006X.74.6.1055

Martire, L. M., Schulz, R., Helgeson, V. S., Small, B. J., & Saghafi, E. M. (2010). Review and meta-analysis of couple-oriented interventions for chronic illness. *Annals of Behavioral Medicine, 40*, 325–342. doi:10.1007/s12160-010-9216-2

McCarthy, B. W., & Thestrup, M. (2008). Couple therapy and the treatment of sexual dysfunction. In A. S. Gurman (Ed.), *Clinical handbook of couple therapy* (4th ed., pp. 591–617). New York, NY: Guilford.

McCrady, B. S., & Epstein, E. E. (2009). *Overcoming alcohol problems: A couples-focused program.* New York, NY: Oxford University Press.

McShall, J. R., & Johnson, M. D. (2015). The association between relationship distress and psychopathology is consistent across racial and ethnic groups. *Journal of Abnormal Psychology, 124*, 226–231. doi:10.1037/a0038267

Meneses, C. W., & Greenberg, L. S. (2011). The construction of a model of the process of couples' forgiveness in emotion-focused therapy for couples. *Journal of Marital and Family Therapy, 37*, 491–502. doi:10.1111/j.1752-0606.2011.00234.x

Meyer, I. (2003). Prejudice, social stress, and mental health in lesbian, gay, and bisexual populations: Conceptual issues and research evidence. *Psychological Bulletin, 129*, 674–697. doi:10.1037/0033-2909.129.5.674

Monson, C. M., & Fredman, S. J. (2012). *Cognitive-behavioral conjoint therapy for PTSD: Harnessing the healing power of relationships.* New York, NY: Guilford.

Nielsen, A. C. (2017). From couple therapy 1.0 to a comprehensive model: A roadmap for sequencing and integrating systemic, psychodynamic, and behavioral approaches to couple therapy. *Family Process, 56*, 540–557. doi:10.1111/famp.12300

Norcross, J. C. (2005). A primer on psychotherapy integration. In J. C. Norcross & M. R. Goldfried (Eds.), *Handbook of psychotherapy integration* (2nd ed., pp. 3–23). New York, NY: Oxford University Press.

Norcross, J. C., & Beutler, L. E. (2000). A prescriptive eclectic approach to psychotherapy training. *Journal of Psychotherapy Integration, 10*, 247–261. doi:10.1023/A:1009444912173

Norcross, J. C., Pfund, R. A., & Prochaska, J. O. (2013). Psychotherapy in 2022: A Delphi poll on its future. *Professional Psychology: Research and Practice, 44*, 363–370. doi:10.1037/a0034633

O'Leary, K. D., & Turkewitz, H. (1981). A comparative outcome study of behavioral marital therapy and communication therapy. *Journal of Marital and Family Therapy, 7*, 159–169. doi:10.1111/j.1752-0606.1981.tb01366.x

Organization of Economic Cooperation and Development. (2011). *Marriage and divorce rates.* Retrieved from http://www.oecd.org/els/family/SF_3_1_Marriage_and_divorce_rates.pdf

Orlinksky, D. E., & Ronnestad, M. H. (2005). *How psychotherapists develop: A study of therapeutic work and professional growth.* Washington, DC: American Psychological Association.

Prigerson, H. G., Maciejewski, P. K., & Rosenheck, R. A. (2000). Preliminary explorations of the harmful interactive effects of widowhood and marital harmony on health, health service use, and health care costs. *The Gerontologist, 40*, 349–357. doi:10.1093/geront/40.3.349

Qualls, S. H. (2003). Aging and cognitive impairment. In D. K. Snyder & M. A. Whisman (Eds.), *Treating difficult couples: Helping clients with coexisting mental and relationship disorders* (pp. 370–391). New York, NY: Guilford.

Raley, R. K., Sweeney, M. M., & Wondra, D. (2015). The growing racial and ethnic divide in U.S. marriage patterns. *The Future of Children, 25*, 89–109. doi:10.1353/foc.2015.0014

Robles, T. F., Slatcher, R. B., Trombello, J. M., & McGinn, M. M. (2014). Marital quality and health: A meta-analytic review. *Psychological Bulletin, 140*, 140–187. doi:10.1037/a0031859

Sexton, T. L., Ridley, C. R., & Kleiner, A. J. (2004). Beyond common factors: Multilevel-process models of therapeutic change in marriage and family therapy. *Journal of Marital and Family Therapy, 30*, 131–149. doi:10.1111/j.1752-0606.2004.tb01229.x

Shadish, W. R., & Baldwin, S. A. (2003). Meta-analysis of MFT interventions. *Journal of Marital and Family Therapy, 29*, 547–570. doi:10.1111/j.1752-0606.2003.tb01694.x

Shumway, S. T., Wampler, R. S., Dersch, C., & Arredondo, R. (2004). A place for marriage and family services in employee assistance programs (EAPs): A survey of EAP client problems and needs. *Journal of Marital and Family Therapy, 30*, 71–79. doi:10.1111/j.1752-0606.2004.tb01223.x

Snyder, D. K. (1999). Affective reconstruction in the context of a pluralistic approach to couple therapy. *Clinical Psychology: Science and Practice, 6*, 348–365. doi:10.1093/clipsy/6.4.348

Snyder, D. K., & Balderrama-Durbin, C. (2012). Integrative approaches to couple therapy: Implications for clinical practice and research. *Behavior Therapy, 43*, 13–24. doi:10.1016/j.beth.2011.03.004

Snyder, D. K., Balderrama-Durbin, C., Cigrang, J. A., Talcott, G. W., Slep, A. M. S., & Heyman, R. E. (2016). Help-seeking among airmen in distressed relationships: Promoting relationship well-being. *Psychotherapy, 53*, 1–12. doi:10.1037/pst0000045

Snyder, D. K., Castellani, A. M., & Whisman, M. A. (2006). Current status and future directions in couple therapy. *Annual Review of Psychology, 57*, 317–344. doi:10.1146/annurev.psych.56.091103.070154

Snyder, D. K., Gasbarrini, M. F., Doss, B. D., & Scheider, D. M. (2011). Intervening with military couples struggling with issues of sexual infidelity. *Journal of Contemporary Psychotherapy, 41*, 201–208. doi:10.1007/s10879-011-9177-1

Snyder, D. K., & Halford, W. K. (2012). Evidence-based couple therapy: Current status and future directions. *Journal of Family Therapy, 34*, 229–249. doi:10.1111/j.1467-6427.2012.00599.x

Snyder, D. K., Mangrum, L. F., & Wills, R. M. (1993). Predicting couples' response to marital therapy: A comparison of short- and long-term predictors. *Journal of Consulting and Clinical Psychology, 61*, 61–69. doi:10.1037/0022-006X.61.1.61

Snyder, D. K., & Mitchell, A. E. (2008). Affective-reconstructive couple therapy: A pluralistic, developmental approach. In A. S. Gurman (Ed.), *Clinical handbook of couple therapy* (4th ed., pp. 353–382). New York, NY: Guilford.

Snyder, D. K., Simpson, J. A., & Hughes, J. N. (Eds.) (2006). *Emotion regulation in couples and families: Pathways to dysfunction and health.* Washington, DC: American Psychological Association.

Snyder, D. K., & Whisman, M. A. (Eds.) (2003). *Treating difficult couples: Helping clients with coexisting mental and relationship disorders.* New York, NY: Guilford.

Snyder, D. K., & Whisman, M. A. (2004). Treating distressed couples with coexisting mental and physical disorders: Directions for clinical training and practice. *Journal of Marital and Family Therapy, 30*, 1–12. doi:10.1111/j.1752-0606.2004.tb01218.x

Snyder, D. K., & Wills, R. M. (1989). Behavioral versus insight-oriented marital therapy: Effects on individual and interspousal functioning. *Journal of Consulting and Clinical Psychology, 57*, 39–46. doi:10.1037/0022-006X.57.1.39

Snyder, D. K., Wills, R. M., & Grady-Fletcher, A. (1991a). Long-term effectiveness of behavioral versus insight-oriented marital therapy: A four-year follow-up study. *Journal of Consulting and Clinical Psychology, 59*, 138–141. doi:10.1037/0022-006X.59.1.138

Snyder, D. K., Wills, R. M., & Grady-Fletcher, A. (1991b). Risks and challenges of long-term psychotherapy outcome research: Reply to Jacobson. *Journal of Consulting and Clinical Psychology, 59*, 146–149. doi:10.1037/0022-006X.59.1.146

Sprenkle, D. H., & Blow, A. J. (2004). Common factors and our sacred models. *Journal of Marital and Family Therapy, 30*, 113–129. doi:10.1111/j.1752-0606.2004.tb01228.x

Sprenkle, D. H., Davis, S. D., & Lebow, J. L. (2009). *Common factors in couple and family therapy: The overlooked foundation for effective practice.* New York, NY: Guilford.

Stanley, S. M., Rhoades, G. K., Amato, P. R., Markman, H. J., & Johnson, C. A. (2010). The timing of cohabitation and engagement: Impact on first and second marriages. *Journal of Marriage and the Family, 72*, 906–918. doi:10.1111/j.1741-3737.2010.00738.x

Swindle, R., Heller, K., Pescosolido, B., & Kikuzawa, S. (2000). Responses to nervous break-downs in America over a 40-year period: Mental health policy implications. *American Psychologist, 55,* 740–749. doi:10.1037/0003-066X.55.7.740

United Nations, Department of Economic and Social Affairs, Population Division. (2015). *World marriage data 2015* (POP/DB/Marr/Rev2015). New York, NY: Author.

Vaez, E., Indran, R., Abdollahi, A., Juhari, R., & Mansor, M. (2015). How marital relations affect child behavior: Review of recent research. *Vulnerable Children and Youth Studies, 10,* 321–336. doi:10.1080/17450128.2015.1112454

Waite, L. J., & Gallagher, M. (2000). *The case for marriage: Why married people are happier, healthier, and better off financially.* New York, NY: Doubleday.

Whisman, M. A. (1999). Marital dissatisfaction and psychiatric disorders: Results from the National Comorbidity Survey. *Journal of Abnormal Psychology, 108,* 701–706. doi:10.1037/0021-843X.108.4.701

Whisman, M. A. (2007). Marital distress and DSM-IV psychiatric disorders in a population-based national survey. *Journal of Abnormal Psychology, 116,* 638–643. doi:10.1037/0021-843X.116.3.638

Whisman, M. A., & Beach, S. R. H. (2015). Couple therapy and depression. In A. S. Gurman, J. L. Below, & D. K. Snyder (Eds.), *Clinical handbook of couple therapy* (5th ed., pp. 585–605). New York, NY: Guilford.

Whisman, M. A., Beach, S. R. H., & Snyder, D. K. (2008). Is marital discord taxonic and can taxonic status be assessed reliably? Results from a national, representative sample of married couples. *Journal of Consulting and Clinical Psychology, 76,* 745–755. doi:10.1037/0022-006X.76.5.745

Whisman, M. A., Sheldon, C. T., & Goering, P. (2000). Psychiatric disorders and dissatisfaction with social relationships: Does type of relationship matter? *Journal of Abnormal Psychology, 109,* 803–808. doi:10.1037/0021-843X.109.4.803

Wills, R. M. (2003). Bereavement and complicated grief. In D. K. Snyder & M. A. Whisman (Eds.), *Treating difficult couples: Helping clients with coexisting mental and relationship disorders* (pp. 392–415). New York, NY: Guilford.

2

Systematic and Culturally Sensitive Assessment of Couple Distress

Christina M. Balderrama-Durbin, Douglas K. Snyder, Richard E. Heyman, and Stephen N. Haynes

The assessment of couple distress requires a systematic, dynamic, and culturally sensitive approach. Couple distress or "relationship distress with spouse or intimate partner" as it is referred to in the *Diagnostic and Statistical Manual of Mental Disorders* (5th ed., *DSM-5*; American Psychiatric Association [APA], 2013, p. 716; also, a Z code in the *ICD-10*; World Health Organization [WHO], 1992) involves clinically significant relationship impairment in behavioral, cognitive, and affective domains of relationship functioning. Each of these domains necessitates systematic assessment attuned to cultural influences to facilitate a comprehensive couple assessment.

Couple assessment shares numerous basic principles with the assessment of individuals including that (a) the assessment methods be empirically linked to targeted problems and constructs thought to be functionally related; (b) selected assessment methods demonstrate evidence of reliability, validity, clinical utility, and cost-effectiveness; and (c) findings be linked within a conceptual framework of the presumed causes for distress, as well as to clinical intervention strategies. The assessment of couple distress is unique in that assessments (a) focus on relationship processes and interactions between individuals, (b) allow for direct observation of target complaints related to communication and other interpersonal exchanges, and (c) must be sensitive to the potential challenges inherent in establishing a collaborative alliance in a conjoint context (Snyder, Heyman, Haynes, & Balderrama–Durbin, 2018).

This chapter is a primer covering the following areas: (a) the prevalence of couple distress and its comorbidity with individual emotional, behavioral, and physical health problems; (b) a conceptual framework with accompanying specific, empirically supported assessment strategies and techniques (e.g., clinical interview, behavioral observation, and self-report methods) for examining relationship functioning across diverse domains (i.e., behavioral, cognitive, and affective); (c) cultural considerations in the assessment; and (d) assessment recommendations and future directions.

The Handbook of Systemic Family Therapy: Volume 3, First Edition.
Edited by Karen S. Wampler and Adrian J. Blow.
© 2020 John Wiley & Sons Ltd. Published 2020 by John Wiley & Sons Ltd.

Prevalence and Implications of Couple Distress

Couple distress is prevalent in both community and clinical populations. Approximately 40–50% of marriages in the United States end in divorce (Kreider & Ellis, 2011). Additionally, one-third of currently married individuals report being in a distressed relationship (Whisman, Beach, & Snyder, 2008).

Not only is couple distress prevalent, but it is also linked to individual emotional and physical well-being. A national survey found that compared with happily married persons, maritally distressed partners were 3 times more likely to have a mood disorder, 2.5 times more likely to have an anxiety disorder, and 2 times more likely to have a substance use disorder (Whisman, 1999). Relatedly, marital distress is overrepresented among those with past-year mental health service utilization (Schonbrun & Whisman, 2010). Moreover, couple distress—particularly negative communication—can have adverse effects on cardiovascular, endocrine, immune, neurosensory, and other physiological systems that contribute to physical health problems (Kiecolt-Glaser & Newton, 2001). The negative effects of couple relationship distress are not confined to the adult partners. Meta-analytic studies show a reliable association between couple relationship distress and negative parent–child interactions. Parents in distressed couple relationships, compared with those in satisfied relationships, are (a) less likely to use positive parenting practices such as acceptance, support, and consistent and appropriate discipline and (b) more likely to use harsh, inconsistent, and abusive parenting (Erel & Burman, 1995).

Conceptual Framework for Couple Assessment

The systematic assessment of couple distress necessitates a conceptual framework that extends beyond individual considerations and evaluates the broader relational and sociocultural context from which couple distress emerges. A multitrait, multilevel assessment model should be used to guide assessment domains (namely cognitive, affective, and behavioral) that operate at multiple ecological levels (individual, dyad, nuclear family, extended family, community, and cultural systems) (see Snyder, Cavell, Heffer, & Mangrum, 1995). The relevance of any specific facet of this model varies considerably across couples. The multitrait, multilevel model serves only as a guide for initial areas of inquiry. It is necessary to examine the unique relations of components of distress for each couple as opposed to relying on global heuristics.

The primary aim of operating within such a framework is to identify important causal relationships both within and between levels and domains of couple distress. For example, a given problem (e.g., avoidance in conflict) can have unique causes (e.g., history of physical abuse) that can affect subsequent treatment interventions. Or a different problem such as parenting disagreements may originate from a mismatch in partners' expectations regarding parenting roles resulting from family-of-origin modeling and broader cultural norms. Similarly, some common targets for intervention (e.g., forgiveness) might be harmful in specific couple contexts (e.g., relationships with emotional or physical abuse) (McNulty & Fincham, 2012).

Finally, assessment must be an ongoing and recursive process throughout treatment. Couple distress is dynamic (changing over time), conditional (varying across contexts and domains), and reciprocal (having bidirectional influences).

Assessment for diagnosis and screening

The *DSM-5* and *ICD-11* (proposed) criteria (see Heyman & Slep, 2019) for diagnosis of couple distress are based on the presence of both a "signature problem symptom" (i.e., pervasive unhappiness with the relationship, thoughts of divorce/separation that are more than transitory) and at least one "harm criterion." These harm criteria include (a) higher likelihood of reciprocating or escalating negativity during conflict and of withdrawal; (b) negative attributional patterns; (c) low sense of efficacy that the relationship can improve; (d) intense or persistent levels of anger, contempt, sadness, or apathy/emotional detachment; or (e) degraded physical health, interpersonal interaction, or performance in major life activities.

When a couple presents for therapy with a primary complaint of relationship dissatisfaction, screening for general couple distress is unnecessary, although in many instances and contexts, screeners (interview or self-report) for couple distress aid in diagnostic clarification. For screening purposes, a brief structured diagnostic interview (e.g., Heyman, Feldbau–Kohn, Ehrensaft, Langhinrichsen-Rohling, & O'Leary, 2001) may be used to assess overall relationship distress and partner violence. Couple distress can also be detected using brief measures designed to distinguish clinic from community couples. An example is a 10-item screening scale (the MSI-B; Whisman, Snyder, & Beach, 2009) derived from the Marital Satisfaction Inventory—Revised (MSI-R) (Snyder, 1997). An alternative screening measure is the Kansas Marital Satisfaction Scale (KMSS) (Schumm et al., 1986) comprising three Likert items assessing satisfaction with marriage as an institution, the marital relationship, and the character of one's spouse. A third option is a set of three Couple Satisfaction Index (CSI) scales constructed using item response theory and comprising 32, 16, and 4 items each (Funk & Rogge, 2007). In general, abbreviated scales of global relationship satisfaction are adequate as initial screening measures in primary care or general psychiatric settings but lack the ability to distinguish reliably among finer gradations of relationship distress among partners presenting for couple therapy.

In a therapeutic setting, clinicians can observe reciprocal problem behaviors. Structured observations are a valuable assessment method for the purposes of initial screening and diagnosis of relationship problems, expression of positive and negative feelings, and efforts to resolve conflicts. The Rapid Marital Interaction Coding System (Heyman, 2004) and Rapid Couples Interaction Scoring System (Krokoff, Gottman, & Hass, 1989) are observational methods that are particularly useful for initial screening and diagnosis of couple distress. Even if a formal coding system is not used, clinicians' familiarity with the behavioral indicators of maladaptive communication patterns and other behaviors that covary with couple distress should inform the screening of couple distress.

We advocate a sequential strategy for progressively more detailed assessment for couples presenting with relationship distress. With a sequential strategy, even when a person is presenting for individual treatment, an initial clinical inquiry is used to determine whether relationship problems might contribute to individual difficulties. If indicated, either a brief structured interview or self-report screening measure (e.g., the 10-item MSI-B or the 4-item CSI scale) is used to screen for relationship distress. For those individuals reporting moderate to high levels of distress, follow-up with more detailed assessment methods to differentiate among levels and sources or domains of distress is warranted. Such methods are discussed in greater detail below.

Primary Domains of Couple Distress

For purposes of treatment planning, couple case conceptualizations must extend beyond global sentiment to assess specific sources and levels of relationship difficulties. We continue here with a discussion of construct domains that are particularly relevant to couple distress—including relationship behaviors, cognitions, and affect—as well as individual and broader cultural factors. We follow this with a discussion of assessment methods and techniques for evaluating specific constructs in these domains. (See Snyder et al., 2018, for more detailed review and comparison of couple distress measures.)

Relationship behaviors

Empirical research examining the behavioral components of couple distress has emphasized two aspects: (a) the rates and the reciprocity of positive and negative behaviors during conflict and (b) communication behaviors related to emotional expression and decision making. Regarding the former, distressed couples are distinguished from nondistressed couples by multiple characteristics, including (a) higher rates of negative verbal and nonverbal exchanges (e.g., disagreements, criticism, hostility); (b) higher levels of reciprocity in negative behavior (i.e., the tendency for negativity in Partner A to be followed by negativity in Partner B); (c) lengthier chains of negative behavior once initiated; (d) higher ratio of negative to positive behaviors, independent of their separate rates; and (e) lower rates of positive verbal and nonverbal behaviors, for example, approval, empathy, smiling, and positive touch (Weiss & Heyman, 1997). Findings also generally suggest a stronger linkage for negativity, compared with positivity, to overall couple distress.

Numerous studies have explicated specific communication behaviors that exacerbate or impede the resolution of couple conflicts. Resolution becomes challenging when partners have difficulties in expressing thoughts and feelings related to specific relationship concerns and deficits in decision-making strategies. Specifically, Gottman (1994) observed that the expression of criticism and contempt, along with defensiveness and withdrawal, predicted long-term distress and risk for relationship dissolution. Christensen and Heavy (1990) found that distressed couples were more likely than nondistressed couples to demonstrate a demand ↔ withdraw pattern, wherein one partner attempts to engage in communication while the other partner withdraws from communication.

Listed below are specific questions related to relationship behaviors, along with some sample assessment methods. In subsequent sections we describe these related methods in greater detail.

Conflict intensity and duration   How frequent and intense are the couple's conflicts? How rapidly do initial disagreements escalate into major arguments? For how long do conflicts persist without resolution? Both interview and self-report measures may yield useful information regarding rates and intensity of negative exchanges as well as patterns of conflict engagement. A commonly used self-report measure specific to communication includes the Communication Patterns Questionnaire

(CPQ) (Christensen, 1987). Couples' conflict resolution patterns may be observed directly by instructing partners to discuss problems of their own choosing that represent both moderate and high disagreement and then either formally or informally coding these interactions using one of the behavioral coding systems described later in this chapter.

Conflict domains   What are the common areas of conflict or distress? For example, interactions regarding finances, children, sexual intimacy, use of leisure time, or household tasks; involvement with others including extended family, friends, or coworkers; and differences in preferences or core values are typical areas of concern (e.g., Heyman, Hunt-Martorano, Malik, & Slep, 2009). In addition to the clinical interview, numerous self-report measures sample sources of distress across a variety of relationship domains. Among those having evidence of both reliability and construct validity for a number of diverse populations are the Frequency and Acceptability of Partner Behavior Inventory (FAPBI) (Doss & Christensen, 2006) and the MSI-R (Snyder, 1997).

Conflict resolution strategies   What resources and deficits do partners demonstrate in problem identification and conflict resolution strategies? Do they engage couple issues at adaptive levels (i.e., neither avoiding nor dwelling on relationship concerns)? Do partners balance their expression of feelings with decision-making strategies? Are problem resolution efforts hindered by inflexibility or imbalances in power? Do partners offer each other support when confronting stressors from within or outside their relationship? Most of the interactional tasks developed for use in couple research have emphasized problem solving and conflict resolution to the exclusion of tasks designed to elicit more positive relationship behaviors such as emotional or strategic support, shared values, and admiration. To sample a wider variety of dyadic behaviors, both clinicians and researchers should include tasks specifically designed to sample potential positive as well as negative exchanges. For example, couples might be asked to discuss a time when one partner's feelings were hurt by someone outside their relationship (e.g., a friend or coworker) to assess behaviors expressing understanding and caring (Mitchell et al., 2008).

Relationship cognitions

Cognitive processes also play a role in moderating the impact of specific behaviors on relationship functioning. For example, findings indicate that distressed couples often exhibit a bias toward selectively attending to negative partner behaviors and relationship events while ignoring or minimizing positive events (Sillars, Roberts, Leonard, & Dun, 2000). Compared with nondistressed couples, distressed partners also tend to blame each other for problems and to attribute each other's negative behaviors to broad and stable traits (Bradbury & Fincham, 1990). Distressed couples are also more likely to have unrealistic standards and assumptions about how relationships should work and lower expectancies regarding their partner's willingness or ability to change their behavior in some desired manner (Epstein & Baucom, 2002). Based on these findings, assessment of relationship cognitions should emphasize the following lines of inquiry described below.

Relationship appraisals   Do partners demonstrate an ability to accurately observe and report both positive and negative relationship events? Weiss (1980) described "sentiment override," whereby global feelings about the partner lead to selective attention to and recall of partner's behavior. In therapy, the provider can compare directly observed behavior against partners' descriptions and interpretations of these same exchanges. Partners' response sets when completing self-report relationship measures can also be assessed; for example, the Conventionalization (CNV) scale on the MSI-R (Snyder, 1997) assesses the tendency to distort relationship appraisals in an overly positive direction.

Relationship attributions   What interpretation or meaning do partners ascribe to relationship events? Clinical interviews are particularly useful for eliciting partners' subjective interpretations of their own and each other's behaviors; such interpretations and attributions are also frequently expressed during conflict resolution or other interactional tasks. To what extent are partners' negative relationship behaviors attributed to stable, negative aspects of the partner rather than to external or transient events? Self-report measures assessing relationship attributions include the Relationship Attribution Measure (RAM) (Fincham & Bradbury, 1992).

Relationship standards and expectancies   What beliefs and expectancies do partners hold regarding both their own and the other person's ability and willingness to change in a manner anticipated to be helpful to their relationship? What standards do they hold for relationships generally? For example, the Relationship Belief Inventory (Eidelson & Epstein, 1982) can be used to identify dysfunctional beliefs about intimate relationships that may contribute to difficulties in a couple's own relationship.

Relationship affect

Paralleling findings regarding behavior exchange, research indicates that distressed couples are distinguished from nondistressed couples by higher overall rates, duration, and reciprocity of negative relationship affect and, to a lesser extent, by lower rates of positive relationship affect. Nondistressed couples show less reciprocity of positive affect, potentially reflecting partners' willingness or ability to express positive sentiments spontaneously independent of their partner's affect (Gottman, 1999). By contrast, partners' influence on each other's negative affect has been reported for both proximal and distal outcomes. For example, Pasch, Bradbury, and Davila (1997) found that partners' negative mood prior to discussion of a personal issue predicted lower levels of emotional support during a subsequent exchange. From a longitudinal perspective, couples who divorce are distinguished from those who remain married by partners' premarital levels of negative affect (especially contempt) and by the persistence of negative reciprocity over time (Cook et al., 1995). The undercontrol and overcontrol of emotion can have a detrimental impact on relationship functioning. With these findings in mind, assessment of couple distress should evaluate the following domains.

Reciprocity of affect   To what extent do partners express and reciprocate negative and positive feelings about their relationship and each other? Partners' reciprocity of affect is best evaluated by observing structured or unstructured samples of couple interactions. Although much of the couple literature emphasizes negative emotions, positive emotions such as smiling, laughter, expressions of appreciation or respect, comfort or soothing, and similar expressions are equally important to assess.

Emotion regulation What ability does each partner have to express his or her feelings in a modulated manner? Problems with emotion self-regulation may be observed either in overcontrol of emotions (e.g., an inability to access, label, or express either positive or negative feelings) or in undercontrol of emotions (e.g., the rapid escalation of anger into intense negativity approaching rage, progression of tearfulness into sobbing, or deterioration in quality of thought secondary to emotional overload). Unregulated negativity culminating in either verbal or physical aggression can be assessed through self-report and partner report using the Revised Conflict Tactics Scale (CTS2) (Straus, Hamby, Boney-McCoy, & Sugarman, 1996).

Affect flexibility and generalization To what extent does partners' negative affect generalize across occasions? Generalization of negative affect can be observed in partners' inability to shift from negative to either neutral or positive affect during an interview or in interactional tasks or in reports of distress across most or all domains of relationship functioning assessed using self-report.

General considerations

The separation of assessment from treatment represents a false dichotomy. The process of couple therapy requires continuous assessment of moment-to-moment fluctuations in affect and cognitions within sessions, as well as sustained progress toward behavior change and resolution of presenting problems between and across sessions. Continuous assessment enables the therapist to evaluate the appropriateness of current treatment strategies and suggest changes in either the content or modality of interventions. Similarly, assessment directed exclusively at information gathering in the absence of therapeutic benefit not only fails to advance the couple's conceptual understanding and motivation toward resolving relationship difficulties, but it may heighten resistance and impede subsequent treatment progress. Assessment should feel beneficial to both clients and providers. Therapeutic assessment (Finn & Tonsager, 1997) requires collaboration with the couple in framing relevant questions, reviewing test findings, generating a tentative formulation of factors contributing to relationship difficulties, establishing initial treatment goals, and deciding on therapeutic strategies.

Therapeutic assessment can be achieved through a thoughtful selection of specific and palatable assessments that broaden the partners' awareness of their own couple dynamics that can ultimately shape their interactions in a positive direction. In this framework, the goal of the initial couple interview is not only to gather information for the purpose of treatment selection; an additional aim is to empower the couple to initiate change and build on positive expectancies. The assessment process itself should be one that provides the couple with some benefit. An exclusive or primary emphasis on identifying presenting problems can magnify partners' defensiveness, antagonisms, and hopelessness.

Thus, couple assessment strategies—whether they emphasize informal or structured self-report or observational methods—should complement one another in serving dual purposes of generating information and helping the partners to construct a more optimistic formulation of their current difficulties, how they came about, and how they can be remediated.

Linking assessment to treatment planning

Case conceptualization is a critical clinical skill that lies at the heart of assessment and treatment planning. It is where all the pieces get put together and the linkages are made. For some couples, brief communication skills training may result in sustained improvement, whereas, for others, major restructuring of family organization and boundaries may be essential to successful intervention. Psychoeducational interventions and behavioral parent training may be critical for some couples, whereas cognitive interventions that challenge irrational fears may be crucial to restoring emotional equilibrium for others. For some couples, interpretation of developmental origins of conflicts involving intimacy and emotional vulnerability may comprise a potent intervention, whereas, for others, the same approach may elicit heightened defensiveness or cognitive deterioration. A more detailed discussion of couple therapy considerations are described by Snyder and Balderrama-Durbin (2020, vol. 3) of this handbook.

Importance of Cultural Considerations in Couple Assessment

As described previously, a multitrait, multilevel framework of couple assessment facilitates understanding of how these primary assessment domains (behavioral, cognitive, and affective) operate at various levels (individual, dyad, nuclear family, extended family, community, and cultural systems). This section emphasizes the role of culture, individual differences, and diversity considerations in couple assessment. We adopt the definition of *culture* from Haynes, Kaholokula, and Tanaka-Matsumi (2018) and the Center for Advanced Research on Language Acquisition (CARLA, 2019) as "the shared patterns of behaviors and interactions, cognitive constructs, and affects that are learned through a process of socialization and that distinguish members of a group from members of another group." Although the construct of culture is often associated with ethnicity, culture can also subsume multiple interacting and overlapping dimensions of diversity and individual differences such as race, gender and sex, religion/spirituality, sexual orientation, disability and economic status, age and occupation, and geographic location, among others.

A focus on culture highlights the multidimensional complexity and importance of differences across persons in couple assessment. Consider the likely cultural differences between an older, economically secure, suburban-dwelling, professional Asian American couple compared with a younger, economically disadvantaged, urbandwelling, nonprofessional European American couple. This one example invokes five dimensions of culture—and as many as 120 possible combinations of aspects of culture. Hence, one can readily discern the challenges that clinicians face in engaging in culturally sensitive couple assessment and in planning culturally sensitive interventions from the assessment data.

Cultural considerations in couple assessment are important because culture can influence meaningful differences in couples' values, beliefs, expectations, goals, patterns of interaction, and the social and family context of the relationship (such as the role of a couple's extended family) (Haynes et al., 2018). The challenge is to use assessment methods and strategies and render clinical judgments that are culturally appropriate for each couple. As noted in Haynes et al. (2018), the validity of measures of couple functioning is more likely to vary across dimensions of culture than the validity of many other measures, such as working memory or visual-spatial abilities.

The interactive, multidimensional, and continuous nature of *culture* requires that the assessor always be sensitive to dimensions of diversity and individual differences in couple assessment. Do the assessment methods and instruments used include the elements of couple functioning that are appropriate for the couple's age, ethnicity, religious values, social setting, and other important dimensions? The assessor also needs to be sensitive to important differences within a specific dimension or group (e.g., ethnicity); for example, couples of African American heritage may exhibit different attitudes, behaviors, and goals as a function of their age, acculturation, religious affiliation, or economic status. Culturally uninformed or biased assessment can lead to ineffective or harmful treatment decisions.

Finally, it is critical to consider measurement equivalence when selecting culturally sensitive measures in couple assessment. Measurement equivalence is the degree to which the content, psychometric evidence (e.g., convergent/discriminant validity, reliability, item performance, factor structure), and the meanings of a measure are similar across dimensions of individual difference such as ethnicity or age. A full discussion of measurement equivalence is beyond the scope of the present chapter (see Ercikan and Lyons-Thomas, 2013; Haynes, Smith, & Hunsley, 2019, for extended discussions of this topic); however, it is important to recognize that a new instrument based only on translation and back-translation of an otherwise well-established instrument provides no information regarding the validity of the new instrument, standardization data, norms, or test equivalence. (Also, see Haynes et al., 2018, for guidelines in the adoption or development of culturally appropriate tests.)

Comorbid Individual Distress

There is mounting evidence that relationship difficulties covary with, contribute to, and result from individual emotional and behavioral disorders (Snyder & Whisman, 2003). Both clinician reports and treatment outcome studies suggest that individual difficulties render couple therapy more difficult or less effective (e.g., Beach, 2014). Hence, when evaluating couple distress, clinicians should attend to individual emotional or behavioral functioning to address the extent to which either partner exhibits individual emotional or behavioral difficulties potentially contributing to, exacerbating, or resulting in part from couple distress. Questions regarding depressive symptoms, suicidality, anxiety, and alcohol or other substance use as well as inquiry regarding previous treatment of emotional and behavioral disorders should be a standard part of the intake interview. Individual difficulties may influence not only treatment approach but also treatment outcome. For example, depression in one or both partners predicts poorer response to couple therapy (Sher, Baucom, & Larus, 1990; Snyder, Mangrum, & Wills, 1993). Moreover, a presenting problem related to an individual dysfunction predicts premature dropout from couple therapy (Allgood & Crane, 1991).

When the initial clinical interview suggests potential interaction of relationship and individual dysfunction, the practitioner may consider any number of brief, focused measures (e.g., the Beck Depression Inventory-II [BDI-II]; Beck, Steer, & Brown, 1996; the Symptom Checklist-90-Revised [SCL-90-R]; Derogatis & Savitz, 1999). When such screening measures suggest significant psychopathology, more extensive and formal assessment of psychopathology may be warranted. However, partners entering couple therapy are often reluctant to accept individual psychopathology as a potential contributing factor; hence, formal assessment of individual dysfunction may generate defensiveness or disrupt initial efforts to establish a collaborative therapeutic alliance.

Finally, a functional analysis establishing the direction and strength of causal relations among individual and relationship disorders, as well as their linkage to situational stressors or buffers, is crucial for determining both the content and sequencing of clinical interventions. For example, even well-intended partners can establish a pattern of behavioral accommodations intended to alleviate the afflicted partner's distress (e.g., taking on the sole responsibility of grocery shopping for a partner suffering from panic attacks). Although these accommodations may help ease distress in the short term, they may contribute to increased avoidance in the afflicted partner as well as greater fatigue, relationship strain, or resentment in the accommodating partner in the long term. In many cases, such functional relations are reciprocal—supporting concurrent individual and relational interventions or interventions at either end of the causal chain.

Assessment Methods and Specific Techniques for Evaluating Couple Distress

Assessment strategies for evaluating relationships vary and include the clinical interview, observational methods, and self- and other-report measures. In the sections that follow, we discuss empirically supported techniques within each of these assessment methods. Although specific techniques within any method could target diverse facets of individual, dyadic, or broader system functioning, we emphasize those more commonly used when assessing couples.

The couple assessment interview

The clinical interview is often the initial step for assessing couples. This initial interview is usually conducted with both partners together and has multiple goals (see Balderrama-Durbin, Abbott, and Snyder (in press) for a more detailed discussion of the content of a couple interview). First, the clinical interview is an important method for identifying a couple's concerns, areas of distress and satisfaction, behavior problems, and strengths. Second, it is an important source of information about the couple's commitment, motivation for treatment, and treatment goals. Third, the assessment interview can serve to strengthen the therapeutic alliance. Fourth, it helps the clinician identify potential barriers to subsequent assessment and treatment and the strategies that might be useful for managing or overcoming those barriers. Fifth, it is the main source of historical data on the couple's marriage and previous therapies.

Finally, it is essential for gaining a couple's informed consent about, and cooperation with, the assessment–treatment process.

The initial couple assessment interview helps guide the clinician's selection of additional assessment strategies. Responses during the interview lead to initial hypotheses about ways in which the couple's behaviors, emotions, cognitions, and external stressors contribute to their distress and guide a functional analysis. Clinicians are interested, for example, in finding out what triggers a couple's arguments, which communication patterns lead to their escalation, why positive relationship events are often overlooked by a couple, and how behaviors, cognitions, and emotions are affected by outside stressors. What does one partner do, or not do, that leads the other partner to feel unappreciated or angry or to withdraw from the relationship? These hypotheses contribute to the eventual case formulation that, in turn, affects decisions about the best treatment strategy for a particular couple (see Haynes et al., 2019, for examples of how a couple assessment interview guides subsequent assessment strategies and case formulation). Subsequent interviews throughout the treatment process help the clinician refine the case formulation, identify new barriers and challenges to treatment, clarify treatment goals, and evaluate treatment outcomes and process.

The interview is a versatile couple assessment method because it can provide information across a large variety of domains. For example, it can provide information on the specific behavioral interactions of the couple such as positive and negative behavioral exchanges, problem-solving skills, sources of disagreement, expectations, automatic negative thoughts, beliefs and attitudes about the partner and relationship, and related emotions. Additional areas of strength in the couple's relationship may also be explored—for example, mutual support, emotional and sexual intimacy, leisure activities, shared values and attitudes, and acts of kindness. The couple assessment interview can also provide information on broader family system or cultural factors that might affect the couple's functioning, treatment goals, and response to interventions. Some of the more common concerns include sex, showing appreciation, housekeeping, emotional expression, and spending time together (e.g., Heyman et al., 2009). The initial assessment interview can also provide information on potentially important causal variables for couple distress at an individual level, such as a partner's substance use, mood disorder, or problematic behavior traits. The couple assessment interview should be sensitive to cultural influences and inform the selection of subsequent assessment measures.

Moreover, family-of-origin experiences can significantly contribute to current relationship problems. A "family genogram"—a graphic representation of transgenerational family structures, dynamics, and critical family events—can assist in identifying key relationship patterns either horizontally across the family system or vertically between generations (McGoldrick, Gerson, & Shellenberger, 1999). A family genogram can serve as an interpretive tool to elucidate contrasts and consistencies across partners' extended families of origin.

Various formats for organizing and conducting more extensive assessment interviews with couples have been proposed. For example, Balderrama-Durbin, Abbott, and Snyder (in press) recommended an extended initial conjoint assessment interview lasting about 2 hr. Alternative formats include an initial meeting with the couple together, followed by individual sessions with each partner, followed by another meeting with the couple together. Each of these formats has its advantages and disadvantages; however, regardless of the format, it is critical that there is a clear understanding from the outset about how information learned in an individual (as opposed to dyadic) context will be handled. Individual assessment sessions for some couples may elicit unilateral disclosure of secrets, engender imbalances in the therapist's alliance with each partner or partners' fears of such imbalances, and subsequently detract from a collaborative therapeutic alliance. (See Bass and Quimby, 2006, for a more detailed discussion and specific recommendations regarding confidentiality and privacy in couple therapy.) It is also important to consider cultural customs that may prohibit a partner from being alone with the therapist (i.e., traditions that require the segregation of genders, particularly when in a closed room).

There is a lack of consensus on the optimal format for a couple intake interview (i.e., partners interviewed together, separately, or a combination of both). Indeed, some studies (Haynes, Jensen, Wise, & Sherman, 1981; Whisman & Snyder, 2007) have found that the convergent validity of self-reports about sensitive issues such as sex, infidelity, and violence is higher from individual interview or alternative individual-response formats than conjoint interviews. Also, a client may not disclose violence in an initial couple assessment interview because of embarrassment, minimization, or fear of retribution (see Rathus and Feindler, 2004, for a discussion of the assessment of partner violence). For this reason, it is important to use the interview as a vantage point from which to conduct further assessments using different methods.

Recommended foci of the initial couple assessment interview vary across clinicians but have common elements. For example, Balderrama-Durbin and colleagues (in press) outlined several broad targets and goals of the interview: (a) the structure and organization of the relationship, (b) current relationship difficulties and their development, (c) previous efforts to address relationship difficulties, (d) the personality and characteristics of each partner, (e) deciding whether or not to proceed with couple therapy, and (f) expectations about the therapy process. Other foci frequently included in couple assessment interviews include (a) cultural or ethnic contexts of the relationship (expected roles for each partner, and the role of the extended family), (b) external stressors faced by the couple (e.g., economic stressors or health-related concerns), (c) the couple's communication and problem-solving skills, (d) each partner's level of distress and commitment to continuing the relationship, (e) areas of disagreement and agreement, (f) positive aspects and strengths of the relationship, (g) social support available to each partner and the couple (e.g., involvement in a religious organization), (h) each partner's behavioral traits that may contribute to couple distress, (i) each partner's goals and expectations regarding the relationship, (j) the couple's sexual relationship and prior sexual experiences, and (k) violence in the relationship.

Despite the many strengths of the assessment interview, a major drawback is that very few of the comprehensive formats have undergone rigorous psychometric evaluation. All have face validity but little empirical evidence regarding their temporal reliability, internal consistency, inter-rater agreement, content validity, concurrent and predictive convergent and discriminant validity, sources of error, and generalizability across sources of individual differences such as ethnicity and age. One recent exception is the Relationship Quality Interview (RQI) (Lawrence et al., 2011), a semi-structured interview designed to obtain objective ratings in various domains of couple functioning including (a) quality of emotional intimacy, (b) quality of the couple's sexual relationship, (c) quality of support transactions, (d) the couple's ability to share power, and (e) conflict/problem-solving interactions. Clinicians should also become familiar with the Cultural Formulation Interview for the *DSM-5* (Lewis-Fernández, Aggarwal, Hinton, Hinton, & Kirmayer, 2016) to facilitate attention to both individual- and couple-level diversity characteristics for developing a comprehensive case formulation and planning effective interventions.

Observational methods

As noted earlier, the dyadic context offers the unique opportunity to directly observe partners' communication and other interpersonal exchanges. Analogue behavioral observation is an assessment method that involves a communication task specifically designed, manipulated, or constrained by a clinician to elicit both verbal and nonverbal behaviors of interest in the service of generating hypotheses and testing functional relations in dyadic exchanges (Heyman & Slep, 2004). Detailed descriptions and psychometric reviews of various couple coding systems have been published previously (cf. Heyman, 2001; Kerig & Baucom, 2004). Although these systems vary widely, in general, they target six major classes of behaviors: (a) affect (e.g., humor, affection, anger, criticism, contempt, sadness, anxiety), (b) behavioral engagement (e.g., demands, pressures for change, withdrawal, avoidance), (c) general communication patterns (e.g., involvement, verbal and nonverbal negativity and positivity, information and problem description), (d) problemsolving (e.g., self-disclosure, validation, facilitation, interruption), (e) power (e.g., verbal aggression, coercion, attempts to control), and (f) support/intimacy (e.g., emotional and tangible support, attentiveness).

There are numerous observational coding systems that have demonstrated considerable reliability, validity, and treatment sensitivity (cf. Kerig & Baucom, 2004). A full review of these is beyond the scope of the current discussion. Temporal stability of observed couple behaviors across tasks and settings is largely unknown for existing coding systems; however, the limited evidence indicates that couples' interactions likely vary across topic (e.g., high vs. low conflict), setting (e.g., home vs. clinic or research laboratory), and length of marriage (with longer married couples exhibiting more enduring patterns) (Heyman, 2001).

Concerns have been raised about the clinical utility of analogue behavioral observations (e.g., Mash & Foster, 2001), because nearly all coding systems require extensive observer training to reach adequate levels of inter-observer agreement. However, even if not striving to code behavioral observations in the manner required for scientific study of couple interactions, the empirically informed use of behavioral observations should be standard in clinicians' assessment of couple distress. We recommend that if it seems reasonable and safe to proceed, the clinician should engage in analogue behavioral observation on classes of behaviors that seem most highly connected to the target problem. This is done by choosing a minimum of two topics of interest (at least one topic for Partner A and at least one for Partner B), asking the couple to discuss the selected topic for 5–10 min while the assessor watches silently, and then switching to a new topic and discussing that one. The topic chosen is dependent on the observational area of interest—for example, asking each partner to choose a topic in which she/he desires change in the relationship to assess behavioral engagement or inviting partners to discuss something they would like to change about themselves in the case of assessing support provision. Based on findings from observational research with couples, Heyman (2001, p. 27) suggested that clinicians use behavioral observations in assessing couple distress to address the following:

- How does the conversation start? Does the level of anger escalate? What happens when it does? Does the couple enter repetitive negative exchange loops?
- Do (partners) indicate afterward that what occurred during the conversations is typical? Is their behavior stable (across two or more) discussions?
- Do behaviors differ when it is (one partner's) topic versus (the other's)? Do they label the other person or the communication process as the problem?
- What other communication behaviors—either positive (e.g., support, empathic reflection) or negative (e.g., criticism, sneers, turning away)—appear functionally related to partners' ability to discuss relationship issues effectively?

Self- and other-report methods

There are many benefits to using self-report methods (e.g., questionnaires) in couple assessment. Self-report questionnaires (a) are convenient and relatively easy to administer; (b) are capable of generating a wealth of information across a broad range of domains and levels of functioning germane to clinical assessment or research objectives; (c) lend themselves to collection of data from large normative samples that can serve as a reference for interpreting data from individual respondents; (d) allow disclosure about events and subjective experiences respondents may be reluctant to discuss with an interviewer or in the presence of their partner; and (e) can provide important data concerning internal phenomena opaque to observational approaches including thoughts and feelings, values and attitudes, expectations and attributions, and satisfaction and commitment. Evidence suggests that systematic monitoring and feedback of therapy progress can enhance couple therapy outcomes (Halford et al., 2012).

However, the limitations of traditional self-report questionnaires also bear noting. Specifically, data from self-report instruments can (a) reflect bias (e.g., "sentiment override") in self- and other-presentation in either a favorable or unfavorable direction; (b) be affected by differences in stimulus interpretation and errors in recollection of objective events; (c) inadvertently influence respondents' nontest behavior in unintended ways (e.g., by sensitizing respondents and increasing their reactivity to specific issues); and (d) typically provide few fine-grained details concerning moment-to-moment interactions compared with analogue behavioral observations.

Because of their potential advantages and despite their limitations, self-report questionnaires of couple and family functioning have proliferated. However, relatively few of these measures have achieved widespread adoption. A majority of the measures in this domain demonstrate little evidence regarding the most rudimentary psychometric features of reliability or validity, let alone clear evidence supporting their clinical utility. Self-report questionnaires should be selected based on evidence of clinical utility, validity, and reliability. A mixture of nomothetic (standardized measures) and idiographic (interview and behavioral observation) methods is optimal in assessing couple distress. Bearing in mind the limitations of self-report couple assessments, a variety of measures have been developed to assess couples' behavioral exchanges including communication, verbal and physical aggression, and physical intimacy and demonstrate psychometric soundness (refer to Table 2.1 for a summary of widely used self-report measures in couple assessment).

Table 2.1 Summary of common self-report instruments by assessment domain.

Instrument	Description	Reference
Behaviors/communication		
Conflicts and Problem-Solving Scales (CPS)	Multidimensional measure of couple conflicts that are most likely to affect parenting and child development	Kerig (1996)
Communication Patterns Questionnaire (CPQ)	35 items assessing the temporal sequence of couples' interactions by soliciting partners' perceptions of their communication patterns before, during, and following conflict	Christensen (1987)
Revised Conflict Tactics Scale (CTS2)	39 perpetrator and 39 victim items examining specific acts of physical, psychological, and sexual aggression	Straus et al. (1996)
Frequency and Acceptability of Partner Behavior Inventory (FAPBI)	20 items examining the frequency and acceptability of positive and negative behaviors in four domains (affection, closeness, demands, and relationship violations)	Doss and Christensen (2006)
Cognitive		
Relationship Attribution Measure (RAM)	10 hypothetical situations for which respondents generate responsibility attributions indicating the extent that the partner intentionally behaved negatively, was selfishly motivated, and was blameworthy for the event	Fincham and Bradbury (1992)
Relationship Belief Inventory (RBI)	40 items identifying dysfunctional beliefs about intimate relationships that may contribute to difficulties in a couple's own relationship	Eidelson and Epstein (1982)
Sexual functioning		
Derogatis Sexual Functioning Inventory (DSFI)	254 items comprising 10 scales reflecting such areas as sexual knowledge, range of sexual experiences, sexual attitudes and drive, and psychological symptoms in nonsexual domains	Derogatis and Melisaratos (1979)
Sexual Interaction Inventory (SII)	102 items assessing the frequency of sexual activity and levels of satisfaction, both real and ideal for both self and partner, across 17 behaviors ranging from intercourse to nudity and nonsexual physical intimacy	LoPiccolo and Steger (1974)
Partner support		
Support in Intimate Relationships Rating Scale (SIRRS)	48 items assessing actual and preferred rates of support behaviors within intimate relationships including emotional, physical, informational, and tangible support	Dehle, Larsen, and Landers (2001)

(Continued)

Table 2.1 (Continued)

Instrument	Description	Reference
Relationship satisfaction/quality		
Dyadic Adjustment Scale (DAS)	32 items assessing relationship cohesion, satisfaction, consensus, and affectional expression (A brief 7-item alternative has also been developed)	Spanier (1976) and Hunsley, Best, Lefebvre, and Vito (2001)
Couple Satisfaction Index (CSI)	32 items measuring couple relationship satisfaction (Brief 16- and 4-item alternatives have also been developed)	Funk and Rogge (2007)
Kansas Marital Satisfaction Scale (KMSS)	3 items assessing satisfaction with marriage as an institution, the marital relationship, and the character of one's spouse	Schumm et al. (1986)
Locke–Wallace Marital Adjustment Test (MAT)	15 items assessing overall happiness in the relationship and agreement in key areas of interaction	Locke and Wallace (1959)
Marital Satisfaction Inventory—Revised (MSI-R)	150 items identifying the nature and intensity of relationship distress in distinct areas of interaction. The MSI-R includes two validity scales, one global scale, and 10 specific scales assessing affective and problem-solving communication, aggression, leisure time together, finances, the sexual relationship, role orientation, family of origin, and interactions regarding children (A brief 10-item screening scale has also been developed)	Snyder (1997) and Whisman et al. (2009)

Self-report measures are particularly important in assessing sensitive topics such as aggression and sexual functioning. There are a number of measures designed to evaluate the nature or extent of aggression within the relationship—a topic couples may be reluctant to discuss during an initial conjoint interview (see Ro & Lawrence (2007) for a review of measures on psychological aggression). Similar to individuals with issues of aggression, some individuals may be reluctant to disclose intimate details of their sexual relationship during an initial interview. Numerous measures of sexual attitudes, behaviors, and conflicts have been developed (see Table 2.1).

Measures of relationship adjustment and global satisfaction are plentiful. The two oldest and most widely used are the Locke–Wallace Marital Adjustment Test (MAT) (Locke & Wallace, 1959) and the Dyadic Adjustment Scale (DAS) (Spanier, 1976). The MAT is a 15-item questionnaire that asks partners to rate their overall happiness in their relationship as well as their extent of agreement in key areas of interaction. Displacing the MAT as the most frequent measure of relationship satisfaction is the DAS, a 32-item instrument purporting to differentiate among four related subscales reflecting cohesion, satisfaction, consensus, and affectional expression. A brief (7-item) version of the DAS has also been developed and found to be psychometrically sound (Hunsley et al., 2001).

A close review of the literature suggests several considerations when selecting global relationship satisfaction measures. Despite its widespread use, the psychometric properties of the DAS have important limitations. Factor analyses have failed to replicate its four subscales (Crane, Busby, & Larson, 1991), and the reliability of the affectional expression subscale is relatively weak. The DAS has been used widely for research purposes and has reliably been related to the propensity for divorce as well as distinguished distressed from nondistressed couples; however, guidelines for the DAS caution against using the measure for diagnosis and treatment planning (Spanier, 1976). There is no evidence that the full-length DAS and similar longer global scales offer incremental validity above the briefer and more recent MSI-B and CSI scales that offer higher precision of measurement and greater sensitivity for detecting differences in relationship satisfaction between couples (Balderrama-Durbin, Snyder, & Balsis, 2015).

There is considerable convergence across measures of relationship satisfaction purporting to assess relationship sentiment (constructs such as marital quality, satisfaction, adjustment, happiness, cohesion, consensus, intimacy, and the like; Heyman, Sayers, & Bellack, 1994), and these constructs tend to overlap on item-content level. Moreover, factor analytic studies of multiscale measures often fail to support purported factor structure and meaningful differentiations at the subscale level. Hence, selection among such instruments should be guided by careful examination of item content and empirical findings regarding both convergent and discriminant validity as well as by such practical considerations as use of a screening device for identifying couple distress versus planning specific treatment components and cultural appropriateness.

However, for purposes of case conceptualization and treatment planning, well-constructed multidimensional measures of couple functioning are needed to discriminate among various sources of relationship strength, conflict, satisfaction, and goals. Widely used in both clinical and research settings is the MSI-R (Snyder, 1997), a 150-item inventory designed to identify both the nature and intensity of relationship distress in distinct areas of interaction. The MSI-R includes two validity scales, one global scale, and 10 specific scales assessing relationship satisfaction in such areas as affective and problem-solving communication, aggression, leisure time together, finances, the sexual relationship, role orientation, family of origin, and interactions regarding children. More than 20 years of research have supported the reliability and construct validity of the MSI-R scales. The instrument boasts a large representative national sample, good internal consistency and test–retest reliability, and excellent sensitivity to treatment change. Studies suggest the potential utility of adaptations of the MSI-R for couples whose preferred language is other than English (e.g., Snyder et al., 2004) and for couples from marginalized sexual orientations (e.g., gay and lesbian couples; Means-Christensen, Snyder, & Negy, 2003).

Conclusions and Recommendations

Couple assessment strategies and specific methods should be tailored to partners' unique constellation of presenting difficulties, as well as available resources and capabilities of the couple and the clinician. However, regardless of the specific context, the following recommendations for assessing couples will generally apply:

- Assessment of couple functioning should be standard practice when treating individuals.
- When treating couples, partners should be screened for individual emotional or behavioral difficulties potentially contributing to, exacerbating, or resulting in part from couple distress.

- Assessment foci should progress from broad to narrow—first identifying relationship concerns at the broader construct level and then examining more specific facets of couple distress and its correlates using a finer-grained analysis.
- Assessment should begin with standardized approaches but then progress to individualized methods facilitating functional analysis of factors related to target concerns.
- Within clinical settings, certain domains (communication, aggression, substance use, affective disorders, emotional or physical involvement with an outside person) should always be assessed with every couple.
- Couple assessment should integrate findings across multiple assessment methods. Self- and other-report measures may complement findings from interview or behavioral observation in generating data across diverse domains. However, special caution should be exercised when adopting self- or other-report questionnaires in assessing couple functioning, because most have not undergone careful scrutiny of their psychometric soundness.
- Couple assessment should also be parsimonious. This can be facilitated by choosing evaluation strategies and modalities that complement each other and by following a sequential approach that uses increasingly narrowband measures to target problem areas that have been identified by other assessment techniques.
- Psychometric characteristics of any assessment technique—whether from interview, analogue behavioral observation, or self-report questionnaire—are conditional on the specific population and purpose for which that assessment method was developed. Given that nearly all measures of couple distress were developed and tested on White, middle-class, married couples, their relevance to and utility for assessing ethnic couples, gay and lesbian couples, and low-income couples is unknown.
- Assessment should be linked to theory and an explicit intervention model. Additionally, assessment related to treatment should be ongoing—not only to evaluate change but also to incorporate emerging data regarding hypothesized linkages between target concerns and potential antecedents and consequences.
- Assessors should be familiar with clinically important aspects of individuals' culture, while recognizing that cultural stereotypes are not necessarily valid for any given individual or couple. Similarly, clinicians should integrate data from multiple assessment methods and measures in a culturally sensitive manner.

Future Directions

Although assessment of couples has shown dramatic gains in both its conceptual and empirical underpinnings over the past 30–40 years, much more remains to be discovered. Both clinicians and researchers need to avail themselves of recent technological advances in assessing couples in more dynamic and ecologically valid ways as well as collaborate in promoting further development of empirically based assessment methods. Considering the centrality of couple distress in mental and physical health, we can expect the assessment of couple distress to become a part of more routine clinical practice in both behavioral and medical healthcare settings. Additionally, as we gain a greater understanding of the mediators and moderators of couple therapy (e.g., age, depressive symptoms, gender roles, pretreatment level of distress, commitment, affection and intimacy, therapeutic alliance, and other relationship characteristics), our approach to couple assessment will only become more refined in the pursuit of best practices in couple assessment.

Acknowledgment

Dr. Heyman's preparation of this chapter was supported by the National Institute of Dental and Craniofacial Research (grant 1UH2DE025980).

References

Allgood, S. M., & Crane, D. R. (1991). Predicting marital therapy dropouts. *Journal of Marital and Family Therapy, 17,* 73–79.

American Psychiatric Association. (2013). *Diagnostic and statistical manual of mental disorders* (5th ed.). Washington, DC: Author.

Balderrama-Durbin, C., Snyder, D. K., & Balsis, S. (2015). Tailoring assessment of relationship distress using the Marital Satisfaction Inventory—Brief form. *Couple and Family Psychology: Research and Practice, 4,* 127–135.

Balderrama-Durbin, C. M., Abbott, B. V., & Snyder, D. K. (in press). Couple distress. In M. M. Antony & D. H. Barlow (Eds.), *Handbook of assessment and treatment planning for psychological disorders* (3rd ed.). New York, NY: Guilford Press.

Bass, B. A., & Quimby, J. L. (2006). Addressing secrets in couples counseling: An alternative approach to informed consent. *The Family Journal: Counseling and Therapy for Couples and Families, 14,* 77–80.

Beach, S. R. H. (2014). The couple and family discord model of depression: Updates and future directions. In C. R. Agnew & S. C. South (Eds.), *Interpersonal relationships and health: Social and clinical psychological mechanisms* (pp. 133–155). New York, NY: Oxford University Press.

Beck, A. T., Steer, R. A., & Brown, G. K. (1996). *Manual for the Beck depression inventory-II.* San Antonio, TX: Psychological Corporation.

Bradbury, T. N., & Fincham, F. D. (1990). Attributions in marriage: Review and critique. *Psychological Bulletin, 107,* 3–33.

Center for Advanced Research on Language Acquisition, University of Minnesota. (2019, April 9). *What is culture?* Retrieved from http://carla.umn.edu/culture/definitions.html

Christensen, A. (1987). Detection of conflict patterns in couples. In K. Hahlweg & M. J. Goldstein (Eds.), *Understanding major mental disorder: The contribution of family interaction research* (pp. 250–265). New York, NY: Family Process Press.

Christensen, A., & Heavy, C. L. (1990). Gender and social structure in the demand/withdraw pattern of marital conflict. *Journal of Personality and Social Psychology, 59,* 73–81.

Cook, J., Tyson, R., White, J., Rushe, R., Gottman, J. M., & Murray, J. (1995). The mathematics of marital conflict: Qualitative dynamic mathematical modeling of marital interaction. *Journal of Family Psychology, 9,* 110–130.

Crane, D. R., Busby, D. M., & Larson, J. H. (1991). A factor analysis of the dyadic adjustment scale with distressed and nondistressed couples. *American Journal of Family Therapy, 19,* 60–66.

Dehle, C., Larsen, D., & Landers, J. E. (2001). Social support in marriage. *The American Journal of Family Therapy, 29,* 307–324.

Derogatis, L. R., & Melisaratos, N. (1979). The DSFI: A multidimensional measure of sexual functioning. *Journal of Sex and Marital Therapy, 5*, 244–281.

Derogatis, L. R., & Savitz, K. L. (1999). The SCL-90-R, Brief Symptom Inventory, and matching clinical rating scales. In M. E. Maruish (Ed.), *The use of psychological testing for treatment planning and outcomes assessment* (2nd ed., pp. 679–724). Mahwah, NJ: Erlbaum.

Doss, B. D., & Christensen, A. (2006). Acceptance in romantic relationships: The frequency and acceptability of partner behavior inventory. *Psychological Assessment, 18*, 289–302.

Eidelson, R. J., & Epstein, N. (1982). Cognition and relationship maladjustment: Development of a measure of dysfunctional relationship beliefs. *Journal of Consulting and Clinical Psychology, 50*, 715–720.

Epstein, N. B., & Baucom, D. H. (2002). *Enhanced cognitive-behavioral therapy for couples: A contextual approach*. Washington, DC: American Psychological Association.

Ercikan, K., & Lyons-Thomas, J. (2013). Adapting tests for use in other languages and cultures. In K. F. Geisinger, B. A. Bracken, J. F. Carlson, J.-I. C. Hansen, N. R. Kuncel, S. P. Reise, & M. C. Rodriguez (Eds.), *APA handbooks in psychology. APA handbook of testing and assessment in psychology, vol. 3. Testing and assessment in school psychology and education* (pp. 545–569). Washington, DC: American Psychological Association.

Erel, O., & Burman, B. (1995). Interrelatedness of marital relations and parent-child relations: A meta–analytic review. *Psychological Bulletin, 118*, 108–132.

Fincham, F. D., & Bradbury, T. N. (1992). Assessing attributions in marriage: The Relationship Attribution Measure. *Journal of Personality and Social Psychology, 62*, 457–468.

Finn, S. E., & Tonsager, M. E. (1997). Information-gathering and therapeutic models of assessment: Complementary paradigms. *Psychological Assessment, 9*, 374–385.

Funk, J. L., & Rogge, R. (2007). Testing the ruler with item response theory: Increasing precision of measurement for relationship satisfaction with the Couple Satisfaction Index. *Journal of Family Psychology, 21*, 572–583.

Gottman, J. M. (1994). *What predicts divorce? The relationship between marital processes and marital outcomes*. Hillsdale, NJ: Erlbaum.

Gottman, J. M. (1999). *The marriage clinic: A scientifically-based marital therapy*. New York, NY: Norton.

Halford, W. K., Hayes, S., Christensen, A., Lambert, M., Baucom, D. H., & Atkins, D. C. (2012). Toward making progress feedback an effective common factor in couple therapy. *Behavior Therapy, 43*, 49–60.

Haynes, S. N., Jensen, B. J., Wise, E., & Sherman, D. (1981). The marital intake interview: A multimethod criterion validity assessment. *Journal of Consulting and Clinical Psychology, 49*, 379–387.

Haynes, S. N., Kaholokula, J. K., & Tanaka-Matsumi, J. (2018). Psychometric foundations of psychological assessment with diverse cultures: What are the concepts, methods, and evidence? In C. Frisby & W. O'Donohue (Eds.), *Cultural competence in applied psychology: Theory, science, practice, and evaluation* (pp. 441–472). New York, NY: Springer.

Haynes, S. N., Smith, G., & Hunsley, J. R. (2019). *Scientific foundations of clinical assessment* (2nd ed.). New York, NY: Taylor and Francis/Routledge.

Heyman, R. E. (2001). Observation of couple conflicts: Clinical assessment applications, stubborn truths, and shaky foundations. *Psychological Assessment, 13*, 5–35.

Heyman, R. E. (2004). Rapid marital interaction coding system (RMICS). In P. K. Kerig & D. H. Baucom (Eds.), *Couple observational coding systems* (pp. 67–94). Mahwah, NJ: Erlbaum.

Heyman, R. E., Feldbau–Kohn, S. R., Ehrensaft, M. K., Langhinrichsen-Rohling, J., & O'Leary, K. D. (2001). Can questionnaire reports correctly classify relationship distress and partner physical abuse? *Journal of Family Psychology, 15*, 334–346.

Heyman, R. E., Hunt-Martorano, A. N., Malik, J., & Slep, A. M. S. (2009). Desired change in couples: Gender differences and effects on communication. *Journal of Family Psychology, 23*, 474–484.

Heyman, R. E., Sayers, S. L., & Bellack, A. S. (1994). Global marital satisfaction vs. marital adjustment: Construct validity and psychometric properties of three measures. *Journal of Family Psychology, 8,* 432–446.

Heyman, R. E., & Slep, A. M. S. (2004). Analogue behavioral observation. In E. M. Heiby & S. N. Haynes (Eds.), *Comprehensive handbook of psychological assessment, vol. 3: Behavioral assessment* (pp. 162–180). New York, NY: Wiley.

Heyman, R. E., & Slep, A. M. S. (2019). Relational diagnoses and beyond. In B. Friese (Ed.), *APA handbook of contemporary family psychology* (pp. 19–34). Washington, DC: American Psychological Association Press.

Hunsley, J., Best, M., Lefebvre, M., & Vito, D. (2001). The seven-item short form of the dyadic adjustment scale: Further evidence for construct validity. *American Journal of Family Therapy, 29,* 325–335.

Kerig, P. K. (1996). Assessing the links between interparental conflict and child adjustment: The Conflicts and Problem-Solving Scales. *Journal of Family Psychology, 10,* 454–473.

Kerig, P. K., & Baucom, D. H. (Eds.) (2004). *Couple observational coding systems.* Mahwah, NJ: Erlbaum.

Kiecolt-Glaser, J. K., & Newton, T. L. (2001). Marriage and health: His and hers. *Psychological Bulletin, 12,* 472–503.

Kreider, R. M., & Ellis, R. (2011). *Number, timing, and duration of marriages and divorces: 2009* [Current Population Reports, P70–125]. Washington, DC: US Census Bureau.

Krokoff, L. J., Gottman, J. M., & Hass, S. D. (1989). Validation of a global rapid couples interaction scoring system. *Behavioral Assessment, 11,* 65–79.

Lawrence, E., Barry, R. A., Brock, R. L., Bunde, M., Langer, A., Ro, E., … Dzankovic, S. (2011). The relationship quality interview: Evidence of reliability, convergent and divergent validity, and incremental utility. *Psychological Assessment, 23,* 44–63.

Lewis-Fernández, R., Aggarwal, N. K., Hinton, L., Hinton, D. E., & Kirmayer, L. J. (Eds.) (2016). *DSM–5 handbook on the cultural formulation interview.* Arlington, VA: American Psychiatric Publishing, Inc.

Locke, H. J., & Wallace, K. M. (1959). Short marital adjustment and prediction tests: Their reliability and validity. *Marriage and Family Living, 21,* 251–255.

LoPiccolo, J., & Steger, J. C. (1974). The sexual interaction inventory: A new instrument for assessment of sexual dysfunction. *Archives of Sexual Behavior, 3,* 585–595.

Mash, E. J., & Foster, S. L. (2001). Exporting analogue behavioral observation from research to clinical practice: Useful or cost defective? *Psychological Assessment, 13,* 86–98.

McGoldrick, M., Gerson, R., & Shellenberger, S. (1999). *Genograms: Assessment and intervention* (2nd ed.). New York, NY: Norton.

McNulty, J. K., & Fincham, F. D. (2012). Beyond positive psychology? Toward a contextual view of psychological processes and well–being. *American Psychologist, 67,* 101–110.

Means-Christensen, A. J., Snyder, D. K., & Negy, C. (2003). Assessing nontraditional couples: Validity of the marital satisfaction inventory–revised (MSI-R) with gay, lesbian, and cohabiting heterosexual couples. *Journal of Marital and Family Therapy, 29,* 69–83.

Mitchell, A. E., Castellani, A. M., Herrington, R. L., Joseph, J. I., Doss, B. D., & Snyder, D. K. (2008). Predictors of intimacy in couples' discussions of relationship injuries: An observational study. *Journal of Family Psychology, 22,* 21–29.

Pasch, L. A., Bradbury, T. N., & Davila, J. (1997). Gender, negative affectivity, and observed social support behavior in marital interaction. *Personal Relationships, 4,* 361–378.

Rathus, J. H., & Feindler, E. L. (2004). *Assessment of partner violence: A handbook for researchers and practitioners.* Washington, DC: American Psychological Association Press.

Ro, E., & Lawrence, E. (2007). Comparing three measures of psychological aggression: Psychometric properties and differentiation from negative communication. *Journal of Family Violence, 22,* 575–586.

Schonbrun, Y. C., & Whisman, M. A. (2010). Marital distress and mental health care service utilization. *Journal of Consulting and Clinical Psychology, 78,* 732–736.

Schumm, W. R., Paff-Bergen, L. A., Hatch, R. C., Obiorah, F. C., Copeland, J. M., Meens, L. D., & Bugaighis, M. A. (1986). Concurrent and discriminant validity of the Kansas Marital Satisfaction Scale. *Journal of Marriage and the Family, 48,* 381–387.

Sher, T. G., Baucom, D. H., & Larus, J. M. (1990). Communication patterns and response to treatment among depressed and nondepressed maritally distressed couples. *Journal of Family Psychology, 4,* 63–79.

Sillars, A., Roberts, L. J., Leonard, K. E., & Dun, T. (2000). Cognition during marital conflict: The relationship of thought and talk. *Journal of Social and Personal Relationships, 17,* 479–502.

Snyder, D. K. (1997). *Manual for the marital satisfaction inventory–revised.* Los Angeles, CA: Western Psychological Services.

Snyder, D. K., & Balderrama-Durbin, C. M. (2020). Current status and challenges in systemic family therapy with couples. In K. Wampler & A. J. Blow (Eds.), *The handbook of systemic family therapy: Systemic family therapy with couples (3).* Hoboken, NJ: Wiley.

Snyder, D. K., Cavell, T. A., Heffer, R. W., & Mangrum, L. F. (1995). Marital and family assessment: A multi-faceted, multilevel approach. In R. H. Mikesell, D. D. Lusterman, & S. H. McDaniel (Eds.), *Integrating family therapy: Handbook of family psychology and systems theory* (pp. 163–182). Washington, DC: American Psychological Association.

Snyder, D. K., Cepeda-Benito, A., Abbott, B. V., Gleaves, D. H., Negy, C., Hahlweg, K., & Laurenceau, J. P. (2004). Cross-cultural applications of the Marital Satisfaction InventoryRevised (MSI-R). In M. E. Maruish (Ed.), *Use of psychological testing for treatment planning and outcomes assessment* (3rd ed., pp. 603–623). Mahwah, NJ: Erlbaum.

Snyder, D. K., Heyman, R. E., Haynes, S. N., & Balderrama–Durbin, C. (2018). Couple distress. In J. Hunsley & E. Mash (Eds.), *A guide to assessments that work* (2nd ed., pp. 489–514). New York, NY: Oxford University Press.

Snyder, D. K., Mangrum, L. F., & Wills, R. M. (1993). Predicting couples' response to marital therapy: A comparison of short- and long-term predictors. *Journal of Consulting and Clinical Psychology, 61,* 61–69.

Snyder, D. K., & Whisman, M. A. (2003). *Treating difficult couples: Helping clients with coexisting mental and relationship disorders.* New York, NY: Guilford Press.

Spanier, G. B. (1976). Measuring dyadic adjustment: New scales for assessing the quality of marriage and similar dyads. *Journal of Marriage and the Family, 38,* 15–28.

Straus, M. A., Hamby, S. L., Boney-McCoy, S., & Sugarman, D. B. (1996). The revised Conflict Tactics Scales (CTS2): Development and preliminary psychometric data. *Journal of Family Issues, 17,* 283–316.

Weiss, R. L. (1980). Strategic behavioral marital therapy: Toward a model for assessment and intervention. In J. P. Vincent (Ed.), *Advances in family intervention, assessment, and theory* (Vol. 1, pp. 229–271). Greenwich, CT: JAI Press.

Weiss, R. L., & Heyman, R. E. (1997). A clinical-research overview of couples interactions. In W. K. Halford & H. J. Markman (Eds.), *Clinical handbook of marriage and couples intervention* (pp. 13–41). New York, NY: Wiley.

Whisman, M. A. (1999). Marital dissatisfaction and psychiatric disorders: Results from the National Comorbidity Survey. *Journal of Abnormal Psychology, 108,* 701–706.

Whisman, M. A., Beach, S. R. H., & Snyder, D. K. (2008). Is marital discord taxonic and can taxonic status be assessed reliably? Results from a national, representative sample of married couples. *Journal of Consulting and Clinical Psychology, 76,* 745–755.

Whisman, M. A., & Snyder, D. K. (2007). Sexual infidelity in a national survey of American women: Differences in prevalence and correlates as a function of method of assessment. *Journal of Family Psychology, 21,* 147–154.

Whisman, M. A., Snyder, D. K., & Beach, S. R. H. (2009). Screening for marital and relationship discord. *Journal of Family Psychology, 23,* 247–254.

World Health Organization. (1992). *The ICD-10 classification of mental and behavioural disorders: Clinical descriptions and diagnostic guidelines.* Geneva, Switzerland: Author.

Part II

Problems in the Couple Relationship

3

Prevention of Couple Distress
Education, Enrichment Programs, and Premarital Counseling

Ryan G. Carlson, Andrew P. Daire,
and Christopher J. Hipp

Couple distress leads to numerous challenges for couples at both the individual and systemic levels (Snyder, Heyman, & Haynes, 2005). Individuals who are engaged in stressful couple relationships are more prone to experience psychological distress, such as depression and anxiety (Whisman, 2007). The bidirectional relationship between couple and individual distress has led some researchers to examine couple therapy as a treatment for individual problems (e.g., Isakson et al., 2006).

Systemically, couple distress often results in relationship dissolution, creating further problems (Røsand, Slinning, Røysamb, & Tambs, 2014). Children of parents who divorce experience a 16% greater likelihood of getting a divorce themselves as an adult, a process that Amato referred to as *multigenerational transmission of union instability* (Amato & Patterson, 2016). Additionally, children whose parents are in unhealthy relationships attend school less frequently, earn poorer grades, and demonstrate more unhealthy coping skills compared with children of parents in healthy relationships (Hadfield, Amos, Ungar, Gosselin, & Ganong, 2018; Lee & McLanahan, 2015; Sigle-Rushton, Lynstad, Andersen, & Kravdal, 2014).

Causes of relational stress vary between couples. However, scholars have identified the time of relationship formation, including partner selection, commitment, and intentional decision making, as important predictors of later relationship success (Owen, Rhoades, & Stanley, 2013; Stanley et al., 2017). As a result, couple and family therapists have implemented preventive interventions, such as premarital education (PE), as a means to help couples become more intentional about their futures together. Evidence supporting the effectiveness of PE (Stanley, Amato, Johnson, & Markman, 2006), combined with the adverse experiences of relationship dissolution on children, prompted the US federal government to begin supporting broader relationship enhancement efforts, more commonly referred to as marital and relationship education (MRE) (Hawkins, Amato, & Kinghorn, 2013). MRE programs receiving federal support aim to provide relationship skills training to help economically disadvantaged

The Handbook of Systemic Family Therapy: Volume 3, First Edition.
Edited by Karen S. Wampler and Adrian J. Blow.
© 2020 John Wiley & Sons Ltd. Published 2020 by John Wiley & Sons Ltd.

couples develop and sustain healthy relationships. MRE programs have reached a broad audience over the past two decades, and hundreds of studies examined program effectiveness. In this chapter, we will provide an overview of MRE programs, including their adaptation to target environmental stressors associated with being marginalized and of low income (experienced by many of the couples targeted to participate in federally funded MRE programs) and discuss MRE as a preventative intervention for couples. We also present a brief overview of current MRE research, challenges to MRE implementation, and future directions for the prevention science field.

Individual and couple distress within relationships

Over the past 50 years, the growing research discipline of psychoneuroimmunology provided a deeper understanding of the physiological impact of stress on individuals (Tausk, Elenkov, & Moynihan, 2008), resulting in a clearer understanding of the relationship between stress and physiological functioning, including the connectivity among the central nervous system (CNS), peripheral nervous system, endocrine system, and immune response system. While the physiological details of this complex process are beyond the scope of this chapter, publications exist that provide a comprehensive and understandable review of these mechanisms (seeKiecolt-Glaser, McGuire, Robles, & Glaser, 2002; Littrell, 2008). However, in this section, we aim to provide the reader with a detailed understanding of stress responses in individuals along with how stress responses can impact couple functioning. We will also address how these stressors may be ameliorated for ethnically diverse and low-income couples who attend MRE.

Stress responses are a person's behavioral, psychological, and physiological reactions to threats that one does not readily feel capable to handle. Stress can originate from an event such as an exam, a traumatic event, or anticipation of something threatening or distressful. Examples of behavioral responses to stress include restlessness, sweaty palms, and irritability. Psychological responses include feeling overwhelmed, anxious, becoming problem focused, and feelings of sadness or depression. A relatively easy way to understand physiological stress response is that it occurs at two levels, short-term response and long-term response, which both originate in the CNS. The *short-term stress response* prepares the body for the concentrated physiological response to a perceived or real threat, which is familiar to most as fight or flight. During fight or flight, the sympathetic-adrenal-medulla (SAM) pathway engages, which is when the hypothalamus triggers the autonomic nervous system to activate the adrenal medulla to release catecholamines, including epinephrine and norepinephrine (Sherman, Bunyan, Creswell, & Jaremka, 2009), that lead to commonly known stress (or anxiety). These stress symptoms include increases in heart rate, blood pressure, blood glucose, blood (vasodilation) to major muscles, and decreases in blood flow (vasoconstriction) to some organs (Dum, Levinthal, & Strick, 2016; Maack, Buchanan, & Young, 2015). The hormones released in this process assist in readying the body to most effectively fight or flight from the stress (Dum et al., 2016). However, chronic or long-term stress responses include activation of the hypothalamic–pituitary–adrenocortical (HPA) axis, where the hypothalamus releases a corticotropin-releasing hormone (CRH) that works in concert with vasopressin, also released from the hypothalamus, to initiate the pituitary gland's release of adrenocorticotropic hormone (ACTH). In the adrenal cortex, ACTH initiates the release of glucocorticoid cortisol (Nicolson, 2008; Tausk et al., 2008). These chronic stress responses may have a negative effect on the individual that results in a reduced ability to cope with daily life events.

The fight-or-flight response observed in acute stress serves a protective role although it does have some depressive impact on the immune system. However, chronic stress, through long-term elevated levels of cortisol, depresses the immune system and inhibits the reactivity of the humoral and cell-mediated immune systems. Cortisol decreases the amount of circulating white blood cells, slows and decreases the movement of leukocytes to the site of infections, inhibits fibroblast growth at site of injuries, inhibits production of T-cell-derived cytokines essential for effective immune responses, and prevents the release of proteolytic enzymes critical in the body's response to fight infections (Guyton & Hall, 1996; Kudielka & Kirschbaum, 2007). This wear and tear on the immune system is referred to as allostatic load. Kudielka and Kirschbaum (2007) defined allostatic load as "the cost of chronic exposure to elevated or fluctuating endocrine or neural responses resulting from chronic or repeated challenges that the individual experiences as stressful linking subjective perception of stress to the development of disease" (p. 6). In this allostatic load model (see McEwen, 1998; McEwen & Stellar, 1993), primary mediators, which are the release of certain hormones, lead to secondary outcomes. Secondary outcomes include physiological effects such as high blood sugar, high blood pressure, and then tertiary outcomes, which result in disease conditions. Allostatic load provides insight into understanding the physiological response and impact of chronic stress, including marital stress, on the body and its association with poorer health outcomes. Some readers might find this level of detail regarding stress and stress response daunting for a chapter on the prevention of couple distress. However, the impact of individual stress spills over into the couple relationship and influences couple functioning.

Physiological stress response and couple functioning

Almost 25 years ago, Malarkey, Kiecolt-Glaser, Pearl, and Glaser (1994) published a study on how marital conflict alters pituitary and adrenal hormones. Specifically, marital conflict in a lab environment resulted in decreased blood serum levels of prolactin and increased levels of epinephrine, norepinephrine, ACTH, and growth hormone. However, these studies that occur in lab environments are activating the acute stress response, yet more recent research indicates that long-term and chronic stress has a more deleterious impact on overall immune response (Bauer-Wu, 2002; Kiecolt-Glaser et al., 2002; Kimmel et al., 2000; Tausk et al., 2008). These chronic stressors influence relationships through stress spillover, and in this way, contextual life stressors impact the couple and parenting (Bodenmann & Randall, 2020, vol. 3; Larson & Almeida, 1999; Neff & Karney, 2009; Westman, 2001). "In general, positive responses (e.g., providing support, making allowances for a spouse's negative behavior) should work to contain the negative influence of stress on a marriage, whereas negative responses (e.g., engaging in negative reciprocity) are likely to exacerbate the transmission of stress between partners" (Neff & Karney, 2007, p. 594). This is supported in Neff and Broady's (2011) study that found that newlywed couples who experienced stress early in their marriage and reported more supportive behaviors along with stronger problem-solving behaviors had less stress long term and greater marital adjustment. Individual personality and stress coping abilities influence global judgments about relationships and quality of partner interactions (Neff & Karney, 2009). Neff and Karney stated, "the processing of daily experiences may be influenced not only by intimates' stable abilities, but also by their current *capacity* to utilize the skills necessary for the adaptive processing of relationship information" (p. 435).

Conjointly, healthy relationship functioning may serve to mitigate some of the negative effects associated with environmental stressors (i.e., contextual stressors) that many couples, especially those who are low-income, experience. Thus, the cycle created through the spillover effect becomes clearer, whereas contextual stressors outside of the relationship contribute to relationship stress, creating additional individual stress. This is particularly salient for poor and historically marginalized ethnic minorities due to already high levels of contextual stressors and relationship stress. Relationship enhancement interventions, such as premarital and marital education programs, teach couples skills to help overcome relational health stressors.

Relationship Education (Premarital and Marital)

Premarital education

Religious organizations have traditionally been the predominant force in providing couples PE to promote healthy marriages (Wilmoth & Smyser, 2012). PE aims to help couples prevent later marital problems through improving communication, relationship satisfaction, and couple commitment (Fawcett, Hawkins, Blanchard, & Carroll, 2010; Stanley, 2001; Stanley, Amato, et al., 2006). Hawkins, Higginbotham, and Hatch (2016) reported the first forms of formal MRE dating back to the 1930s in Philadelphia. By the 1950s, programs concentrating on promoting PE began to take shape as government officials and community leaders recognized the need for formal conceptualization of premarital methods to increase relationship sustainment and reduce the destructive factors associated with relationship dissolution (Hawkins et al., 2016).

Currently, relationship education (RE) research has provided support for the importance of building strong marital relationships (Fawcett et al., 2010; Halford et al., 2017) to increase relationship stability (Stanley, Amato, et al., 2006) while also decreasing the negative intrinsic (e.g., mental and/or physical health problems) and extrinsic (e.g., family dissolution) effects of divorce or relationship breakdown. National governments (Markman & Ritchie, 2015) and state and community agencies (Wilmoth & Smyser) as well as private professionals and online RE modules (Simpson, Leonhardt, & Hawkins, 2018) have contributed to the growing use of PE. Such programs emphasize common problems premarital couples may potentially encounter in marriage and relationship skills (e.g., communication skills) to assist in gaining strategies to reduce the risk of negative effects on the relationship (Markman, Rhoades, Stanley, Ragan, & Whitton, 2010; Williamson, Altman, Hsueh, & Bradbury, 2016). Additionally, couples who attend PE are more likely to attend marital counseling when later problems occur (Williamson, Trail, Bradbury, & Karney, 2014).

PE programs have evolved to include MRE programs that focus on the pre- and postmarital ceremony and relationship issues related to the transition to marriage. PE became the springboard for programs that involve the process of choosing a potential marital partner (e.g., Premarital Interpersonal Choices and Knowledge [PICK]; Van Epp, Futris, Van Epp, & Campbell, 2008) and programs focused on the marital relationship after marriage (e.g., Within Our Reach Program; Stanley et al., 2006). While PE programs help couples anticipate later marital problems, MRE curricula teach couples skills to address existing challenges. MRE aims to help couples sustain healthy relationships by providing them with the skills and tools that promote marriage satisfaction (Bradford, Stewart, Pfister, & Higginbotham, 2016; Carlson, Barden, Daire, & Greene, 2014; Scott, Rhoades, Stanley, Allen, & Markman, 2013).

Differences Between relationship education and traditional therapy

There are several differences between RE interventions and traditional therapy approaches to treatment. One major difference involves the educational and credentialing processes between the two disciplines. Marriage education providers traditionally include individuals from the religious community (i.e., heads of churches, mosques, and synagogues), laypersons, and couples who have completed the required RE training. Therefore, RE providers typically work within the bounds of the specified manual(s) or curricula of their training to disseminate the information. Thus, the individuals or couples providing RE interventions receive certification specific to the program. On the other hand, traditional therapy professionals have completed degree programs and licensing requirements to perform therapeutic interventions by state licensing boards and/or national certification associations that promote education associated with families, couples, and marriages while also providing further therapeutic treatment for problems that could arise from or are occurring in combination with RE (Markman & Ritchie, 2015).

Secondly, several researchers have made distinctions between educationally based marital interventions and traditional couple therapy approaches (e.g., Bradford, Hawkins, & Acker, 2015; Goldenberg, Stanton, & Goldenberg, 2017; Markman & Rhoades, 2012). Wetzler, Frame, and Litzinger (2011) distinguished between MRE and therapy services through the lens of the target populations of each treatment type. MRE has traditionally targeted *healthy couples* and provided skills that promote continued growth and development of the couple throughout their marriage while reducing the risk of marital distress. Traditional therapy focuses on *distressed couples* and the specific distressing issue(s) within the couple's relationship dynamics (Goldenberg, Stanton, & Goldenberg). For example, MRE interventions promote communication skills and role development within a relationship that are generalized to a large portion of society (Williamson et al., 2016). Therapeutic interventions, on the other hand, are tailored to the specific couple and the particular issue being experienced (Goldenberg et al., 2017). The existing literature on the implementation of MRE and therapeutic interventions also includes the various settings and presentation style in which couples seek MRE and/or couple therapy. Halford, Markman, and Stanley (2008) described the role of MRE as a prevention of the possible problems associated with marriage development. Therefore, MRE can be implemented within individual, small group, or large group formats. On the other hand, therapy provides couples with interventions for current issues and problems that have occurred within the confines of the relationship. In this context, therapists focus on the specific details that pertain to that couple and develop a treatment plan with that couple that matches their specific presenting issue. Halford (2011) described MRE as a preemptive strike against the pitfalls of marriage, while couple therapy interventions are used when couples become trapped in those pitfalls.

MRE provides a foundation for couples to begin examining their relationship dynamics, while they gather information on skills to use if certain issues arise later in the relationship. Couple therapy utilizes therapeutic interventions to assist couples as they navigate distress presently occurring in the relationship. While several researchers have examined the distinguishing characteristics between the two relationship platforms, other researchers remain interested with the overlap of different characteristics between the two modalities (Karam, Antle, Stanley, & Rhoades, 2015; Markman & Rhoades, 2012). Additionally, government support for MRE programs has drastically increased the quantity and quality of research surrounding the benefits of educational interventions for future marital/relationship quality.

Marital and relationship education (MRE) programs

RE is typically implemented in a group psychoeducation format (Hawkins, Carroll, Doherty, & Willoughby, 2004). Facilitators can be trained professionals, or laypersons from the community, and are trained to follow guidelines of the curriculum developers. MRE workshops generally take place on consecutive weeknights, or during weekends, for the duration of the curriculum. For example, a 12-hr program utilizing the PREP (Markman, Stanley, & Blumberg, 2010) curriculum may meet over four weeknights, for 3 hr each night. Workshops might also occur in weekend-retreat-style format, where couples spend the weekend away at a hotel. While there is not consensus, or data, to support one workshop format over another (Carlson, Daire, & Bai, 2014), designing schedules that meet the flexible needs of the target consumer is important. Moreover, RE techniques can be adapted to meet the needs of the intended target audience. For example, Markman and Rhoades (2012) discussed the benefits of trained clinicians incorporating RE into traditional psychotherapy approaches with couples.

Government funding in the United States for MRE began in the early 2000s, but the foundation for such funding was established in 1996 with federal approval to reauthorize spending for Temporary Assistance for Needy Families (TANF). Once reauthorized, TANF monies could be used to support healthy relationships for low-income families (Knox, Cowan, Cowan, & Bildner, 2011). As such, the federal government approved the first round of federal Healthy Marriage and Responsible Fatherhood grantees in 2003, with the most recent round of funding supporting grantees through 2020. Federal funding for MRE significantly enhanced the number of people providing RE, the number of people who had access to these services, the quantity and quality of evaluations for RE, the number of professionals trained in various curricula, and the interdisciplinary collaborations aimed at discussing best practices and sharing innovative ideas.

As a result, it is difficult to measure the impact that the US government support has had on the field of RE over the past 15–20 years. Marital and relationship education, often used interchangeably with relationship education, couple and relationship education, or marriage education, has evolved into community-based interventions that have been implemented with ethnically diverse, and low-income, couples and individuals across multiple community partnerships. We use the term marital relationship education (MRE), as this term reflects the broad and inclusive nature that MRE has evolved into over the past decade. However, the MRE literature is not consistent on use of terminology. The broad applications for MRE are inclusive of multiple family contexts, such as people who are in long-term committed relationships, either married or unmarried; those in noncommitted relationships; people not in a relationship at all; people with or without children; and emerging adults and teenagers. Additionally, while traditional MRE programs catered to financially stable White couples (Stanley, Amato, et al., 2006) who may not have been experiencing major relationship stressors, federal support for MRE has enabled and promoted financially under-resourced and ethnically diverse families, couples, and individuals to receive relationship support.

Relationship education for specific populations

In addition to the aforementioned federal funding for the Healthy Marriage Initiative, the Administration for Children and Families, Office of Family Assistance, also supported specific programs and resources for various groups through the African-American Healthy Marriage Initiative (ACF, 2003), Hispanic Healthy Marriage Initiative (Torres, Hyra, & Bouchet, 2013), and Native American Healthy Marriage Initiative (Administration for Native Americans [ANA], n.d.). Currently, the Healthy Marriage and Responsible Fatherhood Initiative supports the Healthy Marriage and Relationship Education Grant Program, the New Pathways for Fathers and Families, and the Responsible Fatherhood Opportunities for Reentry and Mobility, which "are part of Health and Human Services' community-based efforts to promote strong, healthy family formation and maintenance, responsible fatherhood and parenting, and reentry opportunities for fathers returning from incarceration" (see https://www.acf.hhs.gov/ofa/programs/healthy-marriage/about). Such support resulted in the development of MRE curricula for specific populations, particularly for African American, Hispanic, Native American, and incarcerated/reentry populations. These programs addressed the distinct cultural needs of these populations after recognizing that most MRE programs were developed by and for White, middle-class, educated, and nonminority populations (Bernal & Saez-Santiago, 2006; Daire et al., 2012; Ooms, 2007; Torres et al., 2013). Following the various federal initiatives for specific populations can be confusing. We placed these initiatives, and a link to more information about each, in Table 3.1.

Ooms (2007) outlined culturally specific themes for curricula serving African American populations (e.g., the legacy of slavery, effects of matriarchy, impact of racial discrimination), Latinos (e.g., family tensions accommodating to American culture, traditional cultural values, issues of discrimination and immigration), and Native Americans (e.g., particular tribal context, addressing distrust in government-sponsored programs, validity of traditional tribal marriages). Dixon (2014) provided a more in-depth presentation of culturally specific needs and considerations for African American couples, including identification of macro and micro factors that impact African American marriage and relationships. Dixon stated:

> At the macro level is the role that broader sociohistorical and cultural factors play in shaping African-American relationships, marriages, and families. At the micro level is the idea that people are shaped by their experiences in their families: with teachers, friends, and associates; in communities; and in relationship with intimate others. (p. 338)

Table 3.1 Initiatives and resources for relationship education for specific populations.

Specific initiative	Focus	Source for more information
Health and Human Services, Administration for Children and Families: Strengthening Families Curriculum Resource Guide	<ul><li>Information on the target populations of different curriculum</li><li>Overview of the information covered in different curricula</li><li>Contact information (if available) for further information on the program</li></ul>	https://hmrfcurriculum.acf.hhs.gov
National Healthy Marriage Resource Center	<ul><li>Local and nationwide marriage and relationship program search</li><li>Curricula information and overview of multiple MRE programs</li></ul>	http://www.healthymarriageinfo.org
National Resource Center for Healthy Marriage and Families	<ul><li>Research and statistics on national trends</li><li>Resource information on services unique to the needs of specific families</li><li>Resource center search that includes information on building relationship and family success, MRE program research, and domestic violence</li><li>Information on becoming an MRE</li></ul>	https://www.healthymarriageandfamilies.org
Healthy Marriage Initiative (HMI)	<ul><li>Links to information associated with the HMI</li><li>Provides research and information about the purposes of HMI</li></ul>	https://www.acf.hhs.gov/ofa/resource/the-healthy-marriage-initiative-hmi
African-American Healthy Marriage Initiative (AAHMI)	<ul><li>Focus on African American dynamics of marriage and relationships</li></ul>	http://www.aahmi.net/focus.html
Hispanic Healthy Marriage Initiative (HHMI)	<ul><li>Provides reports on results of research associated with the HHMI</li></ul>	https://www.acf.hhs.gov/opre/research/project/hispanic-healthy-marriage-initiative-grantee-implementation-evaluation

Program	Description	Link
Native American Healthy Marriage Initiative (NAHMI)	• Information involving the distribution of funds from the federal government • Focused on supporting Native American individuals and families	https://www.acf.hhs.gov/ofa/programs/tribal
Healthy Marriage and Responsible Fatherhood (HMRF)	• Promotes the exploration of curriculum that enhance marital strength and family cohesion	https://www.acf.hhs.gov/ofa/programs/healthy-marriage
New Pathways for Fathers and Families (New Pathways)	• Provides resources for the promotion of responsible fatherhood through information and curriculum that focuses on fatherhood	https://www.acf.hhs.gov/ofa/programs/healthy-marriage/responsible-fatherhood
Responsible Fatherhood Opportunities for Reentry and Mobility (ReFORM)	• Explains the distribution of funds to promote reentry of incarcerated fathers into healthy and strong households to promote family sustainment	https://www.acf.hhs.gov/ofa/programs/healthy-marriage/prisoner-reentry

Hispanic- and Latino-focused MRE curricula and adaptations of traditional curricula for these populations addressed language and idioms, traditional cultural values (i.e., familismo, personalismo, respeto, confianza, marianismo, and machismo), effects of racial and ethnic discrimination, and immigration status (Torres et al., 2013). Additionally, these adaptations also addressed implementation issues including recruitment and retention with particular consideration given to the influence of immigration and documentation status. Beach and colleagues (2011) examined the influence of cultural adaptations to the PREP curriculum specifically for African American couples. Couples who received culturally sensitive and prayer-focused PREP adaptations outperformed couples in the control group, and those receiving prayer-focused PREP resulted in the largest improvements in their relationships.

Another important population for MRE has been with incarcerated men and women. With over 50% of male and 60% of female incarcerated adults being parents, the need existed for interventions to strengthen family engagement and connectedness, parenting and co-parenting, and overall successful reintegration into society after release (Harcourt, Adler-Baeder, Rauer, Pettit, & Erath, 2017). Spouses and partners suffer financially, socially, and psychologically due to partner incarceration. Children with incarcerated fathers also suffer greater emotional problems, poverty, poorer learning outcomes, and overall life stressors (Herman-Stahl, Kan, & McKay, 2008). Additionally, underrepresented minority children are more impacted by parental incarceration, with research showing the adverse effects of father incarceration on children and families (Arditti, 2016; Geller, Cooper, Garfinkel, Schwartz-Soicher, & Mincy, 2012; Wakefield, 2015). MRE interventions for incarcerated individuals address marriage and relationship strengthening, healthy relationship skills development, and positive and engaged parenting skills. These interventions have demonstrated some success in strengthening positive relationships and relationship satisfaction (Einhorn, Williams, Stanley, Markman, & Eason, 2008; Harcourt et al., 2017). The aforementioned areas of improvement are important because inmates who successfully reintegrate in their family and their role as a parent post-incarceration have lower recidivism rates (Berg & Huebner, 2011; Visher & Travis, 2003). However, many challenges exist in implementing MRE programs with incarcerated populations including distance between inmates and their partners and children, coordinating between multiple agencies, and recruitment and retention including barriers to participation due to limited resources and increased obstacles (Herman-Stahl et al., 2008).

Relationship education research support

A potential limitation and area of criticism for MRE curricula surrounds being evidenced based (i.e., empirically validated) or research based (i.e., based on research but not empirically validated). Numerous curricula were developed in response to federal funding that supported demonstration grants all around the United States (see Table 3.2 for a list of selected curricula; while there are several curricula available, we limited our list to those programs specifically mentioned in this chapter). Additionally, many community-based and faith-based organizations manualized what they had been doing as official curricula, while others were developed by university researchers or alongside researchers. It is important for users to utilize curricula that were normed on their population of interest, as well as consider literacy

Table 3.2 Selected marital and relationship education programs.

Name	Target population	Length	Format	For more information
Prevention and Relationship Education Program (PREP) (Allen, Rhoades, Markman, & Stanley, 2015; Markman, Stanley, & Blumberg, 2010)	• Premarital • Individuals • Military couples • Fathers • Christian • Incarceration	• 2-30 hrs programs	• Didactic and experiential • Normally in group format	https://www.prepinc.com/default.aspx
PREPARE/ENRICH (Bowling, Hill, & Jencius, 2005; Olson, 2002; Prepare/Enrich, 2017)	• Premarital • Married • Christian • Parenting • Preadoption and foster couples	• Variable depending on the amount of categories included in the assessments	• Assessment and didactic	https://www.prepare-enrich.com
Premarital Interpersonal Choices and Knowledge (PICK) (Bradford et al., 2016; Van Epp, 2006)	• Military • Christian • Young adult	• 5 sessions (40–50 minutes long)	• Didactic	http://www.lovethinks.com/singles
Facilitating Open Couple Communication, Understanding, and Study (FOCCUS) (Markey, Micheletto, & Jirgal, 1997)	• Premarital • Couples • General version • Christian	• 4-step process with special content available (e.g., couples with children, interfaith marriages)	• Assessment and didactic	http://www.foccusinc.com/index.aspx

level of the curricula, cost, and training, along with research or empirical data supporting use of the particular curriculum.

Research support for MRE programs has demonstrated mixed, yet promising results. Early research findings typically evaluated premarital programs and included less diverse, homogeneous samples. Findings included support for such approaches as promoting positive communication and improving relationship satisfaction (Giblin, Sprenkle, & Sheehan, 1985; Halford, Markman, Kline, & Stanley, 2003). Government support for RE has resulted in more than 300 published studies (and counting) that include rigorous randomized controlled trials with national samples (e.g., Hsueh et al., 2012; Wood, McConnell, Moore, Clarkwest, & Hsueh, 2010), as well as smaller community-centered, pre–post designs (e.g., Carlson, Barden, Daire, & Swartz, 2014; Carlson, Rappleyea et al., 2017) and several meta-analyses (Blanchard, Hawkins, Baldwin, & Fawcett, 2009; Hawkins, Blanchard, Baldwin, & Fawcett, 2008; Hawkins & Erickson, 2015; Hawkins & Fackrell, 2010). While results appear promising, they are mixed and the findings should be considered with caution. Following is a brief review of some of the primary findings from MRE studies to date.

Federal funding supported two national randomized controlled trials: the first called Building Stronger Families (BSF) (Wood et al., 2010) targeted unwed couples with young children, and the second called Supporting Healthy Marriage (SHM) Hsueh et al., 2012) targeted married couples with children. See Table 3.3 for a comparison of these two studies and their respective methodologies. Findings from the BSF study indicated no positive intervention effects. However, one site, Family Expectations in Oklahoma City, was an outlier. Treatment in Oklahoma did have a positive effect on couples who remained romantically involved, with results showing improved relationship quality, better conflict management, higher quality co-parenting, and improved father involvement. The primary difference between Oklahoma and the remaining sites was that people in Oklahoma received a higher dosage because there was less overall program attrition. Conversely, there were small positive treatment effects for SHM couples who demonstrated higher levels of marital happiness, less marital distress, more warmth and support, more positive communication, and fewer negative behaviors during spousal interaction than control couples. The majority of the eight SHM sites experienced less attrition than BSF programs, which likely contributed to the positive effects.

Several smaller pre–post design studies evaluated outcomes from community-centered relationship enhancement programs. These MRE studies examined program effects for the local population and many found that participants improved overall in their self-reported relationship satisfaction, communication, parenting, and individual distress symptoms (Adler-Baeder et al., 2016; Barton et al., 2017; Bradford et al., 2014). Due to scheduling challenges of implementing MRE for couples, some programs provided MRE for individuals (either in a relationship or not, but attending alone nonetheless). Individual-oriented RE resulted in improved individual distress symptoms (Carlson, Rappleyea et al., 2017), parenting quality (Carlson, Barden, Daire, & Swartz, 2014), and reduced conflict-related behaviors (Antle et al., 2013; Carlson, Wheeler, & Adams, 2018; Visvanathan, Richmond, Winder, & Koench, 2014). Thus, providing relationship skills training to individuals may benefit both members of a couple, even if only one attends.

While initially thought to be a preventive approach better suited for couples with minor relationship issues, MRE research results indicated that couples who are more

Table 3.3 MRE randomized controlled studies with national samples.

Study	Population	Content	Dosage	Attrition
Building Stronger Families (BSF) (Wood et al., 2010)	• Eight locations across the United States • Sample size: 5,102 couples (10,204 individuals)	• Relationship education • Case management • Booster sessions • Control condition	• 12-month intervention length • Intended to provide between 30 and 42 hr of group sessions	• 15 months after initial applying for the program, an 87% response rate was produced • 15-month sample: Treatment group: 2,218 couples (4,436 individuals) Control group: 2,207 couples (4,414 individuals) • Total: 4,425 couples (8,850 individuals)
Supporting Healthy Marriage (SHM) (Hsueh et al., 2012)	• Eight locations across the United States (7 states) • Sample size: 6,298 couples (12,596 individuals)	• Marriage and relationship education • Booster sessions • Case management • Control condition	• 12-month intervention length • Group format: 3–20 couples per workshop Weekly group sessions lasted 2–5 hr • Workshops ranged from 6 to 15 weeks in length • 20–30 hr of relationship education	• 12 months after initial study entry, an 86% response rate was produced • 12-month sample: 5,395 couples (10,790)

distressed, or who are experiencing greater risk factors (Halford, Sanders, & Behrens, 2001), may receive the most benefits (Amato, 2014; Carlson, Rappleyea et al., 2017; Gubits, Lowenstein, Harris, & Hsueh, 2014; Rhoades, 2015). Amato (2014) created a risk index from a subgroup of people who participated in the BSF study. Results suggested that participants with greater risk experienced more benefits than those with lower risk across all BSF sites. Gubits and colleagues conducted a subgroup analysis from the SHM study and examined outcomes for those identified as reporting high distress on baseline measures. Results indicated greater effects for those with higher distress levels. Carlson and colleagues created dichotomous groups of high and low risk based on cutoff scores and then compared outcomes between groups. They found that those in the high-risk groups experienced significantly better results. These combined findings are noteworthy because they provide some evidence that MRE is more than a preventative intervention for nondistressed couples. While it is not entirely clear why distressed couples seem to benefit more than nondistressed, it is possible that the structure of the curricula tools help couples stay on track and this provides positive momentum. There may also be a ceiling effect, meaning that well-adjusted couples have less room for improvement than their more distressed counterparts. Additionally, MRE programs provide couples who are experiencing significant distress hope for the future of their relationship (Hawkins, Allen, & Yang, 2017). Further, MRE programs appear to mitigate the effects of negative mood associated with financial stressors for married couples (McCormick, Hsueh, Merrilees, Chou, & Cummings, 2017).

Mechanisms and processes of change   MRE scholars have focused more recent efforts on understanding predictors of change (e.g., Adler-Baeder et al., 2010), as well as mechanisms and processes of change. While group predictors, other than distress levels, have largely not been identified, important process mechanisms have. For example, facilitators who are warm and clear in their delivery contribute to more positive outcomes (Higginbotham & Myler, 2011). Establishing a strong alliance between couples in MRE groups is important (Owen, Antle, & Barbee, 2013), with men benefiting more from the alliance than women (Quirk, Owen, Inch, France, & Bergen, 2014). Additionally, curricula that are between 9 and 20 hr in duration demonstrate the largest effects (Hawkins, Stanley, Blanchard, & Albright, 2012). MRE facilitation influences outcomes as well. Facilitators who manage their time well, effectively utilize self-disclosure skills, and are perceived by participants as clearly explaining the curriculum material predict more positive change (Higginbotham & Myler, 2011). An awareness of the process factors that contributes to positive effects will help practitioners be intentional about program implementation.

Challenges to MRE program implementation

As the MRE field has evolved, scholars and practitioners have considered factors that may support refining program delivery, as well as create sustainable efforts to provide MRE that may last beyond government support. This type of programmatic research is known as implementation science and, for MRE, includes (a) effective recruitment and retention, (b) identifying program participants who may benefit most from MRE, and (c) understanding dynamics, such as facilitator characteristics and group alliance, that might moderate participant outcomes.

Identifying people who should participate in MRE, also known as recruitment, has been one of the most significant challenges to implementing programs with low-income and ethnically diverse populations. There are many reasons that recruitment is a challenge, including contextual stressors facing economically disadvantaged couples. Contextual stressors include unreliable transportation, shift-style jobs with varying schedules, lack of employment, limited social support, and no childcare (Karney & Bradbury, 2005). To overcome these stressors, many programs utilized varying recruitment strategies that include active and passive methods. Active strategies typically involve partnerships with community organizations so that MRE program staff can meet with potential participants and tell them directly of the program services. Passive strategies involve word-of-mouth referrals or people calling from fliers identified in the community. Active strategies tend to yield greater numbers of referrals, while passive strategies tend to result in fewer referrals, but more people who remain in the program (Carlson et al., 2012).

Retaining people who enroll in MRE program services is another challenge. There are many factors that may influence retention, such as the relationship that staff develop with participants (e.g., Owen, Rhoades, Stanley, & Markman, 2011) or even the number of times and which member of the couple program staff call to provide program information (Carlson, Fripp et al., 2014). Additionally, group dynamics and MRE workshop facilitator characteristics may influence retention (Higginbotham & Myler, 2011; Ketring et al., 2017). Many MRE programs also provide case management style services not only to help people navigate the many challenges to remaining in MRE programs but also to reinforce the material learned, as well as connect them with local resources. People who experience greater stressors appear to benefit most from the case management services provided (Carlson et al., 2016). Retaining participants in MRE programs, especially low-income and ethnically diverse participants, requires thoughtful intentionality.

MRE inclusion and exclusion criteria   Federally funded MRE programs tailored recruitment strategies to target couples and individuals representing a variety of backgrounds and cultures. The inclusion criteria has been broad, with the primary emphasis on economically disadvantaged participants. However, programs have been very careful and deliberate in screening participants for issues that are contraindicated for a relationship enhancement intervention. For example, individuals experiencing active psychoses, or untreated substance abuse, would not be appropriate for MRE. Further, MRE practitioners and researchers have been careful to screen for intimate partner violence (IPV) within couple relationships. Many programs partnered with domestic violence advocates and developed detailed screening protocol (e.g., Daire, Carlson, Barden, & Jacobson, 2014) to understand the context of any presenting IPV. The prevalence of power and control behaviors between a victim and victimizer is a primary concern, and other treatment options should be considered in such cases. However, when IPV is not the result of power and control, MRE may be an indicated treatment, especially individual-oriented MRE.

Individual-oriented MRE has been found to reduce IPV (Carlson et al., 2018), leading some to consider this approach as a preventive effort against family violence (Rhoades & Stanley, 2011). MRE programs that target individuals may provide a safer forum for addressing IPV as this reduces concerns that a victim may be placed in a compromising scenario. MRE programs have been instrumental in advancing the family therapy field with respect to issues of screening and assessing for IPV. While a more detailed focus on IPV is outside the scope of this chapter, interested readers can pursue additional resources (e.g., Carlson et al., 2017; Whiting, Bradford, Vail, Carlton, & Bathje, 2009).

Special Topics in Relationship Education

RE curricula address various topics for couples, with some topics specific to the target population. For example, individual-oriented curricula, such as PREP's *Within Our Reach*, emphasize partner selection, or choosing wisely. Other specialized topics may include issues specific to diverse populations, such as military couples or those from specific cultural backgrounds, as well as addressing faith-based populations. Following, we provide a brief overview and some examples of MRE specialized topics.

Global MRE issues

While the United States makes up only 4.4% of the world's population and North Americans making up 12%, Asia makes up 60% and Africa comprises 17%. Although these two continents total over 75% of the world's population, MRE has quite a minimal presence, although marriage proves important culturally. Some in sub-Saharan African countries espouse to sociocultural practices related to marriage that are different than those found in the United States. This includes early marriage for young girls, lobola (bride price), polygamy (husband having multiple wives), polygyny (husband consults with wife or her family to take on subsequent wives), and women holding less power or decision making in marriage (Al-Krenawi, 1999; Ngazimbi, Daire, Soto, Carlson, & Munyon, 2013; Timaeus & Reynar, 1998). Marriage aids in social status for African women along with the ability for homeownership and protection from exploitation (Ngazimbi, Daire, Carlson, & Munyon, 2017).

Marriages in the United States are focused on early development of love and individual satisfaction where many African marriages are arranged and involve family negotiations on lobola or dowry with love and commitment developing afterward (Ngazimbi et al., 2013, 2017). However, satisfaction is an important concept although not as large a divorce consideration as in the United States. Also, Ngazimbi et al. (2013) found a significant correlation between marital expectations and marital satisfaction in African immigrants living in the United States, but not for US-born individuals. However, no research was found on the examination of MRE in African populations.

Recent changes in divorce rates in Asian countries are slowly bringing the need for marital interventions to the forefront (Huang, 2005; Jones & Yueng, 2014). Huang (2005) identified six influences on marriage and the increased divorce rates in Asian countries: (a) rapid economic growth, urbanization, and the changing cultural norms in Asian societies; (b) enhanced choice through educational/employment opportunities for Asian women; (c) loosening of social control over marriage; (d) divorce laws in most Asian countries having become more lenient; (e) growing individualism; and (f) rise of "romantic love" and the gradual decline in arranged marriages. Considerable attention was given to Asian marriages with the October 2014 (volume 35, issue 12)

Journal of Family Issues: Marriage in Asia special issue. Although none of the articles provided any detailed information of MRE in Asia, Huang (2005) provided a comprehensive overview of MRE programs that exist in Singapore, Taiwan, China, Malaysia, Japan, and India.

MRE has been supported by governments and implemented in countries across the globe. For example, the Australian government has provided support for relation enhancements since the 1960s (Halford & Simons, 2005). About 30% of Australians planning to marry attended some form of PE. MRE has been studied extensively in European countries, such as Germany, Switzerland, and Norway (Bodenmann, Bradbury, & Pihet, 2009; Hahlweg, Markman, Thurmaier, Engl, & Eckert, 1998; Van Widenfelt, Hosman, Schaap, & van der Staak, 1996). The United Kingdom and Singapore have also supported efforts to provide relationship enhancements. Despite some cultural advances in MRE utilization across various countries, more international research is needed regarding MRE's effectiveness and implementation strategies.

Relationship education and religion

Prior to federal funding, the majority of couples who sought RE before marriage received such information through religious outlets (Maybruch, Pirutinsky, & Pelcovitz, 2014). Religious-based RE occurs in the context of promoting marriage through religious doctrine (Kor, Mikulincer, & Pirutinsky, 2012; Lubis, 2011) and/or preestablished programs (e.g., PREP). While religious options for obtaining MRE abound (Doss, Rhoades, Stanley, & Markman, 2009), the content, quality, and length of such RE by religious leaders remain inconsistent (Baucom, Hahlweg, Atkins, Engl, & Thurmaier, 2006; Schumm et al., 2010; Stanley, 2001). For example, Baucom et al. reported instances of as little as 15 minutes with clergy to discuss the couple's perspectives of their relationship, while Wilmoth and Smyser (2012) observed an average of 4 hr of PE that focused on preparations for the wedding. As a result of these inconsistencies, community- and research-based MRE programs have partnered with religious-based facilitators to promote beneficial MRE.

Lopez, Riggs, Pollard, and Hook (2011) perpetuated Stanley et al.'s (1995) four reasons why religious institutions create the cornerstone of MRE dissemination. Within the confines of religious institutions, the importance of relationship sustainment goes hand in hand with RE. Religious organizations promote the marital union as a lifelong commitment that coincides with MRE's focus on relationship cohesion. Secondly, the majority of couples are married in religious ceremonies. Thirdly, the morals and values perpetuated by the religious institution are consistent with the morals and values of the couples being married in that organization; therefore, integrating MRE that encompasses those morals and values aligns with the couple's goals for their relationship. Finally, religious institutions are ingrained in society and provide numerous educational resources to the community it serves.

Historically, religious-based MRE focused on the beliefs and values of the specific religious institution in which the MRE was occurring. Recently, religious leaders have recognized the importance of quality MRE provided to couples seeking support and knowledge. Therefore, new research coalesces religious doctrine into evidence-based MRE.

Future directions for prevention of couple distress and relationship education programs

Government support for MRE programs is not likely to continue indefinitely. Therefore, it is vital for this relatively young field to consider cost-effective, sustainable approaches to maintaining the gains developed over the past two decades. For example, MRE scholars (e.g., Markman & Rhoades, 2012) suggested that more information is needed to understand exactly what mechanisms within MRE create change. Such information would help programs and practitioners develop more tailored responses to MRE, including adapting aspects of MRE approaches into traditional couple therapy approaches.

Innovative MRE implementation will also contribute to sustainability. Most MRE programs are provided in large group formats, which are expensive and require significant resources to conduct. While large group formats have the potential to be cost-effective, they typically result in high attrition, which increases the overall cost per participant. However, there is emerging evidence demonstrating the effectiveness of online MRE programs (e.g., Doss et al., 2016; Doss, Roddy, Nowlan, Rothman, & Christensen, 2018). This is significant because online administration is cost-effective, can reach a broad audience, and allows couples to complete the programming at a time that works best for them.

Finally, MRE practitioners and researchers need to emphasize the public health benefits of promoting and supporting the relational health for those in the community, especially marginalized couples. Positive relational health has systemic benefits that transcend the couple's relationship. For example, healthy relationships may serve as a protective factor for those who have experienced adverse childhood experiences (Wheeler, 2017), reducing the physical correlates associated with these risks and breaking the cycle for future generations. Additionally, while positive relational health cannot on its own remove environmental stressors associated with low economic status, couples may be more prone to cope with these stressors and reduce the negative correlates associated with them. Research will continue to advance the field through a more in-depth understanding of how positive relational health benefits couples and their families.

References

Adler-Baeder, F., Bradford, A., Skuban, E., Lucier-Greer, M., Ketring, S., & Smith, T. (2010). Demographics predictors of relationship and marriage education participants' pre- and post-program relational and individual functioning. *Journal of Couple and Relationship Therapy, 9*(2), 113–132. doi:10.1080/15332691003694885

Adler-Baeder, F., Garneau, C., Vaughn, B., McGill, J., Harcourt, K. T., Ketring, S., & Smith, T. (2016). The effects of mother participation in relationship education on co-parenting, parenting, and child social competences: Modeling spillover effects for low-income minority preschool children. *Family Process, 57*(1), 113–130. doi:10.1111/famp.12267

Administration for Children and Families. (2003). *African American healthy marriage initiative roundtable "why marriage matters" summary report.* Retrieved from http://www.aahmi.net/docs/roundtable.pdf

Administration for Native Americans. (n.d.). *Fast facts: Native American healthy marriage initiative (NAHMI) administration for children and families healthy marriage initiative.*

Retrieved from http://web.archive.org/web/20060926154142/http://www2.acf.hhs. gov/programs/ana/documents/NAHMI_fast_facts.pdf

African American Healthy Marriage Initiative website. (n.d.) *African American Healthy Marriage Initiative (Aahmi.net)*. Retrieved from http://www.aahmi.net/mission.html#fs

Al-Krenawi, A. (1999). Women of polygamous marriages in primary health care centers. *Contemporary Family Therapy, 2*(3), 417–430.

Allen, E. S., Rhoades, G. K., Markman, H. J., & Stanley, S. M. (2015). PREP for strong bonds: A review of outcomes from a randomized control trial. *Contemporary Family Therapy: An International Journal, 37*(3), 232–246.

Amato, P. R. (2014). Does social and economic disadvantage moderate the effects of relation-ship education on unwed couples? An analysis of data from the 15-month Building Strong Families evaluation. *Family Relations, 63*(3), 343–355. doi:10.1111/fare.12069

Amato, P. R., & Patterson, S. E. (2016). The intergenerational transmission of union instability in early adulthood. *Journal of Marriage and Family, 79*(3), 723–738.

Antle, B., Sar, B., Christensen, D., Karam, E., Ellers, F., Barbee, A., & van Zyl, M. (2013). The impact of the within my reach relationship training on relationship skills and out-comes for low-income individuals. *Journal of Marital and Family Therapy, 39*(3), 346–357. doi:10.1111/j.175-0606.2012.00314.x

Arditti, J. A. (2016). A family stress-proximal process model for understanding the effects of parental incarceration on children and their families. *Couple and Family Psychology: Research and Practice, 5*(2), 65–88. doi:10.1037/cfp0000058

Barton, A. W., Beach, S. R., Lavner, J. A., Bryant, C. M., Kogan, S. M., & Brody, G. H. (2017). Is communication a mechanism of relationship education effects among rural African Americans? *Journal of Marriage and Family, 79*(5), 1450–1461. doi:10.1111/jomf.12416

Baucom, D. H., Hahlweg, K., Atkins, D. C., Engl, J., & Thurmaier, F. (2006). Long-term prediction of marital quality following a relationship education program: Being positive in a constructive way. *Journal of Family Psychology, 20*(3), 448–455.

Bauer-Wu, S. M. (2002). Psychoneuroimmunology part I: Physiology. *Clinical Journal of Oncology Nursing, 6*(3), 167–170.

Beach, S. R. H., Hurt, T. R., Franklin, K. J., Fincham, F. D., McNair, L. M., & Stanley, S. M. (2011). Enhancing marital enrichment through spirituality: Efficacy data for prayer focused relationship enhancement. *Psychology of Religion and Spirituality, 33*(3), 201–216. doi:10.1037/a0022207

Berg, M. T., & Huebner, B. M. (2011). Reentry and the ties that bind: An examination of social ties, employment, and recidivism. *Justice Quarterly, 28*(2), 382–410.

Bernal, G., & Saez-Santiago, E. (2006). Culturally centered psychosocial interventions. *Journal of Community Psychology, 34*(2), 121–132. doi:10.1002/jcop.20096

Blanchard, V. L., Hawkins, A. J., Baldwin, S. A., & Fawcett, E. B. (2009). Investigating the effects of marriage and relationship education on couples' communication skills: A meta-analytic study. *Journal of Family Psychology, 23*(2), 203–214. doi:10.1037/a0015211

Bodenmann, G., Bradbury, T. N., & Pihet, S. (2009). Relative contributions of treatment-related changes in communication skills and dyadic coping skills to the longitudinal course of marriage in the framework of marital distress prevention. *Journal of Divorce & Remarriage, 50*, 1–21. doi:10.1080/10502550802365391

Bodenmann, G., & Randall, A. K. (2020). General and health-related stress and couples' cop-ing. In K. S. Wampler & A. J. Blow (Eds.), *The handbook of systemic family therapy: Systemic family therapy with couples (3)*. Hoboken, NJ: Wiley.

Bowling, T. K., Hill, C. M., & Jencius, M. (2005). An overview of marriage enrichment. *The Family Journal, 13*(1), 87–94.

Bradford, A. B., Adler-Baeder, F., Ketring, S. A., Bub, K. L., Pittman, J. F., & Smith, T. A. (2014). Relationship quality and depressed affect among a diverse sample of relationally unstable relationship education participants. *Family Relations, 63*, 219–231. doi:10.1111/fare.12064

Bradford, A. B., Hawkins, A. J., & Acker, J. (2015). If we build it, they will come: Exploring policy and practice implications of public support for couple and relationship education for lower income and relationally distressed couples. *Family Process*, 54(4), 639–654.

Bradford, K., Stewart, J. W., Pfister, R., & Higginbotham, B. J. (2016). Avoid falling for a jerk(ette): Effectiveness of the premarital interpersonal choices and knowledge program among emerging adults. *Journal of Marital & Family Therapy*, 42(4), 630–644.

Carlson, R. G., Barden, S. M., Daire, A. P., & Greene, J. (2014). Influence of relationship education on relationship satisfaction for low-income couples. *Journal of Counseling & Development*, 92(4), 418–427.

Carlson, R. G., Barden, S. M., Daire, A. P., & Swartz, M. (2014). Examining parental alliance for low-income participants who attended relationship education with or without a partner. *Journal of Couple and Relationship Therapy*, 13(2), 153–170. doi:10.1080/1533269 1.2013.871615

Carlson, R. G., Case Pease, J. Wheeler, N. J., Liu, X., McDonald, J., & Strawn, L. (2016). Characteristics of couples who attend family services counselor visits in relationship education. *Marriage & Family Review*, 53, 48–64. doi:10.1080/01494929.2016.1204407

Carlson, R. G., Daire, A. P., & Bai, H. (2014). Examining relationship satisfaction and individual distress for low-to-moderate income couples in relationship education. *The Family Journal*, 22(3), 282–291.

Carlson, R. G., Daire, A. P., Munyon, M. D., Soto, D., Bennett, A., Marshall, D., & McKinzie, C. (2012). Examining recruitment follow-up phone calls and their influence on attendance for husbands and wives in a marriage and relationship education program. *Marriage & Family Review*, 48(1), 82–95. doi:10.1080/01494929.2011.627493

Carlson, R. G., Fripp, J., Munyon, M., Daire, A. P., Johnson, J., & DeLorenzi, L. (2014). Examining passive and active recruitment methods for low-income couples in relationship education. *Marriage & Family Review*, 50(1), 76–91. doi:10.1080/01494929.201 3.851055

Carlson, R. G., Rappleyea, D. L., Daire, A. P., Harris, S. M., & Liu, X. (2017). The effectiveness of couple and individual relationship education: Distress as a moderator. *Family Process*, 56(1), 91–104. doi:10.1111/famp.12172

Carlson, R. G., Rogers, T. L., Wheeler, N. J., Kelchner, V., Griffith, S.-A. M., & Liu, X. (2017). The continuum of conflict and control relationship scale (CCC-RS): Psychometrics for a measure designed to discriminate among types of intimate partner violence. *Measurement and Evaluation in Counseling and Development*, 50(3), 155–169. doi:10.10 80/07481756.2017.1320945

Carlson, R. G., Wheeler, N. J., & Adams, J. (2018). The influence of individual-oriented relationship education on equality and conflict-related behaviors. *Journal of Counseling & Development*, 96(2), 144–154. doi:10.1002/jcad.12188

Daire, A. P., Carlson, R. G., Barden, S. M., & Jacobson, L. (2014). Intimate partner violence (IPV) protocol readiness model. *The Family Journal*, 22(2), 170–178.

Daire, A. P., Harris, S. M., Carlson, R. G., Munyon, M. D., Rappleyea, D. L., Beverly, M. G., & Hiett, J. (2012). Fruits of improved communication: The experiences of Hispanic couples in a relationship education program. *Journal of Couple & Relationship Therapy: Innovations in Clinical and Educational Interventions*, 11(2), 112–129.

Dixon, P. (2014). AARMS: The African-American relationships and marriage strengthening curriculum for African American relationship courses and programs. *Journal of African American Studies*, 18(3), 337–352.

Doss, B. D., Cicila, L. N., Georgia, E. J., Roddy, M. K., Nowlan, K. M., Benson, L. A., & Christenson, A. (2016). A randomized controlled trial of the web-based OurRelationship program: Effects on relationship and individual functioning. *Journal of Consulting and Clinical Psychology*, 84(4), 285–296. doi:10.1037/ccp0000063

Doss, B. D., Rhoades, G. K., Stanley, S. M., & Markman, H. J. (2009). Marital therapy, retreats, and books: The who, what, when, and why of relationship help-seeking. *Journal of Marital & Family Therapy, 35*(1), 18–29.

Doss, B. D., Roddy, M. K., Nowlan, K. M., Rothman, K., & Christensen, A. (2018). Maintenance of gains in relationship and individual functioning following the online OurRelationship program. *Behavior Therapy, 50,* 73–86. doi:10.1016/j.beth.2018.03.011

Dum, R. P., Levinthal, D. J., & Strick, P. L. (2016). Motor, cognitive, and affective areas of the cerebral cortex influence the adrenal medulla. *PNAS Proceedings of the National Academy of Sciences of the United States of America, 113*(35), 9922–9927.

Einhorn, L., Williams, T., Stanley, S. M., Markman, H. J., & Eason, J. (2008). PREP inside and out: Marriage education for inmates. *Family Process, 47*(3), 341–356.

Fawcett, E. B., Hawkins, A. J., Blanchard, V. L., & Carroll, J. S. (2010). Do premarital education programs really work? A meta-analytic study. *Family Relations, 59*(3), 232–239. doi:10.1111/j.1741-3729.2010.00-598.x

Geller, A., Cooper, C., Garfinkel, I., Schwartz-Soicher, O., & Mincy, R. (2012). Beyond absenteeism: Father incarceration and child development. *Demography, 49*(1), 49–76.

Giblin, P., Sprenkle, D. H., & Sheehan, R. (1985). Enrichment outcome research: A meta-analysis of premarital, marital and family interventions. *Journal of Marital and Family Therapy, 11*(3), 257–271.

Goldenberg, I., Stanton, M., & Goldenberg, H. (2017). *Family therapy: An overview* (9th ed.). Boston, MA: Cengage Learning.

Gubits, D., Lowenstein, A. E., Harris, J., & Hsueh, J. (2014). *Do the effects of a relationship education program vary for different types of couples? Exploratory subgroup analysis in the Supporting Healthy Marriage evaluation* (OPRE Report No. 2014-22). Washington, DC: Office of Planning, Research and Evaluation, Administration for Children and Families, U. S. Department of Health and Human Services.

Guyton, A. C., & Hall, J. E. (1996). *Textbook of medical physiology* (9th ed.). Philadelphia, PA: W. B. Saunders.

Hadfield, K., Amos, M., Ungar, M., Gosselin, J., & Ganong, L. (2018). Do changes to family structure affect child and family outcomes? A systemic review of the instability hypothesis. *Journal of Family Theory & Review, 10*(1), 87–110.

Hahlweg, K., Markman, H. J., Thurmaier, F., Engl, J., & Eckert, V. (1998). Prevention of marital distress: Results of a German prespective longitudinal study. *Journal of Family Psychology, 12*(4), 543–556. doi:10.1037/0893-3200.12.4.543

Halford, K. W., Markman, H. J., Kline, G. H., & Stanley, S. (2003). Best practice in couple relationship education. *Journal of Marital and Family Therapy, 29*(3), 385–406.

Halford, K. W., Sanders, M. R., & Behrens, B. C. (2001). Can skills training prevent relationship problems in at-risk couples? Four-year effects of a behavioral relationship education program. *Journal of Family Psychology, 15*(4), 750–768.

Halford, W. K. (2011). *Marriage and relationship education: What works and how to provide it.* New York, NY: Guilford.

Halford, W. K., Markman, H. J., & Stanley, S. (2008). Strengthening couples' relationships with education: Social policy and public health perspectives. *Journal of Family Psychology, 22*(4), 497–505.

Halford, W. K., Rahimullah, R. H., Wilson, K. L., Occhipinti, S., Busby, D. M., & Larson, J. (2017). Four year effects of couple relationship education on low and high satisfaction couples: A randomized clinical trial. *Journal of Consulting and Clinical Psychology, 85*(5), 495–507.

Halford, W. K., & Simons, M. (2005). Couple relationship education in Australia. *Family Process, 44*(2), 147–159.

Harcourt, K. T., Adler-Baeder, F., Rauer, A., Pettit, G. S., & Erath, S. (2017). Relationship education for incarcerated adults. *Family Process, 56*(1), 75–90. doi:10.1111/famp.12164

Hawkins, A. J., Allen, S. E., & Yang, C. (2017). How does couple and relationship education affect relationship hope? An intervention-process study with lower income couples. *Family Relations, 66*(3), 441–452. doi:10.1111/fare.12268

Hawkins, A. J., Amato, P. R., & Kinghorn, A. (2013). Are government-supported healthy marriage initiatives affecting family demographics? A state-level analysis. *Family Relations, 62*(3), 501–513.

Hawkins, A. J., Blanchard, V. L., Baldwin, S. A., & Fawcett, E. B. (2008). Does marriage and relationship education work? A meta-analytic study. *Journal of Consulting and Clinical Psychology, 76*, 723–734. doi:10.1037/a0012584

Hawkins, A. J., Carroll, J. S., Doherty, W. J., & Willoughby, B. (2004). A comprehensive framework for marriage education. *Family Relations, 53*(5), 547–558.

Hawkins, A. J., & Erickson, S. E. (2015). Is couples and relationship education effective for lower income participants? A meta-analytic study. *Journal of Family Psychology, 29*(1), 59–68. doi:10.1037/fam0000045

Hawkins, A. J., & Fackrell, T. A. (2010). Does relationship and marriage education for lower-income couples work? A meta-analytic study of emerging research. *Journal of Couple & Relationship Therapy, 9*(2), 181–191. doi:10.1080/15332691003694927

Hawkins, A. J., Higginbotham, B. J., & Hatch, D. J. (2016). Can media campaigns increase participation in premarital education? The case of the Utah Healthy Marriages Initiative. *Journal of Couple & Relationship Therapy, 15*(1), 19–35.

Hawkins, A. J., Stanley, S. M., Blanchard, V. L., & Albright, M. (2012). Exploring programmatic moderators of the effectiveness of marriage and relationship education programs: A meta-analytic study. *Behavior Therapy, 43*, 77–87.

Herman-Stahl, M., Kan, M. L., & McKay, T. (2008). *Incarceration and the family: A review of research and promising approaches for serving fathers and families.* Prepared for US DHHS—Office of the Assistant Secretary for Planning and Evaluation—ACF/OFA.

Higginbotham, B. J., & Myler, C. (2011). The influence of facilitator and facilitation characteristics on participants' ratings of stepfamily education. *Family Relations, 59*(1), 74–86. doi:10.1111/j.1741-3792.2009.00587.x

Hsueh, J., Alderson, D. P., Lundquist, E., Michalopoulos, C., Gubits, D., & Fein, D. (2012). *The Supporting Healthy Marriage evaluation: Early impacts on low-income families, technical supplement* (OPRE Report No. 2012-27). Washington, DC: Office of Planning, Research and Evaluation, Administration for Children and Families, US Department of Health and Human Services.

Huang, W. (2005). An Asian perspective on relationship and marriage education. *Family Process, 44*(2), 161–173.

Isakson, R., Hawkins, E., Harmon, S., Slade, K., Martinez, J., & Lambert, M. (2006). Assessing couple therapy as a treatment for individual distress: When is referral to couple therapy contraindicated? *Contemporary Family Therapy: An International Journal, 28*(3), 313–322.

Jones, G. W., & Yueng, W. J. (2014). Marriage in Asia. *Journal of Family Issues, 35*(12), 1567–1583.

Karam, E. A., Antle, B. F., Stanley, S. M., & Rhoades, G. K. (2015). The marriage of couple and relationship education to the practice of marriage and family therapy: A primer for integrated training. *Journal of Couple & Relationship Therapy, 14*(3), 277–295.

Karney, B. R., & Bradbury, B. N. (2005). Contextual influences on marriage: Implications for policy and intervention. *Current Directions in Psychological Science, 14*(4), 171–174.

Ketring, S. A., Bradford, A. B., Davis, S. Y., Adler-Baeder, F., McGill, J., & Smith, T. A. (2017). The role of the facilitator in couple relationship education. *Journal of Marital and Family Therapy, 43*(3), 374–390.

Kiecolt-Glaser, J. K., McGuire, L., Robles, T. F., & Glaser, R. (2002). Psychoneuroimmunology: Psychological influences on immune function and health. *Journal of Consulting and Clinical Psychology, 70*(3), 537–547.

Kimmel, P. L., Peterson, R. A., Weihs, K. L., Shidler, N., Simmens, S. J., Alleyne, S., ... Phillips, T. M. (2000). Dyadic relationship conflict, gender, and mortality in urban hemodialysis patients. *Journal of the American Society of Nephrology, 11*(8), 1518–15225.

Knox, V., Cowan, P. A., Cowan, C. P., & Bildner, E. (2011). Policies that strengthen fatherhood and family relationships: What do we know and what do we need to know? *Annals of the American Academy of Political & Social Science, 635*, 216–235. doi:10.1177/0002716210394769

Kor, A., Mikulincer, M., & Pirutinsky, S. (2012). Family functioning among returnees to Orthodox Judaism in Israel. *Journal of Family Psychology, 26*(1), 149–158.

Kudielka, B. M., & Kirschbaum, C. (2007). Biological bases of the stress response. In M. Absi (Ed.), *Stress and addiction: Biological and psychological mechanisms* (pp. 3–15). Cambridge, MA: Elsevier.

Larson, R. W., & Almeida, D. M. (1999). Emotional transmission in the daily lives of families: A new paradigm for studying family process. *Journal of Marriage and the Family, 61*(1), 5–20.

Lee, D., & McLanahan, S. (2015). Family structure transitions and child development. *American Sociological Review, 80*(4), 738–763.

Littrell, J. (2008). The mind-body connection. *Social Work in Health Care, 46*(4), 17–37.

Lopez, J. L., Riggs, S. A., Pollard, S. E., & Hook, J. N. (2011). Religious commitment, adult attachment, and marital adjustment in newly married couples. *Journal of Family Psychology, 25*(2), 301–309. doi:10.1037/a0022943

Lubis, S. A. (2011). Islamic counseling: The services of mental health and education for people. *Religious Education, 106*(5), 494–503.

Maack, D. J., Buchanan, E., & Young, J. (2015). Development and psychometric investigation of an inventory to assess fight, flight, and freeze tendencies: The fight, flight, and freeze questionnaire. *Cognitive Behaviour Therapy, 44*(2), 117–127.

Malarkey, W. B., Kiecolt-Glaser, J. K., Pearl, D., & Glaser, R. (1994). Hostile behavior during marital conflict alters pituitary and adrenal hormones. *Psychosomatic Medicine, 56*(1), 41–51.

Markey, B., Micheletto, M. P., & Jirgal, S. A. (1997). *FOCUSS: Facilitating open couple communication, understanding, and study.* Omaha, NE: FOCUSS, Inc.

Markman, H. J., & Rhoades, G. K. (2012). Relationship education research: Current status and future directions. *Journal of Marital & Family Therapy, 38*(1), 169–200.

Markman, H. J., Rhoades, G. K., Stanley, S. M., Ragan, E. P., & Whitton, S. W. (2010). The premarital communication roots of marital distress and divorce: The first five years of marriage. *Journal of Family Psychology, 24*(3), 289–298.

Markman, H. J., & Ritchie, L. L. (2015). Couples relationship education and couples therapy: Healthy marriage or strange bedfellows? *Family Process, 54*(4), 655–671.

Markman, H. J., Stanley, S. M., & Blumberg, S. L. (2010). *Fighting for your marriage: A deluxe revised edition of the classic best-seller for enhancing marriage and preventing divorce.* San Francisco, CA: Jossey-Bass.

Maybruch, C., Pirutinsky, S., & Pelcovitz, D. (2014). Religious premarital education and marital quality within the Orthodox Jewish community. *Journal of Couple & Relationship Therapy, 13*(4), 365–381.

McCormick, M. P., Hsueh, J., Merrilees, C., Chou, P., & Cummings, E. M. (2017). Moods, stressors, and severity of marital conflict: A daily diary study of low-income families. *Family Relations, 66*(3), 425–440. doi:10.1111/fare.12258

McEwen, B. S. (1998). Protective and damaging effects of stress mediators. *New England Journal of Medicine, 338*(3), 171–179.

McEwen, B. S., & Stellar, E. (1993). Stress and the individual: Mechanisms leading to disease. *Archives of Internal Medicine, 153*(18), 2093–2101.

Neff, L. A., & Broady, E. F. (2011). Stress resilience in early marriage: Can practice make perfect? *Journal of Personality & Social Psychology, 101*(5), 1050–1067.

Neff, L. A., & Karney, B. R. (2007). Stress crossover in newlywed marriage: A longitudinal and dyadic perspective. *Journal of Marriage and Family, 69*(3), 594–607.

Neff, L. A., & Karney, B. R. (2009). Stress and reactivity to daily relationship experiences: How stress hinders adaptive process in marriage. *Journal of Personality and Social Psychology, 97*(3), 435–450.

Ngazimbi, E. E., Daire, A. P., Carlson, R. G., & Munyon, M. D. (2017). Analysis of marital expectations in African immigrants and United-States-born married couples. *The Qualitative Report, 23*(3), 831–848.

Ngazimbi, E. E., Daire, A. P., Soto, D., Carlson, R. G., & Munyon, M. (2013). Marital expectations and marital satisfaction between African immigrant and United States born married couples. *Journal of Psychology in Africa, 23*(2), 317–322.

Olson, D. H. (2002). *PREPARE/ENRICH counselors' manual.* Life Innovations, Inc.: Minneapolis, MN.

Ooms, T. (2007). *Adapting healthy marriage programs for disadvantaged and culturally diverse populations: What are the issues? Center for Law and Social Policy Brief: Couples and Marriage Series*, March 2007, Brief No. 10. (pp. 1–12). Washington, DC: Center for Law and Social Policy.

Owen, J., Antle, B., & Barbee, A. (2013). Alliance and group cohesion in relationship education. *Family Process, 52*, 465–476.

Owen, J., Rhoades, G. K., & Stanley, S. M. (2013). Sliding versus deciding in relationships: Associations with relationship quality, commitment, and infidelity. *Journal of Couple & Relationship Therapy, 12*, 135–149. doi:10.1080/15332691.2013.779097

Owen, J. J., Rhoades, G. K., Stanley, S. M., & Markman, H. J. (2011). The role of leaders' working alliance in premarital education. *Journal of Marital and Family Therapy, 25*(1), 49–57. doi:10.1037/a0022084

Prepare/Enrich, Llc. (2017). *Pepare/Enrich.* Retrieved from https://www.prepare-enrich.com/

Quirk, K., Owen, J., Inch, L. J., France, T., & Bergen, C. (2014). The alliance in relationship education programs. *Journal of Marital and Family Therapy, 40*(2), 178–192. doi:10.1111/jmft.12019

Rhoades, G. K. (2015). The effectiveness of the within our reach relationship education program for couples: Findings from a federal randomized trial. *Family Process, 54*(4), 672–685.

Rhoades, G. K., & Stanley, S. M. (2011). Using individual-oriented relationship education to prevent family violence. *Journal of Couple & Relationship Therapy, 10*(2), 185–200. doi:10.1080/153322691.2011.562844

Røsand, G. B., Slinning, K., Røysamb, E., & Tambs, K. (2014). Relationship dissatisfaction and other risk factors for future relationship dissolution: A population-based study of 18,523 couples. *Social Psychiatry &Psychiatric Epidemiology, 49*(1), 109–119.

Schumm, W. R., Walker, A. B., Nazarinia, R. R., West, D. A., Atwell, C., Barko, A., & Kriley, A. (2010). Predicting the short- and long-term helpfulness of premarital counseling: The critical role of counseling quality. *Journal of Couple & Relationship Therapy, 9*(1), 1–15.

Scott, S. B., Rhoades, G. K., Stanley, S. M., Allen, E. S., & Markman, H. J. (2013). Reasons for divorce and recollections of premarital intervention: Implications for improving relationship education. *Couple and Family Psychology, 2*(2), 131–145.

Sherman, D. K., Bunyan, D. P., Creswell, J. D., & Jaremka, L. M. (2009). Psychological vulnerability and stress: The effects of self-affirmation on sympathetic nervous system responses to naturalistic stressors. *Health Psychology, 28*(5), 554–562.

Sigle-Rushton, W., Lynstad, T. H., Andersen, P. L., & Kravdal, Ø. (2014). Proceed with caution? Parents' union dissolution and children's educational achievement. *Journal of Marriage & Family, 76*(1), 161–174.

Simpson, D. M., Leonhardt, N. D., & Hawkins, A. J. (2018). Learning about love: A meta-analytic study of individually-oriented relationship education programs for adolescents and emerging adults. *Journal of Youth and Adolescence, 47*(3), 477–489.

Snyder, D. K., Heyman, R. E., & Haynes, S. N. (2005). Evidence-based approaches to assessing couple distress. *Psychological Assessment, 17*(3), 288–307.

Stanley, S. M. (2001). Making a case for premarital education. *Family Relations, 50*(3), 272–280.

Stanley, S. M., Amato, P. R., Johnson, C. A., & Markman, H. J. (2006). Premarital education, marital quality, and marital stability: Findings from a large, random household survey. *Journal of Family Psychology, 20*(1), 117–126. doi:10.1037/0893-3200.20.1.11

Stanley, S. M., Markman, H. J., Jenkins, N., Rhoades, G. K., Noll, L., & Ramos, L. (2006). *Within our reach leader manual.* Denver, CO: PREP, Inc.

Stanley, S. M., Markman, H. J., St. Peters, M., & Leber, D. B. (1995). Strengthening marriages and preventing divorce: New directions in prevention research. *Family Relations, 44*, 392–401.

Stanley, S. M., Rhoades, G. K., Scott, S. B., Kelmer, G., Markman, H. J., & Fincham, F. D. (2017). Asymmetrically committed relationships. *Journal of Social and Personal Relationships, 34*(8), 1241–1259. doi:10.1177/0265407516672013

Tausk, F., Elenkov, I., & Moynihan, J. (2008). Psychoneuroimmunology. *Dermatologic Therapy, 21*, 22–31.

Timaeus, I. M., & Reynar, A. (1998). Polygynists and their wives in sub-Saharan Africa: Analysis of five demographic and health surveys. *Population Studies, 52*(2), 145–162.

Torres, L., Hyra, A., & Bouchet, S. (2013). *HHMI grantee implementation evaluation: Hispanics and family-strengthening programs: Cultural strategies to enhance program participation* (OPRE Report No. 2013-19). Washington, DC: Office of Planning, Research and Evaluation, Administration for Children and Families, US Department of Health and Human Services.

Van Epp, J. C. (2006). *How to avoid marrying a jerk.* New York, NY: McGraw-Hill.

Van Epp, M. C., Futris, T. G., Van Epp, J. C., & Campbell, K. (2008). The impact of the PICK a partner relationship education program on single army soldiers. *Family and Consumer Science Research Journal, 36*(4), 328–349.

Van Widenfelt, B., Hosman, C., Schaap, C., & van der Staak, C. (1996). The prevention nof relationship distress for couples at risk: A controlled evaluation with nine-month and two-year follow-ups. *Family Relations, 45*(2), 156–165.

Visher, C. A., & Travis, J. (2003). Transitions from prison to community: Understanding individual pathways. *Annual Review of Sociology, 29*, 89–113.

Visvanathan, P. D., Richmond, M., Winder, C., & Koench, C. H. (2014). Individual-oriented relationship education: An evaluation study in community-based settings. *Family Process.* doi:10.1111/famp.12116

Wakefield, S. (2015). Accentuating the positive or eliminating the negative? Paternal incarceration and caregiver-child relationship quality. *Journal of Criminal Law & Criminology, 104*(4), 905–927.

Westman, M. (2001). Stress and strain crossover. *Human Relations, 54*(6), 717–751.

Wetzler, S., Frame, L., & Litzinger, S. (2011). Marriage education for clinicians. *American Journal of Psychotherapy, 65*(4), 311–336.

Wheeler, N. (2017). *Exploring relationship quality as a dyadic mediator of adverse childhood experiences and health for economically disadvantaged couples* (Dissertation). Retrieved from: http://stars.library.ucf.edu/etd/5380

Whisman, M. A. (2007). Marital distress and DSM-IV psychiatric disorders in a population-based national survey. *Journal of Abnormal Psychology, 116*(3), 638–643.

Whiting, J. B., Bradford, K. B., Vail, A., Carlton, E. T., & Bathje, K. (2009). Developing a domestic violence protocol for marriage education: Critical components and cautions. *Journal of Couple & Relationship Therapy*, *8*(2), 181–196. doi:10.1080/15332690902813844

Williamson, H. C., Altman, N., Hsueh, J., & Bradbury, T. N. (2016). Effects of relationship education on couple communication and satisfaction: A randomized controlled trial with low-income couples. *Journal of Consulting and Clinical Psychology*, *84*(2), 156–166.

Williamson, H. C., Trail, T. E., Bradbury, T. N., & Karney, B. R. (2014). Does premarital education decrease or increase couples' later help-seeking? *Journal of Family Psychology*, *28*(1), 112–117. doi:10.1037/a0034984

Wilmoth, J. D., & Smyser, S. (2012). A national survey of marriage preparation provided by clergy. *Journal of Couple & Relationship Therapy*, *11*(1), 69–85.

Wood, R. G., McConnell, S., Moore, Q., Clarkwest, A., & Hsueh, J. (2010). *The building strong families project. Strengthening unmarried parents' relationships: The early impacts of building strong families*. Administration for Children and Families, Office of Family Assistance. Mathematica Policy Research.

4

Treating Common Couple Concerns

Lee M. Williams

Working with couples can be both a rewarding and challenging clinical experience. Part of that challenge comes from the variety of issues that couples may present in therapy. This chapter will identify common concerns that couples may bring to therapy, as well as possible strategies for addressing these concerns. Therefore, it is hoped that the chapter will be beneficial in terms of thinking both about assessment and intervention for couples.

The chapter will be organized around 8 C's: communication, conflict resolution, commitment, contract, caring, character, culture, and children. Birchler, Doumas, and Fals-Stewart (1999) proposed the first 7 C's as important factors that could impact marital functioning. The eighth C, children, has been added by the author to reflect the important influence that children can have on a couple's relationship. This chapter builds on the work of Birchler and his colleagues by providing an updated perspective on the 8 C's, including the integration of concepts from models that have grown in prominence over the past two decades.

The 8 C's allow clinicians to integrate ideas from a variety of theoretical perspectives. Because the chapter focuses on couples, the concepts and interventions will be primarily based on couple-focused therapies, particularly those with empirical support such as emotionally focused therapy (EFT) (Johnson, 2004, 2015), integrative behavioral couple therapy (IBCT) (Christensen, Dimidjian, & Martell, 2015), and the Prevention and Relationship Enhancement Program (PREP) (Markman, Stanley, & Blumberg, 2010). However, clinicians can also draw upon other family systems models (e.g., structural, strategic, Bowen, narrative) to inform their work. Clinicians can also integrate knowledge from other sources, including research, clinical literature, or even their own insights. For example, research by John Gottman and his colleagues has been extremely influential in our understanding of couples. Therefore, several concepts and interventions based on Gottman's research have been integrated into the chapter. In essence, the 8 C's can be a file cabinet for organizing a wealth of information the clinician may possess about couple relationships.

Clinicians typically use a variety of approaches to collect information during assessment, including clinical observation (e.g., communication samples), relationship

The Handbook of Systemic Family Therapy: Volume 3, First Edition.
Edited by Karen S. Wampler and Adrian J. Blow.
© 2020 John Wiley & Sons Ltd. Published 2020 by John Wiley & Sons Ltd.

histories, genograms, interview questions, and assessment instruments (Edwards, Williams, Speice, & Patterson, 2020, vol. 1). The 8 C's can help clinicians organize the wealth of assessment information they have collected, giving them insight into the key areas of growth and strengths for each couple (Edwards et al., 2020, vol. 1). If important information is missing from one or more of the C's, the therapist can do further assessment to uncover possible concerns or strengths in those areas. Thus, using the 8 C's can facilitate a more thorough assessment, giving the therapist confidence that the key domains of couple functioning have been considered. Furthermore, the 8 C's can be used to structure the feedback given to couples.

Communication

Couples frequently come into therapy complaining that they have issues with communication. Teaching couples communication skills is an important element in many models of couple therapy, including IBCT (Christensen et al., 2015) and cognitive-behavioral couple therapy (CBCT) (Baucom, Epstein, Kirby, & LaTaillade, 2015). Communication skills are also an integral part of approaches that focus on marriage education or enrichment, such as PREP (Markman et al., 2010) or Relationship Enhancement (Scuka, 2016). Communication skills typically focus on teaching individuals how to present issues in an effective manner and become better listeners.

Common problems in communication

Couple communication can be surprisingly complex, with multiple things happening almost simultaneously. The speaker must first formulate what message he or she wants to communicate. This message can be expressed both verbally and nonverbally. The listener must attend to both the verbal and nonverbal signals before deciphering the meaning of the speaker's message. Problems or miscommunication can arise at any of these points.

External and internal processors   Communication problems can arise if a couple have different styles with regard to how formulated the message must be before they articulate it (Williams & Tappan, 1995). Some individuals are external processors, meaning they will begin to share what they are thinking before they have arrived at the final answer. Talking things out helps them determine what they are thinking and feeling. In contrast, internal processors are not likely to share anything out loud until they have figured out what they want to say. They may even mentally rehearse exactly what they want to say.

Neither style is right or wrong, but problems can arise if individuals do not understand their mate's different processing style. For example, internal processors may feel confused by what appear to be contradictions in what external processors are saying. What they do not recognize is that what is said in the beginning are initial drafts, which are subject to change as external processors continue to explore their thoughts and feelings. External processors sometimes feel frustration with internal processors when they do not respond right away. They may misinterpret their mate's initial silence as a lack of concern or interest in the topic rather than a need to process things first. Internal processors, in turn, do not like the pressure of coming up with a response before they have had time to figure out what they are thinking or feeling.

Educating couples on the concept of external and internal processing can be a helpful first step in reducing conflict. External processors are encouraged to recognize that internal processors may need time to contemplate things before talking, while internal processors are reminded that talking things out is the external processor's way of figuring things out. It is also helpful if both individuals explicitly state when they are internally or externally processing. For example, external processors can ask their mates to be a sounding board as they try to process something. Conversely, internal processors can reassure their mates that their initial silence does not mean the topic is being ignored, but they are taking time to formulate their response.

The Four Horsemen   How partners communicate their messages to one another can influence how receptive the other is, especially if the topic has the potential to create conflict. In his research on couples, Gottman (1999) found that frequently using criticism, contempt, defensiveness, or stonewalling when addressing issues is a predictor of divorce or relationship disruption. Gottman referred to these as the "Four Horsemen of the Apocalypse." When individuals use criticism, they attack their partner's character rather than focusing on just the behavior. This may lead to partners becoming defensive (e.g., make excuses, counter blame), another of the Four Horsemen. Contempt is demonstrated when individuals put their partner down verbally or nonverbally, treating them as being inferior. For example, an individual may roll his or her eyes in contempt, as if to say, "How could I have married someone so stupid!" Criticism and contempt may eventually lead the partner to psychologically shut down through stonewalling, the fourth of the horsemen.

Couples can be taught a variety of skills to reduce the Four Horsemen (Gottman, 1999; Gottman & Gottman, 2015). The antidote to criticism is to teach individuals to use "I" statements. "I" statements encourage individuals to state how they feel about their partner's behavior ("I'm frustrated that you left your dirty dishes in the sink last night") rather than attack their character ("You are such a slob!"). "I" statements also remind individuals to take responsibility for how they feel rather than blame their partner for their feelings, which will likely make the partner more receptive to the individual's message. To reduce defensiveness, individuals are encouraged to take some responsibility for the problem. Building a culture of respect and appreciation for one another is the antidote for contempt. Individuals are taught to develop a "habit of mind" where they focus on being more aware of the positives in the relationship. This is accomplished by having individuals get into the practice of looking for and vocalizing appreciation for the positive things their partner does. The best way to prevent stonewalling is to help couples manage conflict before it escalates to the point where individuals become flooded with negative emotions.

Minimize distractions   Being distracted can interfere with communication because individuals cannot accurately interpret a message if they do not receive all its parts. Individuals can be distracted by external stimuli (e.g., watching TV, children arguing in the background) or by internal distractions (e.g., preoccupied with a task, focusing on making a rebuttal rather than listening). Therefore, encouraging individuals to set aside distractions can be helpful in communicating. It also helps if the listener gives the speaker signs that he or she is listening, such as making eye contact or accurately restating what the speaker said.

Addressing filters   Individuals often use past experiences to help them understand or interpret the meaning of a speaker's message. These past experiences create filters that may shape the interpretation of what the partner says or does (Markman et al., 2010). For example, Elizabeth asks her partner Jada, "Are you making dinner?" If Elizabeth has a history of being critical of Jada around doing household chores, then Jada may assume there is implied criticism behind the question (i.e., "Why haven't you made dinner yet?"). In some cases, these filters may lead individuals to misinterpret the intent behind the speaker's message. Elizabeth may have simply wanted to know if Jada had plans to make dinner or if Jada might want her to make dinner instead.

Therapists can improve couple communication by identifying filters that distort their communication. For example, Anton grew up being told by his mother that he was just like his father, whom she clearly hated. Over time, Anton developed a filter that looked for rejection. This filter became problematic for Anton in his marriage to Hawley, who became increasingly frustrated by Anton feeling unloved by her. However, her expressions of frustration were interpreted as a sign of rejection, further reinforcing Anton's filter. The therapist helped Anton and Hawley recognize the presence of the filter and how to challenge it.

Speaker–Listener Technique

Another way to improve communication is to teach couples the Speaker-Listener Technique (Markman et al., 2010) or something similar to it. The Speaker-Listener Technique is particularly helpful for discussing a topic that may create conflict. Using the Speaker-Listener Technique, individuals take turns being in the respective roles of speaker and listener. When the speaker has the floor, he or she is instructed to speak for himself or herself and avoid mind reading what the other may be thinking. The speaker is also encouraged to use the "I" statements described earlier, as well as keep statements brief. This allows the listener the opportunity to paraphrase what the speaker has said to confirm understanding. The listener is told to focus on paraphrasing the speaker's message rather than offering a rebuttal. Couples are told that the goal of paraphrasing is to confirm that the individual understands what the partner is saying, which is different from agreeing with what the partner is saying. When addressing problems, couples are encouraged to first understand where each person is coming from before moving too quickly into problem solving (Gottman & Gottman, 2015; Markman et al., 2010).

Conflict Resolution

Conflict is often the precipitating factor that brings couples into therapy. How a couple relates around the problem is frequently just as important as the problem itself. Therefore, the therapist must not only understand the nature of the problem but also how the couple relates to one another around the problem.

Vicious cycles

A common element behind many couple therapy approaches is to identify and disrupt dysfunctional interactional patterns (Davis, Lebow, & Sprenkle, 2012). These interactional patterns often take the form of a vicious cycle. A common vicious cycle is for one individual to feel hurt or abandoned by the other. In response to this hurt, the individual becomes angry and critical of the partner. However, the expression of anger or criticism results in the partner withdrawing, which further reinforces the individual feeling hurt or abandoned.

Identifying and altering these vicious cycles is often vital to the success of couple therapy. For example, an EFT therapist initially identifies the couple's vicious cycle in terms of reactive or secondary emotions such as anger and then eventually in terms of primary emotions such as hurt or fear (Johnson, 2004, 2015). In IBCT, the therapist identifies patterns of interaction that lead to polarizations over couple differences (Christensen et al., 2015). Likewise, the Gottman approach encourages couples to map out the anatomy of a fight, including the underlying emotional sensitivities for each partner (Gottman & Gottman, 2015).

Identifying the vicious cycle helps individuals take responsibility for their part of the problem, which can move couples away from a nonproductive blaming stance. Consistent with the concept of unified detachment in IBCT (Christensen et al., 2015), identifying the cycle helps couples better understand their dynamics, allowing them to view their relationship in a more objective way. Couples can be encouraged to view the cycle as the adversary, rather than each other.

The therapist's approach for altering the cycle of interaction may vary from theory to theory. For example, the EFT therapist will seek to alter the cycle by having clients express their primary emotions, as well as their disowned parts and needs (Johnson, 2004, 2015). Similarly, the IBCT therapist will encourage partners to express the softer or more vulnerable emotions behind their anger (Christensen et al., 2015). In CBCT, the therapist strives to alter the cognitions that drive the cycle (Baucom et al., 2015). Regardless of the approach, the therapist's goal is to disrupt the vicious cycle and allow a positive cycle to be implemented.

Emotional dysregulation

There is the potential for couples to become flooded with negative emotions as conflict escalates. When flooding occurs, individuals think much more negatively about their relationship and are most likely to say and do things that are destructive to the relationship.

Therefore, helping couples manage flooding when it arises is critical so that they do not do further damage to the relationship. The most common technique is to teach couples to recognize when they are becoming flooded and take a time-out (Gottman & Gottman, 2015; Markman et al., 2010). Couples are instructed to discontinue their argument or disagreement until both are no longer flooded. This typically takes at least 20 minutes, but can take longer for others, especially if they ruminate about the argument (Gottman, 1999). Thus, individuals may benefit from learning techniques to self-soothe so they can more quickly recover (Gottman & Gottman, 2015). It is important that couples resume the conversation at some point so that the time-out is not viewed as an avoidance strategy. It is recommended that whoever asks for the timeout is responsible for reinitiating the conversation. Using the Speaker-Listener Technique described earlier can be helpful when discussing topics that might lead to flooding.

Concepts from dialectical behavior therapy (DBT) have also been integrated into an approach for working with couples where one partner has borderline personality disorder or struggles with emotional dysregulation (Fruzzetti & Payne, 2015). A DBT approach with couples centers on a transactional view where emotional dysregulation on one partner's part can lead to invalidation from the other, which then fuels further emotional dysregulation. A chain analysis is done to help couples dissect their argument and determine skills they can use in the future to avoid a similar conflict. Some of these skills include using mindfulness to build awareness and reduce judgments, resisting urges for making destructive comments, accurately expressing one's primary emotions, and offering validation.

Relationship aggression

Therapists working with couples must always be mindful of the possibility of relationship aggression. Best practice suggests that therapists evaluate for relationship aggression at the outset of therapy using more than one technique (Bradford, 2010; Schacht, Dimidjian, George, & Berns, 2009). For example, using an instrument like the Revised Conflict Tactics Scales (Straus, Hamby, Boney-McCoy, & Sugarman, 1996) to screen for relationship aggression is recommended. In addition, during assessment, the therapist should meet with each partner individually to inquire about relationship aggression. Although there is evidence supporting the effectiveness of couple therapy in treating domestic violence (Stith, McCollum, Amanor-Boadu, & Smith, 2012), there will be some couples where conjoint therapy is contraindicated due to the nature and severity of the violence. See Stith, Spencer, and Mittal (2020, vol. 3) for a more detailed discussion regarding domestic violence in couples.

Resolvable versus perpetual problems

When addressing couple conflict, it may be important to distinguish between resolvable and perpetual problems (Gottman & Silver, 1999). Resolvable problems, as the name implies, are problems that can be solved or remedied. Once addressed, the couple does not need to revisit the problem again. However, couples also can have conflict over perpetual problems, which are problems that will rarely go away. These are problems that need to be managed rather than solved. Perpetual problems arise for all couples because there will be some ways in which two people in a relationship will be fundamentally different from one another. Perpetual problems arise over differences in values, preferences, temperament or personality, or other qualities not likely to change. As a result, individuals must learn to accept these differences (hopefully with a bit of good humor) so that frustration does not escalate into major conflict. Research suggests that 69% of a couple's conflicts will arise from perpetual problems (Gottman, 1999).

For resolvable problems, couples may find it helpful to use a problem-solving framework similar to one taught in PREP (Markman et al., 2010). The couple begins by clearly identifying the problem they are trying to solve. The couple next engages in brainstorming to generate a range of possible solutions. During brainstorming, the couple is encouraged to think outside the box and be as creative as possible in generating ideas and resist evaluating their ideas to avoid hindering creativity. In the next step, couples consider the pros and cons of each idea, eventually selecting which idea to implement. Often the solution will require compromise, with each partner taking some responsibility for implementing the agreed-upon solution. Finally, the couple evaluates the success of the solution after trying it for a time, deciding if they are happy with the outcome or want to consider other options.

As noted earlier, managing perpetual problems requires developing acceptance. From an IBCT perspective (Christensen et al., 2015), one might accept a partner by appreciating the value of their trait or behavior. For example, someone who spends money to enjoy life in the moment may appreciate his or her partner's discipline around saving money for future retirement. Acceptance also can be cultivated by seeing the behavior in the larger context of the person's life or understanding the deeper meaning of the behavior for the individual. Similarly, Gottman and Gottman (2015) believe that exploring the existential meaning ("dreams within conflict") is important when addressing perpetual problems. Alexander and his wife Libby were having conflict over their budget, including how much to set aside for savings each month. Libby felt saving a certain percentage of money each month was important for their future security, especially when contemplating retirement. Alexander, a paraplegic, resisted his wife's suggestion that they save such a large percentage of their income. Alexander told Libby that he knew he had a shortened lifespan due to the health concerns associated with him being a paraplegic. So, he questioned why he was saving for a future he might not see. He questioned why he should not be allowed to spend some money now to enjoy the present. Exploring the existential meaning behind their positions allowed the couple to talk about finances in a different way, which opened the door to negotiating a budget they could both accept. The concept of radical acceptance from DBT can also be applicable (Fruzzetti & Payne, 2015). Radical acceptance means that individuals accept reality for what it is rather than what they think it should be. Rather than thinking that their partner "should" be a particular way, individuals accept that "it is what it is."

Commitment

Commitment can help sustain couples through difficult times. Unfortunately, by the time some couples come to therapy, their commitment to the relationship has eroded. It is not uncommon for one or both partners to be seriously contemplating divorce. This section addresses how to manage couples where one or both are ambivalent about the relationship, as well as how to build commitment.

Working with ambivalence

One approach that a therapist can use with couples where one or both are considering ending the marriage is to conduct a marital or relationship evaluation (Patterson, Williams, Edwards, Chamow, & Grauf-Grounds, 2018). The goal of the evaluation is to help couples understand why the relationship is struggling and what steps might be necessary to resolve the issues. Metaphorically, an evaluation is similar to getting a diagnostic workup on a car that is not properly functioning. Like their car, individuals may know that their marriage is not working properly, but they may not know why it is not working and what it will take to remedy the problem. The marital or relationship evaluation helps answer these questions for the couple.

During the evaluation, the couple is not asked or expected to commit to working on the relationship. Rather, the couple can decide if they want to work on the relationship based on what they learn from the evaluation. For the partner invested in staying, the evaluation will provide insight on how he or she might begin to save the relationship. For the ambivalent partner, the evaluation will help the individual evaluate how difficult it will be to repair the relationship, which can inform the decision as to whether to invest in working on the relationship. In addition, the evaluation may identify issues that the individual may be vulnerable to repeating in subsequent relationships. For example, Rosa was burned out and angry at having to take care of her partner Steven, leading her to seriously contemplate divorce. The evaluation revealed that this was a repetitive pattern in her relationships. Rosa would get into relationships where she would overfunction as a caretaker, eventually becoming burned out and resentful. She would subsequently leave the relationship out of frustration. Rosa was cautioned that she was likely to repeat this pattern in future relationships and that she might as well work on altering this pattern in her current marriage.

Another approach called discernment counseling (Doherty, Harris, & Wilde, 2015) has been developed for working with mixed-agenda couples, those where one is invested in saving the marriage, while the other has serious doubts about continuing it. The goal of discernment counseling is to facilitate the couple deciding which one of three options to pursue. These options include divorce or separation, attempt to reconcile through couple therapy, or maintaining the status quo. The therapist devotes half the session to meeting with the partner considering divorce and the other half with the partner wanting to save the marriage. Conversations with the ambivalent partner focus on making a good decision and identifying his or her contribution to the problems. For the person invested in saving the marriage, the therapist makes sure the individual understands the partner's complaints, as well as steps he or she can do to attempt to save the marriage. For both individuals, the therapist emphasizes each taking responsibility for their contribution to the marriage's decline, along with identifying the couple's interactional pattern. Discernment counseling lasts from one to five sessions, with the therapist and couple deciding after each session whether to have a subsequent session. The reader is referred to Harris and Hall (2020, vol. 3) to read more about treating ambivalent couples.

Building commitment

For couples seeking therapy, often the most important intervention for building commitment is to instill hope. By the time couples come to therapy, many have lived with their distress for some time and have become demoralized. It is difficult to remain committed to any endeavor if it is perceived as a lost cause. Building hope can help instill a renewed desire to see the relationship improved.

Therapists can build hope in a number of ways. For example, therapists can note the couple's strengths, which can be leveraged to bring about change. Couples where each person takes personal responsibility for change rather than blaming their partner can be told that this is often a predictor of success in therapy. Doing a relationship history of the couple's courtship can also build hope because it reminds couples what drew them together in the first place (Hiebert, Gillespie, & Stahmann, 1993). A couple's relationship history might also reveal resiliency in overcoming previous problems, which might be tapped into for addressing current issues.

PREP describes several things couples can do to build and sustain commitment (Markman et al., 2010). Couples need to take the long-term perspective, recognizing that relationships can go through difficult times. Consistently investing in the relationship through the highs and lows will pay off, much like it does when one regularly invests in the stock market. Couples should focus on the "we" and not the "me." Just focusing on one's own needs will undermine commitment. It is better to work as a team to build the quality of the relationship. Couples should avoid thinking that the grass is always greener on the other side. This will lead individuals to look for or focus on other potential partners, which also undermines commitment.

PREP also encourages individuals to focus on the positive memories associated with their courtship. They can also do the things they first did during their early months and years as a couple. The positive experiences couples shared during their courtship motivated them to want to build a life together and can help them do so again. Finally, individuals are encouraged to make the relationship a priority. Putting effort into the relationship is more likely to lead to improvements, which will strengthen the couple's hope and dedication to improving the relationship.

Caring

Caring refers to the variety of ways in which individuals build and maintain their love and connection with one another. This includes how couples show love for one another, participate in mutually rewarding activities together, and share affection and sexual intimacy with one another (Birchler et al., 1999).

Expressing love

When couples are in continual conflict, efforts to show they love their partner can begin to diminish. Therefore, therapists may want to encourage couples to put more effort into doing caring behaviors (Baucom et al., 2015). For example, individuals can identify behaviors that will make their partner happier and increase the frequency in which these behaviors occur.

The therapist may also want to examine if both individuals are expressing their love or caring in the manner in which their partner desires. Chapman (2010) has described five love languages for expressing love. These love languages include offering words of affirmation to one's partner, providing physical touch, spending quality time with one's partner, giving one's partner gifts, or doing acts of service for the partner. Individuals need to learn what their partner's preferred love languages for receiving love are so they can express their love in this manner. Otherwise, their partners may question the extent to which their mate loves them. For example, Evan told his therapist that he did not think that his wife loved him. When asked why he felt this way, Evan stated that she was not very verbally or physically affectionate. He added that this is how people in his family growing up showed how they loved one other. Melissa insisted she loved her husband, but added that she grew up in a very different family from his. Instead of being verbally or physically affectionate, they demonstrated their love by doing things for one another. Not surprisingly, Melissa said that Evan could do a better job of expressing his love by helping out more with the kids or doing more household chores.

Gottman's research on couples also reveals the importance of individuals responding to the emotional bids for connection that partners make daily (Gottman & Silver, 1999). For example, an individual may comment that he or she had a bad day at work. The partner can respond positively by doing a variety of things, such as showing interest, asking questions, expressing support or empathy, or offering a reassuring hug. Or, they may not respond (turn away) or react negatively to the emotional bid (turn against). As therapists, we can help couples recognize when their partner is making an emotional bid and how to respond. Doing so will help couples build up their emotional bank account, which can protect the relationship during times of stress or conflict.

Differences in meta-emotional styles may contribute to individuals missing opportunities to respond to emotional bids (Gottman & Gottman, 2015). Meta-emotions reflect a person's emotions about emotions. Individuals who value emotions and have a rich vocabulary regarding emotions have a meta-emotional style called "emotion coaching." They also try to understand what their emotions mean, using them as a guide to life. In contrast, emotion dismissing individuals do not tend to value emotions in the same way, preferring to "suck it up and get on with life." They can be impatient with people's negative emotions. Problems around emotional bids can arise if there is a meta-emotion mismatch between two partners. If an emotion coaching individual approaches his or her partner seeking emotional support, the partner may have a difficult time validating the individual's emotions due to his or her emotion dismissing style. The Gottman approach attempts to bridge this mismatch by helping individuals develop greater awareness and language around their emotions, teaching them how to make their emotional bids and needs explicit, asking open-ended questions, and making statements that express interest and empathy (Gottman & Gottman, 2015).

Pleasurable activities

Sharing pleasurable activities is an important way in which couples build and sustain their bond (Markman et al., 2010). In fact, sharing pleasurable activities while dating is a key way in how couples develop a connection. Different factors may lead a couple to stop doing pleasurable activities together. For example, conflict may lead the couple to spend less time together. Sometimes couples with children find it difficult to protect time for their relationship, as well as being busy with other commitments (e.g., work, taking care of elderly parents).

Ideally therapists will assess the extent to which couples protect time for engaging in shared pleasurable activities to see if improvements in this area are needed. Encouraging couples to have a regular date night, for example, can be a helpful step in this direction. Couples can do other pleasurable activities together, such as participating in shared hobbies or interests, traveling, or doing projects together. It is also important that couples learn to savor these moments (Gottman & Gottman, 2015).

Sexual intimacy

Sharing a satisfying sexual relationship is another way couples can feel connected. Therefore, it is important that therapists assess the couple's sexual relationship to see if it is a strength or potential area of growth. PREP (Markman et al., 2010) recommends that couples do a number of things to enhance and protect their sexual relationship, including incorporating sensuality and romance into their relationship. For example, couples can increase sensuality through physical touch outside of sex (e.g., holding hands, massages, kissing) or building romance through small gestures such as writing love notes or surprising one's partner with a gift. Like other pleasurable activities, couples also need to protect time to nurture their sexual relationship.

Sometimes couples will struggle with their sexual relationship due to sexual disorders. Problems can arise in a number of different areas, including desire, arousal, or having orgasms. The reader can consult Hertlein, Timm, and D'Aniello (2020, vol. 3) to learn more about the assessment and treatment of sexual disorders.

Contract

In business, a contract consists of mutually agreed-upon expectations between two parties. In a similar manner, a contract also exists between two partners in an intimate relationship due to shared expectations. These expectations can center on many elements of the relationship, such as how finances will be managed, the number of children the couple desires, or the division of household chores. Expectations can exist on the macro-level or micro-level (Birchler et al., 1999). Macro-level expectations are general expectations about the relationship (e.g., how to balance autonomy and connection, gender roles), whereas the micro-level focuses on more specific expectations (e.g., if I cook dinner, then you clean the dishes). Some expectations will be explicitly stated, but others may not be. Couples often discuss the number of children they hope to have, but may not discuss other elements of the relationship (e.g., there may be an implicit assumption that individuals will be sexually faithful).

Unclear expectations

One potential contract issue that couples can encounter is around unclear expectations. As couples get to know each other, they learn more about what the other expects from the relationship. This learning process does not always go smoothly, which can result in conflict. Individuals may disappoint their partner if they do not live up to an expectation, which may have never been explicitly stated. Conflict may force a couple to examine these unstated expectations. For couples early in their relationship, making a concerted effort to learn about each other is a way of uncovering these expectations.

To facilitate this process, the therapist may want to introduce questions or tools that encourage couples to explore expectations, especially in areas they may not have considered. Premarital inventories are an excellent tool for doing this for couples preparing for marriage. Three examples of premarital inventories include PREPARE (Olson & Olson, 2016), FOCCUS (Williams, 2016), and RELATE (Loyer-Carlson, 2016). However, the therapist might use other tools that encourage such exploration. For example, PREP has couples answer questions on numerous topics (e.g., love, sexual fidelity, children, work, sharing feelings) to help uncover relationship expectations (Markman et al., 2010). Doing a genogram with individuals may also reveal important expectations associated with one's family of origin (McGoldrick, Gerson, & Petry, 2008).

Conflicting expectations

Another potential source of conflict for couples is differing expectations on how the relationship should be. Couples will need to negotiate a contract with which they both can live, which sometimes requires compromise. One possible approach for negotiating a compromise is the two-circle exercise (Gottman & Gottman, 2015). Two concentric circles are drawn for each person to distinguish between their wants and needs. The inner circle contains the individual's needs, which are difficult to compromise on due to their importance to the individual. However, the outer circle includes the individual's wants, the things in which he or she can be more flexible. In some cases, if the issue is important enough, the couple may find that the issue is a deal-breaker because an acceptable solution cannot be found. For example, Adam and Amy came into therapy due to a conflict around whether to have children. Adam did not want to have children, but Amy did. Amy indicated that if Adam did not want children, then she might end the relationship so she could pursue being a mother with another partner.

Renegotiating a contract

A couple who established a workable contract may find that parts of the contract need to be renegotiated if a major change occurs in their life. For example, the transition to parenthood may require couples to renegotiate elements of their contract. Other important events like returning to school, retirement, or a significant illness may trigger the need to renegotiate a contract. Sometimes conflict arises as the couple attempts to renegotiate their contract. Bill and Deborah were having conflict over the distribution of household chores. Deborah had done the vast majority of the household chores as a stay-at-home wife and mother for much of the marriage, while Bill fulfilled the traditional role of being the economic provider, working long hours as a business professional. Upon Bill's retirement, Deborah was hoping Bill would do more of the housework. However, Bill initially protested, stating that he did not retire so he could do housework. Eventually through compromise, the couple was able to find a suitable solution to the conflict over chores.

Breach of contract

Another potential area of conflict can center on an individual committing what the other perceives as a serious breach or violation of the contract. A common example is an infidelity or affair. The affair may be emotional, sexual, or both. Timm and Herlein (2020, vol. 3) explore how clinicians can help couples navigate an affair or infidelity.

However, a breach of conflict can arise in other ways too. For example, a breach of contract can occur if an individual expects their partner to be emotionally available in a time of dire need (e.g., cancer diagnosis, miscarriage), but the partner is not. These breaches of contract are called attachment injuries in EFT, which also describes an approach that can be used to help couples heal them (Johnson, Makinen, & Millikin, 2001).

Character

Individuals bring in many personal qualities that can impact a relationship. Typically each partner's personal attributes are what attracted the individuals to each other and are strengths for the relationships. However, there may be other personal attributes that challenge the relationship, such as low self-esteem, mental illness, or physical illness. Temperament or personality is another important individual attribute, which has the potential to be either a strength or challenge for the relationship. Past experiences from childhood or previous relationships also have the ability to shape individuals in significant ways, which may have implications for relationships (Birchler et al., 1999).

Personality or temperament

Personality or temperament can be an important factor in how a couple relates to one another. Personality differences have the potential to be complementary or create conflict (e.g., source of a perpetual problem). In some cases, differences in personality have the potential to be both. The differences that once drew the couple together can now become a source of frustration. A polarization process may kick in, where conflict emerges as each tries to get the other to change (Christensen et al., 2015). Developing acceptance around personality differences may be essential for some couples.

Sometimes therapists can aid couples in better understanding their partner by educating them about temperament or personality. Individuals may perceive their partner's behavior as a personal deficit or evidence of a lack of caring, when in reality it is tied to temperament or personality. For example, Marcus felt his wife Carol did not care for him because she was frequently busy doing errands, housework, and other chores rather than spending time with him. Furthermore, he had observed that when she did have downtime, she would do solitary activities such as reading or being in the garden. The therapist working with the couple felt that the Myers–Briggs framework (Keirsey, 1998) might help Marcus understand that Carol's behavior was better explained by her personality type rather than a lack of caring. The Myers–Briggs looks at four dimensions of personality (introversion and extraversion, sensing and intuition, thinking and feeling, judging and perceiving). As a judger, Carol felt she should get all of her work done before she could relax and play. Due to her extensive responsibilities, Carol often felt there was little time to play. As an introvert, Carol needed solitary time (e.g., reading, gardening) to charge her batteries. This was in direct contrast to her husband, who was extraverted and had a strong need for social interaction with his wife and others. Marcus was also more of a perceiver, who did not understand Carol's need to consistently put work before play. However, Marcus was willing to do more to help with Carol's responsibilities so she would feel greater freedom to spend time with him. Carol was also encouraged to learn to set aside her responsibilities sometimes so she could enjoy time with her husband.

Self-esteem

Healthy self-esteem is important not only to an individual's well-being, but it can also facilitate positive relationships. Conversely, individuals with low self-esteem can experience problems in relationships such as jealousy or difficulties with intimacy.

Individuals may also be especially sensitive to criticism, leading them to become angry or withdrawn due to feelings of inadequacy. In more severe cases, individuals may be depressed or abuse substances due to the negative thoughts and emotions associated with their low self-esteem.

Self-esteem and the relationship may influence each other in a bidirectional manner. Just as building positive self-esteem may be helpful in building a successful relationship, building a successful relationship may help individuals improve their self-esteem, knowing that they are valued and loved by another. However, in more severe cases of low self-esteem, individual therapy may be necessary as an adjunct to couple therapy. Individuals with extremely low self-esteem may have suffered some traumatic events during childhood. Experiencing physical abuse, sexual abuse, emotional abuse, or neglect can all contribute to individuals internalizing a negative self-concept. Processing the previous abuse or traumatic experiences may help the individual develop a different perspective about him or herself, thereby improving self-esteem.

Mental and physical illness

Mental and physical illness can have a profound impact on a couple's relationship (e.g., Crowe, 2004; McDaniel, Doherty, & Hepworth, 2014; Pais & Dankoski, 2011; Rolland, 2018; Whisman & Beach, 2015). For example, mental or physical illness may impede individuals' daily functioning, including their ability to work. This may create a significant shift in roles for the couple, requiring that the couple renegotiate parts of their contract. If individuals are unable to work due to their physical or mental illness, then this can have significant financial consequences. The cost of treatment (e.g., medical or therapy bills, medications) can also add to the financial burden a couple experiences.

Mental or physical illness can impact relationships in other ways too. The irritability associated with pain or mental illness (e.g., depression, bipolar) can create conflict for couples. For example, Charles complained that severe back pain caused by a war injury made him irritable, making the couple more prone to bickering. Surgery to repair his injury was successful, resulting in a significant reduction in his pain and irritability and a subsequent improvement in marital quality. In another case, Seo-yun complained that every fall and winter, her husband Lance would become "Mr. Nasty." Upon further assessment, the therapist discovered that Lance suffered from a rather serious case of seasonal affective disorder. Mental and physical illness can also reduce a couple's ability to do pleasurable activities together. Denzel stopped doing activities with his wife due to his severe back pain, which contributed to her feeling neglected by Denzel. Sexual difficulties can also arise around mental or physical illness. For example, individuals with depression often suffer from low sexual desire. The side effects from medications to treat mental or physical illness (e.g., antidepressants) can also impair sexual functioning.

The therapist may want to do several things to help minimize the negative impact that mental or physical illness can have upon a couple. First, the therapist may need to provide psychoeducation to address any missing knowledge or misconceptions about the illness. For example, Elijah did not understand his partner's compulsions around wanting to gamble. Rather, he assumed her gambling represented a total disregard for him and the relationship. Second, the therapist should assess if the individuals are seeking out treatment and if the treatment is working. In some cases, the therapist may need to make referrals for treatment, explore reasons for avoiding treatment, or address possible treatment noncompliance (e.g., not taking medications). Third, the therapist may need to facilitate the couple communicating about the illness and its impact. Some couples may avoid talking about important concerns related to the illness (Rolland, 2018). For others, a partner's anxiety over whether the mate is properly managing his or her illness can lead to the expression of criticism or even hostility (McDaniel et al., 2014). Both criticism and hostility, along with emotional overinvolvement, can create high expressed emotion, which is linked with a greater risk of relapse for those with severe mental illness (Butzlaff & Hooley, 1998). Fourth, the therapist will want to address any vicious cycles around mental or physical illness. For example, Steven's drinking would make Thomas upset, leading him to criticize and argue with Steven. Unfortunately, Steven coped with the conflict in the couple's relationship by drinking more. The bidirectional influence of relationship functioning with mental and physical illness is one of the reasons that couple therapy has been recommended as a modality for treating a number of disorders (Baucom, Belus, Adelman, Fischer, & Paprocki, 2014; Denton & Brandon, 2011). Fifth, the therapist may find it helpful to externalize the disorder (White & Epston, 1990). This encourages the couple to join together in fighting a common adversary, rather than fight each other. Sixth, the therapist will want to assess and perhaps enhance both partners' coping skills. For example, self-care activities can offer caregivers some respite and reduce the likelihood of depression, burnout, and resentment. Finally, the couple's level of external support should be evaluated and strengthened, if necessary (Pais & Dankoski, 2011). Other chapters in this volume (e.g., Blow, Nelson Goff, Farero, & Ruhlmann, 2020, vol. 3; Klostermann & O'Farrell, 2020, vol. 3; Wittenborn, Baucom, Leifker & Lachmar, 2020, vol. 3) offer a more extensive discussion of couple therapy related to specific mental or physical illnesses.

Past experiences

Birchler et al. (1999) noted that experiences from childhood or other formative relationships might influence how individuals think, feel, or behave in relationships. For example, experiencing childhood sexual abuse could impact an adult's views of sexuality. Therefore, it may be helpful to include at least a brief assessment of each partner's family of origin to identify potential issues that may be impacting the relationship.

   Therapists should also be mindful of how previous intimate relationships can shape an individual's view of the relationship. For example, Alberto was fearful that Maria was having an affair, which she adamantly denied. Alberto admitted that he had no evidence to suggest that Maria was actually having an affair, but was nonetheless fearful that she was having an affair because his two previous wives had been unfaithful.

Culture

Cultural factors can play a significant role in a couple's relationship in three ways (Birchler et al., 1999). First, cultural factors may shape how the couple relates to one another. Second, cultural factors may influence the couple's relationship with their environment (e.g., extended families, society). Third, cultural factors may impact a therapist's ability to understand the couple.

Cultural factors can arise from multiple sources, such as race/ethnicity, nationality, religion, socioeconomic status, or sexual orientation. For one couple, an important cultural difference was being raised in a rural versus an urban area. This shaped not only where they wanted to live but also the lifestyle they wanted to provide for their children. The various cultural backgrounds can intersect to create unique blends of influences for individuals. Some important considerations for managing cultural factors in couple therapy are described next. Singh (2020) also devotes a chapter to working with intercultural couples (Chapter 22, Volume 3).

Cultural differences and couple dynamics

Cultural factors shape each person's values, beliefs, or worldviews, which in turn can shape how individuals relate to their partners (Maynigo, 2017). These differences have the potential to create misunderstandings and conflict for the couple. Yet, at the same time, cultural differences can also enrich the couple.

Cultural differences can manifest in a number of different ways (Bustamante, Nelson, Henriksen, & Monakes, 2011; Maynigo, 2017). Cultural differences can impact how couples communicate with one another. For example, cultural differences can exist with regard to how direct or indirect one can be or the extent to which it is acceptable to express emotions. Conflict might also emerge over cultural differences on how individuals relate to their extended family. For example, the couple may disagree over how involved they should be with their extended families, as well as how private the couple's lives are with regard to extended family. Cultural differences can emerge in other areas as well, such as parenting, gender roles, or the religious socialization of children.

Therapists can help couples recognize when cultural differences may be impacting the relationship. This may help depersonalize the conflict, recognizing that their partner's views or behaviors are a product of cultural socialization (rather than a personal deficiency). In addition to any insights the therapist can offer, it is helpful if couples become invested in learning about each other's cultural backgrounds (Seshadri & Knudson-Martin, 2013). This will help the couple become what Killian (2015) refers to as the "culturally conscious couple." Exploration of each other's cultural backgrounds goes better if individuals can take a curious rather judgmental stance. Conflict is likely to arise if anyone is attacked for his or her cultural beliefs or practices or feels pressured to change. For example, Diana felt resentment that her fiancé Adrian insisted that she join his church if the couple were to get married. Recognizing the problems that this had caused, Adrian later told Diana that she could return to her church if she desired. When learning about each other's cultural background, it can be helpful to look for commonalities rather than just focus on their differences (Bustamante et al., 2011; Seshadri & Knudson-Martin, 2013). Couples often discover things they share in common as they learn more about each other.

Cultural differences and acceptance

Cultural factors can impact the level of acceptance that the couple experiences from their environment, including extended family and society (Maynigo, 2017; Seshadri & Knudson-Martin, 2013). Some individuals experience rejection from their families because they married someone outside the accepted group. With time, some families eventually come to accept the couple, whereas others continue to reject or marginalize the couple. In addition to being emotionally painful, rejection by one or both extended families can create a void in terms of social support. Encouraging couples to build a strong community of social support outside of extended family may be especially helpful for these couples.

Some couples can experience prejudice and discrimination because of their cultural backgrounds. As a result, some couples experience minority stress (LeBlanc, Frost, & Wight, 2015). Much like any other stress, minority stress has the potential to negatively impact the couple. For example, frustration arising from being discriminated against might be displaced to the relationship, causing friction or conflict.

Cultural differences and the therapist

Cultural factors can also impact how the therapist relates to the couple (Poulsen & Thomas, 2011). Therapists must be mindful of how their assumptions about intimate relationships may be different from the couple's. For example, couples that have immigrated from another country may have different values based on their level of acculturation. International students who return to their home country after training in the United States may find that much of what they have learned is relevant, but may still need to adapt what they have learned to fit the cultural context of their home country (Guvensel, Dixon, Parker, McDonald, & O'Hara, 2015).

Children

Couples with children must navigate how to raise their children together. Conflict can emerge over parenting, particularly if the couple has different approaches to discipline. One parent may be lenient with the children, whereas the other parent may be strict. Like other areas, there is a potential for a vicious cycle to emerge. The lenient parent may become more lenient to compensate for what he or she perceives as the other parent being too harsh. The other parent becomes even stricter to compensate for the other parent being too lenient. The therapist can help stop this vicious cycle by reminding both parents that they each have a responsibility to nurture and set limits with their children.

Couples can also fall into an overfunctioning and underfunctioning dynamic with regard to parenting. One mate may feel that he or she has primary responsibility for the parenting and criticizes the other partner for not being more involved as a parent. The partner may withdraw in response to the criticism or feelings of inadequacy around parenting, reinforcing to the overfunctioner that he or she must be the "responsible" parent. Challenging this dynamic may require attention in a number of different areas. For example, the overfunctioner may need to make requests for help, but avoid beginning the conversation with harsh criticism or contempt (Gottman & Silver, 1999). The therapist will also want to explore what prevents the underfunctioning parent from taking a more active role. Sometimes gender socialization is an important factor to consider. Traditional gender socialization reinforces that the primary responsibility for parenting belongs to the mother and that the male's primary responsibility is being the economic provider for the family. Helping couples critically examine these gender messages may help the couple be more flexible in their gender roles (Montgomery, Chaviano, Rayburn, & McWey, 2017). For example, the therapist may want to emphasize the importance of fathers to children extends beyond just being an economic provider (Wilson & Prior, 2011). The therapist may also need to help men to develop new competencies outside their traditionally socialized role so they feel more confident in parenting (Knudson-Martin & Mahoney, 2005).

For couples where individuals are bringing preexisting children into the relationship, a number of potential challenges may arise (Michaels, 2011; Papernow, 2015). For example, couples must balance the time they devote to developing and strengthening their relationship with the demands of raising children. It is also not uncommon for children to become jealous of the attention the parent is giving to the new partner. This can result in a dynamic where the new mate can feel like an outsider with regard to the children and the partner and the other parent can feel caught between the children and the new mate (Papernow, 2015). The therapist can do a number of different things to address this dynamic, including normalizing the challenge, helping partners develop empathy for each other's experience, encouraging all of the subsystems (e.g., biological parent and child, stepparent and child, couple) to have one-on-one time together to strengthen relationships, and possibly looking at preexisting vulnerabilities that can be activated through this dynamic. For example, a parent who was the peacemaker in his or her family of origin may especially struggle with being caught in the middle between the new mate and the children.

Couples bringing children into a relationship must also develop a parental plan for the roles that each will have with the children (Michaels, 2011; Papernow, 2015). Problems can arise if the stepparent is put into the parental role prematurely. For remarried couples, the stepparent will ideally first develop a relationship with the children before assuming a parental role, which Papernow (2013) succinctly calls "connection before correction." Brimhall (2020, vol. 3) provides a more extensive discussion of issues that remarried couples may encounter.

Future Directions

Family therapy has traditionally been oriented to teaching therapists theoretical models or approaches (Sprenkle, Davis, & Lebow, 2009). Assessment is done through the lens of a particular model, and treatment follows the steps or process outlined by the theory. These models offer the therapist a useful guide for assessing, conceptualizing, and treating clients, including couples. Furthermore, some of these models (e.g., EFT, IBCT) have been subject to empirical evaluation and have some empirical support for their effectiveness.

This chapter has taken a different approach by organizing the assessment and treatment couples by the 8 C's rather than a specific theoretical model. In some ways, the 8 C's could be considered an integrative framework because it allows the therapist to incorporate ideas from multiple theoretical models. In addition, the 8 C's allow the clinician to integrate knowledge from other sources, including research and even the therapist's own clinical insights. Although the 8 C's have strong heuristic value, further research should be done to confirm that these are indeed the most important areas of functioning that should be addressed with couples.

The 8 C's framework invites the question as to whether an integrative model is a better approach compared to having an allegiance to a specific model. The 8 C's may offer an advantage because it can accommodate a more comprehensive perspective on couples. Because different models often focus on different things, there may be areas that are overlooked or not emphasized when only using one model. In addition, the 8 C's allow the clinician to take the best ideas from each model and integrate them into a treatment approach for promoting change.

However, the flexibility of the 8 C's could also be problematic, especially if the clinician borrows ideas or interventions from multiple sources in a haphazard manner. This chapter has attempted to integrate concepts and interventions in a thoughtful manner, drawing primarily from research and theoretical models with empirical support. Nonetheless, the effectiveness of using this approach needs to be empirically tested. While it is hoped that the 8 C's will give the clinician maximum flexibility in tailoring his or her approach to specific needs of their clients, it is also possible that interventions will be less effective when isolated from the model in which they were derived. It is unclear if interventions from empirically supported approaches can be mixed and matched and still yield the same effectiveness as they did in the original models. These are questions that future research will hopefully answer.

Conclusion

The 8 C's described in this chapter provide a helpful framework for organizing assessment and treatment for common couple concerns. The 8 C's can help the therapist assess a couple's strengths and areas of growth in several important areas of functioning. The 8 C's are a flexible framework for integrating concepts and interventions from a variety of models, as well as research and the therapist's own clinical insights.

Although the 8 C's have been described as discrete categories, in reality an issue may straddle more than one C. For example, cultural factors may shape the couple's contract, expectations around parenting, or how they communicate about these issues. Also, there is the potential for vicious cycles of conflict to emerge around issues in the C's (e.g., character, co-parenting children). The 8 C's can help the therapist be mindful of the multifaceted nature of the couple's issues.

References

Baucom, D. H., Belus, J. M., Adelman, C. B., Fischer, M. S., & Paprocki, C. (2014). Couple-based interventions for psychopathology: A renewed direction for the field. *Family Process, 53*, 445–461. doi:10.1111/famp.12075

Baucom, D. H., Epstein, N. B., Kirby, J. S., & LaTaillade, J. J. (2015). Cognitive-behavioral couple therapy. In A. S. Gurman, J. L. Lebow, & D. K. Snyder (Eds.), *Clinical handbook of couple therapy* (5th ed., pp. 23–60). New York, NY: Guilford Press.

Birchler, G. R., Doumas, D. M., & Fals-Stewart, W. S. (1999). The seven C's: A behavioral systems framework for evaluating marital distress. *The Family Journal, 7*, 253–264.

Blow, A. J., Nelson Goff, B. S., Farero, A. M., & Ruhlmann, L. M. (2020). Posttraumatic stress and couples. In K. S. Wampler & A. J. Blow (Eds.), *The handbook of systemic family therapy: Systemic family therapy with couples (3)*. Hoboken, NJ: Wiley.

Bradford, K. (2010). Screening couples for intimate partner violence. *Journal of Family Psychotherapy, 21,* 76–82. doi:10.1080/08975351003618650

Brimhall, A. S. (2020). Therapy with remarried and blended families. In K. S. Wampler & A. J. Blow (Eds.), *The handbook of systemic family therapy: Systemic family therapy with couples (3)*. Hoboken, NJ: Wiley.

Bustamante, R. M., Nelson, J. A., Henriksen, R. C., Jr., & Monakes, S. (2011). Intercultural couples: Coping with culture related stressors. *The Family Journal, 19,* 154–164. doi:10.1177/1066480711399723

Butzlaff, R. L., & Hooley, J. M. (1998). Expressed emotion and psychiatric relapse. *Archives of General Psychiatry, 55,* 547–552.

Chapman, G. D. (2010). *The 5 love languages: The secret to love that lasts.* Chicago, IL: Northfield Publishing.

Christensen, A., Dimidjian, S., & Martell, C. R. (2015). Integrative behavioral couple therapy. In A. S. Gurman, J. L. Lebow, & D. K. Snyder (Eds.), *Clinical handbook of couple therapy* (5th ed., pp. 61–94). New York, NY: Guilford Press.

Crowe, M. (2004). Couples and mental illness. *Sexual and Relationship Therapy, 19,* 309–318. doi:10.1080/14681990410001715436

Davis, S. D., Lebow, J. L., & Sprenkle, D. H. (2012). Common factors of change in couple therapy. *Behavior Therapy, 43,* 36–48.

Denton, W. H., & Brandon, A. R. (2011). Couple therapy in the presence of mental disorders. In J. L. Wetchler (Ed.), *Handbook of clinical issues in couple therapy* (2nd ed., pp. 41–55). New York, NY: Routledge.

Doherty, W. J., Harris, S. M., & Wilde, J. L. (2015). Discernment counseling for "mixed-agenda" couples. *Journal of Marital and Family Therapy, 42,* 246–255. doi:10.1111/jmft.12132

Edwards, T. M., Williams, L. W., Speice, J., & Patterson, J. E. (2020). Multilevel assessment. In K. S. Wampler, R. B. Miller, & R. B. Seedall (Eds.), *The handbook of systemic family therapy: The profession of systemic family therapy (1)*. Hoboken, NJ: Wiley.

Fruzzetti, A. E., & Payne, P. (2015). Couple therapy and borderline personality disorder. In A. S. Gurman, J. L. Lebow, & D. K. Snyder (Eds.), *Clinical handbook of couple therapy* (5th ed., pp. 606–634). New York, NY: Guilford Press.

Gottman, J. M. (1999). *The marriage clinic: A scientifically-based marital therapy.* New York, NY: W. W. Norton & Company.

Gottman, J. M., & Gottman, J. S. (2015). Gottman couple therapy. In A. S. Gurman, J. L. Lebow, & D. K. Snyder (Eds.), *Clinical handbook of couple therapy* (5th ed., pp. 129–157). New York, NY: Guilford Press.

Gottman, J. M., & Silver, N. (1999). *The seven principles for making marriage work.* New York, NY: Three Rivers Press.

Guvensel, K., Dixon, A. L., Parker, L. K., McDonald, C. P., & O'Hara, C. (2015). International relevance and applicability of United States-based marriage and family therapy training in Turkey. *Contemporary Family Therapy, 37,* 426–441. doi:10.1007/s10591-9349-3

Harris, S. M., & Hall, E. L. (2020). Therapy with individuals and couples as they decide to continue or end the relationship. In K. S. Wampler & A. J. Blow (Eds.), *The handbook of systemic family therapy: Systemic family therapy with couples (3)*. Hoboken, NJ: Wiley.

Hertlein, K., Timm, T. M., & D'Aniello, C. (2020). Integrating couple therapy into work with sexual dysfunctions. In K. S. Wampler & A. J. Blow (Eds.), *The handbook of systemic family therapy: Systemic family therapy with couples (3)*. Hoboken, NJ: Wiley.

Hiebert, W. J., Gillespie, J. P., & Stahmann, R. F. (1993). *Dynamic assessment in couple therapy.* New York, NY: Lexington Books.

Johnson, S. M. (2004). *The practice of emotionally focused couple therapy: Creating connection* (2nd ed.). New York, NY: Routledge.

Johnson, S. M. (2015). Emotionally focused couple therapy. In A. S. Gurman, J. L. Lebow, & D. K. Snyder (Eds.), *Clinical handbook of couple therapy* (5th ed., pp. 97–128). New York, NY: Guilford Press.

Johnson, S. M., Makinen, J., & Millikin, J. (2001). Attachment injuries in couple relationships: A new perspective on impasses in couple therapy. *Journal of Marital and Family Therapy, 27*, 145–156.

Keirsey, D. (1998). *Please understand me II: Temperament character intelligence.* Del Mar, CA: Prometheus Nemesis Book Company.

Killian, K. D. (2015). Couple therapy and intercultural relationships. In A. S. Gurman, J. L. Lebow, & D. K. Snyder (Eds.), *Clinical handbook of couple therapy* (5th ed., pp. 512–528). New York, NY: Guilford Press.

Klostermann, K., & O'Farrell, T. J. (2020). Alcohol and other substance use disorders. In K. S. Wampler & A. J. Blow (Eds.), *The handbook of systemic family therapy: Systemic family therapy with couples (3)*. Hoboken, NJ: Wiley.

Knudson-Martin, C., & Mahoney, A. R. (2005). Moving beyond gender: Processes that create relationship equality. *Journal of Marital and Family Therapy, 31*, 235–258.

LeBlanc, A. J., Frost, D. M., & Wight, R. G. (2015). Minority stress and stress proliferation among same-sex and other marginalized couples. *Journal of Marriage and Family, 77*, 40–59. doi:10.1111/jomf.12160

Loyer-Carlson, V. L. (2016). RELATE assessment. In J. J. Ponzetti, Jr. (Ed.), *Evidence-based approaches to relationship and marriage education* (pp. 148–162). New York, NY: Routledge.

Markman, H. J., Stanley, S. M., & Blumberg, S. L. (2010). *Fighting for your marriage: A deluxe revised edition of the classic best seller for enhancing marriage and preventing divorce* (3rd ed.). San Francisco, CA: Jossey-Bass.

Maynigo, T. P. (2017). Intercultural couples and families. In S. Kelly (Ed.), *Diversity in couple and family therapy: Ethnicities, sexuality, and socioeconomics* (pp. 309–336). Santa Barbara, CA: Praeger.

McDaniel, S. H., Doherty, W. J., & Hepworth, J. (2014). *Medical family therapy and integrated care* (2nd ed.). Washington, DC: American Psychological Association.

McGoldrick, M., Gerson, R., & Petry, S. (2008). *Genograms: Assessment and intervention* (3rd ed.). New York, NY: W. W. Norton & Company.

Michaels, M. L. (2011). Remarital issues in couple therapy. In J. L. Wetchler (Ed.), *Handbook of clinical issues in couple therapy* (2nd ed., pp. 189–204). New York, NY: Routledge.

Montgomery, J. E., Chaviano, C. L., Rayburn, A. D., & McWey, L. M. (2017). Parents at-risk and their children: Intersections of gender role attitudes and parenting practices. *Child and Family Social Work, 22*, 1151–1160.

Olson, A. K., & Olson, D. H. (2016). Discoveries about couples from PREPARE and ENRICH. In J. J. Ponzetti, Jr. (Ed.), *Evidence-based approaches to relationship and marriage education* (pp. 123–136). New York, NY: Routledge.

Pais, S., & Dankoski, M. E. (2011). What's love got to do with it: Couple, illness, and MFT. In J. L. Wetchler (Ed.), *Handbook of clinical issues in couple therapy* (2nd ed., pp. 57–73). New York, NY: Routledge.

Papernow, P. L. (2013). *Surviving and thriving in stepfamily relationships: What works and doesn't work.* New York, NY: Routledge.

Papernow, P. L. (2015). Therapy with couples in stepfamilies. In A. S. Gurman, J. L. Lebow, & D. K. Snyder (Eds.), *Clinical handbook of couple therapy* (5th ed., pp. 467–488). New York, NY: Guilford Press.

Patterson, J., Williams, L., Edwards, T. M., Chamow, L., & Grauf-Grounds, C. (2018). *Essential skills in family therapy: From the first interview to termination* (3rd ed.). New York, NY: Guilford Press.

Poulsen, S. S., & Thomas, V. (2011). Awareness of culture: Clinical implications for couple therapy. In J. L. Wetchler (Ed.), *Handbook of clinical issues in couple therapy* (2nd ed., pp. 207–224). New York, NY: Routledge.

Rolland, J. S. (2018). *Helping couples and families navigate illness and disability*. New York, NY: Guilford Press.

Schacht, R. L., Dimidjian, S., George, W. H., & Berns, S. B. (2009). Domestic violence assessment procedures among couple therapists. *Journal of Marital and Family Therapy, 35*, 47–59.

Scuka, R. F. (2016). Relationship enhancement program and mastering the mysteries of love. In J. J. Ponzetti, Jr. (Ed.), *Evidence-based approaches to relationship and marriage education* (pp. 165–179). New York, NY: Routledge.

Seshadri, G., & Knudson-Martin, C. (2013). How couples manage interracial and intercultural differences: Implications for clinical practice. *Journal of Marital and Family Therapy, 39*, 43–58. doi:10.1111/j1752-0606.2011.00262.x

Sprenkle, D. H., Davis, S. D., & Lebow, J. L. (2009). *Common factors in couple and family therapy: The overlooked foundation for effective practice*. New York, NY: Guilford Press.

Stith, S. M., McCollum, E. E., Amanor-Boadu, Y., & Smith, D. (2012). Systemic perspectives on intimate partner violence treatment. *Journal of Marital and Family Therapy, 38*, 220–240. doi:10.1111/j.1752-0606.2011.00245.x

Stith, S. M., Spencer, C. M., & Mitta, M. (2020). Couple violence: In-depth assessment and systemic interventions. In K. S. Wampler & A. J. Blow (Eds.), *The handbook of systemic family therapy: Systemic family therapy with couples (3)*. Hoboken, NJ: Wiley.

Straus, M. A., Hamby, S. L., Boney-McCoy, S., & Sugarman, D. B. (1996). The revised conflict tactics scales (CTS2): Development and preliminary psychometric data. *Journal of Family Issues, 17*, 283–316.

Timm, T. M., & Herlein, K. (2020). Affair recovery in couple therapy. In K. S. Wampler & A. J. Blow (Eds.), *The handbook of systemic family therapy: Systemic family therapy with couples (3)*. Hoboken, NJ: Wiley.

Whisman, M. A., & Beach, S. R. H. (2015). Couple therapy and depression. In A. S. Gurman, J. L. Lebow, & D. K. Snyder (Eds.), *Clinical handbook of couple therapy* (5th ed., pp. 585–605). New York, NY: Guilford Press.

White, M., & Epston, D. (1990). *Narrative means to therapeutic ends*. New York, NY: W. W. Norton & Company.

Williams, L. (2016). FOCCUS and REFOCCUS: Preparing and sustaining couples for marriage. In J. J. Ponzetti, Jr. (Ed.), *Evidence-based approaches to relationship and marriage education* (pp. 137–147). New York, NY: Routledge.

Williams, L., & Tappan, T. (1995). The utility of the Myers-Briggs perspective in couple counseling: A clinical framework. *American Journal of Family Therapy, 23*, 367–371.

Wilson, K. R., & Prior, M. R. (2011). Father involvement and child well-being. *Journal of Paediatrics and Child Health, 47*, 405–407.

Wittenborn, A. K., Baucom, B. R. W., Leifker, F. R., & Lachmar, E. M. (2020). Affective and anxiety disorders. In K. S. Wampler & A. J. Blow (Eds.), *The handbook of systemic family therapy: Systemic family therapy with couples (3)*. Hoboken, NJ: Wiley.

5

Couple Violence
In-Depth Assessment and Systemic Interventions
Sandra M. Stith, Chelsea M. Spencer,
and Mona Mittal

A number of overarching issues face all therapists treating couples, especially couples who have experienced intimate partner violence (IPV). First, IPV is generally recognized as a gendered problem; even though women and men are each potentially violent, the system of patriarchy and the uneven size and strength of men and women make it important to address gender inequities and to seek just and equitable relationships to reduce the potential for violence after treatment ends (Paivinen & Holma, 2017). Family therapy scholars have highlighted the importance of addressing the issue of gender equity in therapy (e.g., Dickerson, 2013; Knudson-Martin, 2013). In this chapter, we highlight systemic interventions and the importance of careful screening for appropriateness of conjoint treatment. We place this work in the context of the work of these important family scholars and advocate that victim safety is critical and that systemic interventions not be offered in any way that endangers victims.

Prevalence

IPV is a serious public health issue impacting about 30–38% of women worldwide throughout their lifetime (World Health Organization [WHO], 2013). In the United States, approximately 37% of women and 30% of men have experienced IPV in their lifetime (Smith et al., 2017). Certain subgroups report greater experiences of IPV compared with other groups. For example, in the United States, significantly more Black non-Hispanic women (44%) and multiracial non-Hispanic women (54%) report lifetime experiences of rape, physical violence, or stalking by an intimate partner compared with White non-Hispanic women (35%) (Black et al., 2011). Approximately 55% (95% CI 36.1–73.8) of HIV-positive women in the United States are survivors of lifetime IPV (Machtinger, Wilson, Haberer, & Weiss, 2012). Women who identify as sexual minorities are also at an increased risk of experiencing IPV, with 61.1% of women identifying as bisexual and 43.8% of women identifying as lesbian reporting IPV victimization in their lifetime, compared with 35% of women identifying as heterosexual (Walters, Chen, & Breiding, 2013). For men, 37.3% who identify

The Handbook of Systemic Family Therapy: Volume 3, First Edition.
Edited by Karen S. Wampler and Adrian J. Blow.
© 2020 John Wiley & Sons Ltd. Published 2020 by John Wiley & Sons Ltd.

as bisexual, 29.0% who identify as heterosexual, and 26.0% who identify as gay report IPV victimization in their lifetime (Walters et al., 2013). These data suggest that IPV affects all genders but that the risks are higher for women, minorities, and sexual minorities.

Health consequences of IPV

There is an extensive body of literature on the health consequences of IPV (Bonomi, Anderson, Rivara, & Thompson, 2009; Campbell et al., 2002; Coker, Smith, Bethea, King, & McKeown, 2000). IPV victimization has negative mental and physical health consequences for both men and women (Ansara & Hindin, 2010; Kamimura, Christensen, Tabler, Ashby, & Olson, 2014), although the majority of research has focused on health consequences for female victims. IPV is a leading cause of injury among women (Hewitt, Bhavsar, & Phelan, 2011). Women who have experienced IPV experience more physical health consequences such as back pain, abdominal pain, central nervous system issues, gynecological problems, and digestive issues than women who have not been victims of IPV (Campbell et al., 2002). Female victims have been found to be more likely to be overweight, smoke cigarettes, binge drink, and report experiencing stress, depression, and problems with emotions (Bosch, Weaver, Arnold, & Clark, 2017). Female victims are also at a higher risk for contracting STDs and HIV infection (Campbell et al., 2002; Li et al., 2014; Wingood, DiClemente, & Raj, 2000). Abused women experience greater anxiety and suicide attempts and engage in higher alcohol and drug use as compared with non-abused women (Devries et al., 2013; Mapayi et al., 2013; McKinney, Caetano, Rodriguez, & Okoro, 2010).

Risk factors

Theoretical perspectives on IPV have shifted from single-factor to multifactor frameworks. IPV is not simply caused by an individual's belief system or psychological functioning, but results from the interaction between various characteristics of the individual and their environment. Dutton's nested ecological theory (Dutton, 1995) of IPV identified risk factors for IPV across four ecological levels, that is, macro, exo, micro, and ontogenic levels. We have extended that work to identify and empirically validate risk factors for IPV across the four ecological levels (Stith, Rosen et al., 2004; Stith et al., 2014). The strongest risk markers for IPV perpetration in the general population include prior physical IPV victimization, stalking perpetration, prior psychological abuse perpetration, borderline personality disorder, anger issues, and having attitudes that approve of violence (Stith, Smith et al., 2004). The strongest risk markers for IPV victimization are prior physical IPV perpetration and/or victimization, prior psychological abuse perpetration and/or victimization, and the perpetrator's use of power and control in the relationship (Stith, Smith et al., 2004). It is important to note that these findings indicate that risk markers related to the relationship (which included past experiences of abuse in the relationship) were the strongest risk markers for IPV perpetration and victimization compared with risk markers related to contextual factors, family-of-origin factors, and individual factors.

A recent study by Spencer and colleagues (2017), which is especially important for therapists working with couples where IPV has occurred, or for therapists assessing for IPV, examined mental health factors as risk markers for IPV. This meta-analysis included results from 207 studies and found that depression, anxiety, PTSD, antisocial personality disorder, and borderline personality disorder were all significant risk markers for IPV perpetration and victimization for both men and women. Combining samples of men and women, it was found that anxiety and PTSD were significantly stronger risk markers for IPV victimization than IPV perpetration, which suggests that it would be important to assess for anxiety and PTSD when working with victims of violence (Spencer et al., 2017). Antisocial personality disorder and borderline personality disorder were stronger risk markers for IPV perpetration than IPV victimization, which suggests that treating these disorders may aid in the reduction of IPV.

Studies have also examined differences in strength of risk markers for IPV perpetration and victimization between men and women. Overall, the research has found that men and women share more similarities than differences in regard to risk markers for IPV perpetration and victimization (Spencer, Cafferky, & Stith, 2016; Spencer, Stith, & Cafferky, 2018). When examining gender differences as risk markers for IPV perpetration, alcohol abuse, demand/withdraw relationship patterns, and violence in one's family of origin were significantly stronger risk markers for male IPV perpetration compared with female IPV perpetration (Spencer et al., 2016). When examining gender differences in IPV victimization, depression is a significantly stronger risk marker for IPV victimization for women than for men, which may suggest that depression may be a more prevalent consequence of IPV victimization for women than men (Spencer et al., 2017; Spencer et al., 2018). Alcohol use, child abuse in one's family of origin, and sexual IPV victimization were stronger risk markers for IPV victimization for women compared with men. Further, older age was a stronger protective factor against IPV victimization for men than it was for women (Spencer et al., 2018).

When examining subpopulations, research has found that some risk markers for IPV perpetration and victimization may be stronger in some populations than others and there may be some specific risk markers of importance for certain populations. Research has examined risk markers for IPV perpetration and victimization for same-sex couples (Kimmes et al., 2017). A meta-analytic review (Kimmes et al., 2017) found that there were statistically significant risk markers for IPV in same-sex relationships also found in heterosexual couples, such as alcohol use, anger, child abuse in family of origin, and perpetrating psychological abuse (Cafferky, Mendez, Anderson, & Stith, 2018; Spencer et al., 2016; Stith, Smith et al., 2004). This meta-analysis also examined risk markers specific to same-sex relationships, such as levels of "outness" (i.e., openness to others about their sexual identity), internalized homophobia (i.e., involuntary beliefs by lesbians and gay men that include self-loathing), stigma consciousness, HIV status, and relationship fusion, with results highlighting internalized homophobia as an important risk marker to assess when examining IPV in same-sex couples (Kimmes et al., 2017).

IPV typologies

Researchers have acknowledged the importance of distinguishing between different types of perpetrators of violence (Johnson & Ferraro, 2000). One of the most recognized typologies of IPV is Michael Johnson's typology of domestic violence (Johnson,

1995, 2007, 2008). According to Johnson's typology, there are four distinct categories of IPV: intimate terrorism, common couple violence/situational couple violence, violent resistance, and mutual violence control (Johnson & Ferraro, 2000; Johnson & Leone, 2005). Intimate terrorism is characterized by one partner using violence as a means to control and exert power over their partner and is typically characterized by chronic violence that is more likely to lead to injuries (Kelly & Johnson, 2008). It is important to note that researchers have emphasized that couple treatment is not appropriate when intimate terrorism is present (Stith, McCollum, & Rosen, 2011) due to the danger of the offender getting angry about victim disclosures during therapy (Holtzworth-Munroe, 2001). Common couple violence, or situational couple violence, is another type of violence that is characterized by violence that is often (but not always) bidirectional, which may occur less frequently, may be less severe, and is typically the result of escalating conflict surrounding a specific context or situation (Johnson, 1995; Kelly & Johnson, 2008). Couples experiencing situational couple violence are most appropriate for conjoint treatment (Stith et al., 2011). Violent resistance is a type of IPV that involves the primary victim using violence against the perpetrator in order to regain some control in the relationship (Johnson, 2008). The fourth type of IPV in Johnson's typology is mutual violent control, which is characterized by both partners in the relationship using violence to obtain power and control of one another (Johnson & Ferraro, 2000). This type of IPV is the least common category of IPV. Conjoint therapy is not considered appropriate in couples experiencing violent resistance or mutual violent control (Stith, McCollum, & Amanor-Boadu, 2012).

Another proposed typology of IPV includes proactive versus reactive categories (Chase, O'Leary, & Heyman, 2001; Ross & Babcock, 2009; Tweed & Dutton, 1998). Proactive offenders are characterized by using violence as a means to control their partners and by initiating unprovoked acts of violence and premediated acts of aggression against their partners (Merk, deCastro, & Koops, 2005; Ramirez & Andreu, 2006; Tweed & Dutton, 1998). The proactive offender category is most highly associated with acts of aggression toward their partners that are associated with domination, intimidation, and control over one's intimate partner. This category is similar to Johnson's intimate terrorist, which is not considered appropriate for conjoint treatment (Stith et al., 2011). The other category in this typology is the reactive offender. Reactive offenders are more highly characterized by using impulsive acts of violence, unplanned acts of violence against their partners, and violent acts that are associated with anger, instability, and emotional reactivity (Chase et al., 2001; Ramirez & Andreu, 2006; Ross & Babcock, 2009). The reactive batterer category is associated with impulsive acts of violence toward their partners that stem from conflict, anger, and an inability to control their own emotions. This type of offender may be appropriate for conjoint treatment.

A number of different measures have been used to help clinicians determine the type of violence a couple is experiencing. Friend, Cleary Bradley, Thatcher, and Gottman (2011) tested the effectiveness of Jory's (2004) Intimate Justice Scale for clinical assessment of IPV. Results of this study support the efficacy of the screening tool to distinguish between situationally violent, characterologically violent, and nonviolent couples. Characterologically violent couples are similar to couples where the offender is considered to be an intimate terrorist. Severe emotional and physical abuse is used to dominate and control a partner (Friend et al., 2011). Characterologically violent offenders are also more likely to display antisocial or borderline personality traits than offenders in situationally violent relationships. Future research is needed to enhance practitioners' use of this tool or others.

Current research in effectiveness of batterer intervention programs

The most common interventions for the problem of IPV include shelter or victim services for women and batterer intervention programs (BIPs) for men (Holmgren, Holma, & Seikkula, 2015). Since the foundational work on IPV in the 1970s, group programs for men have become common in the United States and Western Europe. More recently they have also become common in Africa, Asia, and Central and South America. Although BIPs are mandated in most US states, research on the effectiveness of these programs continues to be discouraging. For example, Feder and Wilson (2005) conducted a meta-analysis of the effectiveness of BIPs and indicated that the mean effect for official reports showed a modest benefit but when victim reports were included, the BIPs showed no enhanced benefit. Babcock, Green, and Robie (2004) also found limited effect for BIPs (Duluth model versus cognitive-behavioral therapy [CBT]) in their meta-analytic research. A more recent 2013 meta-analytic review examining 19 research reports, including 49 effect sizes from a sample of 18,941 batterers in the United States and Spain, reported that treatment showed a nonsignificant positive impact on recidivism and that intervention type was not a significant moderator of recidivism (Arias, Ramon, & Vilarino, 2013).

Increasingly researchers are beginning to consider targeted treatment for different types of IPV or for individuals with different co-occurring disorders (Cantos & O'Leary, 2014; Holmgren et al., 2015). In a recent publication, Cantos and O'Leary (2014) suggest that "there is very little evidence to justify the current legal system practice of mandating all perpetrators to psychological interventions addressing power and control issues" (p. 204). One approach that has been suggested has been to refer offenders with mental health diagnoses to mental health treatment. However, Gondolf (2009), who conducted a quasi-experimental study referring a subgroup of offenders to mental health treatment, found that the high dropout rate led to no differential effectiveness for offenders with mental health issues who were referred to mental health treatment in addition to BIP and those who were not referred to mental health treatment.

Several studies have been conducted that begin to show evidence of impact by specific targeted treatments. One intervention that may have some positive impact on program completion is based on motivational enhancement (Scott, King, McGinn, & Hosseini, 2011). In a quasi-experimental trial of a 6-week motivational enhancement intervention along with a 12-week program for batterers resistant to treatment, resistant batterers were more likely to complete treatment (84%) compared with resistant clients in a standard 18-week treatment (47%) or nonresistant clients in standard 18-week intervention (47%). These findings suggest that using motivational enhancement techniques may reduce dropout rate. Another study tested the effectiveness of a computer-tailored intervention seeking to increase participants' readiness to change as an adjunct to usual care for offenders (Levesque, Ciavatta, Castle, Prochaska, & Prochaska, 2012). This study found that the BIP participants who attended usual care plus a computer intervention based on the transtheoretical model of change were more likely to be in the action stage after treatment and had less documented violence and physical injury at the end of treatment. Finally, a randomized control trial (Zarling, Lawrence, & Marchman, 2015) tested the efficacy of a group-based acceptance and commitment therapy intervention for partner aggression compared with a support and discussion control group. The acceptance and commitment therapy program seeks to increase psychological flexibility, acceptance of difficult emotions, and decrease in attachment to thoughts and increase identification of values and committed actions. Overall, the results indicated that acceptance and commitment therapy led to significant reduction in physical and psychological aggression. These interventions (i.e., motivational enhancement, an intervention based on the transtheoretical model, and acceptance and commitment therapy) take offender treatment a new direction and move beyond CBT and Duluth models and are positive and strength based.

Controversy and validity of controversy regarding conjoint treatment

Historically, IPV has been viewed as a private family matter, and it continues to be viewed as a private matter in many countries. For example, China has a long history of traditional male-dominated culture (Zhao, 2000) and has been heavily influenced by Confucian philosophy that advocates for patriarchal beliefs and rigid gender roles (Tang & Lai, 2008). Although, in 2015, a new law was passed in China making violence against women illegal (Palmer, 2017), services and support for victims are just beginning. Another example of a country that has only recently begun to consider violence against wives as a crime is Iran. Despite the high prevalence of IPV in Iran, there is no official social, legal, or financial support for women who are in violent marriages (Safaee & Emamei, 2012). A battered woman's personal reputation and the reputation of her family of origin are damaged by divorce; many women fear living alone, losing custody of their children; and stigmas around divorced women often take precedence over their own well-being and safety (Amin, 2000). The continued development and testing of efficacy of systemic interventions for IPV may be useful in collectivist countries like China and Iran, where family stability often takes precedence over victim safety.

As result of the feminist movement in the United States and Great Britain, IPV began to be viewed as a crime and as a gendered issue. Although we continue to see IPV as a gendered issue, as mentioned earlier, it is critical to determine which type of violence is occurring and to ensure that treatment matches client needs. Most state standards in the United States mandate a specific type of gender-specific treatment for all offenders and are opposed to conjoint or systemic treatment of couple violence. This opposition comes from a view of all IPV as resulting from male power and control. If the IPV emerges from male power and control, systemic treatment might result in victim blaming. Conjoint treatment may also suggest that the female partner may have done something that led to her male partner's violence. In fact, engaging both partners conjointly in a type of couple therapy that encourages open sharing about difficult issues but that does not teach skills or offer support can increase danger to victims (Holtzworth-Munroe, 2001). However, this does not mean that we should not treat these couples conjointly, but rather that therapists must offer safe and effective treatment for appropriately selected couples.

We advocate for systemic interventions, designed to address conflict and increase conflict resolution skills for couples who choose to stay together and who have experienced situational couple violence. Just treating one partner, when both partners are likely to use violence and/or escalate conflict, is not likely to reduce violence. In many of these cases, the violence can be conceptualized as a relational issue and ideally is treated relationally. In fact, in our meta-analytic work, we found the strongest predictor of IPV perpetration was past IPV victimization and the strongest predictor of IPV victimization was past IPV perpetration (Stith, Smith et al., 2004; Stith et al., 2014). Thus, whether the systemic intervention occurs after the gender-specific intervention ordered by the court or as the only intervention for carefully screened couples, systemic intervention, at some point in time, is crucial for couples who choose to stay together. In fact, not offering systemic treatment to couples who do stay together sets them up for potentially more violence in the future.

In-depth assessment of appropriateness for conjoint treatment

Although IPV is a pervasive problem, it is often a hidden problem. O'Leary, Vivian, and Malone (1992) found that while only 6% of women seeking couple therapy indicated that violence was occurring, when asked to complete a standardized assessment, 53% reported that their husbands had physically assaulted them at some point in time. More recently, research by the same team indicated that between 36 and 58% of couples presenting for couple treatment (not with IPV as a presenting problem) have experienced IPV (Jose & O'Leary, 2009). Therefore, it is critical that all couples seeking treatment, not just those seeking therapy for IPV, participate in a thorough assessment process separately from their partner in which each person completes a written assessment regarding IPV. We recommend the Revised Conflict Tactics Scales (CTS2) (Straus, Hamby, Boney-McCoy, & Sugarman, 1996). This measure asks each partner about physical, psychological, or sexual acts they carried out and about acts their partners carried out. Regardless of whether or not a therapist uses this specific scale, it is critical that the therapist learns from each partner about the history of violence and the potential for violence in the relationship. Clinicians seeking to determine appropriate treatment should compare each partner's responses on the measure to determine congruity of reporting between partners' reports of violence in the relationship. Including Jory's Intimate Justice Scale (Jory, 2004) can also help clinicians determine the type of violence a couple is experiencing. Pretreatment assessment also includes assessment of substance use disorders and other mental health disorders. The Alcohol Use Disorders Identification Test (AUDIT) (http://whqlibdoc.who.int/hq/2001/who_msd_msb_01.6a.pdf) is a 10-item screening tool developed by the World Health Organization. It can be used to help the clinician determine whether or not alcohol use disorder treatment should be completed before conjoint treatment. This is important given the association between alcohol use disorders and increase prevalence of IPV.

Inclusion and exclusion criteria

While inclusion and exclusion criteria differ between interventions, some general guidelines include excluding couples from conjoint treatment if there is a clear victim and the victim appears fearful and/or unable or unwilling to speak freely in sessions. These types of couples tend to be characteristic of those experiencing intimate terrorism. Couples are also excluded if the primary aggressor minimizes or does not report violence reported by the partner. This can be determined by contradictory reports by each partner on the CTS2 (Straus et al., 1996). In these cases, it is not possible to address the IPV without endangering a victim if the offender does not admit to or minimizes the violence. Couples or partners are generally referred to targeted treatments of other mental health disorders or substance abuse if these issues are identified in the assessment. Some people are able to participate in both programs concurrently and some need to complete the other treatment first. For example, participants whose violence tends to be related to excessive use of alcohol, who are able to manage or eliminate their use of alcohol through an addiction program taken concurrently with the couple program, can participate in both programs concurrently. However, if the individual with the alcohol problem continues to relapse and the violence continues to occur with the relapse, the addiction program needs to be successfully completed before beginning the couple program. Also, some systemic treatment programs described in this chapter specifically address substance abuse or trauma in addition to IPV.

Current research on the effective treatment of couple violence

There is a growing body of literature on the effectiveness of couple-based interventions for IPV. Findings of a recent systematic review and meta-analysis show that couple therapy for IPV has a significant impact on violence reduction (Karakurt, Whiting, van Esch, Bolen, & Calabrese, 2016). The authors pooled data from 6 studies for a combined sample size of 470 participants. Results indicated that there was a significant reduction in IPV among intervention participants. While additional research is needed in this area, emerging evidence suggests that couple therapy is a viable treatment for certain types of IPV. In the section below we present some established relational IPV interventions and some interventions with preliminary evidence of treatment efficacy. Most of these programs are designed to reduce low or moderate levels of situational couple violence and to improve relationship functioning.

Discussion of systemic treatment models and effectiveness

Domestic Violence-Focused Couples Therapy Domestic Violence-Focused Couples Therapy (DVFCT) is an 18-week program developed for carefully screened couples who choose to stay together after experiencing situational couple violence (Stith et al., 2011). The program is delivered either in a single-couple format or a multi-couple format. Co-therapists deliver the program. The primary objectives of the program are to end all forms of violence (physical, psychological, and sexual), to build conflict resolution skills, and to enhance couple relationships among those couples who choose to stay together or who share custody of children.

DVFCT is based on a solution-focused treatment model, and therapists are encouraged to build on client strengths and help them develop nonviolent conflict resolution strategies (McCollum, Stith, & Thomsen, 2011). An important aspect of the program is the development and continued practice of a negotiated time-out designed to help couples de-escalate when they began to become reactive (Rosen, Matheson, Stith, & McCollum, 2003).

To enhance safety, each client (or each gender-specific group) meets with one of the two therapists before and after each conjoint session. During this pre- and post-meeting session, the therapist assesses for safety and provides support to individual clients. The first six conjoint sessions focus on honoring the problem, developing a vision of a healthy relationship, providing an overview of issues regarding IPV (e.g., cycle of violence, definition of abuse), teaching and practicing mindfulness strategies, developing a negotiated time-out, and considering the impact that drug or alcohol abuse has on the problem (if appropriate.) After the first 6 weeks, the pre- and post-safety assessment continues. In addition, each session begins with a mindfulness activity, and individual/group themes and needs (e.g., communication skills, building on successes, etc.) are addressed. Published research on the program (Stith, Rosen, McCollum, & Thomsen, 2004) indicated that marital aggression (both male and female) was significantly lower at six-month follow-up than at pretest. Even though most couples who participated in the research aspect of the program were US-born Caucasian couples, clients who had emigrated from other countries or who did not identify as Caucasian did participate in the program. Therefore, the authors conducted a qualitative study examining the perceptions of non-US-born or non-Caucasian clients on the importance of racial/ethnic matching with therapists (Horst et al., 2012). Themes emerging from this work highlighted the way culture is multi-faceted and complex. Although clients emphasized that violence is a human problem, not limited to any particular ethnic group, they also emphasized the importance of therapists' demonstrating cultural awareness and competence. A clear finding from this work is the importance of therapists enhancing their cultural awareness and sensitivity. More research is needed in this area.

Behavioral Couples Therapy   Behavioral Couples Therapy (BCT) is an evidence-based dyadic intervention for individuals seeking treatment for alcohol or drug abuse (O'Farrell & Clements, 2012). Studies examining the impact of BCT have also looked at how reducing alcohol or drug abuse is also effective in reducing IPV (O'Farrell, Fals-Stewart, Murphy, Stephan, & Murphy, 2004). According to O'Farrell, Van Hutton, and Murphy (1999), BCT was an effective treatment for reducing IPV, where 61.3% of couples had experienced IPV in their relationship prior to receiving BCT and only 18.7% experienced IPV two years after receiving BCT. The main purpose of BCT is to build support for abstinence and to improve relationship functioning among married or cohabiting people seeking treatment by helping couples change their substance-related interactions. In the BCT model, help is enlisted from the non-substance-abusing partner to act as a support for the recovery of the substance-abusing individual. BCT has two components: substance abuse or alcohol-focused interventions to directly develop support for abstinence and relationship-focused interventions aimed at improving positive feelings, shared activities, and constructive communication (O'Farrell & Clements, 2012). During the intervention, the substance-abusing patient and their partner are seen together for 12 weekly outpatient couple sessions in addition to the patient participating in 20-individual, 12-step facilitation sessions for treatment of substance abuse (Ruff, McComb, Coker, & Sprenkle, 2010). The couple-based sessions are used to (a) negotiate a verbal recovery contract between the two partners that involves a daily sobriety trust discussion during which the substance-abusing partner affirms not to use substances that day and their partner provides support for this intent, (b) teach effective communication skills such as active listening and expressing feelings, (c) enhance relationship satisfaction and increase positive interactions by engaging in shared pleasurable activities and behaviors, and (d) teach conflict resolution and problem-solving skills (O'Farrell & Fals-Stewart, 2006). Content of the individual sessions is drawn from the Individual Drug Counseling Manual (Mercer & Woody, 1999) and is consistent with the Alcoholics

Anonymous philosophy. Evidence for this program's efficacy and effectiveness in increasing abstinence, reducing substance abuse, and improving relationship functioning, including reducing IPV, comes from several large, federally funded clinical trials (O'Farrell & Clements, 2012). Findings of a recent review show that BCT significantly improves relationship adjustment among couples with effect sizes ranging from 0.31 to 1.55. The gains in relationship functioning extend to 1- and 2-year follow-ups (Ruff et al., 2010). Studies of BCT for both male and female substance-abusing study participants show greater reductions in IPV after BCT compared with individual treatment. However, more work is needed to understand the mechanisms behind these changes (O'Farrell & Clements, 2012).

Couples Abuse Prevention Program   Couples Abuse Prevention Program (CAPP) was developed by LaTaillade, Epstein, and Werlinich (2006) to address risk factors for partner aggression among couples dealing with low-to-moderate physical and psychological violence. These risk factors include beliefs that justify aggression, communication skill deficits, and poor emotion regulation. The CAPP intervention sessions focus on psychoeducation about different types of IPV, risk factors for IPV, impact of IPV on the health and well-being of individuals and couples, anger management training, cognitive restructuring, problem-solving training, and strategies to help couples deal with trauma from previous relationships. CAPP is a cognitive-behavioral couple treatment. The treatment is delivered over 10 90-min sessions or 20 45-min sessions to individual couples depending on their availability. The treatment begins with an assessment of individual and couple functioning and of the safety of individual partners in the relationship. Conjoint treatment is deemed appropriate if there are no safety concerns.

In the first session of CAPP, the clinician provides an overview of the intervention protocol and provides information on the session structure and expectations during the intervention phase (e.g., homework assignments), gathers information on the clients' relationship history, and develops intervention goals with an agreement that the main goal of CAPP is to help couples have an aggression-free relationship. Session 2 is focused on a review of client goals, teaching clients about cognitive-behavioral constructs, communication, and strategies for anger management. In sessions 3–4, the focus is on teaching and practicing communication skills (e.g., expressive and listening skills) and on practicing anger management skills (e.g., cognitive restructuring techniques). Sessions 5–7 emphasize problem-solving techniques with a focus on learning to resolve conflict without aggression. In addition, clients are coached into combining communication and problem-solving skills and in applying them. Gender roles, cultural influences, family history, and other beliefs influencing aggression among couples are also explored. In sessions 8–10, clients focus on maintenance of new knowledge and skills learned by continuing to practice their new communication and problem-solving skills. There is also an emphasis on recovery from past relationship trauma and on increasing couple-based positive activities, on providing each other support, and on learning to be a team.

The CAPP model was evaluated in a clinical trial where couples were randomized into the CAPP intervention or treatment as usual (TAU) (therapy using different family systems models). Results indicated an increase in relationship satisfaction and trust in partner and reductions in psychological aggression, negative attributions, and anxiety in both treatment groups. No differences were seen in physical aggression. Lastly, CAPP couples showed a decrease in negative communication by both male and female partners, whereas TAU couples did not report this change (Hrapczynski, Epstein, Werlinich, & LaTaillade, 2011; Kahn, Epstein, & Kivlighan, 2014; LaTaillade et al., 2006).

Strength At Home Couples   Through a collaborative agreement with the Centers for Disease Control and Prevention, Taft and colleagues (2014) developed and tested a military specific IPV prevention program called Strength At Home Couples (SAH-C). This is a 10-session cognitive behavioral couple-based intervention designed to prevent IPV in returning male service members and their partners. The intervention is informed by a social information processing model for IPV perpetration among military populations (Taft, Walling, Howard, & Monson, 2011) and incorporates components of CBT for IPV (Murphy & Scott, 1996), anger management, assertiveness training for veterans (Grace, Niles, Quinn, & Taft, n.d.), and relational treatment of PTSD (Monson & Fredman, 2012).

The primary focus of the intervention is to help couples develop effective conflict resolution skills, increase intimacy and closeness in their relationships, and improve their communication. Sessions 1–3 are focused on PTSD psychoeducation as well as on the relationship between trauma exposure, deployment, and relationship difficulties. Sessions 4–6 focus on conflict management by teaching couples to identify and effectively manage relationship difficulties and conflict. Sessions 7–9 emphasize the importance of basic communication skills such as active listening, giving assertive messages, and identifying and expressing emotions. Couples are encouraged to practice these skills both in and out of sessions. Couples review changes made during the intervention and develop plans for the future in the last session. The intervention is carried out in groups with 3–5 couples in each group and is delivered weekly for 2 hr each week for 10 weeks.

Study feasibility and preliminary estimates of efficacy were determined through a pilot study with nine couples. Six couples were assigned to the SAH-C, and three couples were assigned to a comparison supportive therapy (ST) group-based couple intervention. Recruitment for the pilot study was very challenging. Study results were promising for reductions in IPV among SAH-C participants. None of the male partners engaged in physical IPV toward their female partner during the 30-month follow-up assessment after completing SAH-C, and female partners who completed SAH-C also evidenced reductions in physical IPV use, whereas females receiving ST evidenced large increases in their physical IPV (Taft, Murphy, & Creech, 2016).

Creating Healthy Relationships Program   The Creating Healthy Relationships Program (CHRP) (Cleary Bradley, Friend, & Gottman, 2011) is a psychoeducational intervention program for low-income couples who are parents and who exhibit situational violence. The CHRP is based on more than three decades of research with over 3,000 couples and is built on the sound relationship house theory (Gottman, 1994; Gottman & Silver, 2000; Shapiro & Gottman, 2005). The foundation of the house, which has seven floors, is made up of friendship, fondness, and admiration that together provide a strong foundation for intimate relationships. The model emphasizes constructive conflict management skills, ways to create emotional intimacy, and a culture of respect. It covers five content areas: managing stress, managing conflict, establishing connections in the family with partners and children, creating shared meaning, and maintaining intimacy. The program materials were developed to meet the needs of a population with low literacy levels.

The CHRP intervention is group based. Groups consist of 6–8 couples who meet weekly for 2 hr. The program is 22 weeks long (44 hr in total), and the program content is delivered by a dyad consisting of a female and a male clinician. The sessions are structured such that they begin with a video of couples participating in a mock talk show focused on the topic of the week. The group participants share their thoughts and opinions after watching the video. This is followed by a didactic research-based educational presentation on the topic. The couples then practice the relationship skills being taught.

Treatment efficacy data are drawn from a trial with 115 couples who were randomized into a treatment and a no-treatment control group. Data were collected pre-intervention and between 0 and 6 months after treatment completion. Forty-one out of the 115 couples were lost to follow up between the 2 assessment time periods. Results indicate that the couples in the treatment group showed an improvement in relationship satisfaction scores and a reduction in relationship conflict between baseline and post-intervention assessment. However, no significant differences were found between the treatment and control group in the level of violence, although the treatment group tended toward lower violence (p < 10; Cleary Bradley & Gottman, 2012).

No Kids in the Middle   The program *No Kids in the Middle,* which takes a multifamily approach, was developed by Van Lawick and Visser (2015a, 2015b) in the Netherlands and described in the book chapter written by Van Lawick, Visser, Stith, and Spencer (in press). The program was designed to reduce destructive parental conflicts in families experiencing high conflict divorce and to reduce the damaging influence that the high conflict may have on the children in these families. Parent-focused therapy is used in this program in order to decrease destructive conflicts between parents.

No Kids in the Middle uses a multifamily group approach. This program includes two intake sessions, a network information session, and eight (2-hr) parent treatment sessions with parallel child sessions. A key component of this intervention is the engagement and open dialogue between the therapists, parents, and children and the social support networks of both of the parents (Van Lawick & Visser, 2015b). Conducting the parallel children's group aids in reminding the parents that the main goal of the program is to improve the safety and overall well-being of the children. At the same time, it is important to provide the children an opportunity to share their experiences and to support one another. In this program, parents are asked to participate in experiential exercises that involve writing a new narrative about their separation in which the co-parent is not demonized, empathizing with the position of children, and focusing on own behavior rather than focusing on the behavior of the co-parent. In this program, parents are also encouraged to help one another in finding more constructive ways of resolving conflict and to highlight what each parent wishes for the children in the future.

The goal of No Kids in the Middle is to increase parents' understanding of one another's point of view and to increase acceptance of each other's differences. The ultimate goal of this model is not parent reconciliation. This program also aims to aid in parents' ability to identify triggers that have strong associations with negative affect between the partners, which can lead to intense arguments or conflict between partners. By aiding in the parents' ability to identify cognitive, behavioral, and emotional triggers, it can provide strategies that can de-escalate conflicts between parents. It is also important to note that social supports, or social networks, of both parents are involved in the intervention through homework assignments that involve social networks, as well as inviting each parent's social network to participate in evaluating treatment (Van Lawick & Visser, 2015a).

The evaluation of this program involved a multicenter study in the Netherlands and in Belgium. The authors compared questionnaires filled out by both the parents and the children prior to the intervention with questionnaires filled out at the end of the intervention, approximately 12 weeks later. Parents reported that their conflicts were more constructive after treatment and that the frequency and intensity of conflicts were lowered after they completed treatment. There were no significant differences between men and women found. Children also reported that they witnessed less conflict between parents after treatment. Although the program did not specifically measure IPV before or after treatment, the reduction in frequency and intensity of conflict suggests a reduction in psychological IPV.

Programs designed for specific situations

The systemic interventions reviewed here vary from programs specifically targeting couples who have experienced situational IPV (e.g., Stith et al., 2011) to those specifically targeting alcohol problems in couples, which lead to reduced IPV (O'Farrell et al., 2004), to those that are trauma informed and are designed for a military audience (e.g., Taft et al., 2016), and to other programs that are prevention-focused treatment for low-income families (Cleary Bradley & Gottman, 2012) and prevention-focused treatment for high conflict co-parenting divorced couples (Van Lawick & Visser, 2015b) (see Table 5.1). While more research is clearly needed, preliminary evidence suggests that conjoint treatment has a potential to reduce conflict, reduce IPV, and enhance relationships among high conflict or situationally violent couples.

Coordinated Community Response

Coordinated community response refers to a variety of formal programs/domestic violence agencies that involve interlinked community services responding to IPV that include the legal/criminal justice system, the police, government agencies, social services (e.g., shelters for victims, victim advocates, child services, counseling services), healthcare providers, and other programs (Shorey, Tirone, & Stuart, 2014). Coordinated community response programs were first developed in order to attempt to reduce levels of IPV in communities through coordinated services throughout the community by improving effectiveness of systems responding to IPV, delineating IPV-related services across agencies, delivering victim services, protecting victims of IPV, and sanctioning the perpetrators of IPV (Adler, 2002; Klevens, Baker, Shelley, & Ingram, 2008).

Most of the research on coordinated community response programs has been on the individual components of coordinated community response programs with the majority of research being on advocacy services, which often involves victim advocates aiding abused women obtain community resources and explore legal options (Shorey et al., 2014). Besides advocacy services, other individual components of coordinated community response programs include counseling services, criminal justice services, education and vocational services, and healthcare services (Shorey et al., 2014).

Table 5.1 Overview of systemic treatment models for IPV.

Program	Format	Approach	Objectives	Components and interventions	IPV outcome
Domestic Violence-Focused Couples Therapy Stith et al. (2011)	Single-couple or multi-couple group	Solution focused	End all forms of violence, enhance conflict resolution skills, and enhance couple relationship	Six mostly separate sessions focusing on developing skills for nonviolent relationships. 12 conjoint sessions addressing specific needs	After treatment, both male and female partners indicated lower levels of all forms of IPV
Behavioral Couples Therapy (BCT) O'Farrell and Fals-Stewart (2006))	Couple sessions and individual session for substance-abusing partner	Behavioral	Reduce substance abuse and enhance the couple relationship	12 couple sessions focusing on sobriety contracting, enhancing communication skills, increasing positive interactions, and improving conflict resolution skills. Substance user also receives 20 sessions focused on substance use	After treatment, there were lower levels of IPV experienced in the couple relationships
Couples Abuse Prevention Program (CAPP) LaTaillade et al. (2006)	Couple sessions	Cognitive behavioral	Reduce risk factors for IPV including changing attitudes accepting IPV, reducing communication skill deficits, and poor ability to regulate emotions	10 couple sessions providing psychoeducation on IPV, anger management, communication, problem solving, gender roles, family histories, and strategies to cope and heal from prior trauma	Trends toward reduced physical aggression. Reductions in psychological aggression, negative attributions, from pretest to posttest
Strength At Home Couples Taft et al. (2016).	Multi-couple groups	Cognitive behavioral; trauma informed, military specific	Prevent IPV in returning service members and their partners through increasing relationship intimacy, enhancing conflict resolution skills, and improving communication	10 couple sessions (3 on trauma, deployment, and relationship difficulties, 3 on conflict management, 3 on communication skills, and one on reviewing changes and creating a plan for the future)	After treatment, reduction of IPV was reported

| Creating Healthy Relationships Program
Cleary Bradley and Gottman (2012). | Multi-couple groups | Psychoeducation | Enhance conflict management skills, create emotional intimacy between partners, and create a culture of respect between low-income partners experiencing situational IPV | 22 weekly sessions that focus five content areas: improving stress management, increase conflict management, establish connections, create shared meanings between partners, and improve intimacy between partners | After treatment, couples reported improved relationship satisfaction and a reduction in relationship conflict compared to pre-intervention |
| No Kids in the Middle
Van Lawick and Visser (2015b) | Multifamily groups, as well as parallel child session | Cognitive behavioral | Reduce parental conflicts in high conflict divorce, and to reduce potential damage to children related to parental conflicts | 2 intake sessions, one network session, and 8 parent sessions creating dialogue, increase parents' understanding of the other's view, identify triggers enhancing constructive conflict resolution skills | After treatment, parents reported less destructive conflict, reduction in the frequency and intensity of conflict, and children reported less conflict between parents |

Shorey et al.'s (2014) review of the literature on coordinated community response programs related to victims of IPV found that advocacy services have had a positive impact on a victim's ability to access additional services and reduced re-victimization rates. However, there have been mixed findings in regard to the effectiveness of coordinated community response programs (Klevens et al., 2008). It appears as though the effectiveness of coordinated community response programs is dependent on each individual site. Research has found that in locations with coordinated community response programs that have been established in communities for 6 years, compared with those that have been established for 3 years, women were less likely to report IPV victimization (Post, Klevens, Maxwell, Shelley, & Ingram, 2010). This might suggest that it takes time for these programs to make an impact in their community. It is important to note that the mixed findings of effectiveness of coordinated community response programs may be a result of the difficulty measuring and demonstrating system changes implemented as a result of the coordinated community response program (Kreuter, Lezin, & Young, 2000; Salazar, Emshoff, Baker, & Crowley, 2007).

Clinical Training and Supervision of Clinicians Working with IPV

Education and training about IPV are not just important for therapists working with couples who seek treatment due to the violence in their relationship, but for all clinicians and therapists. Research has found that between 36 and 58% of couples initiating couple therapy have experienced physical IPV in the current relationship (Jose & O'Leary, 2009), which indicates that nearly all clinicians working with couples will work with couples who have experienced physical IPV. Therapists who are not working directly with couples will still work with perpetrators or victims of IPV in their career. For example, substance abuse counselors may not be working with couples directly, but substance use is a risk marker for IPV perpetration and victimization (Cafferky et al., 2018). It is important to ensure that clinical students and trainees understand the importance of careful assessment of IPV in all clients seeking therapy. IPV is common among couples seeking therapy, and therapists need to be trained to carefully screen all couples for IPV.

Working with IPV can be stressful. According to Scerri, Vetere, Abela, and Cooper (2017),

> stress can come from hearing stories of cruelty and neglect; disappointment when the violence continues even after therapy; risk of an inflated sense of responsibility around our work, particularly in the absence of personal and organizational support for our work; and navigating the tensions around introducing systemic/therapeutic ideas into a conservative legal system with no tradition of acknowledging the role of emotion or passion in people's thinking and behavior (p. 122).

Providing supervision in which trainees feel safe and open to discuss concerns is critical to helping trainees learn to work with IPV. In addition, clinicians who are not under supervision should not practice in isolation and be part of a team to be able to process this difficult and important work.

Directions for Future Research

Throughout this chapter, we have offered guidance for systemic clinical practice in the area of IPV prevention and intervention. However, more research is clearly needed to help clinicians determine the most effective ways to treat couples who have experienced IPV. There are some challenges in researching effective treatments of IPV, which highlights the importance of additional research on this topic. One challenge present in IPV research is treatment dropout. It is a possibility that the subset of participants who drop out of treatment may be at greater risk for continued IPV in the relationship and those who complete treatment are more invested in treatment, thus skewing success rates for research purposes. Another challenge IPV research faces is how studies measure violence after treatment has been completed. It is important for researchers to use long-term follow-ups to examine if the decrease in violence was long lasting. Although this is a challenge for most research, it is imperative that IPV research attempts to gain follow-ups from participants to see if the violence in the relationship ended, or was reduced, long term. It is also important to examine victim-reported accounts of IPV, rather than solely on perpetrator-reported accounts of IPV in the relationship or rather than relying on arrest records. It is also important for IPV treatment outcome research to measure IPV as more than only physical acts of violence. Examining psychological and sexual IPV is just as necessary to determine successful treatment as it is to examine counts of physical IPV.

For IPV treatment research, large-scale clinical trials are lacking, and randomized assignments comparing various treatment approaches are not available. We also need more research on culturally specific treatment approaches. If a treatment model developed in the United States, with primarily US-born clients, has demonstrated some level of effectiveness, it is not necessarily appropriate to deliver the model in other countries or to other cultural groups without careful adaptation to cultural norms. Research conducted internationally, with various subgroups and with participants from various nations, is critical for determining best practice in each setting. While it is clear that IPV occurs in all types of relationships, research is lacking on systemic treatment of IPV in same-sex relationships or in relationships in which at least one partner identifies as transgender or gender nonconforming. Research on therapeutic approaches "that represent the full gamut of gender, relationships, and forms of IPV is needed for the development of more individually tailored and sensitive interventions" (Paivinen & Holma, 2017). We strongly advocate for more research on this important issue.

Suggestions for Policy Changes

In order for more research to be conducted and more innovative systemic methods to be developed and tested in the United States with the wide variety of types of IPV, policy changes need to be made: "U.S. state guidelines that absolutely exclude conjoint approaches are overly restrictive, considering the poor evidence of effectiveness for current gender-specific groups. Further, the theoretical foundations of most men-only groups assume unilateral, male-to-female violence, which does not fit at least one-third of court-involved cases and leaves treatment needs of couples experiencing problematic relationship dynamics unmet" (Armenti & Babcock, 2016, p. 109). State standards throughout the United States often treat all types of offenders the same way, assuming the violence is male to female, and based on power and control (Barocas, Emery, & Mills, 2016). Changing state standards for offender programs would allow for testing alternative approaches to IPV interventions: "As the field operates now, even programs that are shown through rigorous research to be safe and promising are either forbidden or cautioned against by statute" (Barocas et al., 2016, p. 945). We view this as a main need for policy change in regard to treatment of IPV.

In order to advocate for policy reform, it is important for systemic clinicians to become a part of the coordinated community approach. For example, collaborating with formal entities within the community they are serving is a great way to be involved in policy change. Systemic clinicians may collaborate with local (either their local community or state-level) domestic violence shelters, treatment centers providing batterer intervention programming, law enforcement, and medical professionals. This can allow for positive communication between these programs, which can aid in collaboration toward policy changes that may allow for systemic treatment of IPV. It is necessary for systemic clinicians to be involved and have a "seat at the table" during these discussions and changes regarding policy. As state standards are revised and policies are instituted, systemic clinicians can advocate for and address any possible concerns in order to allow for ongoing research and testing.

References

Adler, M. A. (2002). The utility of modeling in evaluation planning: The case of the coordination of domestic violence services in Maryland. *Evaluation and Program Planning, 25*(3), 203–213.

Amin, A. F. (2000). *Violence against women.* Sanandaj, Islamic Republic of Iran: Women's Participation Research Center of Kurdistan Providence.

Ansara, D. L., & Hindin, M. J. (2010). Psychosocial consequences of intimate partner violence for women and men in Canada. *Journal of Interpersonal Violence, 26*(8), 1628–1645.

Arias, E., Ramon, A., & Vilarino, M. (2013). Batterer intervention programmes: A meta-analytic review of effectiveness. *Psychosocial Intervention, 22*(2), 153–160.

Armenti, N., & Babcock, J. (2016). Conjoint treatment for intimate partner violence: A systematic review and implications. *Couple and Family Psychology: Research and Practice, 5*(2), 109–123.

Babcock, J. C., Green, C. E., & Robie, C. (2004). Does batterers' treatment work? A meta-analytic review of domestic violence treatment. *Clinical Psychology Review, 23,* 1023–1053. doi:10.1016/j.cpr.2002.07.001

Barocas, B., Emery, D., & Mills, L. G. (2016). Changing the domestic violence narrative: Aligning definitions and standards. *Journal of Family Violence, 31,* 941–947. doi:10.1007/s10896-016-9885-0

Black, M. C., Basile, K. C., Breiding, M. J., Smith, S. G., Walters, M. L., Merrick, M. T., ... Stevens, M. R. (2011). *The National Intimate Partner and Sexual Violence Survey (NISVS): 2010 summary report.* Retrieved from https://www.cdc.gov/violenceprevention/pdf/nisvs_report2010-a.pdf

Bonomi, A. E., Anderson, M. L., Rivara, F. P., & Thompson, R. S. (2009). Health care utilization and costs associated with physical and nonphysical only intimate partner violence. *Health Services Research, 44*(3), 1052–1067.

Bosch, J., Weaver, T. L., Arnold, L. D., & Clark, E. M. (2017). The impact of intimate partner violence on women's physical health: Findings from the Missouri behavioral risk factor surveillance system. *Journal of Interpersonal Violence, 32*(22), 3402–3419.

Cafferky, B. M., Mendez, M., Anderson, J. R., & Stith, S. M. (2018). Substance use and intimate partner violence: A meta-analytic review. *Psychology of Violence, 8*(1), 110–131. doi:10.1037/vio0000074

Campbell, J., Jones, A. S., Dienemann, J., Kub, J., Schollenberger, J., O'campo, P., … Wynne, C. (2002). Intimate partner violence and physical health consequences. *Archives of Internal Medicine, 162*(10), 1157–1163.

Cantos, A. L., & O'Leary, K. D. (2014). One size does not fit all in treatment of intimate partner violence. *Partner Abuse, 5*, 204–236.

Chase, K. A., O'Leary, K. D., & Heyman, R. E. (2001). Categorizing partner-violent men within the reactive-proactive typology model. *Journal of Consulting and Clinical Psychology, 69*(3), 567–572.

Cleary Bradley, R. P., Friend, D. J., & Gottman, J. M. (2011). Supporting health relationships in low-income, violent couples: Reducing conflict and strengthening relationship skills and satisfaction. *Journal of Couple and Relationship Therapy, 10*, 97–116.

Cleary Bradley, R. P., & Gottman, J. M. (2012). Reducing situational violence in low-income couples by fostering healthy relationships. *Journal of Marital and Family Therapy, 38*(Suppl. 1), 187–198. doi:10.1111/j.1752-0606.2012.00288

Coker, A. L., Smith, P. H., Bethea, L., King, M. R., & McKeown, R. E. (2000). Physical health consequences of physical and psychological intimate partner violence. *Archives of Family Medicine, 9*(5), 451.

Devries, K. M., Mak, J. Y., García-Moreno, C., Petzold, M., Child, J. C., Falder, G., & Pallitto, C. (2013). The global prevalence of intimate partner violence against women. *Science, 340*(6140), 1527–1528.

Dickerson, V. (2013). Patriarchy, power, and privilege: A narrative poststructural view of work with couples. *Family Process, 52*, 102–114.

Dutton, D. G. (1995). *The domestic assault of women: Psychological and criminal justice perspectives.* Vancouver, BC: UBC Press.

Feder, L., & Wilson, D. (2005). A meta-analytic review of court-mandated batterer intervention programs: Can courts affect abusers' behavior? *Journal of Experimental Criminology, 1*, 239–262.

Friend, D. J., Cleary Bradley, R. P., Thatcher, R., & Gottman, J. M. (2011). Typologies of intimate partner violence: Evaluation of a screening instrument for differentiation. *Journal of Family Violence, 26*, 551–563. doi:10.1007/s10896-011-9392-2

Gondolf, E. W. (2009). Outcomes from referring batterer program participants to mental health treatment. *Journal of Family Violence, 24*, 577–588.

Gottman, J. M. (1994). *What predicts divorce? The relationship between marital processes and marital outcomes.* Hillsdale, NJ: Erlbaum.

Gottman, J. M., & Silver, N. (2000). *The seven principles for making marriage work: A practical guide from the country's foremost relationship expert.* New York, NY: Three Rivers Press.

Grace, M., Niles, B., Quinn, S., & Taft, C. T. (n.d.). *Anger management manual: National Center for PTSD.* VA Boston Healthcare System. Unpublished manual.

Hewitt, L. N., Bhavsar, P., & Phelan, H. A. (2011). The secrets women keep: Intimate partner violence screening in the female trauma patient. *Journal of Trauma and Acute Care Surgery, 70*(2), 320–323.

Holmgren, H., Holma, J., & Seikkula, J. (2015). Programs for partner violent men: Shared goals with different strategies. *Partner Abuse, 6*(4), 461–476. doi:10.1891/1946-6560.6.4.461

Holtzworth-Munroe, A. (2001). Standards for batterer treatment program: How can research inform our decisions? *Journal of Aggression, Maltreatment & Trauma, 5*, 165–180.

Horst, K., Mendez, M., Culver Turner, R., Amanor Boadu, Y., Minner, B., Cook, J., … McCollum, E. (2012). Ethnic or racial matching in couples treatment for domestic violence. *Contemporary Family Therapy, 34*(1), 57–71.

Hrapczynski, K. M., Epstein, N. B., Werlinich, C. A., & LaTaillade, J. J. (2011). Changes in negative attributions during couple therapy for abusive behavior: Relations to changes in satisfaction and behavior. *Journal of Marital and Family Therapy, 38*, 117–132.

Johnson, M. P. (1995). Patriarchal terrorism and common couple violence: Two forms of violence against women. *Journal of Marriage and Family, 57*, 283–294. doi:10.2307/353683

Johnson, M. P. (2007). Domestic violence: The intersection of gender and control. In L. L. O'Toole, J. R. Schiffman, & M. K. Edwards (Eds.), *Gender violence: Interdisciplinary perspectives* (2nd ed., pp. 257–268). New York, NY: New York University Press.

Johnson, M. P. (2008). *A typology of domestic violence: Intimate terrorism, violent resistance, and situational couple violence.* Boston, MA: Northeastern University.

Johnson, M. P., & Ferraro, K. J. (2000). Research on domestic violence in the 1990s: Making distinctions. *Journal of Marriage and the Family, 62*, 948–963.

Johnson, M. P., & Leone, J. M. (2005). The differential effects of intimate terrorism and situational couple violence: Findings from the national violence against women survey. *Journal of Family Issues, 26*(3), 322–349. doi:10.1186/s12889-015-1649-x

Jory, B. (2004). The intimate justice scale: An instrument to screen for psychological abuse and physical violence in clinical practice. *Journal of Marital and Family Therapy, 30*, 29–44.

Jose, A., & O'Leary, K. D. (2009). Prevalence of partner aggression in representative and clinic samples. In K. D. O'Leary & E. M. Woodin (Eds.), *Psychological and physical aggression in couples: Causes and interventions* (pp. 15–35). Washington, DC: American Psychological Association.

Kahn, S., Epstein, N. B., and Kivlighan, D. (2014). *Couples therapy: Does it improve individual ad relational well-being in couples experiencing mild to moderate aggression?* Unpublished manuscript, Department of Family Science, University of Maryland, College Park.

Kamimura, A., Christensen, N., Tabler, J., Ashby, J., & Olson, L. M. (2014). Prevalence of intimate partner violence and its impact on health: Female and male patients using a free clinic. *Journal of Health Care for the Poor and Underserved, 25*(2), 731–745.

Karakurt, G., Whiting, K., van Esch, C., Bolen, S. D., & Calabrese, J. R. (2016). Couples therapy for intimate partner violence: A systematic review and meta-analysis. *Journal of Marital and Family Therapy, 42*(4), 567–583.

Kelly, J. B., & Johnson, M. P. (2008). Differentiation among types of intimate partner violence: Research update and implications for intervention. *Family Court Review, 46*, 476–499.

Kimmes, J. G., Mallory, A. B., Spencer, C., Beck, A. R., Cafferky, B., & Stith, S. M. (2017). A meta-analysis of risk markers for intimate partner violence in same-sex relationships. *Trauma, Violence, & Abuse.* Advance online publication. doi:10.1177/1524838017708784

Klevens, J., Baker, C. K., Shelley, G. A., & Ingram, E. M. (2008). Exploring the links between components of coordinated community responses and their impact on contact with intimate partner violence services. *Violence Against Women, 14*(3), 346–358.

Knudson-Martin, C. (2013). Why power matters: Creating a foundation of mutual support in couple relationships. *Family Process, 52*, 5–18.

Kreuter, M. W., Lezin, N. A., & Young, L. A. (2000). Evaluating community-based collaborative mechanisms: Implications for practitioners. *Health Promotion Practice, 1*, 49–63.

LaTaillade, J. J., Epstein, N. B., & Werlinich, C. A. (2006). Conjoint treatment of intimate partner violence: A cognitive behavioral approach. *Journal of Cognitive Psychotherapy, 20*, 393–410.

Levesque, D., Ciavatta, M., Castle, P., Prochaska, P., & Prochaska, J. (2012). Evaluation of a stage-based, computer-tailored adjunct to usual care for domestic violence offenders. *Psychology of Violence, 2*, 368–384.

Li, Y., Marshall, C. M., Rees, H. C., Nunez, A., Ezeanolue, E. E., & Ehiri, J. E. (2014). Intimate partner violence and HIV infection among women: A systematic review and meta-analysis. *Journal of the international AIDS society, 17*(1), 18845.

Machtinger, E. L., Wilson, T. C., Haberer, J. E., & Weiss, D. S. (2012). Psychological trauma and PTSD in HIV-positive women: A meta-analysis. *AIDS and Behavior, 16*(8), 2091–2100.

Mapayi, B., Makanjuola, R. O. A., Mosaku, S. K., Adewuya, O. A., Afolabi, O., Aloba, O. O., & Akinsulore, A. (2013). Impact of intimate partner violence on anxiety and depression amongst women in Ile-Ife, Nigeria. *Archives of Women's Mental Health, 16*(1), 11–18.

McCollum, E. E., Stith, S. M., & Thomsen, C. J. (2011). Solution-focused brief therapy in the conjoint couples treatment of intimate partner violence. In C. Franklin, T. S. Trepper, E. E. McCollum, & W. Gingerich (Eds.), *Solution-focused brief therapy: A handbook of evidence-based practice* (pp. 183–195). New York, NY: Oxford University Press.

McKinney, C. M., Caetano, R., Rodriguez, L. A., & Okoro, N. (2010). Does alcohol involvement increase the severity of intimate partner violence? *Alcoholism: Clinical and Experimental Research, 34*(4), 655–658.

Mercer, D. E., & Woody, G. E. (1999). *An individual drug counseling approach to treat cocaine addiction. The collaborative cocaine treatment study model.* Therapy Manuals for Drug Abuse. Rockville, MD: National Institute of Drug Abuse.

Merk, W., deCastro, B. O., & Koops, W. (2005). The distinction between reactive and proactive aggression: Utility for theory, diagnosis, and treatment. *European Journal of Developmental Psychology, 2*(2), 197–220.

Monson, C. M., & Fredman, S. J. (2012). *Cognitive-behavioral conjoint therapy for posttraumatic stress disorder: Therapist's manual.* New York, NY: Guildford Press.

Murphy, C. M., & Scott, E. (1996). *Cognitive-behavioral therapy for domestically assaultive individuals. A treatment manual.* Unpublished manuscript, University of Maryland, Baltimore County.

O'Farrell, T. J., & Clements, K. (2012). Review of outcome research on marital and family therapy in treatment for alcoholism. *Journal of Marital and Family Therapy, 38*(1), 12–144.

O'Farrell, T. J., & Fals-Stewart, W. (2006). *Behavioral couples therapy for alcoholism and drug abuse.* New York, NY: Guilford Press.

O'Farrell, T. J., Fals-Stewart, W., Murphy, C. M., Stephan, S. H., & Murphy, M. (2004). Partner violence before and after couples-based alcoholism treatment for male alcoholic patients: The role of treatment involvement and abstinence. *Journal of Consulting and Clinical Psychology, 72*, 202–217.

O'Farrell, T. J., Van Hutton, V. M., & Murphy, C. M. (1999). Domestic violence before and after alcoholism treatment: A two-year longitudinal study. *Journal of Studies on Alcohol, 60*, 317–321.

O'Leary, K. D., Vivian, D., & Malone, J. (1992). Assessment of physical aggression against women in marriage. The need for multi-modal assessment. *Behavioral Assessment, 14*, 5–14.

Paivinen, H., & Holma, J. (2017). Towards gender awareness in couple therapy and in treatment of intimate partner violence. *Journal of Gender-Based Violence, 1*(2), 221–234. doi:1 0.1332/239868017X15090095287019

Palmer, M. (2017). *Domestic violence and mediation in contemporary China.* UCD Working Papers in Law, Criminology & Socio-Legal Studies Research Paper.

Post, L. A., Klevens, J., Maxwell, C. D., Shelley, G. A., & Ingram, E. (2010). An examination of whether coordinated community responses affect intimate partner violence. *Journal of Interpersonal Violence, 25*(1), 75–93.

Ramirez, J. M., & Andreu, J. M. (2006). Aggression, and some related psychological constructs (anger, hostility, and impulsivity): Some comments from a research project. *Neuroscience and Biobehavioral Reviews, 30*, 276–291.

Rosen, K. H., Matheson, J., Stith, S. M., & McCollum, E. E. (2003). Negotiated time-out: A de-escalation tool for couples. *Journal of Marital and Family Therapy, 29*(3), 291–298.

Ross, J. M., & Babcock, J. C. (2009). Proactive and reactive violence among intimate partner violent men diagnosed with antisocial and borderline personality disorder. *Journal of Family Violence, 24,* 207–617.

Ruff, S., McComb, J., Coker, C. J., & Sprenkle, D. H. (2010). Behavioral couples therapy for the treatment of substance abuse: A substantive and methodological review of O'Farrell, Fals-Stewart, and colleagues' program of research. *Family Process, 49*(4), 439–456.

Safaee, S. H., & Emamei, A. (2012). *Family law.* Tehran, Iran: University of Tehran.

Salazar, L. F., Emshoff, J. G., Baker, C. K., & Crowley, T. (2007). Examining the behavior of a system: An outcome evaluation of a coordinated community response to domestic violence. *Journal of Family Violence, 22*(7), 631–641.

Scerri, C. S., Vetere, A., Abela, A., & Cooper, J. (2017). *Intervening after violence: Therapy for couples and families.* Cham, Switzerland: Springer.

Scott, K., King, C., McGinn, H., & Hosseini, N. (2011). Effects of motivational enhancement on immediate outcomes of batterer intervention. *Journal of Family Violence, 26,* 139–149.

Shapiro, A., & Gottman, J. M. (2005). Effects of a marriage on a psycho-communicative-educational intervention with couples undergoing the transition to parenthood. *Journal of Family Communication, 5,* 102–111.

Shorey, R. C., Tirone, V., & Stuart, G. L. (2014). Coordinated community response components for victims of intimate partner violence: A review of the literature. *Aggression and Violent Behavior, 19*(4), 363–371.

Smith, S. G., Chen, J., Basile, K. C., Gilbert, L. K., Merrick, M. T., Patel, N., ... Jain, A. (2017). *The National Intimate Partner and Sexual Violence Survey (NISVS): 2010–2012 state report.* Atlanta, GA: National Center for Injury Prevention and Control, Centers for Disease Control and Prevention. Retrieved from https://www.cdc.gov/violenceprevention/pdf/NISVS-StateReportBook.pdf

Spencer, C., Cafferky, B., & Stith, S. M. (2016). Gender differences in risk markers for perpetration of physical partner violence: Results from a meta-analytic review. *Journal of Family Violence, 31*(8), 981–984. doi:10.1007/s10896-016-9860-9

Spencer, C., Mallory, A. B., Cafferky, B. M., Kimmes, J. G., Beck, A. R., & Stith, S. M. (2017). Mental health factors and their links to IPV perpetration and victimization: A meta-analysis. *Psychology of Violence.* Advance online publication. doi:10.1037/vio0000156

Spencer, C., Stith, S. M., & Cafferky, B. (2018). Risk markers for physical intimate partner violence victimization: A meta-analysis. *Aggression and Violent Behavior.* Advanced online publication. doi:10.1016/j.avb.2018.10.009.

Stith, S. M., Cafferky, B., Bird, N., Lawson, N., Smith, E., Luu, S., Mallory, A., & Barros Gomez, P. (2014). *Overview of a meta-analytic review of risk markers for IPV.* International Family Violence and Child Victimization Research Conference, Portsmouth, NH.

Stith, S. M., McCollum, E., & Rosen, K. (2011). *Couple therapy for domestic violence: Finding safe solutions.* Washington, DC: American Psychological Association.

Stith, S. M., McCollum, E. E., & Amanor-Boadu, Y. (2012). Systemic perspectives on intimate partner violence treatment. *Journal of Marital and Family Therapy, 38*(1), 220–240.

Stith, S. M., Rosen, K. H., McCollum, E. E., & Thomsen, C. J. (2004). Treating intimate partner violence within intact couple relationships: Outcomes of multi-couple versus individual couple therapy. *Journal of Marital and Family Therapy, 30*(3), 305–318.

Stith, S. M., Smith, D. B., Penn, C. E., Ward, D. B., & Tritt, D. (2004). Intimate partner physical abuse perpetration and victimization risk factors: A meta-analytic review. *Aggression and Violent Behavior, 10,* 65–98. doi:10.1016/j.avb.2003.09.001

Straus, M. A., Hamby, S. L., Boney-McCoy, S., & Sugarman, D. B. (1996). The Revised Conflict Tactics Scales (CTS2): Development and preliminary psychometric data. *Journal of Family Issues, 17*, 283–316.

Taft, C. T., Howard, J., Monson, C. M., Walling, S. M., Resnick, P. A., & Murphy, C. M. (2014). "Strength at home" intervention to prevent conflict and violence in military couples: Pilot findings. *Partner Abuse, 5*(1), 41–57.

Taft, C. T., Murphy, C. M., & Creech, S. K. (2016). *Trauma-informed treatment and prevention of intimate partner violence*. Washington, DC: American Psychological Association.

Taft, C. T., Walling, S. M., Howard, J. M., & Monson, C. (2011). Trauma, PTSD, and partner violence in military families. In S. M. Wadsworth & D. Riggs (Eds.), *Risk and resilience in U.S. military families* (pp. 195–212). New York, NY: Springer Science + Business Media.

Tang, C. S., & Lai, B. P. (2008). A review of empirical literature on the prevalence and risk markers of male-on-female intimate partner violence in contemporary China, 1987–2006. *Aggression and Violent Behavior, 13*(1), 10–28.

Tweed, R. G., & Dutton, D. G. (1998). A comparison of impulsive and instrumental subgroups of batterers. *Violence and Victims, 13*(3), 217–230.

Van Lawick, J., & Visser, M. (2015a). *Kinderen uit de Knel. Een interventie voor gezinnen verwikkeld in een vechtscheiding*. Amsterdam, the Netherlands: SWP.

Van Lawick, J., & Visser, M. (2015b). No kids in the middle: Dialogical and creative work with parents and children in the context of high conflict divorces. *Australian and New Zealand Journal of Family Therapy, 36*, 33–50.

Van Lawick, J., Visser, M., Stith, S. M., & Spencer, C. (in press). Violence in families: Systemic practice and research. In M. Ochs, M. Borcsa, & J. Schweitzer (Eds.), *Systemic Research and Practice, Springer European Family Therapy Association Series*

Walters, M. L., Chen, J., & Breiding, M. J. (2013). *The National Intimate Partner and Sexual Violence Survey (NISVS): 2010 findings on victimization by sexual orientation*. Atlanta, GA: National Center for Injury Prevention and Control, Centers for Disease Control and Prevention. Retrieved from https://www.cdc.gov/violenceprevention/pdf/nisvs_sofindings.pdf

Wingood, G. M., DiClemente, R. J., & Raj, A. (2000). Adverse consequences of intimate partner abuse among women in non-urban domestic violence shelters. *American Journal of Preventive Medicine, 19*(4), 270–275.

World Health Organization. (2013). *Responding to intimate partner violence and sexual violence against women: WHO clinical and policy guidelines*. Geneva: Author.

Zarling, A., Lawrence, E., & Marchman, J. (2015). A randomized controlled trial of acceptance and commitment therapy for aggressive behavior. *Journal of Consulting and Clinical Psychology, 83*(1), 199–212.

Zhao, Y. (2000). Domestic violence in China: In search of legal and social responses. *UCLA Pacific Basin Law Journal, 18*(2), 211–251.

6

Working with Queer Couples

Katie M. Heiden-Rootes, Sheila M. Addison, and J. Douglas Pettinelli

A comprehensive volume on systemic family therapy (SFT) requires a stand-alone chapter on work with couples in which one or both partners identify as lesbian, gay, bisexual, transgender, and queer (LGBTQ) because the language used throughout SFT research, education, and practice *constricts possibilities for couple therapy practice*. The language of SFT both centers and sanctions particular performances of gender and sexual orientation (Tilsen, 2013), via its reliance on binary categories of gender (male/female) and sexual orientation (gay/straight). Thus, the field's language constrains ideas about what the act of being coupled in an intimate, sexual relationship can look like, as well as how therapists can support or intervene in such relationships. For example, the use of terms such as "heterosexual couple" or "lesbian/gay couple" is common in SFT literature. Such language assumes both partners share a sexual identity and fit into a gender binary, when, in fact, bisexual, pansexual, and non-binary people are erased by this framing.

Globally, the SFT field is coming to grips with the reality of an emerging "new normal" of gender and sexual diversity. Based on the most recent estimates, over two million "mixed-orientation" marriages exist in the United States (Buxton, 2004), in which heterosexual or lesbian/gay people partner with a bisexual person or where different-gender partners agree to remain married when one member comes out as lesbian or gay. If we include dating/unmarried relationships of youth and adults, the number swells further (Crofford, 2017). The more we unpack the assumptions in the language, the more we see that "boxes" are in fact cages whose labels no longer describe those we try to hold within them. Theory, education, and research in couple therapy are isomorphic to this global shift, raising the uncomfortable truth that we too are experiencing the limits of our language for identifying effective practice with LGBTQ people.

In an effort to move SFT beyond the gender and sexual binary, we hope to offer a useful summary of the state of the field and an invitation to a more culturally humble (Hook, Davis, Owen, Worthington, & Utsey, 2013) perspective on couple therapy with LGBTQ people. Finally, we reflexively turn our inquiry back on ourselves, making us curious about our own growth edges, uncomfortable about the assumptions

The Handbook of Systemic Family Therapy: Volume 3, First Edition.
Edited by Karen S. Wampler and Adrian J. Blow.
© 2020 John Wiley & Sons Ltd. Published 2020 by John Wiley & Sons Ltd.

we make regarding seemingly heterosexual and cisgender couples, and aroused by the vast opportunities represented by our relative ignorance. We hope this chapter is an encouragement offering preliminary answers regarding best practices—the "known unknowns," as it were (Luft, 1969)—and an impetus for inquiry to build a more just and affirming SFT practice.

Language and some definitions

The language of sexual and gender identity has undergone rapid and frequent changes in recent decades, which continues even as we write this chapter. Some relevant terms are summarized in Table 6.1, along with synonyms clinicians may hear from clients themselves and terms that are wise to avoid, unless they are specifically used by particular clients for self-description.

  We assume language will continue to evolve, so the terms used in this chapter should not be considered definitive and immutable but part of an ongoing conversation. For more perspective on the rapid shifts of language describing sexual and gender minorities, see Serano's (2016) writing on the "activist language merry-go-round" (p. 246) and the search for the "perfect word" (p. 283).

Queer people and couples are everywhere

On a global level, estimates suggest only 10% of the world population across 20 countries live where same-gender couples are able to legally marry (Pew Research Center, 2019). Estimates in partnering of LGBTQ people vary by definition of partnership (e.g., marriage, cohabitation, domestic partnerships, dating) and by sexual orientation. The 2010 US census found 1% of households were headed by same-gender couples (US Census Bureau, 2011). Between 30 and 60% of gay men reported currently being partnered or in a committed romantic relationship (Carpenter & Gates, 2008; Kurdek, 1996; Oswald, 2002). For lesbian women the partnership rates appear to be higher at 50–60%. The US federal government does not track same-gender legal marriage; however estimates suggest between 0.3 and 1% of legal marriages were same-gender couples and about 25% of all same-gender couples were legally married (Fisher et al., 2016). No estimates could be found on transgender, gender nonconforming, bisexual, pansexual, or queer-identified people and their partnership rates.

Significant Factors Affecting Queer Couples

Minority stress and coupling

Minority stress, a central organizing theory for understanding health disparities for LGBTQ people (Hendricks & Testa, 2012; Meyer, 2003), emphasizes the daily and chronic nature of marginalization for LGBTQ people and its impact on their physical and mental health (Meyer, 2003). Meyer postulates that stressors fall on a range from distal to proximal. Distal minority stressors are interpersonal and external events, such as family and peer rejection, homophobic harassment, victimization due to bullying and violence, and homelessness. Proximal minority stressors are internal and are

Table 6.1 Definition of terms and language commonly used in LGBTQ spaces.

Term		Meaning	Other terms	Terms *not* to use
Sexual orientation		A person's sense of how to describe themselves based on which gender(s) attracts them for the purposes of sexual, romantic, affective, and/or intimate partnership or fantasy	Sexual identity	Sexual preference, lifestyle
	Sexual minority	A person whose sexual orientation is not heterosexual (straight)	Queer+	Abnormal, invert, sexual deviant
	Heterosexual	Feeling attracted mostly or only to people not of one's own gender	Straight	Normal
	Gay	Feeling attracted mostly or only to people of one's own gender (used more often for men)	Gay man, MLM (men loving men), gay woman, queer+	"A gay," homosexual, "a homosexual"
	Lesbian	Feeling attracted mostly or only to people of one's own gender (used only for women)	WLW (women loving women)	"A gay," homosexual, "a homosexual"
	Bisexual	Feeling attracted to people of one's own gender, and to people not of one's own gender	Bi, pansexual, omnisexual, plurisexual	Confused, in a phase
	Asexual	Not feeling sexually attracted to people of any gender	Ace	Sexually frigid, sexually immature
	Sexual fluidity	Experiencing change in one's attractions over time, or at different times or circumstances		Confused, in a phase
	Queer+	An umbrella term used to describe all people who are sexual minorities. It is sometimes used to describe all sexual and gender minorities. The term was formerly an anti-gay slur and not all people are comfortable with it	Sexual minority, sexual and gender minority	Abnormal, invert, sexual deviant

(*Continued*)

Table 6.1 (Continued)

	Term	Meaning	Other terms	Terms not to use
	Queer couple	A couple in which one or both partners identify as a sexual minority	Same-gender couple, gay/lesbian couple, bi-including couple, trans-including couple (where applicable)	Same-sex couple (when one member is transgender), gay/lesbian couple (when one or both members are bisexual)
	Different-gender couple	A couple in which both partners identify as different genders	Mixed-gender couple	Heterosexual couple (when one or both members are bisexual)
	Queer affirmative therapy	Therapy that explicitly affirms that being a sexual minority is a normal part of human sexual diversity and is not inherently pathological, that sexual minorities are valued members of the community entitled to dignity and respect, that experiencing same-gender desire and acting on that desire with one or more consenting partners is an acceptable form of sexual expression, and that sexual minorities can have happy, healthy partner and family relationships	Affirmative therapy, gay affirmative therapy, lesbian affirmative therapy, bi-affirmative therapy	
Gender identity	Cisgender	A person's internal sense of their own gender, independent of the gender they were assigned at birth		Sex preference, gender preference, lifestyle
		When a person's gender identity is the same as the gender they were assigned at birth	Cis	Normal
	Transgender	When a person's gender identity is different from the gender they were assigned at birth	Trans, gender minority	"A transgender," transgendered, gender deviant, abnormal, gender confused, drag queen, homosexual, gay

Term	Description	Affirming terms	Non-affirming terms
Gender fluid	Experiencing changes in one's gender over time, or at different times or circumstances.	Genderqueer	confused, delusional, in a phase
Non-binary	A person's gender identity does not fit well into the male–female binary	Genderqueer	Confused, delusional, in a phase, he–she
Agender	Not feeling a particular sense of gender identity.	Genderqueer	Confused, delusional, sexually immature
Gender creative	A term used by some experts for childhood and adolescent gender development to describe children who are exploring gender in fluid, non-binary, or nontraditional ways	Gender expansive, transgender—only when a child is *insistent, persistent, and consistent* about asserting a gender different from the one they were assigned at birth	Gender confused, gay
Transsexual	A person who has undergone medical procedures including gender confirmation surgery/surgeries to align their physical characteristics more closely with their gender identity (considered outdated in some circles)	Transgender person, person who has transitioned	Tranny, gender bender, drag queen
Gender minority Trans-including couple	A person whose gender identity is not cisgender A couple where one or more partners identify as transgender	Transgender	Sexual minority, homosexual, gay Transgender couple (when one member is cisgender), queer couple (when both members are heterosexual)

experiences that perpetuate the feelings of marginalization, for example, internalized homophobia (Meyer, 2003; Rostosky & Riggle, 2017). Minority stressors—both distal and proximal—put chronic pressure on LGBTQ individuals with the effect of increasingly worse mental health outcomes (Hendricks & Testa, 2012; Meyer, 2003) and decreased relationship quality in romantic same-gender partnerships (Balsam & Szymanski, 2005; Doyle & Molix, 2015; Mohr & Daly, 2008; Otis, Rostosky, Riggle, & Hamrin, 2006).

The degree of minority stress for a queer couple is a product of their social and cultural environments. The present social condition for LGBTQ people is inconsistent and both geographically and politically bound. In the United States, Canada, and Japan, recent surveys show increased social acceptance of LGBT people. For example, same-gender marriages were legalized in the United States in 2014, and since this time acceptance of same-gender marriages has had majority support (62%; Pew Research Center, 2017). Yet even in the United States, the state, city, and neighborhood can significantly change the degree of protection for LGBTQ rights and acceptance of queer and trans-including couples (Bruni, 2017). This may explain why many LGBTQ people and same-gender partnered couples live in metropolitan (as opposed to rural) areas where some protections may exist within city limits (The Williams Institute, 2013).

In countries such as Russia, Iran, and China, little to no change in social acceptance of LGBTQ people and same-gender coupling is evident (Flores & Park, 2018). Instead polarization seems to be occurring globally with the most accepting countries (e.g., Iceland, Netherlands, Sweden) becoming more accepting and the least accepting countries (e.g., Ghana, Kenya, Bangladesh) becoming even less accepting (Flores & Park, 2018). In Latin America, the Inter-American Court of Human Rights issued a statement in 2018 urging the 20 countries who are members of the American Convention to legalize same-gender marriage and allow for gender affirming medical interventions and a swift process for changing names and gender for citizens (Berezowsky Ramirez, 2018). Only 3 of the 20 countries have LGBTQ rights laws on the books, meaning this progress could spell change in Latin America.

The news of increased social acceptance in some areas of the world is tempered by increases in the elections of more far-right or conservative leadership in countries around the globe (e.g., Brazil, United States). As more recent events in the United States have shown, state and federal policies are vulnerable to sudden dramatic shifts due to leadership, as exemplified in federal efforts to enshrine religiously based discrimination against same-gender couples and define transgender people out of existence (Human Rights Watch, 2018). LGBT-directed hate crimes increased in 2016 in the United States (Dashow, 2017), as did reports of disproportionate verbal, physical, and sexual victimization by peers of LGB youth in schools in the United States (Centers for Disease Control and Prevention [CDC], 2016). Depression, anxiety, substance abuse, and suicidal behaviors are associated with peer victimization in LGB adolescents (CDC, 2016), with negative long-term implications for health in adulthood (Meyer, 2015). Transgender people, particularly people of color, are at the highest risk of violence and murder (Human Rights Campaign, 2018) in recorded history. As the visibility of LGBTQ people increases, minority stress due to stigma and victimization may also increase impacting couple relationships.

In a meta-analysis of 32 studies on same-gender relationships and minority stress, the single biggest effect on relationship well-being was internalized homophobia of partners (Cao et al., 2017). The effects of minority stress may be mitigated by increased resources for coping and social support, such as those provided by romantic partners (Baams, Bos, & Jonas, 2014), family (Heiden-Rootes, Wiegand, & Bono, 2018), friends, and community (Ariel & McPherson, 2000). Knowing more about whether and how this occurs for couples is central to identifying both vulnerabilities and strengths when working with them in couple therapy. In one longitudinal study on minority stress and dating partnerships, parent attachment security for LGBQ young adults (ages 16–20) predicted beginning to date at older ages, fewer symptoms of psychological distress, and more positive partnering relationships (Starks, Newcomb, & Mustanski, 2015).

Couple therapists need to consider the language used in intake forms and assessment questions that are based on binary and static assumptions of sexual orientation and gender. More inclusive questions provide the means for developing a richer conceptualization of couple therapy clients. For example,

> *Richard[1] and Mark attended couple therapy to address the lack of trust between the partners and differences in sexual interest. The therapist asked during the first session: "Mark, tell me about your previous serious romantic relationships—are there any that stand out as significant?" Mark and Richard smiled knowingly, and Richard said: "Tell her about the woman you nearly married before me."*
>
> *Mark laughed and said, "Look I fell in love with my best friend Darla. I'm gay. She's gay for god's sake! But we seemed like a perfect fit in every other way. So we tried it out. And for a while it was fun, exciting really, and nearly perfect. Though everyone around us thought we were crazy. I was accused of trying to get back in the closet to please my mother. It ended after a few months when I knew I missed being with a man and Darla missed women. But we are still friends and it was an adventure."*
>
> *The therapist followed up with questions about what Mark learned about himself in that relationship and how it informed him now with Richard. Mark talked about experiencing emotional intimacy with Darla and his hopes for creating a deeper emotional connection with Richard.*

This case illustrates how language of a question can create an opportunity to hear about this client's unexpected, though significant, dating experiences. In addition, the therapist frames the experience not as pathological, but as informative to the current relationship. Mark's experience outside of the straight/gay binary becomes a strength for the couple and the therapeutic process.

At the same time, even well-researched assessment tools can create roadblocks to couple therapy because of the assumptions built into their framing:

> *Anne (a cisgender woman) and Sparrow (a non-binary person) came to therapy with a therapist using Gottman Couples Method Therapy, which involves a four-session assessment and feedback process, along with the use of a battery of assessment tools to get at individual history and couple process dynamics.*
>
> *At Sparrow's individual assessment meeting, the therapist asked how the assessment packet went for them. "Honestly it was upsetting in spots," confessed Sparrow. "There were questions that assumed that Anne and I are in a monogamous relationship, and that put me on edge. I started looking at all of the questionnaires wondering if they were relying on assumptions about male and female gender roles, and I was afraid of how you might score them as a result. I kept worrying that I'd run into questions that would make me feel uncomfortable in my gender, and I considered not coming back."*

Family

Queer and trans-including couples may find themselves managing relationships with families of origin differently depending on the degree of family rejection and how "out" they are to extended family. Family of origin can be a significant source of support for LGBTQ people and queer couples (LaSala, 2013). Yet families can also be sources of rejection and thus stress, which may manifest as depression for LGBTQ youth (Meyer, Teylan, & Schwartz, 2015; Ryan, Huebner, Diaz, & Sanchez, 2009; Snapp, Watson, Russell, Diaz, & Ryan, 2015) and adults (Heiden-Rootes et al., 2018). Given the potential for family rejection to be aggressive or lead to cutoff, being "out" to the family as a whole or to key family members may not be possible for all LGBTQ people.

Partners in queer couples may vary in their degree of "outness" (e.g., how long each has internally identified as a sexual minority and to whom who they are out in their personal lives such as work, family, and community members; Otis et al., 2006). This can set the stage for conflict in the couple about how each family of origin treats the other partner. In qualitative interviews, bisexual-identified mothers in different-gender partnerships reported not talking about their bisexuality with their families citing past rejection, fear of judgment or rejection in the present, and feeling pressure to fulfill heteronormative norms (e.g., marry and have a baby with their cisgender male partner) (Goldberg, Allen, Ellawala, & Ross, 2017).

This couple dialogue in therapy illustrates the impact of extended family attitudes:

> *"Your mother has never forgiven me for 'making you trans,'" Ethan observed bitterly to his wife Tracy.*
>
> *"She knows you didn't make me trans," Tracy replied defensively. "She's still just going through her process about all this. She was only just getting used to the idea of me being married to a trans man when I dropped a second bomb on her that her 'son' was really her daughter."*
>
> *"But she thinks you got the idea of being trans from me," argued Ethan. "And she's never welcomed me into your family like she did your sister's wife."*

Perhaps in response to family rejection, queer and trans-including couples may create a "family of choice" made up of friends and often other LGBTQ people (Ariel & McPherson, 2000) who serve as a "protective circle" (Blumer & Murphy, 2011, p. 283; Oswald, 2002). The definition of family is broad and offers a buffer to the negative impact of stigma and prejudice (Blumer & Murphy, 2011; Oswald, 2002). Yet traditional couple therapy tools, such as the genogram, rarely account for such "fictive kin" and thus exclude them from assessment as part of a couple's larger system. For example,

> *"How do I show this couple's ex-girlfriend on their genogram?" the student asked their instructor. "She still lives in their home, and takes their kids to school every morning, and they call her 'Aunt Raisa,' but there's no examples of a relationship like that in our genogram book."*

Researchers have identified strengths including intentionality of relationships, family cohesion (Green, Bettinger, & Zacks, 1996), and role flexibility (Oswald, 2002) in gay and lesbian-headed families. Legal same-gender marriage in the United States and other countries have offered a significant improvement in legal protections and rights (Kim & McKenry, 2002), increased trust and security for couples (Cherlin, 2004), and offered much needed family recognition (Ocobock, 2013). At the same time, partnering and parenthood may mean that couples spend less time with their wider community (Ocobock, 2018), potentially leaving the couple feeling isolated and unsupported.

Identity and intersectionality

Seeing LGBTQ people as only defined by their sexual or gender identities misses the intersectional nature of the human experience (see Almeida & Tubbs, 2020, vol. 1). "Social identities and inequality are interdependent for groups, such as Black lesbians, not mutually exclusive" (Bowleg, 2008, p. 312). Race and socioeconomic status are both areas of intersectional identity that show some significant impacts on experiences of marginalization and family histories for LGBTQ people. For example, in research with homeless LGBTQ youth, the risk identified for homelessness is not simply "rejecting families" but "conditional families" given the additional experiences of inconsistent housing, food security, and parent substance abuse (Robinson, 2018). In the realm of religion, some LGBTQ people report rejection in their family's church while growing up (Gibbs & Goldbach, 2015) and in religiously affiliated colleges they attended (Heiden-Rootes, Wiegand, Thomas, Moore, & Ross, 2018), while others describe experiences of affirmation and care in religious institutions (Lease, Horne, & Noffsinger-Frazier, 2005). Each partner then may have very unique experiences given their social location that adds a multiplicity of relevant current and historical contexts for a couple. Couple therapists may be tempted to downplay these differences and focus on the shared sexual or gender identity, if this exists. However, thickening the story with intersectional understandings of the couples experience will open up dialogue about relationship well-being, satisfaction, family-of-origin acceptance, and dynamics in the couple relationship.

Common Therapy Issues for Queer Couples

Online connection and conflict

The near ubiquity of the Internet and smartphones in many places has meant that a transgender man in Lagos, Nigeria, and a transgender woman in Christchurch, New Zealand, can access many of the same sources of information and online support as a non-binary person in Topeka, Kansas. This has allowed youth, people in rural and suburban areas, and those living in more conservative or even repressive countries to self-identify, seek health information (Magee, Bigelow, DeHaan, & Mustanski, 2012), feel connected to a community, and find readily available romantic and sexual partners (Blackwell, Birnholtz, & Abbott, 2015). For LGBTQ people, this may influence their experience of dating and sexual opportunities, most of which are mediated through social media and apps in many communities (Blackwell et al., 2015). While these tools provide more readily available connection and access, they also allow for micro-segregation by identity, race, age, and so forth, while also facilitating discrimination along those same axes of identity. For couples who are similar by sexual identity but differ by another culture group, social media and apps for dating or hooking up may produce new areas for conflict and disconnection in the "real world":

> *Jamal teared up as he tried to explain his position on non-monogamy to his boyfriend Greg. "What you don't get," he started, "is what it's like for me to go on those apps. 'No beans, no rice, no chocolate, no spice'—you think those dudes are on a diet or something? They don't want to be bothered with black dudes like me, so they put that on their profiles. Meanwhile you make your profile visible for 10 minutes and you've got 30 guys cruising you because you're tall and white and have a good body."*
>
> *"What if I just find guys who are interested in having threesomes?" offered Greg. "I don't want you to go on the apps if it makes you feel bad."*
>
> *"How am I supposed to trust that anybody you bring home is really interested in me?" responded Jamal. "I know they're there to get with you and I could probably go sleep on the couch and they wouldn't notice."*

Couple dynamics

Couple dynamics may be more similar to heterosexual individuals in couple relationships (Kurdek, 2006), with some notable exceptions. Gottman and colleagues (2003) offered some of the first observational research on same-gender couple dynamics noting fundamental differences compared to different-gender couples. Specifically, Gottman et al. (2003) noted same-gender couples ($n = 73$) were less belligerent and domineering, used more humor, and demonstrated more positive affect overall when initiating and discussing a topic of conflict. In a review of research on same-gender couples, Rostosky and Riggle (2017) noted several key strengths including high levels of intimacy, commitment, egalitarian practices, and respect for individual practices.

Queer couples though are not perfect and there is a danger in over-romanticizing them as a means of "fixing" a marginalized group that is coping with the negative effects of minority stress (Green & Mitchell, 2015). Totenhagen, Randall, and Lloyd (2018) assessed stress over time for same-sex couples finding that greater levels of internalized homophobia predicted greater daily stress, more severe conflict, and poorer relationship quality. Gender roles and activities for same-sex couples are often not well defined and may contribute to the stress on the relationship (Addison & Coolhart, 2009; Green & Mitchell, 2015). It should be noted that this may also allow for more flexibility in the relationship and lead to a greater reliance on individual strengths, as opposed to strict gender-defined roles (Rostosky & Riggle, 2017).

Bisexual individuals seem to experience increased difficulties in forming and maintaining intimate relationships as compared with gay and heterosexual individuals (Klesse, 2011; Li, Dobinson, Scheim, & Ross, 2013). This may be due to biphobia experienced with gay, lesbian, and heterosexual individuals (Balsam & Mohr, 2007; Koh & Ross, 2006) and with their own partners (Addison & Coolhart, 2009). The research is inconsistent about access to support for bisexual individuals through their intimate couple relationships (Feinstein, Latak, Bhatia, Davila, & Eaton, 2016) or the larger queer community (Balsam & Mohr, 2007; Feinstein, Dyar, & London, 2017). Bisexual individuals may also differ widely in their degree of outness as a product of who they partner with and the degree of acceptance from their families of origin (Goldberg et al., 2017).

Very little research exists on couple dynamics with transgender and gender nonbinary individuals and their partners. What does exist is largely focused on gender transition and its impact on the couple's relationship (Garamel, Reisner, Laurenceau, Nemoto, & Operario, 2014; Meier, Sharp, Michonski, Babcock, & Fitzgerald, 2013). In both studies, higher relationship quality was associated with better psychological outcomes for the transgender partner after gender transition (Garmael et al., 2014; Meier et al., 2013). Generally, SFT clinicians note, "we know that trans people engage in healthy and happy relationships and face challenges, some that are just like everyone else's and others that are specific to being trans" (Iantaffi & Benson, 2018, p. 196).

For couple therapists the implications are twofold. First, queer and trans-including couples will have specific couple dynamic issues (e.g., biphobia of a partner, varied degrees of outness between partners, body changes due to gender transition) related to being trans or bisexual or in a same-gender relationship. This requires a couple therapist to name and address these issues in a way that communicates understanding and respect. Second, queer and trans-including couples are also just people trying to live and create a loving relationship. The goal then is to not associate *all* couple dynamic problems with being a queer and trans-including couple, and yet, not diminish the impact of living in a society, community, and, in some cases, a family that continues to stigmatize them.

Intimate partner violence

The highest lifetime prevalence rates of intimate partner violence (IPV) were for bisexual, cisgender women (56.9%), and men (37.3%) (Walter, Chen, & Breiding, 2013). Bisexual women were 2.6 times more likely to report IPV than heterosexual women (32.3%). Lesbian women (40.4%) also reported more IPV than heterosexual women, but this difference was not statistically significant (Walter et al., 2013). Gay men (25.2%) reported lifetime IPV at similar rates to heterosexual men (28.7%) (Walter et al., 2013). In a summary of findings for transgender people, Brown and Herman (2015) reported a range from 31.1 to 50.0% of lifetime prevalence of IPV. IPV in queer couples disrupts old, gendered frameworks, particularly in same-gender female couples (Hassouneh & Glass, 2008).

This may lead to assumptions in SFT about who we think we should be asking about violence and if or how we can intervene given the lack of research on therapeutic approaches to domestic violence for same-gender couples. Brown and Herman (2015) outline barriers faced by LGBTQ people in seeking assistance and note that several of these barriers apply to SFT practice. They suggest that SFTs be aware of their own ignorance and assumptions as they work with these couples: (a) the risk of rejection if they seek help and "out" themselves to providers and social service agencies, (b) a lack of LGBTQ-friendly resources for IPV, and (c) experiences of homophobia or transphobia with the people who are supposed to be helping and supporting them.

Consensual non-monogamy

In the United States, over 20% of single adults report having engaged in consensual non-monogamy at some point in their lives (Haupert, Gesselman, Moors, Fisher, & Garcia, 2017), but much higher rates, anywhere from 32 to 70%, have been identified in gay male couples (Levine, Herbenick, Martinez, Fu, & Dodge, 2018; Shernoff, 2006). Blumstein and Schwartz's (1983) foundational study indicated that over a third of lesbian women said their relationship allowed for sex outside the couple.

As with most aspects of transgender people's intimate and sexual relationships, their participation in consensual non-monogamy relationships remains largely unexplored, in part, likely, because most survey research continues to rely on binary categories of gender and cissexist assumptions. However, Malpas (2012) hints delicately at the "sophisticated arrangements" (p. 75) negotiated by some couples when one partner transitions and later overtly suggests that when a couple wants to stay together, but the non-transitioning partner is not bisexual, consensual non-monogamy may provide a way for both to avoid dissatisfaction and get their sexual needs met. Although culturally competent practice with consensual non-monogamy is important to working with queer and trans-including couples, all couple therapists should develop a working knowledge of these types of relationships, as they are not exclusive to LGBTQ people.

Aging

Older LGBTQ people experience higher rates of disability, depression, and loneliness, as compared with heterosexual peers (Fredriksen-Goldsen et al., 2011). Many find themselves relying on partners and friends for support (Fredriksen-Goldsen et al., 2011), given disconnection from their family of origin, and having children (Guasp, 2011). In other studies, older LGBTQ people described barriers to building new friendships due to discrimination by peers in their aging communities (Cronin & King, 2014). Partners may bear the burden of caregiving for an ill or disabled partner with little support from others. For those experiencing disability and illness, the stress on a single partner or small social network may be overwhelming for caregivers and the aging LGBTQ person. Perhaps not surprisingly, gay and lesbian older adults describe aging and increased disability as fracturing connection with their larger LGBTQ social circles and with intimate partners (Barrett, Whyte, Comfort, Lyons, & Crameri, 2015).

Legal marriage can add economic and social resources for LGBTQ older adults, which is associated with improved mental and physical health and increased experiences of stigma (Goldsen et al., 2017). Aging queer couples may be caught between the cultural shifts—where younger individuals are more accepting than their peers of same-gender coupling—and yet benefiting from the support and resources that come with legal marriage and partnering. The implication is the need to assess health of both partners and the support networks of the queer couple for identifying vulnerabilities to isolation and relationship dissolution.

Divorce and relationship dissolution

Only a few research studies exist on what predicts relationship dissolution for queer couples. We could find no studies that are inclusive of bisexual and trans/gender-non-binary partners. Predictors of dissolution among male and female same-gender couples who are childless were similar to heterosexual individuals in couple relationships (e.g., presence of high conflict, low positive affect, and poor communication; Kurdek, 1991, 1996). Observational and self-report data from same-gender cohabiting, childless couples by Gottman and colleagues (2003) found reduced likelihood of relationship dissolution 12 years later when couples demonstrated higher levels of empathy. In one study, lesbian women who were parents ($n = 73$) saw a 31% dissolution rate and reported reasons for this to be due to differences in parenting style, increased distance or disconnection, low sexual intimacy, and finding points of impasse or incompatibility in the relationship (Gartrell, Deck, Rodas, Peyser, & Banks, 2006). Goldberg and Garcia (2015) in a sample of adoptive same- and different-gender parents found lower rates of dissolution for same-gender couples with children—8% overall for same-gender couples, 12% for lesbian women in particular. These rates were similar to heterosexual-identified adoptive parents. They attributed the differences to perhaps a more accepting social context where same-gender couples now experience less minority stress as parents than in decades previous.

Parenting

LGBTQ people create families with children in many different ways including biological, adoption, foster care, and surrogacy. Becoming parents is often linked to the historical, social, legal, and political climate supporting the rights of LGBTQ parents and their families. Currently, 2–3.7 million children are being raised in a home with a LGBTQ parent (Gates, 2015). Approximately 200,000 children live in same-gender couple homes. LGBTQ people are more likely to adopt and take in foster care children, and, in particular, same-gender couples and racial/ethnic minority LGBTQ people are more likely to foster and adopt children (Gates, 2015). Having children is associated with lower income for LGBTQ parents (Gates, 2015) and "the stressors on [queer] families can then be complicated by the impact of heterosexism and cissexism from society, extended family, other biological parents, and even the children themselves depending on their ages" (Addison & Coolhart, 2015, p. 439).

Consistent research findings show gay, lesbian, (Farr, Forssell, & Patterson, 2010), bisexual (Goldberg & Kuvalanka, 2012), and transgender (Stolzer, Herman, & Hasenbush, 2014) parents raise well-adjusted children. Recent US Supreme Court rulings legalized same-gender couple adoption in all 50 states. Yet decisions about placement and custody of children and openness of healthcare providers in assisting queer couples to become parents occur locally. Not all states in the United States or provinces and countries internationally have laws protecting LGBTQ people from discrimination in various social settings (e.g., schools, employment, healthcare, etc.). The outcomes are experiences of rejection, barriers to LGBTQ-affirming services, and inconsistent enforcement of laws protecting LGBTQ people and parents, if they exist. This may create worry and concern about becoming parents (Appell, 2011) and put added strain on the couple relationship. In working with queer couples with children, the issues of permanency of the family and community acceptance for their family structure seem paramount to understand as potentially added stress on the couple relationship. Though much like the issues in couple dynamics, queer couples are still parents who will have similar concerns and stressors as other parents. This case example illustrates the unique ways queer couples become parents and renegotiate roles producing both a new relationship and a baby:

Camila (cisgender woman) and Anna (formerly known as John, transgender woman) presented in couple therapy with concerns about if and how to remain a couple while Anna was going through her gender transition (male to female). Camila desperately wanted a baby and worried about the impact of hormones on Anna's fertility. During the first sessions, the couple agreed to attempt to conceive a baby during the next two menstrual cycles

while Anna was beginning her social gender transition. Conception was successful and soon thereafter Anna began a testosterone regiment. As both partners began to change in appearance—one with a pregnant belly and the other with a feminizing look—both worried openly about if the other found them attractive. Couple therapy continued for discussing sexual attraction, desire, and emotional connection between the couple. In addition, the transition for Anna was discussed including her expectations, concerns, and changes she was noticing. A healthy baby was born and the couple took an extended break from therapy to focus on being new parents. When the couple returned six months later, Anna and Camilla reported they had decided to divorce because Camilla was sure now that she was only attracted to men or masculine features and was finding it more and more difficult to be sexually and affectionately close to her now more feminine partner. There was sadness for both partners and many tears with baby snoozing in the car seat between them on the couch. The couple therapist elicited Anna's deep love and respect for Camilla given her support during the transition. Camilla joked that they could now share clothes and was thankful they would remain connected as parents and friends. The couple therapist remarked that this seemed like a successful relationship, despite the dissolution, given what all they had birthed—a baby and Anna—in the process.

Systemic Therapy for Working with Queer Couples

We surveyed the field looking for model-specific intervention research that included LGBTQ-identified partners or same-gender couples, but ultimately found only two published clinical trials. Neither study indicated whether any couples were mixed-orientation or trans-including, and the samples were not ethnically or racially diverse. We were surprised to find no studies on queer or trans-including couples by some of the leading couple therapy approaches, such as emotionally focused couple therapy, even though it has one of the more robust bodies of outcome research (ICEEFT, 2018). Our findings are described below, followed by a review of writing on clinical theory that is applicable to couple therapy with queer couples.

Model-based outcome research

As of early 2018, only two published papers of clinical trials of couple therapy models, Behavioral Couples Therapy (BCT) and Gottman Couples Method Therapy (GCMT), with queer couples (Fals-Stewart, O'Farrell, & Lam, 2009; Garanzini et al., 2017) were identified. Fals-Stewart et al. (2009) compared (a) individual treatment as usual for alcohol use to (b) BCT + individual treatment for alcohol for same-gender couples. Couples who received BCT showed decreased partner drinking and improved relationship satisfaction. However, female same-gender couples in both groups saw their satisfaction erode at roughly the same rate, raising questions about if BCT was sufficient to address their relationship issues. The loss in relationship gains made through BCT for mixed-gender couples were previously questioned (e.g., Gottman, 1999; Johnson, 2004). As a result, a degree of caution should be taken in applying BCT given that gains made may not hold up over time.

More recently, Garanzini et al. (2017) studied the use of GMCT with same-gender couples presenting for help with a variety of relationship problems and co-occurring problems of substance abuse, suicidality, emotional abuse, and both minor and major domestic violence. Although therapy lasted, on average, about the same amount of time as in studies of mixed-gender couples, the researchers produced twice the effect size of most couple treatments. Couples improved, on average, twice as much as couples in previous research studies even those with couples with seemingly serious comorbidities. The authors speculated the emphasis on playfulness, friendship, and shared values may be core to many same-gender couples' successful relationships (e.g., Gottman et al., 2003; Riggle et al., 2016).

Clinical theory for working with queer couples

Despite the paucity of outcome studies, a remarkable amount of theoretical and conceptual writing on working with queer couples has emerged over the past three decades. Most of the published articles and books address gay and lesbian individuals, though some also address bi- and trans-including couples (e.g., Bigner & Wetchler, 2012). Still, some do not consider specific models for couple work, focusing more on themes arising in therapy content rather than suggesting a particular intervention process or lens for assessment (Giammattei & Green, 2012). While others draw on a variety of couple therapy models, including affirmative therapy integrated with a couple/systems model (Rutter, 2012), emotionally focused couple therapy (Hardtke, Armstrong, & Johnson, 2010), general attachment-focused couple therapy (e.g., Chapman & Caldwell, 2012; Tunnell, 2012), cognitive-behavioral models (Deacon, Reinke, & Viers, 1996; Martell, Safren, & Prince, 2004), and family systems or relational approaches (e.g., Belous, 2015; Connolly, 2012; Greenan & Tunnell, 2003; Treyger, Ehlers, Zajicek, & Trepper, 2008). Rather than consider each theory in turn, we picked three compelling theoretical approaches based on conceptual language and ideas.

First, Rutter (2012) recommends systemic sex therapy, the integrative approach formulated by Weeks, Gambescia, and Hertlein (2015), as a good fit with gay affirmative therapy practices (discussed below in the individual psychotherapy section) for work with gay male couples. Rutter notes how the mix of family systems, solution-focused, narrative, cognitive, and feminist approaches provide a valuable theoretical lens for understanding the experiences of gay men. This integrative approach "affirm[s] the struggle" of same-gender couples, but also "openly accept[s] the unique sex lives of gay men" (2012, p. 38). Incorporating systemic sex therapy's integrative approach allows for diverse interventions such as the use of a sexual genogram, narrative deconstruction questions, and gender role analysis.

Belous (2015), by contrast, suggests integrating contextual family therapy (Boszormenyi-Nagy, Grunebaum, & Ulrich, 1991) with gay affirmative practices to provide a strengths-based framework, a systemic focus, and multicultural considerations for the assessment and intervention process. The model's focus on justice, trustworthiness, and relational ethics offers a language for queer couples and therapists to address injuries both between partners and within a heterosexist cultural context. For example, the impact of social stigma on same-gender couples can be addressed by reframing it in terms of its impact on the couple's sense of justice and the trustworthiness of others. This may be helpful when working with a couple who have conflict over how "out" they want to be about their relationship. Belous also highlights contextual family therapy's stance of "multidirectional partiality" as particularly powerful for therapists because it "involves the crediting and acknowledgement of past injuries, and current predicament of the client" (p. 273).

Finally, Hardtke et al. (2010) and Allan and Johnson (2017) propose the use of emotionally focused couple therapy because it offers a grounding in attachment theory and addresses the dialectical tension between intrapsychic and interpersonal processes. The therapist highlights the tension between the individual's needs and the needs of the couple. When working with couples who regularly experience social stigma and rejection including in their own upbringing with caregivers, "genuineness, unconditional positive regard, and empathy may be regarded as treatment interventions in of themselves" (p. 323). Allan and Johnson (2017) suggest that for gay men, the rejection of gender-nonconforming or "gay" behavior by caregivers may be a kind of mis-attunement. "Therapists working with gay men who have had their view of self and other repeatedly violated by homonegativity need to assess the attachment significance of these events" (Allan & Johnson, 2017, p. 10), meaning a couple therapist will need to consider the degree to which social stigma impacted a LGBTQ person's ability to trust the world and love themselves. This has significant implications for being in relationship with an intimate partner and maintaining a sense of self in the process.

Queering Couple Therapy Practice and Training

Three key areas were identified in psychotherapy research for application to couple therapy practice with queer couples: (a) centering queer voices in psychotherapy practice, (b) integrating LGBTQ + affirmative practices, and (c) reflexive ethical practices for integrating language and deconstructing binary assumptions.

Centering queer voices

A growing body of research in individual psychotherapy is focusing on understanding the experiences of LGBTQ clients of the therapeutic process, the therapist's approach, and the therapist's affirmation of LGBTQ people. Key findings from this literature stand out as applicable to couple therapy. First, LGBTQ adults described the positive and healing benefits of having therapists affirm their sexuality and gender identity (Berke, Maples-Keller, & Richards, 2016; Israel, Gorcheva, Burnes, & Walther, 2008). Unfortunately, many also described encounters with therapists who minimized or showed hostility toward their identity, harming their experience of therapy (Berke et al., 2016; Eady, Dobinson, & Ross, 2011). After three decades of calls for training therapists to work in affirmative and informed ways with LGBTQ clients, there continues to be a significant lack of attunement in psychotherapy to the importance of building these skills and addressing therapists' biases.

Couple therapists working with queer couples potentially have the added task of affirming two different identities that may be a source of conflict or fear for both the clients and the therapist. For example, biphobia may cause a partner to fear their bisexual partner will cheat on them with a partner of a different gender; a therapist with biphobic stereotypes of their own may communicate those beliefs to the bisexual partner at the expense of therapeutic joining, setting up a coalition between the therapist and the other partner:

"I'm feeling really stuck with this couple," Jennifer related to her consultation group. "They're fighting a lot about getting married. The female partner says she really wants it, but I think her intensity is really a defense she's not ready to admit to."

"What makes you say that?" asked a colleague." "Well I see why her boyfriend isn't ready to move forward," said Jennifer. "First she needs to decide who she really wants to be with, men or women, and I think it's easier for her to make him the bad guy for not marrying her than it is for her to look at her own unresolved sexuality."

Finally, bisexual clients expressed the desire for both interest in who they are and tempered, neutral reactions when they come out to their therapists (Eady et al., 2011). They reported intrusive and excessive questions about identity and sexual practices (Eady et al., 2011). It seems that in a quest to understand and affirm an identity, the therapist may become voyeuristic as their own curiosity takes over. In couple therapy, this may occur more readily where the couple's sex life is part of the dynamic in the relationship:

Marsha and Danielle are seeking couple therapy because of the impact of Marsha's depression on their relationship, which includes a dwindling sex life. When the therapist asks about their current sex life and what they would prefer it to be like, Danielle provides details about how often sex occurs, what activities she enjoys, and the changes she's observed in Marsha's patterns of initiation and arousal. Marsha is visibly uncomfortable as Danielle talks.

When the therapist inquires about Marsha's discomfort, Marsha says quietly, "Why do you need to know? This is so weird to talk about with a perfect stranger? Are you gay? How does telling you any of this help us out?" The therapist shifts in the seat internally wondering the same questions and if self-disclosure would be useful at this moment. Instead, the therapist chooses to address the underlying concern: "Marsha, it seems you're worried I may be either judging you two or asking questions based on my own curiosity—am I getting it?"

Marsha relaxes and describes the rejection she felt when she tried to talk to her heterosexual sister about her concerns over her diminishing libido. She worries other straight people will either do the same or become "creepy dudes" who take a voyeuristic attitude toward "lesbian sex."

The queer couple needs to feel safe both from judgment and from feeling like they are sexual objects to be investigated in the therapy room.

Affirmative practices

LGTBQ affirmative therapy is described as follows:

The integration of knowledge and awareness by the therapist of the unique developmental cultural aspects of LGBTQ individuals, therapist's own self-knowledge, and the translation of this knowledge and awareness into effective and helpful therapy skills at all stages of the therapeutic process. (Bieschke, Perez, & DeBord, 2007, p. 408)

In a review of 15 years of research and 49 studies conducted on the effectiveness of LGBQ affirmative therapy, O'Shaughnessy and Speir (2018) concluded there was an overfocus on gay men and little could be concluded about what works for lesbian, bisexual, and queer-identified clients. None of the studies inquired about the experience of queer couples in therapy together or how affirmative therapy practices may shift with couples or families. In the 21 qualitative studies reviewed, "it was also clear, in more than half the studies, that therapist knowledge alone was insufficient, and that clients were looking for therapists to have a more holistic attitude towards LGBQ identity and influence in knowing when and how to integrate knowledge about sexual identity into clinical work" (p. 93).

Becoming "affirming" of LGBTQ people and their partners in therapy may unintentionally produce a preference for cisgender or cisgender "passing" bodies (i.e., cisnormativity; Serano, 2016) and queer couples who look and act like heterosexual individuals in monogamous relationships (i.e., homonormativity; Duggan, 2002). LGBQ clients report microaggressions in individual psychotherapy when attempts were made to overidentify with LGBQ clients while expressing heteronormative bias (Shelton & Delgado-Romero, 2011). For example, in couple therapy, this may look like a therapist assuming a queer couple desires to be legally married in the future and seeing this as a sign of a problem in the relationship if the couple is not focused on becoming legally married. The couple experiences this as a microaggression because their therapist is assessing the quality and value of the relationship based on how well it conforms to a relationship ideal that is dyadic, monogamous, cohabitating, and legally married—a standard developed by and for heterosexuals.

Affirmative queer couple therapy then becomes the context within which the couple can enact power and position themselves as experts on their own lives (Tilsen, 2013) and their relationship. For example, when it comes to talking about sex, a couple therapist needs to affirm and understand that sex for LGBTQ couples may not center on (or even include) penis–vagina intercourse or penetration at all. Iantaffi and Benson (2018) recommend decentering gendered language for sexual anatomy for trans-including couples by asking questions like: "How have you figured out how to talk about your bodies and relationship in a way that works for you?" (p. 209). Questions like this open room for the couple to speak about their own bodied experiences and assumes the couples ability to adapt and create pleasure.

Reflexive ethical practices

To work with couples, generally, is to work with sexuality (Timm, 2009). To work with queer couples is to work with sexuality that pushes the arousal and experiential boundaries of the average couple therapist. Intrapsychic homophobic and transphobic reactions that create feelings of anxiety, disgust, and arousal may be surprising and unwanted or even disavowed by the clinician. Mismanaged anxiety in the therapist may undermine therapy processes meant to create an alliance, promote safety, and facilitate repair in the therapeutic relationship (Shamoon, Lappan, & Blow, 2017).

Attraction to clients is discussed in psychotherapy and training literature (Ladany et al., 1997; Pope, Keith-Spiegel, & Tabachnick, 1986). However, arousal and disgust about the imagery and fantasy occurring for a therapist are still relatively unexplored (Butler, 2011), and thus little is offered therapists in terms of tools for confronting and deconstructing these feelings.

Anything outside our practiced norms of sex can become the erotic "other" creating desire and arousal (Perel, 2007) if it is not killed first by homophobic, erotophobic judgment and shame creating disgust (Tilsen, 2013). Arousal then may be present for heterosexual and LGBTQ-identified therapists. Heterosexual therapists may be particularly reluctant to openly discuss their arousal or disgust given concerns about supervisor or colleague judgment. The end result could be "therapy that is adapted to the needs of the therapist rather than the needs of the patient" (Winnicott, 1949, p. 74) and supervision that skirts the issue of the therapist's and supervisor's own experiences of arousal or disgust:

> *Keisha, a cisgender student therapist, and her different-gender couple were in session with her supervisor behind a one-way mirror. Ariel, a cisgender woman, reports she previously lived with a woman for 11 years. As Ariel answers Keisha's questions about her former relationship, her cisgender male partner Darrel seems disengaged or bored.*
>
> *During a mid-session break, the supervisor asks about how Keisha feels in the room with Ariel and Darrel. Keisha said she feels really good and smiles broadly. The supervisor asks how Ariel's previous sexual relationship might be connected to the couple's clinical concern: Ariel's recent miscarriage and her troubled relationship with Darrel's parents. Keisha reflects and concludes "it's probably not connected" but adds she's trying to be "affirmative" by being curious and open.*
>
> *The supervisor wonders how Ariel and Darrel might be experiencing the session, given the lack of connection to their presenting problem, and reminds Keisha that her focus needs to be on the couple's needs, not on her own curiosity or her desire to be seen as affirming. Keisha acknowledges that Darrel seemed "checked out" while during her "girl talk" with Ariel. Returning to the session, Keisha asks the couple what topic they would like to address with their remaining time. Darrel immediately brings up an argument he and Ariel had over his mother's questions about the recent miscarriage.*

Sexual self-of-the-therapist development

Most SFT therapists and students, from our experience, express the desire to be open, accepting, and empathic to clients who sit across from them. While most are also internally and secretly battling the voices of judgment and disgust about queer love and trans/gender-nonconforming bodies, taboos against talking openly about this struggle persist due in part to fear of judgment from professors, supervisors, and colleagues. Research on unconscious bias suggests that merely becoming aware of how common it is to have biases, and the fact of holding a particular stereotype or bias, does nothing to reduce biased behavior or attitudes; in fact, it can increase them. Rather like breaking a habit, specific, considered action to counteract bias is needed to create change (Devine, Forscher, Austin, & Cox, 2012). SFT needs to continue to work to incorporate this knowledge into its training generally, and couple therapy best practices in particular, so clinicians can get support in working to undermine beliefs and responses that can interfere with queer- and trans-affirming therapy.

We contend that most attempts to create reflective exercises about bias with students or supervisees misses the body-level experiences of arousal and disgust while also not addressing the socialized negativity about queer sexuality and bodies. Butler (2011, p. 63) questioned: *Can we really disconnect our bodies from these discussions when we put on the cloak of "therapist"?* This a significant barrier to training and educating therapists to interact with and effectively work with queer couples. A key competency for SFTs should be developing comfort in the sexual self-of-the-therapist, so there can be open psychological and relational space for examining and addressing homophobic, transphobic, erotophobic, homonormative, and heteronormative biases. The sexual self-of-the-therapist is the one we wish did not exist in therapy spaces, and yet when our bodies are present, so is our sexual self. Arousal and disgust are often surprising as it moves up from the level of body to the consciousness mind. Comfort with this part of ourselves in the room means we are able to acknowledge the arousal or disgust, the accompanying thoughts and feelings, and then set it aside for examination post-therapy session with a trusted colleague or supervisor. We cannot eradicate this innate experience, but we can become accepting and thoughtful about it so it does not become yet another impediment to competent care for queer couples.

Body-level awareness and exploration of the self are unlikely to occur in an evaluative setting like an academic program or administrative supervision as hierarchy does not often allow for the sexual self-of-the-therapist to emerge and be explored. Instead we need to look to experiences outside these contexts where therapists can be both supported and challenged to develop reflexive self-inquiry while fostering curiosity about and belief in the possibilities created by expanding one's sexual and gender frame of reference.

This kind of experience is a common practice as part of postgraduate training in sex therapy: the Sexual Attitude Reassessment (SAR) (Sitron & Dyson, 2009). This intensive group process involves self-examination and group discussion in response to sexually explicit materials and media. The idea is to examine beliefs and feelings that emerge during the course of the SAR so the therapist can consider how to reintegrate them into a more clinically helpful framework for working with sexual and gender diversity. While the sexual content of the SAR may be inconsistent with some individuals' and cultures' values or boundaries, for the purpose of developing basic clinical competence with queer and trans-including couples, alternative and less sexually explicit material could be used.

In addition, if a therapist is morally opposed to LGBTQ identities and same-gender couple relationships, they may not be qualified to work effectively with these clients. This creates an ethical dilemma for the mental health professions, all of which emphasize the importance of both practicing within one's scope of competence, but also nondiscrimination against members of targeted groups (Caldwell, 2011). "Whether the reason for refusal is the therapist's religious belief or their level of competence," Caldwell writes, "the end result can be that members of an already-oppressed group are told that they can be turned away from care simply because they are part of that group" (p. 51).

Taking a relational ethic

A relational ethic (Boszormenyi-Nagy et al., 1991) is not new to SFT as a field, but has more recently been suggested for use in clinical practice with queer youth (Tilsen, 2013). It is "founded on the principle of equitability, that is, that everyone is entitled to have his or her welfare interests considered by other family members" (Boszormenyi-Nagy, et al., 1991, p. 204). A relational ethic also requires the therapist, with their inherent structural power, to consider and address experiences of minority stress with LGBTQ clients (Meyer, 2003, 2015). Addison (2017) emphasizes the importance of directly broaching the marginalized and privileged identities of each partner and the therapist in couple therapy. She recommends therapist take the lead in introducing such topics to avoid colluding with the dominant culture that expects us to maintain silence around privilege, power, and difference. Supervisors and faculty need to assume this responsibility as well and proactively make their own gender and sexual identity available as topics of reflection and discussion with their trainees and students.

A relational ethic compels SFTs to review the use of language on websites and intake forms. The current language in clinical circles often conflates LGBTQ identities with clinical "concerns" or "issues," implying that to be queer or trans is to have issues and be concerned. SFTs should instead frame their work with queer and trans couples in positive and affirming terms, being careful to accurately convey their degree of familiarity and comfort with LGBTQ relationships. For example, "I am a Sex Positive, LGBTQ-affirming couple therapist" avoids falsely equating queerness with diagnoses like depression and anxiety. However, the label "affirming" is earned through focused personal and professional work, and feedback from LGBTQ people, rather than used out of a general desire to appear open. SFTs who desire to be truly affirming should invest in continuing education, books, SAR events, and consultation groups that offer honest feedback.

Consider how the design of your office space, waiting area, and website can materially contribute to a positive and affirming stance toward queer and trans couples. In making your affirmative stance boldly visible, you too are coming out as a therapist and will need to become comfortable with how this influences the way others see you.

Future Directions

Research

Clearly, the state of outcome research on couple therapy with queer and trans-including couples is lacking. The SFT field is still adapting to the increased demand for empirical evidence for treatment effectiveness; at the same time, clinical research continues without consideration of queer and trans-including minority couples. Today, it should not be acceptable, if indeed it ever was, to leave these couples out of studies on the outcomes of SFT. Whether focused on a specific model's outcomes, the common factors of effective relationship therapy, or process research to inform interventions, researchers should commit to recruiting queer and trans-including couples as subjects and specifically reporting their findings on these subgroups.

We suggest some specific questions that would benefit both practitioners and queer and trans-including couples were they to be answered: (a) What couple processes before, during, and after the social and/or medical transition of a partner contribute to healthy individual and relational adjustment? How can current and emerging models of couple therapy address the needs of these couples around transition? (b) Are there differences between bisexuals' same-gender relationships and relationships where both partners identify as gay or lesbian? Do any of these differences have implications for couple therapy? (c) How does the trans or cis status of the therapist influence factors like the therapeutic alliance, the impact of interventions, and the progress toward trans-including couples' goals? (d) Similarly, does the sexual identity of the therapist matter when providing couple therapy to queer couples? (e) Given the importance of an intersectional view of queer and trans-including couples, how do other privileged and marginalized identities—race, class, age, religion, immigration, dis/ability, body size, and so forth—that clients bring to conjoint therapy impact their needs from relational work? How can the various conjoint treatment models incorporate an intersectional view and adapt to better address these needs? How do therapists' multiple privileged and marginalized identities impact their delivery of couple therapy? (f) What do queer and trans-including couples need from conjoint therapy in terms of addressing reproductive choices, family formation, and parenting? How can couple therapists effectively meet those needs? (g) Given the field's interest in adult attachment as a lens for understanding intimate partner dynamics, how is attachment impacted by injuries due to family denial of and rejection due sexual or gender identity, since these identities are so integral to experiences of adult love and attraction? (h) How can the tools we use for research, intake, and assessment in CFT better account for diverse genders, sexual identities, and relationship forms? What best practices for collecting demographic information are emerging in other fields such as sociology and education? (i) If we change the binary, heteronormative, cisnormative, monogamy-focused language we use in our work with clients, what new ways of talking about gender, sexuality, and relationships will emerge? What will we potentially learn about our clients, and ourselves, if we make these changes?

SFT education

SFT masters and doctoral programs vary widely in the degree to which they incorporate critical and queer theories that deconstruct traditional theories of couple and family therapy (McDowell, Emerick, & Garcia, 2014). In the tradition of liberation-based healing practices (Hernández, Almeida, & Vecchio, 2005), our SFT programs are in need of liberation from the usual performances of gender and sexuality in clinical education and practice (McDowell et al., 2014). Liberation needs to begin early in the first courses and supervision experiences where students are asked to study critical theories (e.g., critical race theory, queer theory) that allow for holding tension between seemingly opposing ideas or identities (McDowell et al., 2014) and encourage thinking about gender and sexuality *as performed* rather than fixed and innate (Tilsen, 2013). "Performance," a concept from queer theory, allows for movement, possibility, flexibility, and context-dependent behavior. Ironically, context-dependent behavior and the presence of constant change are foundational systemic principles that seem absent in SFT education and training on sexuality, gender, and couple relationships.

Working with queer couples requires sexuality education grounded in a position of relational ethic and cultural humility. Isomorphically, supervision in SFT should be a space for opening up dialogue and resisting the taboo of talking about arousal, disgust, and reactions to LGBTQ people and queer couples. Faculty should consider the limits of their own training and readiness (Corturillo, McGeorge, & Carlson, 2016) and the ability of their SFT programs to prepare therapists to work with queer couples and then commit to explicitly training students to embody the qualities that make for a safe therapeutic environment for LGBTQ clients and their partners (Nguyen, Grafsky, & Piercy, 2016)—and, we would add, students, faculty, and staff.

Nguyen et al. (2016) offer an example of a student agreement for seeing LGBTQ and other diverse clients that may serve as a template for SFT programs. McGeorge and Stone Carlson (2016) recommend clear and explicit affirmative policies in SFT programs and associated counseling clinics including "(a) anti-harassment policies that prohibit homophobic language, (b) statements that communicate the program's LGB affirmative stance and the expectation that students work affirmatively with

LGB clients, and (c) remediation policies to address situations when students struggle to be affirming of their LGB clients, classmates, and faculty" (p. 9). We would suggest adding language that encompasses the umbrella of sexual orientation and gender diversity. For LGBTQ students, a big welcome sign could be explicit symbols (e.g., rainbows, transgender flag) on the program page, backed up by robust faculty diversity, program policies, and curriculum descriptions that promote affirmative practice and a collegial and affirming atmosphere for sexual and gender minority students.

Family and health policy

The voices of SFT experts are sorely needed to highlight the significant contributions of identity affirmation and relationships on the health of LGBTQ people. It is abundantly clear that devaluation and discrimination contribute significantly to minority stress, which in turn harms the well-being of individuals and couples. But laws protecting the civil rights of LGBTQ people are a patchwork, both within the United States and around the world. Earlier this year, Pakistan passed a sweeping law protecting the rights of citizens to identify as male, female, or both and forbidding discrimination based on gender identity (Hashim, 2018), and Canada added "gender identity or expression" to its anti-discrimination laws with mixed reviews from professionals and the public (Winsa, 2017). The United States remains polarized, with some states offering anti-transgender discrimination laws while others advance overtly transphobic "bathroom bills" depicting transgender people as potential sexual predators. Therefore, those concerned with the well-being of queer couples should be active in efforts to create a more welcoming and inclusive culture in which they can thrive and reduce exposure to stigma that induces minority stress. Similarly, SFT professionals and organizations could lend their expertise to the efforts to reduce barriers to changing names and gender markers on identifying documents and removing gendered language from laws covering marriage, divorce, reproduction, and parenting.

Meanwhile, queer and consensual non-monogamy relationships exist in a virtually infinite combination of forms, from triads and quads to more complex "polycules" of all kinds. These relationships have not benefited from marriage equality, and our culture's default assumption of "one person, one partner"—what Veaux and Rickert (2014) call "couple privilege"—comes into play in everything from the ubiquitous "plus one" invitation to eligibility for health insurance and parental rights. Again, SFT professionals should acknowledge the real harm this causes our non-monogamous clients and take a stand calling for these relationships to be seen as socially and legally legitimate.

Concluding Thoughts

As a field SFT is in a unique position to provide the kind of care needed for queer couples. Our systemic frame and relational ethic calls into question what is in fact "internalized" and wonder, instead, how homophobia, transphobia, and bi-erasure invaded the worlds of queer couples. That is, if we equip ourselves with new language that stretches our systemic family theories of therapy and, dare we say, queer our assumptions, we may be well poised to offer significant contributions to the well-being of queer couples.

Note

1   All vignettes in this chapter are inspired by actual cases but are composites rather than exact descriptions with significant changes to identities of couples. Though the dynamics described are close to the original situations, the details of the cases have been altered significantly to protect confidentiality and meet ethical guidelines.

References

Addison, S. M. (2017). Queer intersectional couple therapy. In M. D. Reiter & R. J. Chenail (Eds.), *Constructivist, critical, and integrative approaches to couples counseling* (pp. 138–180). New York, NY: Routledge/Taylor & Francis Group.

Addison, S. M., & Coolhart, D. (2009). Integrating socially segregated identities: Queer couples and the question of race. In M. Rastogi & V. Thomas (Eds.), *Multicultural couple therapy* (pp. 51–75). New York, NY: SAGE.

Addison, S. M., & Coolhart, D. (2015). Expanding the therapy paradigm with queer couples: A relational intersectional lens. *Family Process, 54*(3), 435–453. doi:10.1111/famp.12171

Allan, R., & Johnson, S. M. (2017). Conceptual and application issues: Emotionally focused therapy with gay male couples. *Journal of Couple & Relationship Therapy, 16*(4), 286–305. doi:10.1080/15332691.2016.1238800

Almeida, R. V., & Tubbs, C. Y. (2020). Intersectionality. In K. S. Wampler, R. B. Miller, & R. B. Seedall (Eds.), *The handbook of systemic family therapy: The profession of systemic family therapy (1)*. Hoboken, NJ: Wiley.

Appell, A. R. (2011). Legal issues in lesbian and gay adoption. In D. M. Brodzinsky & A. Pertman (Eds.), *Adoption by lesbians and gay men: A new dimension in family diversity* (pp. 36–58). New York, NY: Oxford University Press.

Ariel, J., & McPherson, D. W. (2000). Therapy with lesbian and gay parents and their children. *Journal of Marital and Family Therapy, 26*, 421–432.

Baams, L., Bos, H. M. W., & Jonas, K. J. (2014). How a romantic relationship can protect same-sex attracted youth and young adults from the impact of expected rejection. *Journal of Adolescence, 37*(8), 1293–1302. doi:10.1016/j.adolescence.2014.09.006

Balsam, K. F., & Mohr, J. J. (2007). Adaptation to sexual orientation stigma: A comparison of bisexual and lesbian/gay adults. *Journal of Counseling Psychology, 54*(3), 306.

Balsam, K. F., & Szymanski, D. M. (2005). Relationship quality and domestic violence in women's same-sex relationships: The role of minority stress. *Psychology of Women Quarterly, 29*(3), 258–269.

Barrett, C., Whyte, C., Comfort, J., Lyons, A., & Crameri, P. (2015). Social connection, relationships, and older lesbian and gay people. *Sexual and Relationship Therapy, 30*(1), 131–142. doi:10.1080/14681994.2014.963983

Belous, C. K. (2015). Couple therapy with lesbian partners using an affirmative-contextual approach. *The American Journal of Family Therapy, 43*(3), 269–281. doi:10.1080/0192 6187.2015.1012234

Berezowsky Ramirez, D. (2018). *Latin America could lead the way for LGBT rights in 2018.* Retrieved from https://www.hrw.org/news/2018/02/06/latin-america-could-lead-way-lgbt-rights-2018

Berke, D. S., Maples-Keller, J. L., & Richards, P. (2016). LGBTQ perceptions of psychotherapy: A consensual qualitative analysis. *Professional Psychology: Research and Practice, 47*(6), 373–382. doi:10.1037/pro0000099

Bieschke, K. J., Perez, R. M., & DeBord, K. A. (2007). *Handbook of counseling and psychotherapy with lesbian, gay, bisexual, and transgender clients.* Washington, DC: American Psychological Association.

Bigner, J. J., & Wetchler, J. L. (Eds.) (2012). *Handbook of LGBT-affirmative couple and family therapy.* New York, NY: Routledge.

Blackwell, C., Birnholtz, J., & Abbott, C. (2015). Seeing and being seen: Co-situation and impression formation using Grindr, a location-aware gay dating app. *New Media & Society*, *17*(7), 1117–1136.

Blumer, M. L., & Murphy, M. J. (2011). Alaskan gay males' couple experiences of societal non-support: Coping through families of choice and therapeutic means. *Contemporary Family Therapy*, *33*(3), 273.

Blumstein, P., & Schwartz, P. (1983). *American couples: Money, work, sex.* New York, NY: William Marrow and Company Inc.

Boszormenyi-Nagy, I., Grunebaum, J., & Ulrich, D. (1991). Contextual therapy. *Handbook of Family Therapy*, 2, 200–238.

Bowleg, L. (2008). When Black+ lesbian+ woman≠ Black lesbian woman: The methodological challenges of qualitative and quantitative intersectionality research. *Sex Roles*, *59*(5–6), 312–325.

Brown, T., & Herman, J. (2015). *Intimate partner violence and sexual abuse among LGBT people.* Los Angeles, CA: The Williams Institute.

Bruni, F. (2017). *The worst (and best) places to be gay in America. The New York Times.* Retrieved from https://www.nytimes.com/interactive/2017/08/25/opinion/sunday/worst-and-best-places-to-be-gay.html

Butler, C. (2011). Breaking taboos: Acknowledging therapist arousal and disgust. *Psychotherapy and Politics International*, *9*(1), 61–66.

Buxton, A. P. (2004). Works in progress: How mixed-orientation couples maintain their marriages after the wives come out. *Journal of Bisexuality*, *4*(1–2), 57–82.

Caldwell, B. E. (2011). The dilemma: Can a religious therapist refuse to treat gay and lesbian clients. *Family Therapy Magazine*, *10*(5), 50–52.

Cao, H., Zhou, N., Fine, M., Liang, Y., Li, J., & Mills-Koonce, W. R. (2017). Sexual minority stress and same-sex relationship well-being: A meta-analysis of research prior to the US Nationwide legalization of same-sex marriage. *Journal of Marriage and Family*, *79*(5), 1258–1277.

Carpenter, C., & Gates, G. J. (2008). Gay and lesbian partnership: Evidence from California. *Demography*, *45*(3), 573–590.

Pew Research Center (2019). *Same-sex marriage around the world.* Retrieved from https://www.pewforum.org/fact-sheet/gay-marriage-around-the-world/.

Centers for Disease Control and Prevention. (2016). *First national study of lesbian, gay, and bisexual high school students' health.* NCHHSTP Newsroom. Retrieved from https://www.cdc.gov/nchhstp/newsroom/2016/lgb-youth-report-press-release.html

Chapman, D. M., & Caldwell, B. E. (2012). Attachment injury resolution in couples when one partner is trans-identified. *Journal of Systemic Therapies*, *31*(2), 36–53. doi:10.1521/jsyt.2012.31.2.36

Cherlin, A. J. (2004). The deinstitutionalization of American marriage. *Journal of Marriage and Family*, *66*(4), 848–861.

Connolly, C. (2012). Lesbian couple therapy. In J. J. Bigner & J. L. Wetchler (Eds.), *Handbook of LGBT-affirmative couple and family therapy* (pp. 43–56). New York, NY: Routledge.

Corturillo, E. M., McGeorge, C. R., & Carlson, T. S. (2016). How prepared are they? Exploring couple and family therapy faculty members' training experiences in lesbian, gay, and bisexual affirmative therapy. *Journal of Feminist Family Therapy*, *28*(2–3), 55–75. doi:10.1080/08952833.2016.1179549

Crofford, M. L. (2017). Bisexual inclusive couples therapy: Assessment and treatment with bisexuals in mixed orientation relationships. *Sexual and Relationship Therapy, 33*(1–2), 1–11. doi:10.1080/14681994.2017.1412420

Cronin, A., & King, A. (2014). Only connect? Older lesbian, gay, and bisexual (LGB) adults and social capital. *Ageing & Society, 34*(2), 258–279. doi:10.1017/S0144686x12000955

Dashow, J. (2017). *New FBI data shows increased reported incidents of anti-LGBTQ hate crimes in 2016.* Retrieved from: https://www.hrc.org/blog/new-fbi-data-shows-increased-reported-incidents-of-anti-lgbtq-hate-crimes-i

Deacon, S. A., Reinke, L., & Viers, D. (1996). Cognitive-behavioral therapy for bisexual couples: Expanding the realms of therapy. *American Journal of Family Therapy, 24*(3), 242–258.

Devine, P. G., Forscher, P. S., Austin, A. J., & Cox, W. T. L. (2012). Long-term reduction in implicit race bias: A prejudice habit-breaking intervention. *Journal of Experimental Social Psychology, 48*(6), 1267–1278. doi:10.1016/j.jesp.2012.06.003

Doyle, D. M., & Molix, L. (2015). Social stigma and sexual minorities' romantic relationship functioning: A meta-analytic review. *Personality and Social Psychology Bulletin, 41*(10), 1363–1381. doi:10.1177/0146167215594592

Duggan, L. (2002). *The incredible shrinking public: Sexual politics and the decline of democracy.* Boston, MA: Beacon Press.

Eady, A., Dobinson, C., & Ross, L. E. (2011). Bisexual people's experiences with mental health services: A qualitative investigation. *Community Mental Health Journal, 47*(4), 378–389. doi:10.1007/s10597-010-9329-x

Fals-Stewart, W., O'Farrell, T. J., & Lam, W. K. K. (2009). Behavioral couple therapy for gay and lesbian couples with alcohol use disorders. *Journal of Substance Abuse Treatment, 37*(4), 379–387. doi:10.1016/j.jsat.2009.05.001

Farr, R. H., Forssell, S. L., & Patterson, C. J. (2010). Parenting and child development in adoptive families: Does parental sexual orientation matter? *Applied Developmental Science, 14*(3), 164–178.

Feinstein, B. A., Dyar, C., & London, B. (2017). Are outness and community involvement risk or protective factors for alcohol and drug abuse among sexual minority women? *Archives of Sexual Behavior, 46*(5), 1411–1423.

Feinstein, B. A., Latak, J. A., Bhatia, V., Davila, J., & Eaton, N. R. (2016). Romantic relationship involvement as a minority stress buffer in gay/lesbian versus bisexual individuals. *Journal of Gay & Lesbian Mental Health, 20*(3), 237–257. doi:10.1080/19359705.2016.1147401

Fisher, R., Gee, G., & Looney, A. (2016). *Joint filing by same-sex couples after windsor: Characteristics of married tax filers in 2013 and 2014.* Washington, DC: Department of the Treasurey, Office of Tax Analysis. Retrieved from https://www.treasury.gov/resource-center/tax-policy/tax-analysis/Documents/WP-108.pdf

Flores, A. R. & Park, A. (2018). *Polarized progress: Social acceptance of LGBT people in 141 countries 1980–2014.* Retrieved from https://williamsinstitute.law.ucla.edu/wp-content/.../Polarized-Progress-April-2018.pdf

Fredriksen-Goldsen, K. I., Kim, H.-J., Emlet, C. A., Muraco, A., Erosheva, E. A., Hoy-Ellis, C. P., … Petry, H. (2011). *The aging and health report: Disparities and resilience among lesbian, gay, bisexual, and transgender older adults.* Perth, Australia: GRAI (GLBTI Retirement Association Inc.) and Curtin Health Innovations Research Institute, Curtin University.

Garamel, K. E., Reisner, S. L., Laurenceau, J. P., Nemoto, T., & Operario, D. (2014). Gender minority stress, mental health, and relationship quality: A dyadic investigation of transgender women and their cisgender male partners. *Journal of Family Psychology, 28*(4), 437–447.

Garanzini, S., Yee, A., Gottman, J., Gottman, J., Cole, C., Preciado, M., & Jascula, C. (2017). Results of Gottman method couples therapy with gay and lesbian couples. *Journal of Marital and Family Therapy, 43*(4), 674–684. doi:10.1111/jmft.12276

Gartrell, N., Deck, A., Rodas, C., Peyser, H., & Banks, A. (2006). The National lesbian family study: Interviews with mothers of 10-year-olds. *Feminism & Psychology, 16*, 175–192. doi:10.1177/0959-353506062972

Gates, G. J. (2015). Marriage and family: LGBT individuals and same-sex couples. *The Future of Children, 25*(2), 67–87.

Giammattei, S. V., & Green, R. (2012). LGBTQ couple and family therapy. In J. J. Bigner & J. L. Wetchler (Eds.), *Handbook of LGBT-affirmative couple and family therapy* (pp. 1–22). New York, NY: Routledge.

Gibbs, J. J., & Goldbach, J. (2015). Religious conflict, sexual identity, and suicidal behaviors among LGBT young adults. *Archives of Suicide Research, 19*(4), 472–488. doi:10.1080/13811118.2015.1004476

Goldberg, A. E., Allen, K. R., Ellawala, T., & Ross, L. E. (2017). Male-partnered bisexual women's perceptions of disclosing sexual orientation to family across the transition to parenthood: Intensifying heteronormativity or queering family? *Journal of Marital and Family Therapy, 44*(1), 150–164. doi:10.1111/jmft.12242

Goldberg, A. E., & Garcia, R. (2015). Predictors of relationship dissolution in lesbian, gay, and heterosexual adoptive parents. *Journal of Family Psychology, 29*(3), 394.

Goldberg, A. E., & Kuvalanka, K. A. (2012). Marriage (in) equality: The perspectives of adolescents and emerging adults with lesbian, gay, and bisexual parents. *Journal of Marriage and Family, 74*(1), 34–52.

Goldsen, J., Bryan, A. E., Kim, H. J., Muraco, A., Jen, S., & Fredriksen-Goldsen, K. I. (2017). Who says I do: The changing context of marriage and health and quality of life for LGBT older adults. *The Gerontologist, 57*(suppl-1), S50–S62. doi:10.1093/geront/gnw174

Gottman, J. M. (1999). *The marriage clinic: A scientifically based marital therapy.* New York, NY: W. W. Norton & Co.

Gottman, J. M., Levenson, R. W., Gross, J., Frederickson, B. L., McCoy, K., Rosenthal, L., … Yoshimoto, D. (2003). Correlates of gay and lesbian couples' relationship satisfaction and relationship dissolution. *Journal of Homosexuality, 45*(1), 23–43.

Green, R., Bettinger, M., & Zacks, E. (1996). Are lesbian couples fused and gay male couples disengaged? Questioning gender straightjackets. In J. Laird & R. Lifton (Eds.), *Lesbians and gays in couples and families* (pp. 185–230). San Francisco, CA: Jossey-Bass.

Green, R. J., & Mitchell, V. (2015). Gay, lesbian, and bisexual issues in couple therapy. In A. S. Gurman, J. L. Lebow, & D. K. Snyder (Eds.), *Clinical handbook of couple therapy* (5th ed., pp. 489–511). New York, NY: Guilford.

Greenan, D. E., & Tunnell, G. (2003). *Couple therapy with gay men.* New York, NY: Guilford Press.

Guasp, A. (2011). *Lesbian, gay, & bisexual people in later life.* London, UK: Stonewall.

Hardtke, K. K., Armstrong, M. S., & Johnson, S. (2010). Emotionally focused couple therapy- A full-treatment model well-suited to the specific needs of lesbian couples. *Journal of Couple & Relationship Therapy, 9*(4), 312–326. doi:10.1080/15332691.2010.515532

Hashim, A. (2018, May 9). *Pakistan passes landmark transgender rights law.* Al Jazeera. Retrieved 10 May 2018.

Hassouneh, D., & Glass, N. (2008). The influence of gender role stereotyping on women's experiences of female same- sex intimate partner violence. *Violence Against Women, 14*, 310–325.

Haupert, M. L., Gesselman, A. N., Moors, A. C., Fisher, H. E., & Garcia, J. R. (2017). Prevalence of experiences with consensual nonmonogamous relationships: Findings from two national samples of single Americans. *Journal of Sex & Marital Therapy, 43*(5), 424–440.

Heiden-Rootes, K., Wiegand, A., & Bono, D. (2018). Sexual minority adults: A national survey on depression, religious fundamentalism, parent relationship quality & acceptance. *Journal of Marital and Family Therapy, 45*(1), 106–119.

Heiden-Rootes, K., Wiegand, A., Thomas, D., Moore, R. M., & Ross, K. A. (2018). A national survey on depression, internalized homophobia, college religiosity, and climate of acceptance on college campuses for sexual minority adults. *Journal of Homosexuality*, 1–17. doi: 10.1080/00918369.2018.1550329

Hendricks, M. L., & Testa, R. J. (2012). A conceptual framework for clinical work with transgender and gender nonconforming clients: An adaptation of the minority stress model. *Professional Psychology: Research and Practice*, *43*(5), 460.

Hernández, P., Almeida, R., & Vecchio, D. D. (2005). Critical consciousness, accountability, and empowerment: Key processes for helping families heal. *Family Process*, *44*(1), 105–119.

Hook, J. N., Davis, D. E., Owen, J., Worthington, E. L., Jr., & Utsey, S. O. (2013). Cultural humility: Measuring openness to culturally diverse clients. *Journal of Counseling Psychology*, *60*(3), 353.

Human Rights Campaign. (2018). *A time to act: Fatal violence against transgender people in America in 2017*. Retrieved from http://hrc-assets.s3-website-us-east-1.amazonaws.com//files/assets/resources/A_Time_To_Act_2017_REV3.pdf

Human Rights Watch. (2018). *Religious exemptions and discrimination against LGBT people in the US*. Retrieved from https://www.hrw.org/report/2018/02/19/all-we-want-equality/religious-exemptions-and-discrimination-against-lgbt-people

Iantaffi, A., & Benson, K. (2018). Sex is for every body: Trans-affirming sex therapy. In S. Green & D. Flemons (Eds.), *Quickies: The handbook of brief sex therapy* (3rd ed., pp. 196–215). New York, NY: W.W. Norton & Company.

ICEEFT. (2018). *EFT publications – Articles*. Retrieved from https://iceeft.com/eft-publications-articles

Israel, T., Gorcheva, R., Burnes, T. R., & Walther, W. A. (2008). Helpful and unhelpful therapy experiences of LGBT clients. *Psychotherapy Research*, *18*(3), 294–305.

Johnson, S. M. (2004). *The practice of emotionally focused couple therapy: Creating connection* (2nd ed.). New York, NY: Routledge.

Kim, H. K., & McKenry, P. C. (2002). The relationship between marriage and psychological well-being: A longitudinal analysis. *Journal of Family Issues*, *23*(8), 885–911.

Klesse, C. (2011). Shady characters, untrustworthy partners, and promiscuous sluts: Creating bisexual intimacies in the face of heteronormativity and biphobia. *Journal of Bisexuality*, *11*(2–3), 227–244. doi:10.1080/15299716.2011.571987

Koh, A. S., & Ross, L. K. (2006). Mental health issues: A comparison of lesbian, bisexual and heterosexual women. *Journal of Homosexuality*, *51*, 33–57.

Kurdek, L. A. (1991). The dissolution of gay and lesbian couples. *Journal of Social and Personal Relationships*, *8*(2), 265–278.

Kurdek, L. A. (1996). The deterioration of relationship quality for gay and lesbian cohabiting couples: A five-year prospective longitudinal study. *Personal Relationships*, *3*(4), 417–442.

Kurdek, L. A. (2006). Differences between partners from heterosexual, gay, and lesbian cohabiting couples. *Journal of Marriage and Family*, *68*(2), 509–528.

Ladany, N., O'Brien, K. M., Hill, C. E., Melincoff, D. S., Knox, S., & Petersen, D. A. (1997). Sexual attraction toward clients, use of supervision, and prior training: A qualitative study of predoctoral psychology interns. *Journal of Counseling Psychology*, *44*(4), 413.

LaSala, M. C. (2013). Out of the darkness: Three waves of family research and the emergence of family therapy for lesbian and gay people. *Clinical Social Work Journal*, *41*(3), 267–276.

Lease, S. H., Horne, S. G., & Noffsinger-Frazier, N. (2005). Affirming faith experiences and psychological health for Caucasian lesbian, gay, and bisexual individuals. *Journal of Counseling Psychology*, *52*(3), 378.

Levine, E. C., Herbenick, D., Martinez, O., Fu, T. C., & Dodge, B. (2018). Open relationships, nonconsensual nonmonogamy, and monogamy among US adults: Findings from the 2012 National survey of sexual health and behavior. *Archives of Sexual Behavior*, *47*, 1439–1450.

Li, T., Dobinson, C., Scheim, A. I., & Ross, L. E. (2013). Unique issues bisexual people face in intimate relationships: A descriptive exploration of lived experience. *Journal of Gay & Lesbian Mental Health*, *17*(1), 21–39. doi:10.1080/19359705.2012.723607

Luft, J. (1969). *Of Human Interaction*. Palo Alto, CA: National Press.

Magee, J. C., Bigelow, L., DeHaan, S., & Mustanski, B. S. (2012). Sexual health information seeking online: a mixed-methods study among lesbian, gay, bisexual, and transgender young people. *Health Education & Behavior*, *39*(3), 276-289. Chicago.

Malpas, J. (2012). Can couples change gender: Couple therapy with transgender people and their partners. In J. J. Bigner & J. L. Wetchler (Eds.), *Handbook of LGBT-affirmative couple and family therapy* (pp. 69–85). New York, NY: Routledge.

Martell, C. R., Safren, S. A., & Prince, S. E. (2004). *Cognitive-behavioral therapies with lesbian, gay, and bisexual clients*. New York, NY: Guilford Press.

McDowell, T., Emerick, P., & Garcia, M. (2014). Queering couple and family therapy education. *Journal of Feminist Family Therapy*, *26*(2), 99–112. doi:10.1080/08952833.2014.893805

McGeorge, C. R., & Stone Carlson, T. (2016). The state of lesbian, gay, and bisexual affirmative training: A survey of faculty from accredited couple and family therapy programs. *Journal of Marital and Family Therapy*, *42*(1), 153–167.

Meier, S. C., Sharp, C., Michonski, J., Babcock, J. C., & Fitzgerald, K. (2013). Romantic relationships of female-to-male trans men: A descriptive study. *International Journal of Transgenderism*, *14*(2), 75–85. doi:10.1080/15532739.2013.791651

Meyer, I. H. (2003). Prejudice, social stress, and mental health in lesbian, gay, and bisexual populations: Conceptual issues and research evidence. *Psychological Bulletin*, *129*(5), 674–697.

Meyer, I. H. (2015). Resilience in the study of minority stress and health of sexual and gender minorities. *Psychology of Sexual Orientation and Gender Diversity*, *2*(3), 209–213.

Meyer, I. H., Teylan, M., & Schwartz, S. (2015). The role of help-seeking in preventing suicide attempts among lesbians, gay men, and bisexuals. *Suicide and Life-Threatening Behavior*, *45*(1), 25–36. doi:10.1111/sltb.12104

Mohr, J. J., & Daly, C. A. (2008). Sexual minority stress and changes in relationship quality in same-sex couples. *Journal of Social and Personal Relationships*, *25*(6), 989–1007.

Nguyen, H. N., Grafsky, E. L., & Piercy, F. P. (2016). MFT program policies on referral of LGBT clients. *Contemporary Family Therapy*, *38*(3), 307–317.

Ocobock, A. (2013). The power and limits of marriage: Married gay men's family relationships. *Journal of Marriage and Family*, *75*(1), 191–205.

Ocobock, A. (2018). Status or access? The impact of marriage on lesbian, gay, bisexual, and queer community change. *Journal of Marriage and Family*, *80*(2), 367–382.

O'Shaughnessy, T., & Speir, Z. (2018). The state of LGBQ affirmative therapy clinical research: A mixed-methods systematic synthesis. *Psychology of Sexual Orientation and Gender Diversity*, *5*(1), 82.

Oswald, R. F. (2002). Resilience within the family networks of lesbians and gay men: Intentionality and redefinition. *Journal of Marriage and Family*, *64*(2), 374–383.

Otis, M. D., Rostosky, S. S., Riggle, E. D. B., & Hamrin, R. (2006). Stress and relationship quality in same-sex couples. *Journal of Social and Personal Relationships*, *23*(1), 81–99. doi:10.1177/0265407506060179

Perel, E. (2007). *Mating in captivity: Unlocking erotic intelligence*. New York, NY: Harper.

Pew Research Center. (2017). *Changing attitudes on gay marriage*. Retrieved from http://www.pewforum.org/fact-sheet/changing-attitudes-on-gay-marriage

Pope, K. S., Keith-Spiegel, P., & Tabachnick, B. G. (1986). Sexual attraction to clients: The human therapist and the (sometimes) inhuman training system. *American Psychologist*, *41*(2), 147.

Riggle, E. D., Rothblum, E. D., Rostosky, S. S., Clark, J. B., & Balsam, K. F. (2016). "The secret of our success": Long-term same-sex couples' perceptions of their relationship longevity. *Journal of GLBT Family Studies, 12*(4), 319–334.

Robinson, B. A. (2018). Conditional families and lesbian, gay, bisexual, transgender, and queer youth homelessness: Gender, sexuality, family instability, and rejection. *Journal of Marriage and Family, 80*(2), 1–14. doi:10.1111/jomf.12466

Rostosky, S. S., & Riggle, E. D. B. (2017). Same-sex couple relationship strengths: A review and synthesis of empirical literature (2000–2016). *Psychology of Sexual Orientation and Gender Diversity, 4*(1), 1–13. doi:10.1037/sgd0000216

Rutter, P. A. (2012). Sex therapy with gay male couples using affirmative therapy. *Sexual and Relationship Therapy, 27*(1), 35–45. doi:10.1080/14681994.2011.633078

Ryan, C., Huebner, D., Diaz, R. M., & Sanchez, J. (2009). Family rejection as a predictor of negative health outcomes in white and Latino lesbian, gay, and bisexual young adults. *Pediatrics, 123*(1), 346–352.

Serano, J. (2016). *Outspoken: A decade of transgender activism & trans feminism.* Oakland, CA: Switch Hitter Press.

Shamoon, Z. A., Lappan, S., & Blow, A. J. (2017). Managing anxiety: A therapist common factor. *Contemporary Family Therapy, 39*(1), 43–53.

Shelton, K., & Delgado-Romero, E. A. (2011). Sexual orientation microaggressions: The experience of lesbian, gay, bisexual, and queer clients in psychotherapy. *Journal of Counseling Psychology, 58*(2), 210.

Shernoff, M. (2006). Negotiated nonmonogamy and male couples. *Family Process, 45*(4), 407–418. doi:10.1111/j.1545-5300.2006.00179.x

Sitron, J. A., & Dyson, D. A. (2009). Sexuality attitudes reassessment (SAR): Historical and new considerations for measuring its effectiveness. *American Journal of Sexuality Education, 4*(2), 158–177.

Snapp, S. D., Watson, R. J., Russell, S. T., Diaz, R. M., & Ryan, C. (2015). Social support networks for LGBT young adults: Low cost strategies for positive adjustment. *Family Relations, 64*(3), 420–430.

Starks, T. J., Newcomb, M. E., & Mustanski, B. (2015). A longitudinal study of interpersonal relationships among lesbian, gay, and bisexual adolescents and young adults: Mediational pathways from attachment to romantic relationship quality. *Archives of Sexual Behavior, 44*(7), 1821–1831.

The Williams Institute, School of UCLA Law. (2013). *Infographic: % of Same-gender couples raising children in top metro areas (MSA).* Retrieved from: https://williamsinstitute.law. ucla.edu/research/census-lgbt-demographics-studies/infographic-msas-may-2013

Tilsen, J. (2013). *Therapeutic conversations with queer youth: Transcending homonormativity and constructing preferred identities.* Lanham, MD: Jason Aronson, Incorporated.

Timm, T. M. (2009). "Do I really have to talk about sex?" Encouraging beginning therapists to integrate sexuality into couples therapy. *Journal of Couple & Relationship Therapy, 8*(1), 15–33.

Totenhagen, C. J., Randall, A. K., & Lloyd, K. (2018). Stress and relationship functioning in same-sex couples: The vulnerabilities of internalized homophobia and outness. *Family Relations, 67*(3), 399–413.

Treyger, S., Ehlers, N., Zajicek, L., & Trepper, T. (2008). Helping spouses cope with partners coming out: A solution-focused approach. *American Journal of Family Therapy, 36*(1), 30–47.

Tunnell, G. (2012). Gay male couple therapy: An attachment-based model. In J. J. Bigner & J. L. Wetchler (Eds.), *Handbook of LGBT-affirmative couple and family therapy* (pp. 25–42). New York, NY: Routledge.

US Census Bureau. (2011). *Same-sex couple households: American community survey briefs.* Retrieved from https://www.census.gov/prod/2011pubs/acsbr10-03.pdf

Veaux, F., & Rickert, E. (2014). *More than two: A practical guide to ethical polyamory*. Portland, OR: Thorntree Press.

Walter, M. L., Chen, J., & Breiding, M. J. (2013). *The National intimate partner and sexual violence survey (NISVS): 2010 findings on victimization by sexual orientation*. Atlanta, GA: National Center for Injury Prevention and Control.

Weeks, G., Gambescia, N., & Hertlein, K. M. (2015). *A clinician's guide to systemic sex therapy*. New York, NY: Routledge.

Winnicott, D. W. (1949). Hate in the counter-transference. *International Journal of Psycho-Analysis, 30*, 69–74.

Winsa, P. (2017, January 15). *He says freedom, they say hate. The pronoun fight is back*. Toronto Star.

7

Clinical Work with Intercultural Couples

Reenee Singh, Kyle D. Killian, Dharam Bhugun, and Shu-Tsen Tseng

The growth of immigration, changes in social mores and expectations, and advances in global technology have contributed to an increase in intercultural marriages and relationships worldwide, including interracial, interfaith, interethnic, and international partnerships (Bhugun, 2017a). In the United Kingdom, 2.3 million people are living with or married to somebody from a different ethnic group, and 1 in 10 relationships is intercultural. The figures for London are even higher, and it is predicted that by 2030, 50% of people living there will be foreign born (2011 Census), which will increase the number of intercultural intimate relationships. In the United States, almost 4 in 10 (39%) Americans who have married since 2010 have been to those from different religious groups (Murphy, 2015). In the United Kingdom, one might hypothesize that if 1 in 10 relationships in England and Wales is between people of two different ethnic/cultural groups, it is likely that many of these will be interfaith relationships (Singh, 2017).

With regard to the Australian context, the growth of immigration, changes in social and political ideologies, and advances in global technology have reduced boundaries, increased cultural exchange in human relationships, and prompted a trend toward an increase in intercultural pairings, including interracial, interfaith, and interethnic partnerships (Bhugun, 2017a; Luke & Carrington, 2000; Owen, 2002). According to the Australian Bureau of Statistics (ABS, 2017), about 28% percent of couples were Anglo-Australian-born with overseas-born partners. The changes in the cultural demographics of Australia are likely to impact family structures, behaviors, and practices that may not occur in monocultural families. Consequently, intercultural relationships are emerging as an important family dynamic in Australian society. The rise in intercultural relationships presents new dimensions to relationship dynamics, which can be challenging as well as rewarding for intercultural couples and children.

The term intercultural encompasses the different notions of ethnic, interethnic, racial, interracial, religious, interfaith, and country of birth. In the Western literature

The Handbook of Systemic Family Therapy: Volume 3, First Edition.
Edited by Karen S. Wampler and Adrian J. Blow.
© 2020 John Wiley & Sons Ltd. Published 2020 by John Wiley & Sons Ltd.

on intercultural couples, the term "intercultural" refers to the interactions between members of different cultural groups (Ting-Toomey, 1999). An intercultural couple is regarded as two adults in a relationship who have significant differences in nationalities, race, religion, ethnicity, and language (McFadden & Moore, 2001; Perel, 2000; Sullivan & Cottone, 2006). However, intercultural relationships carry different meanings across cultures and contexts. For example, in India, "intercultural" refers to relationships where the partners come from different caste backgrounds and communities. In other countries, partners might identify as intercultural if they come from different class backgrounds or if they are from the same ethnic background but grew up in different countries. Similarly, couples from the same religious background may identify as intercultural because of the difference in the strength of their religious beliefs. In some countries/cultures, unions between those of different faiths are considered intercultural, while in others, different class backgrounds or political values and beliefs constitute cultural differences. Here, the notion of *intersectionality* (the intersection of different identities) is important, as sometimes differences might go hand in hand and at other times, similarity at one level, for example, social class, might override other racial and cultural differences. When we refer to intercultural couples, we are describing both heterosexual and gay and lesbian couples while acknowledging that gay and lesbian couples may have additional specific issues around intersectionality. Further, same-sex couples tend to have intercultural relationships in higher numbers than straight couples. An analysis of the 2010 US Census data (Queer Voices, 2016) found that 20.6% of same-sex couples were interracial or interethnic, compared with 18.3% of straight unmarried couples and 9.5% of straight married couples.

Renewed interest in couple relationships across racial and cultural divides is evidenced in media responses to Prince Harry and Megan Markle's marriage and in the recent number of films on this topic (e.g., *A United Kingdom, Loving, Victoria and Albert*, and *The Big Sick*). It is important to emphasize the strengths and resiliencies in intercultural couple relationships and not to pathologize them or to assume that all the difficulties in an intercultural couple relationship have to do with cultural differences. However, we recognize that intercultural couples may face unique challenges, and there is a growing need for clinicians working in multicultural contexts to acknowledge such challenges and help couples work through them.

Research Overview

Until recently, the literature on intercultural relationships focused on psychosocial challenges, such as barriers to communication (Perel, 2000; Waldman & Rubalcava, 2005), conflicts over parenting (Ho, 1990; Romano, 2001), and differences in cultural values (Garcia, 2006; Hsu, 2001; Waldman & Rubalcava, 2005). Research seemed to suggest that not only did intercultural couples struggle with the differences between them, but they also suffered from societal discrimination and racism. Until 1967, marrying somebody from a different racial group was seen as miscegenation and outlawed in 16 states in the United States. Interracial sexual relationships were illegal in Nazi Germany and during apartheid in South Africa. In some countries, it is especially difficult for couples to marry across religious divides. For example, no religious intermarriages can be performed legally in Israel. In India, the Special Marriage Act was instituted in 1954 to sanction the possibility of marrying across religion. However, intercaste and interreligious marriages are still taboo areas, evidenced by the recent high rate of honor killings among South Asian communities (United Nations Population Fund, 2000).

In a discursive analysis, Killian (2001a) focused on dominant and marginalized discourses used by interracial couples in the United States. At the time, monocultural couples were still seen as the norm by wider society, with discourses of homogamy and color blindness prevailing. Killian found that White partners perceived Black partners' reactions to society's racism as being *hypersensitive*. He used the expression "crossing borders" (Killian, 2001b, 2013) to describe interracial couples in the United States visiting all White or all Black segregated neighborhoods and to symbolize interracial partners' divergent social locations. Some couples, fearing consequences from being seen as a couple, would utilize strategies such as disassociating from one another and restricting their itineraries (Killian, 2003).

Research has also focused on the nature of relationships between intercultural couples, attitudes toward interracial marriages, issues faced by children in the relationship, and cross-cultural comparisons of parenting styles (Bratawidjaja, 2007; Renzaho, 2011). While some studies assume that more intercultural relationships end in divorce compared with monocultural relationships, recent studies have challenged this view (Bhugun, 2017a; Irastorza & DeVoretz, 2009; Kenney & Kenney, 2012). Most studies on intercultural marriages and relationships have been carried out in the clinical domain, approaching the issues from a deficit perspective, focusing on cultural difference as the source of conflict and stress for intercultural couples (Bratter & King, 2008; Hsu, 2001; Perel, 2000). Although it may be true that intercultural couples face many challenges and are subject to negative assumptions from society, they also experience benefits. Falicov (1995) identified several opportunities and positive impacts of cultural differences on intercultural couples, such as mutual adaptation and accommodation that can lead to increased cultural sensitivity, understanding and tolerance of diversity, personal transformation, and mutual acculturation. In fact, recent studies (Bhugun, 2017a; Caballero, Edwards, & Puthussery, 2008; Crippen, 2008, 2011; Heller & Wood, 2000; Killian, 2013; Singla, 2015; Tseng, 2016) have identified new strengths-based factors impacting the experiences of intercultural couples, including that the blending of cultures can enrich interactions and inclusion of both cultures in the relationship can help partners move beyond seeing cultural differences as a bone of contention.

Seshadri and Knudson-Martin's (2013) grounded theory study of intercultural couples revealed that although couples experienced most issues as cultural issues, topics of race were only problematic during their interactions with "others" outside of the relationship. Based on their research, they advocate a strengths-based model for working with intercultural couples. In her study exploring cultural dissonance among intercultural couples and families, Crippen (2011) identified transformative opportunities for intercultural couples and Children. These included the enhancement of cultural competencies through development of a broader frame of reference, increased cultural sensitivity and tolerance for diversity; access to other models of parenting and the opportunity to confront and negotiate imprinted cultural values. Parenting in another language provides an opportunity to learn or create a different style of parenthood than that which was modeled in childhood (p. 7).

Transformative opportunities for children included cultural belonging through a sense of connectedness, increased cultural literacy and adaptability from an expanded worldview and multilingualism, and cultural empathy through increased cultural awareness from the experience of belonging to an intercultural family. Other potential strengths among intercultural couples have been identified as curiosity about differences (Ting-Toomey, 1999) and egalitarianism (Yancey & Lewis, 2009). In a qualitative study, Bhugun (2017a) concluded that the benefits and opportunities of intercultural relationships extend beyond couples themselves to their children as well. Intercultural couples enjoy the richness of both worlds, learning another model of parenting, a holistic family life, and cultural competency. Intercultural couples were fascinated by the rich experiences of traveling to their migrant partner's country, meeting their extended families, and participating in the local social and food culture. Exposure to their partners' world, people, and other cultural entities gave them cultural ascendency and competency over those in monocultural relationships. They described the positive cultural attributes they gained such as sensitivity to, empathy and tolerance of cultural dynamics, adaptability and flexibility, and open-mindedness. The benefits for their children were described as unique experiences unknown to children from monocultural families, including the best of both of their parents' world and culture, job opportunities, adaptability, tolerance, acceptance, open-mindedness, non-materialism, and food culture.

Using a qualitative, thematic narrative analysis, Tseng (2016) explored how intercultural couples in Taiwan view their cultural differences and how they impact on their lives. Five married couples were interviewed. Each couple talked about where they came from, how they would describe their cultural backgrounds, what influenced them to start their relationships, how they experienced their cultural differences and adapted to each other, their experiences of interacting with other people as a couple, their ideas about what constitutes a good relationship, and the challenges/enjoyment of being in an intercultural relationship. Emerging themes included language and communication styles, gender and power differences, life cycle adaptations, child-rearing, extended family, and food. Interestingly, although language barriers between intercultural couples often hinder couples' communication and understanding of each other, in some situations, the language barriers also help couples think more carefully before verbally expressing themselves to their partners.

An ongoing multisite research study (Ugazio, Fellin, & Singh, 2017), based on Ugazio's (2013) theory of semantic polarities, explores the semantic cohesion between samples of monocultural and intercultural couples. The sample comprises 15 monocultural couples (both partners from the same country, i.e., British or Italian) and 15 intercultural couples where one partner is a migrant from the United Kingdom, Europe, the United States, or Australia and the other is from Asia, Africa, or Latin America. The migrant partner has not lived in a Western country before the age of 12, and the couple has been cohabiting for at least a year. The data will comprise extracts from clinical recorded sessions and will be analyzed using the family semantics grid (Ugazio & Castelli, 2015). The research questions explore whether there are greater differences in the semantics between intercultural couples and monocultural couples, and if so, how intercultural couples negotiate and manage these semantics. For example, could this involve the migrant partner accommodating to the Western partner's semantic? Preliminary findings suggest that there are indeed greater differences in the semantics between intercultural couples and monocultural couples. Semantics of freedom and belonging seem to be more prevalent between intercultural couples as compared to monocultural couples.

Significant themes and processes for intercultural couples

Through the review of literature, recurring interrelated themes emerged, which we also see reflected in our clinical practice. These themes will be illustrated using examples from our clinical practice and qualitative research. It is interesting to note that these themes appear to be universal, reflected in the cultural contexts of the United Kingdom, the United States, Australia, and Taiwan:

> *Yasmin and Ben[1] sought premarital couple's therapy, before making a decision about whether to get married or not. Yasmin is a Palestinian Arab woman and Ben is Jewish European. Yasmin's ancestors had to flee Palestine and settle in Jordan as a result of the conflict between Israel and the Palestine. In the first therapy session, they described a recent incident when they were at a party together, with Ben's friends and relatives. One of Ben's friends talked about how the Israelis had wanted the British to leave Israel. Yasmin was upset by this comment and Ben could not understand why. When they talked about the incident, Yasmin explained that she was upset, not only because it was uncomfortable to be the only outsider at a Jewish gathering but also because Ben's friend had designated Palestine as "that area" and described it as a "social construct." Yasmin talked about how her ancestors had lost everything when they had been "kicked out of Palestine." Ben's friend's denying the existence of Palestine felt to Yasmin like a denial of a home and an identity. Yasmin spoke poignantly about how she valued the importance of Ben's homeland Israel and was merely asking for a similar recognition of her own history. The incident at the party could be thought of as a microcosm of the couple's relationship.*

In this case, the couple's differences about how home was defined emerged early on their relationship. With other couples, conflicts about home and whose territory they are living in may occur at different points in the family life cycle. They may erupt later on in their couple relationship, especially when they have children together, and must make decisions about the best country to raise their children in or whose values/traditions to privilege. The decision about whose territory to live in may also become salient when their parents are aging or when it is time to decide which country to retire in.

Where one or both partners in an intercultural couple are migrants, the loss of their home or country of origin may be associated with sadness or grief. Papadopoulos (2002) aptly describes the sense of "nostalgic disorientation" faced by refugees and forced migrants when they have to leave their homes and move to another country. They miss the sights, sounds, tastes, and smells of home, without being consciously aware of what they are missing. Similarly, Falicov (2014) used the idea of ambiguous loss to depict this feeling of disorientation and confusion. These feelings may be compounded by difficulties settling in the host country, problems with visas, and experiences of racism. Political events like Brexit (the United Kingdom planning to exit the European Union) and recent immigration policies in the United States can have a profound impact on intercultural couples' sense of safety and belonging in the home country. In the case of other couples, the migrant partner(s) may embrace the new country and the notion of multiple homes. Hence, the clinician working with intercultural couples should put aside their own assumptions and start with an exploration of the unique significance and meaning of home to each partner in an intercultural couple.

Power and gender

As addressed in the previous section, one way in which power differences between partners in intercultural couples may be played out is through the choice of where to live. Bhugun (2017a) coined the term "righteousness of privilege" to describe another aspect of the power differences between intercultural parents. Bhugun (2017a) found that the issue of power may not be evident or acknowledged until it is brought up, usually by the migrant partner. Partners/parents from the host culture may assume that they have the privilege of truth regarding parenting practices. Some migrant partners described feeling powerless from being treated as outsiders regarding their parenting practices (Bhugun, 2017a). For example, most of the time, immigrant partners report that in their culture and country, newborn children sleep with the parents in the same bed but are disappointed when their host partners insist that the children should sleep in separate rooms. The immigrant partners may feel powerless because the sleeping pattern of the host culture is imposed on them. One example is the Australian host parent who claims to be "always right" because of their beliefs that children should not sleep with their parents and that they should be left to "sleep-cry." In this example, parenting practices from the host culture are accorded the status of "truths."

Killian (2015) found that problems can arise when partners explicitly or implicitly value their culture of origin over that of their partners. Frequently, the partner with greater accompanying power and privilege (e.g., higher status of country of origin, lighter skin, upper to upper middle class, or some intersection of these locations) presumes that the majority of his or her cultural customs, traditions, and values should become the template for the couple system and, if children are created, for the new family system. The more privileged partner can view his/her culture's way of seeing the world, managing conflicts, and raising the next generation as "best" or beyond reproach, expecting the other partner to make a case for why his or her values, traditions, and rituals should be included in the first world order. Alternatively, partners may "sacrifice" their families' histories, identities, and traditions in order to "get along" in the present.

Different cultures may also have vastly different ideas about gendered roles and expectations, and partners who are migrant men or those from minority ethnic groups may be positioned as sexist or dominating. Similarly, women from the host culture may be seen as dominating, opinionated, or "bossy." The ways in which intercultural couples negotiate gender and power differ from one couple to another. Tseng (2016) found that two of the couples in her sample – the French/Taiwanese and the Japanese/Taiwanese couples – arrived at an unusual way of negotiating their cultural, gender, and power differences. In the case of the first couple, the French husband was permanently abroad running his business. When the Taiwanese wife was with him abroad, she depended on him totally, both financially and with regard to interacting with the outside world. However, after she moved back to Taiwan for their children's education and work, her husband had to depend on her when he came home to visit them. This gave her a sense of frustration and hopelessness, because even though she was the one who had all the power, when the couple was in Taiwan, she actually preferred to be led by her husband while retaining financial autonomy. The Taiwanese/Japanese couple also struggled with power negotiations. The Taiwanese husband did not want to be involved in the decision making at home but would then complain about decisions his wife had made. His Japanese wife also expressed her frustration at being in charge. Tseng (2016) speculated that the ambivalence of these two wives in her sample may have to do with the cultural values of their Eastern culture. Traditionally, Eastern women are taught to follow their husband's decisions. Thus, when they were in charge, some wives may feel uneasy because (a) power comes with duty and pressure, (b) their husband's status in others' eyes may decrease, (c) having power over their husband in some areas may unsettle the couple dynamics, or (d) being looked after more by her husband may be interpreted as an indication of love from their husbands.

In the context of parenting, Bhugun (2017a) found that male partners appear to exercise more power than their female partners regarding discipline and socialization processes of the children. Interestingly, gender power in males appeared to be linked to religious values and beliefs. In the intercultural context, some immigrant partners submit to their host partner's lack of understanding of their culture because of their religious values:

> He says he understands my culture, but sometimes there are things that he could never really understand. That's when I think our faith comes in and... "Okay, I have to let go." It's painful, but...

The above quotation from a research participant points to the difficulty in reconciling differences in religion and faith, differences that may be more painful to accommodate to than cultural differences.

However, gender and power are not one-way dimensional processes in intercultural relationships. Some migrant male partners may also lose power when it comes to gender roles in the intercultural family. Although men and women have defined roles in certain ethnic cultures, the inference is that men are still regarded as the authority in the family and ultimate decision makers in family processes. This view of power status could be compromised as a result of marrying into a Euro-American culture, which promotes and values equal gender power and rights. For example, most migrant male partners from ethnic cultures do not cook, wash, and put women's clothes on the clothes line. But in Australia, they have started to cook, wash, and hang clothes out to sustain a healthy relationship and family, as well as an adaptive process in the host society. It appears that the shift in power dynamics is also related to the fact that most women work in either full-time or part-time jobs and therefore their husbands have to share the family and parenting responsibilities. Further, the lack of parenting support from extended family members in Australia, as opposed to the support in ethnic families back home, forces men to share in family and parental roles. Interestingly though, the partners from the ethnic cultures revert to their defined roles when they go back to their countries of origin.

Language and communication styles

Singh and Dutta (2010, p. 98) described the issues of bilingualism in the case of an intercultural couple, where Ahmed, the man, was Moroccan and Pat, the woman, was Australian:[2]

When they first met, they spoke to each other in French, in which they were both fluent. However, after they had children, Ahmed wanted to bring up his children to speak Arabic. The language spoken at home thus excluded Pat, who had imagined, before the children were born, that their family life would be conducted in French. Language was used in this couple and family to mark power differences and to exclude one member of the family.

Language barriers were a common theme in Tseng's (2016) research with intercultural couples. When facing language barriers, depending on whose country is the host country, intercultural couples may face a number of options: using a third language that they both know, one learning their partner's (host country) language, learning each other's language, or creating their own language. One of the participants in her research, the Japanese wife of Taiwanese/Japanese couple, was sent to learn Mandarin by her husband's family the day after she arrived in Taiwan. After spending 17 years in Taiwan and having learned to speak Mandarin fluently, her Taiwanese husband still preferred to talk to her in English, as this is the language they used to communicate in, when they first met in Canada. Moreover, he was frustrated by his wife's low level of proficiency in Mandarin and the difficulties in sustaining an intelligible conversation. Although his wife was happy to form her own group of Taiwanese friends, she still expressed her frustration at not being supported by her husband when she spoke Mandarin.

In another case, where the husband was French and the wife Taiwanese, they created their own language. His Mandarin was poor and she could only speak some basic English. However, their own creation with the aid of sounds and nonverbal language helped them to communicate, like using "bobo" to represent a car and "bobo key" to represent a car key. Although this couple had been together for 21 years, they both still felt they could not converse about important topics—such as their children's education and politics—with each other. The Taiwanese wife seemed to have lowered her expectation of their marriage, as she sometimes felt they were "like good flat mates, but at least we seldom argue."

Sometimes, speaking in the language of the host culture can represent an escape from their own country and language for the migrant partner. One such case was of an intercultural couple living in the United Kingdom, where the husband was a migrant from Guatemala and the wife was English. The wife had made an effort to learn Spanish, but her husband wanted to speak to her and the children only in English. This was a man who had experienced his childhood as abusive and wanted to distance himself from his family of origin, culture, and language.

In her groundbreaking research, Burck (2005) highlighted the possibilities that speaking a foreign language can create—for example, the ability to experience an emotion like anger in a foreign language, but not in one's native tongue. Distancing oneself from one's mother tongue can thus be a liberating experience for some migrants. Just as language differences can create dilemmas for intercultural couples, differences in communication styles can also create barriers in intercultural relationships. Communication styles have been found to be different in different cultures, with Western cultures privileging direct and often assertive styles of communication and Eastern cultures relying more on indirect communication (Bhugun, 2017a; Falicov, 1995; Tamura & Lau, 1992). Clinical work with intercultural couples can help them to recognize the different communication styles that they employ. Further, nonverbal and representational therapeutic techniques such as cultural genograms, ecomaps, and culturegrams may be of great value in bridging verbal impasses that intercultural couples can find themselves in. Such techniques will be explored more fully in a subsequent section.

Constructions of love, intimacy, and couplehood

In a marriage between a Bangladeshi woman born and brought up in the United Kingdom and her spouse who was born and brought up in Bangladesh, differences about the meaning of romantic love prevailed. The wife, who was far more Westernized than her husband, struggled to communicate her romantic feelings, needs for intimacy, and desires to her Bengali-speaking husband. "How do I find Bengali words in which to say, 'I love you?'" she asked her psychotherapist.

In many cultures and religions, arranged marriages are the norm, and premarital sex is prohibited. Marrying outside one's own community, religion, and culture could be associated with a sense of loss, dishonor, and betrayal and may impact the couples' sexual and intimate relationship. Further, the couple may come to their relationship with completely different templates of love, intimacy, and togetherness, originating from their different cultural backgrounds. Partners from migrant or minority ethnic backgrounds, where the couple is often embedded within extended family relationships (Gabb & Singh, 2015b), may not be able to understand the construction of the couple as the primary dyad within the family. In non-Western cultures, the primary "dyad" could comprise the father–son, mother–daughter, or other dyads based on social rather than biological ties. Relying solely on the couple relationship for emotional needs and support could result in feelings of loneliness and isolation. Having a community of other intercultural or mixed couples can help in overcoming the feelings of being alienated by providing a sense of connectedness (Singh, 2014). The dilemmas that are posed for partners who have grown up with different constructions of "family" and coupleness are illustrated in the vignette below:

Tanvir and Isabella (see Note 2), a professional couple in their early forties, came to see me (RS) as they had reached an impasse in their couple relationship, which was affecting their children, Hassan (9) and Rania (6). Tanvir was from a Pakistani Muslim background and Isabella was from a Spanish Catholic background. Both were born and brought up in the United Kingdom. They had been together for 15 years.

The couple had struggled at many points in their relationship. They had married against considerable parental opposition. Tanvir had wanted Isabella to convert to Islam, but her parents, who were staunch Catholics, had refused. Tanvir had agreed to get married in a registry office, but, on the day of the wedding, had not been able to rebel against his parents' wishes and had left Isabella waiting at the registry office, furious. The couple broke up at this point, but got together again, six months later, with Isabella reluctantly agreeing to convert and to bring up the children they planned to have within the Muslim faith.

A few years later, their relationship had almost broken down over Tanvir and his family insisting on having Hassan circumcised. Isabella, once again, finally gave in. However, in the last six months, things had reached a crisis over Tanvir's conviction that Isabella was infatuated with his 27-year-old cousin, who was visiting from Pakistan. Isabella denied this vociferously while admitting that she was going through a "midlife crisis" and needed reassurance about her attractiveness to men. Tanvir secretly installed a CCTV camera in the house and recorded "evidence" of the flirtation between Isabella and his cousin.

Tanvir and Isabella met before the terrible happenings of 9/11 in the United States and the bombings in London (July 2005). Particularly after Brexit, the couple and their two children experienced racism and Islamophobia, within the school, and even from Isabella's relatives, who viewed Tanvir's family with hostility and suspicion. In my work, I tried to open up a space where having these difficult conversations was possible. I drew on Killian's (2013) ideas about particularizing the universal and universalizing the particular.

In Tanvir and Isabella's family, how did the wider—universal—discourses of Islamophobia impact on their couple and parenting relationship? Isabella poignantly recounted how, as a family, they had stopped watching television during difficult times, as the news reminded them of the religious differences between them, which could become politicized. Similarly, they struggled to understand how they might cope with the (particular) racist bullying that Hassan encountered as located not only within their school contexts but as a symptom of a wider universal social malaise? How could they find ways to protect Hassan and intervene in the school system?

Honor, guilt, and shame have different meanings and are privileged differently in different religions and cultures. Tanvir and Isabella had endured a lot in their couple relationship but the one thing that their love couldn't conquer was related to a radical difference in gendered beliefs and values. Although Tanvir didn't believe that Isabella had been unfaithful to him, he had lost trust and honor through her actions of shaming him by flirting with a younger member of his extended clan. Isabella could not understand how her actions, which she saw as an expression of her "freedom" as a Western woman, could have such disastrous consequences. The impasse that opened up between them led her to then see Tanvir as the Muslim "other" and her family and friends reinforced her positioning of him as an oppressor. Tanvir fought hard against this description, angry at being stereotyped, and pointing out that he had been liberal throughout their relationship.

Reverse and reciprocal acculturation

Reverse acculturation is described as the cultural practice wherein a country's fully acculturated minority member introduces the heritage culture to the majority host society (Kim & Park, 2009). In the context of intercultural relationships, reverse acculturation is manifested in multiple domains such as use of language, identity, food, values, behaviors, cultural knowledge, and social affiliation and activities. Reverse acculturation is attributed to both the individual and society. From the individual perspective, reverse acculturation occurs when partners from the minority group reinforce their cultural heritage in the relationship and parenting processes in the host society. From a societal perspective, the cultural exchange is manifested at the center of the host society itself, wherein the society accepts cultural coexistence (Kim & Park, 2009). Narratives into the experiences of intercultural couples clearly demonstrate that reverse acculturation is occurring because of shifts in the global culture toward a more cosmopolitan culture, which values the coexistence of inherent differences and greater tolerance of diversity (Bhugun, 2016). Accordingly, the heterogeneous global culture and the willingness on their part to embrace aspects of other cultures enhance their lifestyle and opportunities and that of their children in both the heritage country and host culture.

Bhugun (2016) found that immigrant partners, most of the time, valued both their ethnic heritage and the host culture by expressing strong sentiments and willingness for integration between their native home and host culture, including traditions, beliefs, values, and connections. Reinforcement and incorporation of the migrant heritage culture were evidenced in partners from both the ethnic minority and dominant group. All the partners from the ethnic minority group were strongly in favor of reinforcing their home cultural values and goals such as respect, discipline, strong family, work ethic, education, and community engagement for their children. However, while valuing the integration of the two cultures, intercultural couples also emphasized the importance of the diaspora communities in the host country that allow them and their children to have continued association and connections with their home culture and community.

Bhugun (2016) posited another dimension of acculturation, "reciprocal acculturation," where some partners from the dominant culture in the host society were also influenced by, supported, preferred, and adopted their partner's minority group cultural processes, especially values and goals. Thus, instead of the minority partner accommodating to the partner from the host culture's beliefs, it is the partner from the host culture who adopts the partner from the minority culture's beliefs and values.

According to the host partners, there were important values in their own upbringing that were now missing, while the influence of the host culture was predominant. Acculturation evolved as a reciprocal process wherein both immigrant and host partners exchanged certain cultural preferences. Intercultural couples described the influence Asian food had on the way they eat and live their lives, and how globalization and the emergence of China as a world economic and cultural power influenced them to encourage their children and themselves to learn their immigrant partner's Chinese language and culture, so that they could benefit from the Chinese global job opportunities.

The acculturation process has also led to an important shift in parenting styles from an authoritarian to authoritative parenting style. Immigrant partners described preferences for the Australian cultural concept of independence and authoritative parenting styles because according to them, it makes the children happier. Asian participants, in particular, reported that they did not like the authoritarian parenting style of their parents regarding discipline and educational expectations. They felt sad and lacked self-confidence because of their parents', particularly their father's, authoritarian style of parenting when it came to educational achievements. Communication and enabling expression of feelings from children seemed to be elusive among some ethnic minority groups. They did not want their children to go through the same experiences and feelings and wanted to reverse these cultural attitudes.

The themes outlined thus far are a summary from the literature and our own clinical and research experiences. A discussion of these interrelated themes highlights the need for clinicians working with intercultural couples to be open and reflexive and to interrogate their own assumptions about couplehood, gender, parenting, language, and the meaning of home and acculturation.

Clinical needs of children in intercultural families

Although living in a mixed family can provide a richness of experience, the opportunities for cultural creativity, and transformational experiences, it also poses unique challenges for children and young people. Perhaps the most common challenge for children and young people who are the product of an intercultural union is the difficulty in reconciling different aspects of their identities. Llerena-Quinn and Bacigalupe (2009) discussed how difficulties between intercultural parents can begin from the moment they choose a name for their firstborn child. For the parents and for the child, a name is an important indicator of identity. Children are sometimes teased in schools about their ethnic first names or surnames. A dual heritage child who may have been able to "pass" as White may feel disappointed by their name as it may give away their ethnic origins. At other times, a child could be visibly Black but have a White name that they feel they do not express the fullness of their identity. The problems about names and visibility may become even more pronounced in step, blended families when there are a number of different surnames—and ethnic identities—within the same family unit. One child in such a family may look visibly different from the others, which may bring up themes of inclusion or exclusion. In adopted families where one or more children are transracially adopted, the themes of belonging and inclusion may be particularly acute for the children.

When there is conflict between the parents and/or between the parents and grandparents or extended families about the choice of names, religion, and parenting practices, children can present with symptoms. Symptoms such as depression, anxiety, eating disorders, and self-harm may be a way of signaling to their teachers or mental health professionals about the troubled relationships at home:

> *Indra and David (see Note 2) presented to therapy because they were concerned about their 13-year-old daughter, Lina, who was self-harming. Indra was from a conservative Hindu Gujarati family and had married David despite considerable opposition from her parents. Lina's birth had been particularly difficult for the couple as they had no support from Indra's family. Lina had always felt torn between her parents and between her English, Christian self and Hindu Gujarati self. She felt that her mother favored her brother and was overly strict with her. The birth of Lina's brother, Vijay, had led to a reconciliation between Indra and her extended family. Lina felt that she was not valued enough by her relatives to have managed to effect such a reconciliation. She was deeply concerned about the conflict between her parents and the differences in their beliefs about adolescence and about how to parent her. Indra tended to be strict and did not approve of Lina's choice of clothes and music. David was seen as more permissive, and Lina's symptoms of cutting were a way of expressing confusion and an overriding need to communicate with her parents so that they could present a united front.*

Working with intergenerational issues and conflicts

The above vignette illustrates the possible difficulties when parents do not accept their adult children's choices of partner. It is common for some parents of adult children to accept the relationship/marriage when the grandchildren are born, although conflict about religious or cultural differences can arise again during transitions and attendant rituals such as a Christening or a Bar Mitzvah. In other instances, especially when the family is deeply religious, the parents may not accept their adult children's spouse or partner at all, even after the birth of the grandchildren. In such cases, the adult children may be faced with the dilemmas of having to make a choice between their partners and their parents, or to live parallel lives, between the two families. This can become especially problematic when the (grand)parents are aging and expect their aging children to look after them. When working with such intergenerational dilemmas, it is wise to prepare the intercultural couple/family through premarital therapy and psychoeducation for the possible challenges ahead. The couple should be prepared for the possibility of cutoff from their families of origin and the effect that such a loss could have on the couple and parenting relationship.

What Are the Ingredients of Successful Intercultural Relationships?

Killian (2015) makes a helpful distinction between culturally *conscious* and culturally *inclusive* intercultural couples. Both kinds of couples have found a way to negotiate and even celebrate the differences between them. Culturally conscious couples are partners who demonstrate an evolved sense of political and cultural awareness of and sensitivity to both self and the other partner (Killian, 2015). Partners' daily experiences in their relationships with each other, peers, extended family members, and the larger society are discussed, and their relative statuses and locations based on the ecosystems of race, gender, and class are also explored on occasion. For example, partners descended from Northern Europe may work hard to understand xenophobia and racism as complex structures in which they are both implicated and embedded (Twine & Steinbugler, 2006). Such conversations require learning how to speak about culture, ethnocentrism, racism, and strategies of antiracism. "Cultural literacy" is a practice and stance that "facilitates ongoing self-education and enables members" of intercultural couples to "translate [cultural and] racial codes, decipher [cultural and] racial structures" (Twine & Steinbugler, 2006, p. 344), and unpack the cultural chauvinism and hegemony ensconced in interactions at all systemic levels. Intercultural partners vary in extent of cultural literacy and may demonstrate contradictions in their literacy from conversation to conversation.

Culturally inclusive intercultural couples do not subscribe to the discourse of homogamy, which suggests that partners need to be the same or similar in backgrounds for the relationship to be a success (Killian, 2013). Culturally inclusive couples resist ethnocentrism and cultural chauvinism. They do so by embracing and weaving into their relationship key aspects of each partner's cultural history and identity and by positively valuing differences. Partners in intercultural relationships do not necessarily transcend or escape the social relations of power, xenophobia, racism, homophobia, classism, and sexism that monocultural couples frequently fall into. Respectful, valuing, and even revolutionary couple relations demand much from both partners, highlighting apparent contradictions both within couples and in our larger society. Even partners who are socially conscious and sensitively "fighting the good fight" toward an alternative kind of intimate relationship/community can also struggle with radical divergences in privilege and power between them. Intercultural couples have work to do in creating a more equalitarian, mutual, and intimate relationship. Therapists should not mount uncritical (and hegemonic) defenses of intercultural relationships founded on an assumption that love and prejudice are "mutually exclusive and counter-posed to one another" (Sexton, 2002, p. 95). Love, respect, and intimacy, though attainable, are necessarily hard won. Clinicians who acknowledge the possibility that intimate partners might love one another and also demonstrate conscious and unconscious prejudices toward one another can help partners become aware of words and actions that are hurtful, whether intentional or unintentional. Love and prejudice can coexist within the same relationship, and it is sometimes the task of the clinician working with intercultural couples to provide a safe context in which the partners can explore the unsaid, without fear of being judged as racist by their partner or the therapist.

Bhugun (2017a) found that in order to make their relational and parenting experiences a positive journey, intercultural couples/parents negotiated their cultural differences by developing several conflict resolution and management strategies. The management strategies are conceptualized into three spheres: (a) individual sphere, (b) couple's/parents' sphere, and (c) child's sphere. These three spheres overlap and enable insights into the interactions between the three domains that are dependent on each other for successful experiences of the phenomenon. Strategies in the individual sphere include respect, flexibility, patience and perseverance, acceptance and tolerance, and open-mindedness. Strategies in the couple's/parents' sphere include communication, compromise, spheres of influence, asymmetric decision making, cultural literacy and embracing a partners' culture, having a plan, and preparedness for minority feelings. Strategies for the child's sphere include not imposing culture on child, encouraging multiculturalism, listening and respecting children, consistency in parenting, and teaching children values (see Figure 7.1). Intercultural couples believed that their mutual efforts of developing and adopting coping strategies within the intercultural context greatly enhanced their relationships and parenting skills.

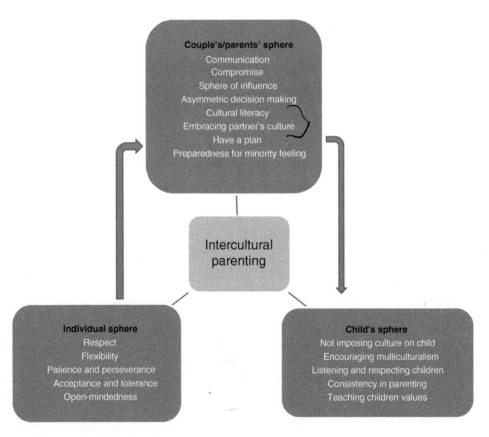

Figure 7.1 Conflict resolution and management strategies of intercultural couples/parents. Reprinted with permission D. Bhugun (2017c, pp. 454–477). Copyright by Wiley.

Clinical Implications: Assessment and Treatment

Falicov (2016) pointed to the complexity of practice with intercultural couples. She posits that for intercultural couples there is a difference in cultural content (values and beliefs), as well as sociopolitical and economic inequalities. These two levels interact and impact on interactional processes. As systemic practitioners, we are trained to intervene at the level of process, but when working with intercultural couples, we have to be mindful of the level of content as well in regard to differences in values and beliefs, as well as socioeconomic and power differences. Further, Falicov (2016) stressed that we must not assume that every intercultural couple will have difficulties nor that all their struggles are because of the intercultural differences. The first stage of clinical practice with intercultural couples involves a thorough and culturally appropriate assessment.

Assessment

Intercultural couples in therapy often encounter a commonly held assumption that their problems directly stem from the cultural and racial differences between them (Killian, 2013). Clinicians should not assume that this is the case but conduct an assessment to see what their presenting issues actually are. Interventions are more likely to be therapeutic if clinicians (a) affirm the significance of the strategies couples employ to survive in a social context that actively supports monocultural couple and family formations and (b) tentatively and sensitively facilitate a conversation about the ways in which culture, gender, race, class, and other axes of power inform practices in the couple, family, and therapeutic relations. Therapists can help intercultural partners discuss culture, gender, and class differences by administering questionnaires that identify commonalities and differences in cultural beliefs and values, and the degree to which the partners value and are inclusive of each other's cultural identities, creating cultural genograms (Hardy & Laszloffy, 1995; Keiley et al., 2002), and conducting internalized other interviewing (Tomm, 1999) and ethnographic debriefing (Cole & Mullaney, 1996).

Cultural assumptions and beliefs inventory

The 44-item Cultural Assumptions and Beliefs Inventory (CABI) (Killian, 2013) can help identify differences, creating a means for deeper understanding in the couple by measuring partners' attitudes and values in seven domains: emotional expressiveness, family-of-origin closeness, individualism versus collectivism, gender roles, religiosity, worldview, and time orientation (i.e., future [the value of planning ahead], present [spur-of-the-moment spontaneity], and past [a greater emphasis on traditions and history]). The CABI can be administered in less than 10 min as part of an initial assessment or in the first session of therapy. By comparing partners' scores on each of these seven subscales, helping professionals can detect differences in cultural assumptions and beliefs that may underlie divergent values and points of view in a couple's life together. Significant differences in scores in the seven domains are correlated with increased conflict and poorer dyadic adjustment. In reviewing partners' scores on the

CABI, therapists can invite couples to start a conversation about the similarities and differences in the partners' cultural assumptions and beliefs.

Index of cultural inclusion

Therapists can administer the Index of Cultural Inclusion (ICI) (Killian, 2013) to get a sense of partners' degree of interest in and acceptance of their own and each other's cultural traditions and values. ICI contains 23 items, measuring four dimensions: partner's perception of how much his/her cultural identity is valued by the other partner, partner's degree of interest in or awareness of his/her own familial and cultural history and traditions, how clear and positive (e.g., sense of belonging, a source of strength) a partner's ethnic or cultural identity is, and how much the internal conflict and confusion is associated with a partner's ethnic or cultural identity. This instrument quickly takes a snapshot of how partners feel about their cultural selves; whether partners feel that their ethnic/cultural histories, values, and traditions are valued in their relationship; and how much either partner is aware of his or her own familial and cultural history. The ICI measures the degree to which partners value culture and history in themselves and in each other and whether partners value culture or history as resources in the relationship or want to "start from scratch."

Cultural genogram

A pictorial display of a couple's family history, including social, psychological, and medical history, a family genogram (McGoldrick, Gerson, & Petry, 2008) permits therapists and clients to examine intergenerational patterns and to identify clients' strengths, resources, and risk factors. Genograms are diagrams that show patterns that connect (Bateson, 2000) through displaying members' names in a family lineage and the nature of the relationships (openness, intensity, etc.) among them. A genogram helps a clinician to create a map of the family structure across at least three generations and to note and update the family picture as it develops. Genograms can be powerful tools for promoting intercultural couples' awareness of each partner's heterogeneous roots. Via cultural genograms (Hardy & Laszloffy, 1995; Keiley et al., 2002), partners can discuss their cultural backgrounds, recount beliefs carried by family members in generations past, and convey their feelings regarding family rituals and legacies. Genograms are also an opportunity to bring into view contradictions among historical narratives originating both in each partner's family of origin and in the larger society (i.e., what is discussed and what has been omitted, by whom and for what purposes). Specific family themes, such as heterogamous relationships, cultural ancestry, and the circumstances under which partners' ancestors entered the country can be coded with colors and/or symbols that carry meaning for each partner. Family photographs, cultural artifacts, and recreating a cultural ritual in the therapy room can add to the experience (Hardy & Laszloffy, 1995). The cultural genogram brings to light information that partners may not currently know or may have been reticent to share. Couples whose members view differences positively will probably enjoy the process of sharing cultural genograms. However, some clients, especially those who are "starting from scratch" with their current relationship, may feel that a therapist is "digging too deep"; they may be uncomfortable with revealing personal information out of family loyalty and/or because they have learned in their families of origin to maintain silence with regard to emotionally charged issues. Moreover, it is important to remember that a couple's presenting problem(s) may not be associated with cultural differences nor related to generations past. Therefore, this technique is most helpful when it aids therapists in addressing couples' expressed needs.

Culturegram

This is an assessment tool that originates in Berlin and Cannon's (2013) work. A culturegram is a diagram that provides a chance for intercultural couples to do some thinking about the differences in their family beliefs, values, traditions, and legacies. Partners are asked to focus on a general theme, for example, gendered beliefs in their families. One partner is asked to draw a circle and within the circle write the answers to the questions of where they are from and what cultural/ethnic heritage they identify with. They are then instructed to draw spokes from the circle and on each spoke write a belief or value that they picked up from their families of origin. A circle at the end of each spoke depicts how the belief has been adopted or modified in the current relationship.

After each partner has completed the exercise, they are asked to compare and contrast their culturegrams:

> *The culturegram can be used as a way of understanding and depicting family scripts. Family scripts are stories about how families ought to be, and roles within families, that are passed down from one generation to another.*

According to Byng-Hall (1985), family scripts could be replicative or corrective. When using a culturegram to investigate family scripts, the spokes depict the values and beliefs that are carried down over generations. The circle attached to the spoke could be thought of as replicative or corrective aspects of the family script:

> *Helen and Rebecca (see Note 2) are a same-sex couple. Helen is a Canadian Protestant and Rebecca is Israeli Jewish. A culturegram was used to explore gender and women's roles in each of their families of origin and how these had been adapted in their relationship (see Figure 7.2).*
>
> *In Helen's family, women were homemakers, who did not work outside the house. Rebecca's mother is a doctor, and Rebecca came from a lineage of powerful matriarchal women who had held jobs outside the home. Helen and Rebecca had thus inherited vastly different ideas about women's place outside their homes, from their families of origin. However, interestingly, in their own relationship (one coming from a replicative script and the other from a corrective script), they both valued professional achievement. They wondered if this negotiation about gendered roles in their relationship may have been different if they were in a heterosexual relationship.*
>
> *The other aspects of their culturegrams had to do with women's influence within the home and women's adoption of societal ideas about beauty and body weight. With the help of a culturegram, Helen and Rebecca understood how they had both arrived at feminist understandings of their world and their relationship, from different vantage points. This helped them to appreciate the strengths and creative power in their relationship.*

Rebecca and Helen's culturegrams: Gender and power

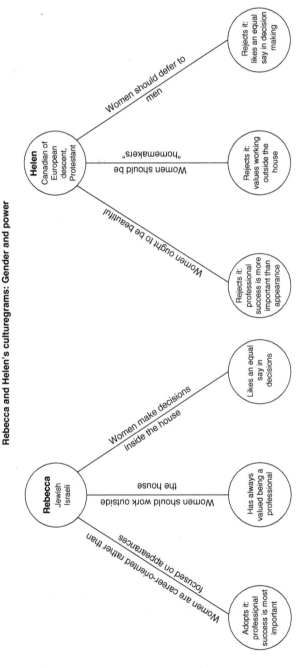

Figure 7.2 Rebecca and Helen's culturegrams: gender and power. Adapted with permission Reibstein and Singh (2018). Copyright by Reenee Singh.

Emotion maps

Devised by the sociologist Jacqui Gabb, and imported into family therapy by Gabb and Singh (2015a), the emotion map is a visual representational research method. After drawing a floor plan of their homes, participants/clients are asked to use emojis to represent incidents from their home. For example, an argument in the kitchen may be depicted with angry or sad faces. Different colored emojis represent different people in the couple/family system.

The emotion map relies on the use of physical space and emotions. As intercultural partners may have different ways of expressing their own emotion, and understanding the other partner's emotions, emotion maps are a useful way to explore events that have transpired at home, before the clinical assessment session. It also helps to understand each partner's understanding of what coupleness means (Gabb & Singh, 2015b).

Internalized other interviewing

This technique can assist therapists working with partners whose social locations, histories, and daily experiences significantly differ (Deacon & Davis, 2001; Tomm, 1999; Vasconcelos & Neto, 2003). It emerged from postmodern ideas about co-constructing realities and meanings and is useful in entering into a partner's culture (Paré, 2001) and engendering empathy and understanding between partners. The clinician asks one partner to speak to the other's experience as if he or she was the other partner, and then vice versa. The clinician starts by telling the couple that this exercise is not a test to see how accurate each partner is. Instead, it is a way for a partner to achieve an awareness of what life is like for his/her partner. For example, the therapist addresses the husband by his wife's name and asks him, "What is your experience of [husband's name]? Who is he as a person? If a complete understanding of him required 30 steps, how many steps have you taken to understand him and your relationship together?" When the therapist has finished asking questions of the internalized other, he or she may ask the partners to guess what percentage of the internalized other's answers matched or overlapped with the actual experience of the other partner. The goal is not to attain a perfect match, but to increase overlap over time between one partner's actual experience and the other partner's experience of the internalized other.

Ethnographic debriefing

Ethnographic interviews are another way of making therapy more sensitive to clients' experiences and perceptions (Langer & Furman, 2005; Wu, Enders, & Domokos-Cheng Ham, 1997). Via a periodic debriefing of clients, clinicians can learn what constitutes helpful, productive therapy through the clients' own words. Ethnographic interviews with clients' families provide a between-session mechanism to assist therapists in collecting their thoughts and access "multiple slices of reality," which can keep clinicians and supervisors in sync with client families (Cole & Mullaney, 1996). When clinicians are confused about what is happening in the therapy room or have limited previous experiences with a given population, clinicians and supervisors can acknowledge or admit their confusion and/or ignorance and choose to seek information from clients. This can result in a more sensitive therapy. Ethnographic debriefing provides space for partners in intercultural relationships to make explicit their concerns and goals, which may have gone unheard or may not have been clearly articulated in the therapy room, so that future sessions can be "more appropriate and on target" from their perspective (Cole & Mullaney, 1996).

Treatment

Victoria and Steve (see Note 1) came in for premarital therapy. Their conflicts centered on how Victoria felt like an outsider when they were with Steve's family and friends. Victoria is of dual heritage: her mother is Zimbabwean, and her father is English. She grew up in Zimbabwe and has lived in the United Kingdom since she was 15. Steve is White, middle class, and English. He was educated at an independent school, and his friends tend to be a homogeneous group with regard to culture and class.

Steve talked about how their home is their haven and how safe and comforted he feels with Victoria there. However, when they are with his family, Victoria's sense of being marginalized and the microaggressions that she experiences against her lead to growing tensions between the partners. Over the course of 12 sessions of systemic couple therapy, Steve learned how to protect Victoria from his family and friends and to ally himself more firmly with her when they were together outside the home. He was coached to speak to his parents alone and to encourage them to be more welcoming to Victoria.

Drawing on Falicov's ideas of separate cultural spaces (2014), Victoria and Steve realized that it was possible for Steve to sometimes visit his family and friends without Victoria. In addition, they developed a group of like-minded friends that they could both relate to. Through the interventions of a cultural genogram and internalized other interviewing, Steve was able to understand Victoria's identity issues and how she was positioned in racialized discourses.

From a self-reflexive position, I (RS) drew on my experiences of having experienced racism in my own interracial marriage. I appreciated the importance of Victoria needing Steve's protection and her sense that he was by her side. Based on my own experiences, I suggested that he indicate to Victoria, in a nonverbal manner (e.g., by looking at her or holding her hand) during an uncomfortable moment, that he was allied primarily with her, rather than his family and friends. Intercultural couple therapy thus offered Victoria and Steve a way of finding separate cultural spaces (Falicov, 2014), as well as safe ways of being together, in the outside world.

Intercultural couples experience both challenges and benefits at different stages of their relationship. It is therefore imperative that practitioners explore both these dynamics to strengthen their clients. Further, intercultural couples are influenced by internal and external contexts. It is therefore important for the practitioners to explore couples' experiences from both external and internal contexts. For example, internal contexts are related to the perceptions of one's identity from an individual, couple, child, family, and religious perspective. It is therefore recommended that practitioners make every effort to understand how couples locate their cultural differences, with the help of the assessment tools outlined in the previous section. External contexts relate to outside factors that impact on the relationship and parenting. For example, some of the external challenges impacting on couples relate to societal attitudes, including attitudes of friends and extended family members toward their relationship, difficulties encountered by and with children and extended family, and racism and exclusion toward all members of their family.

Internal and external domains of family dynamics can often be the source of stress that impact negatively on couples and parenting. Some of the significant stressors relate to (a) cultural differences among couples, such as language barriers, communication styles, parenting beliefs, values and practices, customs and traditions and socialization processes; (b) societal attitudes such as racism and disapproval; (c) power relations regarding language, gender, insider/outsider status; and (d) contextual influences such as extended families and the environment. It is therefore crucial for counselors/therapists to explore and identify those stressors and guide their clients accordingly to resolve these differences.

It is also noteworthy for practitioners to understand that some of the challenges intercultural couples and parents experience may also be experienced by non-intercultural couples and parents, such as concerns for safety, health, education, socialization processes, and power dynamics. Therefore, the provision of services and interventions needs to be balanced or measured between cultural needs and individual contextual needs, as opposed to the "intercultural" aspect only.

The implications for practice mentioned above align with a set of competencies recently adopted by the American Counseling Association (ACA, 2015) for clinical work with intercultural couples and multiracial families. The purpose of the ACA set of competencies is to serve as a resource and framework for how clinicians can competently provide services to members of the multicultural population. Counselors and the helping professionals working with multicultural population and requiring cultural competencies may find it valuable to draw on the set of competencies of the ACA model.

Some of the common therapeutic approaches that can be used in intercultural and mixed families' domains are:

- Narrative therapy (Kim, Prouty, & Roberson, 2012; Molina, Estrada, & Burnett, 2004)
- Cognitive-behavioral therapy (Beck, Rush, Shaw, & Emery, 1979)
- Solution-focused therapy (de Shazer et al., 1986)
- Strengths-based therapy (Bustamante, Nelson, Henriksen Jr., & Monakes, 2011)
- Emotionally focused therapy (EFT) (Greenberg & Johnson, 1988)

According to Molina et al. (2004), narrative therapy is conducive to the needs of intercultural clients. When using the narrative approach, counselors/therapists help clients to tell a story of their experiences, in order to have an understanding of the deeper meaning of their intercultural experiences, and also to make new meaning of the experiences (Molina et al., 2004). With intercultural couples, narrative therapy can be used to co-construct culturally inclusive narratives and to help the couple/family develop a shared and coherent multicultural identity.

When using the cognitive-behavioral therapy approach, counselors/therapists can help clients to identify unrealistic beliefs and expectations, negative perceptions, and subconscious negative thoughts about themselves and others in their environment (Beck et al., 1979). Therapists/counselors can use this approach to guide intercultural couples to build positive attributes about their intercultural perceptions and experiences. Reibstein and Sherbersky's (2012) Exeter model makes use of both cognitive-behavioral and systemic approaches to treat couples where one partner is depressed. It is more recently being adapted for clinical practice with intercultural couples (Reibstein & Singh, in press).

Solution-focused therapy, also known as solution-focused brief therapy, is an effective model that counselors/therapists can use to empower intercultural clients. De Shazer et al. (1986) described this approach as "utilizing what clients bring with them to help them meet their needs in such a way that they can make satisfactory lives for themselves" (p. 207). Solution-focused therapy falls under the social constructionism metatheory given that its philosophy and belief reinforce the fact that language is used to construct the reality of clients (Franklin, 1998). This approach has been used in previous studies of couple therapy, multiracial families, and immigrants (Cheung, 2005; Choi & Akdeniz, 2014; Fong & Urban, 2014).

EFT is a short-term form of therapy that focuses on adult relationships and attachment/bonding. The therapist and clients look at patterns in the relationship, and the therapist encourages couples to look at their current emotional issues and then help them discover feelings and emotions that they may not realize they have. EFT focuses on the present time to makes changes in the here and now. There are three steps in EFT: (a) The therapist helps to de-escalate the couple's or family member's negative cycle of interactions and help them see and understand what is happening in their relationship. (b) In restructure interactions, the therapist helps couples discuss their fears in the relationship. Clients learn to turn toward each other and discuss their needs and they become more open and responsive to each other. (c) In consolidation, the therapist helps clients see how they got into negative patterns and points out how they were able to change those patterns and can continue these types of conversations in the future (Greenberg & Goldman, 2008; Greenberg & Johnson, 1988).

Intercultural couples enjoy many benefits and opportunities in their relational experiences such as richness and best of both world for couples, parents, and children; cultural competency; holistic family life; other models of parenting; job opportunities for children; extended family supports; adaptability, tolerance, acceptance, and open-mindedness; and rich food culture, traditions, and customs. As such, counselors/therapists can rely on these aspects of benefits and opportunities as sources of strengths in the relationships to encourage and empower their clients and help them to change any negative thoughts about their experiences. Bratawidjaja's study (Bratawidjaja, 2007) showed evidence that cross-national couples could strive and survive in their relationship that can be used as useful information to encourage and empower clients.

Therapists using the strengths-based approach can guide and encourage couples to reflect on successful coping strategies they have used that helped their differences, thus offering them a sense of hope that their problems can be resolved. Bhugun's study (Bhugun, 2017a) showed that intercultural couples/parents used several approaches to cope with their relationship and parenting differences, such as communication, flexibility, openness to their partner's culture, respect and support for each other, and sometimes cultural deference where one partner defers to the other partner's culture. The strengths-based approach can be used to help intercultural couples/parents deal with challenges in a positive way.

Other specific therapeutic interventions include "particularizing the universal and universalizing the particular" (Killian, 2013). Killian employed the idea of "universalizing the particular" to demonstrate how an interaction between a couple can be linked to happenings in the wider sociopolitical context, for example, an argument over one parent's overprotectiveness in a dual heritage family can be related to recent media coverage of racist attacks in the family's neighborhood. On the other hand, generalizing statements such as "this is what White men are like" can be deconstructed and examined in the context of the couple's particular histories and beliefs.

Falicov (2014) encouraged intercultural couples to create separate cultural spaces. It is often helpful for intercultural couples to understand that they do not have to bring every aspect of their cultural and religious identities together and that it may be appropriate, for example, for one of them to visit the synagogue or mosque without the other (Singh, 2018). Nonverbal and representational methods used in assessment, such as the cultural genogram, emotion map, positioning lines, and internalized other interviewing, can also be used as part of the therapy process (Singh, 2017). Other techniques that are used with monocultural couples, such as the use of circular questions, teaching communication skills, enactments, the use of homework tasks, and building empathic bridges, are also used to good effect with intercultural couples.

How do we position ourselves as psychotherapists working with intercultural couples? Falicov (2014) suggested that the clinical encounter with an intercultural couple requires the clinician to be self-reflexive about their own culture and cultural values. One of our most important tools is the use of ourselves and self-reflexivity. While this is important in working with any couple, the system that is created when working with intercultural couples comprises the three cultures of the both partners and the therapist, thus increasing the possibilities for cultural alliances, splits, and misunderstandings.

The abovementioned theories can be used with couples, but counselors/therapists would find it particularly helpful to enrich and enhance their therapeutic approaches and provide more effective services to their clients by adopting some key strategies such as storytelling, reflecting on coping strategies, creating of cultural spaces, and exercising reflexivity, that is, setting aside their own bias and prior assumptions (Alvesson & Skoldberg, 2000; Bhugun, 2017b; Gabb & Singh, 2015b; Patton, 2002) about intercultural relationships and mixed families; promoting notions of adaptability, flexibility, tolerance, appreciation, acceptance, and open-mindedness; encouraging cultural literacy in the form of psychosocial education; and emphasizing the positives, benefits, and strengths of "interculturalness."

Implications for Policy

Intercultural couples/parents seem to have difficulty in explaining the "mixedness" of their relationship and that of their children in social contexts and official documents. While the adults in the relationship can at least relate their answers to their ethnic background, they describe that their children are often confused about which parent's ethnic group they belong to, even though they are born in the country they live in.

> According to Caballero et al. (2008), the inclusion of the "mixed" category in the 2001 UK census ethnic group question has been not only widely accepted but also influential in shaping other ethnic minority forms, as well as the visibility of a group of people who are labeled "mixed." On a general level, administrative categories are regarded as socially significant and have important consequences for perceptions of the state of the society (p. 55).

Although the notion of being "mixed" is not unproblematic, the argument here is that the standardized census categories cannot fully reflect the subtlety and complexity of the experiences of mixed families and people from mixed backgrounds. It is therefore important to include the "mixed" category in the international census, especially in countries that are becoming increasingly multicultural such as Australia, Canada, Germany, and the United States, to help researchers and policy makers obtain data to identify issues and develop strategies and programs that can effectively address mixed family issues.

The increase in intercultural marriages and relationships requires culturally appropriate service delivery. The following recommendations are noteworthy to enhance service delivery to this specific group of intercultural couples, parents, and families. First, universities and other educational institutions that provide marriage and relationship counseling courses should introduce special modules regarding cultural literacy that focus on intercultural relationships and families. Second, professional helping organizations need to be fully conversant with the cultural implications and needs of this specific intercultural phenomenon and population and provide education, information, and support services that are exclusive and appropriate to the needs of intercultural families. Third, organizations that provide services to this specific group of intercultural couples and parents seem to be too focused on cross-cultural competency as an organizational policy and standards of service. Cross-cultural competency is not an easy approach for the best results because of the enormity of global cultural values and beliefs. As such, cultural awareness and sensitivity are important approaches for consideration and implementation.

Studies in relation to intercultural parenting and relationships found significant mental health implications for immigrant families, especially regarding parenting (Papps, Walker, Trimboli, & Trimboli, 1995; Renzaho, 2011; Renzaho, McCabe, & Sainsbury, 2011; Sims & Omaji, 1999). State regulations regarding the welfare of children and disciplinary practices of parents largely ignore immigrants' and refugees' cultural concepts of parenting, which add additional stressors on immigrants, refugees, and intercultural families, particularly from Africa, the Middle East, and Asia. These immigrant parents are very confused and do not understand the state legislated Western influenced laws and policies regarding child protection and safety and the practice of having children removed from the family (Papps et al., 1995; Renzaho, 2011; Renzaho et al., 2011; Sims & Omaji, 1999). For example, in the State of Queensland, Australia, the Child Protection Act, 1999 Section 5C states additional principles for Aboriginal or Torres Strait Islander children: (a) the child should be allowed to develop and maintain a connection with the child's family, culture, traditions, language, and community, and (b) the long-term effect of a decision on the child's identity and connection with their family and community should be taken into account.

However, despite the fact that nearly 28% of the population of Australia are immigrants with different cultural beliefs and values about parenting, there are no additional principles for children and parenting for immigrants and refugees in the Child Protection Act. It is imperative that child protection services, nationally and state based, implement additional policies specific to immigrant and refugee parents and children regarding child safety. It is important for child safety workers to understand the cultural concepts of parenting and familiarize themselves with the needs and counseling issues of interracial and intercultural couples, parents, and families, especially the implications and needs of immigrants and refugee couples/parents. All government and nongovernment organizations globally need to implement policies with regard to educating professionals, students, supervisees, and service users about intercultural, interethnic, and interracial issues. It is also important for intercultural couples/parents and families to be considered for Focused Psychological Strategies healthcare plans under the Medicare Benefits Scheme of each country.

Conclusion

Intercultural relationships are a growing global phenomenon and therefore warrant special attention from practitioners. It is imperative that the helping professions show cultural sensitivity and respect when dealing with intercultural couples and families. Therapists/counselors would also benefit by challenging negative stereotypes and discourses of intercultural relationships as problematic from exploring, focusing on, and promoting the positive lived experiences as sources of strengths for their clients. This is well reflected in the following quote from a research participant as to what intercultural couples want to achieve in their relationships:

> *When you go into a relationship, you expect differences or obviously you like differences. So that's why you're together and so when differences come up you know as a couple or parent, you communicate, negotiate and you compromise.*

Notes

1   This vignette is based on one of the participant couples in Ugazio, Fellin, and Singh's (2017) research study. The participants in this study have provided informed consent for their story to be used in academic writing/publishing and for research and teaching purposes. Names and identifying details have been changed to protect confidentiality.
2   This vignette is inspired by actual cases but is a composite rather than an exact description. Though the dynamics described are close to the original situations, the details of the cases have been altered significantly to protect confidentiality and meet ethical guidelines.

References

Alvesson, M., & Skoldberg, K. (2000). *Reflexive methodology: New vista for qualitative research.* London, UK: Sage.

American Counseling Association. (2015). *Competencies for counseling the multiracial population: Multi-racial/ethnic counseling concerns (MRECC) interest network of the American counseling association taskforce.* USA: Author.

Bateson, G. (2000). *Steps to an ecology of mind.* Chicago: University of Chicago Press. (Original work published 1972)

Beck, A. T., Rush, A. J., Shaw, B. F., & Emery, G. (1979). *Cognitive therapy of depression.* New York, NY: Guilford Press.

Berlin, R., & Cannon, H. (2013). *Mixed blessings: A guide to multicultural and multiethnic relationships.* Seattle, WA: Mixed Blessings, LLC.

Bhugun, C. D. (2017a). *The experience of intercultural parenting in Australia (PhD Dissertation) Southern Cross University, Australia.*

Bhugun, D. (2016). *Intercultural parenting: A discussion of power relations and reverse acculturation.* IAFOR Proceedings of the Sixth Asian Conference for Cultural Studies 2016. Kobe, Japan.

Bhugun, D. (2017b). Intercultural parenting in Australia: Managing cultural differences. *The Family Journal: Counseling and Therapy for Couples and Families, 25*(2), 187–195.

Bhugun, D. (2017c). Parenting advice for intercultural couples: A systemic perspective. *Journal of Family Therapy, 39*(3), 454–477.

Bratawidjaja, A. (2007). *The experience of being parents of mixed-heritage children: Phenomenological analysis* (Unpublished doctoral dissertation). Kansas State University, Kansas.

Bratter, J. L., & King, R. B. (2008). "But will it last?" marital instability among interracial and same-race couples. *Family Relations, 57*(2), 160–171. doi:10.1111/j.1741-3729. 2008.00491

Burck, C. (2005). *Multilingual living: Explorations of subjectivity.* London, UK: Routledge.

Bustamante, R. M., Nelson, J. A., Henriksen, R. C., Jr., & Monakes, S. (2011). Intercultural couples: Coping with culture-related stressors. *The Family Journal: Counselling and Therapy for Couples and Families, 19*(2), 154–164. doi:10.1177/1066480711399723

Byng-Hall, J. (1985). The family script: A useful bridge between theory and practice. *Journal of Family Therapy, 7,* 301–305.

Caballero, C., Edwards, R., & Puthussery, S. (2008). *Parenting 'mixed' children: Negotiating difference and belonging in mixed race, ethnicity and faith families.* Joseph Rowntree Foundation. Retrieved from https://www.researchgate.net/profile/Chamion_Caballero/ publication/265537866_Parenting_'Mixed'_Children_Difference_and_Belonging_in_ Mixed_Race_and_Faith_Families/links/54b911660cf28faced626ac3.pdf

Cheung, S. (2005). Strategic and solution-focused couple therapy. In M. Harway (Ed.), *Handbook of couples therapy* (pp. 194–210). New York, NY: Wiley.

Child Protection Act. (1999). Queensland Government. Queensland. Australia.

Choi, J. J., & Akdeniz, R. (2014). Solution-focused approach with multicultural families. In J. S. Kim (Ed.), *Solution-focused brief therapy: A multicultural approach* (pp. 133–149). Denver, CO: Sage.

Cole, C. L., & Mullaney, T. J. (1996, November 7). *Using ethnographic interviews as a training technique.* Presentation at the annual meeting of the National Council on Family Relations, Kansas City.

Crippen, C. (2008). *Cross-cultural parenting: Experiences of intercultural parents and constructions of culturally diverse families* (Unpublished doctoral dissertation). Armidale, Australia: University of New England.

Crippen, C. (2011). *Working with intercultural couples and families: Exploring cultural dissonance to identify transformative opportunities.* Retrieved from https://www.counseling. org/resources/library/vistas/2011-V-Online/Article_21.pdf

de Shazer, S., Berg, I. K., Lipchik, E. V. E., Nunnally, E., Molnar, A., Gingerich, W., & Weiner-Davis, M. I. (1986). Brief therapy: Focused solution development. *Family Process, 25*(2), 207–221.

Deacon, S., & Davis, J. C. (2001). Internal family systems theory: A technical integration. *Journal of Systemic Therapies, 20,* 45–58.

Falicov, C. J. (1995). Cross-cultural marriages. In N. Jacobson & A. Gurman (Eds.), *Clinical handbook of couple therapy* (2nd ed., pp. 231–246). New York, NY: Guilford Press.

Falicov, C. J. (2014). *Latino families in therapy* (2nd ed.). New York, NY: Guilford Press.

Falicov, C. J. (2016). *Intercultural couples.* Plenary Presentation. European Family Therapy Association conference. Athens.

Fong, R., & Urban, B. (2014). Solution-focused approach with Asian immigrants. In J. S. Kim (Ed.), *Solution-focused brief therapy: A multicultural approach* (pp. 122–132). Los Angeles, CA: Sage.

Franklin, C. (1998). Distinctions between social constructionism and cognitive constructivism: Practice applications. In C. Franklin & P. Nurius (Eds.), *Constructivism in practice: Methods and challenges* (pp. 57–94). Milwaukee, WI: Families International Press.

Gabb, J., & Singh, R. (2015a). The uses of emotion maps in research and clinical practice with families and couples: Methodological innovation and critical inquiry. *Family Process, 54,* 185–197.

Gabb, J., & Singh, R. (2015b). Reflections on the challenges of understanding racial, cultural and sexual differences in couple relationship research. *Family Process, 37*(2), 210–227.

Garcia, D. R. (2006). Mixed marriages and transnational families in the intercultural context: A case study of African-Spanish couples in Catalonia. *Journal of Ethnic and Migration Studies, 32*(3), 403–433. doi:10.1080/13691830600555186

Greenberg, L. S., & Goldman, R. N. (2008). *Emotion-focused couples therapy: The dynamics of emotion, love, and power.* Washington, DC: American Psychological Association.

Greenberg, L. S., & Johnson, S. M. (1988). *Emotionally focused therapy for couples.* New York, NY: Guilford Press.

Hardy, K. V., & Laszloffy, T. (1995). The cultural genogram: Key to training culturally competent family therapists. *Journal of Marital and Family Therapy, 21,* 227–237.

Heller, P., & Wood, B. (2000). The influence of religious and ethnic differences on marital intimacy: Intermarriage versus intramarriage. *Journal of Marital and Family Therapy, 26,* 241–252.

Ho, M. K. (1990). *Intermarried couples in therapy.* Springfield, IL: Charles C. Thomas.

Hsu, J. (2001). Marital therapy for intercultural couples. In W. S. Tseng & J. Streltzer (Eds.), *Culture and psychology: A guide to clinical practice* (pp. 225–242). Washington, DC: American Psychiatric Publishing.

Irastorza, N., & Devoretz, D. (2009). *Factors affecting international marriage survival: A theoretical approach.* Retrieved from http://www.sfu.ca/~devoretz/lecturenotes/sem9.pdf

Keiley, M. K., Dolbin, M., Hill, J., Karuppaswamy, N., Liu, R., Poulsen, S., ... Robinson, P. (2002). The cultural genogram: Experiences from within a marriage and family therapy training program. *Journal of Marital and Family Therapy, 28,* 165–178.

Kenney, K., & Kenney, K. (2012). Contemporary multiple heritage couples, individuals and families: Issues, concerns, and counselling implications. *Counselling Psychology Quarterly, 25*(2), 99–112.

Killian, K. D. (2001a). Reconstituting racial histories and identities: The narratives of interracial couples. *Journal of Marital and Family Therapy, 27,* 23–37.

Killian, K. D. (2001b). Crossing borders: Race, gender and their intersections in interracial couples. *Journal of Feminist Family Therapy, 13,* 1–31.

Killian, K. D. (2003). Homogamy outlaws: Interracial couples' strategic responses to racism and partner differences. *Journal of Couple and Relationship Therapy, 2,* 3–21.

Killian, K. D. (2013). *Interracial couples, intimacy & therapy: Crossing racial borders.* New York, NY: Columbia University Press.

Killian, K. D. (2015). Couple therapy and intercultural relationships. In A. Gurman, J. Lebow, & D. Snyder (Eds.), *Clinical handbook for couple therapy* (5th ed., pp. 512–528). New York, NY: Guilford.

Kim, H., Prouty, A. M., & Roberson, P. N. E. (2012). Narrative therapy with intercultural couples: A case study. *Journal of Family Psychotherapy, 23*(4), 273–286.

Kim, Y., & Park, S. (2009). Reverse acculturation: A new cultural phenomenon examined through an emerging wedding practice of Korean Americans in the United States. *Family and Consumer Sciences Research Journal, 37*(3), 359–375. doi:10.1177/10777 27X08330758

Langer, C. L., & Furman, R. (2005). Beyond the ethnographic interview: The research poem as a tool for teaching culturally sensitive social work with native Americans. *Arete, 28,* 93–99.

Llerena-Quinn, R., & Bacigalupe, G. (2009). Constructions of difference among Latino/Latina immigrant and non-Hispanic white couples. In T. A. Karis & K. D. Killian (Eds.), *Intercultural couples. Exploring diversity in intimate relationships* (pp. 167–187). London, UK: Routledge.

Luke, C., & Carrington, V. (2000). Race matters. *Journal of Intercultural Studies, 21*(1), 5–24.

McFadden, J., & Moore, J. L., III (2001). Intercultural marriage and intimacy: Beyond the continental divide. *International Journal for the Advancement of Counselling, 23*, 261–268.

McGoldrick, M., Gerson, R., & Petry, S. (2008). *Genograms: Assessment and intervention* (3rd ed.). New York, NY: Norton.

Molina, B., Estrada, D., & Burnett, J. A. (2004). Cultural communities: Challenges and opportunities in the creation of "happily ever after" stories of intercultural couplehood. *The Family Journal: Counselling and Therapy for Couples and Families, 12*(2), 139–147.

Murphy, C. (2015, June 2). *Interfaith marriage is common in the US, particularly among the recently wed. Blog post.* Pew Research Centre Survey.

Owen, J. D. (2002). *Mixed matches: Interracial marriage in Australia.* Sydney, Australia: University of New South Wales Press.

Papadopoulos, R. K. (2002). Refugees, home and trauma. In R. K. Papadopoulos (Ed.), *Therapeutic care for refugees: No place like home* (pp. 9–39). London, UK: Karnac.

Papps, F., Walker, M., Trimboli, A., & Trimboli, C. (1995). Parental discipline in Anglo, Greek, Lebanese, and Vietnamese cultures. *Journal of Cross-Cultural Psychology, 26*(1), 49–64.

Paré, D. A. (2001). Crossing the divide: The therapeutic use of internalized other interviewing. *Journal of Activities in Psychotherapy Practice, 1*, 21–28.

Patton, M. Q. (2002). *Qualitative research and evaluation methods.* Thousand Oaks, CA: Sage.

Perel, E. (2000). A tourist's view of marriage: Cross-cultural couples—Challenges, choices, and implications for therapy. In P. Papp (Ed.), *Couples on the fault line: New directions for therapists* (pp. 187–198). New York, NY: Guilford.

Queer Voices. (2016, February 2). *Huffpost.* Retrieved June 21 2018 from https://www.huffingtonpost.com/2012/04/26/gay-couples-interracial-interethnic-2010-census_n_1456613.html

Reibstein, J., & Sherbersky, H. (2012). Behavioural and empathic elements of systemic couple therapy: The Exeter model and a case study of depression. *Journal of Family Therapy, 34*(3), 271–283.

Reibstein, J., & Singh, R. (2018). Systemic-behavioural connections for a divided world: The intercultural Exeter couples model. *BPS Psychotherapy Section Review: Special issue. Family and Couple Therapy*, 56–71.

Reibstein, J., & Singh, R. (in press). *The intercultural exeter model. An evidence—based practice for creating couple connections.* Oxford: Wiley.

Renzaho, A. M. N (2011). *Parenting in a new culture: A challenge for African migrant families.* Retrieved from www.deakin.edu.au/news/2011/260711africanmigrants.php

Renzaho, A. M. N., McCabe, M., & Sainsbury, W. J. (2011). Parenting, role reversals and the preservation of cultural values among Arabic speaking migrant families in Melbourne, Australia. *International Journal of Intercultural Relations, 35*(4), 416–424. doi:10.1016/j.ijintrel.2010.09.001Document

Romano, R. C. (2001). *Intercultural marriage: Promises and pitfalls.* Yarmouth, ME: Intercultural Press.

Seshadri, G., & Knudson-Martin, C. (2013). How couples manage interracial and intercultural differences: Implications for clinical practice. *Journal of Marital and Family Therapy, 39*(1), 43–58.

Sexton, J. C. (2002). *The politics of interracial sexuality in post–civil rights era U.S.* (Unpublished doctoral dissertation). University of California, Berkeley.

Sims, M. R., & Omaji, A. K. (1999). Migration and parenting: A pilot study. *Journal of Family Studies, 5*(1), 84–96.

Singh, R. (2014). *Love across border control.* Media Diversified.

Singh, R. (2017). Intimate strangers: Working with interfaith couples. Special issue on spirituality. *Australian and New Zealand Journal of Family Therapy, 38*(1), 7–14.

Singh, R. (2018). *Aporias of love and belonging.* Chapter in book based on conference in Malta on Couple Relationships in the 21st Century. Evolving Contexts and Emergent Meanings.

Singh, R., & Dutta, S. (2010). Working with intercultural couples. In R. Singh & S. Dutta (Eds.), *'Race' and culture. Tools, techniques and trainings. A handbook for professionals* (pp. 95–110). London, UK: Karnac.

Singla, R. (2015). *Intermarriage and mixed parenting, promoting mental health and wellbeing: Crossover love.* London, UK: Palgrave Macmillan.

Sullivan, C., & Cottone, R. R. (2006). Culture based couple therapy and intercultural relationships: A review of the literature. *The Family Journal, 14*(3), 221–225.

Tamura, T., & Lau, A. (1992). Connectedness versus separateness: Applicability of family therapy to Japanese families. *Family Process, 31*(4), 319–340.

Ting-Toomey, S. (1999). *Communicating across cultures.* New York, NY: Guilford.

Tomm, K. (1999). Co-constructing responsibility. In S. McNamee & K. J. Gergen (Eds.), *Relational responsibility: Resources for sustainable dialogue* (pp. 129–138). Thousand Oaks, CA: Sage.

Tseng, S.T. (2016). *How do intercultural couples perceive and deal with cultural differences in their relationship over time—A snapshot of three couples in Taiwan* (MSc dissertation) University of Bedfordshire, UK.

Twine, F. W., & Steinbugler, A. (2006). The gap between "whites" and "whiteness": Interracial intimacy and racial literacy. *DuBois Review: Social Science Research on Race, 3,* 341–363.

Ugazio, V. (2013). *Semantic polarities. Stories permitted and forbidden.* London, UK: Routledge.

Ugazio, V., & Castelli, D. (2015). The semantics grid of the therapeutic relationship. *Testing, Psychometrics, and Methodology in Applied Psychology, 22,* 135–159.

Ugazio, V., Fellin, L.C., & Singh, R. (2017). *Semantic cohesion in intercultural couples.* Ongoing research project at the London Intercultural Couples Centre, in conjunction with the Institute of Family Therapy, London.

United Nations Population Fund Report. (2000). *The state of the world population. Lives together, worlds apart. Men and women in a time of change.* New York, NY: United Nations.

Vasconcelos, J. Q. M., & Neto, L. (2003). The "internalized other" interview technique revisited. *Journal of Family Psychotherapy, 14,* 15–26.

Waldman, K., & Rubalcava, L. (2005). Psychotherapy with intercultural couples: A contemporary psychodynamic approach. *American Journal of Psychotherapy, 59*(3), 227–245.

Wu, S., Enders, L. E., & Domokos-Cheng Ham, M. A. (1997). Social constructionist inquiry in family therapy with Chinese Americans. *Journal of Family Social Work, 2,* 111–128.

Yancey, G., & Lewis, R. (2009). *Interracial families: Current concepts and controversies.* New York, NY: Routledge.

Australian Bureau of Statistics (2017, March). *Australian Demographics Statistics.* Canberra, Australia: Author.

Part III

Couple-Involved Therapies to Address Individual Disorders

8

Couple Interventions for Alcohol Use Disorders

Keith Klostermann and Timothy J. O'Farrell

Historically, substance use disorders have been considered personal problems, perhaps best captured in the long-held and often stated axiom among treatment providers: "Alcoholism and drug abuse are individual problems best treated on an individual basis." This viewpoint has held sway in the substance abuse treatment community for much of the last half century (Mann, 2000). Yet, nearly one-third of married individuals meet criteria for an alcohol use disorder at some point in their lifetime (Hassin, Stinson, Ogburn, & Grant, 2007), and relationship problems are linked to worsening alcohol problems (Chatav & Whisman, 2007; Wesley, 2016). More recently, staunch adherence to this individual-focused conceptualization of alcoholism and drug abuse has slowly given way to a greater acceptance and acknowledgment of the family's and significant other's critical role in the development and maintenance of drug and alcohol abuse. As a result, an increasing number of treatment providers and the programs in which they work are intervening with individuals' partners and families as a way to reduce or eliminate substance abuse by one or more of its members.

During the last three decades, the results of numerous clinical studies have demonstrated the efficacy of partner- and family-based treatment approaches for substance use disorders (O'Farrell & Fals-Stewart, 2006). Meta-analytic reviews of randomized clinical trials have concluded that partner- and family-involved treatments produce better outcomes across several domains of functioning (e.g., reduced substance use, improved marital and family functioning) compared with individual-based interventions that focus exclusively on the substance-abusing client (O'Farrell & Clements, 2012; O'Farrell & Fals-Stewart, 2001). In response to these findings, the Joint Commission on Accreditation of Health Care Organizations (JCAHO) standards for accrediting substance abuse treatment programs in the United States now requires that an adult family member, who lives with an identified substance-abusing patient, be included at minimum, in the initial assessment of the treatment process (Brown, O'Farrell, Maisto, Boies, & Suchinsky, 1997).

Enthusiasm for understanding the role significant others and family members may play in the development, maintenance, and treatment of alcoholism and drug abuse has not been limited to researchers or even the broader professional com-

The Handbook of Systemic Family Therapy: Volume 3, First Edition.
Edited by Karen S. Wampler and Adrian J. Blow.
© 2020 John Wiley & Sons Ltd. Published 2020 by John Wiley & Sons Ltd.

munity; the sheer volume of texts, which have appeared on the topics of code-pendency, adult children of alcoholics, addictive personality, enabling, and so forth, is voluminous. For example, an Internet search of a large online book retailer revealed that over 400 books were available presently for purchase on the topic of codependency alone. Moreover, self-help support groups for family members of alcoholics and drug abusers (e.g., Al-Anon) are present in virtually every community in the United States and in many communities around the world. Because relationship problems and substance use disorders so frequently co-occur, it would be very difficult to find clinicians who specialize in the treatment of substance use disorders or relationship problems that have not had to address both sets of issues concurrently (either with the client individually or in the context of client's relationships).

The purpose of this chapter is to (a) discuss how substance abuse affects one's significant relationships (e.g., romantic and familial) and how providers can draw on fundamental principles of couple and family therapy to improve interactions among members; (b) discuss various partner- and family-involved approaches for substance use that focus on prevention, initiation of change, and active treatment; (c) present the models and goals of couple and family therapy that have been used with substance-abusing clients, their partners, and extended family members; and (d) explore possible future directions with respect to partner- and family-involved therapies with substance-abusing clients.

Substance Use and Relationship Functioning: Practical and Conceptual Considerations

Types of couple-based interventions

Wesley (2016) identified three paradigms for conceptualizing couple interventions: (a) partner-assisted, (b) disorder specific, and (c) couple therapy. Each of these approaches focuses on specific changes that are needed to address an area of concern (e.g., substance misuse) while also considering the couple relationship as an important context for manifestation of symptoms. Partner-assisted interventions focus on the client's behavior change goals and the ways in which a partner can assist in this process, given the relationship can potentially serve as a powerful resource in this process (Baucom, Whisman, & Paprocki, 2012). From this vantage, the partner serves as a coach in helping the client make identified changes, especially in between sessions. Disorder-specific interventions focus on creating change in the couple relationship, but only in areas specifically related to the individual disorder (Baucom et al., 2012). As an example, the relationship may serve as a stressor or trigger for relapse. Couple therapy focuses on ameliorating relationship dysfunction across a number of domains. In cases of substance use disorders, an individual's substance use disorder can become a primary source of relationship difficulty for both partners as these issues often serve as triggers and exacerbate substance use; reduction of relationship distress can positively influence substance use (Wesley, 2016). Given the extensive support for couple therapy in treating substance use disorders, this specific type of intervention is described in detail in this chapter.

Prevalence of substance use disorders and comorbidity with relationship problems

Previous studies support the assertion that substance abuse and family problems very often coexist. For example, Klostermann, Kelley, Mignone, Pusateri, and Wills, (2011) contend that levels of relationship distress among alcohol- and drug-abusing dyads, including instability, conflict, sexual dissatisfaction, and psychological distress, are typically high and these couples are more likely to divorce (Lebow, 2005) compared with the general population. Moreover, relationship dysfunction has been found to be predictive of worse prognosis in alcohol and drug abuse treatment (Lemke, Brennan, & Schutte, 2007), and poor response to substance abuse treatment seems to be predictive of ongoing marital difficulty (e.g., Billings & Moos, 1983; Collins, Ellickson, & Klein, 2007).

Substance abuse issues within an intimate relationship are unique to each couple with partners often disagreeing about the extent of alcohol or drug use as well as the related consequences (Morrissette, 2010). The extent of these disagreements may extend beyond these areas and have implications for parenting practices and, by extension, the psychosocial adjustment of children living in these homes (Klostermann & Kelley, 2009). Excessive substance use often has a deleterious impact on intimacy within the relationship and over time results in emotional detachment characterized by distrust, unhappiness, and disappointment (Morrissette, 2010).

Unfortunately, as the individual's substance problem progresses, he or she may become increasingly isolated from other family members, which may make it difficult to engage them later in the treatment process (Halford & Osgarby, 1993). Relatedly, other family members may experience a wide array of emotions (e.g., anger, guilt, fear, embarrassment) as a result of the patient's drinking or drug use and, consequently, reduce or eliminate contact altogether with the substance-abusing person (Collins et al., 2007). In other cases, family members may try to help/rescue the patient initially. The therapeutic implications of this type of isolation are mixed; while some family approaches might consider this type of avoidance to be appropriate and therapeutic, other models might view this behavior as corrosive.

The interplay between substance use and relationship maladjustment

The interconnection between substance use and relationship distress appears to be marked by what can be best described as "reciprocal causality." Alcoholism and drug abuse by an individual appear to contribute causally to the many relationship problems observed in their relational units. Relationships characterized by substance abuse may experience high levels of relationship dissatisfaction, instability, conflict, sexual dissatisfaction, or psychological distress. A number of studies have also found that relationship dysfunction is strongly linked to substance use and appears to be a major contributing factor to relapse among alcoholics and drug abusers after treatment (e.g., Epstein & McCrady, 1998; Halford & Osgarby, 1993; Lemke et al., 2007). Thus, the link between substance use and relationship problems is not unidirectional, with one consistently causing the other, but rather each can serve as a precursor to the other, creating a "vicious cycle" from which couples that include a partner who abuses drugs or alcohol often have difficulty escaping (O'Farrell & Fals-Stewart, 2006).

There are several relational environmental antecedent conditions and reinforcing consequences of substance use. In particular, couple and family problems (e.g., poor communication and problem solving, arguing, financial stressors) often serve as both precursors to and consequences of excessive drinking or drug use (Klostermann, 2006). Unfortunately, the resulting family or partner response may have an unintended effect and inadvertently facilitate continued drinking or drug use once these problematic behaviors have developed. For example, substance abuse often provides more subtle adaptive consequences for the family members, such as eliciting the expression of emotion and affection (e.g., caretaking when a parent or partner is suffering from a hangover; Klostermann & Fals-Stewart, 2008). Moreover, even when recovery from the alcohol or drug problem has begun, marital and family conflicts can, and very often do, precipitate relapses (Halford & Osgarby, 1993; Rotunda, West, & O'Farrell, 2004).

Although the misuse of alcohol and other psychoactive substances by adults often has serious physical, emotional, behavioral, and economic consequences, the short- and long-term negative effects on those who live with these adults are often no less destructive or traumatic (Kelley et al., 2010). Stress and negative affect, which are comparatively high in families with an alcoholic family member, are associated with increased alcohol use in adolescents (Chassin, Curran, Hussong, & Colder, 1996). Thus, it appears that alcohol-abusing parents are less likely than nonalcoholic parents to monitor what their children are doing, which, in turn, may lead to unhealthy associations of their adolescent children with substance-using peers (Connors, Donovan, & DiClemente, 2004).

The strong interrelationship between substance use and relationship interaction suggests interventions that treat the dyadic or larger family systems (versus an exclusive focus on the substance-abusing patient) hold much promise for being effective. Although couple and family therapy approaches take many different forms, they share two overarching objectives that evolve from a recognition of the nature and degree of interrelationship between substance use and family member interaction: (a) harness the power of the family and/or dyadic system to positively support the patient's efforts to eliminate abusive drinking and drug use and, relatedly, (b) alter dyadic and family interaction patterns to promote an environment in the home that is conducive to long-term stable abstinence for the substance-abusing individual.

Intervention Approaches

Given the finding that marital and family treatments have been shown to be clinically effective for a variety of health problems (Goorden et al., 2016), many different marital and family therapy approaches have been developed (or at least modified) for use with substance-abusing patients including strategic family therapy, structural family therapy, cognitive-behavioral family therapy, behavioral couple therapy (BCT), and solution-focused family therapy. Of these, three theoretical perspectives have come to dominate family-based conceptualizations and are thus viewed as the foundation for the family-based treatment strategies most often used with substance-abusing clients: (a) family disease approach, (b) family systems perspective, and (c) behavioral models (Gondoli & Jacob, 1990). Each of these frameworks is briefly reviewed below.

Family disease approach

The best known and most widely used paradigm is the *family disease approach*. From this vantage, alcoholism and other drug abuse are viewed as an illness of the entire family, suffered not only by the substance user but also by the other family members. Consequently, as the term implies, alcoholism and drug abuse are thought of or viewed as a "family disease," which affects all (or nearly all) family members. In fact, adult and child family members of substance abusers often experience medical and psychiatric disorders at a higher rate than the general public (Ray, Mertens, & Weisner, 2007). In particular, family members of substance users are viewed as suffering from the disease of "codependence," which describes the process underlying the various problems observed in the families of individuals who abuse psychoactive substances. Schaef (1986) argues that codependence is a disease that parallels the addiction disease process and is marked by characteristic family symptoms such as external referencing, caretaking, self-centeredness, control issues, dishonesty, frozen feelings, perfectionism, and fear. The cornerstone of codependency theory is enabling, which, as the term implies, is described as any set of behaviors that perpetuate the psychoactive substance use (Koffinke, 1991) and may include activities such as making it easier for the alcoholic or drug abuser to engage in substance use or shielding the substance user from the negative consequences often resulting from substance misuse. However, there is much debate about the use of this term with definitions ranging from its use as a shorthand label for affected family members to it being perceived as a personality disorder that some have argued should be included in the American Psychiatric Association's Diagnostic and Statistical Manual (Kinney, 2009).

Given that the family disease model argues the entire family unit is believed to be sick, the solution is for each family member to recognize that he or she has a disease, to detach from the substance user, and to engage in his or her own program of recovery (e.g., Al-Anon, Alateen, or Adult Children of Alcoholics groups).

Family systems approach

The family systems model views the misuse of alcohol or other drugs as a major organizing principle for patterns of interactional behavior within the family system that acts to stabilize the system (Lipps, 1999). A reciprocal relationship exists between family functioning and substance use, with an individual's drug and alcohol use being best understood in the context of the entire family's functioning. According to family systems theory, substance abuse in either adults or adolescents often evolves during periods in which the individual family member is having difficulty addressing an important developmental issue (e.g., leaving the home) or when the family is facing a significant crisis (e.g., job loss, marital discord). During these periods, substance abuse can serve to (a) distract family members from their central problem, or (b) slow down or stop a transition to a different developmental stage that is being resisted by the family as a whole or by one of its members (Stanton, Todd, & Associates, 1982).

From the family systems perspective, substance use represents an unhealthy attempt to manage difficulties, which over time become homeostatic and regulate family transactions. Because the substance use serves an important function, the therapist seeks to understand its role in the family, explaining how the behavior has come about, and the purpose it serves. Thus, the primary objective of treatment involves restructuring the interaction patterns associated with the substance use, thereby making the drinking or drug use unnecessary in maintaining healthier systemic functioning (O'Farrell & Murphy, 1995).

Behavioral approach

Behavioral family therapy models are heavily influenced by operant and social learning theories in their conceptualization of the substance user within the family context. Simply stated, behavioral approaches assume that family interactions serve to reinforce alcohol- and drug-using behaviors. From this vantage, substance-using behavior is learned in the context of social interactions (e.g., observing peers, parents, role models in the media) and reinforced by contingencies in the individual's environment. Thus, from a behavioral perspective, substance use is maintained, in part, from the antecedents and consequences that are operating in the family environment. Three general reinforcement patterns are typically observed in substance-abusing systems: (a) reinforcement for substance-using behavior in the form of attention or caretaking, (b) shielding the substance user from experiencing negative consequences related to his or her drinking or drug use, and (c) punishing drinking behavior (e.g., McCrady, 1986).

Consistent with the tenants of operant and social learning approaches, treatment emphasizes contingency management designed to reward sobriety, reduce negative reinforcement of drinking or drug use, and increase prosocial behaviors that may be incompatible with substance use. More specifically, the substance user and involved family members are taught techniques to increase positive interactions, to improve problem solving, and to enhance communication skills. Behaviorists believe that the use of these newly developed skills serves to reduce the likelihood of continued drinking or drug use by the substance-using family member.

Integrated treatment approaches for substance abuse and families

A large number of intervention approaches that integrate treatment for substance abuse and the family have been discussed in the empirical and clinical literatures including, but not limited to, structural/strategic family therapy, multidimensional family therapy, behavioral and cognitive-behavioral family therapy, and solution-focused brief therapy. Some models may be perceived as minor variants of other more established approaches, but many would argue that these nuanced differences may be perceived as more palatable by clients, thereby improving engagement (and retention), and strongly influence treatment response and outcomes for a given client and his or her relational unit.

Regardless of the model under consideration, it is helpful to understand the overarching therapeutic goals from the stance of levels of recovery (e.g., Heath & Stanton, 1998), which can be utilized within a couple's therapy model as well. These goals are as follows:

- **Attainment of sobriety.** The dyad has elements and components that are dysfunctional, but healthy change is possible.
- **Adjustment to sobriety.** The relational system is reorganized and incorporates new healthful behaviors by the substance-abusing client and other romantic partners and family members.
- **Long-term maintenance.** The couple supports and maintains a healthy lifestyle conducive to sobriety that does not incorporate drinking or drug use.

Behavioral Couple Therapy

Why BCT?

Previous research has found that including the partner is a powerful predictor of successful treatment (Heinz, Wu, Witkiewitz, Epstein, & Preston, 2009). A marital approach that has received extensive empirical support for the treatment of alcoholism and substance abuse is BCT (Emmelkamp & Vedel, 2006), which has also been referred to as behavioral marital therapy and learning sobriety together. During the last three decades, couple therapy for substance abuse has received extensive empirical scrutiny, with most research focusing on BCT. BCT has its origins in the Counseling for Alcoholics' Marriages (CALM) project, which was developed in the 1980s and served as one of the first manualized behavioral treatments. In general, these studies have compared BCT with some form of traditional individual-based treatment for substance abuse (e.g., coping skills therapy, 12-step facilitation). Results of studies consistently found that participants receiving BCT experienced higher rates of abstinence and fewer drug- or alcohol-related problems (e.g., Epstein, McCrady, & Morgan, 2007; Walitzer & Derman, 2004), had happier relationships (Emmelkamp & Vedel, 2006), and experienced a lower risk of relationship dissolution (e.g., separation, divorce; see Powers, Vedel, & Emmelkamp, 2008) compared with those in the individual treatment condition.

Primary BCT treatment elements

In the early stages of treatment, therapists attempt to shift the focus from negative feelings and interactions about past and possible future substance use to positive behavioral exchanges between partners. In later sessions, emphasis is placed on communication skills training, problem-solving strategies, negotiating behavior change agreements, and continuing recovery strategies. In general, there is an assumption that if couples are happier and can improve communication, there will be a lower chance of relapse (O'Farrell & Clements, 2012).

When using BCT as part of a general intervention package, a therapist treats the substance-abusing patient and his or her intimate partner with the goal of building support for abstinence from within the dyadic system. With the help of the therapist, the partners develop a "recovery contract" or "sobriety contract," in which the couple agrees to engage in a daily "sobriety trust discussion." In this brief exchange, the substance-abusing partner states his or her intent not to drink or use drugs that day. In turn, the partner verbally expresses positive support for the patient's efforts to remain sober. For substance-abusing patients who are medically cleared and willing, daily ingestion of medications designed to support abstinence (e.g., naltrexone, Antabuse), witnessed and verbally reinforced by the patient's partner, may also be included as part of the sobriety trust discussion. The patient's partner tracks each time the sobriety trust discussion is completed on a daily calendar provided by the therapist and is asked to bring it to each session. Ultimately, the purpose of this ritual is to begin the process of restoring trust between partners. In particular, by the time many couples decide to enter couple treatment, the relationship may be characterized by a lack of trust as a result of the substance abuser's lies, deceit, and manipulation regarding the extent of alcohol or drug use.

Importantly, as a condition of the recovery contract, both partners agree not to discuss past drinking or drug use or fears of future substance use when at home (i.e., between scheduled couple therapy sessions) over the course of couple treatment. Instead, partners are asked to reserve such potentially emotionally charged discussions for their weekly couple therapy sessions, which can then be monitored and, if needed, mediated by the therapist. Many contracts also include specific provisions for sober support activities including partners' regular attendance at self-help meetings (e.g., Alcoholics Anonymous, Al-Anon) and community activities (e.g., church groups), which are also marked on a calendar provided during the course of treatment.

At the start of a typical BCT session, the therapist reviews the recovery calendar to ascertain overall compliance with the different aspects of the contract. The calendar provides an ongoing record of progress that is reviewed by the therapist and clients at each session and provides a visual (and temporal) record of problems with adherence to home practice assignments that can be addressed by the therapist and couple. For couples who have difficulty maintaining the calendar, the therapist works with the partners to identify potential barriers as well as strategies that may be implemented to overcome any obstacles. In an effort to ensure the between-session activities are performed correctly, each session, the therapist asks the couple to perform the previously assigned tasks and abstinence trust discussion and provides corrective feedback as needed. This in-session modeling is critical in that if couples are incorrectly performing the assigned tasks (e.g., including a negative component to the abstinence trust discussion), it may diminish one or both partner's enthusiasm or willingness to perform the assigned tasks and reduce the likelihood of weekly progress and, ultimately, goal attainment.

BCT methods used to enhance relationship functioning

In addition to eliminating substance use, BCT also seeks to concurrently improve relationship functioning through the use of standard couple-based behavioral assignments, which are aimed at increasing positive feelings, increasing the number of shared activities, and improving communication; these relationship enhancement factors are viewed as conducive to sobriety. In the *Catch Your Partner Doing Something Nice* (Turner, 1972) activity, each partner is asked to notice and acknowledge one pleasing behavior performed by the other each day. The *Caring Day* assignment (e.g., Liberman, Wheeler, deVisser, Kuehnel, & Kuehnel, 1980) asks each partner to surprise their significant other with a day of special things that show care for their partner, a specific activity the partner will enjoy and not vice versa. Planning and engaging in mutually agreed-upon *Shared Rewarding Activities* (e.g., O'Farrell & Cutter, 1984) is believed to be important because years of alcohol and drug abuse may have resulted in the cessation of conjoint shared, pleasing activities. Thus, this activity must involve both partners, either as a dyad or with their children or other adults, and can be performed at or away from home. Teaching *Communication Skills* (e.g., Gottman, Notarius, Gonso, & Markman, 1976) such as paraphrasing, empathizing, and validating can help the substance-abusing patient and his or her partner better address stressors in the relationship and in their lives as they arise, which also is viewed as reducing the risk of relapses. Fals-Stewart and O'Farrell (2003) completed a study of behavioral family contracting (BFC), a variant of BCT allowing for inclusion of other family members other than just spouses, in opioid-dependent patients. Results showed that those assigned to the BFC plus individual treatment ingested more doses of naltrexone, attended more treatment sessions, and remained abstinent longer in the one-year follow-up.

Couple-based relapse prevention and planning

Relapse prevention (RP) occurs during the final stages of BCT. More specifically, the partners are asked to develop a written plan (i.e., *Continuing Recovery Plan*) designed to promote stable abstinence (e.g., continuation of a daily abstinence trust discussion, attending self-help support meetings) and list contingency plans in the event a relapse occurs (e.g., contacting the therapist, reengaging in self-help support meetings, contacting a sponsor; Klostermann & Fals-Stewart, 2008). A key element for many couples in creating the Continuing Recovery Plan is the negotiation of the posttreatment duration of the skills and techniques learned during treatment. Couples often have difficulty agreeing upon a timeframe for the cessation of the contract activities. Upon completion of BCT, the substance-abusing partner typically wants a life that does not involve structured exercises, whereas the non-substance-abusing partner is often apprehensive and mistrustful about progress made in treatment (i.e., relationship improvement, abstinence) and thus advocates for continued involvement with certain activities (e.g., self-help meeting attendance, abstinence trust discussions). As an example, the substance-abusing partner may express a desire to forgo the daily abstinence trust discussion since treatment is over and he or she has been sober and feels confident about the progress made in treatment. In this situation, partners develop a mutually agreed-to, long-term gradual reduction of the frequency of the activity until it is eliminated (e.g., for the first month, the couple performs the daily abstinence trust discussion, as was done during active treatment; for the second month, the abstinence trust discussion is performed three times per week; for the third month, the abstinence trust discussion is performed once per week; etc.). If problems arise with any of the planned transitions, partners are encouraged to contact their BCT counselor to discuss the best way to proceed.

Session structure and treatment duration

BCT sessions tend to be moderately to highly structured consisting of three main components: (a) review/check-in on previous weeks' substance use (if any), relationship issues, and compliance with home practice assigned the previous week; (b) introduction of new material; and (c) assignment of home practice. For example, a typical BCT session begins with an update on any drinking or drug use that has occurred since the last session. Compliance with different aspects of the recovery contract is reviewed, and any difficulties completing the agreed-upon tasks are discussed and addressed. Relationship or other difficulties that may have arisen during the last week are then addressed during the session, with the goal being problem resolution. The session then transitions to a review of any homework from the previous session. Next, new material is introduced and modeled by the therapist; clients are then asked to rehearse these skills in session since they will be assigned as home practice between sessions. At the end of each session, partners are given specific homework assignments to complete before the next scheduled session.

Traditionally, the substance-abusing patient and his or her partner are seen together in BCT, typically for 15–20 outpatient couple sessions over 5–6 months. Appropriate candidates for BCT are (a) couples in which partners are married or cohabiting for at least one year; (b) couples in which neither partner has a co-occurring psychiatric condition that may significantly interfere with participation in BCT (e.g., schizophrenia, psychosis); and (c) dyads in which only one member of the couple has a current problem with alcoholism or drug abuse. In those cases in which the identified patient is unwilling to engage in treatment, unilateral family therapy (UFT) may be an effective alternative. In UFT, the therapist works exclusively with the non-substance-using partner in helping to engage the identified client into treatment (Edwards & Steinglass, 1995).

During the last three decades, couple therapy for substance abuse has received extensive empirical scrutiny, with most research focusing on BCT. In general, these studies have compared BCT with some form of traditional individual-based treatment for substance abuse (e.g., coping skills therapy, 12-step facilitation). Findings from these studies have been consistent; compared with those who receive individual treatment, those participants assigned to receive BCT (a) experience higher rates of abstinence and fewer drug- or alcohol-related problems (e.g., Epstein et al., 2007; Walitzer & Derman, 2004), (b) have happier relationships (Emmelkamp & Vedel, 2006), and (c) experience a lower risk of relationship dissolution (e.g., separation, divorce; see Powers et al., 2008).

The O'Farrell BCT model has since been modified to address more specific issues such as acceptance and change. One such modification has resulted in alcohol-focused behavioral couple therapy (ABCT), which is geared toward intervening at both a relationship and alcohol abuse level (McCrady et al., 2016). It combines various aspects of BCT discussed above, with specific elements to address drinking, partner coping, and relationship enhancement (refer to McCrady & Epstein, 2015, for a more detailed description of treatment elements and structure). Interventions such as these speak to the importance of assisting both the individual with a substance abuse problem and their partner for sustainable change.

In an effort to better meet the diverse needs of clients and their partners, the standard BCT model has evolved into several offshoot approaches in the general psychotherapy treatment arena. These variations include enhanced cognitive-behavioral therapy (ECBT), self-regulatory couple therapy (SRCT), and integrative behavioral couple therapy (IBCT) (Kelly & Iwamasa, 2005). Each of these approaches is built upon the BCT framework but possesses characteristics that distinguish them from the standard model as well as each other. For example, in ECBT, focus is on partners' selective attention to mates' behavior, problematic expectancies, and implicit and explicit assumptions about intimate relationships. ECBT is a more comprehensive approach by attending to the interactions couples have with extended family and the community along with assessing relational stressors that occur outside the couple itself (Gurman, 2013). The goal of SRCT is to help each partner identify ways to alter his or her own thinking and behavior in the hope of increasing relationship satisfaction (Halford, 1998). Couples in IBCT focus on acceptance of differences with partners approaching and even embracing these. Such a behavioral change reveals a shift in the function and context of partners' behavior (Gurman, 2013). The emphasis in each of these variant approaches is different; the one commonality across all three is the importance of individual accountability and change rather than changing couple interactions (Kelly & Iwamasa, 2005).

Research Findings on BCT

Primary outcomes: effects on substance use and relationship adjustment

Couple therapy for treating alcohol and drug abuse has received extensive empirical scrutiny, with most research focusing on BCT. O'Farrell, Cutter, and Floyd (1985) randomly assigned male alcoholics and their female partners to alcoholism counseling (e.g., 12-step facilitation, disulfiram encouragement), alcoholism counseling plus interactional couple group therapy, or alcoholism counseling plus BCT. While participants in the BCT condition reported relationship benefits during the two-year follow-up, men in all conditions improved significantly as indicated by the number of nondrinking days. McCrady et al. (1986) examined the impact of spouse involvement in behavioral interventions for alcoholism. More specifically, this study compared minimal spouse involvement (MSI), alcohol-focused spouse intervention (AFSI), or BCT in a sample of 37 alcohol-abusing patients and their partners. Findings revealed that BCT was superior to AFSI and MSI in reducing alcohol use and increasing relationship satisfaction at posttreatment and during the 18-month follow-up phase of the study. In a sample of problem drinkers, Walitzer and Derman (2004) compared individual therapy, cognitive-behavioral treatment (CBT), AFSI, and BCT. Although participants in both the BCT and AFSI conditions outperformed those assigned to the CBT condition in terms of drinking outcomes at posttreatment and follow-up, BCT did not produce significantly better relationship satisfaction than AFSI. Furthermore, Vedel, Emmelkamp, and Schippers (2008) enrolled 64 alcohol-disorder patients (male and female) and their partners in BCT or CBT. While drinking outcomes were similar at posttreatment for clients in each condition, participants in the BCT condition reported greater relationship satisfaction. Importantly, improvements in specific objectives of BCT (i.e., positive communication, shared activities, and negotiation of agreements) have been positively correlated with marital satisfaction in couples taking part in BCT. More recently, O'Farrell and Clements (2012) and Rowe (2012) cited meta-analyses and reviews that showed the long-term effectiveness and improvement of relationship functioning with partners who took part in BCT. Meis et al. (2013) published a systematic review of RCTs from 1996 to 2011, which included the examination of adult couple/family intervention for SUD. The review looked at 11 pooled trials comparing BCT and in one study BFT with individualized treatment, specifically follow-up outcomes at posttreatment points. Significant differences at all points were found in favor of BCT/BFT with effect sizes in the 0.46–0.47 range. Furthermore, the 10 trials examining BCT all found slower rates of relapse or slower rates of increase on heavy drinking days. Overall, the systematic review emphasized that intervention effects held up for a longer period of time following BCT versus individual therapy (Stanton, 2015).

Collectively, research has shown that BCT results in equal or great likelihood of client abstinence. Moreover, with few exceptions (see Walitzer & Derman, 2004), BCT has been shown to result in superior outcomes in terms of relationship functioning.

BCT with female substance-abusing clients

Dyadic conflict and relationship stress may have particularly strong links to problematic abuse and relapse for women. For instance, Green, Pugh, McCrady, and Epstein (2008) found that 47% of alcohol-abusing women in substance abuse treatment indicated marital situations (e.g., an argument with her partner) as reasons for drinking. Similarly, Lemke et al. (2007) found that family problems and emotional distress were linked to relapse for alcohol-abusing women. Moreover, in a study of 102 women and their partners, Graff et al. (2009) found that women's attendance at therapy sessions was linked with relationship satisfaction—the greater the satisfaction, the more likely they were to attend. Because relationship factors appear to play a critical role in the maintenance and exacerbation of substance abuse for women, interventions such as BCT, which are specifically designed to address both relationship issues and substance abuse issues concurrently, would seem likely to have particular benefits for substance-abusing women.

In a recent study by McCrady, Epstein, Cook, Jensen, and Hildebrandt (2009), BCT for alcohol use disorders (ABCT) was more effective than individual therapy for alcohol use disorders (ABIT) regarding percentage of days abstinent (PDA) and percentage of days of heavy drinking (PHD). In addition, women with poorer baseline relationship functioning showed greater improvement on PDA during treatment with ABCT than with ABIT. Women with better baseline relationship functioning showed greater improvement during and after treatment on PDH as compared with those who participated in ABIT. ABCT also showed greater benefit for women who had associated Axis I and Axis II disorders (McCrady et al., 2009). A recent study compared IBT with BCT for women with AUDs. BCT had better outcomes, for example, greater abstinence from alcohol and other drugs, and had fewer substance-related problems during most of the follow-up period (Schumm, O'Farrell, Kahler, Murphy, & Muchowski, 2014).

BCT for gay and lesbian couples

Studies consistently report higher drug and alcohol use among lesbian, gay, bisexual, and transgender (LGBT) women (Cochran & Mays, 2009; McCabe, Hughes, Bostwick, West, & Boyd, 2009). For instance, McCabe et al. (2009) found that compared with heterosexual women, LGBT women had greater odds for past-year substance abuse and dependence. These results, based on a national sample, are consistent with findings based on California (Cochran & Mays, 2007) and New York (Meyer, Schwartz, & Frost, 2008) samples. Moreover, other factors that may need to be considered for sexual minorities are sexual minority stress, social and community support/isolation, internalized homophobia, and concealment. More specifically, it may be the case that many LGBT couples do not obtain treatment because they are not out/experience high-internalized homophobia, they fear additional discrimination, they may be unable to obtain insurance via their partners, and so forth. Unfortunately, systematic examinations of LGBT individuals treated with BCT are lacking. Clearly, this is an important area for future investigation.

Intimate partner violence

The results of multiple studies suggest that roughly two-thirds of the married or cohabiting men entering treatment for alcoholism, or their partners, report at least one episode of male-to-female physical aggression in the year prior to program entry. Estimates of physical aggression among men entering substance abuse programs are four times higher than IPV prevalence estimates from nationally representative surveys (e.g., O'Farrell & Murphy, 1995). Mignone, Klostermann, and Chen (2009) found that the likelihood of male-to-female physical aggression was nearly eight times higher on days of drinking than on days of no drinking for married or cohabiting men after completing alcoholism treatment. Kaufmann, O'Farrell, Murphy, Murphy, and Muchowski (2014) tested the hypothesis that alcohol consumption is a risk factor for partner violence with a within-subject analysis, which compared levels of alcohol consumption in violent versus nonviolent conflict events among substance-abusing women and their male partners. Results showed alcohol consumption was greater prior to violent versus nonviolent conflict. Use of drugs in women, but not men, was more likely prior to violent events. A preliminary study revealed that BCT has been associated with a 60% reduction of IPV prevalence and frequency among alcohol- and drug-abusing men and their non-substance-abusing female partners during the year after treatment compared with baseline levels (O'Farrell, Murphy, Stephan, Fals-Stewart, & Murphy, 2004).

Cost Outcomes

O'Farrell, Choquette, Cutter, and Floyd et al. (1996) presented cost outcomes comparing equally intensive, manualized treatments: (a) BCT plus individual counseling, (b) interactional couple therapy plus individual counseling, and (c) individual counseling only. The cost-to-benefit analysis of BCT plus individual alcoholism counseling revealed the following: (a) average costs per case for alcohol-related hospital treatments and jail stays decreased from about $7,800 in the year before to about $1,100 in the 2 years after BCT with cost savings averaging about $6,700 per case, and (b) there is a benefit-to-cost ratio of $8.64 in cost savings for every dollar spent to deliver BCT. None of the positive cost-to-benefit results observed for BCT were found for subjects assigned to the interactional couple therapy plus individual alcoholism counseling condition, in which posttreatment utilization costs increased.

O'Farrell, Choquette, Cutter, and Brown et al. (1996) presented cost outcomes for a second study in which manualized BCT with added couple RP sessions was compared with manualized BCT alone. Costs of treatment delivery and health and legal service utilization were measured for 12 months prior to and 12 months after BCT. Results of cost-to-benefit analyses revealed that both standard BCT and the longer and more costly form of BCT with additional RP sessions showed decreases in healthcare utilization and legal costs after treatment with an average cost savings per case of $5,053 for BCT only and $3,365 for BCT plus RP. The benefit-to-cost ratios for every dollar spent were $5.97 for BCT only and $1.89 for BCT plus RP in cost savings for every dollar spent. Despite the fact that adding RP to BCT led to less drinking and better relationship adjustment, it did not lead to greater cost savings (e.g., decrease in health and legal service utilization) or a more favorable benefit-to-cost ratio than BCT only. In fact, adding RP to BCT nearly doubled the cost of delivering the standard BCT protocol. Moreover, the results of cost-effectiveness analyses indicated that BCT only was more cost-effective than BCT plus RP in producing abstinence from drinking; however, the two treatments were equally cost-effective when marital adjustment outcomes were considered. Since BCT only was less effective clinically compared with BCT plus RP in terms of abstinent days, it was the lower cost of BCT only that produced its greater cost-effectiveness in relation to abstinence.

Barriers to Effective Partner- and Family-Involved Interventions

There are several clinically significant barriers unique to family interventions with substance-abusing patients and their families. One that is commonly found among couples and families with a substance-abusing member is partner violence. In situations where there is a risk of severe violence (i.e., aggression that has the potential to result in serious injury or is life threatening), the immediate intervention goal is safety; in these situations, partner and family therapy is contraindicated (e.g., Klostermann, Kelley, Milletich, & Mignone, 2011). For some families, there may be legal restrictions (i.e., restraining orders, no contact orders) that preclude conjoint family sessions.

Another barrier is the presence of more than one actively substance-abusing family member in the family, particularly if these individuals have formed a drinking or drug use partnership of some type (Klostermann & Fals-Stewart, 2008). These dual-using family systems may support continued use versus abstinence since the shared recreational activity typically involves substance use. Research on family-based approaches for these family configurations is lacking, and it is often recommended that individual therapy be used prior to engaging family members in treatment. There are also important practical and logistical barriers to partner or family intervention; these include (a) geographical distances among family members or among family members and the treatment provider; (b) family members who are divorced, incarcerated, or otherwise separated; (c) coordination of family members' and treatment providers' schedules; and (d) securing reimbursement for services delivered to multiple individuals in the context of formal treatment (Kennedy, Klostermann, Gorman, & Fals-Stewart, 2005). Moreover, other potential barriers include financial considerations where partner cannot afford to take time off for treatment, lack of culturally sensitive services that can cater to underserved populations such as native communities or LGBTQ clients, and fear, stigma, or lack of knowledge about the importance of partner involvement in the recovery process.

Future Directions

Although there is a growing awareness of the efficacy of partner- and family-involved approaches to the treatment of alcoholism and drug abuse, there are several important gaps in both the research literature and clinical practice that reflect the next generation of research in this area. More specifically, the following four areas seem most pressing: (a) dissemination of evidence-based marital and family treatments to community-based treatment programs, (b) application of these approaches with specific populations, (c) examination of the mechanisms of action underlying the positive effects observed, and (d) exploring the use of partner- and family-involved models as part of a stepped care approach.

Dissemination

Although a number of couple, marital, and family approaches have demonstrated research support for their efficacy, many have yet to be widely adopted in community-based alcoholism and drug abuse treatment. McGovern, Fox, Xie, and Drake (2004) examined community addiction providers' (i.e., directors [$n = 21$] and clinicians [$n = 89$]) experiences, beliefs, and readiness to implement a variety of evidence-based practices. Results were mixed; providers reported more readiness to adopt 12-step facilitation, cognitive-behavioral therapy, motivational interviewing, and RP while less ready to implement contingency management, BCT, and pharmacotherapies. McGovern and colleagues concluded that in order for treatments to be successfully disseminated, investigators must clearly demonstrate the relevance of the treatment to clinicians and staff, even if empirical support is already established. Other factors to consider include degree of difficulty in implementation, how closely (or not) the treatment is aligned with the therapist's preferred theoretical orientation or agency counseling approach, cost of providing treatment, and whether or not the treatment fills a perceived area of need for the clinic. Each of these areas may serve as a potential barrier to successful dissemination of the treatment.

Specific populations

Although the body of empirical literature supporting the use of systemic family therapy for substance abuse is substantial, it is critical to also recognize its limitations. Among these are the types of families that are typically the subject of such studies, which usually include largely White, male substance-abusing patients. Studies on the efficacy of marital and family therapy approaches for women with substance use disorders are far less common, although available evidence does suggest that they are efficacious (McCrady et al., 2009). Even fewer studies have examined partner- and family-involved interventions with same-sex couples (Klostermann et al., 2011). Future studies are needed to examine gender orientation-specific factors as well as non-gender orientation-specific factors that may increase substance misuse among gay and lesbian individuals.

Furthermore, a great deal of research has been conducted related to both family therapy and culture and ethnicity, but very little of this has appeared in the family therapy literature on substance abuse. This represents what is likely the most important gap in the extant empirical literature to date. Among major life experiences that must be accounted for when treating families in which a member has a problem with drinking or drug use is how factors such as acculturation and ethnic identity influence the treatment process.

Mechanisms of action

We now have confidence that many treatments are effective (Miller & Wilbourne, 2002), but despite the successful efforts of substance abuse treatment researchers to conduct rigorous clinical trials and spell out in treatment manuals what the treatments consist of, little research has actually investigated what the active ingredients of these treatments are (Longabaugh, 2007). In other words, what are the mechanisms of action that make certain partner- and family-involved approaches curative? If these factors can be identified, then these approaches can be modified to optimize their efficiency and effectiveness.

Partner- and family-involved treatment in the context of stepped care

Despite the demonstrated efficacy of manualized marital and family approaches, there are large individual differences in patient response to treatment. As noted by McKay (2009), even for the most efficacious treatments, there are a certain number of people that do not respond to treatment, yet in an effort to tightly control the intervention, nonresponding patients receive the same amount of manualized treatment as those who respond well. Research on standardized interventions to treat substance abuse disorders is beginning to shift away from a "one-size-fits-all" perspective and move toward adaptive interventions. Adaptive interventions, although standardized, call for different dosages of treatment to be employed strategically with patients and families across time. Given the heterogeneity in familial characteristics and response to treatment, future studies are needed to develop tailored interventions based on treatment algorithms that dictate treatment modifications triggered by the patient's initial response and changes in symptom severity. Thus, more flexible versions of marital and family treatments may be more easily disseminated to community providers and more palatable to patients receiving the intervention.

Conclusion

As has been well documented in scholarly journals and popular media, the emotional, economic, and societal toll of alcoholism and drug abuse is incalculable. The effects of substance use disorders affect not only the clients but also those around them; in fact, those emotionally closest to the substance-abusing client often suffer the most. Couples' approaches have had well-documented success, because these methods examine outcomes across multiple domains of functioning that go well beyond frequency of substance use (e.g., child and family adjustment, family violence, relationship quality). By seeking to foster family environments conducive to abstinence, couple and family approaches have great potential to help individuals and families maintain long-term and even multigenerational healthful change.

References

Baucom, D. H., Whisman, M. A., & Paprocki, C. (2012). Couple-based interventions for psychopathology. *Journal of Family Therapy*, 334, 250–270.

Billings, A. G., & Moos, R. H. (1983). Comparisons of children of depressed and nondepressed parents: A social environmental perspective. *Journal of Abnormal Child Psychology*, 11, 463–485.

Brown, E. D., O'Farrell, T. J., Maisto, S. A., Boies, K., & Suchinsky, R. (1997). *Accreditation guide for substance abuse treatment programs*. Newbury Park, CA: Sage.

Chassin, L., Curran, P. J., Hussong, A. M., & Colder, C. R. (1996). The relation of parent alcoholism to adolescent substance use: A longitudinal follow-up study. *Journal of Abnormal Psychology*, 105, 70–80.

Chatav, Y., & Whisman, M. A. (2007). Marital dissolution and psychiatric disorders: An investigation of risk factors. *Journal of Divorce and Remarriage*, 47, 1–13. doi:10.1300/J087v47n01_01

Cochran, S. D., & Mays, V. M. (2007). Physical health complaints among lesbians, gay men, and bisexual and homosexually experienced heterosexual individuals: Results from the California Quality of Life Survey. *American Journal of Public Health*, 97, 2048–2055.

Cochran, S. D., & Mays, V. M. (2009). Burden of psychiatric morbidity among lesbian, gay, and bisexual individuals in the California Quality of Life Survey. *Journal of Abnormal Psychology*, 118(3), 647–658. doi:10.1037/a0016501

Collins, R. L., Ellickson, P. L., & Klein, D. J. (2007). The role of substance use in young adult divorce. *Addiction*, 102(5), 786–794.

Connors, G. J., Donovan, D. M., & DiClemente, C. C. (2004). *Substance abuse treatment and the stages of change: Selecting and planning interventions*. New York, NY: Guilford.

Edwards, M. E., & Steinglass, P. (1995). Family therapy treatment outcomes for alcoholism. *Journal of Marital and Family Therapy*, 21, 475–509.

Emmelkamp, P. M., & Vedel, E. (2006). *Evidence-based treatment for drug and alcohol abuse*. New York, NY: Taylor and Francis Group.

Epstein, E. E., & McCrady, B. S. (1998). Behavioral couples treatment of alcohol and drug use disorders: Current status and innovations. *Clinical Psychology Review*, 18, 689–711.

Epstein, E. E., McCrady, B. S., & Morgan, T. J. (2007). Couples treatment for drug-dependent males: Preliminary efficacy of a stand alone outpatient model. *Addictive Disorders & Their Treatment*, 6, 21–37.

Fals-Stewart, W., & O'Farrell, T. J. (2003). Behavioral family counseling and naltrexone compliance for male opioid-dependent patients. *Journal of Consulting and Clinical Psychology*, 71(3), 432–442.

Gondoli, D. M., & Jacob, T. (1990). Family treatment of alcoholism. In R. Watson (Ed.), *Drug and alcohol abuse reviews: Vol. 1. Prevention and treatment of drug and alcohol abuse* (pp. 245–262). New York, NY: Humana Press.

Goorden, M., Schawo, S. J., Bouwmans-Frijters, C. A. M., van der Schee, E., Hendriks, V. M., & Hakkaart-van Roijen, L. (2016). The cost-effectiveness of family/family-based therapy for treatment of externalizing disorders, substance use disorders and delinquency: A systematic review. *BMC Psychiatry*, 16, 237. Retrieved from http://ezproxy.medaille.edu/login?url=http://search.ebscohost.com.ezproxy.medaille.edu/login.aspx?direct=true&db=psyh&AN=2016-35089-001&site=ehost-live&scope=site

Gottman, J. M., Notarius, C., Gonso, J., & Markman, H. (1976). *A couples guide to communication*. Champaign, IL: Research Press.

Graff, F. S., Morgan, T. J., Epstein, E. E., McCrady, B. S., Cook, S. M., Jensen, N. K., & Kelly, S. (2009). Engagement and retention in outpatient alcoholism treatment for women. *American Journal on Addictions*, 18, 277–288.

Green, K. E., Pugh, L. A., McCrady, B. S., & Epstein, E. E. (2008). Unique aspects of female-primary alcoholic relationships. *Addictive Disorders & Their Treatment*, 7(3), 169–176.

Gurman, A. S. (2013). Behavioral couples therapy: Building a secure base for therapeutic integration. *Family Process*, 52(1), 115–138.

Halford, W. K. (1998). The ongoing evolution of behavioral couples therapy: Retrospect and prospect. *Clinical Psychology Review*, 18, 613–633.

Halford, W. K., & Osgarby, S. M. (1993). Alcohol abuse in clients presenting with marital problems. *Journal of Family Psychology*, 6(3), 245–254.

Hassin, D. S., Stinson, F. S., Ogburn, E., & Grant, B. F. (2007). Prevalence, correlates, disability, and comorbidity of DSM-IV alcohol abuse and dependence in the United States. *Archives of General Psychiatry*, 64, 830–842.

Heath, A. W., & Stanton, M. D. (1998). Family-based treatment: Stages and outcomes. In R. J. Frances & S. I. Miller (Eds.), *Clinical textbook of addictive disorders* (2nd ed., pp. 496–520). New York, NY: Guilford.

Heinz, A. J., Wu, J., Witkiewitz, K., Epstein, D. H., & Preston, K. L. (2009). Marriage and relationship closeness as predictors of cocaine and heroin use. *Addictive Behaviors*, 34(3), 258–263. doi:10.1016/j.addbeh.2008.10.020

Kaufmann, V. G., O'Farrell, T. J., Murphy, C. M., Murphy, M. M., & Muchowski, P. (2014). Alcohol consumption and partner violence among women entering substance use disorder treatment. *Psychology of Addictive Behaviors*, 28(2), 313–321.

Kelley, M., Klostermann, K., Doane, A. N., Mignone, T., Lam, K. K., Fals-Stewart, W., & Padilla, M. A. (2010). The case for examining and treating the combined effects of parental drug use and intimate parental violence on children in their homes. *Aggression and Violent Behavior*, 15, 76–82.

Kelly, S., & Iwamasa, G. Y. (2005). Enhancing behavioral couple therapy: Addressing the therapeutic alliance, hope, and diversity. *Cognitive and Behavioral Practice*, 12, 102–112.

Kennedy, C., Klostermann, K., Gorman, C., & Fals-Stewart, W. (2005). Treating substance abuse and intimate partner violence: Implications for addiction professionals. *Counselor Magazine*, 6(1), 28–34.

Kinney, J. (2009). *Loosening the grip* (9th ed.). New York, NY: McGraw-Hill.

Klostermann, K. (2006). Substance abuse and intimate partner violence: Treatment considerations. *Substance Abuse Treatment, Prevention, and Policy*, 1, 1–24.

Klostermann, K., & Fals-Stewart, W. (2008). Behavioral couples therapy for substance abuse. *Journal of Behavior Analysis of Offender and Victim*, 1(4), 81–93.

Klostermann, K., & Kelley, M. L. (2009). Alcoholism and intimate partner violence: Effects on children's psychosocial adjustment. *International Journal of Environmental Research and Public Health*, 6(12), 3156–3168.

Klostermann, K., Kelley, M. L., Mignone, T., Pusateri, L., & Wills, K. (2011). Behavioral couples therapy for substance abuse: Where do we go from here? *Substance Use & Misuse*, 46, 1502–1509.

Klostermann, K., Kelley, M. L., Milletich, R. J., & Mignone, T. (2011). Alcoholism and partner aggression among gay, lesbian, and bisexual couples. *Aggression and Violent Behavior*, 16, 115–119.

Koffinke, C. (1991). Family recovery issues and treatment resources. In D. C. Daley & M. S. Raskin (Eds.), *Treating the chemically and their families* (pp. 195–216). Newbury Park, CA: Sage.

Lebow, J. (2005). Family therapy at the beginning of the twenty-first century. In J. Lebow (Ed.), *Handbook of clinical family therapy* (pp. 1–16). Hoboken, NJ: Wiley.

Lemke, S., Brennan, P. L., & Schutte, K. K. (2007). Upward pressures on drinking: Exposure and reactivity in adulthood. *Journal of Studies on Alcohol and Drugs*, 68, 437–445.

Liberman, R. P., Wheeler, E. G., deVisser, L. A., Kuehnel, J., & Kuehnel, T. (1980). *Handbook of marital therapy: A positive approach to helping troubled relationships*. New York, NY: Plenum Press.

Lipps, A. J. (1999). Family therapy in the treatment of alcohol related problems. *Alcoholism Treatment Quarterly*, 17, 13–23.

Longabaugh, R. (2007). The search for mechanisms of change in behavioral treatments for alcohol use disorders: A commentary [Special Issue]. *Alcoholism: Clinical & Experimental Research*, 31, S1.

Mann, K. (2000). One hundred years of alcoholism: The twentieth century. *Alcohol and Alcoholism*, 35, 10–15.

McCabe, S. E., Hughes, T. L., Bostwick, W. B., West, B. T., & Boyd, C. J. (2009). Sexual orientation, substance use behaviors and substance dependence in the United States. *Addiction*, 104, 1333–1345.

McCrady, B. S. (1986). Implications for behavior therapy of the changing alcoholism health care delivery system. *The Behavior Therapist*, 9, 171–174.

McCrady, B. S., & Epstein, E. E. (2015). Couple therapy in the treatment of alcohol problems. In D. K. Snyder & J. Lebow (Eds.), *Clinical handbook of couple therapy* (5th ed., pp. 555–584). New York, NY: Guilford Press.

McCrady, B. S., Epstein, E. E., Cook, S., Jensen, N., & Hildebrandt, T. (2009). A randomized trial of individual and couple behavioral alcohol treatment for women. *Journal of Consulting and Clinical Psychology*, 77(2), 243–256.

McCrady, B. S., Noel, N. E., Abrams, D. B., Stout, R. L., Nelson, H. F., & Hay, W. M. (1986). Comparative effectiveness of three types of spouse involvement in outpatient behavioral alcoholism treatment. *Journal of Studies on Alcohol*, 47(6), 459–467. doi:10.15288/jsa.1986.47.459

McCrady, B. S., Wilson, A. D., Munoz, R. E., Fink, B. C., Fokas, K., & Borders, A. (2016). Alcohol-focused behavioral couple therapy. *Family Process*, 55(3), 443–459.

McGovern, M. P., Fox, T. S., Xie, H., & Drake, R. E. (2004). A survey of clinical practices and readiness to adopt evidence-based practices: Dissemination research in an addiction treatment system. *Journal of Substance Abuse Treatment*, 26, 305–312.

McKay, J. R. (2009). *Treating substance use disorders with adaptive continuing care.* Washington, DC: American Psychological Association.

Meis, L. A., Griffin, J. M., Greer, N., Jensen, A. C., Macdonald, R., Carlyle, M., … Wilt, T. J. (2013). Couple and family involvement in adult mental health treatment: A systematic review. *Clinical Psychology Review*, 33, 275–286.

Meyer, I. H., Schwartz, S., & Frost, D. M. (2008). Social pattern of stress and coping: Does disadvantaged social statuses confer more stress and fewer coping resources? *Social Science Medicine*, 67, 368–379.

Mignone, T., Klostermann, K., & Chen, R. (2009). The relationship between relapse to alcohol and relapse to violence. *Journal of Family Violence*, 24, 497–406.

Miller, W. R., & Wilbourne, P. L. (2002). Mesa grande: A methodological analysis of clinical trials of treatments for alcohol use disorders. *Addiction*, 97, 265–277.

Morrissette, P. J. (2010). Couples at the crossroads: substance abuse and intimate relationship deliberation. *The Family Journal: Counseling and Therapy for Couples and Families*, 18(2), 146–153.

O'Farrell, T. J., Cutter, H. S., & Floyd, F. J. (1985). Evaluating behavioral marital therapy for male alcoholics: Effects on marital adjustment and communication from before to after treatment. *Behavior Therapy*, 16(2), 147–167. doi:10.1016/S0005-7894(85)80042-3

O'Farrell, T. J., Choquette, K. A., Cutter, H. S. G., Brown, E. D., Bayog, R., McCourt, W., … Deneault, P. (1996). Cost-benefit and cost-effectiveness analyses of behavioral marital therapy with and without relapse prevention sessions for alcoholics and their spouses. *Behavior Therapy*, 27, 7–24.

O'Farrell, T. J., Choquette, K. A., Cutter, H. S. G., Floyd, F. J., Bayog, R. D., Brown, E. D., … Deneault, P. (1996). Cost-benefit and cost-effectiveness analyses of behavioral marital therapy as an addition to outpatient alcoholism treatment. *Journal of Substance Abuse*, 8, 145–166.

O'Farrell, T. J., & Clements, K. (2012). Review of outcome research on marital and family therapy in treatment for alcoholism. *Journal of Marital and Family Therapy*, 38, 122–144.

O'Farrell, T. J., & Cutter, H. S. G. (1984). Behavioral marital therapy couples groups for male alcoholics and their wives. *Journal of Substance Abuse Treatment*, 1, 191–204.

O'Farrell, T. J., & Fals-Stewart, W. (2001). Family-involved alcoholism treatment: An update. In M. Galanter (Ed.), *Recent developments in alcoholism, volume 15: Services research in the era of managed care* (pp. 329–356). New York, NY: Plenum Press.

O'Farrell, T. J., & Fals-Stewart, W. (2006). *Behavioral couples therapy for alcoholism and drug abuse.* New York, NY: Guilford Press. Retrieved from http://search.ebscohost.com. ezproxy.medaille.edu/login.aspx?direct=true&db=psyh&AN=2006-12207-000&site=ehost-live&scope=site

O'Farrell, T. J., & Murphy, C. M. (1995). Marital violence before and after alcoholism treatment. *Journal of Consulting and Clinical Psychology*, 63, 256–262.

O'Farrell, T. J., Murphy, C. M., Stephan, S. H., Fals-Stewart, W., & Murphy, M. (2004). Partner violence before and after couples-based alcoholism treatment for male alcoholic patients: The role of treatment involvement and abstinence. *Journal of Consulting and Clinical Psychology*, 72, 202–217.

Powers, M. B., Vedel, E., & Emmelkamp, P. M. (2008). Behavioral couples therapy (BCT) for alcohol and drug use disorders: A meta-analysis. *Clinical Psychology Review*, 28, 952–962.

Ray, G. T., Mertens, J. R., & Weisner, C. (2007). The excess medical cost and health problems of family members of persons diagnosed with alcohol or drug problems. *Medical Care*, 45(2), 116–122.

Rotunda, R. J., West, L., & O'Farrell, T. J. (2004). Enabling behavior in a clinical sample of alcohol-dependent clients and their partners. *Journal of Substance Abuse Treatment*, 26, 269–276.

Rowe, C. L. (2012). Family therapy for drug abuse: review and updates: 2003–2010. *Journal of Marital and Family Therapy*, 38, 59–81.

Schaef, A. W. (1986). *Co-dependence: Misunderstood—Mistreated*. San Francisco, CA: Harper & Row.

Schumm, J. A., O'Farrell, T. J., Kahler, C. W., Murphy, M. M., & Muchowski, P. (2014). A randomized clinical trial of behavioral couples therapy verses individually based treatment for women with alcohol dependence. *Journal of Consulting and Clinical Psychology*, 82(6), 993–1004.

Stanton, M. D. (2015). Family therapy. In M. Galanter, H. D. Kleber, & K. T. Brady (Eds.), *The American Psychiatric Publishing textbook of substance abuse treatment* (5th ed., pp. 479–495). Arlington, VA: American Psychiatric Publishing, Inc. Retrieved from http://search.ebscohost.com.ezproxy.medaille.edu/login.aspx?direct=true&db=psyh&AN=2015-18397-033&site=ehost-live&scope=site

Stanton, M. D., Todd, T. C., & Associates (1982). *The family therapy of drug abuse and addiction*. New York, NY: Guilford.

Turner, J. (1972, October). *Couple and group treatment of marital discord*. Paper presented at the Sixth Annual Meeting of the Association for Advancement of Behavior Therapy, New York, NY.

Vedel, E., Emmelkamp, P. M., & Schippers, G. M. (2008). Individual cognitive-behavioral therapy and behavioral couples therapy in alcohol use disorder: A comparative evaluation in community-based addiction treatment centers. *Psychotherapy and Psychosomatics*, 77(5), 280–288.

Walitzer, K. S., & Derman, K. H. (2004). Alcohol-focused spouse involvement and behavioral couples therapy: Evolution of enhancements to drinking reduction treatment for male problem drinkers. *Journal of Consulting and Clinical Psychology*, 72, 944–955.

Wesley, K. C. (2016). The use of behavioural couple therapy and couple-based interventions in the treatment of substance use disorders. *Addiction Research & Theory*, 24(2), 89–92.

9

Couple-Based Interventions for the Treatment of Depressive and Anxiety Disorders

Andrea K. Wittenborn, Brian R.W. Baucom,
Feea R. Leifker, and E. Megan Lachmar

Depressive disorders are the largest contributor to global medical disability, and anxiety disorders rank sixth (World Health Organization [WHO], 2017). In a given year, the proportion of the global population with depressive disorders is 4.4%, while the proportion with anxiety disorders is 3.6%. Together, depressive and anxiety disorders cost the global economy about $1.15 trillion annually (Chisholm et al., 2016) and carry significant social and familial costs. Depressive disorders, which we will refer to as depression unless discussing a specific depressive diagnostic classification, is characterized by persistent sadness, cognitive dysfunction, and somatic symptoms, and anxiety disorders involve excessive fear and worry. However, depression and anxiety also share a number of symptoms (e.g., irritability, difficulty concentrating, sleep problems; American Psychiatric Association [APA], 2013). In the United States, only one-third of people diagnosed with depression seek treatment (Waitzfelder et al., 2018). Patients with depression and co-occurring relationship problems who receive individually focused treatment report lower rates of remission compared with those without relationship problems (Denton et al., 2010). Depression has been labeled a "we-disease" to call attention to the interdependence of both partners as suffering patients (Acitelli & Badr, 2005), a process that is similar among partners experiencing anxiety (Beach & Whisman, 2012). Longitudinal findings indicate that depression and anxiety impede the quality of couple relationships and poor relationships contribute to depression and anxiety, thereby maintaining a vicious cycle of poor mental health and relationships (Davila, Karney, Hall, & Bradbury, 2003; Zaider, Heimberg, & Iida, 2010).

Our goal in this chapter is to first describe the empirical literature on the relationship between depression, anxiety, and relationship problems. Given the significant overlap in etiology among depression and anxiety, we approach the discussion of anxiety and depression from a dimensional perspective in which we describe underlying mechanisms relevant to couple relationships. We then discuss findings on the relationship between the underlying mechanisms of disorder and relationship distress. Next, we provide an

---

The Handbook of Systemic Family Therapy: Volume 3, First Edition.
Edited by Karen S. Wampler and Adrian J. Blow.
© 2020 John Wiley & Sons Ltd. Published 2020 by John Wiley & Sons Ltd.

overview of the evidence for couple-based interventions for depression and anxiety. Finally, we suggest future directions for research and highlight the need to understand how couple-based interventions target the underlying mechanisms of disorder.

Associations Between Depression, Anxiety, and Couple Distress

Depressive and anxiety disorders are strongly associated with increased relationship distress (McLeod, 1994; Whisman, 1999, 2007). This association exists for both women and men (McLeod, 1994; Whisman, 1999) and is often bidirectional (e.g., Davila et al., 2003). For example, poor relationship quality is associated with future development of mood and anxiety symptoms (e.g., Overbeek et al., 2006). That is, close relationships contribute to one's sense of worth and often signal the presence of social support that is protective against the negative effects of stressful life events (Cohen & Willis, 1985). It may be that as relationship quality is reduced, so too are the ameliorative effects of being in a relationship, thus putting one at risk for psychopathology. Conversely, the presence of depression and anxiety may also put one at risk for the development of relationship distress, due in large part to characteristics of the disorders spilling over into the relationship.

Once depressive or anxiety disorders are present, positive interpersonal relationships are highly important for recovery from the disorder. For example, in individual treatment of generalized anxiety disorder (GAD), treatment outcomes decline as marital tension increases (Durham, Allan, & Hackett, 1997) or in the presence of hostile criticism from one's partner (Zinbarg, Lee, & Yoon, 2007). Also of note, interpersonal functioning is not always improved following individual treatments for anxiety or depression, even if the disorder itself remits (e.g., Atkins, Dimidjian, Bedics, & Christensen, 2009), thereby setting the individual up for relapse.

Several specific domains of relationship functioning seem to be impacted by mood and anxiety disorders, including communication and sexual functioning. Initial work examining associations among depressive symptoms and communication behaviors during couple conflict have resulted in inconsistent conclusions. Several studies linked greater severity of depressive symptoms to higher levels of maladaptive communication behaviors, such as higher levels of aggression (Biglan et al., 1985), more frequent reassurance seeking (e.g., Joiner, Metalsky, Katz, & Beach, 1999), and less effective problem solving (Christian, O'Leary, & Vivian, 1994), while other research has failed to find a link between variability in communication behaviors that was uniquely attributable to depressive symptoms (e.g., Baucom et al., 2007; Schmaling & Jacobson, 1990). More recent work suggests that these inconsistent findings are likely related to the importance of acute sad mood and sex as moderators of the depression–communication behavior association. For example, Rehman and colleagues (Rehman, Ginting, Karimiha, & Goodnight, 2010) found that higher levels of depressive symptoms were associated with higher levels of negative communication behaviors only following an acute sad mood induction among depressed wives. Finally, associations between being diagnosed with depression and enacting higher levels of criticism and aggression have been found to be stronger among couples with depressed wives than among couples with depressed husbands (e.g., Gabriel, Beach, & Bodenmann, 2010).

Most work examining symptoms of anxiety and communication behaviors in romantic relationships focuses on social anxiety disorder. Greater symptoms of social anxiety are associated with greater desire to avoid conflict, actual avoidance of conflict, greater overreliance on others, and less assertion (Davila & Beck, 2002). Relative to individuals without social anxiety disorder, individuals with social anxiety disorder enact lower levels of positive behavior when interacting with their romantic partners in general and higher levels of negative behavior during conflict with their romantic partners (Wenzel, Graff-Dolezal, Macho, & Brendle, 2005).

Turning to sexual functioning, major depressive disorder and higher levels of depressive symptoms are well-established correlates of lower levels of sexual interest and sexual satisfaction and less frequent intercourse (e.g., del Mar Sánchez-Fuentes, Santos-Iglesias, & Sierra, 2014; Kennedy, 2008). In addition, antidepressant medications can further impair sexual functioning (Kennedy, Rizvi, Fulton, & Rasmussen, 2008). While the link between sexual functioning and anxiety is less well studied than with depression, anxiety seems to have a similarly negative impact. Among a small sample of women with panic disorder, women and their male partners endorsed less frequent sexual intercourse and less sexual desire compared with couples in the control condition (Van Minnen & Kampman, 2000). In this same sample, panic disorder was also associated with increased odds of meeting criteria for either hypoactive sexual desire disorder or sexual aversion disorder compared to women in the control group. However, the association between anxiety and sexual functioning or satisfaction may be limited to heterosexual couples, as Beaber and Werner (2009) found an association between anxiety and sexual dysfunction among heterosexual women, but not women in same-sex relationships. It is possible that anxiety may reduce sexual functioning due to increased negative cognitions (such as fears of failure and increased focus on performance). Indeed, in a sample of undergraduate students and their partners, social anxiety was associated with greater fear of intimacy and less satisfaction with sexual communication, which in turn predicted lower sexual satisfaction (Montesi et al., 2013).

Using data from the National Comorbidity Survey, Whisman (1999) examined the presence of specific anxiety and mood disorders when controlling for the presence of comorbid disorders on the association with relationship distress. He determined that the presence of multiple disorders increased risk for relationship distress. Thus, more severe symptomatology may be most strongly associated with relationship distress. This highlights the need to consider the associations between underlying mechanisms of mood and anxiety disorders, as well as their unique associations with relationship distress.

Crosscutting Mechanisms of Depressive and Anxiety Disorders

While categorical classification systems are still used for clinical diagnosis of mental disorders, the empirical understanding of disorders is shifting to a dimensional perspective that acknowledges multiple etiologies (Wittenborn, Rahmandad, Rick, & Hosseinichimeh, 2016). Dimensional views emphasize that in contrast to the discrete categories of disorders proposed in classification systems, mental illness actually occurs across a continuum of symptom severity and is caused by multiple interacting factors. Dimensional approaches gained significant momentum when the National Institute of Mental Health's (NIMH) Research Domain Criteria framework was initiated in 2009 (Clark, Cuthbert, Lewis-Fernández, Narrow, & Reed, 2017). The NIMH Research Domain Criteria framework focuses on dimensional psychological constructs that are relevant to mental disorders and human behavior. In contrast to characterizing disorders by symptoms, dimensional frameworks focus on multifactorial causes of mental illness. A dimensional approach to mental illness offers many advantages, including a more accurate understanding of etiology, artifactual comorbidities, and personalized treatment. Depression and anxiety are driven by similar complex mechanisms including attentional and interpretation bias, rumination, behavior avoidance, emotion regulation, attachment security, and neuroticism (i.e., Brown & Barlow, 2009). In fact, a unified protocol or transdiagnostic treatment of depression and anxiety has been created (Barlow et al., 2017), and studies indicate significant support for treating both conditions through identical modalities (i.e., Titov et al., 2011).

Attentional and interpretation bias

Attentional and interpretation bias is one of the mechanisms linked with symptoms, severity, course, and recurrence of depression and anxiety (Baert, De Raedt, & Koster, 2010; Disner, Shumake, & Beevers, 2017; Mathews & MacLeod, 2005). Attentional bias is defined as a focus toward negative information, such as when individuals with depressive disorders selectively direct attention toward sad faces (Gotlib, Krasnoperova, Yue, & Joormann, 2004). Interpretation bias is the negative interpretation of neutral or ambiguous stimuli (Grey & Mathews, 2009). Individuals with greater depression and anxiety symptom severity have been shown to exhibit sustained attention to negative information (Baert et al., 2010).

Attentional and interpretation bias and relationship distress Distorted cognitions, including biases in attention to and interpretation of relationship behaviors, are consistently and strongly associated with the development and maintenance of relationship distress (e.g., Baucom, Epstein, Sayers, & Sher, 1989; Bradbury, Fincham, & Beach, 2000). The degree to which partners perceive one another's behaviors is important to how they will interpret the behavior. On average, partners only agree on behaviors that occurred in the relationship about half the time (e.g., Christensen & Nies, 1980). Because individuals with anxiety show greater attention to threat than non-anxious individuals (e.g., Bar-Haim, Lamy, Perigamin, Bakermans-Kranenburg, & van IJzendoorn, 2007; Cisler & Koster, 2010), they may selectively attend to their environment and partners' behaviors differently than non-anxious partners. For example, individuals with anxiety disorders may have excessive concerns about their safety when out in public and attend to potential internal or external cues that signal a threat. This may cause them to appear distracted or decline to participate in activities with their partner, potentially negatively affecting the relationship. Within the relationship, individuals with anxiety may also selectively attend to signs of threat, such as cues that their partner is angry or does not care about them.

Once a behavior is perceived (or, for that matter, the absence of a behavior is perceived), individuals make explanations, or attributions, about their partners' behaviors. Individuals with anxiety and depression tend to make more negative attributions about situations and others' behaviors (e.g., Luten, Ralph, & Mineka, 1997). For example, they may interpret not receiving affection when their partner returns home as a potential signal that they did something wrong or their partner does not care about them. Over time, making more frequent and severe negative attributions can lead to less relationship satisfaction (Fincham, Harold, & Gano-Phillips, 2000). As relationship distress sets in, individuals also become more prone to making negative attributions, which may further increase relationship distress (Fincham et al., 2000).

Rumination

Rumination is a crosscutting mechanism of depression and anxiety described as repetitive thoughts surrounding the symptoms, causes, and future consequences of depressed mood (Nolen-Hoeksema, 1991). This includes frequent thoughts about disappointments, inadequacies, mistakes, and negative feelings (Davis & Nolen-Hoeksema, 2000). Rumination is an extensively studied vulnerability factor for depression and anxiety and contributes to more severe and prolonged episodes (Nolen-Hoeksema, 2000; Trick, Watkins, Windeatt, & Dickens, 2016). Research reveals that thought suppression can lead to increased rumination (Wenzlaff & Luxton, 2003). Additionally, effects of negative rumination increase when under stress (Vrshek-Schallhorn, Velkoff, & Zinbarg, 2018; Wenzlaff & Luxton, 2003).

Rumination and relationship distress   Largely studied in the context of depression and relationships, rumination seems to have a direct negative effect on intimate relationships. Joiner (2000) referred to rumination as the "cognitive motor" driving interpersonal problems (e.g., excessive reassurance seeking) among individuals with depression. Subsequent research seems to confirm this. Kuehner and Buerger (2005) found that increased rumination was associated with reduced relationship satisfaction among currently and formerly depressed individuals. Rumination has also been prospectively linked to relationship satisfaction, such that tendency to ruminate is associated with reduced relationship satisfaction several months later (Pearson, Watkins, Kuyken, & Mullan, 2010). Furthermore, rumination moderates the association between depression and relationship satisfaction, such that among people who ruminate more, there is a stronger link between depression and relationship functioning (Whitton & Kuryluk, 2013). While the link between anxious rumination and marital satisfaction has not yet been studied, it likely impacts the relationship in a similar manner.

In terms of relationship behaviors, rumination is associated with less tendency to forgive a partner following a relationship transgression (Kachadourian, Fincham, & Davila, 2005). It is possible that more ruminative individuals perseverate to a greater extent than less ruminative individuals on negative relationship events. This could in turn make them less likely to engage in conflict resolution behaviors. Rumination is also associated with difficulty with interpersonal problem solving (Lyubomirsky & Nolen-Hoeksema, 1995), which may further impair individuals' abilities to resolve conflicts as they arise in relationships.

Behavioral avoidance

Behavioral avoidance is an innate coping strategy commonly used by those with depression and anxiety and is defined as avoiding particular experiences to reduce negative feelings and thoughts. However, this avoidance may lead to the development and maintenance of anxiety and depressive symptoms (Holahan, Moos, Holahan, Brennan, & Schutte, 2005; Ottenbreit, Dobson, & Quigley, 2014). There has also been a link uncovered between rumination, maladaptive emotion regulation strategies, and both cognitive and behavioral avoidance (Dickson, Ciesla, & Reilly, 2012; Quigley, Wen, & Dobson, 2017).

Behavioral avoidance and relationship distress   Behavioral avoidance is a hallmark symptom of anxiety disorders. Because individuals often avoid situations, places, or people that cause them anxiety, this may result in restricting the couple's environment and activities. As these symptoms prevent anxious individuals from going places, engaging in social situations, and/or making decisions, this might cause conflict or negatively impact relationships (Baucom, Stanton, & Epstein, 2003).

Emotion regulation

Emotion regulation is defined as how individuals process and express emotions, such as the magnitude of emotional response to a stimulus (Gross, 2013). This involves over-regulation (e.g., inhibiting emotional arousal) and under-regulation (e.g., enhancing emotional arousal; Wittenborn, Faber, & Keiley, 2012). This also includes strategies such as rumination, distraction, cognitive reappraisal, suppression, and acceptance, among others (Liu & Thompson, 2017). Individuals with depression have been found to lack inhibition when processing negative material (Joormann & Gotlib, 2010). In turn, this reduction in inhibition is associated with greater rumination (Joormann & Gotlib, 2010). There is also evidence that differences among culture and gender exist for emotion regulation in its relation to depression; for example, women across cultures are more likely to ruminate and use anger suppression (Kwon, Yoon, Joormann, & Kwon, 2013).

Both anxiety and depression have been associated with greater overall negative affect, while diminished positive affect has been more strongly linked to depression than anxiety (Watson, Clark, & Carey, 1988). Additionally, those diagnosed with depression have greater instability of negative affect (Houben, Van Den Noortgate, & Kuppens, 2015) or blunted responses to both positive and negative stimuli (Bylsma, Morris, & Rottenberg, 2008). Anxiety and depression are associated with irritability, anger, and hostility (APA, 2013; Painuly, Sharan, & Mattoo, 2005).

Emotion regulation and relationship distress   Less effective emotion regulation and a greater tendency to experience higher levels of negative affect are characteristic of depressive and anxiety disorders, and depression is additionally associated with frequent enactment of hostile and critical behaviors toward romantic partners (Painuly et al., 2005). Impaired emotion regulation has been hypothesized as a common mechanism by which negative affect and hostility may be related to depressive and anxious symptoms. Recent work supports this supposition while also demonstrating that certain emotion regulation strategies are implicated in links involving depressive and anxious symptoms. More specifically, Desrosiers, Vine, Klemanski, and Nolen-Hoeksema (2013) found reappraisal to be associated with lower levels of depressive and anxious symptoms and nonacceptance of emotional experiences to be significantly associated only with depressive symptoms. Difficulties with emotion regulation have been shown to explain the relationship between depression and withdrawn behaviors in couple relationships (Holley, Haase, Chui, & Bloch, 2018).

Attachment insecurity

A perceived lack of social support is known to have a direct effect on psychopathology, and attachment relationships encompass a special form of social support from an intimate partner (Thoits, 2011). Adult attachment relationships are close relationships with a romantic partner from whom comfort can be sought during times of need (Bowlby, 1988). Partners build stable bonds and positive views of self and others when their attachment figures reliably and sensitively respond to bids for proximity and support (Feeney, 2016). When partners are frequently unavailable, unresponsive, and insensitive during stressful times, negative views of self and others are formed and felt security erodes. When a secure connection between partners is not maintained, it can also increase partners' vulnerability to mental disorders. Quality of attachment bonds has been found to predict prospective symptoms of depression and anxiety (Lee & Hankin, 2009).

Attachment insecurity and relationship distress Research demonstrates a relationship between attachment insecurity, relationship distress, and depression and anxiety. Among heterosexual couples, attachment mediates the relation between depressive symptoms and marital distress (Heene, Buysse, & Van Oost, 2005). These researchers also found that attachment avoidance and security were significant moderators of the association between depressive symptoms and distress among women, suggesting that a strong relationship between depression and distress only held among women who self-reported as low in attachment security. Another study compared clinical and control couples and found that patients with depression and their partners reported more marital distress compared with controls and their marital distress was associated with insecure attachment (Heene, Buysse, & Van Oost, 2007). The study also indicated that attachment was a significant mediator of the association between depressive symptoms and marital distress for women. Other studies found similar trends among men (Scott & Cordova, 2002). Compared with depressive disorders, there has been less research on attachment insecurity, relationship distress, and anxiety disorders, though available findings indicate similar results (e.g., Cassidy, Lichtenstein-Phelps, Sibrava, Thomas, & Borkovec, 2009).

Neuroticism

Neuroticism is a personality trait defined by the experience of negative emotions, low self-esteem, and sensitivity to stress (Costa & McCrae, 1987). Neuroticism is a cross-cutting mechanism associated with the development and severity of depression and anxiety (i.e., Hakulinen et al., 2015). Rumination and emotion regulation strategies have been found to be mediating variables in the relationship between neuroticism and symptoms of depression and anxiety (Roelofs, Huibers, Peeters, Arntz, & van Os, 2008; Yoon, Maltby, & Joormann, 2013). In addition, neuroticism has also been linked with adverse couple relationship outcomes, such as declines in relationship satisfaction (Fisher & McNulty, 2008). Studies have also revealed age-related decreases in neuroticism over time (Roberts, Walton, & Viechtbauer, 2006).

Neuroticism and relationship distress A meta-analysis suggests that neuroticism has a small to medium association with lower relationship stability and satisfaction among both husbands and wives (Karney & Bradbury, 1995). Of all personality traits in the big five model, neuroticism has the strongest link with relationship functioning among both heterosexual (Karney & Bradbury, 1995; Kurdek, 1997) and same-sex couples (Kurdek, 1997). Not only does neuroticism affect an individual's level of relationship satisfaction, but a recent meta-analysis shows that partners of individuals higher in neuroticism also have lower relationship satisfaction (Malouff, Thorsteinsson, Schutte, Bhullar, & Rooke, 2010). Further, the amount of neuroticism each partner exhibits contributes to the couple's overall level of satisfaction (Kurdek, 1997).

Couple-Based Interventions for Depressive and Anxiety Disorders

While there is significant value in considering the active mechanisms of disorders to improve the efficiency and effectiveness of treatment, frameworks and supporting research for a mechanism-based understanding of mental illness and its treatment have only recently emerged (Insel et al., 2010; Wittenborn et al., 2016). Thus, the empirical literature revealing the processes by which couple-based interventions target etiological mechanisms is currently limited. As a result, we review the general clinical findings on couple-based interventions for depression and anxiety. Since there are many prior reviews of couple-based interventions for depression (e.g., Beach, Dreifuss, Franklin, Kamen, & Gabriel, 2008; Beach, Whisman, & Bodenmann, 2014), we provide a general overview of the extensive literature and describe studies on couple-based interventions for anxiety disorders in more detail.

Couple therapy for depressive disorders

Couple-based interventions for depression grew out of the pioneering research in the late 1980s and 1990s (e.g., Whisman, 1999) establishing robust associations between higher levels of marital distress, higher levels of negative affect, higher levels of depressive symptoms, and increased risk for meeting diagnostic criteria for major depressive disorder (see Gupta, Coyne, and Beach (2003) for a review). Initial work focused on the efficacy of behaviorally and cognitively based couple therapies for improving symptoms of depression. In this form of couple-based intervention, couples present with concerns primarily related to their romantic relationship, and the "identified client" in the treatment is the relationship itself rather than the psychological health and well-being of either of the partners per se (e.g., Baucom, Whisman, & Paprocki, 2012). Existing reviews of this literature conclude that behaviorally based couple therapy is an efficacious treatment for depression and may be a preferable intervention for co-occurring relationship distress and depression relative to empirically supported individual interventions for depression (e.g., Barbato & D'Avanzo, 2008; Baucom, Belus, Adelman, Fischer, & Paprocki, 2014; Beach & Whisman, 2012).

Three clinical trials have also examined emotionally focused therapy (EFT), an attachment and affect regulation based treatment for couples experiencing co-occurring depression and relationship distress (Denton, Wittenborn, & Golden, 2012; Dessaulles, Johnson, & Denton, 2003; Wittenborn et al., 2019). The most recent trial explored mechanisms of change across weekly sessions and follow-up. Results suggest that EFT directly targets depressive symptoms and relationship satisfaction and the temporal changes in each outcome vary by couple. For some couples, improvements in relationship satisfaction leads to improvements in depression, the opposite is true for others, and still other couples report change in both outcomes simultaneously.

Couple therapy for anxiety disorders

Work examining couple-based interventions for anxiety disorders has tested the efficacy of both couple therapies and partner-assisted interventions for improving symptoms of anxiety. Couple therapy emphasizes improving the romantic relationship, while partner-assisted interventions focus on leveraging the romantic relationship to improve the psychological symptoms of one of the partners in it (e.g., Baucom et al., 2012). The "identified patient" in partner-assisted interventions is one of the two partners, and treatment decisions are guided by a focus on improving the target individual's psychological well-being.

Several studies have examined the effect of couple therapy on anxiety and marital satisfaction. Chernen and Friedman (1993) tested behavioral marital therapy (BMT) among a sample of patients with panic disorder and agoraphobia (PDA) and their partners. Interventions included communication training, problem solving, and working to improve couples' behavioral exchanges (e.g., Jacobson & Margolin, 1979). Chernen and Friedman (1993) found that, among distressed couples, BMT improved relationship satisfaction and PDA symptoms. However, it had little effect on symptoms among already satisfied couples. Among a sample of individuals with symptoms of phobia and/or obsessive–compulsive disorder, Cobb, McDonald, Marks, and Stern (1980) randomly assigned couples to marital therapy or partner-assisted exposure therapy. Marital therapy consisted of problem solving, agreeing on contracts and goals, sexual skills training, and communication training. Exposure treatment outperformed marital therapy, and marital therapy did not significantly reduce psychopathology.

More recent forms of couple therapy have also been helpful in reducing symptoms of anxiety. For example, when testing the efficacy of the OurRelationship program, an online intervention based on the principles of integrative behavioral couple therapy (IBCT; Christensen & Jacobson, 1998), Doss and colleagues (2016) found that after completing the intervention, couples' anxiety symptoms improved. Couples participating in the intervention were community couples who did not need to have a prior diagnosis of an anxiety disorder. However, that same intervention has been adapted to help treat GAD. By including GAD-specific psychoeducation, mindfulness, and emphasizing change in the GAD symptoms (rather than relationship change only), Benson, Doss, and Christensen (2018) found that both GAD symptoms and relationship satisfaction improved posttreatment.

Partner-assisted therapy for anxiety disorders

Partner-assisted interventions for anxiety have been created for PDA, but not any other anxiety disorders. Partner-assisted interventions for PTSD commonly use partner-assisted gradual exposure (e.g., Arrindell, Emmelkamp, & Sanderman, 1986; Cobb, Mathews, Childs-Clarke, & Blowers, 1984; Emmelkamp et al., 1992; Hand, Angenendt, Fischer, & Wilke, 1986; Mathews, Teasdale, Mundby, Johnston, & Shaw,

1977). In partner-assisted exposure, the symptomatic partner and their partner engage in a series of planned outings that gradually increase in the degree in which they elicit fear or anxiety. The non-anxious partner might actively assist their partner (e.g., use relaxation techniques, help with cognitive restructuring) or may just assist by simply accompanying their partner on the exposure. In a review of the research, Byrne, Carr, and Clark (2004) concluded that partner-assisted therapy results in symptomatic improvement in 23–45% of cases. While most treatments to date generally use partners to assist in exposure (and attend treatment sessions), a few studies have examined additional partner-based interventions. For example, Arnow, Taylor, Agras, and Telch (1985) provided individuals with four sessions of partner-assisted exposure therapy for PDA, followed by eight sessions of couple relaxation training or couple communication training. Barlow, Mavissakalian, and Hay (1981) conducted group therapy sessions with couples and, unlike other studies, focused on cognitive restructuring as well as exposure and saw reductions in patient and partner-rated symptoms of PDA.

Reviews of the literature generally show that individual and partner-assisted interventions for PDA are relatively comparable in effectiveness (Byrne et al., 2004; Daiuto, Baucom, Epstein, & Dutton, 1998). Diauto and colleagues (1998) highlight a small nonsignificant trend for individual exposure to be more effective than the partner-assisted exposure in reducing symptoms of PDA. It is worth noting that some of the studies showing that spouse-assisted treatment outperforms individual treatment (e.g., Barlow, O'Brien, & Last, 1984; Cerny, Barlow, Craske, & Himadi, 1987) include additional therapeutic elements in the treatment. These researchers added cognitive restructuring to partner-assisted exposure for PDA, which may contribute to improved outcomes. For example, the use of a partner to assist in cognitive restructuring may facilitate identification of distorted thoughts, help individuals challenge these thoughts, or aid in generating alternative thoughts the anxious partner may not have otherwise identified. As mentioned above, to date, partner-assisted interventions have only been tested among individuals with PDA. However, given the promising results, the use of a partner to aid in exposure and cognitive restructuring could be helpful for individuals meeting criteria for other anxiety disorders.

In a review of the literature, Byrne et al. (2004) conclude there is mixed evidence suggesting that individuals with better relationship functioning tend to show a better treatment response in couple treatment for PDA. More directly, couples' abilities to openly communicate about the fears and anxiety experienced by the partner with PDA seemed to improve treatment outcomes (Craske, Burton, & Barlow, 1989). This is also consistent with findings by Arnow and colleagues (1985) suggesting that communication training improved outcomes when compared with couple relaxation training. It could be that the symptomatic partner's ability to communicate their fear allows them to receive support from their partner, potentially improving treatment outcomes. Additionally, it may be that partners' accurate knowledge of the symptomatic partner's levels of fear is important to help facilitate gradual exposure. That is, if partners are not aware of the degree of fear the anxious partner is experiencing, they may push their partner too fast on approaching certain items on their fear hierarchy. Pushing partners to reduce their avoidance too soon and approach a place or situation they are not ready for could reduce the effectiveness of the exposure or even possibly have a negative impact on treatment outcomes.

Future Directions

Targeting cross-cutting mechanisms to improve treatment outcomes

Recent research suggests that mental disorders described in the *Diagnostic and Statistical Manual (DSM)* (APA, 2013) are often split into small categories with significant overlap and sometimes trivial variation (Sauer-Zavala et al., 2017). Emerging evidence supports a dimensional basis for psychiatric classification in which constructs with broad applicability across disorders, such as attentional biases and attachment security, may help guide the development of more efficient and effective interventions that directly target underlying mechanisms of disorder. One method by which to do this is to develop approaches that personalize treatment to a given patient (Wittenborn et al., 2016). Personalized treatment may be guided by a patient's demographics, symptoms, or other factors. More research in this area is needed. Another way in which interventions have been designed to target underlying mechanisms is through transdiagnostic treatment. Transdiagnostic approaches target underlying mechanisms that are relevant to the development and maintenance of mental illness spanning multiple disorders (Barlow et al., 2017). Close intimate relationships are known to play a significant role in prevention, recovery, and maintenance as they relate to mental illness (Whisman, 2001; Whisman & Baucom, 2012). Interpersonal health is also linked to better physical health and well-being (Jaremka, Glaser, Malarkey, & Kiecolt-Glaser, 2013; Robles, Slatcher, Trombello, & McGinn, 2014). As a result, intimacy has been suggested as an important transdiagnostic problem (Wetterneck & Hart, 2012). Research is needed to understand the potential effects of couple-based interventions on common mechanisms of depression and anxiety.

Diverse couples

With few exceptions (e.g., Beaber & Werner, 2009; Lee, Cohen, Hadley, & Goodwin, 1999), clinical research examining couple-based interventions for partners suffering from depression and anxiety has predominately included couples who identify as being white, middle class, heterosexual, and early to middle adulthood. There is an urgent need to understand best practices for partners who identify as minority in regard to their race and ethnicity, socioeconomic status, and sexual orientation. It is also important to understand couple interventions for aging adults, particularly given the evolving roles of aging partners that often include caretaking responsibilities. Adaptations for these populations or the development of novel interventions are needed to eliminate disparities and achieve health equity.

Implementation science

Prior research on couple-based interventions for depressive and anxiety disorders has focused primarily on efficacy trials with some expansion into effectiveness research. Implementation trials are an important next step in future research on couple therapy for depression and anxiety. Implementation research sheds light onto how effective interventions are translated into real-world practice settings (Proctor et al., 2009). There is a significant gap between care that is known to be effective and care that is available in community settings. On average, it takes 17 years for care that is found to be effective in university laboratory settings to be available in the community (Morris,

Wooding, & Grant, 2011). Studies that help reduce the evidence to treatment gap by understanding useful approaches to large-scale clinical trainings on evidence-based practices are crucial to reducing the suffering of millions of Americans (Proctor et al., 2009). Emerging research on the experience of learning EFT for couples indicates a promising start for future research (e.g., Sandberg & Knestel, 2011). EFT has a long history of offering intensive training across the world, and more research on implementation strategies for moving additional evidence-based treatments into local systems is needed.

Mobile technologies for mental health interventions

The provision of mental health intervention through mobile technologies, known by the abbreviation mHealth, is a promising area for future research on couple-based interventions for depression and anxiety. Over 95% of adults living in the United States own a mobile phone, a rate that exceeds ownership of desktop and laptop computers and spans a wide range of demographic groups (Pew Research Center, 2018). Mobile technologies offer opportunities to expand the reach of couple-based interventions, enhance patient engagement, expand delivery options, and maintain gains following termination (Clough & Casey, 2015; Price et al., 2014). mHealth may be especially useful for engagement and treatment delivery among patients with depression given the significant functional and motivational impairment that create barriers to attending health visits (Lépine & Briley, 2011). Prior research has focused primarily on mental health screening (Kim et al., 2016) and intervention (van't Hof, Cuijpers, & Stein, 2009) for individuals with less attention given to couple-based interventions. Future studies might examine adjunctive mHealth assessment and interventions combined with traditional approaches, adaptations of traditional assessment and interventions for mobile platforms, or innovative uses of technology to assess and intervene in novel ways.

Conclusions

Depressive and anxiety disorders are the most burdensome mental health conditions and rank highly among the most burdensome of all health conditions. Couple-based interventions offer effective methods for treating couples in which one or both partners are experiencing symptoms of depression and anxiety. While research to date has made substantial contributions in identifying effective ways to intervene among couples with depression and anxiety, further research is needed. Future research must better understand the etiological mechanisms of disorder and the ways in which evidence-based couple interventions target underlying mechanisms. We must commit to studying the delivery of couple-based interventions for diverse couples, including relevant cultural adaptations. Such research has the potential to help reduce the suffering of millions of people across the globe.

References

Acitelli, L. K., & Badr, H. J. (2005). My illness or our illness? Attending to the relationship when one partner is ill. In T. A. Revenson, K. Kayser, & G. Bodenmann (Eds.), *Decade of behavior. Couples coping with stress: Emerging perspectives on dyadic coping* (pp. 121–136). Washington, DC: American Psychological Association. doi:10.1037/11031-006

American Psychiatric Association (2013). *Diagnostic and statistical manual of mental disorders (DSM-5®)*. Author.

Arnow, B. A., Taylor, C. B., Agras, W. S., & Telch, M. J. (1985). Enhancing agoraphobia treatment outcome by changing couple communication patterns. *Behavior Therapy*, 16, 452–467. doi:10.1016/S0005-7894(85)80024-1

Arrindell, W. A., Emmelkamp, P. M. G., & Sanderman, R. (1986). Marital quality and general life adjustment in relation to treatment outcome in agoraphobia. *Advanced Behavior Research and Therapy*, 8, 139–185. doi:10.1016/0146-6402(86)90002-0

Atkins, D. C., Dimidjian, S., Bedics, J. D., & Christensen, A. (2009). Couple discord and depression in couples during couple therapy and in depressed individuals during depression treatment. *Journal of Consulting and Clinical Psychology*, 77, 1089. doi:10.1037/a0017119

Baert, S., De Raedt, R., & Koster, E. H. (2010). Depression-related attentional bias: The influence of symptom severity and symptom specificity. *Cognition and Emotion*, 24, 1044–1052. doi:10.1080/02699930903043461

Barbato, A., & D'Avanzo, B. (2008). Efficacy of couple therapy as a treatment for depression: A meta-analysis. *Psychiatric Quarterly*, 79, 121–132. doi:10.1007/s11126-008-9068-0

Bar-Haim, Y., Lamy, D., Perigamin, L., Bakermans-Kranenburg, M. J., & van IJzendoorn, M. H. (2007). Threat-related attentional bias in anxious and non-anxious individuals: A meta-analytic study. *Psychological Bulletin*, 133, 1–24. doi:10.1037/0033-2909.133.1.1

Barlow, D. H., Farchione, T. J., Sauer-Zavala, S., Latin, H. M., Ellard, K. K., Bullis, J. R., … Cassiello-Robbins, C. (2017). *Unified protocol for transdiagnostic treatment of emotional disorders: Therapist guide*. Oxford, UK: Oxford University Press.

Barlow, D. H., Mavissakalian, M., & Hay, L. R. (1981). Couples treatment of agoraphobia: Changes in marital satisfaction. *Behavior Research and Therapy*, 19, 245–255. doi:10.1016/0005-7967(81)90008-5

Barlow, D. H., O'Brien, G. T., & Last, C. G. (1984). Couples treatment of agoraphobia. *Behavior Therapy*, 14, 41–58. doi:10.1016/S0005-7894(84)80040-4

Baucom, B. R., Eldridge, K., Jones, J., Sevier, M., Clements, M., Markman, H., … Christensen, A. (2007). Contributions of marital distress and depression to communication patterns in distressed couples. *Journal of Social and Clinical Psychology*, 26, 689–707. doi:10.1521/jscp.2007.26.6.689

Baucom, D. H., Belus, J. M., Adelman, C. B., Fischer, M. S., & Paprocki, C. (2014). Couple-based interventions for psychopathology: A renewed direction for the field. *Family Process*, 53, 445–461. doi:10.1111/famp.12075

Baucom, D. H., Epstein, N., Sayers, S., & Sher, T. G. (1989). The role of cognition in marital relationships: Definitional, methodological, and conceptual issues. *Journal of Consulting and Clinical Psychology*, 57(1), 31–38. doi:10.1037/0022-006X.57.1.31

Baucom, D. H., Stanton, S., & Epstein, N. B. (2003). Anxiety disorders. In D. K. Snyder & M. A. Whisman (Eds.), *Treating difficult couples: Helping couples with coexisting mental and relationship disorders* (pp. 57–87). New York, NY: Guilford.

Baucom, D. H., Whisman, M. A., & Paprocki, C. (2012). Couple-based interventions for psychopathology. *Journal of Family Therapy*, 34, 250–270. doi:10.1111/j.1467-6427.2012.00600.x

Beaber, T. E., & Werner, P. D. (2009). The relationship between anxiety and sexual functioning in lesbians and heterosexual women. *Journal of Homosexuality*, 56, 639–654. doi:10.1080/00918360903005303

Beach, S. R., & Whisman, M. A. (2012). Affective disorders. *Journal of Marital and Family Therapy*, 38, 201–219. doi:10.1111/j.1752-0606.2011.00243.x

Beach, S. R. H., Dreifuss, J. A., Franklin, K. J., Kamen, C., & Gabriel, B. (2008). Couple therapy and the treatment of depression. In A. S. Gurman (Ed.), *Clinical handbook of couple therapy* (4th ed., pp. 545–566). New York, NY: Guilford Press.

Beach, S. R. H., Whisman, M. A., & Bodenmann, G. (2014). Couple, parenting, and interpersonal therapies for depression in adults: Toward common clinical guidelines within a stress generation framework. In I. A. Gotlib & C. Hammen (Eds.), *Handbook of depression* (3rd ed., pp. 552–570). New York, NY: Guilford Press.

Benson, L. A., Doss, B. D., & Christensen, A. (2018). Online intervention for couples affected by generalized anxiety disorder. *The European Journal of Counseling Psychology*, 7, 1–13. doi:10.5964/ejcop.v7i1.108

Biglan, A., Hops, H., Sherman, L., Friedman, L., Arthur, J., & Osteen, V. (1985). Problem-solving interactions of depressed women and their husbands. *Behavior Therapy*, 16, 431–451. doi:10.1016/S0005-7894(85)80023-X

Bowlby, J. (1988). *A secure base: clinical applications of attachment theory.* London, UK: Routledge.

Bradbury, T. N., Fincham, F. D., & Beach, S. H. (2000). Research on the nature and determinants of marital satisfaction: A decade in review. *Journal of Marriage and Family*, 62, 964–980. doi:10.1111/j.1741-3737.2000.00964.x

Brown, T. A., & Barlow, D. H. (2009). A proposal for a dimensional classification system based on the shared features of the DSM-IV anxiety and mood disorders: Implications for assessment and treatment. *Psychological Assessment*, 21, 256. doi:10.1037/a0016608

Bylsma, L. M., Morris, B. H., & Rottenberg, J. (2008). A meta-analysis of emotional reactivity in major depressive disorder. *Clinical Psychology Review*, 28, 676–691. doi:10.1016/j.cpr.2007.10.001

Byrne, M., Carr, A., & Clark, M. (2004). The efficacy of couples-based interventions for panic disorder with agoraphobia. *Journal of Family Therapy*, 26, 105–125. doi:10.1111/j.1467-6427.2004.00273.x

Cassidy, J., Lichtenstein-Phelps, J., Sibrava, N. J., Thomas, C. L., Jr., & Borkovec, T. D. (2009). Generalized anxiety disorder: Connections with self-reported attachment. *Behavior Therapy*, 40, 23–38. doi:10.1016/j.beth.2007.12.004

Cerny, J. A., Barlow, D. H., Craske, M. G., & Himadi, W. G. (1987). Couples treatment of agoraphobia: A two year follow up. *Behavior Therapy*, 18, 401–415. doi:10.1016/S0005-7894(87)80007-2

Chernen, L., & Friedman, S. (1993). Treating the personality disordered agoraphobic patient with individual and marital therapy. *Journal of Anxiety Disorders*, 7, 163–177. doi:10.1016/0887-6185(93)90014-C

Chisholm, D., Sweeny, K., Sheehan, P., Rasmussen, B., Smit, F., Cuijpers, P., & Saxena, S. (2016). Scaling-up treatment of depression and anxiety: A global return on investment analysis. *The Lancet Psychiatry*, 3, 415–424. doi:10.1016/S2215-0366(16)30024-4

Christensen, A., & Jacobson, N. S. (1998). *Acceptance and change in couple therapy: A therapist's guide to transforming relationships.* New York, NY: W. W. Norton & Company. ISBN: 0393702901

Christensen, A., & Nies, D. C. (1980). The spouse observation checklist: Empirical analysis and critique. *The American Journal of Family Therapy*, 2, 69–79. doi:10.1080/01926188008250357

Christian, J., O'Leary, K., & Vivian, D. (1994). Depressive symptomatology in maritally discordant women and men: The role of individual and relationship variables. *Journal of Family Psychology*, 8, 32–42. doi:10.1037/0893-3200.8.1.32

Cisler, J. M., & Koster, E. H. W. (2010). Mechanisms of attentional biases toward threat in the anxiety disorders: An integrative review. *Clinical Psychology Review*, 30, 203–216. doi:10.1016/j.cpr.2009.11.003

Clark, L. A., Cuthbert, B., Lewis-Fernández, R., Narrow, W. E., & Reed, G. M. (2017). Three approaches to understanding and classifying mental disorder: ICD-11, DSM-5, and the National Institute of Mental Health's research domain criteria (RDoC). *Psychological Science in the Public Interest*, 18, 72–145. doi:10.1177/1529100617727266

Clough, B. A., & Casey, L. M. (2015). The smart therapist: A look to the future of smartphones and mHealth technologies in psychotherapy. *Professional Psychology: Research and Practice*, 46, 147. doi:10.1037/pro0000011

Cobb, J., McDonald, R., Marks, I., & Stern, R. (1980). Marital versus exposure therapy: Psychological treatments of co-existing marital and phobic obsessive problem. *Behavioural Analysis and Modification*, 4, 3–17.

Cobb, J. P., Mathews, A. M., Childs-Clarke, A., & Blowers, C. M. (1984). The spouse as co-therapist in the treatment of agoraphobia. *British Journal of Psychiatry*, 144, 282–287.

Cohen, S., & Willis, T. A. (1985). Stress, social support, and the buffering hypothesis. *Psychological Bulletin*, 98, 310–357. doi:10.1037/0033-2909.98.2.310

Costa, P. T., & McCrae, R. R. (1987). Neuroticism, somatic complaints, and disease: Is the bark worse than the bite? *Journal of Personality*, 55, 299–316. doi:10.1111/j.1467-6494.1987.tb00438.x

Craske, M. G., Burton, T., & Barlow, D. H. (1989). Relationships among measures of communication, marital satisfaction, and exposure during couples treatment of agoraphobia. *Behavior Research and Therapy*, 27, 131–140. doi:10.1016/0005-7967(89)90071-5

Daiuto, A. D., Baucom, D. H., Epstein, N., & Dutton, S. S. (1998). The application of behavioral couples therapy to the assessment and treatment of agoraphobia: Implications of empirical research. *Clinical Psychology Review*, 18, 663–687.

Davila, J., & Beck, J. G. (2002). Is social anxiety associated with impairment in close relationships? A preliminary investigation. *Behavior Therapy*, 33, 427–446. doi:10.1016/S0005-7894(02)80037-5

Davila, J., Karney, B. R., Hall, T. W., & Bradbury, T. N. (2003). Depressive symptoms and marital satisfaction: Within-subject associations and the moderating effects of gender and neuroticism. *Journal of Family Psychology*, 17, 557–570. doi:10.1037/0893-3200.17.4.557

Davis, R. N., & Nolen-Hoeksema, S. (2000). Cognitive inflexibility among ruminators and nonruminators. *Cognitive Therapy and Research*, 24, 699–711. doi:10.1023/A:1005591412406

del Mar Sánchez-Fuentes, M., Santos-Iglesias, P., & Sierra, J. C. (2014). A systematic review of sexual satisfaction. *International Journal of Clinical and Health Psychology*, 14, 67–75. doi:10.1016/S1697-2600(14)70038-9

Denton, W. H., Carmody, T. J., Rush, A. J., Thase, M. E., Trivedi, M. H., Arnow, B. A., … Keller, M. B. (2010). Dyadic discord at baseline is associated with lack of remission in the acute treatment of chronic depression. *Psychological Medicine*, 40, 415–424. doi:10.1017/S0033291709990535

Denton, W. H., Wittenborn, A. K., & Golden, R. N. (2012). Augmenting antidepressant medication treatment of depressed women with emotionally focused therapy for couples: A randomized pilot study. *Journal of Marital and Family Therapy*, 38, 23–38. doi:10.1111/j.1752-0606.2012.00291.x

Desrosiers, A., Vine, V., Klemanski, D. H., & Nolen-Hoeksema, S. (2013). Mindfulness and emotion regulation in depression and anxiety: Common and distinct mechanisms of action. *Depression and Anxiety*, 30, 654–661. doi:10.1002/da.22124

Dessaulles, A., Johnson, S. M., & Denton, W. H. (2003). Emotion-focused therapy for couples in the treatment of depression: A pilot study. *The American Journal of Family Therapy*, 31, 345–353. doi:10.1080/01926180390232266

Dickson, K. S., Ciesla, J. A., & Reilly, L. C. (2012). Rumination, worry, cognitive avoidance, and behavioral avoidance: Examination of temporal effects. *Behavior Therapy*, 43, 629–640. doi:10.1016/j.beth.2011.11.002

Disner, S. G., Shumake, J. D., & Beevers, C. G. (2017). Self-referential schemas and attentional bias predict severity and naturalistic course of depression symptoms. *Cognition and Emotion*, 31, 632–644. doi:10.1080/02699931.2016.1146123

Doss, B. D., Cicila, L. N., Georgia, E. J., Roddy, M. K., Nowlan, K. M., Benson, L. A., & Christensen, A. (2016). A randomized controlled trial of the web-based OurRelationship program: Effects on relationship and individual functioning. *Journal of Consulting and Clinical Psychology*, 84, 285–296. doi:10.1037/ccp0000063

Durham, R. C., Allan, T., & Hackett, C. A. (1997). On predicting improvement and relapse in generalized anxiety disorder following psychotherapy. *British Journal of Clinical Psychology*, 36, 101–119. doi:10.1111/j.2044-8260.1997.tb01234.x

Emmelkamp, P. M. G., van Dyck, R., Bitter, M., Heins, R., Onstein, E. J., & Eisen, B. (1992). Spouse-aided therapy with agoraphobics. *British Journal of Psychiatry*, 160, 51–56.

Feeney, J. A. (2016). Adult romantic attachment: Developments in the study of couple relationships. In J. Cassidy & P. R. Shaver (Eds.), *Handbook of attachment: Theory, research, and clinical applications* (pp. 456–481). New York, NY: Guilford Press.

Fincham, F. D., Harold, G. T., & Gano-Phillips, S. (2000). The longitudinal association between attributions and marital satisfaction: Direction of effects and role of efficacy expectations. *Journal of Family Psychology*, 14, 267–285. doi:10.1037/0893-3200.14.2.267

Fisher, T. D., & McNulty, J. K. (2008). Neuroticism and marital satisfaction: The mediating role played by the sexual relationship. *Journal of Family Psychology*, 22, 112. doi:10.1037/0893-3200.22.1.112

Gabriel, B., Beach, S. R., & Bodenmann, G. (2010). Depression, marital satisfaction and communication in couples: Investigating gender differences. *Behavior Therapy*, 41, 306–316. doi:10.1016/j.beth.2009.09.001

Gotlib, I. H., Krasnoperova, E., Yue, D. N., & Joormann, J. (2004). Attentional biases for negative interpersonal stimuli in clinical depression. *Journal of Abnormal Psychology*, 113, 127.

Grey, S. J., & Mathews, A. M. (2009). Cognitive bias modification–priming with an ambiguous homograph is necessary to detect an interpretation training effect. *Journal of Behavior Therapy and Experimental Psychiatry*, 40, 338–343. doi:10.1016/j.jbtep.2009.01.003

Gross, J. J. (2013). Emotion regulation: Taking stock and moving forward. *Emotion*, 13, 359. doi:10.1037/a0032135

Gupta, M., Coyne, J. C., & Beach, S. R. (2003). Couples treatment for major depression: Critique of the literature and suggestions for some different directions. *Journal of Family Therapy*, 25, 317–346. doi:10.1111/1467-6427.00253

Hakulinen, C., Elovainio, M., Pulkki-Råback, L., Virtanen, M., Kivimäki, M., & Jokela, M. (2015). Personality and depressive symptoms: Individual participant meta-analysis of 10 cohort studies. *Depression and Anxiety*, 32, 461–470. doi:10.1002/da.22376

Hand, I., Angenendt, J., Fischer, M., & Wilke, C. (1986). Exposure and in-vivo with panic management for agoraphobia: Treatment rational and long term outcome. In I. Hand & H. Wittchen (Eds.), *Panic and phobias: Empirical evidence of theoretical models and long term effects of behavioral treatments* (pp. 104–127). Berlin, Germany: Springer-Verlag.

Heene, E., Buysse, A., & Van Oost, P. (2007). An interpersonal perspective on depression: The role of marital adjustment, conflict communication, attributions, and attachment within a clinical sample. *Family Process*, 46, 499–514. doi:10.1111/j.1545-5300.2007.00228.x

Heene, E. L., Buysse, A., & Van Oost, P. (2005). Indirect pathways between depressive symptoms and marital distress: The role of conflict communication, attributions, and attachment style. *Family Process*, 44, 413–440. doi:10.1111/j.1545-5300.2005.00070.x

Holahan, C. J., Moos, R. H., Holahan, C. K., Brennan, P. L., & Schutte, K. K. (2005). Stress generation, avoidance coping, and depressive symptoms: A 10-year model. *Journal of Consulting and Clinical Psychology*, 73, 658. doi:10.1037/0022-006X.73.4.658

Holley, S. R., Haase, C. M., Chui, I., & Bloch, L. (2018). Depression, emotion regulation, and the demand/withdraw pattern during intimate relationship conflict. *Journal of Social and Personal Relationships*, 35, 408–430.

Houben, M., Van Den Noortgate, W., & Kuppens, P. (2015). The relation between short-term emotion dynamics and psychological well-being: A meta-analysis. *Psychological Bulletin*, 141, 901. doi:10.1037/a0038822

Insel, T., Cuthbert, B., Garvey, M., Heinssen, R., Pine, D. S., Quinn, K., … Wang, P. (2010). Research domain criteria (RDoC): Toward a new classification framework for research on mental disorders. *American Journal of Psychiatry*, 167, 748–751. doi:10.1176/appi.ajp.2010.09091379

Jacobson, N. S., & Margolin, G. (1979). *Marital therapy: Strategies based on social learning and behavior exchange principles.* New York, NY: Brunner/Mazel.

Jaremka, L. M., Glaser, R., Malarkey, W. B., & Kiecolt-Glaser, J. K. (2013). Marital distress prospectively predicts poorer cellular immune function. *Psychoneuroendocrinology,* 38(11), 2713–2719. doi:10.1016/j.psyneuen.2013.06.031

Joiner, T., Metalsky, G., Katz, J., & Beach, S. (1999). Depression and excessive reassurance–seeking. *Psychological Inquiry,* 10, 269–278. doi:10.1207/S15327965PLI1004_1

Joiner, T. E. (2000). Depression's vicious scree: Self-propagating and erosive properties in depression chronicity. *Clinical Psychology: Science and Practice,* 7, 203–218. doi:10.1093/clipsy.7.2.203

Joormann, J., & Gotlib, I. H. (2010). Emotion regulation in depression: Relation to cognitive inhibition. *Cognition and Emotion,* 24, 281–298. doi:10.1080/02699930903407948

Kachadourian, L. K., Fincham, F., & Davila, J. (2005). Attitudinal ambivalence, rumination, and forgiveness of partner transgressions in marriage. *Personality and Social Psychology Bulletin,* 31, 334–342. doi:10.1177/0146167204271595

Karney, B. R., & Bradbury, T. N. (1995). The longitudinal course of marital quality and stability: A review of theory, method, and research. *Psychological Bulletin,* 118, 3–34.

Kennedy, S. H. (2008). Core symptoms of major depressive disorder: Relevance to diagnosis and treatment. *Dialogues in Clinical Neuroscience,* 10, 271.

Kennedy, S. H., Rizvi, S., Fulton, K., & Rasmussen, J. (2008). A double-blind comparison of sexual functioning, antidepressant efficacy, and tolerability between agomelatine and venlafaxine XR. *Journal of Clinical Psychopharmacology,* 28, 329–333. doi:10.1097/JCP.0b013e318172b48c

Kim, J., Lim, S., Min, Y. H., Shin, Y. W., Lee, B., Sohn, G., ... Shin, S. Y. (2016). Depression screening using daily mental-health ratings from a smartphone application for breast cancer patients. *Journal of Medical Internet Research,* 18, e216. doi:10.2196/jmir.5598

Kuehner, C., & Buerger, C. (2005). Determinants of subjective quality of life in depressed patients: The role of self-esteem, response styles, and social support. *Journal of Affective Disorders,* 86, 205–213. doi:10.1016/j.jad.2005.01.014

Kurdek, L. A. (1997). Relation between neuroticism and dimensions of relationship commitment: Evidence from gay, lesbian, and heterosexual couples. *Journal of Family Psychology,* 11, 109–134. doi:10.1037/0893-3200.11.1.109

Kwon, H., Yoon, K. L., Joormann, J., & Kwon, J. H. (2013). Cultural and gender differences in emotion regulation: Relation to depression. *Cognition & Emotion,* 27, 769–782. doi:10.1080/02699931.2013.792244

Lee, A., & Hankin, B. L. (2009). Insecure attachment, dysfunctional attitudes, and low self-esteem predicting prospective symptoms of depression and anxiety during adolescence. *Journal of Clinical Child and Adolescent Psychology,* 38, 219–231. doi:10.1080/15374410802698396

Lee, M. R., Cohen, L., Hadley, S. W., & Goodwin, F. K. (1999). Cognitive-behavioral group therapy with medication for depressed gay men with AIDS or symptomatic HIV infection. *Psychiatric Services,* 50, 948–952. doi:10.1176/ps.50.7.948

Lépine, J. P., & Briley, M. (2011). The increasing burden of depression. *Neuropsychiatric Disease and Treatment,* 7, 3. doi:10.2147/NDT.S19617

Liu, D. Y., & Thompson, R. J. (2017). Selection and implementation of emotion regulation strategies in major depressive disorder: An integrative review. *Clinical Psychology Review,* 57, 183–194. doi:10.1016/j.cpr.2017.07.004

Luten, A. G., Ralph, J. A., & Mineka, S. (1997). Pessimistic attributional style: Is it specific to depression versus anxiety versus negative affect? *Behaviour Research and Therapy,* 35, 703–719. doi:10.1016/S0005-7967(97)00027-2

Lyubomirsky, S., & Nolen-Hoeksema, S. (1995). Effects of self-focused rumination on negative thinking and interpersonal problem solving. *Journal of Personality and Social Psychology,* 69, 176–190. doi:10.1037/0022-3514.69.1.176

Malouff, J. M., Thorsteinsson, E. B., Schutte, N. S., Bhullar, N., & Rooke, S. E. (2010). The five factor model of personality and relationship satisfaction of intimate partners: A meta-analysis. *Journal of Research in Personality*, 44, 124–127. doi:10.1016/j.jrp.2009.09.004

Mathews, A., & MacLeod, C. (2005). Cognitive vulnerability to emotional disorders. *Annual Review of Clinical Psychology*, 1, 167–195. doi:10.1146/annurev.clinpsy.1.102803.143916

Mathews, A. M., Teasdale, J., Mundby, M., Johnston, D., & Shaw, P. (1977). A home based treatment program for agoraphobia. *Behavior Therapy*, 8, 915–924. doi:10.1016/S0005-7894(77)80161-5

McLeod, J. (1994). Anxiety disorders and marital quality. *Journal of Abnormal Psychology*, 103, 767–776. doi:10.1037/0021-843X.103.4.767

Montesi, J. L., Conner, B. T., Gordon, E. A., Fabuer, R. L., Kim, K. H., & Heimberg, R. G. (2013). On the relationship among social anxiety, intimacy, sexual communication, and sexual satisfaction in young couples. *Archives of Sexual Behavior*, 42, 81–91. doi:10.1007/s10508-012-9929-3

Morris, Z. S., Wooding, S., & Grant, J. (2011). The answer is 17 years, what is the question: Understanding time lags in translational research. *Journal of the Royal Society of Medicine*, 104, 510–520. doi:10.1258/jrsm.2011.110180

Nolen-Hoeksema, S. (1991). Responses to depression and their effects on the duration of depressive episodes. *Journal of Abnormal Psychology*, 100, 569.

Nolen-Hoeksema, S. (2000). The role of rumination in depressive disorders and mixed anxiety/depressive symptoms. *Journal of Abnormal Psychology*, 109, 504. doi:10.1037/0021-843X.109.3.504

Ottenbreit, N. D., Dobson, K. S., & Quigley, L. (2014). An examination of avoidance in major depression in comparison to social anxiety disorder. *Behaviour Research and Therapy*, 56, 82–90. doi:10.1016/j.brat.2014.03.005

Overbeek, G., Volleberg, W., de Graaf, R., Scholte, R., de Kemp, R., & Engels, R. (2006). Longitudinal associations of marital quality and marital dissolution with the incident of DSM-III-R disorders. *Journal of Family Psychology*, 20, 284–291. doi:10.1037/0893-3200.20.2.284

Painuly, N., Sharan, P., & Mattoo, S. K. (2005). Relationship of anger and anger attacks with depression. *European Archives of Psychiatry and Clinical Neuroscience*, 255, 215–222. doi:10.1007/s00406-004-0539-5

Pearson, K. A., Watkins, E. R., Kuyken, W., & Mullan, E. G. (2010). The psychosocial context of depressive rumination: Ruminative brooding predicts diminished relationship satisfaction in individuals with a history of past major depression. *British Journal of Clinical Psychology*, 49, 275–280. doi:10.1348/014466509X480553

Pew Research Center. (2018). *Mobile fact sheet*. Retrieved from http://www.pewinternet.org/fact-sheet/mobile

Price, M., Yuen, E. K., Goetter, E. M., Herbert, J. D., Forman, E. M., Acierno, R., & Ruggiero, K. J. (2014). mHealth: A mechanism to deliver more accessible, more effective mental health care. *Clinical Psychology & Psychotherapy*, 21, 427–436. doi:10.1002/cpp.1855

Proctor, E. K., Landsverk, J., Aarons, G., Chambers, D., Glisson, C., & Mittman, B. (2009). Implementation research in mental health services: An emerging science with conceptual, methodological, and training challenges. *Administration and Policy in Mental Health and Mental Health Services Research*, 36, 24–34. doi:10.1007/s10488-008-0197-4

Quigley, L., Wen, A., & Dobson, K. S. (2017). Avoidance and depression vulnerability: An examination of avoidance in remitted and currently depressed individuals. *Behaviour Research and Therapy*, 97, 183–188. doi:10.1016/j.brat.2017.07.015

Rehman, U. S., Ginting, J., Karimiha, G., & Goodnight, J. A. (2010). Revisiting the relationship between depressive symptoms and marital communication using an experimental paradigm: The moderating effect of acute sad mood. *Behaviour Research and Therapy*, 48, 97–105. doi:10.1016/j.brat.2009.09.013

Roberts, B. W., Walton, K. E., & Viechtbauer, W. (2006). Patterns of mean-level change in personality traits across the life course: A meta-analysis of longitudinal studies. *Psychological Bulletin*, 132, 1. doi:10.1037/0033-2909.132.1.1

Robles, T. F., Slatcher, R. B., Trombello, J. M., & McGinn, M. M. (2014). Marital quality and health: A meta-analytic review. *Psychological Bulletin*, 140, 140–187. doi:10.1037/a0031859

Roelofs, J., Huibers, M., Peeters, F., Arntz, A., & van Os, J. (2008). Rumination and worrying as possible mediators in the relation between neuroticism and symptoms of depression and anxiety in clinically depressed individuals. *Behaviour Research and Therapy*, 46, 1283–1289. doi:10.1016/j.brat.2008.10.002

Sandberg, J. G., & Knestel, A. (2011). The experience of learning emotionally focused couples therapy. *Journal of Marital and Family Therapy*, 37, 393–410. doi:10.1111/j.1752-0606.2011.00254.x

Sauer-Zavala, S., Gutner, C. A., Farchione, T. J., Boettcher, H. T., Bullis, J. R., & Barlow, D. H. (2017). Current definitions of "transdiagnostic" in treatment development: A search for consensus. *Behavior Therapy*, 48, 128–138. doi:10.1016/j.beth.2016.09.004

Schmaling, K., & Jacobson, N. (1990). Marital interaction and depression. *Journal of Abnormal Psychology*, 99, 229–236.

Scott, R. L., & Cordova, J. V. (2002). The influence of adult attachment styles on the association between marital adjustment and depressive symptoms. *Journal of Family Psychology*, 16, 199. doi:10.1037//0893-3200.16.2.199

Thoits, P. A. (2011). Mechanisms linking social ties and support to physical and mental health. *Journal of Health and Social Behavior*, 52, 145–161. doi:10.1177/0022146510395592

Titov, N., Dear, B. F., Schwencke, G., Andrews, G., Johnston, L., Craske, M. G., & McEvoy, P. (2011). Transdiagnostic internet treatment for anxiety and depression: A randomised controlled trial. *Behaviour Research and Therapy*, 49, 441–452. doi:10.1016/j.brat.2011.03.007

Trick, L., Watkins, E., Windeatt, S., & Dickens, C. (2016). The association of perseverative negative thinking with depression, anxiety and emotional distress in people with long term conditions: A systematic review. *Journal of Psychosomatic Research*, 91, 89–101. doi:10.1016/j.jpsychores.2016.11.004

Van Minnen, A., & Kampman, M. (2000). The interaction between anxiety and sexual functioning: A controlled study of sexual functioning in women with anxiety disorders. *Sexual and Relationship Therapy*, 15, 47–57. doi:10.1080/14681990050001556

van't Hof, P., Cuijpers, P., & Stein, D. J. (2009). Self-help and internet-guided interventions in depression and anxiety disorders: a systematic review of meta-analyses. *CNS Spectrums*, 14, 34–40. doi:10.1017/S1092852900027279

Vrshek-Schallhorn, S., Velkoff, E. A., & Zinbarg, R. E. (2018). Trait rumination and response to negative evaluative lab-induced stress: Neuroendocrine, affective, and cognitive outcomes. *Cognition and Emotion*, 33, 1–14. doi:10.1080/02699931.2018.1459486

Waitzfelder, B., Stewart, C., Coleman, K. J., Rossom, R., Ahmedani, B. K., Beck, A., ... Simon, G. E. (2018). Treatment initiation for new episodes of depression in primary care settings. *Journal of General Internal Medicine*, 1–9. doi:10.1007/s11606-017-4297-2

Watson, D., Clark, L. A., & Carey, G. (1988). Positive and negative affectivity and their relation to anxiety and depressive disorders. *Journal of Abnormal Psychology*, 97, 346. doi:10.1037/0021-843X.97.3.346

Wenzel, A., Graff-Dolezal, J., Macho, M., & Brendle, J. R. (2005). Communication and social skills in socially anxious and nonanxious individuals in the context of romantic relationships. *Behaviour Research and Therapy*, 43, 505–519. doi:10.1016/j.brat.2004.03.010

Wenzlaff, R. M., & Luxton, D. D. (2003). The role of thought suppression in depressive rumination. *Cognitive Therapy and Research*, 27, 293–308. doi:10.1023/A:1023966400540

Wetterneck, C. T., & Hart, J. M. (2012). Intimacy is a transdiagnostic problem for cognitive behavior therapy: Functional Analytical Psychotherapy is a solution. *International Journal of Behavioral Consultation and Therapy*, 7, 167.

Whisman, M. A. (1999). Marital dissatisfaction and psychiatric disorders: Results from the National Comorbidity Study. *Journal of Abnormal Psychology*, 108, 701–706. doi:10.1037/0021-843X.108.4.701

Whisman, M. A. (2001). Marital adjustment and outcome following treatments for depression. *Journal of Consulting and Clinical Psychology*, 69, 125. doi:10.1037/0022-006X.69.1.125

Whisman, M. A. (2007). Marital distress and DSM-IV psychiatric disorders in a population-based national survey. *Journal of Abnormal Psychology*, 116, 638–643. doi:10.1037/0021-843X.116.3.638

Whisman, M. A., & Baucom, D. H. (2012). Intimate relationships and psychopathology. *Clinical Child and Family Psychology Review*, 15, 4–13. doi:10.1007/s10567-011-0107-2

Whitton, S. W., & Kuryluk, A. D. (2013). Intrapersonal moderators of the association between relationship satisfaction and depressive symptoms: Findings from emerging adults. *Journal of Social and Personal Relationships*, 30, 750–770. doi:10.1177/0265407512467749

Wittenborn, A. K., Faber, A. J., & Keiley, M. K. (2012). An attachment and affect regulation based multiple couple group intervention for couples transitioning to marriage/commitment. *Journal of Couple and Relationship Therapy*, 11, 189–204. doi:10.1080/15332691.2012.692941

Wittenborn, A. K., Liu, T., Ridenour, T. A., Lachmar, E. M., Mitchell, E. A., & Seedall, R. B. (2019). Randomized controlled trial of emotionally focused couple therapy compared to treatment as usual for depression: Outcomes and mechanisms of change. *Journal of Marital and Family Therapy*, 45, 395–409.

Wittenborn, A. K., Rahmandad, H., Rick, J., & Hosseinichimeh, N. (2016). Depression as a systemic syndrome: Mapping the feedback loops of major depressive disorder. *Psychological Medicine*, 46, 551–562. doi:10.1017/S0033291715002044

World Health Organization. (2017). *Depression and other common mental disorders: Global health estimates.* Geneva, Switzerland: Author.

Yoon, K. L., Maltby, J., & Joormann, J. (2013). A pathway from neuroticism to depression: Examining the role of emotion regulation. *Anxiety, Stress & Coping*, 26, 558–572. doi:10.1080/10615806.2012.734810

Zaider, T. I., Heimberg, R. G., & Iida, M. (2010). Anxiety disorders and intimate relationships: A study of daily processes in couples. *Journal of Abnormal Psychology*, 119, 163. doi:10.1037/a0018473

Zinbarg, R. E., Lee, J. E., & Yoon, K. L. (2007). Dyadic predictors of outcome in a cognitive-behavioral program for patients with generalized anxiety disorder in committed relationships: A "spoonful of sugar" and a dose of non-hostile criticism may help. *Behavior Research and Therapy*, 45, 699–713. doi:10.1016/j.brat.2006.06.005

10

Posttraumatic Stress and Couples

Adrian J. Blow, Briana S. Nelson Goff,
Adam M. Farero, and Lauren M. Ruhlmann

Even before the term posttraumatic stress disorder (PTSD) was originally printed in the *Diagnostic and Statistical Manual of Mental Disorders, Third Edition (DSM-III)* (American Psychiatric Association [APA], 1980), researchers and clinicians had been working to understand the effects from exposure to traumatic events, to identify those individuals most vulnerable to the repercussions from trauma, and to understand the factors that enhance the outcomes of resilience, growth, and recovery in certain survivors. Almost in tandem, others identified that individual trauma survivors were not alone in the turmoil of their daily symptoms—partners, children, and other individuals close to trauma survivors also lived with the burden of PTS/D, often in silence along with the survivors (Figley, 1989a, 1989b; Solomon et al., 1992).

Today, we recognize the psychological, emotional, behavioral, cognitive, and biological symptoms of PTS/D that make up the individual effects from trauma and the potential range of trauma symptoms, from acute to chronic (Ford, Grasso, Elhai, & Courtois, 2015). The level of functioning of the individual trauma survivor has been widely studied and clinically described, particularly since the term "PTSD" was identified. The *DSM-V* (APA, 2013) categorizes PTSD symptoms into four clusters: *re-experiencing* (e.g., flashbacks, intrusive memories), *arousal* (e.g., hypervigilance, anger outbursts), *changes in cognitions and mood* (e.g., negative thoughts and feelings, feeling isolated), and *avoidance* (e.g., avoiding trauma-related stimuli or reminders of the event). When these symptoms are present, they permeate the lives of many trauma survivors, whether or not they meet the full criteria for PTSD.

Symptoms of posttraumatic stress create a difficult living situation for trauma survivors and their family members, as the symptoms associated with trauma and PTS/D are pernicious and highly disruptive. PTSD places considerable strain on the partner of the individual living with PTSD. Not only are the partners affected by the partner's trauma symptoms, but they may also have to overcompensate in other areas, such as household chores, childcare, or other tasks. These partners may also develop symptoms related to living with a traumatized individual. Secondary traumatic stress (STS) can be traced back to the early work of Figley and others (Figley, 1989a, 1989b), which focused primarily on Vietnam veteran partners. In the years since, several

The Handbook of Systemic Family Therapy: Volume 3, First Edition.
Edited by Karen S. Wampler and Adrian J. Blow.
© 2020 John Wiley & Sons Ltd. Published 2020 by John Wiley & Sons Ltd.

clinicians and researchers have sought to conceptualize and empirically validate this term—to provide direct evidence for the secondary effects of trauma. Researchers have addressed STS from several different clinical and empirical approaches, providing the foundation from which we can begin to understand that the repercussions of trauma and PTS/D are not isolated and individual, but are systemic and interpersonal. As Figley (1995, 2002) stated, living with and caring for someone with PTS/D can be traumatizing to the partner, children, and other family members. In this chapter, we will argue that intervening in intimate relationships is an essential element in helping ameliorate PTS/D symptoms in individuals and to stem the degenerative effects that can occur.

PTS/D symptoms can send the wrong message to a partner, the message that an individual wants to be left alone and does not want to talk about what happened in the past or what is currently happening, in terms of PTS/D symptoms. This is because PTS/D symptoms do not manifest as warm approachable emotions. Rather, they are often emotions like anger or avoidance that serve to drive loved ones away. Even though these emotions may be present, it does not mean that an individual does not wish to talk about their experiences. In fact, these individuals may be longing for a place to tell their loved one what is happening. However, a partner may interpret these emotions negatively and feel hurt and shut out by their loved one with PTSD. This dynamic leads to more relational distance, misunderstandings, and isolation and ultimately to more arguing and tension.

Trauma Exposure and Trauma Type

Some prevalence estimates suggest that upward of 75–90% of the population will experience a potentially traumatic event (Kessler et al., 2017; Kilpatrick et al., 2013), with many people experiencing multiple traumas over the course of their lifetime (Contractor, Brown, & Weiss, 2018; Karam et al., 2014). The aggregate of repeat trauma exposure (i.e., polytraumatization; Contractor et al., 2018; Sullivan, Contractor, Gerber, & Neumann, 2017) is associated with increased emotional distress, functional impairment, posttraumatic stress symptom severity, and depression (Briere, Agee, & Dietrich, 2016; Contractor et al., 2018; Karam et al., 2014). Studies show that there is a dose–response relationship between cumulative trauma and psychological distress, such that each additional trauma exposure is predictive of exacerbated posttraumatic stress and psychosocial impairment (Briere et al., 2016; Contractor et al., 2018; Turner & Lloyd, 1995).

Equally important to trauma load in understanding survivors' posttraumatic adaptation is the type of trauma experienced. For example, interpersonal traumas (e.g., assault, physical abuse, sexual abuse, intimate partner violence [IPV]) are associated with more severe posttraumatic stress symptoms, affective dysregulation, anxious attachment patterns, and interpersonal challenges than non-interpersonal trauma (Alisic, Boeije, Jongmans, & Kleber, 2012; Briere et al., 2016; Forbes et al., 2014; McCall-Hosenfeld, Winter, Heeren, & Liebschutz, 2014; Taft, Resick, Watkins, & Panuzio, 2009). Interpersonal trauma is particularly poignant because it threatens survivors' understanding and sense of safety, both within themselves and in the context of close relationships, which can subsequently contribute to distorted beliefs and increased psychosocial distress (Alisic et al., 2012; Sullivan et al., 2017).

Betrayal trauma theory (Freyd, Klest, & Allard, 2005; Sivers, Schooler, & Freyd, 2002) elucidates such findings further by suggesting that the degree to which a traumatic experience constitutes a betrayal by a significant or trusted other affects how survivors process and integrate their experience into their working narratives or schemas. Further, according to this theory, survivors of interpersonal trauma face a dual threat from both the direct (e.g., compromised sense of safety, more severe symptomology) and indirect effects of victimization (Freyd, 1996; Freyd et al., 2005). Specifically, survivors of interpersonal trauma are at a greater risk for "betrayal blindness," an increased vulnerability to making unsound decisions about who to trust in relationships, which may make them increasingly susceptible to future re-victimization (Freyd, 1996).

Recognizing that the phenomenology of polytraumatization and betrayal trauma were fundamentally distinct from other forms of victimization, the field of traumatology adopted the term "complex trauma" to characterize traumatic experiences that are chronic, varied, and perpetuated across time, generally perpetrated by significant or trusted others at developmentally sensitive periods in survivors' lives (Ford & Courtois, 2009; van der Kolk, Roth, Pelcovitz, Sunday, & Spinazzola, 2005). Research suggests there are unique complex trauma sequelae—complex PTSD (CPTSD)—differentiated from traditional PTSD by exaggerated symptoms of posttraumatic stress and affective dysregulation, a diminished sense of self/identity disturbance, high dissociative tendencies, pronounced psychosomatic symptoms, and severe disruptions in interpersonal relations and the capacity for emotional intimacy (Cloitre, Garvert, Brewin, Bryant, & Maercker, 2013; Cloitre, Garvert, Weiss, Carlson, & Bryant, 2014; Elhai, Naifeh, Forbes, Ractliffe, & Tamburrino, 2011; Elklit, Hyland, & Shevlin, 2014; Ford & Courtois, 2009; van der Kolk et al., 2005). Moreover, results from 20 population surveys in the World Health Organization World Mental Health Survey Initiative have identified a risk threshold of PTSD survivors associated with four or more traumatic life events as indicative of a "complex" clinical presentation, indicated by increased functional impairment and greater symptom morbidity, compared to traditional cases of PTSD (Karam et al., 2014).

Although not recognized within the *DSM-V* (APA, 2013), CPTSD is included in the World Health Organization's 11th revision of the *International Classification of Diseases (ICD-11)* (WHO, 2018) based on this growing body of research supporting its etiological and symptomatic discretion from other trauma-related disorders (e.g., Cloitre et al., 2013, 2014; Elhai et al., 2011; Elklit et al., 2014; Hyland et al., 2017; Karam et al., 2014; Karatzias et al., 2017). CPTSD also has implications for working with couples and families, as "disruptions in relationships" is one of the three additional CPTSD symptom clusters. Dorahy et al. (2013) described CPTSD as "a *relational disorder* with its antecedents in relational trauma and its consequences in relational disconnectedness" (p. 72). Thus, the interpersonal experience and manifestation of complex traumatic stress poses a significant threat to the strength and stability of relational attachment bonds. Although additional research is needed to develop a more comprehensive understanding of complex trauma in the context of couple relationships, preliminary findings allude to heightened vulnerability among dyads coping with this unique type of traumatic stress.

Theoretical Rationale for Trauma-Informed Systemic Interventions

While much of the empirical, theoretical, and clinical literature on trauma and PTS/D has focused almost exclusively on the individual trauma survivor, some progress has been made to recognize the systemic effects of trauma, including the recognition that PTS/D could result from indirect exposure to the trauma, from learning about the trauma experiences or being exposed to the symptoms of the primary trauma survivor (APA, 2013). Incorporating a partner or support person in treatment provides a key opportunity for members of the system to support the primary trauma survivor in his/her recovery process while at the same time providing support/knowledge to the partner in negotiating the ups and downs of trauma recovery. Ignoring the systemic effects of trauma and PTS/D may be neglecting effective and critical paths for healing (Blow, Fraser Curtis, Wittenborn, & Gorman, 2015).

As described by Ford et al. (2015), social support systems can serve as a protective buffer, providing some of the necessary components to protect individuals from the negative effects of trauma. However, support systems also may be vulnerable to the stress and trauma symptoms experienced by primary trauma survivors, possibly leading to secondary trauma and relationship impairment, as well as other negative outcomes. This may be due to symptoms of trauma effectively pushing people away if an individual is displaying angry outbursts or withdrawing without explanation. How those critical relationships are impacted, either directly or indirectly, are what we focus on next through the current theoretical models that describe the systemic effects of trauma and PTS/D.

Social support and trauma

Early literature on stress and coping presented the original buffering hypothesis for social support and well-being (Cohen, 2004; Cohen & Wills, 1985; Thoits, 1982, 1995). The shift then to studying trauma and traumatic stress/PTSD and social support in the field is not surprising. Previous research on trauma and social support has focused on structural (i.e., the presence of social relationships) and functional (i.e., specific resources provided from one's social relationships) social support, and on perceived resources and stressors from individuals in the social network, primarily as social support affects PTSD symptom levels (James, Van Kampen, Miller, & Engdahl, 2013; King, King, Fairbank, Keane, & Adams, 1998; Platt, Keyes, & Koenen, 2014). Two previous meta-analyses of risk factors related to PTSD indicated the lack of social support to be a strong predictor of PTSD symptoms (Brewin, Andrews, & Valentine, 2000; Ozer, Best, Lipsey, & Weiss, 2003).

In a sample from the National Epidemiologic Survey on Alcohol and Related Conditions, diversity of social support seemed to be more critical to PTSD outcomes than the perceived amount of support the person receives (Platt et al., 2014). Although social support has been found to be the strongest and most consistent protective factor that reduces the risk for PTSD (Brewin et al., 2000; Ford et al., 2015), the couple relationship, as a primary social support component, has not been acknowledged as a key factor in trauma treatment and recovery. In fact, Riggs (2000) stated that the systemic treatment of trauma and traumatic stress is merely considered adjunct or peripheral to individual interventions.

The Couple Adaptation to Traumatic Stress (CATS) model

The Couple Adaptation to Traumatic Stress (CATS) Model (Nelson Goff & Smith, 2005) was one of the first family systems frameworks to outline the interpersonal effects of trauma in the context of couple systems (see Nelson Goff, Ruhlmann, Dekel, & Huxman, 2020, vol. 4, for further description of family-based models of trauma and PTS/D). The CATS Model (Nelson Goff & Smith, 2005; Oseland, Gallus, & Nelson Goff, 2016) provides a description of the mechanisms by which traumatic stress influences individual and couple functioning and dyadic interaction. The individual biopsychosocial trauma symptoms (e.g., PTSD symptoms) affect not only the individual trauma survivor but also his/her partner because of the close connection and intimacy of the marital/couple relationship. The partner's parallel (i.e., vicarious or secondary) trauma symptoms (STS) may mutually impact the coping methods of the trauma survivor and the relationship functioning of the couple (see Nelson Goff & Smith, 2005; Oseland et al., 2016). The CATS Model suggests that the effects of traumatic stress, specifically in the context of the spousal or couple relationship, involves both individual and relational factors in recognizing the full effects and consequences of trauma, which involve a cyclical and mutual process within the couple relationship (Nelson Goff & Smith, 2005; Oseland et al., 2016).

The modifications to the original CATS Model (Oseland et al., 2016) add a more specific outline of the couple functioning components, including communication as a primary element, as well as three additional components that coincide with Herman's (1997) triphasic model of trauma: safety and stability, traumatic process, and connection. Based on these components, Oseland and colleagues outlined the specific interpersonal components in each section, grounded in theoretical knowledge and empirical support gleaned since the publication of the original CATS Model (Nelson Goff & Smith, 2005). The revised CATS Model introduced a clinical intervention framework by organizing into three treatment phases—according to Herman's (1997) triphasic trauma treatment model. The revised CATS Model was intended to provide a pragmatic guide for clinical interventions with traumatized couples. The CATS Model continues to inform thinking on both research and intervention on trauma, PTS/D, and couple relationship functioning.

Attachment theory as conceptualized in emotionally focused therapy (EFT) and application to trauma

Attachment theory was developed by Bowlby (1969) and is focused on the bonds that exist between a caregiver and a child. Attachment theory has been applied to adult intimate relationships (e.g., Hazan & Shaver, 1987; Johnson, 2002a; Johnson & Williams Keeler, 1998), with trauma being a key factor that is disruptive to attachment bonds. Traumatic experiences can wreak havoc on the attachment bonds of an individual, especially when trauma is interpersonal (e.g., sexual trauma, physical violence). From this standpoint, individuals may have a difficult time trusting other people. The symptoms of trauma (e.g., avoidance, hypervigilance) also create distance in attachment within intimate relationships. Trauma survivors may have difficulties in sharing what is going on when they are triggered, even with loved ones, and over time, these walls create distance in relationships.

Emotionally focused therapy (EFT) suggests that as a part of trauma recovery, bonds in intimate relationships need to be restructured with a safe and available significant other, as a part of trauma recovery, because of the effects of trauma on both the traumatized individual and on the relationship. Johnson (2002a) emphasized that many traumatic experiences occur within a relational context and the consequences often are transmitted across other interpersonal relationships. Johnson and Williams Keeler (1998) described the emotional responses and patterns of distance, defense, and distrust that occur in couples in which a partner has a history of trauma that negatively affects their relationship functioning. As Johnson (2002a) stated, "if a person's connection with significant others is not part of the coping and healing process, then, inevitably, it becomes part of the problem and even a source of retraumatization" (p. 7). The negative impact of numbing, avoidance, and other symptoms of the individual trauma survivor(s) produces a reciprocal pattern of mutual distance and disconnection between partners, reducing the interpersonal attachment necessary for healthy dyadic functioning (Johnson, 2002a). However, the connection that partners develop for one another also could provide a resource in healing from trauma through the development of a safe, stable, and secure bond between partners that promotes mutual attachment and connection. Thus, attachment within intimate relationships is a critical aspect in recognizing the systemic effects of trauma in couples (Johnson, 2002a; Nelson Goff & Smith, 2005; Oseland et al., 2016).

Ambiguous loss and intimate couple relationships

Ambiguous loss is a concept that has gained importance in the trauma literature (Boss, 2004), but which may not be equated with other losses such as death, yet they have negative impacts on relationships. Ambiguous loss is characterized by an unclear or uncertain loss, such as when someone is missing for years but no body is found. Ambiguous losses are psychological losses, losses that change a relationship and lead to grief, but often not to resolution of grief due to the ambiguities of the loss (Boss, 2004). In relation to trauma, losses do occur, but unlike loss from a death, losses due to traumatic events are unclear in that trauma changes individuals in a way that can be confusing or ambiguous. In this sense, even though an individual may still be physically present, she/he has been changed completely. For example, a soldier returns from a war deployment where he witnessed several highly traumatic events; he is changed by these events, and even though he is still physically present when he returns home, he is psychologically absent (or psychologically different). He is completely changed by the traumatic experiences. This loss, according to Boss, is stressful, because it is not clearly defined and its resolution is not always possible. For those in a relationship with trauma survivors, there is no specific or tangible loss that leads to mourning and then to resolution. When the traumatized soldier returns from war, a partner at home has to adjust considerably to the changes in his/her loved one and get to know him/her all over again. These trauma adjustments lead to mixed (ambiguous) feelings (e.g., my husband is not dead, but he has changed). As individuals deal with ambiguous loss caused by trauma, there are several considerations. One is that trauma work is often done with individuals and not with a collective group such as a family/couple relationship (López-Zerón & Blow, 2017). This is something that needs to change in that not only does a traumatic event change an individual, but the treatment for the individual leads to changes as well. Even if we conceptualize these changes as growth, as occurs in the posttraumatic growth literature, it is still a growth that affects relationships. For this reason, including partners is important in trauma-based clinical interventions. Finally, growing through a trauma is a painful, often lengthy, process, which can last weeks to months or even years. The process of recovery from trauma is optimized if the couple can grow together, supporting each other through their recovery process. Partners need to be able to live with this process while at the same time working to provide optimal support and also deal with their own losses, which can be difficult for both partners (Boss, 2004).

The work by Monson, Taft, and Fredman (2009) also described the idea of ambiguous loss for military couples. Caregivers who are often partners are faced with supporting their loved one on multiple levels. While the partner still loves the individual, she/he now must adapt to someone with PTS/D, a disorder often characterized by angry outbursts or emotional detachment while at the same time having to be a key source of support for the individual with PTS/D. Adjusting to these losses for the partner can create further problems in the couple relationship, leading to a spiraling or reciprocal pattern of problems, where the PTS/D symptoms are exacerbated and the relationship problems worsen. This can lead to lower support for the individual with PTS/D and possibly a higher presence of PTS/D symptoms. (See the work of Dekel, Goldblatt, Keidar, Solomon, and Polliack (2005), which describes the perspective of a wife of a veteran with PTSD.)

Cognitive models of trauma and relationships

The cognitive-behavioral interpersonal model describes various cognitive, behavioral, and emotional challenges associated with PTS/D that contribute to relationship distress (Dekel & Monson, 2010). Although this model has yet to be studied as a whole, several studies have provided insight into a variety of mechanisms that help explain the connection between the experience of trauma and ensuing interpersonal difficulties.

The CBT-interpersonal model explains that as cognitive processes are disrupted by PTS/D, these disruptions then contribute to and perpetuate PTS/D and associated couple relationship problems. The experience of trauma can have a detrimental influence on a variety of belief systems as they relate to the trauma survivor and his/her partner, including trust, power/control, intimacy, and esteem (Janoff-Bulman, 1992; McCann & Pearlman, 1990). For example, trauma survivors are more likely to experience an attentional bias toward environmental threats, meaning that they may be particularly sensitive to their environment and may perceive danger or threats where none exist. This can lead trauma survivors to be distrusting of people with whom they interact, including their partners. Along with this distrust, trauma survivors may use controlling behavior with their partners, which ultimately damages the relationship and lowers satisfaction. These are especially present in survivors traumatized by trusted individuals, as with betrayal traumas, described previously (Freyd et al., 2005; Sivers et al., 2002).

Similar to cognitions, PTS/D-related behaviors also have the potential to harm the interpersonal relationships of trauma survivors. One key behavioral mechanism is the avoidance of trauma-related stimuli. In fact, emotional numbing has been identified as the most consistent PTSD symptom cluster that negatively affects relationship functioning (Campbell & Renshaw, 2018). In an effort to avoid negative emotions related to the trauma, trauma survivors may avoid self-disclosure with their partner, particularly if experiences related to the trauma are extremely painful or shameful (DiMauro & Renshaw, 2018; Monk & Nelson Goff, 2014). The breakdown in communication and emotional expression can then diminish the couple's intimacy and closeness. PTS/D is also characterized by inhibited conflict management and problem-solving skills, which are theorized to contribute to aggressive behaviors toward a romantic partner. PTS/D symptom severity, especially hyperarousal (Jordan et al., 1992; Taft, Street, Marshall, Dowdall, & Riggs, 2007), is positively correlated with violent behavior (Byrne & Riggs, 1996, 2002; Glenn et al., 2002; Riggs, Byrne, Weathers, & Litz, 1998), which negatively affects interpersonal functioning.

Cognitions (appraisal) also play a role in how a partner may perceive a traumatic experience and related symptoms. For example, Renshaw and Campbell (2011) found that partners were less distressed in their relationships when they believed that their service member partner had experienced difficult traumatic experiences while on deployment. However, the partners interpreted PTS/D symptoms differently if they perceived deployment experiences as not that stressful. These findings suggest that partner perceptions of trauma symptoms and causes of trauma symptoms are an important consideration in how the couple unit as a whole adapts to these symptoms. Thus, the CBT-interpersonal model provides insight into how trauma-related symptoms may perpetuate the reciprocal relationship between PTS/D and relationship problems.

Empirical Evidence of Trauma, PTS/D, and Interpersonal Relationships

In addition to the theoretical models, there has been an increase in empirical study of the interpersonal effects of trauma and PTSD in couples or the reciprocal interaction between the two (see Blow et al., 2013; Campbell & Renshaw, 2016; Erbes, Meis, Polusny, & Compton, 2011; Monk & Nelson Goff, 2014; Monson et al., 2009; Nelson Goff, Crow, Reisbig, & Hamilton, 2007; Renshaw & Campbell, 2011; Renshaw, Rodebaugh, & Rodrigues, 2010; Renshaw, Rodrigues, & Jones, 2008; Taft, Watkins, Stafford, Street, & Monson, 2011). A Google Scholar search on "couples and trauma" demonstrates the increase: only 15,000 citations were found between 1970 and 1999, with 58,500 citations from 2000 to 2017—an increase of almost four times the number of 1970–1999 citations. When searching "PTSD and couples," the increase is even more striking: 1,370 citations from 1970 to 1999, with 16,500 citations since 2000. Next, we review the research that provides support for the reciprocal interaction between PTS/D and interpersonal functioning, including problems in relationship functioning, as well as positive outcomes for couples.

Service member and veteran populations

Much of the literature on psychological trauma and PTS/D stems from research on military service member and veteran (SMV) populations. The association between symptoms of PTSD and relationship difficulties is well established in military couples (Allen, Rhoades, Stanley, & Markman, 2010; Erbes et al., 2012; Gewirtz, Polusny,

DeGarmo, Khaylis, & Erbes, 2010; Lambert, Engh, Hasbun, & Holzer, 2012; Riggs et al., 1998). For example, in one study, Allen and colleagues (2010) studied 434 Army couples and the relationship between PTSD in husbands and marital outcomes. They concluded that higher PTSD symptoms were associated with lower marital satisfaction, lower confidence in the relationship, less positive bonding in the relationship, a weakened parenting alliance, higher levels of negative communication, and a lower commitment to the relationship for both partners. The interaction of PTSD and relationship difficulties can set off a series of negative spirals for couples in which symptoms of PTSD exacerbate relationship functioning; in turn, relationship difficulties exacerbate symptoms of PTSD (Blow et al., 2015).

PTSD in SMV populations has been associated with decreased marital satisfaction, increased verbal aggression, communication difficulties, and heightened levels of sexual dissatisfaction and other intimacy difficulties (Cook, Riggs, Thompson, Coyne, & Sheikh, 2004; Dekel & Solomon, 2006). In a meta-analysis of 31 studies, trauma symptoms were negatively associated with relationship quality, and compared with civilian populations, the effect was stronger in military couples (Taft et al., 2011). In particular, PTSD symptoms, such as emotional numbing, sleep problems, and avoidance, are disruptive to positive relationship functioning (Cook et al., 2004; Nelson Goff et al., 2007). Post-9/11 SMVs have reported more difficulty readjusting to family and civilian life when compared with veterans who served in previous wars (Morin, 2011), which may be due to the greater demands placed on today's military and military families (Karney & Crown, 2007). Members of different branches of the military, such as National Guard members, may be affected differently given different deployment conditions and work environments after a deployment ends (Blow et al., 2013; Gorman, Blow, Ames, & Reed, 2011).

There is growing evidence that partners of veterans have increased incidence of psychological problems (Calhoun, Beckham, & Bosworth, 2002; Gorman et al., 2011; Mansfield et al., 2010), and in cases where the veteran has PTSD, partners' lives become organized by the diagnosis, which ultimately affects their independence (Dekel et al., 2005). Murphy, Palmer, and Busuttil (2016) described a "burden of mental illness" in their study of caregiving partners of UK veterans diagnosed with PTSD. Diehle, Brooks, and Greenberg (2017) provided a systematic review of 27 studies investigating PTSD symptoms in partners of veterans, finding strong evidence for STS in the partners of help-seeking veterans diagnosed with PTSD. Symptomatology in the partner can potentially affect the primary trauma survivor's symptoms, reinforcing the cyclical nature of stress and trauma, which could result in both individual and relational damage (Nelson Goff & Smith, 2005; Oseland et al., 2016).

PTS/D, depression, and anxiety in SMV samples are linked with decreased relationship satisfaction and impaired interpersonal functioning (Allen et al., 2010; Caska et al., 2014; Caska & Renshaw, 2011; Renshaw et al., 2008). SMVs with depression or PTSD are nearly five times more likely to experience relational and readjustment problems than soldiers without these diagnoses (Sayers, Farrow, Ross, & Oslin, 2009). Many SMVs experience high levels of emotional reactivity and relational uncertainty (Caska et al., 2014), which may result in interpersonal hostility (Knobloch-Fedders, Caska-Wallace, Smith, & Renshaw, 2017; Marshall, Panuzio, & Taft, 2005; Teten et al., 2010), withdrawal from the partner (i.e., emotionally shutting down, disconnecting; Knobloch-Fedders et al., 2017; Nelson Goff et al., 2006), impaired communication (Knobloch & Theiss, 2012; Nelson Goff et al., 2006), and unstable relationships. Knobloch and Theiss (2012) found that military couples often have difficulty communicating and connecting, which may result in isolation and with-drawal between partners. These patterns of isolation and disconnection can threaten the interpersonal connections and exacerbate intrapersonal symptoms, like PTS/D and STS. While strong interpersonal relationships may buffer the negative effects of military-related stress and trauma (Blow, Farero, Ganoczy, Walters, & Valenstein, 2018; Campbell & Renshaw, 2013; Taft et al., 2011), the intrapersonal and interper-sonal effects from trauma often threaten the very relationships that are crucial for resilience, healing, and recovery for survivors.

Nonmilitary traumas

In a national sample study conducted by Kilpatrick et al. (2013), trauma exposure was high (89.7%), with lifetime prevalence and 12-month prevalence at 8.3 and 4.7%, respectively. Nonmilitary traumas have also been directly connected with poor psy-chological and physical health (Felitti et al., 1998), yet the empirical research on the relationship between nonmilitary trauma and couple and family functioning is quite limited (D'Andrea, Sharma, Zelechoski, & Spinazzola, 2011; Felitti et al., 1998). Trauma experienced in early childhood increases the risk of experiencing depression, anxiety, and PTS/D later in life (Gilbert et al., 2009; Kaufman, Plotsky, Nemeroff, & Charney, 2000). Specifically, childhood trauma is linked with future difficulties with emotional processing and regulation (Etkin & Wager, 2007), with recent findings suggesting that such trauma actually inhibits individuals' ability to respond well to emotional conflict later in life (Marusak, Martin, Etkin, & Thomason, 2015). Thus, childhood trauma can have a significant impact on intimate relationships in adulthood.

Children who experience abuse (encompassing physical, sexual abuse, and neglect) are at risk for a number of problems in adulthood, many of which may negatively affect interpersonal relationships. Adults who experienced child abuse are more likely to struggle with substance abuse (Gilbert et al., 2009; Simpson & Miller, 2002) and engage in more high-risk sexual behaviors (Steel & Herlitz, 2005). Female victims of childhood sexual abuse are more likely to be re-victimized through sexual or physical violence in adulthood (Classen, Palesh, & Aggarwal, 2005). These women also report worse outcomes in couple functioning, including less relationship satisfaction, impaired communication, and reduced trust in their romantic partners (DiLilio & Long, 1999). Experiencing physical abuse and witnessing domestic violence as a child are each associated with the perpetration of physical and psychological partner abuse for some (Bevan & Higgins, 2002; Chapple, 2003).

Risk for intimate partner violence

The potential for increased risk of IPV in individuals with PTSD, both as victims and as perpetrators of the violence, has received extensive empirical focus (Marshall et al., 2005; Sherman, Sautter, Jackson, Lyons, & Han, 2006; Taft et al., 2005, 2007, 2011). One study indicated that military couples' risk for violence in their relation-ships is up to three times higher compared with nonmilitary samples (Marshall et al.,

2005). It is thought that violent behaviors are related to trauma symptoms and PTSD (Taft et al., 2007). Smith, Smith, Violanti, Bartone, and Homish (2015) found that the rate of IPV perpetration in a large national US sample was higher in those with a PTSD diagnosis (12.7%) than those without (4.9%). A systematic research review (Trevillion et al., 2015) of male veterans with PTSD who reported incidents of physical violence against female partners in the past year found a rate that was over twice (27.5%) the rate of the Smith et al. study. Finley, Baker, Pugh, and Peterson (2010) reported three patterns of IPV related to PTSD, namely, IPV due to anger, dissociation, and sleep-related disturbances, indicating a need to recognize different causes of IPV in couples with a trauma history.

Victims of IPV in adulthood experience adverse relationship outcomes. One study examined the effects of a history of IPV victimization on individuals' current romantic relationships (Hellemans, Loeys, Dewitte, De Smet, & Buysse, 2015), and results showed that a history of being victimized through IPV was associated with worse outcomes in mental well-being, interpersonal attachment, relationship satisfaction, sexual satisfaction, sexual dysfunction, and sexual communication. These findings applied to both men and women but were more marked in women. In another study, women who were victims of sexual trauma reported higher levels of negative communication and IPV in their romantic relationships (Jones, Kashy, Villar-Loubet, Cook, & Weiss, 2013). These studies illustrate the significant effects that IPV and sexual assault have on both individual well-being and their ability to have healthy intimate relationships later in life.

It is also necessary to recognize that in some cases, IPV is bidirectional. While most of the existing literature examines male-to-female IPV, female-to-male as well as mutual violence has also been identified within couples (Teten, Sherman, & Han, 2009). Misca and Forgey (2017) provided a comprehensive review of research on combat-related trauma in military and veteran populations, indicating the role of PTSD in bidirectional IPV, and they discuss this as a critical risk factor for both perpetration and victimization.

In spite of the growing literature on individual trauma, research on PTS/D and interpersonal relationships still lags behind. This has changed somewhat in the last decade as more studies have been conducted that show that problems created in couple relationships by PTS/D lead to reciprocal cycles in relationships where PTS/D symptoms exacerbate relationship problems and these relationship problems exacerbate PTS/D symptoms. This leaves couples "caught in vicious cycles of deteriorating relationships and mental health" (Blow et al., 2015, p. 262).

Posttraumatic growth and resilience in couples

Posttraumatic growth Despite the negative impact that trauma can have on individuals and couples, some are able to respond positively. Two terms in the trauma literature that describe this phenomenon of successfully navigating adversity are posttraumatic growth and resilience. Posttraumatic growth is a term coined in the 1990s by clinical psychologists Tedeschi and Calhoun (1996). Their review of literature on positive psychology led them to conclude that after experiencing trauma, some individuals report positive growth in the following three areas of their lives: (a) self-perception, (b) interpersonal relationships, and (c) philosophy of life. This opened the door for an influx of studies in recent years on how people experience growth as a result of a variety of traumatic experiences, including bereavement, cancer and other diseases, natural disasters, rape, and military combat, among others. An earthquake analogy can be used to describe posttraumatic growth (Tedeschi & Calhoun, 2004), with the earthquake being the traumatic event experienced. After an individual's life and view of the world is "shattered" by trauma, she/he is left to "rebuild" by seeking meaning and understanding of the traumatic experience. Posttraumatic growth occurs when an individual's view of self and the world is rebuilt in a way that protects against future repercussions from the trauma.

Recently, the study of posttraumatic growth has expanded to the study of couples, particularly couples dealing with cancer (Zwahlen, Hagenbuch, Carley, Jenewein, & Buchi, 2010), specifically breast cancer survivors and their partners (Ávila, Coimbra, Park, & Matos, 2017; Manne et al., 2004; Moore et al., 2011). Couple outcomes have been explored as predictors of posttraumatic growth. Findings indicated that posttraumatic growth is positively associated with marital intimacy and commitment (Hagedoorn, Kreicbergs, & Appel, 2011; Moore et al., 2011).

Just as partners can experience secondary traumatization (Nelson Goff & Smith, 2005), partners of trauma survivors may experience secondary posttraumatic growth through their interactions with their partners, and one partner's experiences with posttraumatic growth can influence the other partner (Canevello, Michels, & Hilaire, 2016; Manne et al., 2004). Studies indicate that certain factors, such as partner responsiveness and support, as well as emotional expressiveness, may serve as possible mechanisms for mutual posttraumatic growth in partners (Canevello et al., 2016; Manne et al., 2004; Weiss, 2004).

Resilience Closely related to posttraumatic growth, resilience is the ability to return to normal functioning following trauma with the relative absence of negative symptoms (Lepore & Revenson, 2006). Although similar to posttraumatic growth, resilience does not include the shattering of world assumptions and associated distress, which initiates the development of posttraumatic growth (Tedeschi & Calhoun, 2004). Like posttraumatic growth, resilience has been examined in the context of romantic relationships. Qualities of resilient individuals that enable them to successfully navigate relationship challenges include the ability to cope with life challenges, regulate their emotions, and find positive meaning in challenges (Ong, Bergeman, & Chow, 2010; Skodol, 2010; Tugade & Fredrickson, 2004). Resilience can be a resource in romantic relationships, which helps couples overcome relationship difficulties and is linked with greater relationship satisfaction (Bradley & Hojjat, 2017; Melvin, Gross, Hayat, Jennings, & Campbell, 2012). It is associated with several characteristics, including self-efficacy, optimism, creative problem solving, and positive relationship expectations (Hjemdal et al., 2011; Huber, Navarro, Womble, & Mumme, 2010; Skodol, 2010). Other aspects of resilience associated with higher relationship satisfaction include positive adaptation style and self-confidence with conflict management (Huber et al., 2010; Neff & Broady, 2011). Recent findings also suggest that resilience mediates the relationship between social support and marital satisfaction (Bradley & Hojjat, 2017). As individuals and couples demonstrate the characteristics of resilience, they not only respond well individually after a trauma, but they experience stronger interpersonal relationships. The positive impact from resilience and posttraumatic growth has important implications for clinical interventions for PTSD and trauma in couples.

Interventions for PTS/D and Couples: Toward More Systemic Treatment

Baucom and colleagues (Baucom, Belus, Adelman, Fischer, & Paprocki, 2014) described three ways to conceptualize the inclusion of intimate partners in treatment when there is a major mental health concern like PTSD. First, *partner-assisted interventions* focus on helping the individual with the mental health condition, but include the intimate partner in treatment. It should be emphasized that this approach does not target the couple relationship in any way, but instead engages the partner as an additional source of support as the individual with the mental health condition works on treatment goals. The second kind of couple work they described is *disorder-specific interventions*, which include work with both the individual mental health condition and the couple relationship, but only in as much as it relates to the mental health concern. The relationship is modified to accommodate the changes needed in the mental health recovery process. Third, Baucom et al. (2014) described interventions that target *changes in the couple relationship*. These interventions occur in cases where there is significant couple distress in addition to the mental health symptoms. In the trauma literature, we could find evidence mainly for the second approach, although it is likely that the relationship is also the target of intervention in many cases as PTS/D is highly correlated with relationship distress, as previously described. There was limited evidence in working with individual PTS/D symptoms in the presence of a partner, as is suggested in partner-assisted interventions (Baucom et al., 2014). This is largely an unexplored area, but we believe is one of promise, especially given the promising individual interventions for trauma, such as Internal Family Systems Therapy (Schwartz, 1995) and Eye Movement Desensitization and Reprocessing (EMDR) Therapy (Shapiro, Kaslow, & Maxfield, 2011).

There is more research focused on PTSD-specific couple interventions, although it is in its infancy. The main approaches will be described below. Conjoint clinical interventions research has resulted in promising outcomes, but these studies have almost exclusively focused on SMV couples, and some of them have poor designs and small samples (e.g., Monson et al., 2012; Sautter, Armelie, Glynn, & Wielt, 2011; Sautter, Glynn, Cretu, Senturk, & Vaught, 2015; Sautter, Glynn, Thompson, Franklin, & Han, 2009; Weissman et al., 2018).

Although research suggests that trauma survivors want family-focused clinical programs and services (Erbes, Polusny, MacDermid, & Compton, 2008; Khaylis, Polusny, Erbes, Gewirtz, & Rath, 2011; Meis et al., 2013), interpersonal interventions are limited, particularly evidence-based trauma treatment programs that address the mutual effects of trauma and relational functioning (see Wadsworth et al. 2013). The need for more systemic services also has been emphasized by families (Fischer et al., 2015) and even federal agencies (Institute of Medicine, 2014), recognizing the critical aspects of trauma in relationship functioning and interpersonal relationships in providing a positive buffer from traumatic stress effects on individuals. However, in spite of this preliminary evidence and support, there are simply not enough studies of relational interventions for couples where one or both have significant trauma. Funders have not prioritized this area of intervention. It should also be acknowledged that this work is difficult and complex and requires a great deal of knowledge of both trauma and couple's work. It also requires a setting in which this work can be optimally accomplished. That may be why several studies involving couples and trauma have been carried out in VA settings (see Monson et al., 2012; Weissman et al., 2018).

Cognitive-behavioral couple therapy

Individually focused cognitive-behavioral therapies, such as cognitive processing therapy (CPT) and cognitive-behavioral therapy (CBT), among other variations of this approach, are evidence-based treatments for trauma-related diagnoses for individuals (Cahill, Rothbaum, Resick, & Follette, 2009; Ford et al., 2015; Resick, Williams, Suvak, Monson, & Gradus, 2012). CPT is typically delivered over 12 therapy sessions with the purpose of helping individuals with PTSD rebuild their trauma-related cognitions in a more positive way. The role of the therapist is to help the client develop adaptive strategies for addressing negative cognitions, often with a focus on areas such as control, intimacy, safety, power, and trust (Resick, Monson, & Chard, 2016). CBT approaches have been expanded to include couples interventions and are one of the few theories studied using a couple approach with PTSD (Monson et al., 2011). In a pilot study utilizing cognitive-behavioral conjoint therapy with couples where one of the partners had a PTSD diagnosis, the treatment procedure was divided into three phases: (a) education about PTSD that encourages physical and emotional safety within the relationship, (b) exercises focused on improving relationship functioning, and (c) cognitive restructuring to help the couple resolve cognitions that may lead to the development of PTSD and relationship problems (Monson et al., 2011). Partners in this study reported significantly higher relationship satisfaction and reductions in relational distress (Monson et al., 2011). CBT approaches to treating PTS/D in a couple therapy context show potential to treat both PTS/D symptoms and relationship difficulties (Monson, Schnurr, Stevens, & Guthrie, 2004; Monson et al., 2009, 2011).

Emotionally focused therapy

Emotionally focused therapy (EFT) with trauma survivors involves recognizing the systemic effects of trauma on both partners and creating the potential for the interpersonal relationship to provide a secure base for healing from trauma within the treatment process (Johnson, 2002a, 2002b; Weissman et al., 2018). EFT is one evidence-based approach to working with couples, and it has high potential to treat PTSD in the context of a couple relationship, although more studies are needed (Blow et al., 2015; Weissman et al., 2018). Studies have addressed the utility of EFT in working with PTSD and other related mental health difficulties (Denton, Wittenborn, & Golden, 2012; Dessaulles, Johnson, & Denton, 2003; Halchuk, Makinen, & Johnson, 2010; MacIntosh & Johnson, 2008; Weissman et al., 2018), and it is a promising intervention from these preliminary studies.

Trauma and PTS/D create difficulties in relationships, because intimate relationships require a level of closeness and connection that are likely to exacerbate trauma symptoms (Johnson & Williams Keeler, 1998). EFT helps individuals face these symptoms together, but first a context of safety is created that allows a platform for deeper and more intense emotional work to occur. In EFT, it is possible to set up interactions that support trauma survivors disclosing emotional struggles with their partners, without having to delve into all of the painful specifics of the traumatic experiences. EFT is a couple therapy approach rooted in attachment theory, which helps couples de-escalate relationship conflicts and create safety within the relationship to discuss difficult or painful issues. EFT works to identify and expand emotions within the interpersonal relationship and helps a couple achieve success in not only expressing difficult or painful emotions but also responding to these interactions in ways that are healing and promote recovery. These processes of change help couples interrupt dysfunctional sequences of relating to each other while at the same time creating more positive connections and more positive cycles of relating. In this way then, an intimate relationship turns into a positive support context as opposed to a source of stress. This relationship safe haven is a context where partners can express, explore, and learn to regulate emotions, which are all helpful for improved individual functioning (Blow et al., 2015). The high level of safety along with exploring emotions makes it an ideal approach to work with couples affected by PTSD. (See Blow et al. (2015) for an in depth review of EFT and its use with couples where PTSD is present.)

Important Clinical Considerations

Given the body of literature described here pertaining to the relationship between PTS/D symptoms and relationship functioning, much more study is needed on interventions targeting couples dealing with trauma. More work is needed to identify mechanisms of change for PTSD when it is treated in a couple context. We call for an interdisciplinary approach that would bring researchers together doing this work and increase cross-disciplinary collaboration between professional and theoretical areas. While individually oriented practitioners often recognize the systemic effects of trauma, they may feel unprepared to address or work with dyads and families. While traditional healthcare is shifting to a team-based, holistic, integrative approach to wellness, mental healthcare for trauma still has interdisciplinary conflicts or barriers to collaboration. Until we remove the threats to finding holistic, collaborative interventions, it is likely that trauma survivors and their family members will not receive the systemic care that can be helpful to their recovery (López-Zerón & Blow, 2017).

While we strongly believe that working with PTSD in the context of the couple relationship is a highly promising approach to treatment, this should not occur in a haphazard manner but rather with caution and an abundance of planning. Great care should be taken in all trauma-related clinical interventions. We advocate sharing of traumatic experiences with a partner after much discussion and preparation has occurred about the content of the trauma to be shared, the purpose of sharing, and the capacity of the partner to absorb the information and to respond in an appropriate manner. For example, a male military veteran who shares details about a combat experience that led to the deaths of women and children may end up pushing a partner away with this information. It may be advisable not to share this information at all or only share it after processing it with in individual therapy. It is also advisable to share this information in small increments.

Any therapist who works with trauma will attest that it is not easy work. Sometimes, working with trauma symptoms can end up making them worse before they get better. Further, working on trauma-related symptoms with a partner, without careful planning, can lead to hurt feelings that deepen the wounds of trauma. We advocate that therapists approach this work with careful *assessment* of the trauma histories of both partners. We believe that this treatment works best when it *goes slow* and when therapists are able to manage the symptoms that are stirred up in the work. It is essential that the non-traumatized partner be coached to be an empathic listener and to be responsive and attuned to the needs of the partner with PTS/D. When things go wrong due to the symptom exacerbations, couples need help staying engaged in processing what occurred in the relationship. Finally, it is essential that trauma work with couples be occurring in a context of safety. This work requires vulnerability in trauma survivors, and as a result, therapists should work in the early sessions to establish safety for this work (see Johnson, 2002a). It is contraindicated to do trauma work with couples if this safety does not exist as would be reflected in contexts with IPV, infidelity, or frequent arguing and verbal or emotional abuse.

Conclusion and Future Directions

In this chapter, we have identified great promise for studying the relationship between PTS/D and intimate couple relationships. From this review, it is clear that while a significant amount of research on trauma in couples has occurred, more still needs to be done. In particular, we believe that studying a wider array of interventions for couples where trauma is present is warranted, particularly including different types of interventions and dosages, as well as addressing different categories of trauma, including CPTSD. Finally, specific types of couples, including dual-trauma couples (see Riggs, 2014; Ruhlmann, Gallus, & Durtschi, 2018), unique outcomes based on the gender of the trauma survivor (e.g., female veterans with PTSD, male physical and sexual abuse survivors), and the specific relationship factors and mechanisms that contribute to both exacerbated trauma outcomes and posttraumatic growth and resilience in couples are areas needing additional focus. It is clear that the impact of trauma and PTS/D within the couple context is not isolated but creates reciprocal patterns of interaction that can create further damage to the individuals and their interpersonal relationships or that can provide an avenue for healing and growth in the context of couple and family functioning.

References

Alisic, E., Boeije, H. R., Jongmans, M. J., & Kleber, R. J. (2012). Supporting children after single-incident trauma: Parents' views. *Clinical Pediatrics*, 51(3), 274–282. doi:10.1177/0009922811423309

Allen, E. S., Rhoades, G. K., Stanley, S. M., & Markman, H. J. (2010). Hitting home: Relationships between recent deployment, posttraumatic stress symptoms, and marital functioning for Army couples. *Journal of Family Psychology*, 24(3), 280–288. doi:10.1037/a0019405

American Psychiatric Association. (1980). *Diagnostic and statistical manual of mental disorders* (3rd ed.). Washington, DC: Author.

American Psychiatric Association. (2013). *Diagnostic and statistical manual of mental disorders* (5th ed.). Arlington, VA: Author.

Ávila, M., Coimbra, J., Park, C., & Matos, P. (2017). Attachment and posttraumatic growth after breast cancer: A dyadic approach. *Psycho-Oncology*, 26(11), 1929–1935. doi:10.1002/pon.4409

Baucom, D. H., Belus, J. M., Adelman, C. B., Fischer, M. S., & Paprocki, C. (2014). Couple-based interventions for psychopathology: A renewed direction for the field. *Family Process*, 53(3), 445–461. doi:10.1111/famp.12075

Bevan, E., & Higgins, D. (2002). Is domestic violence learned? The contribution of five forms of child maltreatment to men's violence and adjustment. *Journal of Family Violence*, 17(3), 223–245. doi:10.1023/A:1016053228021

Blow, A., Fraser Curtis, A., Wittenborn, A., & Gorman, L. (2015). Relationship problems and military related PTSD: The case for using emotionally focused therapy for couples. *Contemporary Family Therapy*, 37, 261–270. doi:10.1007/s10591-015-9345-7

Blow, A., Gorman, L., Ganoczy, D., Kees, M., Kashy, D., Valenstein, M., … Chermack, S. (2013). Hazardous drinking and family functioning in National Guard veterans and spouses postdeployment. *Journal of Family Psychology*, 27, 303–313. doi:10.1037/a0031881

Blow, A. J., Farero, A., Ganoczy, D., Walters, H., & Valenstein, M. (2018). Intimate relationships buffer suicidality in National Guard service members: A longitudinal study. *Suicide & Life-Threatening Behavior*. doi:10.1111/sltb.12537

Boss, P. (2004). Ambiguous loss research, theory, and practice: Reflections after 9/11. *Journal of Marriage and Family*, 66(3), 551–566. doi:10.1111/j.0022-2445.2004.00037.x

Bowlby, J. (1969). *Attachment: Volume I: Attachment and loss*. New York, NY: Basic Books.

Bradley, J., & Hojjat, M. (2017). A model of resilience and marital satisfaction. *Journal of Social Psychology*, 157, 588–601. doi:10.1080/00224545.2016.1254592

Brewin, C. R., Andrews, B., & Valentine, J. D. (2000). Meta-analysis of risk factors for posttraumatic stress disorder in trauma-exposed adults. *Journal of Consulting and Clinical Psychology*, 68(5), 748–766.

Briere, J., Agee, E., & Dietrich, A. (2016). Cumulative trauma and current posttraumatic stress disorder status in general population and inmate samples. *Psychological Trauma Theory Research Practice and Policy*, 8(4), 439–446. doi:10.1037/tra0000107

Byrne, C., & Riggs, D. (1996). The cycle of trauma; relationship aggression in male Vietnam veterans with symptoms of posttraumatic stress disorder. *Violence and Victims*, 11(3), 213–225. doi:10.1891/0886-6708.11.3.213

Byrne, C., & Riggs, D. (2002). Gender issues in couple and family therapy following traumatic stress. In R. Kimerling, P. Ouimette, & J. Wolfe (Eds.), *Gender and PTSD* (pp. 382–399). New York, NY: Guilford.

Cahill, S., Rothbaum, B., Resick, P., & Follette, V. (2009). Cognitive-behavioral therapy for adults. In E. Foa, M. Friedman, & J. Cohen (Eds.), *Effective treatments for PTSD: Practice guidelines from the International Society for Traumatic Stress Studies* (2nd ed., pp. 139–222). New York, NY: Guilford.

Calhoun, P. S., Beckham, J. C., & Bosworth, H. B. (2002). Caregiver burden and psychological distress in partners of veterans with chronic posttraumatic stress disorder. *Journal of Traumatic Stress*, 15, 205–212. doi:10.1023/A:1015251210928

Campbell, S., & Renshaw, K. (2013). PTSD symptoms, disclosure, and relationship distress: Explorations of mediation and associations over time. *Journal of Anxiety Disorders*, 27(5), 494–502. doi:10.1016/j.janxdis.2013.06.007

Campbell, S., & Renshaw, K. (2016). Military couples and posttraumatic stress: Interpersonally based behaviors and cognitions as mechanisms of individual and couple distress. In S. MacDermid Wadsworth & D. Riggs (Eds.), *War and family life* (pp. 55–75). Cham, Switzerland: Springer International Publishing AG.

Campbell, S. B., & Renshaw, K. D. (2018). Posttraumatic stress disorder and relationship functioning: A comprehensive review and organizational framework. *Clinical Psychology Review*, 65, 152–162. doi:10.1016/j.cpr.2018.08.003

Canevello, A., Michels, V., & Hilaire, N. (2016). Supporting close others' growth after trauma: The role of responsiveness in romantic partners' mutual posttraumatic growth. *Psychological Trauma Theory Research Practice and Policy*, 8(3), 334–342. doi:10.1037/tra0000084

Caska, C., & Renshaw, K. (2011). Perceived burden in spouses of National Guard/Reserve service members deployed during Operations Enduring and Iraqi Freedom. *Journal of Anxiety Disorders*, 25(3), 346–351. doi:10.1016/j.janxdis.2010.10.008

Caska, C., Smith, T., Renshaw, K., Allen, S., Uchino, B., Birmingham, W., & Carlisle, M. (2014). Posttraumatic stress disorder and responses to couple conflict: Implications for cardiovascular risk. *Health Psychology*, 33(11), 1273–1280. doi:10.1037/hea0000133

Chapple, C. (2003). Examining intergenerational violence: Violent role modelling or weak parental controls? *Violence and Victims*, 18(2), 143–162. doi:10.1891/vivi.2003.18.2.143

Classen, C. C., Palesh, O. G., & Aggarwal, R. (2005). Sexual revictimization: A review of the empirical literature. *Trauma, Violence & Abuse*, 6(2), 103–129. doi:10.1177/1524838005275087

Cloitre, M., Garvert, D. W., Brewin, C. R., Bryant, R. A., & Maercker, A. (2013). Evidence for proposed ICD-11 PTSD and complex PTSD: A latent profile analysis. *European Journal of Psychotraumatology*, 4(1), 20706. doi:10.3402/ejpt.v4i0.20706

Cloitre, M., Garvert, D. W., Weiss, B., Carlson, E. B., & Bryant, R. A. (2014). Distinguishing PTSD, complex PTSD, and borderline personality disorder: A latent class analysis. *European Journal of Psychotraumatology*, 5(1), 25097. doi:10.3402/ejpt.v5.25097

Cohen, S. (2004). Social relationships and health. *American Psychologist*, 59(8), 676–684. doi:10.1037/0003-066X.59.8.676

Cohen, S., & Wills, T. (1985). Stress, social support, and the buffering hypothesis. *Psychological Bulletin*, 98(2), 310–357. doi:10.1037/0033-2909.98.2.310

Contractor, A. A., Brown, L. A., & Weiss, N. H. (2018). Relation between lifespan polytrauma typologies and post-trauma mental health. *Comprehensive Psychiatry*, 80, 202–213. doi:10.1016/j.comppsych.2017.10.005

Cook, J. M., Riggs, D. S., Thompson, R., Coyne, J. C., & Sheikh, J. (2004). Posttraumatic stress disorder and current relationship functioning among World War II ex-prisoners of war. *Journal of Family Psychology*, 18, 36–45. doi:10.1037/0893-3200.18.1.36

D'Andrea, W., Sharma, R., Zelechoski, A. D., & Spinazzola, J. (2011). Physical health problems after single trauma exposure: When stress takes root in the body. *Journal of the American Psychiatric Nurses Association*, 17(6), 378–392. doi:10.1177/1078390311425187

Dekel, R., Goldblatt, H., Keidar, M., Solomon, Z., & Polliack, M. (2005). Being a wife of a veteran with posttraumatic stress disorder. *Family Relations*, 54, 24–36. doi:10.1111/j.0197-6664.2005.00003.x

Dekel, R., & Monson, C. (2010). Military-related post-traumatic stress disorder and family relations: Current knowledge and future directions. *Aggression and Violent Behavior*, 15, 303–309. doi:10.1016/j.avb.2010.03.001

Dekel, R., & Solomon, Z. (2006). Secondary traumatization among wives of Israeli POWs: The role of POWs' distress. *Social Psychiatry and Psychiatric Epidemiology*, 41, 27–33. doi:10.1007/s00127-005-0002-6

Denton, W., Wittenborn, A., & Golden, R. (2012). Augmenting antidepressant medication treatment of women with emotionally focused therapy for couples: A pilot study. *Journal of Marital and Family Therapy*, 38, 23–38. doi:10.1111/j.1752-0606.2012.00291.x

Dessaulles, A., Johnson, S., & Denton, W. (2003). Emotion-focused therapy for couples in the treatment of depression: A pilot study. *American Journal of Family Therapy*, 31, 345–353. doi:10.1080/01926180390232266

Diehle, J., Brooks, S. K., & Greenberg, N. (2017). Veterans are not the only ones suffering from posttraumatic stress symptoms: What do we know about dependents' secondary traumatic stress? *Social Psychiatry and Psychiatric Epidemiology*, 52(1), 35–44. doi:10.1007/s00127-016-1292-6

DiLilio, D., & Long, P. J. (1999). Perceptions of couple functioning among female survivors of child sexual abuse. *Journal of Child Sexual Abuse*, 7(4), 59–76. doi:10.1300/J070v07n04_05

DiMauro, J., & Renshaw, K. D. (2018). Trauma-related disclosure in sexual assault survivors' intimate relationships: Associations with PTSD, shame, and partners' responses. *Journal of Interpersonal Violence*. doi:10.1177/0886260518756117

Dorahy, M., Corry, M., Shannon, M., Webb, K., McDermott, B., Ryan, M., & Dyer, K. (2013). Complex trauma and intimate relationships: The impact of shame, guilt and dissociation. *Journal of Affective Disorders*, 147(1), 72–79. doi:10.1016/j.jad.2012.10.010

Elhai, J., Naifeh, J., Forbes, D., Ractliffe, K., & Tamburrino, M. (2011). Heterogeneity in clinical presentations of posttraumatic stress disorder among medical patients: Testing factor structure variation using factor mixture modeling. *Journal of Traumatic Stress*, 24(4), 435–443. doi:10.1002/jts.20653

Elklit, A., Hyland, P., & Shevlin, M. (2014). Evidence of symptom profiles consistent with posttraumatic stress disorder and complex posttraumatic stress disorder in different trauma samples. *European Journal of Psychotraumatology*, 5(1), 24221. doi:10.3402/ejpt.v5.24221

Erbes, C., Meis, L., Polusny, M., & Compton, J. (2011). Couple adjustment and posttraumatic stress disorder symptoms in National Guard veterans of the Iraq war. *Journal of Family Psychology*, 25, 479–487. doi:10.1037/a0024007

Erbes, C., Meis, L., Polusny, M., Compton, J., & MacDermid Wadsworth, S. (2012). An examination of PTSD symptoms and relationship functioning in U.S. soldiers of the Iraq war over time. *Journal of Traumatic Stress*, 25, 187–190. doi:10.1002/jts.21689

Erbes, C., Polusny, M., MacDermid, S., & Compton, J. (2008). Couple therapy with combat veterans and their partners. *Journal of Clinical Psychology*, 64(8), 972–983. doi:10.1002/jclp.20521

Etkin, A., & Wager, T. D. (2007). Functional neuroimaging of anxiety: A meta-analysis of emotional processing in PTSD, social anxiety disorder, and specific phobia. *American Journal of Psychiatry*, 164(10), 1476–1488. doi:10.1176/appi.ajp.2007.07030504

Felitti, V. J., Anda, R. F., Nordenberg, D., Williamson, D. F., Spitz, A. M., Edwards, V., ... Marks, J. S. (1998). Relationship of childhood abuse and household dysfunction to many of the leading causes of death in adults: The Adverse Childhood Experiences (ACE) Study. *American Journal of Preventive Medicine*, 14(4), 245–258. doi:10.1016/S0749-3797(98)00017-8

Figley, C. (1989a). *Helping traumatized families*. San Francisco, CA: Jossey-Bass.

Figley, C. (Ed.) (1989b). *Treating stress in families*. New York, NY: Brunner/Mazel.

Figley, C. (1995). Compassion fatigue as secondary traumatic stress disorder. In C. Figley (Ed.), *Compassion fatigue: Coping with secondary traumatic stress disorder in those who treat the traumatized* (pp. 1–20). New York, NY: Brunner/Mazel.

Figley, C. (Ed.) (2002). *Treating compassion fatigue*. New York, NY: Brunner-Routledge.

Finley, E. P., Baker, M., Pugh, M. J., & Peterson, A. (2010). Patterns and perceptions of intimate partner violence committed by returning veterans with post-traumatic stress disorder. *Journal of Family Violence*, 25(8), 737–743. doi:10.1007/s10896-010-9331-7

Fischer, E. P., Sherman, M. D., McSweeney, J. C., Pyne, J. M., Owen, R. R., & Dixon, L. B. (2015). Perspectives of family and veterans on family programs to support reintegration of returning veterans with posttraumatic stress disorder. *Psychological Services*, 12(3), 187–198. doi:10.1037/ser0000033

Forbes, D., Lockwood, E., Phelps, A., Wade, D., Creamer, M., Bryant, R. A., ... O'Donnell, M. (2014). Trauma at the hands of another: Distinguishing PTSD patterns following intimate and nonintimate interpersonal and noninterpersonal trauma in a nationally representative sample. *Journal of Clinical Psychiatry*, 75(2), 147–153. doi:10.4088/JCP.13m08374

Ford, J., & Courtois, C. (2009). Defining and understanding complex trauma and complex traumatic stress disorders. In C. Courtois & J. Ford (Eds.), *Treating complex traumatic stress disorders: Scientific foundations and therapeutic models* (pp. 13–30). New York, NY: Guilford.

Ford, J., Grasso, D., Elhai, J., & Courtois, C. (2015). *Posttraumatic stress disorder: Scientific and professional dimensions* (2nd ed.). San Diego, CA: Academic Press.

Freyd, J. (1996). *Betrayal trauma: The logic of forgetting abuse*. Cambridge, MA: Harvard University Press.

Freyd, J., Klest, B., & Allard, C. (2005). Betrayal trauma: Relationship to physical health, psychological distress, and a written disclosure intervention. *Journal of Trauma & Dissociation*, 6(3), 83–104. doi:10.1300/J229v06n03_04

Gewirtz, A., Polusny, M., DeGarmo, D., Khaylis, A., & Erbes, C. (2010). Posttraumatic stress symptoms among National Guard soldiers deployed to Iraq: Associations with parenting behaviors and couple adjustment. *Journal of Consulting and Clinical Psychology*, 78(5), 599–610. doi:10.1037/a0020571

Gilbert, R., Widom, C. S., Browne, K., Fergusson, D., Webb, E., & Janson, S. (2009). Burden and consequences of child maltreatment in high-income countries. *Lancet*, 373(9657), 68–81. doi:10.1016/s0140-6736(08)61706-7

Glenn, D. M., Beckham, J. C., Feldman, M. E., Kirby, A. C., Hertzberg, M. A., & Moore, S. D. (2002). Violence and hostility among families of Vietnam veterans with combat-related posttraumatic stress disorder. *Violence and Victims*, 17, 473–489.

Gorman, L., Blow, A. J., Ames, B., & Reed, P. (2011). National Guard families after combat: Mental health, use of mental health services, and perceived treatment barriers. *Psychiatric Services*, 62(1), 28–34. doi:10.1176/ps.62.1.pss6201_0028

Hagedoorn, M., Kreicbergs, U., & Appel, C. (2011). Coping with cancer: The perspective of patients' relatives. *Acta Oncologica*, 50(2), 205–211. doi:10.3109/0284186x.2010.536165

Halchuk, R., Makinen, J., & Johnson, S. (2010). Resolving attachment injuries in couples using emotionally focused therapy: A three-year follow-up. *Journal of Couple and Relationship Therapy*, 9, 31–47. doi:10.1080/15332690903473069

Hazan, C., & Shaver, P. (1987). Romantic love conceptualized as an attachment process. *Journal of Personality and Social Psychology*, 52(3), 511–524. doi:10.1037/0022-3514.52.3.511

Hellemans, S., Loeys, T., Dewitte, M., De Smet, O., & Buysse, A. (2015). Prevalence of intimate partner violence victimization and victims' relational and sexual well-being. *Journal of Family Violence*, 30(6), 685–698. doi:10.1007/s10896-015-9712-z

Herman, J. (1997). *Trauma and recovery: The aftermath of violence—From domestic abuse to political terror.* New York, NY: Basic Books.

Hjemdal, O., Friborg, O., Braun, S., Kempenaers, C., Linkowski, P., & Fossion, P. (2011). The resilience scale for adults: Construct validity and measurement in a Belgian sample. *International Journal of Testing*, 11(1), 53–70. doi:10.1080/15305058.2010.508570

Huber, C. H., Navarro, R. L., Womble, M. W., & Mumme, F. L. (2010). Family resilience and midlife marital satisfaction. *The Family Journal*, 18(2), 136–145. doi:10.1177/1066480710364477

Hyland, P., Shevlin, M., Elklit, A., Murphy, J., Vallières, F., Garvert, D., & Cloitre, M. (2017). An assessment of the construct validity of the ICD-11 proposal for complex posttraumatic stress disorder. *Psychological Trauma Theory Research Practice and Policy*, 9(1), 1–9. doi:10.1037/tra0000114

Institute of Medicine. (2014). *Treatment for posttraumatic stress disorder in military and veteran populations: Final assessment.* Washington, DC: The National Academies Press. Retrieved from https://www.nationalacademies.org/hmd/Reports/2014/Treatment-for-Posttraumatic-Stress-Disorder-in-Military-and-Veteran-Populations-Final-Assessment.aspx

James, L. M., Van Kampen, E., Miller, R. D., & Engdahl, B. E. (2013). Risk and protective factors associated with symptoms of post-traumatic stress, depression, and alcohol misuse in OEF/OIF veterans. *Military Medicine*, 178(2), 159–165. doi:10.7205/MILMED-D-12-00282

Janoff-Bulman, R. (1992). *Shattered assumptions: Towards a new psychology of trauma.* New York, NY: Free Press.

Johnson, S. (2002a). *Emotionally focused couple therapy with trauma survivors: Strengthening attachment bonds.* New York, NY: Guilford.

Johnson, S. (2002b). Marital problems. In D. Sprenkle (Ed.), *Effectiveness research in marriage and family therapy* (pp. 163–190). Alexandria, VA: The American Association for Marriage and Family Therapy.

Johnson, S., & Williams Keeler, L. (1998). Creating healing relationships for couples dealing with trauma: The use of emotionally focused marital therapy. *Journal of Marital and Family Therapy*, 24, 25–40. doi:10.1111/j.1752-0606.1998.tb01061.x

Jones, D. L., Kashy, D., Villar-Loubet, O. M., Cook, R., & Weiss, S. M. (2013). The impact of substance use, sexual trauma and intimate partner violence on sexual risk intervention outcomes in couples: A randomized trial. *Annals of Behavioral Medicine: A Publication of the Society of Behavioral Medicine*, 45(3), 318–328. doi:10.1007/s12160-012-9455-5

Jordan, B. K., Marmar, C. R., Fairbank, J. A., Schlenger, W. E., Kulka, R. A., Hough, R. L., & Weiss, D. S. (1992). Problems in families of male Vietnam veterans with posttraumatic stress disorder. *Journal of Consulting and Clinical Psychology*, 60, 916–926. doi:10.1037/0022-006X.60.6.916

Karam, E. G., Friedman, M. J., Hill, E. D., Kessler, R. C., McLaughlin, K. A., Petukhova, M., ... Koenen, K. C. (2014). Cumulative traumas and risk thresholds: 12-month PTSD in the World Mental Health (WMH) surveys. *Depression and Anxiety*, 31(2), 130–142. doi:10.1002/da.22169

Karatzias, T., Cloitre, M., Maercker, A., Kazlauskas, E., Shevlin, M., Hyland, P., ... Brewin, C. R. (2017). PTSD and complex PTSD: ICD-11 updates on concept and measurement in the UK, USA, Germany and Lithuania. *European Journal of Psychotraumatology*, 8(sup7), 1418103. doi:10.1080/20008198.2017.1418103

Karney, B. R., & Crown, J. S. (2007). *Families under stress: An assessment of data, theory, and research on marriage and divorce in the military.* Santa Monica, CA: RAND.

Kaufman, J., Plotsky, P. M., Nemeroff, C. B., & Charney, D. S. (2000). Effects of early adverse experiences on brain structure and function: Clinical implications. *Biological Psychiatry*, 48(8), 778–790. doi:10.1016/S0006-3223(00)00998-7

Kessler, R. C., Aguilar-Gaxiola, S., Alonso, J., Benjet, C., Bromet, E. J., Cardoso, G., ... Koenen, K. C. (2017). Trauma and PTSD in the WHO World Mental Health Surveys. *European Journal of Psychotraumatology*, 8(sup 5), 1353383. doi:10.1080/20008198.20 17.1353383

Khaylis, A., Polusny, M., Erbes, C., Gewirtz, A., & Rath, M. (2011). Posttraumatic stress, family adjustment, and treatment preferences among National Guard soldiers deployed to OEF/OIF. *Military Medicine*, 176, 126–131. doi:10.7205/MILMED-D-10-00094

Kilpatrick, D. G., Resnick, H. S., Milanak, M. E., Miller, M. W., Keyes, K. M., & Friedman, M. J. (2013). National estimates of exposure to traumatic events and PTSD prevalence using DSM-IV and DSM-5 criteria. *Journal of Traumatic Stress*, 26(5), 537–547. doi:10.1002/jts.21848

King, L. A., King, D. W., Fairbank, J. A., Keane, T. M., & Adams, G. A. (1998). Resilience–recovery factors in post-traumatic stress disorder among female and male Vietnam veterans: Hardiness, postwar social support, and additional stressful life events. *Journal of Personality and Social Psychology*, 74(2), 420–434.

Knobloch, L. K., & Theiss, J. A. (2012). Experiences of U.S. military couples during the post-deployment transition: Applying the relational turbulence model. *Journal of Social and Personal Relationships*, 29(4), 423–450. doi:10.1177/0265407511431186

Knobloch-Fedders, L. M., Caska-Wallace, C., Smith, T. W., & Renshaw, K. (2017). Battling on the home front: Posttraumatic stress disorder and conflict behavior among military couples. *Behavior Therapy*, 48(2), 247–261. doi:10.1016/j.beth.2016.08.014

Lambert, J., Engh, J., Hasbun, A., & Holzer, J. (2012). Impact of posttraumatic stress disorder on the relationship quality and psychological distress of intimate partners: A meta-analytic review. *Journal of Family Psychology*, 26(5), 729–737. doi:10.1037/a0029341

Lepore, S., & Revenson, T. (2006). Resilience and posttraumatic growth: Recovery, resistance, and reconfiguration. In L. Calhoun & R. Tedeschi (Eds.), *Handbook of posttraumatic growth, research and practice* (pp. 24–46). Mahwah, NJ: Routledge.

López-Zerón, G., & Blow, A. (2017). The role of relationships and families in healing from trauma. *Journal of Family Therapy*, 39(4), 580–597. doi:10.1111/1467-6427.12089

MacIntosh, H. B., & Johnson, S. M. (2008). Emotionally focused therapy for couples and childhood sexual abuse survivors. *Journal of Marital and Family Therapy*, 34(298–315). doi:10.1111/j.1752-0606.2008.00074.x

Manne, S., Ostroff, J., Winkel, G., Goldstein, L., Fox, K., & Grana, G. (2004). Posttraumatic growth after breast cancer: Patient, partner, and couple perspectives. *Psychosomatic Medicine*, 66(3), 442–454. doi:10.1097/00006842-200405000-00025

Mansfield, A., Kaufman, J., Marshall, S., Gaynes, B., Morrissey, J., & Engel, C. (2010). Deployment and the use of mental health services among U.S. Army wives. *The New England Journal of Medicine*, 362, 101–109. doi:10.1056/NEJMoa0900177

Marshall, A., Panuzio, J., & Taft, C. (2005). Intimate partner violence among military veterans and active duty servicemen. *Clinical Psychology Review*, 25, 862–876. doi:10.1016/j.cpr.2005.05.009

Marusak, H. A., Martin, K. R., Etkin, A., & Thomason, M. E. (2015). Childhood trauma exposure disrupts the automatic regulation of emotional processing. *Neuropsychopharmacology*, 40(5), 1250–1258. doi:10.1038/npp.2014.311

McCall-Hosenfeld, J. S., Winter, M., Heeren, T., & Liebschutz, J. M. (2014). The association of interpersonal trauma with somatic symptom severity in a primary care population with chronic pain: Exploring the role of gender and the mental health sequelae of trauma. *Journal of Psychosomatic Research*, 77(3), 196–204. doi:10.1016/j.jpsychores.2014.07.011

McCann, I., & Pearlman, L. (1990). Vicarious traumatization: A framework for understanding the psychological effects of working with victims. *Journal of Traumatic Stress*, 3, 131–149. doi:10.1007/BF00975140

Meis, L. A., Schaaf, K. W., Erbes, C. R., Polusny, M. A., Miron, L. R., Schmitz, T. M., & Nugent, S. M. (2013). Interest in partner-involved services among veterans seeking mental health care from a VA PTSD clinic. *Psychological Trauma Theory Research Practice and Policy*, 5(4), 334–342. doi:10.1037/a0028366

Melvin, K., Gross, D., Hayat, M., Jennings, B., & Campbell, J. (2012). Couple functioning and posttraumatic stress symptoms in US army couples: The role of resilience. *Research in Nursing and Health*, 35, 164–177. doi:10.1002/nur.21459

Misca, G., & Forgey, M. A. (2017). The role of PTSD in bi-directional intimate partner violence in military and veteran populations: A research review. *Frontiers in Psychology*, 8, 1394. doi:10.3389/fpsyg.2017.01394

Monk, J. K., & Nelson Goff, B. S. (2014). Military couples' trauma disclosure: Moderating between trauma symptoms and relationship quality. *Psychological Trauma Theory Research Practice and Policy*, 6(5), 537–545. doi:10.1037/a0036788

Monson, C., Fredman, S., Adair, K., Stevens, S., Resick, P., Schnurr, P., ... Macdonald, A. (2011). Cognitive-behavioral conjoint therapy for PTSD: Pilot results from a community sample. *Journal of Traumatic Stress*, 24, 97–101. doi:10.1002/jts.20604

Monson, C., Fredman, S., MacDonald, A., Pukay-Martin, N., Resick, P., & Schnurr, P. (2012). Effects of cognitive-behavioral couple therapy for PTSD: A randomized controlled trial. *Journal of the American Medical Association*, 308(7), 700–709. doi:10.1001/jama.2012.9307

Monson, C., Schnurr, P., Stevens, S., & Guthrie, K. (2004). Cognitive-behavioral couple's treatment for posttraumatic stress disorder: Initial findings. *Journal of Traumatic Stress*, 17, 341–344. doi:10.1023/B:JOTS.0000038483.69570.5b

Monson, C., Taft, C., & Fredman, S. (2009). Military-related PTSD and intimate relationships: From description to theory-driven research and intervention development. *Clinical Psychology Review*, 29(8), 707–714. doi:10.1016/j.cpr.2009.09.002

Moore, A. M., Gamblin, T. C., Geller, D. A., Youssef, M. N., Hoffman, K. E., Gemmell, L., ... Steel, J. L. (2011). A prospective study of posttraumatic growth as assessed by self report and family caregiver in the context of advanced cancer. *Psycho-Oncology*, 20(5), 479–487. doi:10.1002/pon.1746

Morin, R. (2011). *The difficult transition from military to civilian life*. Retrieved from http://www.pewsocialtrends.org/2011/12/08/the-difficult-transition-from-military-to-civilian-life

Murphy, D., Palmer, E., & Busuttil, W. (2016). Mental health difficulties and help-seeking beliefs within a sample of female partners of UK veterans diagnosed with post-traumatic stress disorder. *Journal of Clinical Medicine*, 5(8), 68. doi:10.3390/jcm5080068

Neff, L. A., & Broady, E. F. (2011). Stress resilience in early marriage: Can practice make perfect? *Journal of Personality and Social Psychology*, 101(5), 1050–1067. doi:10.1037/a0023809

Nelson Goff, B., Crow, J., Reisbig, A., & Hamilton, S. (2007). The impact of individual trauma symptoms of deployed soldiers on relationship satisfaction. *Journal of Family Psychology*, 21(3), 344–353. doi:10.1037/0893-3200.21.3.344

Nelson Goff, B., Reisbig, A. M. J., Bole, A., Scheer, T., Hayes, E., Archuleta, K., ... Smith, D. (2006). The effects of trauma on intimate relationships: A qualitative study with clinical couples. *American Journal of Orthopsychiatry*, 76(4), 451–460. doi:10.1037/0002-9432.76.4.451

Nelson Goff, B., & Smith, D. (2005). Systemic traumatic stress: The couple adaptation to traumatic stress model. *Journal of Marital and Family Therapy*, 31, 145–157. doi:10.1111/j.1752-0606.2005.tb01552.x

Nelson Goff, B. S., Ruhlmann, L., Dekel, R., & Huxman, S. (2020). Trauma, posttraumatic stress, and family systems. In K. S. Wampler, M. Rastogi, & R. Singh (Eds.), *The handbook of systemic family therapy: Systemic family therapy and global health issues (4)*. Hoboken, NJ: Wiley.

Ong, A., Bergeman, C., & Chow, S. (2010). Positive emotions as a basic building block of resilience in adulthood. In J. Reich, A. Zautra, J. Hall, J. Reich, A. Zautra, & J. Hall (Eds.), *Handbook of adult resilience* (pp. 81–93). New York, NY: Guilford.

Oseland, L., Gallus, K., & Nelson Goff, B. (2016). Clinical application of the couple adaptation to traumatic stress model: A pragmatic framework for working with traumatized couples. *Journal of Couple and Relationship Therapy*, 15, 83–101. doi:10.1080/15332691.2014.938284

Ozer, E. J., Best, S. R., Lipsey, T. L., & Weiss, D. S. (2003). Predictors of posttraumatic stress disorder and symptoms in adults: A meta-analysis. *Psychological Bulletin*, 129(1), 52–73.

Platt, J., Keyes, K. M., & Koenen, K. C. (2014). Size of the social network versus quality of social support: Which is more protective against PTSD? *Social Psychiatry and Psychiatric Epidemiology*, 49(8), 1279–1286. doi:10.1007/s00127-013-0798-4

Renshaw, K., & Campbell, S. (2011). Combat veterans' symptoms of PTSD and partners' distress: The role of partners' perceptions of veterans' deployment experiences. *Journal of Family Psychology*, 25(6), 953–962. doi:10.1037/a0025871

Renshaw, K., Rodebaugh, T., & Rodrigues, C. (2010). Psychological and marital distress in spouses of Vietnam veterans: Importance of spouses' perceptions. *Journal of Anxiety Disorders*, 24(7), 743–750. doi:10.1016/j.janxdis.2010.05.007

Renshaw, K., Rodrigues, C., & Jones, D. (2008). Psychological symptoms and marital satisfaction in spouses of operation Iraqi freedom veterans: Relationships with spouses' perceptions of veterans' experiences and symptoms. *Journal of Family Psychology*, 22, 586–594. doi:10.1037/0893-3200.22.3.586

Resick, P. A., Monson, C. M., & Chard, K. M. (2016). *Cognitive processing therapy for PTSD: A comprehensive manual*. New York, NY: Guilford.

Resick, P. A., Williams, L. F., Suvak, M. K., Monson, C. M., & Gradus, J. L. (2012). Long-term outcomes of cognitive–behavioral treatments for posttraumatic stress disorder among female rape survivors. *Journal of Consulting and Clinical Psychology*, 80(2), 201–210. doi:10.1037/a0026602

Riggs, D. (2000). Marital and family therapy. In E. B. Foa, T. M. Keane, & M. J. Friedman (Eds.), *Effective treatments for PTSD: Practice guidelines from the International Society for Traumatic Stress Studies* (pp. 280–301). New York, NY: Guilford Press.

Riggs, D. (2014). Traumatized relationships: Symptoms of posttraumatic stress disorder, fear of intimacy, and marital adjustment in dual trauma couples. *Psychological Trauma Theory Research Practice and Policy*, 6(3), 201–206. doi:10.1037/a0036405

Riggs, D., Byrne, C., Weathers, F., & Litz, B. (1998). The quality of the intimate relationships of male Vietnam veterans: Problems associated with posttraumatic stress disorder. *Journal of Traumatic Stress*, 11(1), 87–101. doi:10.1023/A:1024409200155

Ruhlmann, L. M., Gallus, K. L., & Durtschi, J. A. (2018). Exploring relationship satisfaction and attachment behaviors in single- and dual-trauma couples: A pilot study. *Traumatology*, 24(1), 27–35. doi:10.1037/trm0000129

Sautter, F. J., Armelie, A. P., Glynn, S. M., & Wielt, D. B. (2011). The development of a couple-based treatment for PTSD in returning veterans. *Professional Psychology: Research and Practice*, 42(1), 63–69. doi:10.1037/a0022323

Sautter, F. J., Glynn, S. M., Cretu, J. B., Senturk, D., & Vaught, A. S. (2015). Efficacy of structured approach therapy in reducing PTSD in returning veterans: A randomized clinical trial. *Psychological Services*, 12(3), 199–212. doi:10.1037/ser0000032

Sautter, F. J., Glynn, S. M., Thompson, K., Franklin, L., & Han, X. (2009). A couple-based approach to the reduction of PTSD avoidance symptoms: Preliminary findings. *Journal of Marital and Family Therapy*, 35(3), 343–349. doi:10.1111/j.1752-0606.2009.00125.x

Sayers, S., Farrow, V., Ross, J., & Oslin, D. (2009). Family problems among recently returned military veterans referred for a mental health evaluation. *Journal of Clinical Psychiatry*, 70(2), 163–170. doi:10.4088/JCP.07m03863

Schwartz, R. C. (1995). *Internal family systems therapy*. New York, NY: Guilford.

Shapiro, F., Kaslow, F. W., & Maxfield, L. (2011). *Handbook of EMDR and family therapy processes*. Hoboken, NJ: Wiley.

Sherman, M., Sautter, F., Jackson, H., Lyons, J., & Han, X. (2006). Domestic violence in veterans with posttraumatic stress disorder who seek couples therapy. *Journal of Marital and Family Therapy*, 32, 479–490. doi:10.1111/j.1752-0606.2006.tb01622.x

Simpson, T. L., & Miller, W. R. (2002). Concomitance between childhood sexual and physical abuse and substance use problems. A review. *Clinical Psychology Review*, 22(1), 27–77. doi:10.1016/S0272-7358(00)00088-X

Sivers, H., Schooler, J., & Freyd, J. (2002). Recovered memories. In V. Ramachandran (Ed.), *Encyclopedia of the human brain* (Vol. 4, pp. 169–184). San Diego, CA: Academic Press.

Skodol, A. (2010). The resilient personality. In J. Reich, A. Zautra, & J. Hall (Eds.), *Handbook of adult resilience* (pp. 112–125). New York, NY: Guilford.

Smith, K. Z., Smith, P. H., Violanti, J. M., Bartone, P. T., & Homish, G. G. (2015). Posttraumatic stress disorder symptom clusters and perpetration of intimate partner violence: Findings from a U.S. nationally representative sample. *Journal of Traumatic Stress*, 28(5), 469–474. doi:10.1002/jts.22048

Solomon, Z., Waysman, M., Belkin, R., Levy, G., Mikulincer, M., & Enoch, D. (1992). Marital relations and combat stress reaction: The wives' perspective. *Journal of Marriage and Family*, 54, 316–326. doi:10.2307/353063

Steel, J. L., & Herlitz, C. A. (2005). The association between childhood and adolescent sexual abuse and proxies for sexual risk behavior: A random sample of the general population of Sweden. *Child Abuse and Neglect*, 29(10), 1141–1153. doi:10.1016/j.chiabu.2004.10.015

Sullivan, E., Contractor, A. A., Gerber, M. M., & Neumann, C. (2017). Examination of polytrauma typologies: A latent class analysis approach. *Psychiatry Research*, 255, 111–118. doi:10.1016/j.psychres.2017.05.026

Taft, C., Pless, A., Stalans, L., Koenen, K., King, L., & King, D. (2005). Risk factors for partner violence among a national sample of combat veterans. *Journal of Consulting and Clinical Psychology*, 73, 151–159. doi:10.1037/0022-006X.73.1.151

Taft, C., Resick, P., Watkins, L., & Panuzio, J. (2009). An investigation of posttraumatic stress disorder and depressive symptomatology among female victims of interpersonal trauma. *Journal of Family Violence*, 24(6), 407–415. doi:10.1007/s10896-009-9243-6

Taft, C., Street, A., Marshall, A., Dowdall, D., & Riggs, D. (2007). Posttraumatic stress disorder, anger, and partner abuse among Vietnam combat veterans. *Journal of Family Psychology*, 21, 270–277. doi:10.1037/0893-3200.21.2.270

Taft, C., Watkins, L., Stafford, J., Street, A., & Monson, C. (2011). Posttraumatic stress disorder and intimate relationship problems: A meta-analysis. *Journal of Consulting and Clinical Psychology*, 79, 22–33. doi:10.1037/a0022196

Tedeschi, R., & Calhoun, L. (1996). The posttraumatic growth inventory: Measuring the positive legacy of trauma. *Journal of Traumatic Stress*, 9, 455–471. doi:10.1002/jts.2490090305

Tedeschi, R., & Calhoun, L. (2004). Target article: "Posttraumatic growth: Conceptual foundations and empirical evidence". *Psychological Inquiry*, 15(1), 1–18. doi:10.1207/s15327965pli1501_01

Teten, A., Schumacher, J., Taft, C., Stanley, M., Kent, T., Bailey, S., ... White, D. (2010). Intimate partner aggression perpetrated and sustained by male Afghanistan, Iraq, and Vietnam veterans with and without posttraumatic stress disorder. *Journal of Interpersonal Violence*, 25(9), 1612–1630. doi:10.1177/0886260509354583

Teten, A., Sherman, M., & Han, X. (2009). Violence between therapy-seeking veterans and their partners: Prevalence and characteristics of nonviolent, mutually violent, and one-sided violent couples. *Journal of Interpersonal Violence*, 24(1), 111–127. doi:10.1177/0886260508315782

Thoits, P. A. (1982). Conceptual, metholdological, and theoretical problems in studying social support as a buffer against stress. *Journal of Health and Social Behavior*, 23, 145–159.

Thoits, P. A. (1995). Stress, coping, and social support processes: Where are we? What next? *Journal of Health and Social Behavior*, 35, 53–79.

Trevillion, K., Williamson, E., Thandi, G., Borschmann, R., Oram, S., & Howard, L. M. (2015). A systematic review of mental disorders and perpetration of domestic violence among military populations. *Social Psychiatry and Psychiatric Epidemiology*, 50(9), 1329–1346. doi:10.1007/s00127-015-1084-4

Tugade, M. M., & Fredrickson, B. L. (2004). Resilient individuals use positive emotions to bounce back from negative emotional experiences. *Journal of Personality and Social Psychology*, 86(2), 320–333. doi:10.1037/0022-3514.86.2.320

Turner, R. J., & Lloyd, D. A. (1995). Lifetime traumas and mental health: The significance of cumulative adversity. *Journal of Health and Social Behavior*, 36(4), 360–376. doi:10.2307/2137325

van der Kolk, B., Roth, S., Pelcovitz, D., Sunday, S., & Spinazzola, J. (2005). Disorders of extreme stress: The empirical foundation of a complex adaptation to trauma. *Journal of Traumatic Stress*, 18(5), 389–399. doi:10.1002/jts.20047

Wadsworth, S. M., Lester, P., Marini, C., Cozza, S., Sornborger, J., Strouse, T., & Beardslee, W. (2013). Approaching family-focused systems of care for military and veteran families. *Military Behavioral Health*, 1(1), 31–40. doi:10.1080/21635781.2012.721062

Weiss, T. (2004). Correlates of posttraumatic growth in married breast cancer survivors. *Journal of Social and Clinical Psychology*, 23(5), 733–746. doi:10.1521/jscp.23.5.733.50750

Weissman, N., Batten, S. V., Rheem, K. D., Wiebe, S. A., Pasillas, R. M., Potts, W., ... Dixon, L. B. (2018). The effectiveness of emotionally focused couples therapy with veterans with PTSD: A pilot study. *Journal of Couple & Relationship Therapy*, 17(1), 25–41. doi:10.10 80/15332691.2017.1285261

World Health Organization. (2018). *International Classification of Diseases 11th Revision: 06 Mental, behavioural or neurodevelopmental disorders: Disorders specifically associated with stress.* Retrieved from https://icd.who.int/browse11/l-m/en#/http%3a%2f%2fid.who.int%2ficd%2fentity%2f991786158

Zwahlen, D., Hagenbuch, N., Carley, M. I., Jenewein, J., & Buchi, S. (2010). Posttraumatic growth in cancer patients and partners—Effects of role, gender and the dyad on couples' posttraumatic growth experience. *Psycho-Oncology*, 19(1), 12–20. doi:10.1002/pon.1486

11

General and Health-Related Stress and Couples' Coping

Guy Bodenmann and Ashley K. Randall

In couple therapy, the role of stress in relationship functioning is often considered as an internal stress, which is reflected in partners' communication problems, goal discrepancies, or incompatible needs. However, stress from outside the relationship (e.g., workload, stress with the family of origin) often plays an even more important role in couples' functioning and can trigger partners' internal stress (Bodenmann, Ledermann, & Bradbury, 2007).

Couples and families can experience a number of stressors irrespective of their level of functioning, which can be developmental or situational in nature (Gladding, 2014). In the context of couples' therapy, stressors have been commonly categorized as *vertical* and *horizontal* stressors (Gladding, 2014), which are also reflected in Carter and McGoldrick's model (Carter & McGoldrick, 1988). Vertical stressors are multigenerational in nature, whereas horizontal stressors are related to present life (e.g., life cycle transitions, illness, and the current political climate). Furthermore, these stressors can occur across all systems, from the individual to the couple to the immediate or extended family to the community and beyond.

Conceptualizing the role of stress in close relationships is not unique to couple therapy, however. Psychological research has focused on understanding the role of internal stress on relationship functioning (see Randall & Bodenmann, 2009, 2017). Typically, relationship tensions, differences in needs and goals, and inequities and role ambiguity are defined as *internal stressors*, as they have their origin within the relationship (e.g., Harway, 2005). However, health issues (chronic or severe illness, disabilities, etc.) can be considered internal stressors (e.g., Milbury, Badr, Fossella, Pisters, & Carmack, 2013). Irrespective of the type of internal stress, the experience of such stress has been found to be associated with increased relationship tension and dissatisfaction (Randall & Bodenmann, 2009), whereas external stress (stress originating outside the relationship) is positively associated with an increase in dysfunctional communication (e.g., "shutting down") and decrease in intimacy between partners. As such, many mental health providers aim to improve relationship quality by means of communication trainings and increasing intimacy (e.g., Epstein and Baucom, 2002).

The Handbook of Systemic Family Therapy: Volume 3, First Edition.
Edited by Karen S. Wampler and Adrian J. Blow.
© 2020 John Wiley & Sons Ltd. Published 2020 by John Wiley & Sons Ltd.

Although the focus on internal stress is important, research shows that couples also need to learn how to cope with external stressors as these can have a more detrimental effect on individual and relational well-being (Randall & Bodenmann, 2009). External stress originates outside the relationship from sources that have essentially nothing to do with the partner or the relationship, such as workplace, family of origin, and financial stress (Randall & Bodenmann, 2009). Additionally, some couples may be differentially exposed to external stressors due to their minority status (e.g., Meyer, 2003). Furthermore, research on both heterosexual (Buck & Neff, 2012; Neff & Karney, 2009) and same-sex couples (Totenhagen, Randall, Cooper, Tao, & Walsh, 2017) has shown that the experience of external stress can *cross over* (i.e., from one partner to the other) and *spill over* to (i.e., external stress becoming internal stress) one's romantic partner and relationship (Bodenmann, Ledermann et al., 2007). Despite the robust literature on the negative associations between the experience of external stress on relationship well-being (see Randall & Bodenmann, 2009, for a review), there is a lack of therapeutic techniques designed to focus specifically on identifying and coping with external stressors (for exceptions see Bodenmann, Cina et al., 2008; Bodenmann & Shantinath, 2004). However, improving couples' dyadic coping skills can be considered an important focus of intervention, given that communication skills often deteriorate under conditions of stress (Bodenmann & Shantinath, 2004).

Dyadic coping is conceptualized in the Systemic Transactional Model (STM) (Bodenmann, 1995, 2005; Bodenmann, Randall, & Falconier, 2016) as the ways in which both partners perceive a stressful situation by sharing their appraisals ("we-stress") or by realizing the partner's stress experience and engaging in shared coping efforts (i.e., both partners try to deal with the stress together by downregulating each other's negative emotions or supporting the other in his/her problem solving and emotion regulation). Dyadic coping is considered as a temporal process that relies on each partner's stress communication (verbal or nonverbal), the perception and understanding of this stress communication by the other partner, and his/her dyadic coping efforts matching the other's needs. Dyadic coping has been found to explain variance of relationship quality above and beyond individual coping (Papp & Witt, 2010).

Based on the growing literature on couples' stress and coping from around the world (see Falconier, Randall, & Bodenmann, 2016), this chapter will illustrate the current research on the negative association between couple external stress and relationship functioning. To do so, we specifically focus on "common" or shared external stressors and health-related stressors, which have had a growing focus in the literature (e.g., Badr, 2004; Kayser, Watson, & Andrade, 2007; Revenson, Kayser, & Bodenmann, 2005; Vilchinsky, 2019). Our hope is that this knowledge will allow mental health professionals working with couples to (a) understand the implications of stress and coping research, as applied to a variety of couples (e.g., dual career couples, couples in the transition to parenthood, retiring couples, couples dealing with life strain or critical life events, couples struggling with everyday stress and high work–family workload); (b) inform couples, through psychoeducation, about the impact of couple external stress on communication, shared time together, sexuality, and intimacy; and (c) understanding techniques associated with teaching couples dyadic coping skills, conceptualized as a relationship maintenance behavior found effective in combating stress' deleterious effects (Randall & Messerschmitt, 2020).

Theoretical Background on the Role of Stress in Couples' Functioning

Interpersonal view of stress in close relationships

The most widespread definition of stress includes an imbalance between internal and external demands and the capability of the individual to respond to these demands by applying internal or external resources (Lazarus & Folkman, 1984). Historically, stress has been considered as an individual phenomenon, conceptualizing stress as an individual's experience of an event. However, within the last decades, there has been an expansion of this conceptualization to understand stress as a dyadic or interpersonal construct (e.g., Bodenmann, 1995, 2005; Lyons, Mickelson, Sullivan, & Coyne, 1998; Randall & Bodenmann, 2009, 2017). According to Randall and Bodenmann (2009, 2017), the main assumption of the interpersonal view of stress (as a dyadic construct) is that in a close committed relationship the stress of one partner is associated with the other partner's experience of stress due to their interdependence (Kelley & Thibaut, 1978). Furthermore, as noted above, experiences of external stress can spill over, causing internal stress within the relationship (Neff & Karney, 2009). The impact of stress spillover processes can lead to an increase in the likelihood of relationship conflicts, mutual alienation, and decreased relationship satisfaction in the long run (Bodenmann, 2005; Ferguson, 2012).

Stress models and relationship development

Defining stress as an interpersonal construct has been primarily reflected in two theoretical models.

The vulnerability–stress–adaptation model The *vulnerability–stress–adaptation (VSA) model* (Karney & Bradbury, 1995) proposes that the effects of stress on adverse relational outcomes are based on (a) *enduring vulnerabilities* (i.e., stable characteristics making individuals vulnerable to stress), (b) *stressful events* (e.g., life events, stressful circumstances, etc.), and (c) *adaptive processes* (e.g., the ability to provide support to one another) (Karney & Bradbury, 1995). More recently, Totenhagen, Randall, and Lloyd (2018) demonstrated the utility of expanding the VSA model to understand specific vulnerabilities of same-gender couples, given their unique experiences of minority stressors, above and beyond "common" external stressors couples may face. Based on a sample of 81 same-sex couples, Totenhagen et al. (2018) found internalized homophobia (Frost & Meyer, 2009) and low outness to be associated with worse relational functioning, as measured by severity of conflict, relationship quality, and commitment.

The stress–divorce model Bodenmann (1995, 2000, Bodenmann, Charvoz et al., 2007) proposed a *stress–divorce model* that describes the impact of external minor (i.e., everyday stressors) or major (i.e., developmental tasks, critical life events) stressors on partners' relationship functioning. Specifically, the impact of stress on partners' relationship functioning can be observed by the increase in mutual alienation and decrease in communication, which, over time, can lead to relationship dissolution. According to the *stress–divorce model*, stress originating outside the relationship (i.e., external stress) often spills over into the relationship, causing stress within the relationship (i.e., internal stress). Thus, one partner's experience of external stress often becomes dyadic internal stress, affecting both partners individually and the couple as a whole. This stress spillover process can then affect a number of relational processes, which include, but are not limited to, effective communication and shared time together. For example, the increase of external stress can increase couples' dysfunctional communication (i.e., less communication in general, more superficial communication, more solution-oriented communication and less emotional self-disclosure, more verbally aggressive and hostile communication or withdrawal). Furthermore, the increase of dysfunctional communication can also lead to less time shared between partners and increased feelings of mutual alienation (e.g., Bodenmann, Charvoz et al., 2007).

Health-related impact of stress in close relationships

The experience of stress spillover has also been found to have negative associations with health-related outcomes. Specifically, research has shown the deleterious effects of stress on sleep quality (McEwen, 1998), sexual dysfunction (Bodenmann, Ledermann, Blattner, & Galluzzo, 2006), and cardiovascular disease (Charmandari, Tsigos, & Chrousos, 2005). In the long run, these changes on relational functioning are associated with increased rates of relationship dissolution and divorce (Bodenmann, Charvoz et al., 2007; Randall & Bodenmann, 2009). Importantly, however, partners' individual and dyadic coping behaviors are able to alleviate the negative impact of stress on couples' functioning. The better each partner or the couple is able to manage stress, the less effects stress can have on the relationship, and their relationship quality. As such, we argue that strengthening couples' coping resources is associated with enhancing relationship functioning in general.

Empirical Findings on the Role of Stress in Close Relationships

Several studies have documented the assumed processes in the stress–divorce model (e.g., Bodenmann, Charvoz et al., 2007; Falconier, Nussbeck, Bodenmann, Schneider, & Bradbury, 2015; Neff & Karney, 2009; Randall & Bodenmann, 2009; Story & Bradbury, 2004). Specific to the stress–divorce model, research has shown that, when under stress, couples' communication quality drops by 40%. Specifically, negative communication (e.g., blaming, criticism, defensiveness, belligerence, contempt) increases, while positive communication behaviors between partners (e.g., showing interest, care, and affection) decreases.

Across the literature, researchers have found a negative association between external stress and relationship functioning. Many studies show that couple external stress such as economic stress (e.g., Jackson et al., 2016), minority stress (e.g., Otis, Rostosky, Riggle, & Hamrin, 2006; Randall, Totenhagen, Walsh, Adams, & Tao, 2017; Rostosky & Riggle, 2017), racial discrimination (Kerr et al., 2018), and immigration stress (Falconier, Nussbeck, & Bodenmann, 2013) are associated with poor relationship functioning. External stress increases the likelihood of internal stress (relationship tensions, conflicts, health problems) and by this means decreases couples' satisfaction and stability. In sum, the level of stress to which a couple is exposed can have a substantial burden on relationship functioning; however, partners can help mitigate stress' deleterious effects by engaging in (positive) dyadic coping.

Couples' Coping with Stress: The Systemic Transactional Model (STM)

To help combat stress' deleterious effects, it is important to take into consideration not only each partner's individual coping resources, but how partners cope together (i.e., engaging in dyadic coping). Dyadic coping is defined as the way couples cope with stress together as a unit, either by supporting each other, by delegating tasks and duties, or by engaging in joint problem solving or joint emotion regulation (Bodenmann, 1997; Bodenmann et al., 2016). Several dyadic coping models have been proposed since the 1990s (e.g., Lee & Roberts, 2018), which help to conceptualize how partners can cope together in the face of stress. In Bodenmann's (1995, 2005) STM, the stress coping process is viewed as an interplay between both partners, as it is assumed that the stress of one partner is always relevant to the other partner's satisfaction and well-being; thus, stress is conceptualized as a dyadic construct. Due to partners' interdependence, the stress of one partner affects the other, and as such, both partners have an (implicit) interest in managing stress together by combining their coping resources (Bodenmann, 1997; Bodenmann et al., 2016).

Empirical findings on the efficacy of dyadic coping

Dyadic coping has been shown to be a consistent and powerful predictor of relationship satisfaction across cultures (Falconier et al., 2016; Falconier, Jackson, Hilpert, & Bodenmann, 2015; Hilpert et al., 2016) and has been shown to be significantly (positively) associated with relationship quality above and beyond partner's individual coping resources (Herzberg, 2013; Papp & Witt, 2010). Additionally, dyadic coping has been shown to buffer the negative effects of stress on (positive) communication (Bodenmann, Atkins, Schär, & Poffet, 2010; Bodenmann, Ledermann et al., 2007). While dyadic coping has repeatedly found to be a significant (positive) predictor of relationship functioning, it is also important for partners' individual well-being in different-gender (Bodenmann, Meuwly, & Kayser, 2011) as well as same-gender couples (e.g., Randall, Tao, Totenhagen, Walsh, & Cooper, 2017). For example, using a sample of female same-gender couples, Randall and colleagues showed that partner engagement in emotion-focused dyadic coping mitigated the negative association between discrimination stress and depressive symptoms.

Engagement in dyadic coping has also been found to be effective in the context of health issues. Couples' coping together is a powerful predictor of better relationship and health adjustment. This association has been supported in couples dealing with cancer, cardiovascular diseases, other chronic illnesses, or psychological disorders (e.g., Revenson & Lepore, 2012). Additionally, recent research has found that parental dyadic coping was associated with lower internalizing and externalizing child symptoms (Zemp, Bodenmann, Backes, Sutter-Stickel, & Revenson, 2016). Taken together, these findings indicate that strengthening dyadic coping is beneficial for relationship functioning as well as all family members' psychological and physical well-being.

Couple Interventions Aimed at Strengthening Dyadic Coping

Research on stress and coping has important implications for relationship education and interventions with couples and families (Randall, Bodenmann, Molgora, &

Margola, 2010). Stress-related psychoeducation and dyadic coping-oriented interventions, described below, can be useful in any therapeutic approach (systemic, humanistic, cognitive behavioral, emotion focused, etc.) and are not limited to a specific approach. The techniques described below were developed and evaluated in the context of relationship education as well as couple therapy; however, these techniques have a broad scope of application in the context of systemic family therapy, health psychology, clinical psychology, and family science. Importantly, these techniques can be combined with other elements such as communication trainings and cognitive or emotion-focused interventions, and may represent useful techniques in addition to classical intervention elements. Specific examples of such approaches can be found in the *Couples Coping Enhancement Training* (CCET) (Bodenmann & Shantinath, 2004) and the *Coping-Oriented Couple Therapy* (COCT) techniques (Bodenmann, 2010; Bodenmann, Plancherel et al., 2008; Lau et al., 2017).

Psychoeducation

Psychoeducation is an important element in couple therapy, where the couple is taught about the erosive and long-term unperceived impact of stress on the couples' daily life. As partners often do not realize how external stress can impact their communication difficulties and relationship problems, the stress–divorce model is explained to couples, and their awareness for protecting their relationship against couple external stress is strengthened. During the psychoeducation phase, the clinician also introduces the concept of dyadic coping and illustrates its benefit in jointly coping with stress. Practically, the therapist teaches partners how to (a) better communicate their own experienced stress to their partner, (b) understand their partner's stress more accurately, (c) mutually engage in telling and listening during stress-related self-disclosure, and (d) provide adequate support that matches their partner's needs (Bodenmann, 2005, 2010; Bodenmann & Randall, 2012).

3-Phase method

The 3-phase method (Bodenmann, 2007; Bodenmann & Randall, 2013) is a novel communication and support method used in both CCET and COCT. The method is based on principles of cognitive therapy (Beck, Rush, Shaw, & Emery, 1979) and the concept of central hassles (Gruen, Folkman, & Lazarus, 1988) and allows for the exploration of each partner's individual or personal schemas. By the exploring each partner's schemas individually, both partners are part of the discovery process and are engaged as either the speaker or the listener. The therapist prompts both partners at the same time (the speaker and the listener), and his/her job is to facilitate emotional self-disclosure in the speaker and empathic understanding in the listener during the process. The 3-phase method is delivered in a quiet setting where both partners are sitting in front of each other, allowing for the best practice of active listening, while the clinician sitting between the partners a few feet away. The 3-phase method offers a clear structure with regard to the duration of the exercises, roles of both partners (speaker and listener), and setting.

Process of the 3-phase method In the *first phase* of the 3-phase method (20–30 min), the facilitator utilizes the funnel method to support the stressed partner to disclose his/her stress to his/her partner by telling him/her about the stress experience (Bodenmann, 2007, 2010). The goal of this first phase is to get a deeper understanding of why the situation was so stressful for the partner and to gain a deeper insight into the (stressed) partner's functioning. During this sharing, the clinician encourages the stressed partner to explore his/her emotions (e.g., fear, disappointment, feelings of helplessness, shame, etc.) and cognitions ("his [my boss'] reaction showed me that he does not have any respect toward me") surrounding the stress by searching for an explanation why the situation was so demanding ("I was not able to stand up for myself, and let him [the boss] know what I completed on the project. Instead of being acknowledged for what I did, I was only criticized for what I did not do."). The clinician facilitates stress-related emotional self-disclosure by means of open-ended questions ("How was this for you?" "Tell more about your feelings." "Why was this so terrible?"). At the same time, the clinician prompts the (non-stressed) partner to actively listen and try to empathically understand how the partner feels. This insight is viewed as basic for empathic understanding, acceptance of partner's behaviors, and mutual tolerance. While the funnel method allows the stressed partner to deepen their stress disclosure, it also allows the "listening" partner to emotionally connect with their partner in an effort to downregulate their negative emotions and provide emotional support. As such, his/her empathic listening (i.e., the "listening" partner) is the root for adequate provision of (supportive) dyadic coping that increase partners' feeling of we-ness, trust, and mutual attachment. A recent study by Leuchtmann, Horn, Randall, Kuhn, and Bodenmann (2018) showed that the method is very effective.

In the *second phase* of the 3-phase method (10 min), the clinician asks the listening partner how he/she could provide supportive dyadic coping to the stressed partner. Given that partners have already developed a deepened emotional experience by means of the funnel method, support provision is no longer considered superficial or primarily instrumental. As such, the listening partner can authentically express his/ her feelings of understanding, as he/she is emotionally affected by their partner's stress. He/she now usually provides emotion-focused supportive dyadic coping by expressing empathy, encouraging the partner, helping him/her to reframe the situation, or supporting his/her individual coping efforts. Only following emotion-focused supportive dyadic coping are partners invited to provide instrumental support (i.e., giving practical help or advices), if still needed. The clinician validates the partner's dyadic coping behaviors. If the partner is not able to provide adequate support, the therapist offers suggestions as a way to help the partner increase their support of their partner. If partners are not able to engage in self-disclosure or empathic listening due to personal characteristics (e.g., problematic personality traits like narcissism or alexithymia), the therapist does not apply this method based on clinical judgment.

In the *third phase* (5 min), the clinician asks the stress (supported) partner to give feedback about how helpful, effective, and satisfying the partner's supportive dyadic coping was.

Goals of the 3-phase method By means of the 3-phase method, partners learn that external minor daily stressors can cause increased experiences of stress by triggering personal schemata. Schemata-related stress often endures many hours or days and easily spills over to the intimate relationship, empoisoning couple interaction (e.g.,

Neff & Karney, 2009). By engaging in both the speaker and listener roles, the 3-phase method allows both partners to become aware of each other's personally important schema (e.g., "I feel only well when I have complete control over my environment," "I am only okay when I give a great presentation," "I am only appreciated when I am perfect," "I am only valuable when I feel loved," etc.) by exploring emotions, thoughts, and behavioral reactions that emerge when recalling the stressful situation.

It is important to note that in both CCET and COCT, the goal is to improve partners' emotional self-disclosure, empathic listening, and dyadic coping behaviors. This makes the most sense for couples dealing with an elevated general stress levels (e.g., dual earning couples, couples dealing with child-related stress, couples during transitions); however, research has shown that most couples can benefit from stress-related psychoeducation and an enhancement of dyadic coping. The 3-phase method has been found effective for couples coping with different general and health-related stressors (Bodenmann, 2010). The 3-phase method is only applied when a sufficient level of mutual positivity, respect, and commitment between partners is present, as observed by the therapist and stated by both partners, which typically occurs in the later phases of couples' therapy. Behavioral exchange techniques, communication training, and commitment work are used to build this basis (Epstein & Baucom, 2002). The 3-phase method should not be applied to couples with low relationship commitment, those thinking about ending their relationship, or to couples where one partner is diagnosed with a personality disorder, as emotional self-disclosure requires mutual positivity such as respect, interest and openness for the partner's well-being.

Role of the clinician   The clinician oversees the application of the speaker and listener rules and prompts both partners throughout the method, as described above (Bodenmann, 2007, 2010). The clinician's job is to support both partners in the exploration of their schemata by helping him/her to dive deeper into his/her emotions by asking open-ended question. By asking these questions, the clinician helps the speaker (i.e., stressed partner) to engage in deepened emotional self-disclosure regarding the stress situation.

During the three phases, the clinician prompts/coaches both partners simultaneously (the speaker and the listener) by joining both partners with gaze and verbal reinforcement and by prompting them in their specific roles. For the speaker, the clinician prompts him/her to emotionally self-disclose with regard to personal schemata triggered by the stress situation (by asking open-ended questions and reinforcing stress communication). For the listener, the clinician asks him/her from time to time to summarize the important elements of self-exploration that were expressed by the speaker, to emotionally connect (phase one), and to adequately support their partner (phase two).

CCET workshops

CCET aims to help couples identify daily stressors and their impact on couples' functioning while teaching them to cope with these stressors in a more effective way. Additionally, couples are taught to increase their mutual understanding, tolerance, and acceptance of one another. CCET has five major goals: (a) improving individual stress management; (b) enhancing the couple's ability to cope together; (c) sensitizing the couple to issues of mutual fairness, equity, and respect with regard to dyadic coping; (d) improving marital communication (by teaching partners deeper self-disclosure by means of speaker and listener rules); and (e) enhancing problem-solving skills (by means of a structured multistep approach).

CCET workshops can be delivered in a variety of modalities: as a weekend workshop (duration between 8 and 15 hr according to the format) or as an online intervention. Usually, weekend workshops include six to eight couples, with one trainer per two couples in order to coach closely the communication and support exercises. Providers are well trained and licensed (for more information see Johnson, Randall, & Bodenmann, 2018). The efficacy of CCET has been examined with heterosexual couples (see different studies below) and is currently being developed to be piloted with same-sex couples (Randall, Totenhagen, & Bodenmann, 2019).

Effectiveness of Coping-Oriented Couple Approaches

Effectiveness of CCET

CCET (Bodenmann & Shantinath, 2004) is based on cognitive-behavioral therapeutic principles and empirical findings conducted across cultures (see Randall & Bodenmann, 2009; Revenson et al., 2005).

CCET (Bodenmann & Shantinath, 2004) has been found to be effective in various forms of delivery; in different formats varying in dosage (15, 12, 8 hr plus blended learning by means of a DVD; Zemp et al., 2017), also a self-directed approach of CCET (DVD intervention; Bodenmann, Hilpert, Nussbeck, & Bradbury, 2014) showed significant improvements in dyadic coping, conflict communication, and relationship satisfaction in women (with mixed results in men). The efficacy of CCET has been shown in several studies, reporting positive effects on relationship satisfaction, couple communication, and dyadic coping with mean effect sizes of $d = 0.36$ (post), $d = 0.32$ (follow-up after 6 months), and $d = 0.44$ (after a 1-year follow-up; Bodenmann, Pihet, Shantinath, Cina, & Widmer, 2006; Randall et al., 2010). The improvement of dyadic coping has also been found to be associated with reduced depressive symptomatology ($d = -1.3$; Bodenmann, Plancherel et al., 2008) and increased psychological well-being (Pihet, Bodenmann, Cina, Widmer, & Shantinath, 2007).

Effects of CCET were found to be stronger in distressed couples, showing generally high levels of stress or a lower relationship satisfaction (Bodenmann et al., 2014). The improvement of dyadic coping by means of CCET has also been found to be associated with reduced child conduct problems and externalizing symptoms (Bodenmann, Cina, Ledermann, & Sanders, 2008).

Effectiveness of COCT

Similar to the CCET, COCT or couple-focused interventions have a similar focus on the enhancement of dyadic coping skills. The approach is based on the assumption that relationship distress is often a consequence of external stress that triggers unpleasant or problematic personality traits (e.g., rigidity, dominance, intolerance, avarice, anxiety) that develop their destructive potential and exert a detrimental impact on the close relationship (e.g., tensions, arguments, disappointment, disillusion). In the context of cancer, couple-oriented interventions are well documented (Badr & Krebs, 2013) as they are in couples dealing with chronic health conditions and psychopathology (Fischer, Baucom, & Cohen, 2016).

Effectiveness of TOGETHER

TOGETHER is another prevention program designed to enhance dyadic coping in couples dealing with economic stress (Falconier, Kim, & Conway, 2018). TOGETHER is an interdisciplinary prevention program that focuses on financial strain in particular. Specifically, TOGETHER aims to help couples under financial strain improve their financial management, communication, and dyadic coping skills by (a) enhancing awareness of the deleterious consequences of financial strain on individuals' psychological well-being and on couples' relationships; (b) enhancing problem-solving skills and couple's communication about financial issues; (c) enhancing partners' mutual understanding about beliefs, roles, and expectations regarding finances; (d) improving individual and dyadic strategies to cope with financial strain as a couple; and (e) teaching effective ways of handling finances (e.g., financial planning, financial styles, improving financial behaviors, credit use, risk management) (for details, see Falconier et al., 2018). A recent pilot study conducted by Falconier et al. (2018) supports the effectiveness of TOGETHER.

Overall effectiveness of coping-oriented interventions

The research reviewed points to the efficacy and effectiveness of coping-oriented interventions, based on randomized control trials. However, it is challenging to have "pure" control groups to track in follow-up studies. Most studies have been conducted so far with different-gender, middle-aged, and well-educated couples. As such, the generalizability of such coping-oriented approaches to minority couples and those with low SES is limited. Falconier et al. (2018) are the first to investigate effects of coping-oriented interventions in the latter population, with a specific focus on couples coping with financial stressors. Randall, Totenhagen, and Bodenmann (2019) are currently revising the CCET manual with a focus on coping with the experience of sexual minority stressors for sexual minority couples.

Differences Between Coping-Oriented Interventions and Other Approaches

Coping-oriented interventions differ from cognitive-behavioral therapy or emotion-focused couple therapy, in that coping approaches specifically focus on the impact of external stress on couples' functioning, and particularly in its emphasis on the enhancement of couples' dyadic coping resources. While other approaches mainly work on the improvement of communication skills and emotion-focused interaction patterns, CCET and COCT emphasize strengthening mutual understanding, shared support, and intimacy between partners.

Feasibility and application of methods

Coping-oriented interventions are usually well-received by couples. Couples who engage in such interventions learn the negative impact of external stress on their communication and shared time and the importance of coping together with these adversities. The 3-phase method is, however, rather demanding for therapists as well as couples, as stress-related emotional self-disclosure demands the willingness to confide in the partner and to trust that personal vulnerabilities are handled with carefulness. For the listener, the method can be considered demanding as well, as he/she has to accept emotional contagion in order to emotionally understand the partner and be prepared to provide emotional support. The method is successfully used in prevention (CCET) and coping-oriented couple therapy (COCT) with most couples. It is not applicable with couples in escalating crisis, when one partner is diagnosed with psychosis or personality disorders such as antisocial, narcissistic, histrionic, or paranoid personality disorder or suffers from acute PTSD. In all other cases the 3-phase method is applicable, albeit at a later stage in the therapy, for example, in cases of extramarital affairs, severe humiliations, grievances, or trauma. When one partner suffers from a chronic disease or a psychological disorder the 3-phase method is applied as usual.

Discussion

Stress and coping in couples play an important role in relationship education and couple therapy (Randall et al., 2010). Teaching couples about the detrimental effects of stress on individual and relational well-being as well as techniques aimed at improving couples' coping (i.e., dyadic coping skills) is of great importance for mental health professionals working with couples. Despite its importance and international attention (see Falconier et al., 2016), fostering couples' resilience against stress is still neglected in many clinical interventions. Although couple-oriented interventions are proposed in many different health problems, and are becoming more and more recognized, the aspects of stress and dyadic coping remain largely neglected issues that merit further consideration.

The 3-phase method offers an easily adaptable technique that can be widely used and integrated in different therapeutic approaches, above and beyond the traditional communication or problem-solving techniques present in couples' therapy (Gladding, 2014), which aim to improve couples' stress resiliency. As communication deficits, sexual problems, lack of intimacy, and alienation between partners are often consequences of unresolved stress, a focus on these aspects is beneficial in relationship education (e.g., CCET) as well as couples' therapy (e.g., COCT). In most cases, working on improving individual coping skills is not sufficient to combat stress' deleterious effects; the enhancement of dyadic coping is required. As has been shown in this chapter, the 3-phase method, a support-oriented training helping couples to improve their stress-related self-disclosure and their empathic listening and aiming to broaden their mutual support behaviors, is a useful technique that can be applied with a wide range of couples in different stages of their relationship and with regard to various stressors (e.g., daily hassles, financial strain, child-related stress, minority stress, and health-related stress).

Research of the last 20 years indicates that strengthening dyadic coping is beneficial for relationship functioning as well as for all family members' psychological and physical well-being (Falconier et al., 2016). As in systemic family therapy (Minuchin & Nichols, 1998), stress and coping are traditionally considered as an interdependent phenomenon, affecting all family members; as such a therapeutic focus on these two target variables makes considerable sense. Studies on the effectiveness and efficacy of coping-oriented interventions show promising results and illustrate that strengthening couples' coping is valuable above and beyond traditional interventions.

Future directions

Examining the effectiveness of coping-oriented interventions (CCET, COCT, and TOGETHER) has been mainly conducted with different-gender couples coping with "common stressors." A promising area for future research is to expand work with understanding couples' experience of normative stressors (e.g., transition to parenthood) and minority stressors (e.g., same-gender couples, racial minorities, couples dealing with specific rare diseases, etc.). Randall and colleagues have made promising contributions in moving this field in this direction. Furthermore, there is a lack of knowledge regarding the question of which couples may benefit most from interventions targeting stress and coping and how the methods (i.e., 3-phase method) have to be adapted to specific needs (e.g., attachment styles, psychological disorders such as dementia in elderly couples or PTSD, severe health problems, military deployment, etc.). Although coping-oriented interventions seem to be beneficial for most couples, specific modifications of the techniques may be even more promising for clinicians working with distressed couples across cultures.

References

Badr, H. (2004). Coping in marital dyads: A contextual perspective on the role of gender and health. *Personal Relationships*, 11(2), 197–211. doi:10.1111/j.1475-6811.2004.00078.x

Badr, H., & Krebs, P. (2013). A systematic review and meta-analysis of psychosocial interventions for couples coping with cancer: Couples meta-analysis. *Psycho-Oncology*, 22(8), 1688–1704. doi:10.1002/pon.3200

Beck, A. T., Rush, J., Shaw, B. F., & Emery, G. (1979). *Cognitive therapy of depression*. New York, NY: Guilford.

Bodenmann, G. (1995). A systemic-transactional conceptualization of stress and coping in couples. *Swiss Journal of Psychology/Schweizerische Zeitschrift Für Psychologie/Revue Suisse de Psychologie*, 54(1), 34–49.

Bodenmann, G. (1997). Dyadic coping: A systematic-transactional view of stress and coping among couples: Theory and empirical findings. *European Review of Applied Psychology*, 47(2), 137–141.

Bodenmann, G. (2000). *Stress und Coping bei Paaren* [*Stress and coping in couples*. Göttingen, Germany: Hogrefe.

Bodenmann, G. (2005). Dyadic coping and its significance for marital functioning. In T. A. Revenson, K. Kayser, & G. Bodenmann (Eds.), *Couples coping with stress: Emerging perspectives on dyadic coping* (pp. 33–49). Washington, DC: American Psychological Association.

Bodenmann, G. (2007). Dyadic coping and the 3-phase-method in working with couples. In L. VandeCreek (Ed.), *Innovations in clinical practice: Focus on group and family therapy* (pp. 235–252). Sarasota, FL: Professional Resources Press.

Bodenmann, G. (2010). New themes in couple therapy: The role of stress, coping, and social support. In K. Hahlweg, M. Grawe-Gerber, & D. Baucom (Eds.), *Enhancing couples: The shape of couple therapy to come* (pp. 142–156). Cambridge, MA: Hogrefe.

Bodenmann, G., Atkins, D. C., Schär, M., & Poffet, V. (2010). The association between daily stress and sexual activity. *Journal of Family Psychology*, 24(3), 271–279. doi:10.1037/a0019365

Bodenmann, G., Charvoz, L., Bradbury, T. N., Bertoni, A., Iafrate, R., Giuliani, C., ... Behling, J. (2007). The role of stress in divorce: A three-nation retrospective study. *Journal of Social and Personal Relationships*, 24(5), 707–728. doi:10.1177/0265407507081456

Bodenmann, G., Cina, A., Ledermann, T., & Sanders, M. R. (2008). The efficacy of the Triple P-Positive Parenting Program in improving parenting and child behavior: A comparison with two other treatment conditions. *Behaviour Research and Therapy*, 46(4), 411–427. doi:10.1016/j.brat.2008.01.001

Bodenmann, G., Hilpert, P., Nussbeck, F. W., & Bradbury, T. N. (2014). Enhancement of couples' communication and dyadic coping by a self-directed approach: A randomized controlled trial. *Journal of Consulting and Clinical Psychology*, 82(4), 580–591. doi:10.1037/a0036356

Bodenmann, G., Ledermann, T., Blattner, D., & Galluzzo, C. (2006). Associations among everyday stress, critical life events, and sexual problems. *The Journal of Nervous and Mental Disease*, 194(7), 494–501. doi:10.1097/01.nmd.0000228504.15569.b6

Bodenmann, G., Ledermann, T., & Bradbury, T. N. (2007). Stress, sex, and satisfaction in marriage. *Personal Relationships*, 14(4), 551–569. doi:10.1111/j.1475-6811.2007.00171.x

Bodenmann, G., Meuwly, N., & Kayser, K. (2011). Two conceptualizations of dyadic coping and their potential for predicting relationship quality and individual well-being: A comparison. *European Psychologist*, 16(4), 255–266. doi:10.1027/1016-9040/a000068

Bodenmann, G., Pihet, S., Shantinath, S. D., Cina, A., & Widmer, K. (2006). Improving dyadic coping in couples with a stress-oriented approach: A 2-year longitudinal study. *Behavior Modification*, 30(5), 571–597. doi:10.1177/0145445504269902

Bodenmann, G., Plancherel, B., Beach, S. R. H., Widmer, K., Gabriel, B., Meuwly, N., ... Schramm, E. (2008). Effects of coping-oriented couples therapy on depression: A randomized clinical trial. *Journal of Consulting and Clinical Psychology*, 76(6), 944–954.

Bodenmann, G., & Randall, A. K. (2012). Common factors in the enhancement of dyadic coping. *Behavior Therapy*, 43(1), 88–98. doi:10.1016/j.beth.2011.04.003

Bodenmann, G., & Randall, A. K. (2013). Close relationships in psychiatric disorders. *Current Opinion in Psychiatry*, 26(5), 464–467.

Bodenmann, G., Randall, A. K., & Falconier, M. K. (2016). Coping in couples: The systemic-transactional model. In M. K. Falconier, A. K. Randall, & G. Bodenmann (Eds.), *Couples coping with stress: A cross-cultural perspective* (pp. 5–22). New York, NY: Routledge.

Bodenmann, G., & Shantinath, S. D. (2004). The couples coping enhancement training (CCET): A new approach to prevention of marital distress based upon stress and coping. *Family Relations*, 53(5), 477–484.

Buck, A. A., & Neff, L. A. (2012). Stress spillover in early marriage: The role of self-regulatory depletion. *Journal of Family Psychology*, 26(5), 698–708. doi:10.1037/a0029260

Carter, B. E., & McGoldrick, M. E. (1988). *The changing family life cycle: A framework for family therapy*. New York, NY: Gardner Press.

Charmandari, E., Tsigos, C., & Chrousos, G. (2005). Endocrinology of the stress response. *Annual Review of Physiology*, 67(1), 259–284. doi:10.1146/annurev.physiol.67.040403.120816

Epstein, N. B., & Baucom, D. H. (2002). *Enhanced cognitive-behavioral therapy for couples: A contextual approach.* Washington, DC: American Psychological Association.

Falconier, M. K., Jackson, J. B., Hilpert, P., & Bodenmann, G. (2015). Dyadic coping and relationship satisfaction: A meta-analysis. *Clinical Psychology Review, 42,* 28–46. doi:10.1016/j.cpr.2015.07.002

Falconier, M. K., Kim, J., & Conway, C. A. (2018). TOGETHER: A couple's model to enhance relationships and economic stability. In A. Betoni, S. Donato, & S. Molgora (Eds.), *When "we" are stressed. A dyadic approach to coping with stressful events* (pp. 183–204). New York, NY: Nova Science Publisher.

Falconier, M. K., Nussbeck, F., & Bodenmann, G. (2013). Immigration stress and relationship satisfaction in Latino couples: The role of dyadic coping. *Journal of Social and Clinical Psychology, 32*(8), 813–843. doi:10.1521/jscp.2013.32.8.813

Falconier, M. K., Nussbeck, F., Bodenmann, G., Schneider, H., & Bradbury, T. N. (2015). Stress from daily hassles in couples: Its effects on intradyadic stress, relationship satisfaction, and physical and psychological well-being. *Journal of Marital and Family Therapy, 41*(2), 221–235. doi:10.1111/jmft.12073

Falconier, M. K., Randall, A. K., & Bodenmann, G. (Eds.) (2016). *Couples coping with stress: A cross-cultural perspective.* New York, NY: Routledge.

Ferguson, M. (2012). You cannot leave it at the office: Spillover and crossover of coworker incivility: Spillover and crossover of incivility. *Journal of Organizational Behavior, 33*(4), 571–588. doi:10.1002/job.774

Fischer, M. S., Baucom, D. H., & Cohen, M. J. (2016). Cognitive-behavioral couple therapies: Review of the evidence for the treatment of relationship distress, psychopathology, and chronic health conditions. *Family Process, 55*(3), 423–442. doi:10.1111/famp.12227

Frost, D. M., & Meyer, I. H. (2009). Internalized homophobia and relationship quality among lesbians, gay men, and bisexuals. *Journal of Counseling Psychology, 56*(1), 97–109. doi:10.1037/a0012844

Gladding, S. T. (2014). *Family therapy: History, theory, and practice* (6th ed.). Upper Saddle River, NJ: Pearson, Merrill Prentice Hall.

Gruen, R. J., Folkman, S., & Lazarus, R. S. (1988). Centrality and individual differences in the meaning of daily hassles. *Journal of Personality,56*(4),743–762.doi:10.1111/j.1467-6494.1988. tb00475.x

Harway, M. (Ed.) (2005). *Handbook of couple therapy.* New York, NY: Wiley.

Herzberg, P. Y. (2013). Coping in relationships: The interplay between individual and dyadic coping and their effects on relationship satisfaction. *Anxiety, Stress, and Coping, 26*(2), 136–153.

Hilpert, P., Randall, A. K., Sorokowski, P., Atkins, D. C., Sorokowska, A., Ahmadi, K., … Yoo, G. (2016). The associations of dyadic coping and relationship satisfaction vary between and within nations: A 35-nation study. *Frontiers in Psychology, 7,* 1106. doi:10.3389/fpsyg.2016.01106

Jackson, G. L., Trail, T. E., Kennedy, D. P., Williamson, H. C., Bradbury, T. N., & Karney, B. R. (2016). The salience and severity of relationship problems among low-income couples. *Journal of Family Psychology, 30*(1), 2–11. doi:10.1037/fam0000158

Johnson, C., Randall, A. K., & Bodenmann, G. (2018). Couples coping enhancement training enrichment program. In J. Lebow, A. Chambers, & D. Breunlin (Eds.), *Encyclopedia of couple and family therapy.* Cham, Switzerland: Springer Publishing. doi:10.1007/978-3-3 19-15877-8_768-1

Karney, B. R., & Bradbury, T. N. (1995). The longitudinal course of marital quality and stability: A review of theory, methods, and research. *Psychological Bulletin, 118*(1), 3–34. doi:10.1037/0033-2909.118.1.3

Kayser, K., Watson, L. E., & Andrade, J. T. (2007). Cancer as a "we-disease": Examining the process of coping from a relational perspective. *Families, Systems & Health, 25*(4), 404–418. doi:10.1037/1091-7527.25.4.404

Kelley, H. H., & Thibaut, J. W. (1978). *Interpersonal relations: A theory of interdependence.* New York, NY: Wiley.

Kerr, J., Schafer, P., Perry, A., Orkin, J., Vance, M., & O'Campo, P. (2018). The impact of racial discrimination on African American fathers' intimate relationships. *Race and Social Problems*, 10, 1–11. doi:10.1007/s12552-018-9227-3

Lau, K., Tao, C., Randall, A. K., & Bodenmann, G. (2017). Coping oriented couples therapy. In J. Lebow, A. Chambers, & D. Breunlin (Eds.), *Encyclopedia of couple and family therapy* (pp. 1–6). Cham, Switzerland: Springer.

Lazarus, R. S., & Folkman, S. (1984). *Stress, appraisal, and coping.* New York, NY: Springer.

Lee, E., & Roberts, L. J. (2018). Between individual and family coping: A decade of theory and research on couples coping with health-related stress: Couples coping with health-related stress. *Journal of Family Theory & Review*, 10(1), 141–164. doi:10.1111/jftr.12252

Leuchtmann, L., Horn, A. B., Randall, A. K., Kuhn, R., & Bodenmann, G. (2018). A process-oriented analysis of the three-phase method: A therapeutic couple intervention strengthening dyadic coping. *Journal of Couple and Relationship Therapy*, 17(4), 251–275.

Lyons, R. F., Mickelson, K. D., Sullivan, M. J. L., & Coyne, J. C. (1998). Coping as a communal process. *Journal of Social and Personal Relationships*, 15(5), 579–605.

McEwen, B. S. (1998). Protective and damaging effects of stress mediators. *New England Journal of Medicine*, 338(3), 171–179. doi:10.1056/NEJM199801153380307

Meyer, I. H. (2003). Prejudice, social stress, and mental health in lesbian, gay, and bisexual populations: Conceptual issues and research evidence. *Psychological Bulletin*, 129(5), 674–697. doi:10.1037/0033-2909.129.5.674

Milbury, K., Badr, H., Fossella, F., Pisters, K. M., & Carmack, C. L. (2013). Longitudinal associations between caregiver burden and patient and spouse distress in couples coping with lung cancer. *Supportive Care in Cancer*, 21(9), 2371–2379. doi:10.1007/s00520-013-1795-6

Minuchin, S., & Nichols, M. P. (1998). Structural family therapy. In F. M. Dattilio (Ed.), *The Guilford family therapy series. Case studies in couple and family therapy: Systemic and cognitive perspectives* (pp. 108–131). New York, NY: Guilford Press.

Neff, L. A., & Karney, B. R. (2009). Stress and reactivity to daily relationship experiences: How stress hinders adaptive processes in marriage. *Journal of Personality and Social Psychology*, 97(3), 435–450. doi:10.1037/a0015663

Otis, M. D., Rostosky, S. S., Riggle, E. D. B., & Hamrin, R. (2006). Stress and relationship quality in same-sex couples. *Journal of Social and Personal Relationships*, 23(1), 81–99. doi:10.1177/0265407506060179

Papp, L. M., & Witt, N. L. (2010). Romantic partners' individual coping strategies and dyadic coping: Implications for relationship functioning. *Journal of Family Psychology*, 24(5), 551–559. doi:10.1037/a0020836

Pihet, S., Bodenmann, G., Cina, A., Widmer, K., & Shantinath, S. (2007). Can prevention of marital distress improve well-being? A 1 year longitudinal study. *Clinical Psychology & Psychotherapy*, 14(2), 79–88. doi:10.1002/cpp.522

Randall, A. K., & Bodenmann, G. (2009). The role of stress on close relationships and marital satisfaction. *Clinical Psychology Review*, 29(2), 105–115.

Randall, A. K., & Bodenmann, G. (2017). Stress and its associations with relationship satisfaction. *Current Opinion in Psychology*, 13, 96–106.

Randall, A. K., Bodenmann, G., Molgora, S., & Margola, D. (2010). The benefit of stress and coping research in couples for couple therapy. In F. Angeli (Ed.), *Close relationships and community psychology: An international psychological perspective* (pp. 169–186). Milan, Italy: Catholic University.

Randall, A. K., & Messerschmitt, S. (2020). Dyadic coping as relationship maintenance. In B. Ogolsky & J. K. Monk (Eds.), *Relationship maintenance: Theory, process, and context.*

Randall, A. K., Tao, C., Totenhagen, C. J., Walsh, K. J., & Cooper, A. (2017). Associations between sexual orientation discrimination and depression among same-sex couples:

Moderating effects of dyadic coping. *Journal of Couple and Relationship Therapy*, 16(4), 325–345.

Randall, A.K., Totenhagen, C.J., & Bodenmann, G. (2019). *Couples coping enhancement training—Sexual minority stress.* Manuscript in preparation.

Randall, A. K., Totenhagen, C. J., Walsh, K. J., Adams, C. B., & Tao, C. (2017). Coping with workplace minority stress: Associations between dyadic coping and anxiety among women in same-sex relationships. *Journal of Lesbian Studies*, 21(1), 70–87.

Revenson, T. A., Kayser, K., & Bodenmann, G. (Eds.) (2005). *Couples coping with stress: Emerging perspectives on dyadic coping.* Washington, DC: American Psychological Association.

Revenson, T. A., & Lepore, S. J. (2012). Coping in social context. In A. Baum, T. A. Revenson, & J. Singer (Eds.), *Handbook of health psychology* (2nd ed., pp. 193–217). New York, NY: Taylor & Francis Group.

Rostosky, S. S., & Riggle, E. D. (2017). Same-sex relationships and minority stress. *Current Opinion in Psychology*, 13, 29–38. doi:10.1016/j.copsyc.2016.04.011

Story, L. B., & Bradbury, T. N. (2004). Understanding marriage and stress: Essential questions and challenges. *Clinical Psychology Review*, 23(8), 1139–1162. doi:10.1016/j.cpr.2003.10.002

Totenhagen, C. J., Randall, A. K., Cooper, A. N., Tao, C., & Walsh, K. J. (2017). Stress spillover and crossover in same-sex couples: Concurrent and lagged daily effects. *Journal of GLBT Family Studies*, 13(3), 236–256. doi:10.1080/1550428X.2016.1203273

Totenhagen, C. J., Randall, A. K., & Lloyd, K. (2018). Stress and relationship functioning in same-sex couples: The vulnerability of internalized homophobia. *Family Relations*, 67, 399–413.

Vilchinsky, N. (2019). Stress and crisis management. In C. Llewellyn, S. Ayers, C. McManus, S. Newman, K. Petrie, T. Revenson, et al. (Eds.), *Cambridge handbook of psychology, health and medicine*, Cambridge Handbooks in Psychology (pp. 309–313). Cambridge, UK: Cambridge University Press.

Zemp, M., Bodenmann, G., Backes, S., Sutter-Stickel, D., & Revenson, T. A. (2016). The importance of parents' dyadic coping for children: The importance of parents' dyadic coping. *Family Relations*, 65(2), 275–286. doi:10.1111/fare.12189

Zemp, M., Merz, C. A., Nussbeck, F. W., Halford, W. K., Schaer Gmelch, M., & Bodenmann, G. (2017). Couple relationship education: A randomized controlled trial of professional contact and self-directed tools. *Journal of Family Psychology*, 31(3), 347–357. doi:10.1037/fam0000257

Part IV
Special Issues

12

Therapy with Individuals and Couples Deciding to Continue or End Their Relationship

Steven M. Harris and Eugene L. Hall

Systemic family therapists face a number of challenges when working with couples that are uncertain about their commitment to their relationship. Without appropriate assessment procedures in place, systemic family therapists risk overlooking the presence of "commitment uncertainty" (Owen, Rhoades, et al., 2014) in one or both partners. Consider a couple seeking therapy to work through the residual effects of one partner's extramarital affair. The clinician might begin by gathering a significant amount of information about families of origin, significant events in the relationship, and details regarding the affair itself. However, one or both partners could be seriously considering leaving the relationship but may not disclose these thoughts and feelings in therapy, especially if the couple presents together in a first meeting. Oftentimes, marital doubts, divorce ambivalence, or commitment uncertainty within a marriage is never vocalized (Vaughan, 1986). Many therapists mistakenly assume that the couple's presence in therapy indicates a commitment to the relationship: "If you're here, you are committed to the relationship and to therapy."

Research suggests that approximately 30% of all couples presenting for couple therapy may include one or both partners uncertain about their level of commitment to the marriage (Doherty, Harris, & Wilde, 2016). The underlying phenomenon at play with these couples has been described by some as commitment uncertainty (Owen, Rhoades, et al., 2014; Stanley, Rhoades, & Whitton, 2010), while Doherty and colleagues refer to these couples as "mixed-agenda" couples (with one partner leaning in to the marriage/relationship and the other leaning out of it). Trying to engage these couples in traditional couple therapy becomes very difficult when the goal is to help facilitate emotional connection or bonding. One member of the couple is typically ready and willing to implement suggestions for change, but the other is less interested. One does the homework, while the other offers reasons for why the homework could not be completed. This can be frustrating to the couple (certainly disheartening to the partner who wants to see the relationship stay intact) as well as the therapist. This chapter details the unique needs of these mixed-agenda couples, what occupies

The Handbook of Systemic Family Therapy: Volume 3, First Edition.
Edited by Karen S. Wampler and Adrian J. Blow.
© 2020 John Wiley & Sons Ltd. Published 2020 by John Wiley & Sons Ltd.

their minds, and options for engaging them in meaningful and effective ways. While the focus of this chapter will primarily be on mixed-agenda couples, the ideas we present can also be applied in individual therapy to clients who present with divorce ideation. However, we caution that when a therapist meets with individuals in this state, there is a strong propensity to neglect the non-represented partner's perspective surrounding the relationship difficulties and divorce narratives. This can have devastating detrimental effects if the individual that presents for therapy "sells" a divorce narrative without also taking responsibility for his/her contributions to the couple's problems. As systemic family therapists, this cannot be how we engage this population. We must be committed to a systemic way of viewing relational health and divorce ideation.

Two predominant theories associated with commitment uncertainty in couples are presented to outline the major conceptual frameworks grounding our knowledge of this population. Social exchange theory (Emerson, 1976) has been one foundational theory applied to this population. The assumptions and concepts associated with social exchange theory provide an exchange-based understanding of couple relationships and divorce or reconciliation decision making. Attachment theory (Ainsworth & Bowlby, 1991), alternatively, brings a more humanistic perspective of couple relationships. Both provide a nuanced understanding of how systemic researchers and therapists often situate these couples. Current empirical evidence on mixed-agenda couples is summarized, followed by an outline of best practices with intervention and prevention efforts. The chapter concludes with policy suggestions, changes and future directions. The overarching goal of this chapter is to provide systems-oriented therapists knowledge of the underlying dynamics and processes at play in order for them to implement effective clinical practices with couples who are uncertain about the future of their relationship.

Predominant Frameworks and Theoretical Concepts

Social exchange theory

Social exchange theory became one of the first to encompass the complexities of couples who are deciding whether or not to stay together. Derived from the field of behavioral psychology, social psychology, and economics, exchange theory situates the makeup of a couple as two independent entities engaged in an exchange relationship with both seeking to maximize rewards and minimize costs (Sabatelli & Shehan, 2009). The founders of this theory posit that humans are rational beings who understand the importance of interdependence in exchange relationships but are consistently weighing potential alternatives (Blau, 1964). Homeostasis is maintained through expectations derived from previous experiences in relationships and equity as the ratio of cost/reward to expectation (Walster, Walster, & Berscheid, 1978).

Exchange theory allowed early research on couple relationships to examine the dynamic needs and wants of individuals in a relationship, as opposed to viewing behavior as a human's primal needs to procreate or increase the survival rate of their offspring with evolutionary theory (Sabatelli & Shehan, 2009). Social exchange theory encompasses the intangible variables associated with couples deciding whether to stay together for both costs (e.g., conflict, unhappiness) and rewards (e.g., connection, satisfaction) (Blau, 1964; Thibaut & Kelley, 1959). Subsequent research on exchange theory in systemic practice refined the concepts to situate decision making in terms of attractions and barriers to leaving the relationship, as well as alternatives to the relationship (Kurdek, 2000).

A critique of applying social exchange theory to couples who are deciding whether or not to stay together is the emphasis on a basic cost/reward model, which inhibits further integration of more human characteristics (e.g., love, responsibility, commitment) (Donovan & Jackson, 1990). The incorporation of attraction, barriers, and alternatives allows for more human characteristics, providing a systemic look at couple interaction over time (Albrecht & Kuna, 1980). Attraction to the relationship expanded a singular view of rewards (e.g., attraction to partner) to rewards that vary in quality over time (e.g., relationship satisfaction) and those that involve others outside the couple relationship (e.g., well-being of children). Barriers to leaving the relationship expanded the linear view of costs (e.g., conflict) to include structural barriers (e.g., legal contracts) and relational barriers (e.g., care/concern for partner). The concept of greater alternatives contextualizes rewards/attractions and costs/barriers by establishing their basis of comparison (e.g., cultural norms, previous relationship experiences) (Blau, 1964; Levinger, 1979; Thibaut & Kelley, 1959).

Applying social exchange theory to understand couples deciding whether to stay together or separate has both strengths and limitations. The framework provides researchers and clinicians a base from which to assess what is valued and a common method of identifying imbalance in relationships (Sabatelli, Lee, & Ripoll-Núñez, 2018). Several applications of exchange theory to the divorce decision-making process identify love and intimacy as rewards or barriers (e.g., leaving the relationship would leave a person without emotional closeness) (Donovan & Jackson, 1990); however their placement in a basic exchange relationship contradicts the basis of many predominant systemic models for working with couples. In addition, the theory lacks effective incorporation of concepts such as sacrifice and altruism.

Attachment theory

The attachment theory framework informs systemic research and grounds several clinical models for working with couples (Bassard & Johnson, 2016). As developed by John Bowlby and Mary Ainsworth, attachment theory was initially developed to understand the bonding process and importance of affection in mother–child relationships (Bowlby, Ainsworth, & Bretherton, 1992). The results of the early attachment studies led to hypothesizing about the development of internal working models (i.e., ways humans identify how to act and behave in emotionally close/love relationships), which have since been expanded upon in psychological, social scientific, and neuroscientific studies (Bretherton & Munholland, 2008). Mary Ainsworth and Sylvia Bell grounded their strange situation test in this developing theory (Ainsworth & Bell, 1970; Bowlby et al., 1992). The test initially identified three different types of attachment styles: secure, insecure avoidant, and ambivalent/resistant (Ainsworth, Blehar, Waters, & Wall, 1978). Subsequent research identified a fourth attachment style, disorganized/disoriented (Main & Solomon, 1990). All are identified in the test by assessing the onset and duration of separation stress and the ability to regulate emotionally once reunited with an attachment figure (Ainsworth & Bell, 1970).

Researchers have adapted the theory, and subsequent styles of attachment, to construct a framework for understanding adult romantic relationships (Bartholomew & Horowitz, 1991; Hazan & Shaver, 1987; Kitson, 1982). The initial model of adult attachment indicated that the same theoretical concepts important for secure attachment in the infant–caregiver relationship were the same for adult–adult relationships: needing a safe haven, having a secure base, and maintaining proximity with an attachment figure (e.g., intimate partner) (Hazan & Shaver, 1987, 1994). This research posited three adult attachment styles that paralleled the initial three styles of infant attachment. Bartholomew and Horowitz (1991) proposed a four-type model based on their research that incorporated working models into adult attachment style: secure, preoccupied, fearful, and dismissing. Adults are placed into one of four categories based on their levels of dominance and warmth in their romantic relationships.

Attachment theory was applied to relationship stress and divorce shortly after Bowlby and Ainsworth evidenced their theory (Kitson, 1982; Simpson & Rholes, 1994). However, little research has since used attachment theory to better understand divorce and separation (Slade, 2008), including the decision-making process for commitment uncertain couples. Early research investigated connections between attachment styles and salient aspects of partner relationships (e.g., love, commitment, trust). Kitson (1982) found evidence to support lasting feelings of attachment to a former spouse even after they separated. Simpson (1990) identified a correlation between insecure attachment styles and less positive and more negative emotions in romantic relationships for both continuously married and separated couples. Davila and Bradbury (2001) found an association between attachment insecurity in the early stages of marital relationships with both relationship dissatisfaction and divorce. These findings pointed to the presence of an attachment style prior to engaging in a committed relationship. However, inconsistent and noncausal findings indicate the need for a better understanding of couple relationships.

The progression of attachment-based research has prompted researchers to expand the theory to incorporate the dynamic nature and different types of relationships. Diamond, Brimhall, and Elliott (2018) found that attachment style did not vary across relationship type (e.g., continuously married, remarried). Alexandrov, Cowan, and Cowan (2005) developed the Couple Attachment Interview and utilized continuous measures (scores from coding of interview videos of attachment styles vs. categorical types based on self-report measures). In their first study using the Couple Attachment Interview, the researchers found evidence that "continuous codes explained variance in marital quality, over and above categorical codes" (Alexandrov et al., 2005, p. 143). These results indicate the need for advanced measures of and methods for obtaining adult attachment styles in romantic relationships. Kurdek (2002) found validity and reliability issues with the Adult Attachment Inventory and Relationship Scales Questionnaire as comprehensive measures of attachment in adult romantic relationships across heterosexual, gay, and lesbian couples. This author discussed the importance of utilizing closeness and commitment as two distinct relationship outcomes and recommends that attachment styles as variables in research on romantic relationships be understood in the context of how individuals construct internal working models of relationships (Kurdek, 2002).

Building on attachment styles, research has identified several important attachment-based processes and concepts that provide important information on couple relationships. The internal working model allows researchers and systemic therapists to understand how individuals manage their own distress, as well as their partners, by integrating both individual characteristics and past relationship experiences into their working model (Bowlby, 1973; Seedall & Wampler, 2013). One's internal working model of self and one for others informs the behaviors in close relationships that individuals use to connect and/or cue their partner they are distressed, as well as how an individual responds to others' needs (Johnson, 2004).

Emotion is also a central concept of attachment research and interventions (Bassard & Johnson, 2016). In their study of attachment avoidance and emotional congruence, Seedall and Wampler (2012) found that participants with high attachment avoidance reported positive feelings during a discussion with their partner regarding an issue in their relationship. However, these participants showed higher levels of psychophysiological arousal via a measure of their skin conductance levels. This discrepancy indicates the potential that individuals with high attachment avoidance might have "an unwillingness to address the more difficult issues that inevitably arise in relationships, thereby putting long-term relationship satisfaction at risk" (Seedall & Wampler, 2012, p. 956). In a subsequent study, Seedall and Wampler (2016) found that those with high attachment anxiety reported more positive feelings toward their partner during high structured interactions but not low structured interactions. The authors indicate the importance of integrating this finding into clinical work with couples through increased facilitation of couple interactions for those who report higher levels of attachment anxiety.

Of particular importance to couples deciding whether or not to stay together in attachment-based research is the evidence that closeness and commitment are unique aspects of relationships. The complex nature of committed relationships requires a micro examination of their processes. Although singular attachment style categories bring challenges to the research on, and theoretical understanding of, this population, attachment theory brought a needed humanistic perspective of adult romantic relationships (beyond a costs and rewards comparison). The progression of this theory and its application allow for a better foundation of understanding and working with couples uncertain about their commitment.

Dialectic tensions in the divorce or reconciliation decision-making process

At the time this chapter was written, the authors know of only one comprehensive theoretical model of the divorce/reconciliation decision-making process. Allen and Hawkins (2017) propose a preliminary model for organizing the complex intra- and interpersonal factors that influence couples as they determine the future of their relationship. In their article, "Theorizing the Decision-Making Process for Divorce or Reconciliation," the authors first review the extant literature on decision making specific to divorce or reconciliation. Their comprehensive review addresses the important distinctions between rational and interpretive grounding of the frameworks used in these articles. The authors integrate their critique of interpretive frameworks with their proposed model, based on a rational paradigm. Their model is supported by qualitative data from the National Divorce Decision-Making Project (Hawkins et al., 2015). The results of their analysis "suggest that the experience of divorce or reconciliation decision making emerges from a dialectical interaction among a number of polarities that are in parallel and simultaneous process with each other" (Allen & Hawkins, 2017, p. 62).

The conceptual model of divorce or reconciliation decision making explores these dialectical tensions within four primary domains: time, space, logic, and dialogue (Allen & Hawkins, 2017). These "four key interdependent strands of meaning that animate the process" (Allen & Hawkins, 2017, p. 62) provide the configuration needed to organize the complex individual tensions within each and allow for a more nuanced understanding of all the various factors at play (Corbin & Strauss, 2008). These dialectical tensions are summarized in this section to illustrate the range of considerations for couples in the divorce or reconciliation decision-making process, as well as the diverse factors influencing these processes.

The dimension of time in the (dialectical tensions) model represents the present moment that a person exists in, while reflecting on their past and thinking about their future (Allen & Hawkins, 2017). Within this strand exist the tensions between past and future, pivotal and prosaic, absolute and relative, and stability and change. Someone thinking about divorce may weigh past experiences in their relationship with potential future relationships. They may also experience tension between stability and change (e.g., stability of partner, positive or negative change) that can reinforce uncertainty and contribute to more frequent and serious divorce ideation. The divorce ideation processes "are likely nonlinear processes that double back, returning to earlier stages, or go over the same ground multiple times in a non-recursive pattern" (Allen & Hawkins, 2017, p. 63).

Understanding couples in the context of space is another important aspect of theorizing about the divorce decision-making process (Allen & Hawkins, 2017). The authors propose some of the tensions existing in space: public vs. private, personal vs. social, literal vs. figurative, and here vs. there. Highly distressed couples may avoid shared spaces at home or feel challenged by being together in public. A couple may evaluate the state of their relationship, itself, as a space in which they exist. Tensions in these spaces may also lead to ideation about divorce and also may fluctuate over time (Allen & Hawkins, 2017; Hawkins et al., 2017). A couple interacting in social situations as if no problems exist, but continuing to think about divorce with no effort to resolve their problems would be an example of the public vs. private tension.

Allen and Hawkins also include logic and dialogue as two strands in which these dialectical tensions exist (Allen & Hawkins, 2017). Someone contemplating divorce may vacillate between thoughts of separating based on logic vs. those in emotion, and these can range in severity (i.e., soft vs. serious). The logical vs. emotional thoughts can be understood in terms of the two primary theories discussed, social exchange and attachment. Logical thoughts can be the weighing of costs and rewards (e.g., weighing alternatives with barriers to leaving the relationship), while emotional thoughts are when an individual contemplates loss and sadness in the potential absence of their spouse. This is also an example of dialogue, another strand that runs through the dialectical tensions at play in the decision-making process (Allen & Hawkins, 2017). The back and forth within an individual is the internal dialogue. Partners often begin thinking about divorce internally and do not engage others (Allen & Hawkins, 2017; Vaughan, 1986). The model presents several dialectical tensions within the dialogue strand: self vs. others, internal vs. external, proximal vs. distal, and public vs. private.

Allen and Hawkins describe the movement throughout these strands and multiple dialectical tensions as a "balancing act" where they must stabilize "contradictory dimensions as they constantly shift and interact" (Allen & Hawkins, 2017, p. 64). The authors posit growth, entropy, or further ambivalence as potential outcomes of managing the multiple tensions at play in the divorce or reconciliation decision-making processes. Individuals facing mounting pressure when deciding whether or not to stay with their partner may end up growing closer to their partner. However, the tensions might also lead to a further lack of clarity and certainty around their decision (Allen & Hawkins, 2017). The authors acknowledge the need for further theory development in this area by integrating both rational and interpretive aspects into future frameworks, particularly for complex microlevel processes of commitment uncertain or mixed-agenda couples.

Theory in Research and Practice

Relationship ambivalence and commitment uncertainty

Relationship ambivalence and commitment uncertainty are important concepts throughout the body of literature on couples deciding whether or not to stay together. Both can occur prior to a relationship (e.g., dating), during a committed relationship (e.g., marriage), and throughout the process of dissolving a relationship (e.g., divorce) (Doherty, Harris, & Wickel Didericksen, 2016; Knobloch, 2008; Quirk et al., 2016). Often used interchangeably, both concepts represent the mixed and/or contradicting thoughts and feelings of an individual toward their intimate partner relationship (Owen, Rhoades, et al., 2014; Pepper, 1993). However, ambivalence and uncertainty are distinct concepts (Baek, 2010; Owen, Rhoades, et al., 2014). Each independently contributes to our understanding of how best to help commitment uncertain or mixed-agenda couples (Doherty et al., 2016; Owen, Keller, et al., 2014). The complexity of these concepts and the multifaceted ways ambivalence shows up in couple relationships create challenges for therapists seeking to understand the thoughts and feelings of their clients in times of extreme stress (e.g., high potential for divorce or separation). Several independent models of relationship ambivalence and commitment uncertainty exist in the extant literature; however, this section aims to provide a clear depiction of ambivalence and uncertainty as distinct concepts salient to couples who are deciding whether or not to separate or divorce.

Ambivalence can be broadly understood as conflicting or contradictory thoughts and/or feelings a person has toward someone or something (Priester & Petty, 2001). In the context of couple relationships, ambivalence is operationalized as the simultaneous feelings of wanting to stay in the relationship and wanting to leave (Baek, 2010; Pepper, 1993). This paradoxical state can begin to inform the actions of an individual toward their partner (Knobloch, 2008; Weingardt, 2000). These actions might be confusing and bring tension or conflict into the relationship (Pepper, 1993), resulting in lowered relationship quality and commitment to the relationship for both partners (Knobloch, 2008). Relationship ambivalence should also be distinguished from dilemmas that individuals face in couple relationships (Pepper, 1993). Dilemma denotes a more acute need for decision and forces one to evaluate the consequences of leaving vs. staying. For example, a victim of intimate partner violence (IPV) may be forced to compare the potential for further abuse with the perceived costs of a divorce (e.g., further victimization).

Commitment uncertainty can be applied to several aspects of long-term relationships (e.g., investment, willingness to sacrifice) (Owen, Rhoades, et al., 2014). While ambivalence is a state of mixed thoughts and/or feelings, uncertainty is characterized by a lack of information or knowledge (Baek, 2010; Downs, 1957). Commitment uncertainty is also characterized by doubt or lack of confidence in decision making (Owen, Rhoades, et al., 2014). An uncertain partner lacks the information and/or confidence needed to know whether they want to remain committed to their partner. The intensity of commitment uncertainty may also fluctuate, which poses further challenges to clinicians as commitment shifts between sessions may impact therapeutic outcomes (Owen, Keller, et al., 2014). Important to note is that ambiguity might be easily conflated with uncertainty (Owen, Rhoades, et al., 2014); however ambiguity refers to something that is open to more than one interpretation and not necessarily a lack of confidence (Frisch & Baron, 1988).

Integrating an understanding of relationship ambivalence and commitment uncertainty as distinct concepts outside of broader foundational theories is important in conceptualizing a mixed-agenda couple. One partner might weigh certain characteristics of their "ideal" partner (e.g., attractiveness, financial security) over the course of their relationship. In isolation, the use of social exchange theory can provide a grounding for understanding attractive alternatives and personal or structural barriers to leaving. This framework, however, excludes the integration of dynamic feelings and thoughts of ambivalence and uncertainty. Attachment theory also provides a potential map of the needs and wants for one partner contemplating leaving their relationship. Uncertainty has been associated with an avoidant attachment style and ambivalence with an anxious style (Stanley et al., 2010). However, attachment theory posits a singular assessment of needs and wants in one person (Bartholomew & Horowitz, 1991), which is seemingly antithetical to the variable qualities of relationship ambivalence and commitment uncertainty. Although these concepts alone do not constitute a full working framework, the findings across these bodies of literature allude to the need for expansion in our theoretical understanding of and approach to working with couples deciding whether or not to separate.

Divorce ideation

Similar to commitment uncertainty, divorce ideation is a collection of thoughts and feelings associated with a lack of clarity regarding the future of the couple relationship. Divorce ideation, however, refers specifically to times when one partner thinks about divorce as an alternative to remaining in their marriage (Hawkins, Allen, Roberts, Harris, & Allen, 2018). One partner experiencing ambivalence, uncertainty, dilemmas, or any adverse experience for a couple could prompt this type of ideation. For example, having close friends or family members go through a divorce could prompt someone to assess the state of their own marriage. Like ambivalence and uncertainty, divorce ideation is a dynamic process that encompasses a range of complex thoughts and feelings (Hawkins et al., 2018). The ideation process can be influenced by the same factors that impact marital stability (e.g., specific adverse events, long-term problems). However, thinking about divorce has been associated with factors such as length of relationship, religiosity, and age (Booth & White, 1980). These associations are independent of marital satisfaction, indicating an autonomous nature of divorce ideation.

One influence to consider is the culture in which divorce ideation exists. Particularly for countries with high divorce rates (e.g., United States, Russia), thinking about divorce may come to some individuals more easily and/or more frequently because divorce is more common. An experimental study in the United States showed that participants' openness toward reasons for divorce decreased only after each were given educational materials that discussed the seriousness of wedding vows and current divorce rates, but not when solely given information on wedding vows (Stalder, 2012). Further, openness to divorce was negatively associated with how serious one is about wedding vows. These findings point to the importance of incorporating an understanding of social influence on attitudes and feelings toward divorce when working with couples deciding whether or not to separate.

Recent studies have distinguished between different types of ideation (Hawkins et al., 2017, 2018). Those who were thinking about divorce were differentiated by the "type" of thinker they were. The types took three primary forms: soft, serious, and conflicted (Hawkins et al., 2017). The serious thinkers were characterized by frequent thoughts of divorce, "high levels of connection problems (e.g., growing apart) in their marriages and modest levels of instrumental problems (e.g., division of domestic labor)" (Hawkins et al., 2018, p. 2). This group also reported low levels of more serious problems like infidelity and domestic violence but reported the lowest levels of hope for their relationship. The soft thinkers thought about divorce only a few times in the past 6 months, reported a significant amount of problems in their relationship, and generally wanted to work on their marriages (Hawkins et al., 2017). The soft thinkers, however, felt they had clarity in the process, while the serious thinkers reported feeling unclear in their decision-making process (Hawkins et al., 2018). The third group, conflicted thinkers, reported the highest levels of marital problems in terms of frequency and severity. This group contained the most reports of being done with the relationship but the highest on hope comparatively. The variations in how often and how serious people think about divorce point to the need for systemic therapists to normalize divorce ideation for clients (Hawkins et al., 2017).

Reasons for divorcing

Committed couples are impacted by a range of adverse experiences over the course of their relationship that potentially affect their overall relationship quality and/or the likelihood of separating (Karney & Bradbury, 1995; Rauer, Karney, Garvan, & Hou, 2008). Situating the known predictors of relationship dissatisfaction and instability with the reasons couples give for ending a committed relationship provides a nuanced look at how these variables influence the divorce decision-making process. For working with couples thinking about separating, regardless of the clinician's theoretical orientation or modality, identifying and working with the specific problems may be further polarizing to the partners rather than bringing them closer together. The initial goals for clinicians, then, should include assessing for safety, level of commitment, and clarity in the decision-making process for both partners.

The primary finding of importance to this chapter is the incongruence between reported reasons for divorce and research findings on problems that impact relationship stability. Hawkins, Willoughby, and Doherty (2012) found that "growing apart" and "not being able to talk together" were the most common responses couples gave for the reason behind their split. Financial issues and infidelity were the third and fourth most common, respectively. In a comparison study with older vs. younger recently divorced individuals, "grew apart/incompatible" was the most common response for the older group and "personality differences" for the younger group (Moore, 1992). A study of 56 couples who divorced in Israel found that the most common reasons for separating were those inherent to the relationship (e.g., diminishing love, differences in religious beliefs) (Cohen & Finzi-Dottan, 2012). Alternatively, a study by the National Fatherhood Initiative found that "lack of commitment" was most common, followed by "too much conflict and arguing" (Glenn, 2005).

Much of the research on predictors of relationship satisfaction and instability has focused on factors that do not top the list of reasons for separation such as mental health (Idstad et al., 2015), sexual satisfaction (Fisher & McNulty, 2008), the transition to parenthood (Doss, Rhoades, Stanley, & Markman, 2009), substance abuse (Fals-Stewart, Birchler, & O'Farrell, 1999), and social support (Frazier, Tix, & Barnett, 2003). The discrepancy between the broad range of reported reasons for divorce and the research on couple relationships leaves room for a better understanding of what prompts and reinforces divorce ideation specifically. Our understanding of this research highlights the importance of systemic therapists' role in the prevention of unnecessary divorce by seeking to fully understand the nuanced reasons that prompt divorce ideation and how this might diverge from the narrative our clients create during the divorce decision-making process. However, the therapist must balance advancing the welfare of the couple with each partner's autonomy in decision making (American Association for Marriage and Family Therapy [AAMFT], 2015). Thus, a reasonable primary goal for working with this population is to facilitate conversations that could help each partner achieve greater clarity and confidence in their divorce/reconciliation decision making (Harris, Crabtree, Bell, Allen, & Roberts, 2017). In other words, the potential for reconciliation should be maintained by the therapist while simultaneously supporting each partner's decision-making process.

Treatment

Several clinical models are predominant across the field of systemic family therapy, such as emotionally focused therapy (EFT) and the Gottman Method of Relationship Therapy. However, these modalities do not necessarily address the needs of mixed-agenda couples. When used with a mixed-agenda couple before helping them gain clarity and confidence in their decision making, these treatments can then polarize couples or even push one or both partners to end the relationship. When treatment occurs in the absence of commitment uncertainty, these models are shown to be effective and potentially serve as a preventative measure for couples who might otherwise reach the point of separation.

Emotionally focused therapy

EFT is a highly researched and effective couple therapy modality (Wiebe & Johnson, 2016). The EFT model is primarily rooted in attachment theory and places an emphasis on decreasing isolation and increasing love in a couple's relationship (Johnson, 2004). EFT's core assumption is that the accessibility and responsiveness of each partner are the building blocks of a secure adult attachment bond (Johnson, 2004). The primary goals of EFT are to tap into key emotional responses and experience them in therapy, facilitate change in how partners respond to one another, and help the couple feel more secure and connected in their relationship (Johnson & Bradley, 2007).

EFT requires each partner to be committed to the relationship, which would exclude a mixed-agenda couple from treatment. The first step in EFT works to fully understand conflict in a relationship and how this relates to core attachment issues (Johnson & Bradley, 2007; Johnson, Hunsley, Greenberg, & Schindler, 1999). The focus on connecting a couple's primary problems with the attachment needs of each partner is a strength of EFT; however the model's initial focus on problems may not be effective with commitment uncertain couples. Improper assessment of commitment could lead to further polarization or prompting a rash decision to separate. The primary needs of a mixed-agenda couple are clarity and confidence in the treatment goal and in their hoped-for goals for the relationship (Harris et al., 2017), which should occur before moving in too deeply to emotional or experiential couple therapy.

The Gottman Method of Relationship Therapy

The effectiveness of the Gottman Method of Relationship Therapy and its underlying assumptions are also highly evidenced in the literature on distressed couples (Garanzini et al., 2017; Gottman, Ryan, Swanson, & Swanson, 2005; Levenson & Gottman, 1983). The Gottman Method focuses on how partners treat one another (e.g., respect, empathy, affection, and positivity) and how they manage conflict (e.g., maintaining a $5:1$ ratio of positive to negative comments during an argument) (Gottman, Gottman, & DeClaire, 2006). The research of John and Julie Gottman and their colleagues spans decades and utilizes observational and physiological methods to understand the interactional patterns that predict divorce and those that encourage healthy, long-term marriages and relationships (Gottman et al., 1998, 2003; Levenson & Gottman, 1983).

The application of Gottman's research has been effectively translated to both couple therapy and relationship education programs (Babcock, Gottman, Ryan, & Gottman, 2013; Bradley, Drummey, Gottman, & Gottman, 2014; Gottman & Gottman, 2015). Each approach serves as an important intervention for couples in distress and a potential prevention effort to reduce the number of couples who reach the point of deciding whether or not to stay together. Gottman's research found that over 90% of couples would divorce when at least one partner was stonewalling (Gottman, 1994). Although his research is not intended to assess when intervention is no longer possible, the deterministic nature seems to miss opportunities to work with couples who may be stonewalling and on the brink of divorce. Like EFT, Gottman Method is a recommended therapy modality for couples who have decided to work on their relationship.

Discernment counseling

Doherty and Harris (2017) developed the discernment counseling model and protocol for working with commitment uncertainty or what they call "mixed-agenda" couples. The goal of discernment counseling is to help couples gain greater clarity and confidence in their decision making about the future of their marriage/relationship when one or both are thinking about leaving the marriage. This clarity and confidence is based on a deeper understanding of how the option of divorce became a possibility for one or both members of the couple and each person's contribution to the problems in the marriage. By outlining three potential paths that are in front of a couple at this stage (1: Status quo, 2: Separation/Divorce, 3: Reconciliation or rehabilitation of an unhealthy marriage, which includes 6 months of a concerted effort to get the relationship back to a healthy place with divorce off the table), the discernment counselor engages the couple in conversations about what each path requires on the parts of each person in the couple. So, to maintain the status quo in the relationship, what must each person agree to be doing? To successfully negotiate the divorce path, how must each person in the marriage be acting toward one another? And what are the changes and transitions that the couple should prepare for with each other (finances, visitation, co-parenting) and their children (transitions in children's lives introduced by the parents' divorce)? Finally, should the couple choose to reconcile or rehabilitate their relationship, what changes would each individual have to make in the way they relate to one another?

The discernment counselor first helps map out the couple's process and pattern of dysfunctional interactions (pursue/distance, attack/withdraw, withdraw/withdraw, etc.). Then, each person comes to an understanding of their unique and personal role in the couple process while developing a personal agenda for change (PAC), three or four things each person would work on during the 6-month period of reconciliation. At the end of 6 months of couple therapy (if both partners choose path 3), the couple can revisit the conversation about divorcing if they have not experienced an increase in the level of health in the relationship.

Discernment counseling can best be understood as work that happens before engaging in a couple therapy experience. Further, this modality helps to set the agenda for change in couple therapy. Discernment counseling is delivered through a series of sessions with both individual and conjoint conversations with the counselor. The model is heavily focused on engaging the individual specifically around their contribution to the couple pattern. Neither person is allowed to maintain a focus on the psychological deficits of their partner. Many clients come to discernment counseling having "figured out" their partner's contributions to the demise of the marriage (my husband is a narcissist), but are less able to see their own contributions. Further, clients offering psychological assessments of their partner such as this struggle to take responsibility for their role in dysfunctional relationship patterns. Therefore, each person is encouraged to resist the urge to discuss their partner's contribution to the problem. Instead, each individual begins to see how their own behaviors have contributed to the relational "dance," and this is much more likely to help them see how changing their own behavior may result in a change in the marriage. Individuals share with their partner, at the end of each session, what they are learning about their own contributions to the decline in the health of the relationship. Another possible outcome includes realizing that neither divorce nor couple therapy is right at the time (path 1). These couples typically understand that no movement (at least for right now) is best for their situation. These couples are encouraged to put a time limit on their "status quo" agreement and follow up with a discernment counselor at a later time. For those who realize that the best decision is to terminate the relationship (divorce) or to temporarily separate (path 2), they are offered local resources for proceeding down that path in the healthiest and most civil way, so as to reduce the conflict and subsequent trauma that can sometimes attend the divorce process. For more on discernment counseling, see *Helping couples on the brink of divorce: Discernment counseling for troubled relationships* (Doherty & Harris, 2017).

Ethical Issues and Important Considerations

The developers of the most recent version of the AAMFT Code of Ethics (2015) outline six aspirational goals for the field. One of these is that MFTs aspire to embrace "innovation and the advancement of knowledge of systemic and relational therapies" (AAMFT, 2015). Finding ways to treat couples in the throes of deciding to end or work to improve their relationship is indeed an innovative cutting edge with most of the attention being generated in the last couple of years (Doherty & Harris, 2017). Furthermore, our duty to our clients' mandates that we strive to "advance the welfare of families and individuals and make reasonable efforts to find the appropriate balance between conflicting goals within the family system" (AAMFT, 2015). Nowhere else in the world of couple therapy are the goals of individual clients competing quite like they are in situations where mixed-agenda couples present for treatment with one partner leaning into the relationship and the other leaning out. Some of the more obvious and salient ethical challenges when working with this population are outlined below. We realize that not all systemic family therapists adhere to, or are beholding to, the AAMFT-generated Code of Ethics. So, this section will focus on ethical issues generally as it is our belief that ethical and responsible family therapy practices should resemble one another regardless of how association or governmental prescriptions suggests they practice.

Ethical issues

Respecting client autonomy   First and foremost, we believe that systemic family therapists must respect the autonomy and agency of clients to make their own decisions regarding their intimate relationships. As we have presented material on divorce decision making over the last several years, it is not uncommon for an audience member to ask, "What if the couple should never have married in the first place?" Or similarly, "What if you don't believe the couple should be married?" Or the more extreme, "How can I tell them that I don't think they should be married?" To each of these we emphatically respond that is it *not* our job to tell or recommend to adults the decisions they should make regarding the status of their intimate relationships. In working with couples on the brink of divorce, there will always be a temptation to weigh in on what seems to be the easiest, immediate decision. We have heard story after story of clients who, after just a few sessions, were told to divorce because their situation/marriage was "hopeless." These marital death sentences have typically come at the end of a couple therapy experience where the therapist has expressed that he/she is out of suggestions for strengthening or improving the marriage. The therapist typically makes this declaration after exhausting his/her favorite interventions. This, throw-my-hands-up-in-defeat attitude may be soothing for the therapist, but it is extremely disconcerting to at least one of the members of the couple (and sometimes both). Respecting client autonomy in these situations requires a therapist to sit with ambiguity and the unknown. All too often therapists are tempted to embrace a goal of immediate personal happiness at the expense of understanding and challenging couple dynamics where both parties have contributed to a decrease in marital health (Doherty, 2002). Indeed, supporting a "personal happiness" agenda in the short term can be one cause of a couple therapist giving up on a couple's interest in receiving help through couple therapy.

Negotiating confidentiality Systemic family therapists can also experience challenges in maintaining client confidentiality because our clients are often more than just one person. When individuals in a couple are making a divorce decision, they struggle to arrive at a decision with clarity and confidence (Harris et al., 2017). When practicing discernment counseling, the clinician is potentially being asked to be the holder of two different agendas. You are saying to one person, "I support you in your desires to work on the relationship and will guide and counsel you to that end." And to the other you are saying, "I understand your interest in leaving the marriage, I want to help you make the best decision possible." This process can result in multiple shifts and changes in how the couple is thinking about their commitment to the marriage. One week they (or one of the members of the couple) may be convinced that divorce is the answer, while the next week they may be more willing to try some reconciliation efforts. Because of this, it behooves the couple's therapist to sit with the shifting narratives and let each individual deliver their own difficult or even longed-for news. Furthermore, it is not uncommon for couple therapists to have individual phone calls, sessions, or even portions of sessions with couples on the brink of divorce.

Another common experience for couple therapists is to receive information that one of the partners would like to keep confidential. The literature on secret keeping in couple therapy is broad, is varied, and has developed over the years (Fall & Lyons, 2003; Imber-Black, 1993; North, Shadid, & Hertlein, 2018). Some have advocated not keeping secrets (Butler, Harper, & Seedall, 2009), while others have expressed the need for criteria to be met before facilitating disclosure (Fall & Lyons, 2003; North et al., 2018). As far as we know, all governmental laws and association codes of ethics that apply to the practice of any mental health discipline require that the practitioners keep client information confidential. With few exceptions, state statutes mandate we keep everything a client tells us confidential (Jost, 2006). This means we do not get to declare special exceptions to confidentiality even when family secrets, or other information we believe impairs our clinical work, are shared with us. Patient–therapist confidentiality is the cornerstone of modern psychotherapy. Clients need to know they are able to confide in a therapist without fear of their thoughts and concerns being shared without their consent. That does not mean, however, we are relieved from sharing our perspective regarding information provided by one partner when the other was not present. Clinical judgment can be used to convey how we believe this information could impact a relationship on the brink of divorce.

Maintaining competency and the development of new skills Systemic family therapists should, as a matter of practice, keep abreast of new developments in the field through education, training, and supervision. Systemic family therapists should also take great care to ensure the competence of their clinical work when they are in the process of acquiring new clinical skills. With regard to couples in the middle of divorce decision making, we know considerably more today than we knew just 2 years ago. There is a developing literature base in this area from both an empirical (Hawkins et al., 2017) and clinical perspective (Doherty et al., 2016). Systemic family therapists who are familiar with this literature could easily normalize the processes of divorce ideation and commitment uncertainty for their clients. Additionally, there are trainings available for discernment counseling online via the Doherty Relationship Institute (http://dohertyrelationshipinstitute.com). When learning a new clinical approach, we caution novice and experienced therapists to seek out competent supervision as they get more comfortable with a new treatment protocol. We also encourage those being trained in new models to accurately represent their skill level to the public and professional colleagues.

Compassion fatigue and other self of the therapist considerations   The therapist's self is also a potential area of concern. Our personal experiences of divorce, at multiples times in our lives, will affect how we interact with this population. Each of us, for example, develops ideas about and has experiences of our own or our parent's marriage/relationship and whether it has been a healthy or unhealthy union. Whether we were raised in an intact family or one where divorce was experienced will also color the lens with which we view our own clients and their decision-making process. Do we see divorce or separation as a "bad" thing, or was our parent's or our own divorce a godsend that allowed each member of the family to relate to each other in more healthy ways?

Additionally, and speaking from experience of having worked with multiple couples who have been told by their couple therapist they should divorce or should have never married in the first place, we can attest to the fact that therapists can get to a place where they give up on hope for the couple's marriage/relationship long before the couple does. We believe this could be a function of compassion fatigue. Negash and Sahin (2011) warned about the fruits compassion fatigue when they suggest that one manifestation of compassion fatigue is when the therapist gives up hope for change. When a therapist is unaware they are working with a mixed-agenda couple, supporting one partner's narrative about the relationship at the cost of the other's becomes an easy trap. Negash and Sahin (2011) confirm that "when an MFT experiences fatigue, empathy becomes more complicated and difficult to balance. The therapist may relate strongly to one member and not to another" (p. 4). They also caution that compassion fatigue can reduce the standard of care and contribute to depersonalization of the client, which can "lead family therapist to provide advice that is not necessarily appropriate or beneficial" (p. 5). Finally, one other place that fatigue may show up is in a loss of respect for the couple. This can "manifest itself in a loss of empathy, respect, and positive feelings for clients" (Negash & Sahin, 2011, p. 5). With mixed-agenda couples, even the most capable therapist can become frustrated without knowing which agenda to pursue. This makes it imperative that we become skilled at sitting with the ambiguity of a situation and helping our clients make decisions with clarity and confidence before pushing them to make a premature, and often costly, decision.

Continuation of treatment   We also have an ethical, and maybe even moral, obligation to continue treatment only as long as the treatment is beneficial. This ethical issue can arise when, through the course of couple's therapy, there seem to be no therapeutic gains or there is a general lack of progress. Therapists have described this as "losing traction" or "spinning our wheels" in therapy. If happening during the course of traditional couple therapy, it may be a sign that one or both of the partners are not convinced that either a goal of "better connection" or "increased intimacy" is really what they need. This can be a sign of a commitment uncertainty or of a mixed-agenda couple. If this is the case, traditional therapy, which requires a commitment to the relationship as a cornerstone of success (Johnson, 2004), is contraindicated.

Family court system Working with couples that are deciding to divorce will ultimately result in a number of those couples divorcing. Because of this it is wise to have language in consent forms regarding agreements about what information can or cannot be used in court. We recommend following the course of action outlined in the consent form used by the Minnesota Couples on the Brink Project (located at http://www.cehd.umn.edu/fsos/research/mcb/pdf/Intake%20Packet%202016.pdf).

Participants agree to the following:

> *… the parties agree that they will not seek to use in any court proceeding any statements made by the other party or a facilitator at any meeting… they also agree that they will not call as witnesses or seek to obtain for court purposes any of the notes or documents prepared…*

Of course, this will not exempt a clinician from having to respond to a subpoena issued by a judge, but it might prevent an overly zealous lawyer and a hurt client from trying to make a case out of discussions in treatment initially aimed at seeing if repairing the relationship was a possibility at all.

Family violence considerations In the early 1990s, Neil Jacobson, noted psychologist and couple therapy researcher, said, at a meeting of the National Council on Family Relations, "If we stopped providing therapy for couples where there had been some violence, we'd be doing little to no couple therapy" (text paraphrased). He was suggesting that IPV is so pervasive in our marriages and intimate relationships, at least to a degree, that withholding treatment from couples where this was going on would be unhelpful to the many couples who could benefit from treatment. With that said, we can probably do a good job of separating those couples who could benefit from treatment where the IPV has been situational in nature versus those couples where patriarchal terrorism occurs. For more on the distinction between the two, see Michael Johnson's groundbreaking contribution on the topic (1995). As in any couple therapy situation, we must do our best to protect our clients while understanding that we cannot foresee every possible way clients can be harmed by their participation in therapy. One resource for screening couples for the presence of IPV, specifically with mixed agendas, is provided by the Minnesota Couples on the Brink Project. This particular resource consists of four questions designed to assess threat, coercion, and the presence of legal mandates that apply to the couple (restraining orders) in order to verify, as much as possible, that IPV will not be a concern for a couple that chooses to participate in discernment counseling (found at http://www.cehd.umn.edu/fsos/research/mcb/pdf/Screening%20interview%20form-4.pdf).

Policy, Prevention and Practice: Recommendations and Future Directions

The legal system can be a primary resource for couples in the divorce and separation process but many who are merely "thinking" about divorce or separation may never engage with the legal system directly. However, the policies in place may impact one's decision-making process regardless of direct contact with a judge, lawyer, or other court-appointed professional. For couples who are legally married, divorce can be a long and taxing process. Unless both partners agree on the terms, divorce often requires mediators, lawyers, and judges to intervene. Further, divorce requires one party to file a legal petition, which automatically places that partner as the petitioner and the other as the defendant. This inherently places one partner as the "winner" and the other a "loser" since a verdict must be rendered by a judge.

The already ambiguous state of the relationship for couples who are uncertain about their commitment may benefit from a system that embraces patience as a core principle and does not "push" one or both partners to "get on with it" and make a decision. Research has indicated that up to 30% of couples who are going through the divorce process may contain one partner who does not really want the divorce (Doherty, Willoughby, & Peterson, 2011). In 10% of these specific cases, both members of the couple indicated an interest in preventing the divorce but were unsure of the available resources to help them in this endeavor. Of course, not all divorces should be prevented, but there does seem to be a small portion of divorces that could be if proper services were identified and utilized.

Some states have embraced various waiting periods for couples who have filed for divorce. Any policy changes must go beyond waiting periods (which are typically seen as parental in nature) to include offering resources for potential reconciliation. In our experience with couples on the brink of divorce, most only see two paths forward, maintaining the status quo (unacceptable) and divorce (the unknown), and this is not useful unless someone paints for them a picture of what reconciliation efforts might entail. Once couples see that their problems are related to a system of interactions and if each person focused on changing their own behavior, they might get a sense of hope that lasting change is possible. Even slowing down the divorce process by asking couples if they have explored options for reconciliation would be an important policy change.

The reality is that most of the changing that needs to happen is not at a legislative policy level at all or would have to happen at such a high level (i.e., relationship education in high school) and would take such a long time for its potential to be realized that very few policy makers would back it. We believe that the greatest changes can occur in the offices of couple therapists and in the private conversations of those who reach out for help with their troubled marriages (Lind Seal, Doherty, & Harris, 2016). Once regular couple therapists understand they need to adopt a new approach with a new goal for dealing with commitment uncertain (mixed-agenda) couples, then our couples will have the space they need to live in their ambiguity without feeling the need to rush to a decision to divorce. Helping couples make divorce decisions with clarity and confidence should, theoretically, reduce the conflictual nature of divorce and help all those affected by it navigate the waters with less emotional reactivity.

Based on previous research, the duration, frequency, and intensity of each are important in identifying the different types of couples in therapy (Hawkins et al., 2017; Quirk et al., 2016). Clinicians working with couples might incorporate two easily administered assessments into their clinical protocol to identify mixed-agenda couples. The first is a 2-item assessment used in the discernment counseling protocol (Appendix A). Participants fill out a self-assessment instrument that, among other things (i.e., problems checklist, dyadic adjustment, depression, etc.), provides the clinician with the couple's perspective on how "mixed" a couple's agenda is. An additional question assesses the "type" of attitude individuals in the couple have toward "working on" the marriage (Appendix B). This question also aids in assessing a mixed-agenda within couples who seek help or individuals who seek help by themselves.

Future directions

The body of literature on working with couples deciding to stay together or separate remains primarily in theory and conceptual frameworks (Allen & Hawkins, 2017; Amato, 2010). Many studies have examined the predictors of divorce and impact of separating couples on the family (Amato, 2010; Goldberg & Garcia, 2015). However, more research is needed on commitment uncertainty and divorce ideation inside and outside the context of couple therapy. What prompts uncertainty for some individuals and not others? How does current marital policy impact couple relationships? How do individuals navigate commitment uncertainty in couple therapy? What aspects of therapeutic conversations impact uncertainty and divorce ideation? Empirical answers can help prevent unnecessary divorce by informing relevant policy, improve therapy for couples deciding whether or not to separate, and decrease the negative impact of divorce on children and families.

The legalization of same-sex marriage in 2015 highlighted a gap in the literature on same-sex couple relationships. Early research on same-sex relationships showed many similarities and some differences when compared with heterosexual couples (Kurdek, 1991a, 1991b; Lannutti & Cameron, 2002). Same-sex couples face many of the same challenges as heterosexual couples and break up for similar reasons (Kurdek, 1998; Lau, 2012). When separating, however, same-sex couples seem to maintain closer and more amicable relationships during and after the separation process (Bacon, 2012; Harkless & Fowers, 2005). This unique aspect of same-sex committed relationships prior to the legalization of same-sex marriage also remains an understudied area of couple research. Further examination of coupling and uncoupling processes in same-sex committed relationships might produce information salient to all couples who are deciding whether or not to separate.

Lastly, a somewhat unacknowledged aspect of work with couples in this chapter is the presence of children in the couple relationship. Early research on divorce and child well-being found that children of divorce scored worse on mental health outcomes during childhood and into adulthood (Amato, 2000; Amato & Keith, 1991; Cherlin, Chase-lansdale, & Christine, 1998). More recent research, however, has identified high levels of marital conflict prior to the divorce, sibling order, and mental health of the children prior to the divorce as predictors of child and adolescent adjustment to this type of family transition (Roth, Harkins, & Eng, 2014; Storksen, Roysamb, Holmen, & Tambs, 2006). Little is known about children of parents who, at least once, seriously considered separating. For example, conflict prior to and during a separation hinders a child's adjustment (Roth et al., 2014). However, couples may engage in conflict over time but never formally separate. Gaining a better understanding of how commitment uncertainty influences child outcomes could also help guide systemic therapists in their practice.

A. Mixed-Agenda Couple Assessment

When asking for counseling as a couple, the two people in the relationship may be leaning in different directions about whether to stay together or break up. Please circle the number below that is closest to your own "leaning" at the moment.

1	2	3	4	5	6	7	8	9	10

Definitely preserve the relationship   Not sure   Definitely end the relationship

What is your best guess for how your spouse or partner is leaning?

1	2	3	4	5	6	7	8	9	10

Definitely preserve the relationship   Not sure   Definitely end the relationship

Note. Reprinted with permission from Doherty and Harris (2017, p. 52). Copyright 2017 by American Psychological Association.

B. Assessment of Attitudes Toward Divorce

People have different attitudes about divorce or working on their marriage. Check which of these statements most closely fits your own attitude right now. Please read all of them and then pick just one statement:

- ☐ I'm done with this marriage; it's too late now even if my spouse were to make major changes
- ☐ I have mixed feelings about the divorce; sometimes I think it's a good idea and sometimes I'm not sure
- ☐ I would consider reconciling if my spouse got serious about making major changes
- ☐ I don't want this divorce, and I would work hard to get us back together

Note. Reprinted with permission from Doherty et al. (2016, p. 5). Copyright 2016 by Taylor & Francis.

References

Ainsworth, M. D. S., & Bell, S. M. (1970). Attachment, exploration, and separation: Illustrated by the behavior of one-year-olds in a strange situation. *Child Development, 41*(1), 49–67. doi:10.2307/1127388

Ainsworth, M. D. S., Blehar, M. C., Waters, E., & Wall, S. N. (1978). *Patterns of attachment: A psychological study of the strange situation.* Hillsdale, NJ: Erlbaum.

Ainsworth, M. D. S., & Bowlby, J. (1991). An ethological approach to personality development. *American Psychologist, 46*(4), 333–341. doi:10.1037/0003-066X.46.4.333

Albrecht, S. L., & Kuna, P. R. (1980). The decision to divorce: A social exchange perspective. *Journal of Divorce, 3*(4), 339–378. doi:10.1300/J279v03n04

Alexandrov, E. O., Cowan, P. A., & Cowan, C. P. (2005). Couple attachment and the quality of marital relationships: Method and concept in the validation of the new couple attachment interview and coding system. *Attachment and Human Development, 7*(2), 123–152. doi:10.1080/14616730500155170

Allen, S., & Hawkins, A. J. (2017). Theorizing the decision-making process for divorce or reconciliation. *Journal of Family Theory & Review*, 9(1), 50–68. doi:10.1111/jftr.12176

Amato, P. R. (2000). The consequences of divorce for adults and children. *Journal of Marriage and Family*, 62(4), 1269–1287. doi:10.1111/j.1741-3737.2000.01269.x

Amato, P. R. (2010). Research on divorce: Continuing trends and new developments. *Journal of Marriage and Family*, 72(3), 650–666. doi:10.1111/j.1741-3737.2010.00723.x

Amato, P. R., & Keith, B. (1991). Parental divorce and the well-being of children: A meta-analysis. *Psychological Bulletin*, 110(1), 26–46. doi:10.1037/0033-2909.110.1.26

American Association for Marriage and Family Therapy. (2015, January 1). *AAMFT code of ethics*. Retrieved from: https://www.aamft.org/Legal_Ethics/Code_of_Ethics.aspx

Babcock, J. C., Gottman, J. M., Ryan, K. D., & Gottman, J. S. (2013). A component analysis of a brief psycho-educational couples' workshop: One-year follow-up results. *Journal of Family Therapy*, 35(3), 252–280. doi:10.1111/1467-6427.12017

Bacon, J. (2012). Until death do us part: Lesbian rhetorics of relational divorce. *Women's Studies in Communication*, 1409. doi:10.1080/07491409.2012.724523

Baek, Y. M. (2010). An integrative model of ambivalence. *The Social Science Journal*, 47(3), 609–629. doi:10.1016/j.soscij.2010.02.003

Bartholomew, K., & Horowitz, L. M. (1991). Attachment styles among young adults: A test of a four-category model. *Journal of Personality and Social Psychology*, 61(2), 226–244. doi:10.1037/0022-3514.61.2.226

Bassard, A., & Johnson, S. M. (2016). Couple and family therapy: An attachment perspective. In J. Cassidy & P. R. Shaver (Eds.), *Handbook of attachment* (3rd ed., pp. 805–824). New York, NY: The Guilford Press.

Blau, P. (1964). *Power and exchange in social life* (pp. 352). New York, NY: Wiley.

Booth, A., & White, L. (1980). Thinking about divorce. *Journal of Marriage and Family*, 42(3), 605–616. Retrieved from http://www.jstor.org/stable/351904%5Cnhttp://www.jstor.org/stable/351904

Bowlby, J. (1973). *Attachment and loss, vol. II: Separation* (Vol. 2). New York, NY: Basic Books.

Bowlby, J., Ainsworth, M., & Bretherton, I. (1992). The origins of attachment theory. *Reference: Developmental Psychology*, 28(5), 759–775. doi:10.1037/0012-1649.28.5.759

Bradley, R. P. C., Drummey, K., Gottman, J. M., & Gottman, J. S. (2014). Treating couples who mutually exhibit violence or aggression: Reducing behaviors that show a susceptibility for violence. *Journal of Family Violence*, 29(5), 549–558. doi:10.1007/s10896-014-9615-4

Bretherton, I., & Munholland, K. A. (2008). Internal working models in attachment relationships: Elaborating a central construct in attachment theory. In J. Cassidy & P. R. Shaver (Eds.), *Handbook of attachment: Theory, research, and clinical applications* (3rd ed., pp. 102–127). New York, NY: Guildford Press. doi:10.1212/01.WNL.0000152986.07469.E9

Butler, M. H., Harper, J. M., & Seedall, R. B. (2009). Facilitated disclosure versus clinical accommodation of infidelity secrets: An early pivot point in couple therapy. Part 1: Couple relationship ethics, pragmatics, and attachment. *Journal of Marital and Family Therapy*, 35(1), 125–143. doi:10.1111/j.1752-0606.2008.00106.x

Cherlin, A. J., Chase-lansdale, P. L., & Christine, M. (1998). Effects of parental divorce on mental health throughout the life course. *American Sociological Review*, 63(2), 239–249. Retrieved from http://www.jstor.org/stable/2657325

Cohen, O., & Finzi-Dottan, R. (2012). Reasons for divorce and mental health following the breakup. *Journal of Divorce and Remarriage*, 53(8), 581–601. doi:10.1080/10502556.2012.719413

Corbin, J., & Strauss, A. (2008). Practical considerations. In J. Corbin & A. Strauss (Eds.), *Basics of qualitative research (3rd ed.): Techniques and procedures for developing grounded theory* (pp. 19–44). Thousand Oaks, CA: SAGE Publications, Inc. doi:10.4135/9781452230153

Davila, J., & Bradbury, T. N. (2001). Attachment insecurity and the distinction between unhappy spouses who do and do not divorce. *Journal of Family Psychology*, 15(3), 371–393. doi:10.1037//0893-3200.15.3.371

Diamond, R. M., Brimhall, A. S., & Elliott, M. (2018). Attachment and relationship satisfaction among first married, remarried, and post-divorce relationships. *Journal of Family Therapy*, 40, S111–S127. doi:10.1111/1467-6427.12161

Doherty, W. J. (2002). How therapists harm marriages and what we can do about it. *Journal of Couple & Relationship Therapy*, 1(2), 1–17. doi:10.1300/J398v01n02_01

Doherty, W. J., & Harris, S. M. (2017). *Helping couples on the brink of divorce: Discernment counseling for troubled relationships.* Washington, DC: American Psychological Association. doi:10.1037/0000029-000

Doherty, W. J., Harris, S. M., & Wickel Didericksen, K. (2016). A typology of attitudes toward proceeding with divorce among parents in the divorce process. *Journal of Divorce & Remarriage*, 57(1), 1–11. doi:10.1080/10502556.2015.1092350

Doherty, W. J., Harris, S. M., & Wilde, J. L. (2016). Discernment counseling for "mixed-agenda" couples. *Journal of Marital and Family Therapy*, 42(2), 246–255. doi:10.1111/jmft.12132

Doherty, W. J., Willoughby, B. J., & Peterson, B. (2011). Interest in marital reconciliation among divorcing parents. *Family Court Review*, 49(2), 313–321. doi:10.1111/j.1744-1617.2011.01373.x

Donovan, R. L., & Jackson, B. L. (1990). Deciding to divorce: A process guided by social exchange, attachment, and cognitive dissonance theories. *Journal of Divorce*, 13(4). doi:10.1300/J279v13n04

Doss, B. D., Rhoades, G. K., Stanley, S. M., & Markman, H. J. (2009). The effect of the transition to parenthood on relationship quality: An eight-year prospective study. *Journal of Personality and Social Psychology*, 96(3), 601–619. doi:10.1037/a0013969

Downs, A. (1957). *An economic theory of democracy.* New York, NY: Harper.

Emerson, R. M. (1976). Social exchange theory. *Annual Review of Sociology*, 2(1), 335–362. doi:10.1146/annurev.so.02.080176.002003

Fall, K. A., & Lyons, C. (2003). Ethical considerations of family secret disclosure and post-session safety management. *The Family Journal*, 11(3), 281–285. doi:10.1177/1066480703252339

Fals-Stewart, W., Birchler, G. R., & O'Farrell, T. J. (1999). Drug-abusing patients and their intimate partners: Dyadic adjustment, relationship stability, and substance use. *Journal of Abnormal Psychology*, 108(1), 11–23.

Fisher, T. D., & McNulty, J. K. (2008). Neuroticism and marital satisfaction: The mediating role played by the sexual relationship. *Journal of Family Psychology*, 22(1), 112–122. doi:10.1037/0893-3200.22.1.112

Frazier, P. A., Tix, A. P., & Barnett, C. L. (2003). The relational context of social support: Relationship satisfaction moderates the relations between enacted support and distress. *Personality and Social Psychology Bulletin*, 29(9), 1133–1146. doi:10.1177/0146167203254545

Frisch, D., & Baron, J. (1988). Ambiguity and rationality. *Journal of Behavioral Decision Making*, 1(3), 149–157. doi:10.1002/bdm.3960010303

Garanzini, S., Yee, A., Gottman, J. M., Gottman, J. S., Cole, C., Preciado, M., & Jasculca, C. (2017). Results of gottman method couples therapy with gay and lesbian couples. *Journal of Marital and Family Therapy*, 43(4), 674–684. doi:10.1111/jmft.12276

Glenn, N. D. (2005). *With this ring: A national survey on marriage in America.* Retrieved from https://www.fatherhood.org/with-this-ring-survey.

Goldberg, A. E., & Garcia, R. (2015). Predictors of relationship dissolution in lesbian, gay, and heterosexual adoptive parents. *Journal of Family Psychology*, 29(3), 394–404. doi:10.1037/fam0000095

Gottman, J. M. (1994). *What predicts divorce? The relationship between marital processes and marital outcomes.* Hillsdale, NJ: Lawrence Erlbaum Associates.

Gottman, J. M., Coan, J., Carrere, S., Swanson, C., Gottman, J. M., Coan, J., … Swanson, C. (1998). Predicting marital happiness and stability from newlywed interactions. *Journal of Marriage and the Family*, 60(1), 5–22.

Gottman, J. M., Gottman, J. S., & DeClaire, J. (2006). *Ten lessons to transform your marriage: America's love lab experts share their strategies for strengthening your relationship.* Middlebury, VT: Harmony Books.

Gottman, J. M., Levenson, R. W., Gross, J., Frederickson, B. L., McCoy, K., Rosenthal, L., … Yoshimoto, D. (2003). Correlates of gay and lesbian couples' relationship satisfaction and relationship dissolution. *Journal of Homosexuality*, 45(1), 23–43. doi:10.1300/J082v45n01_02

Gottman, J. M., Ryan, K., Swanson, C., & Swanson, K. (2005). Proximal change experiments with couples: A methodology for empirically building a science of effective interventions for changing couples' interaction. *The Journal of Family Communication*, 5(3), 163–190. doi:10.1207/s15327698jfc0503_1

Gottman, J. S., & Gottman, J. M. (2015). *10 principles for doing effective couples therapy.* Norton Series on Interpersonal Neurobiology. New York, NY: W. W. Norton & Company.

Harkless, L. E., & Fowers, B. J. (2005). Similarities and differences in relational boundaries among heterosexuals, gay men, and lesbians. *Psychology of Women Quarterly*, 29(2), 167–176. doi:10.1111/j.1471-6402.2005.00179.x

Harris, S. M., Crabtree, S. A., Bell, N. K., Allen, S. M., & Roberts, K. M. (2017). Seeking clarity and confidence in the divorce decision-making process. *Journal of Divorce & Remarriage*, 58(2), 83–95. doi:10.1080/10502556.2016.1268015

Hawkins, A. J., Allen, S. E., Galovan, A. M., Harris, S. M., Allen, S. M., Roberts, K. M., & Schramm, D. G. (2017). What are they thinking? A national study of stability and change in divorce ideation. *Family Process*, 56(4), 1–17. doi:10.1111/famp.12299

Hawkins, A. J., Allen, S. M., Roberts, K., Harris, S. M., & Allen, S. M. (2018). Divorce ideation. *Encyclopedia of Couple and Family Therapy*, 1–5. doi:10.1007/978-3-319-15877-8_791-1

Hawkins, A. J., Roberts, K., Harris, S. M., Allen, S., Schramm, D., & Galovan, A. (2015). *What are they thinking? A national survey of married individuals who are thinking about divorce.* Provo, UT: Family Studies Center, Brigham Young University.

Hawkins, A. J., Willoughby, B. J., & Doherty, W. J. (2012). Reasons for divorce and openness to marital reconciliation. *Journal of Divorce & Remarriage*, 53(6), 453–463. doi:10.1080/10502556.2012.682898

Hazan, C., & Shaver, P. R. (1987). Romantic love conceptualized as an attachment process. *Journal of Personality and Social Psychology*, 52(3), 511–524. doi:10.1037//0022-3514.52.3.511

Hazan, C., & Shaver, P. R. (1994). Attachment as an organizational framework for research on close relationships. *Psychological Bulletin*, 5(1), 1–22. doi:10.1207/s15327965pli0501

Idstad, M., Torvik, F. A., Borren, I., Rognmo, K., Røysamb, E., & Tambs, K. (2015). Mental distress predicts divorce over 16 years: the HUNT study. *BMC Public Health*. doi:10.1186/s12889-015-1662-0

Imber-Black, E. (1993). *Secrets in families and family therapy: An overview.* New York, NY: W. W. Norton & Co.

Johnson, M. P. (1995). Patriarchal terrorism and common couple violence: Two forms of violence against women. *Journal of Marriage and Family*, 57(2), 283–294. Retrieved from http://www.jstor.org/stable/353683

Johnson, S. M. (2004). *The practice of emotionally focused couple therapy: Creating connection* (2nd ed.). New York, NY: Brunner-Routledge.

Johnson, S. M., & Bradley, B. (2007). Creating loving relationships. In J. H. Bray & M. Stanton (Eds.), *The Wiley-Blackwell handbook of family psychology* (pp. 402–415). Chichester, UK/Malden, MA: Wiley-Blackwell.

Johnson, S. M., Hunsley, J., Greenberg, L., & Schindler, D. (1999). Emotionally focused couples therapy: Status and challenges. *Clinical Psychology: Science and Practice*, 6(1), 67–79. doi:10.1093/clipsy.6.1.67

Jost, T. S. (2006). *Constraints on sharing mental health and substance use treatment information imposed by federal and state medical records privacy laws.* National Center for Biotechnology Information. US National Library of Medicine.

Karney, B. R., & Bradbury, T. N. (1995). The longitudinal course of marital quality and stability: A review of theory, method, and research. *Psychological Bulletin*, 118, 3–34. doi:10.1037//0033-2909.118.1.3

Kitson, G. C. (1982). Attachment to the spouse in divorce: A scale and its application. *Source Journal of Marriage and Family*, 44(2), 379–393. doi:10.2307/351547

Knobloch, L. K. (2008). The content of relational uncertainty within marriage. *Journal of Social and Personal Relationships*, 25(3), 467–495. doi:10.1177/0265407508090869

Kurdek, L. A. (1991a). Correlates of relationship satisfaction in cohabiting gay and lesbian couples: Integration of contextual, investment, and problem-solving models. *Journal of Personality and Social Psychology*, 61(6), 910–922. doi:10.1037/0022-3514.61.6.910

Kurdek, L. A. (1991b). The dissolution of gay and lesbian couples. *Journal of Social and Personal Relationships*, 8(2), 265–278. doi:10.1177/0265407591082006

Kurdek, L. A. (1998). Relationship outcomes and their predictors: Longitudinal evidence from heterosexual married, gay cohabiting, and lesbian cohabiting couples. *Jounral of Marriage and the Family*, 60(3), 553–568. Retrieved from http://www.jstor.org/stable/353528

Kurdek, L. A. (2000). Attractions and constraints as determinants of relationship commitment: Longitudinal evidence from gay, lesbian, and heterosexual couples. *Personal Relationships*, 7, 245–262. doi:10.1111/j.1475-6811.2000.tb00015.x

Kurdek, L. A. (2002). On being insecure about the assessment of attachment styles. *Journal of Social and Personal Relationships*, 19(6), 811–834.

Lannutti, P. J., & Cameron, K. A. (2002). Beyond the breakup: Heterosexual and homosexual post-dissolutional relationships. *Communication Quarterly*, 50(2), 153–170. doi:10.1080/01463370209385654

Lau, C. Q. (2012). The stability of same-sex cohabitation, different-sex cohabitation, and marriage. *Journal of Marriage and Family*, 74(5), 973–988. doi:10.1111/j.1741-3737.2012.01000.x

Levenson, R. W., & Gottman, J. M. (1983). Marital interaction: Physiological linkage and affective exchange. *Journal of Personality and Social Psychology*, 45(3), 587–597.

Levinger, G. (1979). A social exchange view on the dissolution of pair relationships. In R. Burgess & T. Huston (Eds.), *Social exchange in developing relationships* (pp. 169–193). Amsterdam, the Netherlands: Elsevier.

Lind Seal, K., Doherty, W. J., & Harris, S. M. (2016). Confiding about problems in marriage and long-term committed relationships: A National Study. *Journal of Marital and Family Therapy*, 42(3), 438–450. doi:10.1111/jmft.12134

Main, M., & Solomon, J. (1990). Procedures for identifying infants as disorganized/disoriented during the Ainsworth strange situation. *Attachment in the Preschool Years: Theory, Research, and Intervention*, 1, 121–160.

Moore, A. G. (1992). Reasons for divorce: Age and gender differences. *Journal of Women & Aging*, 4(2), 47–60. doi:10.1300/J074v04n02

Negash, S., & Sahin, S. (2011). Compassion fatigue in marriage and family therapy: Implications for therapists and clients. *Journal of Marital and Family Therapy*, 37(1), 1–13. doi:10.1111/j.1752-0606.2009.00147.x

North, J., Shadid, C., & Hertlein, K. M. (2018). Deception in family therapy: Recognition, implications, and intervention. *Australian and New Zealand Journal of Family Therapy*, 39, 38–53. doi:10.1002/anzf.1280

Owen, J., Keller, B., Shuck, B., Luebcke, B., Knopp, K., & Rhoades, G. K. (2014). An initial examination of commitment uncertainty in couple therapy. *Couple and Family Psychology: Research and Practice*, 3(4), 232–238. doi:10.1037/cfp0000030

Owen, J., Rhoades, G., Shuck, B., Fincham, F. D., Stanley, S., Markman, H., & Knopp, K. (2014). Commitment uncertainty: A theoretical overview. *Couple and Family Psychology; Research and Practice*, 3(4), 207–219. doi:10.1037/cfp0000028

Pepper, N. (1993). Indecision regarding a couple relationship a working model for ambivalence. *Australian and New Zealand Journal of Family Therapy*, 14(4), 181–188. doi:10.1002/j.1467-8438.1993.tb00966.x

Priester, J. R., & Petty, R. E. (2001). Extending the bases of subjective attitudinal ambivalence: Interpersonal and intrapersonal antecedents of evaluative tension. *Journal of Personality and Social Psychology*, 80(1), 19–34. doi:10.1037//0022-3514.80.1.19

Quirk, K., Owen, J., Shuck, B., Fincham, F. D., Knopp, K., & Rhoades, G. (2016). Breaking bad: Commitment uncertainty, alternative monitoring, and relationship termination in young adults. *Journal of Couple & Relationship Therapy*, 15(1), 61–74. doi:10.1080/153 32691.2014.975306

Rauer, A. J., Karney, B. R., Garvan, C. W., & Hou, W. (2008). Relationship risks in context: A cumulative risk approach to understanding relationship satisfaction. *Journal of Marriage and Family*, 70(2), 1122–1135. doi:10.1111/j.1741-3737.2008.00554.x.Relationship

Roth, K. E., Harkins, D. A., & Eng, L. A. (2014). Parental conflict during divorce as an indicator of adjustment and future relationships: A retrospective sibling study. *Journal of Divorce & Remarriage*, 55(2), 117–138. doi:10.1080/10502556.2013.871951

Sabatelli, R. M., Lee, H., & Ripoll-Núñez, K. (2018). Placing the social exchange framework in an ecological context. *Journal of Family Theory and Review*, 10(1), 32–48. doi:10.1111/jftr.12254

Sabatelli, R. M., & Shehan, C. L. (2009). Exchange and resource theories. In P. Boss, W. J. Doherty, R. Larossa, W. Schumm, & S. Steinmetz (Eds.), *Sourcebook of family theories and methods* (pp. 385–417). New York, NY: Springer.

Seedall, R. B., & Wampler, K. S. (2012). Emotional congruence within couple interaction: The role of attachment avoidance. *Journal of Family Psychology*, 26(6), 948–958. doi:10.1037/a0030479

Seedall, R. B., & Wampler, K. S. (2013). An attachment primer for couple therapists: Research and clinical implications. *Journal of Marital and Family Therapy*, 39(4), 427–440. doi:10.1111/jmft.12024

Seedall, R. B., & Wampler, K. S. (2016). Couple emotional experience: Effects of attachment anxiety in low and high structure couple interactions. *Journal of Family Therapy*, 38(3), 340–363. doi:10.1111/1467-6427.12113

Simpson, J. A. (1990). Influence of attachment style on romantic relationships. *Journal of Personality and Social Psychology*, 59(5), 971–980. doi:10.1037/0022-3514.59.5.971

Simpson, J. A., & Rholes, W. S. (1994). Stress and secure base relationships in adulthood. In K. Bartholomew & D. Perlman (Eds.), *Attachment processes in adulthood* (Vol. 5, pp. 181–204). London, UK: Jessica Kingsley Publishers.

Slade, A. (2008). *The implications of attachment theory and research for adult psychotherapy. Handbook of Attachment: Theory, Research and Clinical Applications*, 762782.

Stalder, D. R. (2012). The role of dissonance, social comparison, and marital status in thinking about divorce. *Journal of Social and Personal Relationships*, 29(3), 302–323. doi:10.1177/0265407511431179

Stanley, S. M., Rhoades, G. K., & Whitton, S. W. (2010). Commitment: Functions, formation, and the securing of romantic attachment. *Journal of Family Theory & Review*, 2(4), 243–257. doi:10.1111/j.1756-2589.2010.00060.x

Storksen, I., Roysamb, E., Holmen, T. L., & Tambs, K. (2006). Adolescent adjustment and well-being: Effects of parental divorce. *Scandinavian Journal of Psychology*, 47, 75–84. doi:10.1111/j.1467-9450.2006.00494.x

Thibaut, J. W., & Kelley, H. H. (1959). *The social psychology of groups*. New York, NY: Wiley.

Vaughan, D. (1986). *Uncoupling: Turning points in intimate relationship*. New York, NY: Oxford University Press.

Walster, E., Walster, G. W., & Berscheid, E. (1978). *Equity: Theory and research*. Boston, MA: Allyn and Bacon.

Weingardt, K. R. (2000). Viewing ambivalence from a sociological perspective: Implications for psychotherapists. *Psychotherapy: Theory, Research, Practice, Training*, 37(4), 298–306. doi:10.1037/0033-3204.37.4.298

Wiebe, S. A., & Johnson, S. M. (2016). A review of the research in emotionally focused therapy for couples. *Family Process*, 55(3), 390–407. doi:10.1111/famp.12229

13

Therapy for Divorcing Couples
Managing the Transition Out of the Relationship
Scott C Huff, Melinda Stafford Markham, Nicole R. Larkin, and Erin R. Bauer

Although the divorce rate has declined and leveled out in the last few decades (National Center for Health Statistics, 2017), approximately 40–45% of first marriages end in divorce (Kreider & Ellis, 2011b). Divorce is often accompanied by multiple transitions that can be stressful for those involved. While not all changes that accompany divorce are negative (see Hetherington and Kelly, 2002, for a review), adults who divorce are at an increased risk for a number of negative outcomes. Compared with married individuals, those who divorce are more likely to have depressive symptoms, health problems, and even early death (Bierman, Fazio, & Milkie, 2006; Hughes & Waite, 2009; Lorenz, Wickrama, Conger, & Elder, 2006; Sbarra, Law, Lee, & Mason, 2009; Sbarra, Law, & Portley, 2011; Shor, Roelfs, Bugyi, & Schwartz, 2012; Waite, Luo, & Lewin, 2009). For some, divorce has short-term consequences, while for others the consequences are a chronic strain and continue for an extended amount of time (Amato, 2010; Sbarra, Hasselmo, & Bourassa, 2015).

The negative effects of divorce are not limited to the divorcing couple. Approximately 1.2 million children who experience parental divorce each year (Kreider & Ellis, 2011a) are also affected. Children with divorced parents are at an increased risk for academic difficulties (Amato & Anthony, 2014; Frisco, Muller, & Frank, 2007) and both internalizing (Kim, 2011; Weaver & Schofield, 2015) and externalizing problems (Amato & Anthony, 2014; Weaver & Schofield, 2015). Some of the effects of parental divorce can last into adulthood, including decreased psychological well-being (Amato & Sobolewski, 2001), increased likelihood of relationship dissolution (Cui, Fincham, & Durtschi, 2010; Wolfinger, 2005), and adult children feeling less close to their parents, particularly nonresidential fathers (Amato & Patterson, 2017; Amato & Sobolewski, 2001).

Divorce is a process that takes place over time and the legal divorce itself is not directly related to negative effects for children (Amato, 2010). There are, however, a number of strains that can occur with parental divorce that increase children's risk for negative outcomes (Amato, 2010). Some of these risk factors include reduced parental support and monitoring (Emery & Forehand, 1994; Rodgers & Rose, 2002), parental conflict (Grych, 2005), children's reduced contact with nonresidential parents (Kelly, 2007), decline in standard of living (Amato, 2010), and parents entering new romantic relationships (Ivanova, Mills, & Veenstra, 2014; Wochik, Schenck, & Sandler, 2009). These strains moderate children's reactions to their parents' divorce, which affects the duration of the negative consequences (Amato, 2010).

The negative effects of divorce are most pronounced when there are ongoing difficulties, making this a primary area of focus for relationship-focused therapists. Focusing on factors important for enhancing children's adjustment to parental divorce such as cooperative co-parenting (Sigal, Sandler, Wolchik, & Braver, 2011), continued nonresidential parent involvement with the child (Adamsons & Johnson, 2013), and the development and maintenance of positive parent–child relationships (Nielsen, 2017) will benefit those experiencing divorce.

Systemic Clinical Conceptualizations of Divorced and Separated Families

Multiple approaches have been taken to develop models or conceptualizations to work with divorced families. A number of authors have focused on describing the divorce process as a series of stages, influenced by family life cycle theories (Ahrons, 1998; Carter & McGoldrick, 1999; Schwartz & Kaslow, 1997). Sprenkle and Gonzalez-Doupé (1996), for example, focus on three stages: pre-divorce, during the divorce, and post-divorce. Each stage comes with requisite tasks and goals for achieving optimal outcomes. Schwartz and Kaslow (1997) include similar chronological divisions but add additional stages to address specific common difficulties. Their seven stages focus on the emotional divorce, the legal phase, the economic divorce, co-parenting concerns, the community divorce, spiritual and religious considerations, and the psychic divorce. Though presented as chronological stages, authors of these models regularly acknowledge that families are unlikely to progress through the models in an invariant order or even to necessarily have trouble at every stage.

In light of this complexity, an alternative approach has been to typify single major issues and to focus on specific treatment concerns. This may include advancing specific models (e.g., Pietsch, 2002, focused on narrative therapy) or specific underlying problems (e.g., Cohen's, 1998, focus on father's narcissistic personality disorder features). Johnston and Campbell (1988) made a unique contribution in developing a framework for counseling and mediation with high conflict divorced families. Their model is notable for its adherence to systemic principles and its ecological focus. Rather than focusing on stages, they categorize typical problems at *intrapsychic,* *interactional,* or *external* levels. They posit that the most serious difficulties in the divorce process come from combinations of difficulties between different levels. Viewing problems in divorcing couples from these multiple levels is consistent with broader work on co-parenting (not only for divorcing couples) that uses an ecological model to represent the interaction between individual characteristics, relationship characteristics, and environmental characteristics affecting co-parenting relationships (Feinberg, 2003).

Briefly, Johnston and Campbell's (1988) intrapsychic factors are those associated with individual personal reactions to the divorce; interactional factors are related to the relationship between the ex-spouses; and external factors are those that include wider subsystems including legal involvement and extended family. Although developed on a clinical sample of highly conflicted families, their model provides a framework by which to organize the literature on potential difficulties in the divorce process. It should be noted, however, that their conceptualization, as do most discussions of divorce, presumes that couples are not psychotic, dangerously violent, or otherwise inappropriate for conjoint treatment. In such cases, conceptualizations and interventions focused on those problems will likely be favored.

Intrapsychic considerations

Johnston and Campbell (1988) identify several ways that individual factors within divorcing partners, in concert with relational and external factors, can contribute to ongoing problems between ex-partners. Personality disorders have been suggested as an example of intrapsychic characteristics that lead directly to conflict in divorce. Cohen (1998), for example, focuses on fathers with narcissistic personality disorder traits. She notes that such individuals are especially susceptible to problems in divorce from the threat of divorce to their self-concept and will react strongly to maintain their grandiose self-image, leading to conflict. Neff and Cooper (2004) likewise suggest that personality disorders are frequent among couples that struggle to resolve their divorce. Johnston and Campbell (1988), based on a sample of 80 families that they studied in depth, found that 64% of parents had symptoms consistent with an Axis II diagnosis and 27% exhibited personality disorder traits. Importantly, however, they found that for most clients, these symptoms developed alongside the stress of divorce. They thus emphasized that even in the case of personality disorder traits, the context of the situation is critical to understanding its contribution.

Johnston and Campbell go on to discuss two major areas for assessment and intervention related to intrapsychic factors: threats to self-integrity and problems related to loss. They focus their discussion of threats to self-integrity under the term *narcissistic vulnerability*. Similar to a diathesis–stress model (Goforth, Pham, & Carlson, 2011), they posit that individuals have a level of risk of identity disturbance going into divorce. Individuals with low narcissistic vulnerability are less likely to see the divorce as an indication that they are fundamentally flawed, though they may still experience depression or an increased need for validation to make up for negative experience. Highly vulnerable individuals, including those with personality disorders, are likely to experience divorce as a direct threat to their identity. Moreover, they may be particularly likely to fight to appear the better parent or to "win" in court to validate themselves.

Threats to a person's self-integrity might be conceptualized through the concept of differentiation of self. Differentiation of self refers to an individual's ability to maintain a sense of identity, even in stressful situations (Bowen, 1978). Someone with poor differentiation of self is likely to rely on feelings, rather than facts, to make decisions and to shape their identity based on their current relationship. Haber (1990) explicitly tied differentiation of self to difficulties in individuals going through a divorce. He noted that partners with poor differentiation of self will often have boundaries that are so loose and blurred that the spouses cease to identify as individuals and only define themselves as a partner. When this identity fusion is broken because of divorce proceedings, the result can be a traumatic loss of identity to either or both spouses. Frequently, spouses feel they have lost a piece of themselves or feel incomplete. Partners' subsequent efforts to manipulatively maintain the relationship through conflict or to avoid dealing with their overwhelming feelings by cutting off from the other partner are likely to hamper their ability to effectively coordinate with the other partner or to parent individually (Gürmen, Huff, Brown, Orbuch, & Birditt, 2017).

Johnston and Campbell's (1988) second major intrapsychic concern, loss and grief, encompasses the ways that individuals may fail to mourn the loss of the relationship. They note that the experience of loss may create feelings of helplessness, result in individuals masking their hurt with anger, or reactivate past traumas. Each of these can contribute to ongoing difficulties between ex-spouses. This area of concern relates to Schwartz and Kaslow's (1997) discussion of the emotional divorce, wherein each partner, especially if one or both feels abandoned, needs therapeutic support to establish themselves as an individual and to work through feelings of loss, failure, desertion, and loneliness.

Though findings on its real impact are somewhat contradictory, the effects of initiator status on divorce adjustment are one way that working through loss may be evident (Diamond & Parker, 2018; Emery, 2012; Steiner, Durand, Groves, & Rozzell, 2015; Steiner, Suarez, Sells, & Wykes, 2011). The general thinking is that initiators began grieving long before the separation and wanted the divorce more, whereas non-initiators have had less time to mourn and process the loss and are thus at an emotional disadvantage (Baum, 2003; Emery, 2012; Pettit & Bloom, 1984). Non-initiators experience rejection and may have intense emotions surrounding the divorce, while initiators are more likely to experience guilt (Emery, 2012). For women specifically, "separation guilt" may result from initiating the divorce due to societal expectations to care for children and husbands (Baum, 2007). Although initiators are more likely to experience guilt, because initiators are further along in their psychological adjustment, they are also more likely to enter new relationships quicker than non-initiators (Sweeney, 2002). These initiator versus non-initiator issues present further complications to ongoing interactions.

Interactional considerations

Johnston and Campbell (1988) focus on two opposing processes when discussing interactional problems. They note that significant problems might stem from partners adopting significantly negative or overly idealized views of one another. Negative views are likely to be related to drastic changes in perception based on a partner's behavior, such as infidelity. Such events can effectively develop a hostile attribution bias (De Castro, Veerman, Koops, Bosch, & Monshouwer, 2002) that then makes all other interactions difficult due to misunderstanding and a lack of trust (Hopper, 2001). These issues of perception and definition connect closely with family therapy models focused on meaning making, such as solution-focused brief therapy and narrative therapy (de Shazer et al., 2012; White, 1995; White & Epstein, 1990). Pietsch (2002), for example, explicitly connected narrative therapy and divorce transitions, agreeing with Johnston and Campbell that the definitions and stories that are developed in the divorce process are a major component to ongoing relational and individual difficulties.

Johnston and Campbell's discussion of idealization interacts closely with threats to self-integrity and coping with loss. They describe ex-spouses who experience a sudden loss of the relationship as unable to work through pain or the loss of their self-concept. Rather than turning to denigration, they idealize the relationship and wish for further contact with the other partner. Manipulatively creating conflict or engaging in litigation becomes a way to draw the ex-partner into the relationship. Cases of idealization may further lead to patterns of occasionally reuniting to try the relationship again, often to only have it again fail.

It is also in this level that many common family therapy concepts must be considered in connection with the divorce. Triangulation, for example, is a consistent concern in the literature, for both adults and children involved in the divorce (Lebow & Rekart, 2007; Margolin, Gordis, & John, 2001). Consistent with Bowen's (1978) original conceptualization of triangles in family systems, the unstable dyad of divorced partners is highly likely to triangulate in others to make it more stable. Former partners may try to convince friends, helping professionals, court officials, and their children to be on their side. This behavior is indicative of basic anxiety and instability in the dyad. Questions of hierarchy, boundaries, and family adaptation are similarly important systemic concepts to consider in divorcing couples, given the stress the family system is experiencing through the divorce process. Madden-Derdich and Leonard (2002), for example, noted that divorced parents struggle because they lack experience for their new roles, and social norms for their behavior do not exist. The process of both parents coming to develop role definitions based on their own perceptions and their joint interactions creates significant opportunities for misunderstanding and stress.

External considerations

Finally, Johnston and Campbell (1988) point to factors that are external to the couple that may play a role in difficulties during the divorce transition. These may include new partners, cultural norms, and friends' reactions, among other concerns. It is particularly important to recognize interactions between external concerns and other levels. In the case of legal issues, for example, parents with high narcissistic vulnerability may be more apt to pursue litigation to validate their self-concept. At the same time, participating in litigation, as opposed to mediation, is related to decreased parental involvement (Emery, Laumann-Billings, Waldron, Sbarra, & Dillon, 2001). Similarly, in connection to extended family, Myers and Perrin (1993) noted that the parents of custodial parents (i.e., grandparents of the child) might be called upon to support the parent financially or emotionally and thus become involved in the divorce process, perhaps making demands and holding expectations of their child relative to the other parent and thus potentially contributing to conflict. Grandparents may likewise suffer emotionally based on restricted access to their grandchildren due to their child's or the other partner's reaction to the divorce.

Family diversity presents additional considerations in understanding ongoing difficulties. Lesbian, gay, bisexual, and transgender (LGBT) individuals and families, for example, may experience unique concerns. One possible scenario is when the divorce also includes the disclosure of a partner's LGBT orientation (Bigner, 2006). Such disclosures may bring additional feelings of hurt, mistrust, and confusion to the partner being disclosed to. For the disclosing partner, it may bring relief, but also distress or guilt as they potentially damage what was an authentically meaningful relationship. The nature of the disclosure—voluntary compared to being outed—adds additional complexity (Bigner, 2006). Alternatively, the separation or divorce of an LGBT family may present unique problems as well. Especially in situations without legal protection of LGBT relationships, the end of the relationship may present unique problems related to custody where children may not be biologically or legally related to both parents (Allen, 2007). Allen (2007) notes that the loss of a private relationship that was not legally or socially sanctioned may be particularly difficult as it can create feelings of ambiguous loss for partners.

Johnston and Campbell (1988) further describe the ways that helping professionals may unwittingly contribute to ongoing problems when not approaching therapy with divorcing individuals from a systemic lens. For example, an individual therapist may support a client in "holding firm boundaries" with an ex-spouse, not realizing that the client is acting on a reactionary negative view of the ex-spouse because of his infidelity and is thus refusing visitation. In the apparent interest of the client's autonomy and assertiveness, the clinician is not recognizing the client's need to work through hurt and loss to be able to co-parent effectively. Fineman (1988) suggests that this may be more nefarious as helping and legal professionals may encourage difficulties to maintain their clientele.

Systemic Interventions with Divorcing Families

The ecological conceptualization presented naturally lends itself to interventions for specific problems at different levels. At the same time, there are aspects of therapy with divorcing couples that are generalized to work at any level and warrant consideration. These include goal setting, session formats, and ethical and legal concerns.

Two major goals stand out consistently in connection with divorce therapy. First, all individuals going through the divorce should be able to recover and move forward with their lives satisfactorily (Ahrons, 1994; Schwartz & Kaslow, 1997). In stage models, this goal is often a focus of the pre-divorce and post-divorce stages, being supportive of—but secondary to—the goals of the during-divorce stages (Schwartz & Kaslow, 1997; Sprenkle & Gonzalez-Doupé, 1996). It is also most associated with the intrapsychic concerns of Johnston and Campbell (1988). The second goal focuses on reducing the negative impacts on children by reducing conflict and improving co-parental cooperation (Ahrons, 1994; Johnston & Campbell, 1988). Stage models typically focus on this concern in the during-divorce stage. It is generally the major concern of the interactional and external levels of Johnston and Campbell's conceptualization.

Preferred session formats typically stem from the goals of a given case. Individual sessions are often recommended for intrapsychic concerns, while conjoint sessions are preferred for most other problems, if safety permits (Johnston & Campbell, 1988; Schwartz & Kaslow, 1997; Sprenkle & Gonzalez-Doupé, 1996). Notably, given the focus of this chapter on couples' process through the divorce, the involvement of children in sessions is not typically necessary and may be contraindicated if it exposes the children to unmanageable conflict and triangulation. Children will likely benefit from their own therapy, preferably with coordination between therapists to avoid triangulation (Lebow & Rekart, 2007).

Another general consideration relates to legal and ethical issues stemming from working with divorcing couples. Given the close association with the legal system, it is important for therapists to be aware of legal concerns. A thorough discussion of this topic is outside the scope of this chapter and will vary according to local regulations, but a few considerations can be considered. Coordination with attorneys and court is typically preferred (Lebow & Rekart, 2007). However, Schwartz and Kaslow (1997) specifically recommend taking safeguards to avoid being drawn into an evaluator role or testifying on behalf of a client. Doing so is highly likely to be associated with triangulation with one former partner against the other (Bowen, 1978). It also creates significant threats to the therapeutic relationship and alliance. Specifically, making a judgment for one parent over the other is almost certainly going to limit the therapist's ability to effectively work with the parent that has received the negative judgment. It may also be difficult for a therapist in an evaluator role to effectively recognize improvements that both former partners can be making. The American Association for Marriage and Family Therapy Code of Ethics formalizes these recommendations in declaring that marriage and family therapists "avoid providing evaluations for those who are clients, unless otherwise mandated by legal systems" (section 7.6, American Association for Marriage and Family Therapy, 2015) with specific instructions on managing custody evaluations. As previously noted, divorce clients in conflict are likely to engage in triangulating the therapist to join a coalition against the other parent, which needs to be carefully monitored. Lebow and Rekart (2007) recommend consultation with other therapists involved in the case to help manage triangulation.

The remainder of this section presents interventions for divorcing couples based on the various levels in Johnston and Campbell's (1988) conceptualization. A distinction will be made between interventions for the couple and interventions focused on parenting and children. A separate chapter in this handbook discusses interventions designed to help parents and children following divorce (Huff & Hartenstein, 2020, vol. 2). This distinction is ultimately arbitrary, as the systemic nature of divorce means that parenting interventions will be dependent on interventions for the individuals (e.g., resolving grief and improving communication will make parenting easier) and will also help individual's adjustment (e.g., the good of the child is generally the motivation for resolving many individual concerns). Thus, while former partners will occasionally be addressed as parents and some concerns directly related to children will be addressed here, interventions focused on improving parenting, such as co-parenting best practices and avoiding triangulating the child, and intervening with the child can be found in the other chapter.

Intrapsychic

Stemming from individuals' issues, intrapsychic concerns are often resolved on an individual therapy basis. Interventions are generally focused on feelings of loss or on working through threats to clients' self-integrity. To what extent clients' reactions are consistent with grief, trauma, or crisis, techniques associated with these are appropriate. The ABCX crisis model (Hill, 1949), for example, has been applied to clients going through divorce and may provide an avenue of focusing on resources and definitions of the divorce in service of reducing how much of a crisis the client experiences (Sprenkle & Cyrus, 1983). Likewise, Kübler-Ross's (1969) grief process may be instructive (Froiland & Hozeman, 1977; Weisman, 1975). Reframing clients' anger, denial, and other feelings as evidence of grief may help in changing definitions and encouraging cooperation. Likewise, a grief approach may help explain why the first one to 3 years following divorce proceedings are the most variable, with relationships stabilizing thereafter (Drapeau, Gagné, Saint-Jacques, Lépine, & Ivers, 2009; Forehand, Neighbors, Devine, & Armistead, 1994; Sbarra & Emery, 2008; Toews & McKenry, 2001). Given the general lack of social norms or traditions related to divorce, Schwartz and Kaslow (1997) suggest that a divorce ceremony may be a useful exercise for some couples to resolve feelings of grief. This may include taking time to acknowledge the positive aspects of the relationship that are being lost as well as involving the children and family friends as a means of avoiding revising the relationship history or developing camps of friends.

Solution-focused techniques may provide a natural way to address narcissistic vulnerability and feelings of helplessness (Ramisch, McVicker, & Sahin, 2009). Solution-focused therapy treats the client as an expert and emphasizes their strengths, abilities, and opportunities to find solutions (de Shazer et al., 2012). The miracle question (with emphasis on what will be different for the individual, not the ex-spouse) and scaling questions are a natural fit for goals related to improving self-efficacy (Lloyd & Dallos, 2006; Ramisch et al., 2009). Johnston and Campbell (1988) add that, consistent with solution-focused therapy (de Shazer et al., 2012), a generally supportive attitude focused on reinforcing positive behaviors is important to resolving intrapsychic concerns. Naturally, when a client's narcissistic vulnerability is significant, additional care is needed.

Another potential need within the intrapsychic realm is to shift parents' focus away from their own loss and hurt and to recognize the potential for harm to the child (Schwartz & Kaslow, 1997; Whiteside, 1998). Johnston and Campbell (1988) recommend asking explicitly about the child's reactions to the divorce and helping parents to recognize the ways their ongoing conflict affects the child. Systems-focused techniques of discussing circular causation may be particularly effective in these situations to avoid triggering client's defensiveness (Smith-Acuña, 2011). Somewhat paradoxically, in the case of clients with personality disorders and personality disorder traits, it may be necessary to reframe the child's best interests in terms of the client's self-interest. Based on research into working with individuals with personality disorders (Beck & Freeman, 1990), Neff and Cooper (2004) reported positive results from a parent education program with this approach. For example, parents can be helped to recognize that the better their relationship with their ex-spouse, the more information and influence they have when the child is with that parent.

Interactional

Within their relatively narrow discussion of interactional interventions, Johnston and Campbell (1988) emphasize helping clients to develop more realistic views of the ex-partner, as opposed to the idealized or denigrated view adopted in the process of the divorce. The process can be likened to the re-storying process of narrative therapy. Pietsch (2002) and Lebow and Rekart (2007) specifically recommend a narrative approach to help clients reframe the divorce and their divorce story to move forward more productively.

Looking beyond negative perceptions of ex-spouses, systemic treatment models offer significant opportunities to improve relationships between divorced and divorcing couples. Though the general treatment is geared toward couples seeking to improve their relationship and be together (Johnson, 2004). Allan (2016) contends that the first stage of emotionally focused therapy may be valuable to divorcing couples. With its focus on de-escalation, the first stage emphasizes listening to and validating concerns, building empathy for each client and between clients, and recognizing negative cycles. Emotionally focused therapy likewise employs enactments, a systemic technique that focuses directly on interactional difficulties. Enactments can serve both diagnostic and intervention functions as divorcing couples develop healthy patterns of behavior (Allan, 2016; Minuchin, 1974). Given the possibility of conflict to breakout in cases of high conflict divorce, however, care must be taken if enactments become attacking or one-sided (Nichols & Fellenberg, 2000). If the former partners are unable to sustain direct dialogue with one another, it will likely be necessary to keep conversations between each partner and the therapist, seeking reaction from the other former partner afterward. Doing so is designed to help the system maintain a lower level of anxiety until it can sustain more (Crossno, 2011).

Allan also notes the importance in therapy of creating an effective therapeutic alliance. This can be particularly difficult among divorced couples, given that without care, validating one partner's experience may be experienced as a breach of the alliance with the other partner. Thus, a therapist must be careful to validate each individual's experience, without necessarily agreeing with his/her perception or blame of the other partner. Lebow and Rekart (2007) similarly recommend establishing a multipartial alliance (Boszormenyi-Nagy, 1974) that is caring, but focused on fairness. This stance may be compared to detriangulation within a Bowenian approach (Crossno, 2011). By maintaining a fair stance with each partner and strictly avoiding being drawn into coalitions against the other partner, detriangulation is focused on helping clients in conflict develop a relationship with less anxiety and conflict. This is particularly relevant to divorce cases.

External

In discussing external concerns, Johnston and Campbell (1988) make the observation that external concerns often serve as a mask for intrapsychic and interpersonal concerns. Focusing specifically on cultural differences between spouses, they report that problems based on different cultures are most often a reflection of problems like self-esteem, grief, and negative attribution biases. The cultural complaints are used to continue the fight to "win" against the other partner. In such cases, it is critical for therapists to appropriately work through the intrapsychic and interpersonal concerns first. Johnston and Campbell report that once concerns at the other levels have been resolved, the external cultural concerns can typically be managed through basic negotiation and compromise. For example, once an ex-husband has worked through the grief that was also making him feel like his ex-wife was trying to keep the children away from him, it will be much easier for him to negotiate changing visitation schedules so the children can participate in a cultural event with their mother.

Given this warning, however, there are various external concerns that are likely to require or benefit from therapeutic intervention or support. For example, as individuals work through their difficulties with the divorce, their family members or friends may continue to encourage conflict or otherwise meddle in the family. This may be an indication that the family and friends may be experiencing intrapsychic problems of their own and need help to work through grief or other identity injuries. One of the former partner's mothers, for example, may feel that their family identity or her personal identity as a mother has been injured by the "failure" of her child's marriage. To resolve this, she may continually blame and find fault with the other former partner to her child or even her grandchildren. In such cases, a referral to a systemically informed individual therapist or, if appropriate, an invitation to a conjoint session with one or both members of the divorced couple can help to work through the extended family's or friends' difficulties. The divorced couple themselves will likely benefit from coaching on holding appropriate boundaries and not letting others manipulate or unduly influence them. Identity, differentiation of self, and assertiveness-focused interventions will be helpful in this.

Ahrons (1998) provides an important dynamic to address in working through external concerns. In her efforts to destigmatize divorce and help parents be better parents, she has advanced language like "binuclear families" to emphasize the need for the co-parents to conceptualize themselves as a combined unit and to support one another. Clinically, increasing support represents an additional focus separate from reducing conflict and can apply to both the personal relationship and the co-parental relationship. For example, in the case of remarriage, helping the other partner to find ways to show appropriate support can be valuable for them and their children. This support may take the form of acknowledging personally and verbally to the child, if appropriate, that the new partner is another loving adult in the child's life and that remarriage has helped the former spouse to be more effective as a parent.

Clinicians must balance such efforts with effective rules, boundaries, and hierarchy (Minuchin, 1974). Efforts to build support must take into account real questions and concerns about safety and appropriateness, so long as those concerns are not masking unresolved intrapsychic or interpersonal problems. Additionally, boundary ambiguity abounds in divorced families, especially as stepparents join the system (Sweeney, 2010). In lower conflict settings, therapy can focus on helping both parents stay united in their parenting decisions and for the biological parents to remain the key decision makers for their children. For example, when the former spouses remarry, clinicians can help the newly married spouses to recognize the importance of the other biological parent in decision making. At the same time, the ex-spouse's acceptance that the new spouse may need to make in-the-moment parenting decisions for the children will also be essential. Clinically, techniques focused on changing the structure of the family to be more adaptable, such as enactments and making covert patterns more overt, are particularly apt, especially if all relevant members of the system (i.e., new spouses, grandparents, concerned friends) can be present (Aponte & Van Deusen, 1981).

In cases of higher conflict or safety risks to children, support and boundaries need to be appropriately adapted, but not ignored. Additional rules, boundaries, or other constraints may be required and may be part of court orders. For example, a family member or new spouse who is abusive may need to be restricted from a child or require supervision. At the same time, when external factors limit one parent's access to the child, clinicians can help the present parent to still express support or at least avoid complaining about the absent parent to help their own healing process and to reduce the child's experience of loyalty conflict (Wozencraft, Tauzin, & Romero, 2019). For example, if one parent moves away because of work, the remaining parent can continue to encourage contact and support the other parent in being a parent as much as possible.

Psychoeducation and mediation

In many cases, divorcing couples in therapy will also be interacting with other systems designed to minimize the effects of divorce on children and the potential impact on social systems. Many states in the United States, for example, offer or mandate some form of parent education following divorce, though the focus and requirements of each state vary significantly (Pollet & Lombreglia, 2008). Unfortunately, many of these programs are untested or evaluated merely on participant satisfaction (Feng & Fine, 2001; Frieman, Garon, & Garon, 2000; Shifflett & Cummings, 1999). When these programs are evaluated, the research is often not rigorous (Sigal et al., 2011). In general, parent education programs are more effective when they focus on skills and providing information about positive behaviors (Arbuthnot, Poole, & Gordon, 1996; Kramer, Arbuthnot, Gordon, Rousis, & Hoza, 1998; Kurkowski, Gordon, & Arbuthnot, 1994). Importantly, studies have shown systemic impacts from parent education. For example, divorcing parents who participated in divorce parenting education have been found to have reduced co-parenting conflict (Cookston, Braver, Griffin, De Lusé, & Miles, 2007; Fackrell, Hawkins, & Kay, 2011), improved parent–child relationships and parental discipline (Fackrell et al., 2011), and improved child outcomes (Braver, Griffin, & Cookston, 2005; Fackrell et al., 2011).

Divorcing couples can also engage in mediation. Mediation is an alternative dispute resolution process that involves the divorcing couple and a third party who assists the couple to enhance their communication and use effective problem solving and negotiation techniques to reach agreements (Moore, 2014). A wide range of professionals can provide mediation services, including professional mediators, attorneys, psychologists, and social workers (Sbarra & Emery, 2006). Divorcing couples can participate in custody mediation, which is limited to negotiating issues relating to the children, or comprehensive mediation, which includes negotiation over issues relating to children, finances, and property division (Sbarra & Emery, 2006). Professionals interested in providing mediation can find a variety of resources (e.g., Emery, 2004; Friedman, 1993; McKnight & Erickson, 2008) and should consult their particular state or country regarding certification.

Proponents report that mediation promotes better relationships and more collaborative co-parenting relationships (Emery, Matthews, & Kitzmann, 1994; Emery, Matthews, & Wyer, 1991; Emery, Sbarra, & Grover, 2005). The research suggests that these effects are most pronounced in the first 1 or 2 years following the divorce (Kelly, 1991; Sbarra & Emery, 2008). Notably, long-term comparisons between couples that used mediation and couples that litigated their divorce have generally failed to show significant differences (Emery et al., 2001; Sbarra & Emery, 2005). Part of the difficulty in the research on mediation is that selection effects and gender effects continue to make it difficult to accurately understand how helpful it is and if it is more or less helpful for some people (e.g., Camplair & Stolberg, 1990, found mediation to be more positive for women than for men).

Contact refusal and parental alienation

One particular concern that deserves a focus is contact refusal by children following the divorce (Huff, Anderson, Adamsons, & Tambling, 2017). Having a child refuse contact can be stressful and confusing for a parent that may contribute to additional intrapsychic and interactional difficulties. It may also lead to blaming the other parent for turning the child against them. With the terminology and proposed diagnosis of "parental alienation syndrome" gaining some notoriety (Baker, 2006; Gardner, 1991, 1999, 2002), it is valuable to remind therapists and clients that for most clients, contact refusal is a result of complex interactions between several factors, rather than the direct result of one parent's behaviors (Fidler & Bala, 2010). Kelly and Johnston's (2001) research, for example, demonstrated that a combination of abuse, parental deficits, and previous relationship patterns, in addition to alienating behaviors, better accounted for contact refusal than any single explanation (Johnston, Walters, & Olesen, 2005). Beyond this, adolescents have been found to be prone to spontaneous rejection of one parent (Bala, Hunt, & McCarney, 2010; Johnston & Goldman, 2010; Wallerstein & Kelly, 1974, 1976). Children may likewise feel a need to choose a side when interparental conflict makes them feel caught between parents (Afifi & Schrodt, 2003; Maccoby, Buchanan, Mnookin, & Dornbusch, 1993; Wallerstein & Kelly, 1974).

Focusing specifically on parents, these findings suggest that clinicians can take a few concrete steps in the case of contact refusal. First, in line with Kelly and Johnston's (2001) work, parents experiencing contact refusal can take an account of themselves to see if their parenting behavior is in any way contributing to contact refusal. A lack of warmth and attention, for example, may lead to children not wanting to spend time with a parent. Helping parents to reduce conflict and make explicit statements showing support for the other parent is also likely to reduce children's loyalty conflicts and lessen any perceived need for contact refusal. Finally, parents may need support in being patient, as contact refusal may be spontaneous and may likewise resolve itself without intervention (Johnston & Goldman, 2010). Particularly in the case of adolescents, rejection may be a normative development process as they make sense of and react to the divorce.

Case Examples

To illustrate the principles shared in this chapter, we now present a few sample cases of therapy with divorcing couples. Each of these cases is a composition of cases seen by the authors and cases shared in the literature (Johnston & Campbell, 1988; Schwartz & Kaslow, 1997). A case of minor difficulty involved a couple who were referred for therapy by the court system. Their representative with the court reported that they were unable to come to agreements in mediation. The first few sessions bore this out. The wife presented as aloof and disengaged, while the husband was active and talkative, sharing numerous accusations about the wife's behaviors before and after the divorce. Notably, the husband considered himself less emotional about the divorce, though he also reported that his ideal resolution would be his wife calling off the divorce. The wife, meanwhile, reported sadness, but a determination to continue with the process. Given the couple were not prone to major conflict and there did not appear to be any safety concerns, conjoint sessions were used throughout the course of treatment. This was seen as minimizing the risk of triangulation and was useful in keeping the focus on them being able to co-parent their children.

Over the course of the first few sessions, the question of "leaver" and "left" became a central feature, with the wife having been the initiator of the divorce after privately considering it for years. Thus, as was discussed in a session, the husband was left in an emotionally difficult position, trying to manage the blow to his ego and the grief of losing a relationship that he thought was going well. It became clear that the husband's intrapsychic concerns were soothed by blaming his wife and hiding his emotions.

It may have been valuable, given the focus on the husband's personal emotional experience, to have met individually with him or to refer him to an individual therapist. In this case however, making the insight was sufficient to create change. At the beginning of the session following a discussion of his intrapsychic difficulties, the husband reported that he recognized that he had not accepted the divorce previously, but had done so now and was ready for mediation. As he backed away from his accusations, the wife reengaged, and they were able to process the sadness of losing the marriage while still moving forward with the divorce as the preferred option. The few remaining sessions focused on practical elements of the divorce, which were then formalized with a court mediator. The course of treatment presents a clear example of the ways that underlying issues and systemic effects contribute to difficulties. A lone focus on conflict resolution skills or negotiating practical matters would not have been adequate to help the couple and their children.

In a more difficult case, a couple were referred for therapy having spent several years in and out of the court system, it being their only means of finding resolution to most disagreements. Their representative at the court presented himself as strongly sided with the mother, seeing the father as negligent and borderline abusive, both to the mother and to the children. In therapy, they presented as strongly cutoff, with simple answers to questions about their history and feelings leading to shouting disagreements between the two of them in the therapy office. The wife presented herself as just trying to take care of herself and her children. She explicitly reported that she had no trust for her former husband and that she felt threatened by even being in his presence, let alone talking with him (though there was no indication that violence had occurred in the past). The husband cast himself as a victim of parental alienation, reporting that his wife constantly lies and invents new accusations to destroy him personally and his relationship with his children. The children were doing poorly in most domains of their lives. They struggled in school and exhibited a variety of symptoms of emotional distress including disrupted sleep, depressed mood/irritability, and some refusal to connect with their father.

This couple presents multiple levels of difficulty. Given the conjoint therapist's role and efforts to maintain an alliance with both parties, it was difficult to get enough vulnerability to explicitly address intrapsychic concerns. While this could potentially be resolved by meeting individually with the partners, the risk of triangulation and the limited number of sessions required by the court led the therapist to rely on conjoint sessions, focused on improving their interpersonal process. If circumstances allowed, it would be ideal to have each client in individual therapy with coordination between different therapists (including a therapist for the children). In this case, the mother already had a personal therapist and refused to have the conjoint therapist talk to him. It would later come out that she was coordinating her responses to her former husband and the conjoint therapist with her personal therapist, significantly undermining the conjoint work. Thus, she was largely unresponsive to treatment suggestions or interventions from conjoint therapy. This illustrates one of the most significant problems in the case. Throughout the system, the mother had been reasonably successful at convincing others that her position was true, a significant risk without a systemic focus and coordination between professionals. Her position matched closely Johnston and Campbell's (1988) description of extreme denigration as an interactional problem interacting with an external system. Thus, the mother felt repeatedly validated by professionals and saw little reason to compromise with her former husband. Although the father was not completely innocent of the accusations made against him, the negative attribution did not fit his current behaviors and no actual abuse was evident. Unfortunately, the defensiveness that he had developed through the process left him distrustful of helping professionals and unwilling to meet with an individual therapist.

Treatment for this family introduces an important concept related to goals and foci in therapy. While it would be desirable to help every couple work through their issues to the point that they can cooperate and negotiate effectively, what Ahrons (1994) might call "perfect pals" or "cooperative colleagues," this is often outside the realm of the court's expectations or the available time in treatment. Instead, the first and sometimes ultimate goal is to help clients manage their conflict to the point that it is not negatively affecting their children. Using Ahrons' typology, this may mean going from "fiery foes" to "angry associates." In this family's case, the major efforts were to reduce the triangulation in the external systems and to improve their interactional patterns to facilitate better coordination. Detriangulation was managed by talking about concerns with both the clients and the parties that were available to be talked with. This may take the form of systemic reframes, focusing on how everyone shares some responsibility in making things better.

Further, a process of challenging hostile attributions was implemented. Throughout the sessions, a "hub-and-spoke" approach, where the clients typically spoke only to the therapist, not each other, was used to manage the emotion in the room. Only near the end of the treatment were limited enactments used to practice direct communication. Two major efforts in therapy included looking for and creating exceptions to the narrative and developing safe, controlled communication systems. In looking for and creating exceptions, the clients were challenged to name ways that their former spouse could relate to them that would not indicate malice. This may be as small as saying "Hello" at a child's sports event, which became a task for the next session. Although seemingly insignificant, repeated and amplifying efforts have the ability to change dominant stories and reverse hostile attributions. In this case, the couple was initially dismissive of how important it was, but their success at minor tasks gave the therapist a chance to challenge the negative assumptions made and help them continue on to having an actual conversation about pickup arrangements for their next visitation exchange while not in therapy.

Developing controlled communication plans can take a variety of forms. For this couple, the speaker–listener technique was employed as a way to help them manage their conflict and hostile attributions. Having to check their assumptions and do the work to actually understand the other person was instrumental in easing their interactions. Although they were again initially dismissive of the process, given how cumbersome it is, upon reflection they also noted that they were able to coordinate a weekly schedule better than they have ever done before. Ultimately, this couple was semi-successful in achieving the baseline goal of improving their ability to coordinate and compromise without court involvement. They completed their required amount of sessions and were not interested in further treatment.

Conclusion

Overall, we hope the models, information, and recommendations shared within this chapter are useful to therapists and other professionals working with divorcing couples. Though it should be noted that many couples are able to successfully navigate the divorce transition without intervention (Ahrons, 1994; Whiteside, 1998), the potential for negative outcomes to adults, children, and communities should encourage therapists and other stakeholders to better consider ways to support those couples that are struggling to successfully transition out of marriage. Effective intervention can go a long way to minimize the harm to all parties. By way of reference and summary, Table 13.1 provides an overview of many of the principles and techniques shared in this chapter. This chapter provides some direction, but continued research into the effectiveness of techniques and approaches as well as the general systemic processes in divorce will be critical to improving outcomes for all involved.

In reviewing the literature and recommendations, two major themes stand out that deserve special consideration. The first is that therapists and any other professionals involved in work with divorcing couples must have a strong appreciation for the complexity of such cases. These cases often include individuals in significant emotional

Table 13.1 Key principles and strategies when working with divorcing couples.

Key principles and goals	*Key strategies and interventions*
Successful personal divorce transition	Re-storying/meaning making exercises
	Identify and build personal resources
	Processing and expressing grief/sadness
Improve interpersonal relationship	Systemic reframes
	Education on circular causation
	Communication skills training/speaker–listener technique
	Enactments
	Promote support of one another
Reduce conflict	Develop effective boundaries, especially when safety is a concern
	"Hub-and-spoke" therapy to manage conflict
	Enactments to encourage relationship change
Avoiding triangulation	Multipartial alliances
	Detriangulation
	Involve friends and families that contribute to problems
	Education on effects of loyalty conflict on children
	Supervision or consultation for oneself
	Consultation with other involved parties

distress trying to work through difficult decisions with the person who may be responsible for that emotional distress. Numerous systemic and ecological processes are occurring simultaneously; simplistic or linear explanations for behaviors are likely to result in contributing to ongoing difficulties.

The second theme is that the treatment literature is generally lacking empirical support. Compared to divorce in general and the mediation process, therapy with divorcing couples has remarkably little research backing the recommended interventions. This may be related to the complexity of the cases and the general difficulty of recruiting participants who may be suspicious or tired of involvement in divorce systems. The majority of the literature relies on non-systematic clinical impressions. In the best cases, the literature uses theory to guide interventions, but this is not always the case, either. Ultimately, the field and treatment of families will be strongly benefited by a greater emphasis on finding ways to effectively recruit this population and empirically validating treatment recommendations for divorcing couples.

References

Adamsons, K., & Johnson, S. K. (2013). An updated and expanded meta-analysis of nonresident fathering and child well-being. *Journal of Family Psychology*, 27, 589–599. doi:10.1037/a0033786

Afifi, T. S., & Schrodt, P. (2003). "Feeling caught" as a mediator of adolescents' and young adults' avoidance and satisfaction with their parents in divorced and non-divorced households. *Communication Monographs*,70(2),142–173.doi:10.1080/0363775032000133791

Ahrons, C. R. (1994). *The good divorce* (pp. 56). New York, NY: Harper Collins.

Ahrons, C. R. (1998). *The good divorce: Keeping your family together when your marriage comes apart* (2nd ed.). New York, NY: Harper Collins.

Allan, K. R. (2016). The use of emotionally focused therapy with separated or divorced couples. *Canadian Journal of Counselling & Psychotherapy/Revue Canadienne de Counseling et de Psychothérapie*, 50, S62–S79.

Allen, K. R. (2007). Ambiguous loss after lesbian couples with children break up: A case for same-gender divorce. *Family Relations*, 56, 175–183. doi:10.1111/j.1741-3729.2007.00450.x

Amato, P. R. (2010). Research on divorce: Continuing trends and new developments. *Journal of Marriage and Family*, 72, 650–666. doi:10.1111/j.1741-3737.2010.00723.x

Amato, P. R., & Anthony, C. J. (2014). Estimating the effects of parental divorce and death with fixed effects models. *Journal of Marriage and Family*, 76, 370–386. doi:10.1111/jomf.12100

Amato, P. R., & Patterson, S. E. (2017). The intergenerational transmission of union instability in early adulthood. *Journal of Marriage and Family*, 79, 723–738. doi:10.1111/jomf.12384

Amato, P. R., & Sobolewski, J. M. (2001). The effects of divorce and marital discord on adult children's psychological well-being. *American Sociological Review*, 66, 900–921.

American Association for Marriage and Family Therapy. (2015). *AAMFT code of ethics*. Retrieved from https://www.aamft.org/Legal_Ethics/Code_of_Ethics.aspx

Aponte, H. J., & Van Deusen, J. M. (1981). Structural family therapy. In A. S. Gurman & D. P. Kniskern (Eds.), *Handbook of family therapy* (pp. 310–360). New York, NY: Brunner/Mazel.

Arbuthnot, J., Poole, C. J., & Gordon, D. A. (1996). Use of educational materials to modify stressful behaviors in post-divorce parenting. *Journal of Divorce & Remarriage*, 25, 117–137. doi:10.1300/J087v25n01_08

Baker, A. J. L. (2006). The power of stories: Stories about power: Why therapists and clients should read stories about the parental alienation syndrome. *American Journal of Family Therapy*, 34(3), 191–203.

Bala, N., Hunt, S., & McCarney, C. (2010). Parental alienation: Canadian court cases 1989-2008. *Family Court Review*, 48, 164–179. doi:10.1111/j.1744-1617.2009.01296.x

Baum, N. (2003). The male way of mourning divorce: When, what, and how. *Clinical Social Work Journal*, 31, 37–50.

Baum, N. (2007). "Separation guilt" in women who initiate divorce. *Clinical Social Work Journal*, 35, 47–55.

Beck, A. T., & Freeman, A. (1990). *Cognitive therapy of personality disorders*. New York, NY: Guilford.

Bierman, A., Fazio, E. M., & Milkie, M. A. (2006). A multifaceted approach to the mental health advantage of the married: Assessing how explanations vary by outcome measure and unmarried group. *Journal of Family Issues*, 27, 554–582. doi:10.1177/0192513X05284111

Bigner, J. J. (2006). Disclosing gay or lesbian orientation within marriage: A systems perspective. In C. A. Everett, R. E. Lee, C. A. Everett, & R. E. Lee (Eds.), *When marriages fail: Systemic family therapy interventions and issues: A tribute to William C. Nichols* (pp. 85–100). New York, NY: Haworth Press.

Boszormenyi-Nagy, I. (1974). Ethical and practical implications of intergenerational family therapy. *Psychotherapy and Psychosomatics*, 24, 261–268.

Bowen, M. (1978). *Family therapy in clinical practice*. New York, NY: Jason Aronson.

Braver, S. L., Griffin, W. A., & Cookston, J. T. (2005). Prevention programs for divorced non-resident fathers. *Family Court Review*, 43, 81–96. doi:10.1111/j.1744-1617.2005.00009.x

Camplair, C. W., & Stolberg, A. L. (1990). Benefits of court-sponsored divorce mediation: A study of outcomes and influences on success. *Mediation Quarterly*, 7, 199–213. doi:10.1002/crq.3900070303

Carter, B., & McGoldrick, M. (1999). *The expanded family life cycle: Individual, family, and social perspectives* (3rd ed.). Needham Heights, MA: Allyn & Bacon.

Cohen, O. (1998). Parental narcissism and the disengagement of the non-custodial father after divorce. *Clinical Social Work Journal*, 26, 195–215.

Cookston, J. T., Braver, S. L., Griffin, W. A., De Lusé, S. R., & Miles, J. C. (2007). Effects of the dads for life intervention on interparental conflict and coparenting in the two years after divorce. *Family Process*, 46, 123–137.

Crossno, M. A. (2011). Bowen family systems theory. In L. Metcalf (Ed.), *Marriage and family therapy: A practice-oriented approach* (pp. 39–64). New York, NY: Springer.

Cui, M., Fincham, F. D., & Durtschi, J. A. (2010). The effect of parental divorce on young adults' romantic relationship dissolution: What makes a difference? *Personal Relationships*, 18, 410–426. doi:10.1111/j.1475-6811.2010.01306.x

De Castro, B. O., Veerman, J. W., Koops, W., Bosch, J. D., & Monshouwer, H. J. (2002). Hostile attribution of intent and aggressive behavior: A meta-analysis. *Child Development*, 73(3), 916–934.

de Shazer, S., Dolan, Y., Korman, H., Trepper, T., McCollum, E., & Berg, I. K. (2012). *More than miracles: The state of the art of solution-focused brief therapy* (2nd ed.). New York, NY: Taylor & Francis.

Diamond, R. M., & Parker, M. L. (2018). Development of the divorce initiation inventory. *Contemporary Family Therapy*. Advance online publication. doi:10.1007/s10591-018-9463-0

Drapeau, S., Gagné, M. H., Saint-Jacques, M. C., Lépine, R., & Ivers, H. (2009). Post-separation conflict trajectories: A longitudinal study. *Marriage & Family Review*, 45(4), 353–373.

Emery, R. E. (2004). *Renegotiating family relationships: Divorce, child custody, and mediation*. New York, NY: Guildford Press.

Emery, R. E. (2012). *Renegotiating family relationships: Divorce, child custody, and mediation.* New York, NY: Guilford Press.

Emery, R. E., & Forehand, R. (1994). Parental divorce and children's well-being: A focus on resilience. In R. J. Haggerty, L. R. Sherrod, N. Garmezy, & M. Rutter (Eds.), *Stress, risk, and resilience in children and adolescents: Processes, mechanisms, and interventions* (pp. 65–99). New York, NY: Cambridge University Press.

Emery, R. E., Laumann-Billings, L., Waldron, M. C., Sbarra, D. A., & Dillon, P. (2001). Child custody mediation and litigation: Custody, contact, and coparenting 12 years after initial dispute resolution. *Journal of Consulting and Clinical Psychology,* 69(2), 323–332. doi:10.1037//0022-006X.69.2.323

Emery, R. E., Matthews, S. G., & Kitzmann, K. M. (1994). Child custody mediation and litigation: Parents' satisfaction and functioning one year after settlement. *Journal of Consulting and Clinical Psychology,* 62(1), 124–129. doi:10.1037/0022-006X.62.1.124

Emery, R. E., Matthews, S. G., & Wyer, M. M. (1991). Child custody mediation and litigation: Further evidence on the differing views of mothers and fathers. *Journal of Consulting and Clinical Psychology,* 59, 410–418.

Emery, R. E., Sbarra, D., & Grover, T. (2005). Divorce mediation: Research and reflections. *Family Court Review,* 43, 22–37. doi:10.1111/j.1744-1617.2005.00005.x

Fackrell, T. A., Hawkins, A. J., & Kay, N. M. (2011). How effective are court-affiliated divorcing parents education programs? A meta-analytic study. *Family Court Review,* 49, 107–119.

Feinberg, M. E. (2003). The internal structure and ecological context of coparenting: A framework for research and intervention. *Parenting Science and Practice,* 3, 95–131. doi:10.1207/S15327922PAR0302_01

Feng, P., & Fine, M. A. (2001). Evaluation of a research-based parenting education program for divorcing parents. *Journal of Divorce & Remarriage,* 34, 1–23. doi:10.1300/J087v34n01_01

Fidler, B. J., & Bala, N. (2010). Children resisting postseparation contact with a parent: Concepts, controversies, and conundrums. *Family Court Review,* 48, 10–47. doi:10.1111/j.1744-1617.2009.01287.x

Fineman, M. A. (1988). Dominant discourse professional language and legal change. *Harvard Law Review,* 101, 727–774.

Forehand, R., Neighbors, B., Devine, D., & Armistead, L. (1994). Interparental conflict and parental divorce: The individual, relative, and interactive effects on adolescents across four years. *Family Relations,* 387–393.

Friedman, G. J. (1993). *A guide to divorce mediation: How to reach a fair, legal settlement at a fraction of the cost.* New York, NY: Workman Publishing.

Frieman, B., Garon, H., & Garon, R. J. (2000). Parenting seminars for divorcing parents. *Journal of Divorce & Remarriage,* 33(3–4), 129–143. doi:10.1300/J087v33n03_08

Frisco, M. L., Muller, C., & Frank, K. (2007). Parents' union dissolution and adolescents' school performance: Comparing methodological approaches. *Journal of Marriage and Family,* 69, 721–741. doi:10.1111/j.1741-3737.2007.00402x

Froiland, D. J., & Hozeman, T. L. (1977). Counseling for constructive divorce. *Personnel and Guidance Journal,* 55, 525–529.

Gardner, R. A. (1991). Legal and psychotherapeutic approaches to the three types of parental alienation syndrome families: When psychiatry and the law join forces. *Court Review,* 28(1), 14–21.

Gardner, R. A. (1999). Differentiating between parental alienation syndrome and bona fide abuse-neglect. *The American Journal of Family Therapy,* 27(2), 97–107.

Gardner, R. A. (2002). Denial of the parental alienation syndrome also harms women. *The American Journal of Family Therapy,* 30(3), 191–202.

Goforth, A. N., Pham, A. V., & Carlson, J. S. (2011). Diathesis-stress model. In S. Goldstein & J. A. Naglieri (Eds.), *Encyclopedia of child behavior and development* (pp. 502–503). Boston, MA: Springer.

Grych, J. H. (2005). Interparental conflict as a risk factor for child maladjustment: Implications for the development of prevention programs. *Family Court Review*, 43, 97–108.

Gürmen, M. S., Huff, S. C., Brown, E., Orbuch, T. L., & Birditt, K. S. (2017). Divorced yet still together: Ongoing personal relationship and coparenting among divorced parents. *Journal of Divorce & Remarriage*, 58(8), 645–660.

Haber, J. (1990). A family systems model for divorce and the loss of self. *Archives of Psychiatric Nursing*, 4(4), 228–234.

Hetherington, E. M., & Kelly, J. (2002). *For better or for worse: Divorce reconsidered*. New York, NY: Norton & Company.

Hill, R. (1949). *Families under stress: Adjustment to the crises of war separation and reunion*. New York, NY: Harper & Brothers.

Hopper, J. (2001). The symbolic origins of conflict in divorce. *Journal of Marriage and Family*, 63, 430–445.

Huff, S. C., Anderson, S. R., Adamsons, K. L., & Tambling, R. B. (2017). Development and validation of a scale to measure children's contact refusal of parents following divorce. *The American Journal of Family Therapy*, 45, 66–77. doi:10.1080/01926187.2016.1275066

Huff, S. C., & Hartenstein, J. L. (2020). Helping children in divorced and single parent families. In K. S. Wampler & L. M. McWay (Eds.), *The handbook of systemic family therapy: Systemic family therapy with children and adolescents (2)*. Hoboken, NJ: Wiley.

Hughes, M. H., & Waite, L. J. (2009). Marital biography and health at mid-life. *Journal of Health and Social Behavior*, 50, 344–358.

Ivanova, K., Mills, M., & Veenstra, R. (2014). Parental residential and partnering transitions and the initiation of adolescent romantic relationships. *Journal of Marriage and Family*, 76, 465–475. doi:10.1111/jomf.12117

Johnson, S. M. (2004). *The practice of emotionally focused couple therapy: Creating connection*. New York, NY: Brunner-Routledge.

Johnston, J. R., & Campbell, L. E. G. (1988). *Impasses of divorce: The dynamics and resolution of family conflict*. New York, NY: Free Press.

Johnston, J. R., & Goldman, J. R. (2010). Outcomes of family counseling interventions with children who resist visitation: An addendum to Friedlander and Walters (2010). *Family Court Review*, 48, 112–115. doi:10.1111/j.1744-1617.2009.01292.x

Johnston, J. R., Walters, M. G., & Olesen, N. W. (2005). The psychological functioning of alienated children in custody disputing families: An exploratory study. *American Journal of Forensic Psychology*, 23(3), 39–64.

Kelly, J. B. (1991). Parent interaction after divorce: Comparison of mediated and adversarial divorce processes. *Behavioral Sciences & the Law*, 9, 387–398.

Kelly, J. B. (2007). Children's living arrangement following separation and divorce: Insights from empirical and clinical research. *Family Process*, 46, 35–52.

Kelly, J. B., & Johnston, J. R. (2001). The alienated child: A reformulation of parental alienation syndrome. *Family Court Review*, 39(3), 249–266.

Kim, H. S. (2011). Consequences of parental divorce for child development. *American Sociological Review*, 76, 487–511. doi:10.1177/0003122411407748

Kramer, K. M., Arbuthnot, J., Gordon, D. A., Rousis, N. J., & Hoza, J. (1998). Effects of skill-based versus information-based divorce education programs on domestic violence and parental communication. *Family Court Review*, 36(1), 9–31.

Kreider, R. M., & Ellis, R. (2011a). *Living arrangements of children: 2009*. Current Population Reports, pp. 70–126. Washington, DC: US Census Bureau.

Kreider, R. M., & Ellis, R. (2011b). *Number, timing, and duration of marriages and divorces: 2009*. US Department of Commerce, Economics, and Statistics Administration. US Census Bureau.

Kübler-Ross, E. (1969). *On death and dying*. New York, NY: Macmillan Company.

Kurkowski, K. P., Gordon, D. A., & Arbuthnot, J. (1994). Children caught in the middle: A brief educational intervention for divorced parents. *Journal of Divorce & Remarriage*, 20, 139–151. doi:10.1300/J087v20n03_09

Lebow, J., & Rekart, K. N. (2007). Integrative family therapy for high-conflict divorce with disputes over child custody and visitation. *Family Process, 46*, 79–91.

Lloyd, H., & Dallos, R. (2006). Solution-focused brief therapy with families who have a child with intellectual disabilities: A description of the content of initial sessions and the processes. *Clinical Child Psychology and Psychiatry, 11*, 367–386.

Lorenz, F. O., Wickrama, K. A. S., Conger, R. D., & Elder, G. H. (2006). The short-term and decade-long effects of divorce on women's midlife health. *Journal of Health and Social Behavior, 47*, 111–125.

Maccoby, E. E., Buchanan, C. M., Mnookin, R. H., & Dornbusch, S. M. (1993). Postdivorce roles of mothers and fathers in the lives of their children. *Journal of Family Psychology, 7*(1), 24–38. doi:10.1037/0893-3200.7.1.24

Madden-Derdich, D. A., & Leonard, S. A. (2002). Shared experiences, unique realities: Formerly married mothers' and fathers' perceptions of parenting and custody after divorce. *Family Relations, 51*, 37–45. doi:10.1111/j.1741-3729.2002.00037.x

Margolin, G., Gordis, E. B., & John, R. S. (2001). Coparenting: A link between marital conflict and parenting in two-parent families. *Journal of Family Psychology, 15*, 3–21. doi:10.1037/0893-3200.15.1.3

McKnight, M. S., & Erickson, S. K. (2008). *Mediating divorce: A step-by-step manual.* San Francisco, CA: Jossey-Bass.

Minuchin, S. (1974). *Families and family therapy.* Cambridge, MA: Harvard University Press.

Moore, C. W. (2014). *The mediation process: Practical strategies for resolving conflict* (4th ed.). San Francisco, CA: Wiley.

Myers, J. E., & Perrin, N. (1993). Grandparents affected by parental divorce: A population at risk? *Journal of Counseling & Development, 72*, 62–66. doi:10.1002/j.1556-6676.1993.tb02278.x

National Center for Health Statistics. (2017). *National marriage and divorce rate trends.* Retrieved from https://www.cdc.gov/nchs/fastats/marriage-divorce.htm

Neff, R., & Cooper, K. (2004). Parental conflict resolution: Six-, twelve-, and fifteen-month follow-ups of a high-conflict program. *Family Court Review, 42*, 99–114. doi:10.1111/j.174-1617.2004.tb00636.x

Nichols, M. P., & Fellenberg, S. (2000). The effective use of enactments in family therapy: A discovery-oriented process study. *Journal of Marital and Family Therapy, 26*, 143–152.

Nielsen, L. (2017). Re-examining the research on parental conflict, coparenting, and custody arrangements. *Psychology, Public Policy, and Law, 23*, 211–231. doi:10.1037/law0000109

Pettit, E., & Bloom, B. (1984). Whose decision was it? The effects of initiator status on adjustment to marital disruption. *Journal of Marriage and the Family, 46*, 567–595. doi:10.2307/352600

Pietsch, U. K. (2002). Facilitating post-divorce transition using narrative therapy. *Journal of Couple & Relationship Therapy, 1*, 65–81. doi:10.1300/J398v01n01_05

Pollet, S. L., & Lombreglia, M. (2008). A nationwide survey of mandatory parent education. *Family Court Review, 46*, 375–394.

Ramisch, J. L., McVicker, M., & Sahin, Z. S. (2009). Helping low-conflict divorced parents establish appropriate boundaries using a variation of the miracle question: An integration of solution-focused therapy and structural family therapy. *Journal of Divorce & Remarriage, 50*, 481–495. doi:10.1080/10502550902970587

Rodgers, K. B., & Rose, H. A. (2002). Risk and resiliency factors among adolescents who experience marital transitions. *Journal of Marriage and Family, 64*, 1024–1037.

Sbarra, D. A., & Emery, R. E. (2005). The emotional sequelae of nonmarital relationship dissolution: Analysis of change and intraindividual variability over time. *Personal Relationships, 12*(2), 213–232.

Sbarra, D. A., & Emery, R. E. (2006). In the presence of grief: The role of cognitive-emotional adaptation in contemporary divorce mediation. In M. A. Fine & J. H. Harvey (Eds.),

Handbook of divorce and relationship dissolution (pp. 553–574). Mahwah, NJ: Lawrence Erlbaum.

Sbarra, D. A., & Emery, R. E. (2008). Deeper into divorce: Using actor-partner analyses to explore systemic differences in coparenting conflict following custody dispute resolution. *Journal of Family Psychology, 22*(1), 144–152. doi:10.1037/0893-3200.22.1.144

Sbarra, D. A., Hasselmo, K., & Bourassa, K. J. (2015). Divorce and health: Beyond individual differences. *Current Directions in Psychological Science, 24,* 109–113. doi:10.1177/0963721414559125

Sbarra, D. A., Law, R. W., Lee, L. A., & Mason, A. E. (2009). Marital dissolution and blood pressure reactivity: Evidence for the specificity of emotional intrusion-hyperarousal and task-related emotional difficulty. *Psychosomatic Medicine, 71,* 532–540.

Sbarra, D. A., Law, R. W., & Portley, R. M. (2011). Divorce and death: A meta-analysis and research agenda for clinical, social, and health psychology. *Perspectives on Psychological Science, 6,* 454–474.

Schwartz, L. L., & Kaslow, F. W. (1997). *Painful partings: Divorce and its aftermath.* Hoboken, NJ: Wiley.

Shifflett, K., & Cummings, E. M. (1999). A program for educating parents about the effects of divorce and conflict on children: An initial evaluation. *Family Relations, 48*(1), 79.

Shor, E., Roelfs, D. J., Bugyi, P., & Schwartz, J. E. (2012). Meta-analysis of marital dissolution and mortality: Reevaluating the intersection of gender and age. *Social Science & Medicine, 75,* 46–59.

Sigal, A., Sandler, I., Wolchik, S., & Braver, S. (2011). Do parent education programs promote healthy post-divorce parenting? Critical distinctions and a review of the evidence. *Family Court Review, 49,* 120–139. doi:10.1111/j.1744-1617.201

Smith-Acuña, S. (2011). *Systems theory in action: Applications to individual, couples, and family therapy.* Hoboken, NJ: Wiley.

Sprenkle, D. H., & Cyrus, C. L. (1983). Abandonment: The stress of sudden divorce. In C. R. Figley & H. I. McCubbin (Eds.), *Stress and the family: Coping with catastrophe* (Vol. II, pp. 53–89). New York, NY: Brunner/Mazel.

Sprenkle, D. H., & Gonzalez-Doupé, P. (1996). Divorce therapy. In F. P. Piercy, D. H. Sprenkle, & J. L. Wetchler (Eds.), *Family therapy sourcebook* (2nd ed., pp. 181–219). New York, NY: Guilford Press.

Steiner, L. M., Durand, S., Groves, D., & Rozzell, C. (2015). Effect of infidelity, initiator status, and spiritual well-being on men's divorce adjustment. *Journal of Divorce & Remarriage, 56*(2), 95–108. doi:10.1080/10502556.2014.996050.0.01357.x

Steiner, L. M., Suarez, E. C., Sells, J. N., & Wykes, S. D. (2011). Effect of age, initiator status, and infidelity on women's divorce adjustment. *Journal of Divorce & Remarriage, 52,* 33–47. doi:10.1080/10502556.2011.534394

Sweeney, M. M. (2002). Remarriage and the nature of divorce: Does it matter which spouse chose to leave? *Journal of Family Issues, 23,* 410–440. doi:10.1177/0192513X02023003005

Sweeney, M. M. (2010). Remarriage and stepfamilies: Strategic sites for family scholarship in the 21st century. *Journal of Marriage and Family, 72*(3), 667–684.

Toews, M. L., & McKenry, P. C. (2001). Court-related predictors of parental cooperation and conflict after divorce. *Journal of Divorce & Remarriage, 35*(1–2), 57–73.

Waite, L. J., Luo, Y., & Lewin, A. C. (2009). Marital happiness and marital stability: Consequences for psychological well-being. *Social Science Research, 38,* 201–212.

Wallerstein, J. S., & Kelly, J. B. (1974). The effects of parental divorce: The adolescent experience. In E. J. Anthony & C. Koupernik (Eds.), *The child in his family* (pp. 479–505). New York, NY: Wiley.

Wallerstein, J. S., & Kelly, J. B. (1976). The effects of parental divorce: Experiences of the child in later latency. *American Journal of Orthopsychiatry, 46,* 256–269. doi:10.1111/j.1939-0025.1976.tb00926.x

Weaver, J. M., & Schofield, T. J. (2015). Mediation and moderation of divorce effects on children's behavior problems. *Journal of Family Psychology*, 29, 39–48. doi:10.1037/fam0000043

Weisman, R. (1975). Crisis theory and the process of divorce. *Social Casework*, 56, 205–212.

White, M. (1995). *Re-authoring lives*. Adelaide, South Australia: Dulwich Centre Publications.

White, M., & Epstein, D. (1990). *Narrative means to therapeutic ends*. New York, NY: Norton & Company.

Whiteside, M. F. (1998). The parental alliance following divorce: An overview. *Journal of Marital and Family Therapy*, 24, 3–24. doi:10.1111/j.1752-0606.1998.tb01060.x

Wochik, S. A., Schenck, C. E., & Sandler, I. N. (2009). Promoting resilience in youth from divorced families: Lessons learned from experimental trials of the new beginnings program. *Journal of Personality*, 77, 1833–1868. doi:10.1111/j.1467-6494.2009.00602.x

Wolfinger, N. H. (2005). *Understanding the divorce cycle: The children of divorce in their own marriages*. New York, NY: Cambridge University Press.

Wozencraft, T. A., Tauzin, M., & Romero, L. (2019). The relationship between psychological functioning in a college sample and retrospective reports of parental loyalty conflicts and psychological maltreatment. *Journal of Divorce & Remarriage*, 60(2), 104–116.

14

Therapy with Remarried and Stepfamilies

Andrew S. Brimhall

"People who find themselves as members of stepfamilies often seem unprepared for what they experience and surprised at what they encounter" (Ganong & Coleman, 2017, p. 2).

Estimates suggest that one out of every two Americans will spend at least a portion of their lives in a stepfamily relationship (Ganong & Coleman, 2017; Papernow, 2015; Parker, 2011). Similar rates have been reported in countries like Canada and the United Kingdom (Wilson & Smallwood, 2008; Wu & Schimmele, 2005). While national statistics do not exist, some estimates suggest that Asian countries (where stepfamilies are often stigmatized) have also experienced increases (Cherlin, 2017). In China the percentage of all marriages that were classified a remarriage increased from 3% in 1985 to 10% in 2007 (Wang & Zhou, 2010). Despite these numbers, most, as the quote suggests, are unprepared for that experience and are surprised at the challenges they encounter. Andrew Cherlin (1978), in perhaps the most widely cited paper on stepfamilies, offered a potential explanation for the challenges faced by stepfamilies. According to him, stepfamilies lacked guidance, clearly defined roles, and social and institutional support, including proper language that described stepfamily relationships. Based on his insights, he coined the statement that remarriage was an "incomplete institution" (p. 636). Although decades of research have helped establish some "institutional norms" (Coleman & Ganong, 1990; Coleman, Ganong, & Fine, 2000; Sweeney, 2010), the fact that Cherlin's article is still heavily cited reflects the societal struggle many stepfamilies continue to face today.

Given this lack of clearly defined norms, many stepfamilies (and clinicians) often inappropriately apply norms and expectations that are developed for first-time families (Ganong & Coleman, 2017, 2018; Sweeney, 2010). Using these norms to navigate the inherently complicated terrain of stepfamily relationships is like trying to navigate a large bustling city using the map of a smaller rural city; some elements may be the same, but you will eventually end up lost (Papernow, 2018). Rather than improving interactions, these attempts often backfire and make situations worse, perhaps providing some explanation for why divorce rates for stepfamilies are often higher than first-time marriages (Ganong & Coleman, 2017; Teachman, 2008). With increased

The Handbook of Systemic Family Therapy: Volume 3, First Edition.
Edited by Karen S. Wampler and Adrian J. Blow.
© 2020 John Wiley & Sons Ltd. Published 2020 by John Wiley & Sons Ltd.

longevity, the likelihood that clinicians will find themselves working with individuals, couples, and families who have transitioned through several meaningful relationships is increasingly high, especially considering that stepfamilies are quickly becoming the most common family form (McGoldrick & Carter, 2015). Some estimates even suggest that there are now more multinuclear families (a term developed as a more positive alternative to stepfamilies) than nuclear families in the United States and other high-income countries (CDC, 2008; McGoldrick & Carter, 2015). This chapter will discuss the prevalence of stepfamilies, provide some theoretical adaptations clinicians may want to consider, and discuss specific characteristics that are unique to stepfamilies to provide a more detailed map that will aid clinicians when working with these individuals and families, thus reducing surprises they might encounter.

Prevalence and Definitions

A casual review of the stepfamily literature might inaccurately imply that stepfamilies are a relatively new phenomenon—a function of increased divorce rates in the mid- to late 1900s (Ganong & Coleman, 2017). However, historical reviews indicate that large numbers of stepfamilies have existed in every culture (Ihinger-Tallman & Pasley, 1987; Spanier & Furstenberg, 1987). In fact, there is evidence that current remarriage rates are about the same as remarriage rates in the eighteenth-century United States and Europe (Chandler, 1991; Ganong & Coleman, 2017; Noy, 1991). While stepfamilies have always existed, the research involving these families is relatively new. The first North American study on remarriage appeared in 1930 (Waller, 1930), and a 1979 review, published nearly 50 years later, only documented 11 studies (Ganong & Coleman, 2017). Over the next four decades, that number grew from eleven to thousands of publications from scholars in nearly two dozen countries (Ganong & Coleman, 2018).

One of the primary reasons for the explosion in professional interest in stepfamilies was an important demographic shift that occurred in the early 1970s. Until this point in history, the predominate precursor to remarriage was bereavement, not divorce (Ganong & Coleman, 2017; Strow & Strow, 2006). While remarriage after the loss of a spouse is difficult, in many ways, it did not produce the same challenges as remarriage post-divorce (Brimhall & Engblom-Deglmann, 2011; Brimhall, Wampler, & Kimball, 2008; Grinwald & Shabat, 1997; Marwit & Carusa, 1998). Rather than replacing deceased parents (*substitute parents*), stepparents now became *additional parents* (Browning & Artelt, 2012; Ganong & Coleman, 2017; Papernow, 2018). Remarriage post-bereavement allowed many stepfamilies to simply reconstitute the nuclear family, and as a result they often went unrecognized as stepfamilies.

This demographic shift was not isolated to the United States and occurred a few years later in several high-income countries (e.g., Canada, Australia, New Zealand). This shift, in many ways, has changed the landscape of stepfamilies and increased their complexity. It has led to more relationships, increased ambiguity, and additional terms. For example, attempts to develop language that adequately classifies just the stepparents' new role in this complex network of family relationships have resulted in terms such as social parent, acquired parent, added parent, nonparent, or half-parent (Ganong & Coleman, 2017), with some recommending that scholars adopt the term binuclear families to represent post-divorce families as two distinct families who share the child as a common nucleus (Ahrons, 1980). This term has been expanded to include multinuclear families since stepfamilies may include the interweaving of three or more families (McGoldrick & Carter, 2015).

Stepfamily terminology defined

How people and relationships are defined is important because as Ganong and Coleman (2017) write, "the use of language can serve to legitimize certain family forms and place others on the fringe of acceptability ... language helps to shape thinking" (p. 27). Despite some of the negative connotations associated with the term stepfamilies and each of its relational derivatives (stepfather, stepmother, and stepchild), it remains the most commonly used among both behavioral and social scientists (Ganong & Coleman, 2018; Papernow, 2018; Widmer, Romney, & Boyd, 1999). Concerns regarding the term blended families have been raised because, like the idea of a melting pot, it puts undue pressure on families to blend in a way that does not acknowledge the potential diversity of each system—a major critique of the clinical literature involving stepfamilies (Ganong & Coleman, 2017; Papernow, 2018). Also, using blended is awkward and inappropriate when referring to specific relationships (i.e., blended father/mother/child).

Many scholars decided to use the term stepfamily instead of remarriage because stepfamilies are the fastest-growing family form in the United States (Browning & Artelt, 2012) and many of them are formed through cohabitation, not marriage. Those who use remarriage typically use it to distinguish between the couple relationship (remarriage) and the family relationship (stepfamily). While this may place added emphasis on the couple relationship (a relationship that is often overlooked in stepfamily literature), using the term remarriage has the potential of excluding large portions of the population who have not married—a trend that is increasingly common (Browning & Artelt, 2012; Ganong & Coleman, 2018; Papernow, 2018), especially in other high-income countries like Europe, New Zealand, and Australia where the stigma associated with cohabitation is lower (Cherlin, 2017). Therefore, despite its negative associations, the term stepfamily will be used in most instances throughout this chapter.

Stepfamily is typically defined as a family where at least one of the adults within the relationship has a child (or children) from a previous relationship (Cherlin, 2017; Ganong & Coleman, 2018). A stepparent, therefore, is an adult whose romantic partner has a child from a previous relationship, and a stepchild is a child whose parent is partnered with an adult who is not a formal parent either biologically or through adoption (Ganong & Coleman, 2017). As for siblings, children in stepfamilies may have siblings where they share both parents biologically, one parent (typically referred to as half-sibling), or no parents (stepsiblings). Within stepfamilies, family membership and relationships exist even when members do not share a family residence (Ganong & Coleman, 2018) or institutional recognition (i.e., marriage).

Demographic trends

Irrespective of the terms used, demographic trends suggest that (a) men enter stepfamilies more often (and faster) than women, especially if children are involved; (b) religious people tend to marry and remarry more often than nonreligious individuals; (c) older adults enter stepfamilies more often than younger adults and when they do, they typically follow more traditional paths (i.e., marriage); and (d) stepfamilies exist, whether through remarriage or cohabitation, in some form in every country in the world (De Jong Gierveld & Merz, 2013; Ganong & Coleman, 2018). Even in countries where the divorce rate is traditionally low (i.e., Asian countries), remarriage and stepfamilies are on the rise (Kim, 2010; Nozawa, 2015).

Theoretical Adaptations

Despite the growing number of stepfamilies (and other nontraditional families) worldwide, most fundamental theories unique to family therapy were created during a time when the field was trying desperately to establish the importance of viewing individuals and families systemically. Theories were developed for a generic family, and any attempts to create specialized rules to account for different types of families (e.g., stepfamilies, single-parent families, adoptive families) may have diluted the message and undermined progress (Browning & Artelt, 2012). As a result, these theories relied on generalities that were heavily influenced by biases surrounding traditional first-time families and their interactions. Historically, graduate training programs have continued to teach these fundamental theories and very few have curricula designed to help clinicians navigate stepfamilies' unique family structures and the complexities involved in forming and maintaining them (Papernow, 2015, 2018).

This generic application and the lack of training and familiarity with stepfamilies often result in clinicians relying on the same techniques and assumptions they use with first-time families. Not only is this approach ineffective, but it can be destructive (Papernow, 2015; Visher & Visher, 1996). In many cases, our training programs are guilty of distributing inaccurate maps to emerging professionals. While it is beyond the scope of this chapter to provide an adaptation for every theory, specific theories that might be commonly used with stepfamilies will be discussed and important adaptations provided, thus enhancing clinical work with stepfamilies. These include (a) developmental life cycle, (b) structural, and (c) attachment.

Developmental life cycle

From a developmental life cycle perspective, all human behavior should be understood as an individual and family evolve through the family life cycle matrix, paying particular attention to the sociocultural contexts that influence the family's development (McGoldrick, Carter, & Garcia-Preto, 2015). It is through these lenses, and relationships, that individual identity is formed and development occurs. From this model, stress is often greatest during transitional periods because the family is often forced to redefine roles and relationships as they seek to rebalance the family system (McGoldrick et al., 2015). More importantly, many developmental theorists believe that if developmental tasks and emotional issues are not properly addressed during the appropriate stage, these issues will be carried forward and hinder people from transitioning effectively to future relationships and tasks. Stepfamilies face a specific challenge because not only are they trying to accomplish the typical tasks associated with traditional family development but they are also negotiating divorce and forming a stepfamily, tasks that both represent significant detours that place the family on an entirely new trajectory. For this reason, both divorce and forming a stepfamily have both been identified as additional phases to the preexisting family life cycle (McGoldrick & Carter, 2015). These additional phases, and the incongruent timing of everyone's development, can often lead to significant stress. Some even suggest that forming a stepfamily may be one of the most difficult developmental transitions a family must learn to negotiate (McGoldrick & Carter, 2015).

Theoretical adaptations   The fact that the parent–child bond predates the couple relationship is simply one example of how the individual, marital, and family life cycles for stepfamilies are often incongruent (Ganong & Coleman, 2017). Research indicates that romantic partners often report larger age discrepancies in stepfamilies versus first-time families. From a life course perspective, events that occur outside the expected norm create more stress (Bengtson & Allen, 2009). Stepfamilies experience many off-time events, including the marriage itself that may have less support (first-time weddings may receive more support than subsequent marriages). Given that younger people are delaying marriage, individuals tend to be older when they are eligible for remarriage. This is noteworthy because estimates suggest that US women reproduce at similar rates whether they are in a stepfamily or a first-time family (Li, 2006), although this is less likely for stepfamilies where both partners bring children from a previous relationship (Stewart, 2002).

Stepfamilies often receive a strong message from society to do everything possible to function like a nuclear family; in fact many well-intentioned clinicians and self-help authors encouraged stepfamilies to have a child together, asserting that having a shared child would cement family bonds. This led some scholars to facetiously adopt the term concrete babies (Ganong & Coleman, 2017). While this decision may increase family unity in some cases, having a baby in later life is another example of incongruent family development. A stepfamily may experience multiple life course challenges simultaneously. An adolescent may be trying to separate from the family (a normal developmental task) at the same time as the stepfamily is pushing for cohesion to form their new identity, a process that is magnified by having a new child. Older adults may be preparing for retirement while attending little league games. Coupled with other tenets, these additional "out-of-the-norm" developmental stressors add additional strain to the system.

Another challenge is the stress stepfamilies often experience around forming rituals and routines. From a developmental perspective, a vital aspect of forming strong individual and family identities is rituals and routines (Doherty, 1999; Ganong & Coleman, 2017; Pasley & Dollahite, 1995). Given the lack of shared history, stepfamilies are initially void of this identity and often lack the relational glue to keep them together during times of distress (Sherman, Webster, & Antonucci, 2013). In many instances, stepfamilies are often going through these developmental stressors without the relational resources necessary to weather them. One reason living arrangements are so important is the role they play in determining the level of identity formed. More opportunities for shared history are created when people live together versus sporadic visits a few times a year. Researchers find that expectations around stepparent involvement vary greatly depending on whether stepparents are in contact with the stepchild daily, rarely, or never (Ganong & Coleman, 2017).

While forming new identities is vital, stepfamilies need to be sensitive to preexisting identities that were formed through previous family interactions. If they are not

careful, they may unintentionally (or in some cases intentionally) place greater emphasis on forming their new family identity and neglect past identities. And yet, family
systems theory and developmental theorists suggest that when encountering stress
and change families maintain homeostasis by reverting to past identities and rituals to
get through difficult transitions (Pasley & Dollahite, 1995). This creates conflict as
some members of stepfamilies work to form new identities while other members of
the family may try to maintain equilibrium by clinging to the past. Therapists who are
conscientious of developmental and life cycle changes, and the stress they often place
on stepfamily relationships, may consider borrowing from Berry's (2005) acculturation model to help alleviate the stress associated when integrating two cultures, which
will be discussed next.

Developmentally informed clinical recommendations   Berry's (2005) acculturation
model talks about the interaction that occurs when two cultures collide. He describes
four strategies used by the dominant culture. They include multiculturalism, melting
pot, segregation, and exclusion. The strategy employed by the dominant culture will
typically influence which strategy the minority culture uses, which are integration,
assimilation, separation, or marginalization. Ideally the dominant culture adopts a
stance that values the minority culture (multiculturalism), thus creating space for the
minority culture to adopt some elements of the dominant culture while maintaining
important aspects of their own (integration). More often, the dominant culture
expects the minority group to adopt the dominant culture (melting pot) and creates
an environment where the minority culture must fully embrace the dominant culture
and forget their own (assimilation). The term "blended family" is an example of this
pressure for families to assimilate.

   In other cases, the dominant group may actively seek segregation or exclusion,
which often results in the minority group separating from the dominant culture, and
reinforcing their own (separation), or disowning both their own culture and the culture of the dominant group (marginalization). Researchers have found that multicultural strategies typically result in the best overall health for minority cultures (Berry,
Phinney, Sam, & Vedder, 2006).

   Clinicians face a difficult task as they help stepfamilies explore the importance of
integrating both "cultures" (Berry, 2005). Clinicians need to facilitate conversations
around the importance of past experiences and the meaning attached to them, thus
helping family members understand that these experiences are a part of their identity
and not simply an attempt to ostracize. Given their central role in forming identities,
rituals are routines that often connect people to their past. While these preexisting
rituals may be helpful for some members of the family (e.g., children, nonresidential
parent), it may be more difficult for others (e.g., residential parent and stepparents).
While the children (and other extended family members) may be longing for connection to the past, the residential parent and stepparent may be wanting to distance
themselves from the past and strive to form their own identity through new rituals and
routines. Well-intentioned stepfamilies may be surprised that attempts to establish
these new identities may be met with resistance and anger; they often do not realize
that creating new rituals can also represent loss for some family members since it might
mean leaving the past behind (Pasley & Dollahite, 1995). The task is to appropriately
balance the competing needs of developing a new identity while simultaneously

maintaining aspects of the old or at least providing opportunities to grieve and process the losses of the past (Pasley & Dollahite, 1995). By so doing, they may help members of the stepfamily not feel isolated and alone—a common feeling described by stepparents, nonresidential parents, and other extended kin (Browning & Artelt, 2012).

Clinicians should also help stepfamilies understand that the developmental transitions associated with stepfamily formation take time. They should be reminded that this process is not a matter of months but often requires 3–5 years (Browning & Artelt, 2012; Ganong & Coleman, 2017; Papernow, 2013, 2015). Likewise, clinicians should help reinforce the message that integration may not be possible in all situations. Like minority cultures who have been repeatedly oppressed, individuals who have grown up in environments where they were marginalized or given messages that their identity was not valued may be less likely to engage in a process of integration. The pain underlying these experiences typically needs to be processed therapeutically before these individuals may be willing to consider the possibility of integration. Although integration is often the ideal, Papernow (2018) strongly recommends that stepfamilies hear the message that civility, rather than love, should be the initial expectation for new stepfamily relationships.

While not an exhaustive list, this section describes some of the individual, relational, and family life cycle challenges stepfamilies face. Clinicians and family life scholars should help stepfamilies understand the developmental tasks of each life cycle and the potential stressors that come with on-time versus off-time events. Specific attention should be given to the pressure these families experience as they maintain important elements from past relationships while forming new identities. Given the integral role of multiple generations in the family life cycle, negotiating these conversations may require expanding the clinical focus to include nonresidential parents, extended kin, and others that are active in maintaining these identities (McGoldrick & Carter, 2015).

Structural therapy

The hallmark of structural family therapy is the hierarchy and boundaries that exist between subsystems within the family (Minuchin, 1974). From the structural perspective, a family can adapt better to its external environment (the overarching goal of structural therapy) when the family as a whole (a subsystem of the external environment) is able to benefit from the resources available in each of its own subsystems. Families with a complex web of subsystems working together should find itself well prepared to interact with its external environment (Minuchin, Lee, & Simon, 2006). Families where boundaries are either too rigid (some family members are not able to access necessary resources) or too diffuse (a lack of boundaries makes it impossible to differentiate too subsystems) find themselves deprived of the resources necessary to effectively adapt. Within the nuclear family, the parental subsystem is typically seen as the executive subsystem, and parents are encouraged to develop a hierarchal structure that helps situate the parental subsystem at the center of the family interaction (Minuchin et al., 2006). While this hierarchal structure may be beneficial for first-time nuclear families, it may cause significant problems for stepfamilies, where there may be estranged biological parents and stepparents who may not be liked or respected by their new stepchildren.

Theoretical adaptations Like nuclear families, clinicians often identify a strong couple bond as a primary requisite of successful stepfamilies (Ganong & Coleman, 2017). Unlike nuclear families, the couple relationship is not the relationship with the longest history, and as a result they are often trying to form their bond while simultaneously trying to develop relationships with new stepchildren and extended kin and maintain existing ties with children and former partners. This can be challenging especially when third parties (i.e., children, former partners) may actively be trying to dissolve the relationship.

All families, to some degree, face the challenge of maintaining the couple bond in the presence of active parenting. However, this tension is acutely present for stepfamilies where children can actively challenge the legitimacy of one parent (Ganong & Coleman, 2017). Researchers indicate that two-thirds (66%) of stepchildren believe they should be the top priority when conflict exists (Moore & Cartwright, 2005). Stepparents, often based on norms from first-time families, disagree and feel the couple relationship should take priority (Browning & Artelt, 2012; Papernow, 2018). Attachment researchers suggests that individuals are wired to expect that intimate others will not turn their backs on them, especially in their moments of need (Porges, 2011). However, since the parent–child bond is typically stronger than the couple bond, and it has a longer history, parents repeatedly turn their backs on their partners (Papernow, 2018). For partners who expect their partner to "put them first," this can often challenge the supremacy of the couple relationship. Rather than establishing only one hierarchal (or executive) subsystem, stepfamilies should be encouraged to consider two, the couple relationship and the biological parent–child relationship. Acknowledging the central importance of both subsystems may help reduce potential conflicts and decrease competition.

A recent client from a complex stepfamily expressed his dissatisfaction with his wife because, according to their ecclesiastical leader, the marriage should take first priority (a uniformed message based on first-time family biases). As a result, he wanted their bedroom to be their sanctuary. He was repeatedly distressed when he entered their bedroom and saw his wife cuddling her son; to him, she was choosing her son over him and could not understand why she continued to ignore his request. From her perspective, she was simply being an attuned parent who was emotionally responding to her child's need. Ironically, the wife reported a lot of frustration with her husband when he would not spend time with her but instead take his biological children out to lunch during their visitations. According to him, he had such limited time with his children that he wanted to take advantage of that time when it was available. Despite both feeling on the outside in one situation and misunderstood in the other, they failed to realize that they were both experiencing different sides of the same struggle. When they were the outsider, they wanted to establish boundaries around the couple subsystem and make it the priority. When they were in the parent role, they keenly felt the central importance of the parent–child relationship. Clinicians should normalize this struggle and help clients realize that both relationships are critical to successful stepfamilies and an attempt to prioritize one over the other often leads to unnecessary power struggles (Browning & Artelt, 2012; Ganong & Coleman, 2017; Papernow, 2018). Stepfamilies should be strongly encouraged to invest in each subsystem, specifically devoting alone time to the couple and parent–child relationship.

Cultural norms and societal messages create another pattern that can be hard for stepfamilies as they learn to interact with their external environment. Forming a successful stepfamily may require restructuring traditional gender roles (McGoldrick & Carter, 2015), especially for stepmother households. Traditionally, societal messages have placed the woman at the center of the physical and emotional relationships in the home. Russo (1976) introduced the motherhood mandate—a mandate that dictates to women that motherhood is instinctual, that it completes them in a way no other experience can, and that children need them for optimal development (Ganong & Coleman, 2017). The motherhood mandate and other cultural messages about parenting exist in first-time families, but the couple relationship often precedes parenting, giving individuals time to integrate these two roles. In stepfamilies, the parenting role is typically most salient and often incompatible with the partner role, which may result in parents choosing their children because they view themselves as their protector (Weaver & Coleman, 2010). These messages may be even stronger in Eastern cultures (i.e., Japan) where stepparents are not just outsiders to the parent–child relationship, but principles like "oyakoko" (deep-seated values of filial piety) may place them as outsiders to strong grandparent–parent–child relationships (Papernow, 2018; Raymo, Iwasawa, & Bumpass, 2004).

Irrespective of the reasons, stepparents often report feeling like an outsider, which is accompanied by feelings of rejection, loneliness, and invisibility (Brimhall & Engblom-Deglmann, 2011; Ganong & Coleman, 2017; Papernow, 2018). This may be especially hard for stepmothers, who feel the strength of the motherhood mandate clashing with the negative stereotype of the wicked stepmother. They often feel caught between their partner and their partner's children, preferring to focus on the role of partner, but being forced into parenting based on gendered expectations (Ganong & Coleman, 2017). This may often result in the stepmother feeling like she is being exploited rather than a contributing member of the family; this feeling is often enhanced when stepchildren are young, when the stepmother feels less emotionally attached to the children, and when most parenting decisions are handled between her partner and his ex-spouse (McGoldrick & Carter, 2015). Stepfathers also experience a similar challenge as they negotiate the double bind they experience between rescuer and intruder, often pressured by their partners to engage in the disciplining of the stepchildren but often being censured by the stepchildren (or in some cases their partner) for trying to intervene.

Structural-therapy-informed clinical recommendations   Since couples who experience role conflicts are likely to leave the marriage (Browning & Artelt, 2012; Ganong & Coleman, 2017), clinicians must help stepfamilies integrate both roles into one overarching family role, a task that is difficult given strong societal messages (Papernow, 2018). Specifically, clinicians should help stepfamilies understand the loyalty conflicts associated with the fact that the parent–child relationship is the relationship with the longest history (Adler-Baeder, 2007; Skogrand, Dansie, Higginbotham, Davis, & Barrios-Bell, 2011). As a result, couple bonds may be very tenuous and fragile. Rather than establishing rigid boundaries to "protect" the couple relationship, couples should be encouraged to be very intentional in creating their relationship and establishing boundaries that exclude outside parties (e.g., children, ex-partners, in-laws) while also maintaining space for the parent–child relationship. Unlike nuclear families, stepfamilies might be specifically encouraged to have less family time and focus on subsystems within the family like parent–child time and couple time.

New partners also need to understand that positive parent–child relationships are linked to more positive stepparent–stepchild relationships (Jensen, Lippold,

Mills-Koonce, & Fosco, 2017) and that partners' attempts to strengthen the parent–child bond is not a threat to the couple relationship (Papernow, 2018). As a result, clinical work with these families may require intentional work with specific subsystems before inviting the entire system to therapy. At times, prematurely inviting the entire system to therapy can create stress that overwhelms the already fragile system (Browning & Artelt, 2012).

The ability of clinicians to help stepfamilies establish this dual hierarchy might be facilitated if they help individuals understand the physical and emotional impact of partners turning toward, away, and against one another (Gottman & Gottman, 2017). Given the difference in relational histories, parents repeatedly turn away from their partners toward their children. Clinicians should help couples understand the inherent challenge associated with these dynamics and normalize parents' attempts to protect or mediate. Likewise, clinicians need to help parents understand the emotional experience associated with the outsider feeling rejected and alone. Stepparents are more inclined to create space for parent–child interactions if they feel like their partner understands their feelings and validates the pain of feeling rejected and alone (Papernow, 2018). Clinicians may also need to help children and other members of the family system (e.g., extended family, former partners) learn ways to assertively ask for what they need rather than trying to undermine the new couple relationship.

Attachment theory

From an attachment perspective, Bowlby (1979) described how "many of the most intense emotions arise during the formation, the maintenance, the disruption, and the renewal of attachment relationships" (p. 130). The intensity of these emotions centers around the fact that attachment theorists and scholars assert that the ability to form and maintain attachment bonds at every stage of life is as critical to survival as nutrition (Feeney & Monin, 2016). A common challenge faced by stepfamilies is the fact that they are born of loss (Browning & Artelt, 2012; Visher & Visher, 1996). Whether the stepfamily is created post-divorce or post-bereavement, it happens after the disruption of one of the strongest affectional bonds formed, not only between adults but also between parents and children (Feeney & Monin, 2016).

By nature, the very foundation of stepfamilies is built on loss and transition. Failure to recognize these losses or provide the support necessary to mourn them interferes with an individual's ability to engage wholeheartedly in developing and nourishing meaningful stepfamily relationships, especially when past losses continue to serve as barriers (Papernow, 2013). Some scholars even suggest that if losses are not adequately mourned, then the "stepfamily inherits trouble" (Coale Lewis, 1985, p. 16).

A common metaphor used by Papernow (2013, 2015, 2018) to teach the importance of properly healing losses is her bruise theory of feelings. When describing their vulnerability cycle, Scheinkman and Fishbane (2004) suggest that past traumatic events can result in vulnerabilities that "remain sensitive to the touch" (p. 281). The sheer number of losses involved in most stepfamilies, and the various relationships they affect, means that individuals within these situations may be dealing with multiple losses that result in vulnerabilities. Papernow (2018) describes these vulnerabilities as bruises and educates stepfamilies that when somebody hits your healthy arm, it hurts. The level of pain, however, is vastly different if there is a preexisting bruise in the location they hit. If that bruise happens to be a deep bruise, most people will have a strong traumatic response to being touched, even if softly. Brimhall et al. (2008) interviewed individuals who remarried after a divorce. They found that every single participant, irrespective of the reason behind their divorce, described a strong physical and emotional reaction to their new spouse triggered by an experience with their previous partner. In a similar vein, children who witness their parents re-partner may experience yet another level of loss, especially if they were accustomed to spending more time with their parent since the separation/divorce. This may create loyalty binds that often leave the parent feeling torn; if they care for their new partner, children may feel abandoned; if they nurture their child, the new partner might feel deserted.

Theoretical adaptations from attachment theory   While forming attachment bonds is an integral part of any parent–child relationship (Feeney & Monin, 2016), stepfamilies, and the clinicians who work with them, need to be careful not to put undue pressure on family members to form strong attachments, especially in the beginning. One of the expectations that is potentially destructive to stepfamilies is the pressure to interact like a first-time family. Political, religious, and social conservatives often endorse the nuclear family as the ideal environment to enhance both adult and child well-being (Acs, 2007; Ganong & Coleman, 2017). These strong societal messages often pressure stepfamilies to function in the same way as traditional nuclear families; they try to move from unclear families to nuclear families (Simpson, 1994). This may be why the single largest group of adoptive parents in the United States is stepparents (Ganong & Coleman, 2017). This pressure may be especially strong in cultures where family is highly valued and divorce and remarriage are stigmatized (Papernow, 2018). Stepfamilies in these cultures (i.e., Japanese, Chinese, Latinx) may feel especially pressured to "pass" as first-time families (Nozawa, 2015; Papernow, 2015; Tai, 2005; Webber, 2003) since laws in some countries, like Japan, do not allow for joint custody (Nozawa, 2015). These potentially destructive messages are often what propel the unrealistic expectations faced by stepfamilies; one specific myth that often gets propelled is the instant love myth (Brooks, 2013; Hetherington & Kelly, 2002).

The instant love myth is the misconception that stepparents and children should automatically love one another and form close attachment bonds like nuclear families. This often is not the case. In fact, in several instances, especially when stepchildren are older, the parent–child attachment bond may never occur. In some cases, this is merely a function of the life cycle reality described above and should not be interpreted as a failure on the part of the family (McGoldrick & Carter, 2015). Clinicians would do well to understand the distinction between affiliation, affectional bonds, and attachment (Cassidy, 2016).

While most individuals form meaningful relationships with multiple people throughout the course of their lives (affiliation), not all of these relationships rise to the level of affectional or attachment bonds. The specific criteria for affectional bonds are as follows: (a) the relationship is persistent across time, (b) the relationship involves a specific person, (c) the relationship is emotionally significant, (d) the person wants to establish proximity, and (e) separation distress occurs (Cassidy, 2016). The additional criteria necessary to elevate that relationship to an attachment bond is an individual seeks comfort and reassurance from this person during their times of distress. Understanding that forming these relationships is a process hopefully will help dispel the instant love myth and provide stepfamilies the space and time necessary to work toward these types of bonds. Unfortunately, the instant love myth, and some of the systemic challenges facing stepfamilies, often puts undue pressure on some individuals to accelerate relationship growth in ways that are typically detrimental for their development (Browning & Artelt, 2012; Papernow, 2018; Visher & Visher, 1996). Instead, many scholars encourage stepparents to engage in affinity-seeking behaviors, friendly gestures that help build the affiliation between parent and child (Browning & Artelt, 2012; Ganong & Coleman, 2017; Papernow, 2015; Pasley & Dollahite, 1995), ideally working toward either an affectionate or attachment bond.

Unfortunately, for many stepparents, these attempts are either dismissed, ignored, or in some cases openly rejected. If the stepparent is anxiously attached, this form of rejection may be very difficult and they may try harder, often putting more pressure on the relationship. If the stepparent is avoidantly attached, they may not engage initially, but if attempts are made and he/she is then rejected, the stepparent may distance themselves and focus their attention elsewhere. To make matters worse, step-parents often enter a system after the biological parent has been parenting alone for some time. Biological parents who are often exhausted from the demands of parent-ing are looking to share the load with someone else. From an attachment perspective, these competing needs, coupled with the message to interact like a first-time family, can create a system that backfires on unsuspecting stepfamilies. This potential pitfall can be seen in the literature detailing the impact of non-biological parents disciplining stepchildren.

Research has clearly established the fact that early disciplining by stepparents is detrimental (Ganong & Coleman, 2017; Hetherington, Bridges, & Insabella, 1998; Hetherington & Kelly, 2002; Kinniburgh-White, Cartwright, & Seymour, 2010). Many professionals recommend that only after the stepparent has built a warm and caring relationship with their stepchildren should they venture into authoritative par-enting, which includes disciplining (Pasley & Dollahite, 1995). Even then, it is pri-marily recommended for younger children only (Hetherington et al., 1998; Papernow, 2013). Instead stepparents should be placed in a supportive role (e.g., your mother needs you to do the dishes and I'm here to see that it happens) that keeps the primary responsibility for disciplining on the biological parent. The pressure that stepparents feel to intervene early may be influenced by culture. Research suggests that African American stepfathers (Stewart, 2007) and gay stepfathers (Crosbie-Burnett & Helmbrecht, 1993; Lynch, 2005) are more likely to leave discipline to their partners, while Japanese stepparents are expected to replace nonresidential parents as discipli-narians (Nozawa, 2015). It appears that stepparents who adopt a slower approach to disciplining and who continually engage in affinity-seeking behaviors increase the likelihood of forming a stronger bond with their stepchildren.

Attachment-informed clinical recommendations Given the volume and often signifi-cance of the losses experienced by stepfamilies, it may be important to teach stepfami-lies the importance of attachment theory and the fact that persistent attachments exist, even if those relationships were negative, long after separation occurs (McGoldrick & Carter, 2015; Weiss, 1975). If the idea of persistent attachment (even between ex-spouses) is understood, then clinicians can predict the arousal of old emo-tional attachments that may be triggered, both positive and negative, during signifi-cant life transitions (e.g., weddings, graduations). In these cases, it may help to show them video clips of Ed Tronick's still face experiment (Weinberg & Tronick, 1996) to help them realize that the inability to access important attachment figures creates physical and emotional distress. Also, that a consistent inability to access important figures over time may be the cause for bruises/vulnerabilities experienced later (Johnson, Makinen, & Millikin, 2001). This may help reframe children's desire to stay connected to both residential and nonresidential parents as natural. It may also help new partners understand why current partners may react to certain situations in a way that seems more intense than is warranted. Normalizing these reactions may help people process them and prevent them from cutting off emotionally or becoming overly reactive (McGoldrick & Carter, 2015).

Attachment breaks are a consistent part of stepfamily challenges (Papernow, 2018). When past vulnerabilities/bruises are present, it may require more than education and insight. Several resources exist that describe interpersonal processes that help couples and families heal from injuries caused by attachment breaks (Naaman, Pappas, Makinen, Zuccarini, & Johnson–Douglas, 2005; Schade & Sandberg, 2012). The essence of these models is helping parents and partners remain accessible and engaged instead of getting defensive or withdrawing. This can be difficult if they are feeling threatened or attacked. Therefore, it is also essential to train children and partners who feel hurt or betrayed to express their need in a soft and vulnerable way that highlights the underlying attachment need (Papernow, 2015). These processes are important to learn because the most regulating force for both children and partners is attunement by a caring attachment figure (Schore, 2016; Siegel, 2012).

Also, it may help if clinicians reinforce the message that new attachments take time and that stepparents should not be thrown into a disciplinarian role immediately, thus minimizing potential breaks to an attachment process that has not solidified. Rather they should be given time to engage in affinity-seeking behaviors that help strengthen the relationship. Stepparents should be encouraged to spend time with their stepchildren but also reminded that their initial attempts may be rejected. They should be supported in adopting a securely attached position that continues to reach out rather than becoming overanxious or openly avoidant. Understanding the distress described above may also help stepparents be more sensitive to the needs of their stepchildren and realize that their reaction may be born of grief and loss rather than anger and hostility. Either way it helps reinforce the message that the myth of instant love is not only unrealistic but potentially harmful.

Summary

In summary, graduate programs continue to effectively teach important family therapy theories that help clinicians systemically intervene with couples and families. Original attempts to apply theories to a general family are no longer necessary. Training programs and clinicians need to take opportunities to understand some of the unique challenges that face stepfamilies and adapt their models accordingly. While this section was not an exhaustive adaptation of some common theories, it hopefully demonstrated how this tailoring can occur. Also, it is important to note that the challenges described in each theory are not unique to that theory, but simply some examples of common challenges experienced by stepfamilies and how to intervene using that model. While this section included some unique challenges facing stepfamilies, there are others that are important to consider. Likewise, scholars have recommended different levels of intervention depending on the presenting need.

Other Important Differences Unique to Stepfamilies

Most stepfamily professionals agree that understanding the fundamental differences between stepfamilies and first-time families is critical to working effectively with stepfamilies (Browning & Artelt, 2012; Ganong & Coleman, 2017; Papernow, 2018; Visher & Visher, 1996). Visher and Visher (1979, 1988, 1996), pioneers in the field of clinical work with stepfamilies, often maintained that most problems faced by stepfamilies were not the result of psychological problems, but rather a misunderstanding of how stepfamilies differed from first-time nuclear families (Ganong & Coleman, 2017). Based on this belief, they would often advocate for psychoeducation and support as necessary interventions. They believed that helping families understand these unique differences, and providing them the support necessary, would alleviate many of the challenges stepfamilies face and improve family functioning. Papernow (2018), realizing that some psychological problems may exist, expanded the "education as intervention" model by including interpersonal and intrapsychic interventions for times when psychoeducation was insufficient. When working with stepfamilies, all three levels are necessary. Attempts by well-intentioned clinicians to not include educational components into their therapeutic work with stepfamilies are shortsighted and will often make the work harder. Failing to include educational components may be an indication that clinicians (and the stepfamilies they are seeing) have succumbed to the societal pull to treat them as first-time nuclear families, a process the literature refers to as "retreating from complexity" (Goldner, 1982, p. 205).

While several stepfamily scholars have created their own list of specific differences (see Browning & Artelt, 2012; Ganong & Coleman, 2017; Papernow, 2013; Visher & Visher, 1996), most include the same prevailing themes: (a) increased complexity; (b) loss, loyalty conflicts, and lack of control; and (c) lack of social support. This section will discuss these unique differences, helping clinicians and scholars understand the intricacies involved so they can intervene accordingly. Although interrelated, these differences will be discussed individually and suggestions for intervening at each level (psychoeducation, interpersonal, and intrapsychic) will be included.

Difference 1: Increased complexity

In English, there exist kinship terms to acknowledge the possibility of eight dyadic relationships (Bohannan, 1984; Ganong & Coleman, 2017). These include husband–wife, father–daughter, mother–daughter, father–son, mother–son, brother–brother, sister–sister, and brother–sister. This number increases to 22 at a minimum, if partners divorce and each re-partners with an individual with children. In general, stepfamilies have more people, more relationships, and more roles, including more extended kin (Ganong & Coleman, 2017). Just capturing the potential relationships is daunting enough, but when also considering the relationship quality of each relationship, the number becomes staggering. Batchelder (1995) developed relationship orientations that she described as directional attitudes toward another individual. If each person can feel either positive, negative, or neutral, any dyadic relationship results in nine potential relationship orientations. Based on these orientations, she calculates that a nuclear family of 3 has 27 potential orientations. A post-divorce remarriage including a simple stepfamily would increase that number to 89. This does not include multiple partner fertility (Ganong & Coleman, 2017) and more complex stepfamilies that would result in numbers even harder to track. These numbers provide some insight into the level of complexity stepfamilies (and clinicians who work with them) are asked to juggle.

It also helps shed some light on the finding that up to 25% of partners in complex stepfamilies (defined as both parents bringing children from a previous relationship) report different numbers when asked how many children they have (Stewart, 2005). Added to the complexity of relational orientations is the fact that 9–15 different typologies exist for stepfamilies depending on whether children exist from the previous union, custody arrangements, and where the children reside most of the time (Ganong & Coleman, 2017).

A common way that stepfamilies try to reduce the amount of complexity is to reduce the amount of contact with certain relationships. This may include restricting contact with a nonresidential parent or trying to severe those ties completely by pushing for adoption (Ganong & Coleman, 2017). While this may eliminate some complexity, research indicates that these decisions often lead to greater emotional and interpersonal loss and increased conflict because children miss the absent parent (Browning & Artelt, 2012; Papernow, 2013; Visher & Visher, 1996). This process, and the potential outcomes, may be like families who push for closed rather than open adoptions to avoid complexities and ambiguities of adoption (Logan & Smith, 2013).

Given the increased emphasis on joint custody, more stepfamilies are experiencing the challenges associated with sharing two homes (Emery, 2012; Ganong & Coleman, 2017). With complex stepfamilies, they may have a different number of children in their home at any given time. These rotating residences, often referred to as the accordion effect, may contribute to the level of ambiguity stepfamilies experience, especially if each home has a different set of rules and expectations (Papernow, 2015). Ambiguity can be detrimental to the emotional health of an individual, regardless of age or situation, and can lead to feelings of helplessness, depression, and anxiety (Boss, 2006). Being a member of two households can be very difficult, because including more people means sharing control and decision-making power. This can be especially hard if arguments around childcare contributed to the initial divorce (Browning & Artelt, 2012).

Also, uncertainty exists around whether part-time residents should be treated as guests or visitors or held to the same expectations as full-time residents. In cases like these, a residential stepfather who parents with firm boundaries and high expectations might transform into a Disneyland Dad when his biological children visit during the weekend. This is problematic because research indicates that both adults and children in stepfamilies are finely attuned to noticing differences, even those of minor magnitude (Ganong & Coleman, 2017; Mekos, Hetherington, & Reiss, 1996). For children who are often caught in the middle, another dynamic of living in two households is potential power imbalances. This perceived injustice might result in children threatening to live with the other parent if their wishes are not met.

Psychoeducation   Typically, just voicing the complexity for stepfamilies can be helpful (Papernow, 2018). Coupled with conversations about unrealistic expectations clinicians can help validate the overwhelming nature of trying to juggle so many competing needs. It may also be beneficial for clinicians to be familiar with the different types of stepfamilies that exist and understand how different structures may influence family dynamics.

While nuclear families typically can tolerate a certain level of differential treatment between parents and children, the experience for stepfamilies is very different. Stepfamilies must be encouraged to develop consistent rules and expectations across households. Coordination with previous partners is often vital, which can be difficult, especially given that very few relationships share the same level of anger and hostility as the relationship between former partners (Brimhall et al., 2008). When providing psychoeducation, it may be appropriate to have these conversations with the entire system to help everybody gain an appreciation for what the stepfamily is being asked to accomplish. Systemically this may help families understand the stress and pressure they may feel and may help explain why certain aspects of the stepfamily might be experiencing more tension.

Interpersonal   As important as it might be for clinicians to validate and acknowledge the level of complexity experienced by the stepfamily, it may be even more empowering to teach family members how to have these conversations together (Papernow, 2018). Having consistent conversations about the complexities, they encounter open dialogue instead of dismissing it. Often well-intentioned family members, and in some cases the clinicians working with them, may want to reduce the complexity. It may help to encourage them to embrace the complexity rather than trying to remove it. An example of these conversations may be the need partners have to discuss some of the differential treatment they see occurring within the family. Likewise, parents and stepparents may need to be coached as they develop clear and consistent expectations for their children and stepchildren. This may be especially true if they have different styles of parenting. Consistently, research indicates that parents often advocate for warmth and understanding for their children while stepparents from many cultures want more limits and boundaries with stepchildren (Faroo, 2012; Nozawa, 2015; Papernow, 2015; Tai, 2005; Webber, 2003). Parents are often viewed as permissive while stepparents are described as harsh and rigid. Due to the highly sensitized attunement these families experience around differences, clinicians may need to coach them on how to have these conversations in ways that reinforce the relationship, trying to bring both individuals closer to the middle, rather than exacerbating the divisions.

Unlike psychoeducation, these conversations are probably best to have within subsystems. Trying to manage the magnitude of potential variations will often overwhelm a system that does not have the foundation necessary to absorb it. Instead, certain relationships (e.g., biological parent–child, couple, biological parent–stepparent–child) should be the focus. Based on past experiences, these families typically have a strong fear of dissolution. As a result, interventions used with first-time families to restructure a stuck system by creating a certain level of distress may be too much for these families. Instead, they need a strong sense of stability that typically comes through strengthening specific subsystems and then working toward the whole (Browning & Artelt, 2012).

Intrapsychic   Individuals who are strongly advocating for less complexity may have past experiences that felt overwhelming or outside their control. As a result, they may feel very uncomfortable or unsafe with complexity. In these instances, some individual work may be necessary to help them learn how to regulate their emotions and increase their ability to manage the uncertainty that complexity invites. Additionally, individuals who experience high levels of anger toward their ex-spouse may need to do some internal work before engaging in conversations about rules and expectations with former partners. This may also be true of individuals who grew up in very permissive or authoritarian homes. They may have either very inconsistent expectations or be overly harsh. The potential consequences of maintaining these positions should be highlighted and explored.

Difference 2: Loss, loyalty conflicts, and lack of control

The three concerns that typically are the most unique to children in stepfamilies are loss, loyalty conflicts, and a lack of control (Browning & Artelt, 2012). Despite being considered a positive trait, loyalty binds in stepfamilies often leave them vulnerable. In many cases loyalty is the result of a deep respect for another person that leads to a relationship of trust and commitment. It is a feeling that must be earned and not forced. If it is forced, through myths like instant love, then it may backfire and lead to resentment. Children who have experienced multiple transitions through the divorce and remarriage of one or both of their biological parents (Ganong & Coleman, 2017; Papernow, 2018; Visher & Visher, 1996) often experience multiple losses and report feeling a lack of control. An example is a child who was parentified while the family restructured after the divorce who is then replaced by the new stepparent and demoted back to their role as a child. The emotional closeness and responsibility they faced, even if it felt overwhelming at times, is often an unacknowledged loss that occurs. Some research indicates that despite parents reporting the same level of empathy toward their children throughout the process of forming a stepfamily, that children, especially adolescents, reported that their parents had become less empathic (Browning, 1987; Browning & Artelt, 2012).

As competition for these scare resources (i.e., time, love, attention, etc.) becomes more entrenched, then loyalty conflicts may arise. Despite stepparents not being replacement parents, the similarity in roles often creates an environment where it feels like being loyal to one person requires rejecting another (Browning & Artelt, 2012). This sense of loyalty is often enhanced in stepfamilies where children are required to instantly love and accept the stepparent or in cases where the stepchild does not acknowledge their stepparent as a legitimate part of the family. In these instances, they often reinforce their loyalty to the nonresidential parent (whose flaws are often mini-mized) while magnifying the flaws of the stepparent. Stepparents again are encour-aged to not demand loyalty, thus exacerbating the conflict, but rather to maintain a positive presence. Nonresidential parents are encouraged to not engage in any behav-iors that might send a message that they are reinforcing this need from loyalty. Another major loyalty conflict is the unbearable tension the residential parent feels as they are often forced to choose between their children and their new partner. Each of these loyalty conflicts experiences an underlying foundation of loss and lack of control that often deepens the conflict.

Psychoeducation McGoldrick and Carter (2015) discuss how in earlier times, when countries were less industrialized, families lived in larger communities often sur-rounded by extended family. Referred to as community enclaves, children were often raised in environments where multiple adults cared for them and helped raise them to maturity. In these environments, children are often provided the freedom to maintain multiple allegiances, and there is less emphasis on remaining loyal to one adult.

Browning and Artelt (2012) offer a similar analogy of a student with multiple teach-ers/professors. Typically, since there is no unconscious expectation that the student show loyalty to one professor over another, they have the ability and freedom to feel equally fond of each professor. Stepfamilies are encouraged to adopt similar views of parenting. Rather than trying to monopolize loyalty, clinicians should help parents, stepparents, and children all understand the value of creating environments void of loyalty conflicts, where individuals are free to be loyal to multiply people.

Interpersonal This is another instance where specific subsystems may need clinical attention. Clinicians can intentionally invite nonresidential parents to therapy with their children to clearly communicate that isolated loyalty is not necessary and that multiple allegiances are acceptable. Likewise, newly formed couples can be taught to avoid loyalty conflicts between the couple and the parent–child dynamic, knowing that both relationships are central to positive stepfamily development. Once that sub-system is strengthened, clinicians may invite the children into the therapy room to help the residential parent and stepparent clearly state that they view both relation-ships as important and necessary.

Intrapsychic In instances where one of the parents, or subsystems, is trying to monopolize loyalty, then individual sessions may be necessary to explore the possible trauma underlying the need for unquestioned loyalty. Attempts to require loyalty may indicate that a person has felt rejected in the past and feels threatened by com-peting relationships. These individuals may need to therapeutically work through these traumas to lessen the intensity of these threats so they can contribute to an environment of multiple allegiances without fearing they will become insignificant or obsolete.

Difference 3: Lack of social support

Although stepfamilies may no longer be viewed as incomplete institutions (Cherlin, 1978), they still receive limited support from society (Ganong & Coleman, 2017). Because of negative stereotypes that exist around stepmothers and stepfathers, they are often given very few opportunities to discuss their struggles with other individu-als. This can be heightened if they already belong to a marginalized population (i.e., lesbian, gay, bisexual, and transgender [LGBT] community) or if they belong to a community that has a strong nuclear family ideology. For example, in Hong Kong, second wives are often referred to as "worn shoes" (Tai, 2005). Although many cul-tures have stereotypes unique to their community, the portrayal of the stepmother as evil/wicked is common to many. The story of Cinderella, and the 345 derivatives of it (Smith, 1953), can be traced to ninth-century China suggesting it is a global phe-nomenon (Ganong & Coleman, 2017). In fact, an analysis of fairytales ranked step-mothers as one of the top six representations of evil, only behind bears, wolves, giants, ogres, and witches (Wald, 1981). Scholars hypothesize that audiences could not accept the uglier aspects of the human condition and so the stepmother character was invented to protect the pure image of motherhood (Collins, 1988). Stepfathers are often spared from being vilified in fairytales, but they are often portrayed as evil char-acters in books and movies, predators that are likely to abuse their partner's offspring (Claxton-Oldfield & Butler, 1998).

Another example of limited social support is the legal relationship experienced in stepfamilies. Currently in the United States, a child can only have two parents of record (Ganong & Coleman, 2017). If a stepparent was interested in obtaining legal rights for a stepchild, the parental rights of the nonresident parent would first need to be terminated, a policy that creates conflict between co-parents, increases loyalty binds, and fuels hostility between the nonresidential parents and the stepfamily. Other countries (i.e., England and New Zealand) have laws that recognize stepparents as social parents with limited legal rights and responsibilities. Gay and lesbian parents who divorce often find they have more in common with stepparents than their heterosexual counterparts in nuclear families. In both families, irrespective of parent involvement, one adult lacks legal ties to the child/children (Ganong & Coleman, 2017). These laws and policies are not limited to only the United States. In some Eastern countries (e.g., Singapore, Japan), housing policies disadvantage stepfamilies and nonresidential fathers (Komamura, 2015).

Psychoeducation   Attempts should be made to share a more balanced view of stepparents and to describe the myths underlying the evil stepmother who is only interested in her husband's money or the dangerous stepfather who cannot be trusted. Likewise, examples should be provided about how these negative images may influence family interactions.

Interpersonal   Unconscious racial bias is a term used to describe a process in which individuals claim they are not prejudiced toward a particular group of people, and yet their subtle behaviors and interactions suggest they are (Haider et al., 2011). This process may occur within stepfamilies. Attempts by the stepparent to be nice may be misinterpreted as being manipulative. Conversations need to occur between individuals when these microaggressions occur. In the beginning, parents (or clinicians) may need to serve as an interpreter to help increase understanding.

Intrapsychic   Individuals who grew up in marginalized communities associated with negative stereotypes, or those whose intersectionality represents several social locations that have been oppressed (e.g., Black, gay/lesbian, stepmother/stepfather), may be especially vulnerable to these negative stereotypes and the lack of social support. Therapy may need to focus on these vulnerabilities to increase the amount of support they receive (Papernow, 2018).

Summary

These unique differences highlight the unique developmental, structural, and relational processes involved in stepfamilies. They expand on the fact that stepfamilies are typically poorly prepared for the challenges they encounter; they enter stepfamilies with unrealistic expectations mirroring nuclear families; not all family members experience the same level of motivation to make relationships work; and many family members lack the skills necessary to manage this intricately complex relationships (Ganong & Coleman, 2017). Clinical work may require a combination of psychoeducation, interpersonal, and intrapsychic work to help family members navigate the complicated terrain inherent to stepfamily dynamics.

Future Directions for Research and Policy

The stepfamily literature has grown exponentially since that first review in 1979. Since that time, thousands of studies have been devoted to various aspects of the stepfamily experience (Ganong & Coleman, 2018). These studies have moved away from crude comparisons (primarily comparing stepfamilies and first-time families) to very sophisticated models comparing important within group differences (e.g., stepfather vs. stepmother, simple vs. complex).

Additionally, application of theory and theory building has deepened, providing professionals better maps for navigating stepfamily complexities. Based on these developments, certain trends and norms have emerged that perhaps replace Cherlin's (1978) original claim that remarriage is an "incomplete institution." Although these norms represent substantial growth in understanding the dynamics associated with stepfamilies, there are several areas in stepfamily research and policy that need additional attention.

Research Several challenges continue to face stepfamily scholars. First, although research methods and analyses have become increasingly sophisticated, continued attention needs to be spent examining the structural complexity of stepfamilies. Given the variability in stepfamilies, it is important to look for ways to include multiple family members. Subpopulations that are consistently missing from the literature are non-residential parents, stepparents, siblings, and extended kin (Ganong & Coleman, 2017). Research designs and recruitment strategies should look for innovative ways to try and include more family members.

Although the literature is becoming more culturally diverse, scholars need to proactively include underrepresented racial and ethnic minorities. Given some of the familial values and beliefs underlying these communities of interest, it would be important to understand their experiences with stepfamily formation and maintenance. While some longitudinal data exists, more is needed to understand the structural changes experienced by stepfamilies. For example, some scholars hypothesize that the conflict experienced by stepfamilies would decrease if post-divorce families transitioned to remarriage sooner because they would not have time to develop new norms. Others argue that multiple transitions in a short period of time may lead to increased conflict and be detrimental to family relationships (Engblom-Deglmann & Brimhall, 2016; Ganong & Coleman, 2017). Other structural transitions include the loss of a stepparent, whether through divorce or bereavement. Decisions to stay involved typically depend on whether they were ever claimed as family members (Sherman et al., 2013). Finally, a common finding among couples' decision to re-partner is that they slide into it rather than decide (Stanley, Rhoades, Amato, Markman, & Johnson, 2010). In some British and New Zealand studies, scholars found that only 40% of stepfamilies reported discussing issues, including childrearing, before living together (Brown & Robinson, 2012). Even fewer attended any type of formal preparation (Higginbotham, Miller, & Niehuis, 2009). Additional work needs to occur on how to help stepfamilies see the value of both prevention and intervention. While quality programs exist (see Ganong & Coleman, 2017, for overview), additional research is needed to evaluate the effectiveness of these interventions.

Policy Given that estimates predict that one out of every two individuals will spend time in a stepfamily arrangement, laws and policies should be considered that decrease the ambiguous nature of stepfamily relationships. Typically, organizations and other social expectations will follow laws and policy. Clearer laws would help provide clearer research because institutions (like the US census) might more accurately classify relationships. Adopting laws that allowed for more than two parents might help alleviate some of the loyalty conflicts experienced by stepfamilies. Many of these changes have occurred in other countries. Research could help evaluate the impact of these policies and whether they improved family life for stepfamilies.

Conclusion

Stepfamilies have always existed. However, stepfamilies before the 1970s often went unrecognized because remarriage occurred post-bereavement. Stepparents often replaced deceased parents and the family continued to function, at least on the surface, as a reconstituted nuclear family. However, once remarriage post-divorce became the primary pathway to remarriage, stepparents were considered additional parents rather than substitutes. The complexity involved with having multiple parents and partners led to an explosion in stepfamily literature. Both research and clinical understanding have become more sophisticated over the years and have resulted in unique characteristics encountered by stepfamilies. Recommendations were provided for clinicians and family life educators on how to effectively intervene through psychoeducation, through interpersonal processes, and with intrapsychic vulnerabilities. While research has improved, several important limitations still exist and require professionals to continue working toward an in-depth map that accurately depicts the terrain that makes stepfamily life inherently complex.

References

Acs, G. (2007). Can we promote child well-being by promoting marriage? *Journal of Marriage and Family, 69*(5), 1326–1344. doi:10.r1111/j.1741-3737.2007.00450.x

Adler-Baeder, F. (2007). *Smart steps: Embrace the journey.* Auburn, AL: National Stepfamily Resource Center. Retrieved from http://www.stepfamilies.info/smart-steps.php

Ahrons, C. R. (1980). Joint custody arrangements in the postdivorce family. *Journal of Divorce, 3*(3), 189–205. doi:10.1300/J279v03n03_01

Batchelder, M. L. (1995). Adolescents' adaptation to structural changes in family relationships with parental divorce: A combinatorial model. In T. Kindermann & J. Valsiner (Eds.), *Development of person-context relations* (pp. 165–203). Hillsdale, NJ: Erlbaum.

Bengtson, V. L., & Allen, K. R. (2009). The life course perspective applied to families over time. In *Sourcebook of family theories and methods* (pp. 469–504). Boston, MA: Springer.

Berry, J. W. (2005). Acculturation: Living successfully in two cultures. *International Journal of Intercultural Relations, 29*(6), 697–712. doi:10.1016/j.ijintrel.2005.07.013

Berry, J. W., Phinney, J. S., Sam, D. L., & Vedder, P. (2006). *Immigrant youth in cultural transition.* Mahwah, NJ: Lawrence Erlbaum Association.

Bohannan, P. (1984). Stepparenthood: A new and old experience. In R. S. Cohen, B. J. Cohler, & S. H. Weissman (Eds.), *Parenthood: A psychodynamic interpretation* (pp. 204–219). New York, NY: Guilford.

Boss, P. (2006). *Loss, trauma, and resilience: Therapeutic work with ambiguous loss.* New York, NY: W. W. Norton & Company.

Bowlby, J. (1979). *The making and breaking of affectional bonds*. London, UK: Tavistock/ Routledge.

Brimhall, A., Wampler, K., & Kimball, T. (2008). Learning from the past, altering the future: A tentative theory of the effect of past relationships on couples who remarry. *Family Process, 47*(3), 373–387. doi:10.1111/j.1545-5300.2008.00259.x

Brimhall, A. S., & Engblom-Deglmann, M. L. (2011). Starting over: A tentative theory exploring the effects of past relationships on postbereavement remarried couples. *Family Process, 50*(1), 47–62. doi:10.1111/j.1545-5300.2010.01345.x

Brooks, J. (2013). *The process of parenting*. New York, NY: McGraw Hill.

Brown, O., & Robinson, J. (2012). Resilience in remarried families. *South African Journal of Psychology, 42*(1), 114–126. doi:10.1177/008124631204200112

Browning, S. W. (1987). Preference prediction, empathy, and personal similarity as variables of family satisfaction in intact and stepfather families. *Dissertation Abstracts International: Section B. Sciences and Engineering, 47*(11), 4642–4643.

Browning, S. W., & Artelt, E. (2012). *Stepfamily therapy: A 10-step clinical approach*. Washington, DC: American Psychological Association.

Cassidy, J. (2016). The nature of the child's ties. In J. Cassidy & P. Shaver (Eds.), *Handbook of attachment: Theory, research, and clinical applications* (3rd ed., pp. 3–24). New York, NY: Guilford.

Centers for Disease Control.(2008). Births, marriages, divorces, and deaths: Provisional data for 2007. *National Vital Statistics Report, 56*(16). Retrieved from www.cdc.gov/nchs/products/nvsr.htm

Chandler, J. (1991). *Women without husbands: An exploration of the margins of marriage*. London, UK: Macmillan.

Cherlin, A. J. (1978). Remarriage as an incomplete institution. *American Journal of Sociology, 84*, 634–650. doi:10.1086/226830

Cherlin, A. J. (2017). Introduction to the special collection on separation, divorce, repartnering, and remarriage around the world. *Demographic Research, 37*, 1275–1296.

Claxton-Oldfield, S., & Butler, B. (1998). Portrayal of stepparents in movie plot summaries. *Psychological Reports, 82*(3), 879–882. doi:10.2466/pr0.1998.82.3.879

Coale Lewis, H. (1985). Family therapy with stepfamilies. *Journal of Strategic and Systemic Therapies, 4*(1), 13–23. doi:10.1521/jsst.1985.4.1.13

Coleman, M., Ganong, L., & Fine, M. (2000). Reinvestigating remarriage: Another decade of progress. *Journal of Marriage and Family, 62*(4), 1288–1307. doi:10.1111/j.1741-3737.2000.01288.x

Coleman, M., & Ganong, L. H. (1990). Remarriage and stepfamily research in the 1980s: Increased interest in an old family form. *Journal of Marriage and the Family*, 925–940. doi:10.2307/353311

Collins, S. (1988). *Step-parents and their children*. London, UK: Souvenir Press.

Crosbie-Burnett, M., & Helmbrecht, L. (1993). A descriptive empirical study of gay male stepfamilies. *Family Relations, 42*, 256–262. doi:10.2307/585554

De Jong Gierveld, J., & Merz, E.-M. (2013). Parents' partnership decision making after divorce or widowhood: The role of (step) children. *Journal of Marriage and Family, 75*, 1098–1113. doi:10.1111/jomf.12061

Doherty, W. J. (1999). *The intentional family: Simple rituals to strengthen family ties*. New York, NY: Avon Books.

Emery, R. E. (2012). *Renegotiating family relationships: Divorce, child custody, and mediation* (2nd ed.). New York, NY: Guilford.

Englblom-Deglmann, M., & Brimhall, A. S. (2016). Not even cold in her grave: How postbereavement remarried couples perceive family acceptance. *Journal of Divorce & Remarriage, 57*(3), 224–244. doi:10.1080/10502556.2016.1150189

Faroo, F. (2012). *Remarriage in the Malay community: An exploration of expectations and adjustments to stepfamily living*. Singapore: Persatuan Pemudi Islam Singapura (PPIS).

Feeney, B. C., & Monin, J. K. (2016). An attachment-theoretical perspective on divorce. In J. Cassidy & P. Shaver (Eds.), *Handbook of attachment: Theory, research, and clinical applications* (3rd ed., pp. 941–965). New York, NY: Guilford.

Ganong, L., & Coleman, M. (2017). *Stepfamily relationships: Development, dynamics, and interventions* (2nd ed.). New York, NY: Springer.

Ganong, L., & Coleman, M. (2018). Studying stepfamilies: Four eras of family scholarship. *Family Process, 57*(1), 7–24. doi:10.1111/famp.12307

Goldner, V. (1982). Remarriage family: Structure, system, future. In J. C. Hansen & L. Messenger (Eds.), *Therapy with remarried families* (pp. 187–206). Rockville, MD: Aspen.

Gottman, J., & Gottman, J. (2017). The natural principles of love. *Journal of Family Theory & Review, 9*(1), 7–26. doi:10.1111/jftr.12182

Grinwald, S., & Shabat, T. (1997). The "invisible" figure of the deceased spouse in a remarriage. *Journal of Divorce & Remarriage, 26*(3–4), 105–113. doi:10.1300/J087v26n03_09

Haider, A. H., Sexton, J., Sriram, N., Cooper, L. A., Efron, D. T., Swoboda, S., … Cornwell, E. E. (2011). Association of unconscious race and social class bias with vignette-based clinical assessments by medical students. *JAMA, 306*(9), 942–951. doi:10.1001/jama.2011.1248

Hetherington, E. M., Bridges, M., & Insabella, G. M. (1998). What matters, what does not? Five perspectives on the association between marital transitions and children's adjustment. *American Psychologist, 53*, 167–184. doi:10.1037/0003-066X.53.2.167

Hetherington, E. M., & Kelly, J. (2002). *For better or for worse: Divorce reconsidered*. New York, NY: W. W. Norton & Company.

Higginbotham, B. J., Miller, J. J., & Niehuis, S. (2009). Remarriage preparation: Usage, perceived helpfulness, and dyadic adjustment. *Family Relations, 58*(3), 316–329. doi:10.1111/j.1741-3729.2009.00555.x

Ihinger-Tallman, M., & Pasley, K. (1987). Divorce and remarriage in the American family: A historical review. *Remarriage and stepparenting: Current research and theory*, 3–18.

Jensen, T. M., Lippold, M. A., Mills-Koonce, R., & Fosco, G. M. (2017). Stepfamily relationship quality and children's internalizing and externalizing problems. *Family Process.* doi:10.1111/famp.12284

Johnson, S. M., Makinen, J. A., & Millikin, J. W. (2001). Attachment injuries in couple relationships: A new perspective on impasses in couples therapy. *Journal of Marital and Family Therapy, 27*, 145–155. doi:10.1111/j.1752-0606.2001.tb01152.x

Kim, H. (2010). Exploratory study on the factors affecting marital satisfaction among remarried Korean couples. *Families in Society: The Journal of Contemporary Social Services, 91*(2), 193–200. doi:10.1606/1044-3894.3977

Kinniburgh-White, R., Cartwright, C., & Seymour, F. (2010). Young adults' narratives of relational development with stepfathers. *Journal of Personal Relationships, 27*, 1–19. doi:10.1177/0265407510376252

Komamura, A. K. (2015). *Legal issues facing stepfamilies in Japan.* Presented at the conference Toward a Better Future for Children and Adults in Stepfamilies: What Social Policies are Needed for Separated and Repartnered Families? Tokyo, Japan.

Li, J. C. A. (2006). The institutionalization and pace of fertility in American stepfamilies. *Demographic Research, 14*, 237–266. doi:10.4054/DemRes.2006.14.12

Logan, J., & Smith, C. (2013). *After adoption: Direct contact and relationships.* Abingdon, UK: Routledge.

Lynch, J. M. (2005). Becoming a stepparent in gay/lesbian stepfamilies: Integrating identities. *Journal of Homosexuality, 48*(2), 45–60.

Marwit, S., & Carusa, S. (1998). Communicated support following loss: Examining the experiences of parental death and parental divorce in adolescence. *Death Studies, 22*(3), 237–255. doi:10.1080/074811898201579

McGoldrick, M., & Carter, B. (2015). Families transformed by the divorce cycle: Reconstituted, multinuclear, recoupled, and remarried families. In M. M. McGoldrick, B. Carter, & N.

Garcia-Preto (Eds.), *The expanded family life cycle: Individual, family, and social perspectives* (5th ed., pp. 317–335). Boston, MA: Allyn and Bacon.

McGoldrick, M., Carter, B., & Garcia-Preto, N. (2015). Overview: The life cycle in its changing context. In M. M. McGoldrick, B. Carter, & N. Garcia-Preto (Eds.), *The expanded family life cycle: Individual, family, and social perspectives* (5th ed., pp. 1–19). Boston, MA: Allyn and Bacon.

Mekos, D., Hetherington, E. M., & Reiss, D. (1996). Sibling differences in problem behavior and parental treatment in nondivorced and remarried families. *Child Development, 67*(5), 2148–2165. doi:10.1111/j.1467-8624.1996.tb01849.x

Minuchin, S. (1974). *Families & family therapy.* Cambridge, MA: Harvard University Press.

Minuchin, S., Lee, W., & Simon, G. M. (2006). *Mastering family therapy: Journeys of growth and transformation* (2nd ed.). Hoboken, NJ: Wiley.

Moore, S., & Cartwright, C. (2005). Adolescents' and young adults' expectations of parental responsibilities in stepfamilies. *Journal of Divorce & Remarriage, 43*(1–2), 109–128. doi:10.1300/J087v43n01_06

Naaman, S., Pappas, J. D., Makinen, J., Zuccarini, D., & Johnson–Douglas, S. (2005). Treating attachment injured couples with emotionally focused therapy: A case study approach. *Psychiatry: Interpersonal and Biological Processes, 68*(1), 55–77. doi:10.1521/psyc.68.1.55.64183

Noy, D. (1991). Wicked stepmothers in Roman society and imagination. *Journal of Family History, 16*(4), 345–361. doi:10.1177/036319909101600402

Nozawa, S. (2015). Remarriage and stepfamilies. In S. R. Quah (Ed.), *The Routledge handbook of families in Asia* (pp. 345–358). London, UK: Routledge.

Papernow, P. L. (2013). *Surviving and thriving in stepfamily relationships: What works and what doesn't.* New York, NY: Routledge.

Papernow, P. L. (2015). Therapy with couples in stepfamilies. In A. Gurman, J. Lebow, & D. Snyder (Eds.), *Clinical handbook of couple therapy* (5th ed., pp. 467–488). New York, NY: Guilford.

Papernow, P. L. (2018). Clinical guidelines for working with stepfamilies: What family, couple, individual, and child therapists need to know. *Family Process, 57*(1), 25–51. doi:10.1111/famp.12321

Parker, K. (2011). *A portrait of stepfamilies. Pew Social & Demographic Trends.* Retrieved from http://www.pewsocialtrends.org/2011/01/13/a-portrait-of-stepfamilies

Pasley, K., & Dollahite, D. C. (1995). The nine Rs of stepparenting adolescents: Research-based recommendations for clinicians. In D. K. Huntley (Ed.), *Understanding stepfamilies: Implications for assessment and treatment* (pp. 87–98). Alexandria, VA: ACA.

Porges, S. (2011). The polyvagal theory: Neurophysiological foundations of emotions, attachment, communication, and self-regulation. In *Norton series on interpersonal neurobiology* (1st ed., pp. 313–314). New York, NY: Norton.

Raymo, J. M., Iwasawa, M., & Bumpass, L. (2004). Marital dissolution in Japan: Recent trends and patterns. *Demographic Research, 11*(14), 395–419. doi:10.4054/DemRes.2004.11.14

Russo, N. F. (1976). The motherhood mandate. *Journal of Social Issues, 32*(3), 143–153. doi:10.1111/j.1540-4560.1976.tb02603.x

Schade, L. C., & Sandberg, J. G. (2012). Healing the attachment injury of marital infidelity using emotionally focused couples therapy: A case illustration. *The American Journal of Family Therapy, 40*(5), 434–444. doi:10.1080/01926187.2011.631374

Scheinkman, M., & Fishbane, M. D. (2004). The vulnerability cycle: Working with impasses in couple therapy. *Family Process, 43*, 279–299. doi:10.1111/j.1545-5300.2004.00023.x

Schore, A. N. (2016). *Affect regulation and the origin of the self.* New York, NY: Routledge.

Sherman, C. W., Webster, N. J., & Antonucci, T. C. (2013). Dementia caregiving in the context of late-life remarriage: Support networks, relationship quality, and well-being. *Journal of Marriage and Family, 75*(5), 1149–1163. doi:10.1111/jomf.12059

Siegel, D. J. (2012). *The developing mind* (2nd ed.). New York, NY: Guilford.

Simpson, B. (1994). Bringing the unclear' family into focus: Divorce and re-marriage in contemporary Britain. *Man*, 831–851. doi:10.2307/3033971

Skogrand, L., Dansie, L., Higginbotham, B. J., Davis, P., & Barrios-Bell, A. (2011). Benefits of stepfamily education: One-year post program. *Marriage and Family Review, 47,* 146–163. doi:10.1080/01494929.2011.571634

Smith, W. C. (1953). *The stepchild.* Chicago, IL: University of Chicago Press.

Spanier, G. B., & Furstenberg, F. F. (1987). Remarriage and reconstituted families. In M. B. Sussman & S. Steinmetz (Eds.), *Handbook of marriage and the family* (pp. 419–434). Boston, MA: Springer.

Stanley, S. M., Rhoades, G. K., Amato, P. R., Markman, H. J., & Johnson, C. A. (2010). The timing of cohabitation and engagement: Impact on first and second marriages. *Journal of Marriage and Family, 72*(4), 906–918. doi:10.1111/j.1741-3737.2010.00738.x

Stewart, S. D. (2002). Contemporary American stepparenthood: Integrating cohabiting and non-resident stepparents. *Population Research and Policy Review, 20,* 345–364.

Stewart, S. D. (2005). Boundary ambiguity in stepfamilies. *Journal of Family Issues, 26,* 1002–1029.

Stewart, S. D. (2007). *Brave new stepfamilies.* Thousand Oaks, CA: Sage.

Strow, C. W., & Strow, B. K. (2006). A history of divorce and remarriage in the United States. *Humanomics, 22*(4), 239–257. doi:10.1108/08288660610710755

Sweeney, M. M. (2010). Remarriage and stepfamilies: Strategic sites for family scholarship in the 21st century. *Journal of Marriage and Family, 72*(3), 667–684. doi:10.1111/j.1741-3737.2010.00724.x

Tai, L. Y. T. (2005). The making of the second spring: The experiences of remarried persons in Hong Kong. In K. P. H. Young (Ed.), *Marriage, divorce, remarriage* (pp. 191–219). Hong Kong: Hong Kong University.

Teachman, J. (2008). Complex life course patterns and the risk of divorce in second marriages. *Journal of Marriage and Family, 70*(2), 294–305. doi:10.1111/j.1741-3737.2008.00482.x

Visher, E., & Visher, J. S. (1988). *Old loyalties, new ties.* New York, NY: Brunner/Mazel.

Visher, E., & Visher, J. S. (1996). *Therapy with stepfamilies.* New York, NY: Brunner/Mazel.

Visher, E. B., & Visher, J. S. (1979). *Stepfamilies: A guide to working with stepparents and stepchildren.* New York, NY: Brunner/Mazel.

Wald, E. (1981). *The remarried family: Challenge and promise.* New York, NY: Family Services Association of America.

Waller, W. (1930). *The old love and the new; divorce and readjustment.* Philadelphia, PA: Liveright.

Wang, Q., & Zhou, Q. (2010). China's divorce and remarriage rates: Trends and regional disparities. *Journal of Divorce & Remarriage, 51*(4), 257–267.

Weaver, S. E., & Coleman, M. (2010). Caught in the middle: Mothers in stepfamilies. *Journal of Social and Personal Relationships, 27*(3), 305–326. doi:10.1177/0265407510361729

Webber, R. (2003). Making stepfamilies work: Step-relationships in Singaporean stepfamilies. *Asia Pacific Journal of Social Work and Development, 13*(2), 90–112. doi:10.1080/21650993.2003.9755930

Weinberg, M. K., & Tronick, E. Z. (1996). Infant affective reactions to the resumption of maternal interaction after the still-face. *Child Development, 67*(3), 905–914. doi:10.1111/j.1467-8624.1996.tb01772.x

Weiss, R. S. (1975). *Marital separation: Coping with the end of a marriage and the transition to being single again.* New York, NY: Basic Books.

Widmer, E., Romney, A. K., & Boyd, J. (1999). Cognitive aspects of step-terms in American kinship. *American Anthropologist, 101*(2), 374–378. doi:10.1525/aa.1999.101.2.374

Wilson, B., & Smallwood, S. (2008). The proportion of marriages ending in divorce. *Population Trends, 131*(131), 28–36.

Wu, Z., & Schimmele, C. M. (2005). Repartnering after first union disruption. *Journal of Marriage and Family, 67*(1), 27–36. doi:10.1111/j.0022-2445.2005.00003.x

15

Affair Recovery in Couple Therapy
Tina M. Timm and Katherine Hertlein

This chapter is focused on clinical work with couples who have experienced an affair and express a desire to stay together and rebuild their relationship. Some couples begin their affair recovery immediately after the discovery or disclosure of infidelity and are in a relational crisis. Others come to therapy for unrelated issues, but it is quickly apparent that a past betrayal has never healed and is contributing directly to the lack of connection and safety in the relationship. Some couples are very clear about their commitment to stay together right from the beginning, while others are ambivalent but at least willing to see if they can find a path to healing. There are many other types of clinical presentations related to affairs that will not be discussed in this chapter, such as therapy with individuals who are currently having an affair, couples where one partner has affairs and it is accepted by the other partner by virtue of choosing to ignore it, couples who decide to stay together after the revelation of the affair but cease the interpersonal and romantic part of their relationship, or couples whose cultures encourage or support multiple marriages or relationships. Consensual non-monogamy in the form of open sexual or emotional relationships is only included if the relational agreement is violated in some way, thereby resulting in a betrayal of trust.

To say the treatment of infidelity is complex is both a cliché and an understatement. The dilemmas with treatment start with the very definition of infidelity and then only get more complicated from there. There is great variation in the types of affairs, reasons why people have affairs, how they go about having the affair, the meaning of the affair to a particular individual or relationship, the cultural norms and expectations, and of course given all those variables, what to do to help couples grow and heal from the experience if they choose to stay together. While couple therapy always involves a complex set of variables, infidelity often has a higher level of intensity and therefore typically more urgency and angst on the part of the clients and therapist. Unfortunately, most of what we know about affairs and how to treat them is built on a limited amount of research that is fraught with unique data collection barriers (Blow & Hartnett, 2005a, 2005b). Furthermore, any publication that discusses technology and infidelity will already be out of date by the time it is published. Such is the exponential speed of the changing world of technology.

The Handbook of Systemic Family Therapy: Volume 3, First Edition.
Edited by Karen S. Wampler and Adrian J. Blow.
© 2020 John Wiley & Sons Ltd. Published 2020 by John Wiley & Sons Ltd.

Definitional Dilemmas

Most people agree that having sex with another person without the knowledge or consent of the partner constitutes an affair or "cheating." Even within this most agreed-upon definition however, there is great ambiguity—most notably, how to define "sex." Some people define this term very narrowly, perhaps only conceptualizing it as intercourse, while others argue that "sex" and "being sexual," although still individually defined, include a broad array of physical behaviors such as "outercourse" (orgasms without penetration), oral sex, passionate kissing, fondling, and so forth. Often people are unaware of their personal definition until they find themselves in a situation where they feel betrayed and/or find themselves arguing with another person who thinks differently from themselves. Things get even less clear when defining emotional affairs. Where is the line between being friendly and flirtation? When does flirtation become an emotional affair? These boundaries involving people outside of one's primary relationship are sometimes spoken about, but many times assumed. Some people may be defensive about their behavior and insist, "It's not like I had a 'real affair,'" meaning only the ones with physical contact "count." Other people are not defensive as much as just unclear about where the boundaries should be with other people or what their partner's expectations are about fidelity.

How technology has complicated the definition

The new ways in which people can interact through technology have opened additional definitional dilemmas. Often, couples do not discuss these definitions, thus contributing to more misunderstandings and betrayal (Hertlein, 2012). For example, for some, a partner watching pornography online is cheating. For others, it is insignificant. Sometimes it is not the pornography per se, but whether there is secrecy around viewing it. For some individuals certain kinds of pornography are fine, but other types of pornography feel like betrayal. For example, some may be fine with their partner looking at a pornographic film with professional actors, but not live webcams. What about chat rooms? What about sending and receiving photos and videos? While some Internet activity stays only in the virtual world, there are times where it transitions into face-to-face contact. What began as simple curiosity can turn into the need for more erotic experiences and the pushing of boundaries. The lines of what is cheating and what is not get blurry and confusing.

Micro-cheating

A more recent, nuanced controversy in the definition of infidelity is that of "micro-cheating." Micro-cheating includes activities that might not initially be considered full-fledged infidelity, but are potential breaches of trust that could damage relationships or perhaps lead to a more significant betrayal. The behaviors could be seemingly small actions that are easy to dismiss as insignificant and sometimes that's what they are—behaviors that are friendly or flirtatious, but there are still clear boundaries that would never be crossed. Just because someone is texting a coworker does not mean they are cheating. Just because someone is friends with an ex-partner on social media does not mean they are having an affair. However, for some, small decisions and behaviors can lead to a person becoming emotionally or physically focused on someone outside their relationship. For some people, the activities they are engaged in may be consciously or unconsciously keeping their options open or seeing who else is out there who might be more appealing than the current partner. Examples of these may include purposely not wearing one's wedding ring to a certain event, spending additional time with someone one finds attractive, or cruising dating profiles. When other people become a viable option, not everyone is able (or willing) to stop it.

However, when does the concept of micro-cheating potentially become a problem? When taken to the extreme, some couples (or an individual partner) might set oppressive rules in an attempt to hyper-protect relational boundaries. Examples might include never being allowed to have lunch with someone who could be a potential partner or not being allowed to interact on social media with anyone perceived to be a potential threat. This basic lack of trust in a partner, especially in the face of no evidence to warrant it, can be toxic over time. It also feeds into the expectation that our partners are supposed to be our sole source of friendship, energy, entertainment, and passion. Esther Perel (2006) would argue that this is detrimental to long-term relationships. Secure individuals in strong relationships recognize that they live in a world of possible other partners and that this is a good thing. It does not have to be threatening that a partner is attractive or attracted to others. In fact, this can be a source of eroticism.

To navigate these murky areas, Glass (2003) would encourage an individual to consider the following questions: (a) Is there secrecy around the behavior? (b) Is there emotional intimacy? (c) Is there sexual chemistry? Yes to any of these questions is a potential warning sign, and certainly if all three are present, this would be commonly considered an affair. This whole discussion on micro-cheating highlights the definitional challenges of infidelity. Each relationship has a line that establishes the parameters of fidelity to the relationship, and at times, this line can be crossed in an overt and obvious way. At other times, it is a fraying around the edges of the boundary. Ultimately, it is about intent related to the behaviors.

Inclusive partner-based definition

The definition of an affair matters. Clinically the best working definition continues to be that of Blow and Hartnett (2005a), who define it as "a sexual and/or emotional act engaged in by one person within a long-term committed relationship, where such an act occurs outside of the primary relationship and constitutes a breach of trust and/or violation of agreed-upon norms (overt and covert) in that relationship." This definition works well because it is broad and is *relationally* defined. For couples (and their therapists), the more individuals/couples know about their definition and their partner's definition, the less likely they are to hurt each other unknowingly. They also need to have healthy processes in place to engage in productive discussions when agreed-upon definitions of fidelity have been violated:

> *For example, Jamie and Johnson[1], a couple in their 20s, came to therapy because Jamie believed Johnson was cheating on her. Johnson had been having a conversation via Facebook with a coworker and these messages were sent outside of Jamie's awareness. While there was nothing necessarily inflammatory about the messages, both Jamie and Johnson agreed that Johnson did not disclose the conversation to Jamie, thus holding the interaction in secret. While Jamie conceptualized this behavior as cheating and Johnson did not, the couple could come to the agreement that Jamie felt betrayed.*

Prevalence

The prevalence of affairs varies based not just on how it is defined, or the type, but also by how the data are collected. Whisman and Snyder (2007) found that the annual prevalence of married women reporting infidelity when interviewed face-to-face was 1% while it increased to 6% when the data was collected using a computer-assisted interview. Not surprisingly, participants felt more comfortable disclosing when they were allowed to be anonymous. The topic of how many people are having affairs is fraught with controversy with many different rates described. A quick Internet search reveals a wide range of numbers with some maintaining (without evidence) that more than 50% of relationships include infidelity. In a careful review of the literature, Blow and Hartnett (2005b) concluded that infidelity occurs in less than 25% of relationships. This is still a relatively high number and those who present for couple's therapy may include a higher number of infidelity occurrences. The topic of infidelity prevalence highlights the difficulties in researching the topic with definitional issues around infidelity looming large. These types of studies do not have sophisticated mechanisms to assess things like the meanings of extra-relational behaviors on the relationship itself. Most studies are focused on sexual intercourse and data collection on this topic is difficult (see Blow and Hartnett (2005a, 2005b) for an in-depth review of the topic).

Motivations for Affairs

As with any human behavior, affairs are both mitigated and mediated by a variety of individual, relational, transgenerational, and contextual factors that contribute to the personal motivations or reasons why people have affairs. There are a variety of typologies, most of which are derived from theories or clinical experience. For example, Lusterman (1998) identifies eight such motivations including midlife events (developmental crises), entitlement (someone who feels they deserve to have additional sexual partners if they want), sexual identity (unsure of sexual orientation), sexual addiction (more commonly referred to as out of control sexual behaviors now), exploratory (wanting novelty in a new partner), tripod (triangulation of another person into marriage), retaliatory (revenge), and exit (someone consciously or unconsciously wants out of the marriage).

The late Frank Pittman wrote extensively on the topic of affairs and three of his proposed types of affairs (1989) have overlap with Lusterman in that he identifies habitual philandering (multiple affairs/serial infidelity), marital arrangements (similar to tripod—implicitly using an affair to stabilize the marriage), and accidental (a novel, unexpected adventure that was opportunistic but not planned). His fourth type is romantic (a desire to recapture the intensity of being in love).

Brown (2001) has five categories in her typology, all of which speak more to the internal or relational patterns of avoidance:

1 Conflict avoidance, in which a couple cannot stand up to each other because they fear conflict. One or both of the partners have a deep aversion to tension and talking about issues within their marriage. In an effort to force a conversation about the couple's conflict, the offending spouse has an affair where they are easily caught.

2   Intimacy avoidance, in which the partners constantly fight. Within this type of affair, one or both partners unconsciously fear the security and intimacy monogamy can provide and therefore sabotage the relationship.

3   Split self, in which both partners have neglected their own needs to tend to the needs of another (i.e., their spouse). The commonly known "midlife crisis" would fit in this category. Within this affair, the offending spouse feels that since they have spent their life doing the right thing for their spouse, now they deserve to have some fun with someone else.

4   Exit affair, in which one has decided to leave the relationship. This type of affair is used by the offending spouse as an excuse to end the marriage, with the hope that the offended spouse will initiate the divorce proceedings.

5   Last, the entitlement affair, in which a partner has devoted so much time and energy to success that he or she is out of touch with the emotional self. In this type of affair, according to Brown, the offending party feels entitled to whatever he or she wants.

Bagarozzi (2008) proposed types of affairs that have to do with the internal dilemma of escapism. He came up with eight descriptors of affair types:

1   Brief encounters that are the stereotypical one-night stand with a stranger, and as the name suggests, these affairs are brief and unplanned.

2   Periodic premeditated sexual encounters that are affairs that allow a person to be able to act out sexual fantasies with someone else, and these are usually fantasies that the individual's partner/spouse would disapprove or refuse to engage in.

3   Instrumental/utilitarian/employment advantage affairs that are normally used when one spouse believes that having sex with a boss or colleague will improve his or her career.

4   Revenge affairs that serve the purpose of retaliation against a spouse for some wrongdoing, often a relational transgression of some kind.

5   Short-term sexual relationships that are triggered by significant life change events or a developmental crisis or challenge.

6   Paraphiliac affairs that can include behaviors such as voyeurism, exhibitionism, frotteurism, or soliciting partners willing to engage in atypical sexual behaviors. These affairs can have a compulsive quality to them that are conceptualized as being rooted in psychic pain, anxiety, and/or depression.

7   Unconsciously motivated cathartic affairs where someone is attempting to resolve an internal conflict. While they may have a compulsive quality to them, they are not paraphiliac in nature.

8   Long-term relationships that result from an unfulfilling primary relationship. These affairs may include falling in love and plans to stay together if/when the primary relationship dissolves.

Girard, Connor, and Woolley (2018) highlight different types of affairs, which they believe are associated with various types of attachment styles. There are four types of affairs characterized by high attachment anxiety styles: the protest affair (in retaliation for abandonment or rejection by the primary partner), the come-get-me affair (held to feel important), the hedge fund affair (stemming from a belief that one's partner will always leave, thus having to hedge bets with the affair partner), and the romantic fantasy affair (where the affair partner is an escape from the individual's stressful life). There are three types of affairs connected to high attachment avoidance styles: the burned-out affair (where one desires connection and cannot obtain the connection in their primary relationship), the power player affair (where one has learned the only way to be safe in relationships is to be in power), and the compulsive affair (where there is an addiction component and an inability to stop).

Perel (2006, 2017), a current leading voice on the topic of infidelity, does not discuss types of affairs as much as motivations, concluding that perhaps someone who cheats is not turning away from their partner insomuch as they are looking for another *self*. In her view, affairs can reawaken a person, or stave off a feeling of deadness. For some, an affair can unconsciously feel like an antidote to death. As part of "feeling alive," the imagination, anticipation, and build up to an affair can be more exciting than the sexual act itself. Infidelity is not just about sexual desire, but it is about the desire to be noticed, to feel important, to reconnect to who you once were—some of the most powerful aspects that an affair partner provides. In the end, an affair is a confrontation with oneself, a crisis of identit.

Technology and Infidelity

While having affairs is as old as time, the ease with which someone can find partners, erotic content, and information is unprecedented. The ability to find people on the Internet, both previous partners and new potential partners, is virtually just a click away (Hertlein, 2012). The multifaceted more recent ways that one can betray a partner include texting, sexting, emailing, live videos, social media, websites, and chat rooms. Many affairs involve a combination of these modalities including virtual and "real-world" contact, making treatment even more tricky. What is clear is that acts of betrayal that occur online can have the same serious relational consequences as the face-to-face ones (Hertlein & Webster, 2008). In addition to the role of technology as an affair medium, technology also often provides a highly detailed, intimate account of the betrayal. Many affairs are discovered as a result of finding evidence online or on electronic devices, and in some cases, this includes thousands of texts, emails, and so forth. While this often helps partners to feel like they know the truth about what happened, the level of detail included can be highly traumatizing and can cause more severe posttraumatic symptoms:

> *For example, Angela and Roberto, a professional couple in their early 50s, came to treatment to recover from Roberto's infidelity. Roberto had a 2-year affair with a colleague at work, primarily through his cell phone. The affair was discovered through a series of messages stored on the cloud accessed via the family's iPad. As a consequence, Angela felt that she could not trust him even at work situations because of the potential of him running into the affair partner. Angela's hypervigilance was so pronounced that she was unable to believe the tracking device on his phone that said he was at his therapist's office and believed that at those times he was actually meeting with the affair partner instead. In talking with the couple about the fact that there was no more evidence of the affair on Roberto's phone, Angela reported that she would never be able to get to a place where she believed that the affair was over because of how easy it was to delete messages. In another case, Ben and Bonnie, a couple*

married 36 years, came to therapy after the discovery of Ben's multiple affairs. Ben facilitated these affairs through his various cell phones (up to five at any given time). When Bonnie would ask him to get rid of a phone, he would comply, but shortly after replace the phone, citing work reasons, thus further jeopardizing the marriage.

Unfortunately, online infidelity adds yet another complex dilemma—just because there is no evidence of an affair does not mean that it is not happening (Hertlein, Dulley, Cloud, Leon, & Chang, 2017). Partners fearful of being cheated on can engage in frantic electronic monitoring and searching to determine if someone is having an affair, to find additional evidence of an affair, or to continue making sure it does not happen again. They can get stuck in a mental whirlwind, convinced it is there but they are just not able to find it. The ability to open up secret email accounts, have a secret phone, create online personas with fake names, and the like is fairly easy to do and has made it all the more difficult to reassure a partner or find a peaceful recovery post-affair.

Assessment and Treatment of Infidelity

In short, successful affair recovery is about helping the couple to have sustained engagement with the difficult content and process. The overall goal in doing so is to rebuild the relational security. This begins at assessment and continues throughout treatment. It is the therapists' ability to use their expertise to teach the couple what works to heal the relationship, help them to have reparative therapeutic experiences while in session, and reinforce and support their ability to stay engaged with the process between sessions. While this may sound simplistic on paper, it involves complex theoretical integration with specific goals in mind.

Assessment

All good treatment begins with a thorough assessment. We advocate that therapists do one couple therapy session, then two individual sessions, and then a fourth session as a couple again to review the treatment plan. This recommendation is not without controversy as it immediately brings into play the dilemma of what should and should not be disclosed in the individual sessions. There are different schools of thought around seeing individual partners as a part of couple therapy—everything from "Don't ever do it," to seeing them regularly with no restrictions about what can be shared. The biggest issue is what to do with information that may be shared in an individual session that the individual does not want the partner to know as a part of couple therapy. It is a delicate issue for sure, with both ethical and legal implications.

How to handle secrets   In general, the authors believe that knowing more is better than knowing less. If information is pushed underground, it will ultimately sabotage the work. While you do not want to get stuck with a long-term secret, you need as much information as possible so you have the best chance of success. Therefore, the policy of "Do not share any information you would not share with your partner in the room" is not helpful in this regard. Individuals will likely share more fully when their partners are not in the room. They can sometimes say what they are thinking without fear of hurting their partner. Let them know that honesty is essential to the process and ideally anything that is shared in the individual sessions would be integrated into the couple work, if not right away, then as soon as possible. The therapist needs to be clear from the beginning that any secrets that are disclosed in treatment that directly affect the viability of success will need to be revealed but also reassure them that you will assist in that process.

This policy is essential because we need to know for sure that the affair has ended. If it has, that is, straightforward. If it has not, there needs to be a plan. Sometimes the partner knows that the affair has not ended, so this is not a secret. If they do not know, however, the therapist needs as much information as possible to decide how to proceed ethically. If the partner does not want to end the affair, then the therapist would be very clear that it is not recommended to do couple therapy at this time. This stance is supported by others including Lusterman (1998). Until the partner is willing to put both feet back into the primary relationship, the couple therapy has little chance of success. This is framed as an ethical imperative to not do therapy that realistically will be ineffective. If they want to end the affair, a clear plan needs to be made as to when and how this will happen. As part of these conversations, the therapist is trying to discern how willing the person is to work on the relationship. If they do not wish to end the affair, or they already know they want out of the relationship, we would rather know this earlier rather than later. There are times when the person who is having the affair does not really want to save the primary relationship but rather they are coming to couple therapy to safely tell the partner that they want out. There are other times when they want to end the affair, but it is emotionally difficult because of a strong attachment to the affair partner. If this is the case, individual therapy with someone else is recommended to help the client successfully end that relationship. Couple therapy can proceed once the affair has been terminated.

An alternative when there is high ambivalence to being fully committed to treatment is discernment therapy with the couple (see Harris & Hall, 2020, vol. 3), in order to help the leaning out (affair) party decide the course for his/her future in the relationship. Discernment therapy is an excellent way to deal with the dilemmas of secrets in couple therapy. It also allows the same therapist to be both a support for the individuals and an advocate for the relationship, a dynamic that is often missing in therapy where there is a couple therapist and two other individual therapists involved. In discernment counseling, infidelity is one of the "hard" reasons to leave a relationship. Therefore, discernment counseling may be used to determine if a couple wants to engage in affair recovery.

If there are other secrets that are divulged in the individual session, the therapist needs to support them to disclose more to the partner. Examples of this might be related to the affair itself, for instance, a situation in which the individual disclosed most of the information about the affair, but not all of it. The authors encourage them to share all of it as soon as possible with their partner. A thorough disclosure at the beginning, while scary, does two positive things: it lets the partner know (a) that they are willing to come forward with information instead of hiding it and (b) that there is nothing that will be discovered later in treatment. Even though this is a painful process initially, it is much better than having the information come out slowly over time or having more information be discovered after they said they had disclosed everything. There is also something freeing about beginning the reparative process with no secrets. Secrets create a bubble around a person that will not ever allow for full closeness between a couple.

While some therapists choose to not have individual sessions as a part of affair recovery because of discovering secrets, it seems best for therapists to know so that they can facilitate full disclosure, which seems to be the most healing approach for couples. While there is limited research on this approach, Atkins, Eldridge, Baucom, and Christensen (2005) found that ultimately couples who disclosed the affair had higher marital satisfaction than those who did not after engaging in couple therapy.

Assessment specific to each individual   In addition to knowing affair-specific information in the individual session, there are a number of additional areas of assessment that are essential.

Daily functioning   It is essential to assess the daily functioning and emotional consequences of the post-discovery phase. Most crucial would be assessing for suicidality and potential violence or violent thoughts toward the partner or affair partner. Assessing for relational violence is best done in the individual session(s). In situations where violence is present or threatened, the partner may not feel safe disclosing it in couple therapy. If there has been physicality during fights in the past, and both partners describe it similarly, that is, a good sign of honesty. Be sure to ask the question in a broad way, as people have different definitions about what constitutes violence in a relationship. Instead of asking if the partner has ever been *physically abusive*, ask "What is the most physical a fight has ever been between the two of you?" or "Have you ever been afraid that your partner would hurt you?" Also ask if the partner has threatened to hurt anyone else, especially the affair partner. While there may have been comments made about wanting to hurt that person, the therapist must evaluate how credible or likely it is that they will act on the threat. It is not uncommon for the hurt partner to "cyber-stalk" the affair partner trying to find out everything they can about the person online. If it is geographically possible, there are times when the hurt person is driving by the affair partner's house or place of employment. This may be accompanied by thoughts of confronting them and/or hurting them in some way physically or verbally. If there is a history of violence with either partner, or a credible, viable threat to another person, safety plans must be put in place. At a minimum, if relationship violence is ongoing or has occurred in the recent past, this issue should be addressed prior to conjoint therapy. Please see Stith, Spencer, and Mittal (2020, vol. 3) for a full review of violence assessment and safety planning.

Posttraumatic stress symptoms   The discovery of an affair has high emotionality for both partners, but the hurt partner often struggles more with posttraumatic stress (PTS) symptoms (Glass, 2003). While this is disconcerting, and often makes them feel like they are "losing it" or "going crazy," it is important to normalize how common this is. Symptoms of PTS can include intrusive thoughts and/or re-experiencing (e.g., not being able to stop thinking about it, easily "triggered" by things related to the affair), avoidance (e.g., being numb, desperately wanting to not think about it), changes in mood and cognition (e.g., negative emotions and thoughts, self-blame, loss of interest), and arousal and hyperreactivity (e.g., agitation, aggressiveness, difficulty concentrating, hypervigilance, sleep disturbances) (*DSM-5*, 2013; World Health Organization, 2018). Collaboratively come up with healthy coping mechanisms to be able to function and make good decisions from day to day. To this end, ask about how they are sleeping, eating, and functioning at daily tasks (at home and work) and the intensity of the PTS symptoms. Brainstorm coping skills to help with the most pressing concerns. Instill hope that these symptoms diminish over time. Although this initial assessment of the intensity of symptoms is done in the individual session, it is ideal to pull the partner in as soon as possible so they know what is happening and can be an ongoing support, if possible. However, it must always be clear that self-care and affect regulation must primarily be the responsibility of each individual and the partner plays a supportive role.

SUBSTANCE USE   The therapist must also ask directly about drug and alcohol usage. Since substance abuse is not uncommon, it should be a part of any assessment, but even more so during times of stress. At the very least, ask about the frequency and quantity of usage. If usage seems problematic, a plan must be developed to keep all involved safe. The combination of intense emotions and substance use at the very least results in unproductive, potentially destructive conversations and, at worst, increases the likelihood of violence. Couples should be told in no uncertain terms that conversations about the affair should not be attempted under the influence of drugs or alcohol.

SOCIAL SUPPORT   Also, key during this time is external social support. Ask each individual who knows about the affair and who they consider safe to talk to when they need support. This may be friends or family members. Herein lies another dilemma. Once you tell someone, you cannot take back what you have told them. Making good choices in the beginning about who is likely to support you without bias is essential. Especially early in the process, it is good to err on the side of people who care about the relationship and will not try to force a premature decision about the viability of the relationship. Because of the shame often associated with infidelity, partners can be quite isolated. The person who had the affair does not want people to know what they have done and sometimes the hurt person is also protective of them. Sometimes the hurt person fears that they will be judged for staying with the person or judged for thinking about not staying with them. The bottom line is that the therapist cannot be the only support system.

FAMILY OF ORIGIN   It is also important to do a brief history of each partner's family of origin—most notably, who is in the family, what is the level of contact and/or support, is there a history of affairs in the family, and what did they learn about sexuality and relationships growing up and how this has affected their current relationship. This gleans useful information and assesses personal insight into intergenerational and past relationship patterns that have been ongoing or are likely to affect the healing process.

ADDITIONAL CONTEXT   Lastly, it is helpful to know the basic developmental milestones (e.g., At what age did they start dating? Become sexually active?) and formative sexual experiences such as any unwanted or traumatic sexual experiences, as well as the larger contexts in which someone was raised, most notably culture, ethnicity, religion, and geography. All of this information collectively helps to assess the individual history, mental health, self-esteem, and potential reaction of each partner to relational hurts. Knowing these things early in treatment aids in treatment planning.

Assessment specific to the affair   Assessment specific to the affair involves who it was with, how it started, how long it continued, what it entailed, when it ended, how/when it was discovered, and so forth. The therapist also needs to assess the extent to which the internet played a role in facilitating the affair (Hertlein & Blumer, 2013).

In the earlier case with Angela and Roberto, the therapist assessed how long the affair was going on, what the discovery was like for Angela, and how many triggers she had related to the affair because of the detailed information he provided to Angela when she asked for details after the discovery. In addition, the therapist assessed for other areas of infidelity, only to discover that Roberto had an emotional affair prior to the sexual affair that Angela discovered. Some hurt partners want to know only the basics of the affair, who it was with, how long it lasted, what it included (sexual vs. emotional), and if it is over. Others want to know much more as it is only with total disclosure of all the information that they feel they can make a decision about whether or not to stay and or to assess the extent of the betrayal. We support the hurt partner having full disclosure of the information they feel they need to know to move forward and make this stance very clear to both partners at the outset of treatment. The one thing that we caution strongly about though is related to information about *specific* details of what was done sexually with the affair partner. While it may feel like necessary information at the time, there have been many partners who later regretted knowing this information as it made it harder to heal in the long run and resulted in visual images that they could not get out of their minds. When there is an urge to ask questions about specifics, we advise the hurt partner to write all these questions down. Together we can reassess each one later in treatment and whether or not they still have the same need to know. Oftentimes they do not, and partners are glad they waited. For other types of information, the therapist supports the hurt partner's "right" to ask and supports the partner who had the affair to disclose fully even though it may feel scary to do so. The person who had the affair often worries that any additional information beyond what is already known will potentially end the relationship and/or it will hurt their partner more. While this may be true, it is better than trying to heal in the face of the unknown, where hurt partners will assume the worst and can never move on because they do not feel like they know the whole story. If additional information is disclosed, there may be a setback to progress, but in our experience, when these are not disclosed, they inevitably result in large relationship difficulties down the line. A possible metaphor for this would be that the relationship has suffered a gunshot wound and if the bullet is not removed, it will never heal properly. The full disclosure essentially serves to remove the bullet—painful, but necessary—the scar will always remain, but the relationship can heal and even grow stronger (Atkins et al., 2005).

MEANING OF THE AFFAIR   Affair assessment also begins the important task of discerning the specific meaning of the affair to the hurt partner. Without doubt, some factors related to affairs and affair partners result in a more significant level of betrayal (Weeks, Gambescia, & Jenkins, 2003). In one case, the wife was having an affair with her husband's brother. This caused a great deal of pain for the husband both in the relationship with his wife and in the relationship with his brother. Not only is one more likely to see the person again, but also there is betrayal from two people. For some partners, the pain is the same whether it was a one-time occurrence or many months, but in general, the longer it went on, the more the meaning of it changes to incorporate many other questions, including reassessing all the life events that happened during that time, questioning the relationship in general (e.g., did you ever really love me?), and at times self-doubt about their own reality testing (e.g., how could this have been happening and I did not realize it). If there were direct questions asked about the partner having an affair that were historically met with denial, defensiveness, and messaging about there being something wrong with the person who was being suspicious, that all has to be reevaluated and re-assimilated.

For some partners, it hurts less if the affair was "just sex," but not a "real" relationship. The meaning for them is one that discounts the importance of the affair partner and sees the affair as simply a physical act, but they do not feel the primary relationship is threatened by the affair partner. For people in this category, it would be far worse if their partner had actually cared for the other person as that triggers more fears related to attachment. Conversely, another person might be hurt less if the partner actually cared for the affair partner, but it did not become physical. For them, the meaning might incorporate the idea that it is normal to be attracted to other people and potentially fall in love, but we make choices about what to do about acting on those feelings. In this scenario, the hurt would be greater if there had been a sexual relationship. Of course, many affairs do not fall neatly into these categories and they are a combination of physical and emotional. Assessment questions should include "What about the affair was most hurtful?" and "What felt most threatening to the relationship about the affair?" The answers to these questions provide important clues as to how to heal that is specific to each relationship.

Assessment specific to the relationship   Assessment specific to the relationship should include the history (e.g., How did they meet? How did it progress from dating, engagement, marriage?), current status of the relationship (e.g., living together or separated), and if there were any previous attachment injuries in both the current and past relationships. Communication and conflict styles can be observed in session and asked about directly. As early as possible, relational patterns and styles of interactions should be identified. Attachment is also a key part of the relational assessment for infidelity. One tool used commonly is the Experiences in Close Relationships Scale—Revised (Fraley, Waller, & Brennan, 2000). The findings of this inventory are discussed in the context of the couple session to provide a background of what the status may have been prior to the infidelity and to open up a discussion point of what work needs to be done to assist the couple with building their attachment style.

Models of treatment for affair recovery

Unfortunately, the field does not have strong research evidence to related to the treatment of affairs. However, they are theoretical models that are helpful clinically and certainly some common factors between them.

Attachment-based models. One of the hallmarks of infidelity is damage to the trust and security of the relationship. This rupture is often conceptualized as an attachment injury, a relational injury that threatens the core assumption of a relationship. It is a violation of trust resulting from a betrayal or from an abandonment at a moment of intense need or vulnerability (Johnson, Makinen, & Millikin, 2001). Emotionally focused couple therapy (EFT) is an attachment-based model that rebuilds the secure attachment between the partners. EFT has strong empirical support for its effectiveness as a couple therapy model (Johnson, Hunsley, Greenberg, & Schindler, 1999), and the specific attachment injury resolution model (AIRM) treatment protocol (Makinen & Johnson, 2006) has demonstrated success 3 years' posttreatment related to improvements in trust, forgiveness, and relationship satisfaction (Halchuk, Makinen, & Johnson, 2010). The focus on attachment makes EFT an ideal framework to resolve attachment injuries specific to affair betrayal (Cluff Schade & Sandberg, 2012; Johnson, 2005). Research on attachment and infidelity has also shed light on the relationship between attachment and affairs. It is useful to conceptualize the affair through an attachment lens. For example, Allen and Baucom (2004) found that when men have dismissive attachment styles, they are more likely to engage in infidelity while women with a preoccupied attachment style had higher numbers of partners outside of their primary relationship. They also showed a relationship between attachment style and motivations for infidelity (Allen & Baucom, 2004). Those with fearful and preoccupied attachment styles were likely to have more intimacy motivations for infidelity. Dismissive attachment styles were more likely to be associated with the rationale for infidelity as a need for autonomy from the primary relationship (e.g., independence). Allen and Baucom (2004) suggest that attachment style is likely related to the regulation of intimacy in the primary relationship. In another study by Bogaert and Sadava (2002), individuals higher in anxious attachment are more likely to engage in infidelity, and they concluded that this was true for women in particular.

An integration of eye movement desensitization and reprocessing (EMDR) and EFT, both empirically validated forms of treatment of trauma in their own right, may be useful in addressing the trauma-specific symptoms in post-affair recovery (Negash, Carlson, & Linder, 2018). Using a case study, the authors illustrate how EMDR was used successfully within the steps of EFT. A systematic clinical study using therapists trained in both models would be necessary to assess the symptom relief over time.

Timm and Blow (2018) describe a model of affair recovery informed by multiple theories but largely by EFT, with three general phases of treatment: (a) assessment and crisis management, (b) restoring a secure base, and (c) maintenance and affair proofing. As in any work with couples, these phases do not necessarily occur sequentially, and parts of them can occur simultaneously with others (e.g., keeping another affair from happening, or "affair proofing," happens from the very start of treatment). The treatment model is an active and directive process of both individual and couple coaching. The couple often needs help with what to do and sometimes even what to say. The overall goal is to facilitate relationship growth, not just a return to the pre-affair baseline. Such posttraumatic growth requires us to hold onto hope and possibilities for resiliency, helping clients believe and discover that they can get through the difficult moments.

Cognitive-behavioral methods   In their book, *Getting Past the Affair*, Snyder, Baucom, and Gordon (2007) describe a three-stage model of affair recovery based largely on cognitive-behavioral therapy principles. Phase one is the impact stage. This stage helps to orient couples to understand what has happened and manage the initial impact and effects of the affair on the system. Phase two is the exploring context and finding meaning stage where factors that contributed to the affair happening. Lastly, phase three is the moving on stage. This final stage helps couples to reclaim their relationship post-affair. Use of this model with six couples in a replicated case study design found less marital distress and greater forgiveness posttreatment (Gordon, Baucom, & Snyder, 2004).

The importance of forgiveness   Forgiveness is actually a key part in many models of affair recovery (Gordon, Khaddouma, Baucom, & Snyder, 2015; Weeks et al., 2003). The act of forgiving has been shown to have a positive impact on one's physical and mental health (Raj, Elizabeth, & Padmakumari, 2016; Toussaint, Worthington, & Williams, 2015). Clinicians are advised, however, that forgiveness is not a panacea for every relationship problem and will not be the solution for every infidelity issue. In cases of infidelity, it is important that the couple reach several milestones before moving toward forgiveness (Weeks et al., 2003). See Hertlein and Brown (2018) for a review of when and how forgiveness can be offered in treatment.

Using mindfulness   Building on the research of the effectiveness of using mindfulness to improve intimate relationships (Carson, Carson, Gil, & Baucom, 2004), an initial exploration of the use of mindfulness in the treatment of infidelity has shown promise, specifically that the mindfulness skill of being nonreactive was positively related to higher levels of forgiveness (John, Allen, & Coop Gordon, 2015).

Rebuilding trust   John Gottman (2011) has developed a trust revival method for couples who have experienced infidelity. He believes that rebuilding the relationship hinges on the ability to process negative events productively. He outlines trust building with the acronym ATTUNE, each letter representing an essential part of the healing process:

A—Awareness of the partner's negative emotion
T—Turning toward your partner's emotion
T—Tolerance of the emotional experience
U—Understanding the emotion
N—Non-defensive listening to the emotion
E—Empathy toward the emotion

With the many models that are available, the selection of models for a particular case is less clear. For example, the models that frame the affair as a trauma to the relationship may not be a frame that is endorsed by the client. Further, models that rely on attachment and focusing on what went wrong in the relationship may inadvertently communicate blame or responsibility on the part of the noninvolved partner, thus compromising conjoint treatment. Finally, in cases where the affair was carried on by an individual with a personality disorder such as narcissism, it may not be in the couple's best interest (at least not in the case of the noninvolved partner) to rebuild the attachment, as to do so would be unsafe and irresponsible. Clinicians need to understand the client's frame, worldview, and have a good assessment on any underlying pathology prior to proceeding.

Affair Proofing

Affair proofing is putting a plan in place to decrease the possibility of another affair happening. Not surprisingly, it involves sustained conversations about potential contributing factors, individual and relational risk factors, necessary boundaries, and behavioral plans for safety. These conversations also serve to rebuild trust as well since they are developed collaboratively and become a relational contract moving forward. Glass (2003) discusses the concept of "walls and windows" to illustrate both how the boundaries begin to shift toward an affair and of course what needs to be done to prevent future affairs. In secure marriages, the couple creates a healthy wall that represents a boundary around their relationship. Behind the safety of this wall, they can look out of the window together, with no secrets and nothing to hide. As affair behaviors begin to escalate, sometimes in ways that seem inconsequential, the boundaries start to shift. What begins happening is a wall starts to build between the partners in the primary relationship and the window of intimacy opens to the affair partner. As the affair progresses, the affair partner moves to the inside, and the primary partner gets pushed to the outside. Examples of this progression include having inside jokes that are shared only between the affair partners, discussing details about their primary partner and their relationship, and moving on to more intimate subjects that they are not telling their partner, often with the preface that they cannot talk to their partner about things "like this." The process of shutting out the primary partner is complete when the affair partner becomes the "go to partner," meaning the first person they think to call when something important happens. With 24-hr access to people through texting, emailing, and social media, this type of intimacy can be built quickly.

The goal in affair recovery is to reestablish a wall around the primary relationship that puts the affair partner (and any other potential affair partners) on the outside again. In general, Glass (2003) discusses three precautions that are hallmarks to maintaining a secure relationship: (a) not discussing relationship problems with anyone who could be a potential alternative to their partner; (b) if they did talk to someone (family or friend) about their marriage, making sure that the person is a friend to the marriage; and (c) if someone wants to talk about their personal problems with either of them, being cautious and intentional about boundaries. Confidential, intimate conversations have the potential to lead to emotional over-involvement and there needs to be a plan to not let that happen.

In the wake of an affair, the "wall" also needs to include a plan to set clear and consistent boundaries with the affair partner. Sometimes this is easier to do than others. If the affair was a one-night stand with someone they will likely never see again, then the physical boundary is easy. In this digital age, however, clear boundaries need to be set with regard to what constitutes a betrayal. In fact, the couple may still be at odds in the initial part of treatment as to whether an affair occurred. One suggestion is to help the couple agree that one of the partners feels betrayed and to work from that shared stance. As the couple recovers, they can reinvent their relationship to include more clarity regarding what moving forward would constitute betrayal. This may include blocking telephone numbers, deleting email addresses, cutting off any kind of social media, and so forth. If contact is made in any way, the person who had the affair contracts to tell their primary partner immediately. Together they can develop a plan to respond or not respond as the case may be. It is very tempting for the person who had the affair to not tell the partner about things of this nature, especially if things are going well. They know it will be upsetting and will result in difficult conversations. This is where the therapist predicting this is possible and coaching them what to do is so vital, so there is a plan in place if it happens. It is always framed as a way to build trust and intimacy to disclose this type of contact. If the partner finds out about it at a later date, it will be yet another betrayal that was discovered and it may put the viability of the relationship back in question. Vossler (2016) implores couple therapists to ask more thorough questions about technology contact with affair partners and help clients to establish clear boundaries in order to begin building trust in the relationship.

The Post-affair Sexual Relationship

There are a number of ways in which the sexual relationship can be impacted, and it is often the topic therapists feel ill equipped to address. There are times when safety, trust, and closeness are restored and the sexual relationship will fall into place without any direct intervention. However, this is not always the case. The effect of an affair on the couples' sexual relationship is as diverse as every other outcome—based on the history of each person and their relationship. For some, it can enhance the relationship, while for others it can lead to years of difficulties.

It can affect the sexual relationship in any number of ways. One very common issue is the insidious nature of intrusive thoughts. For example, everything is going well during sex, and then out of nowhere a thought pops up, "I wonder if he liked doing this more with her?" or "Is she thinking of her when we do this?" or "I can't believe he was with someone else." The person does not want to be thinking these things, but the thought is there nonetheless, and it may affect the sexual interaction. For some, one thought leads to a whole flurry of thoughts and it quickly spins out of control internally. Depending on the intensity or frequency of the thought, the person having them may feel overwhelmed and start to cry, or alternatively resort to some sort of numbing technique to not feel. Neither is good when a couple is trying to connect. Intrusive thoughts can impact physical functioning as well. Men can have difficulty maintaining an erection when thoughts of the affair start crowding in.

Another presentation post-affair is that there is actually an improvement in the sexual life of the couple. This can happen in healthy and not so healthy ways. For some, the affair has been a wake-up call to recommit and revitalize the relationship. As a result, they prioritize spending time together and often times that includes having more sex. Particularly when the partner who had the affair has been expressing a desire for their sex life to be better for a long time, the hurt partner may finally see the pain of what their dismissiveness has caused and make efforts to repair this. As part of the painful post-affair conversations, the rawness can bring about good conversations about desire and eroticism that have needed to be talked about and it opens new space for exploration and experimentation.

A less healthy presentation of a "better sex life" post-affair is where the hurt partner is frantically trying to keep another affair from happening. While some affairs happen because of a nonexistent or unfulfilling sex life with the primary partner, it is ultimately unhealthy to "do whatever it takes" so the partner will not cheat again. An example of this would be having sex every day, so the partner will have no need to look elsewhere. Of course, this is no guarantee. People can and do have affairs even when they are sexually satisfied in the primary relationship. These behaviors are often driven by insecurity and the need to control the partner's sexual desire and expression. It also privileges quantity over quality, which is a problem in terms of long-term intimacy and connection. A partner also might agree to do things they do not want to do in order to keep the partner from cheating again. This does not come from a centered, grounded relational place; rather it comes from a frantic place where they will compromise their own well-being in order to not be abandoned. The person who had the affair sometimes operates from this frantic place as well, wanting to show to the partner that they are desirable, or wanting to fix things physically in order to avoid the emotional pain.

A third presentation is an unexpected one perhaps. Despite the fact that the affair was painful emotionally, the hurt partner is aware that the thought of their partner being with someone else is actually erotic to them and that has enhanced their sexual relationship. This can be confusing as it is mixed in with a complex set of negative emotions and even admitting it can bring up feelings of shame as if it breaks a societal taboo or is not the response they "should be having" in the wake of being hurt. Others worry that if it is arousing that it somehow sends a message that what the partner did must not have been that bad. As with all affair recovery, it is in the careful processing of the post-affair emotions that couples bring their relationship level to a deeper level of intimacy.

Conclusion

Based on the current prevalence of infidelity, and the ways in which technology continues to provide more ways of blurring sexual and emotional boundaries, therapists will continue to find many couples in their offices trying to recover from issues of betrayal. The field of systemic family therapy should be leading the way in training and studying this topic. While we have a number of theoretical models, we need more research on effective treatment for infidelity including mechanisms of change for specific affair types and symptom presentations. We also need to know more about conceptual aspects of infidelity—types of affairs, motivations to cheat, vulnerabilities, and the like. Due to the complex nature infidelity and wide variation in response to betrayal, some of these can only be thoroughly explored using qualitative research methods. The authors implore that this important topic continue to be explored systemically.

Note

1 Client names and case material discussed in this chapter have been changed as needed to protect confidentiality.

References

Allen, E. S., & Baucom, D. H. (2004). Adult attachment and patterns of extradyadic involvement. *Family Process, 43*(4), 467–488. doi: 10.1111/j.1545-5300.2004.00035.x

American Psychiatric Association.(2013). *Diagnostic and statistical manual of mental disorders* (5th ed.). Arlington, VA: Author.

Atkins, D. C., Eldridge, K. A., Baucom, D. H., & Christensen, A. (2005). Infidelity and behavioral couple Therapy: Optimism in the face of betrayal. *Journal of Consulting and Clinical Psychology, 73*, 144–150. doi:10.1037/0022-006X.73.1.144

Bagarozzi, D. A. (2008). Understanding and treating marital infidelity: A multidimensional model. *American Journal of Family Therapy, 36,* 1–17. doi:10.1080/01926180601186900

Blow, A. J., & Hartnett, K. (2005a). Infidelity in committed relationships I: A methodological review. *Journal of Marital and Family Therapy, 31*(2), 183–216. doi:10.1111/j.1752-0606.2005. tb01555.x

Blow, A. J., & Hartnett, K. (2005b). Infidelity in committed relationships II: A substantive review. *Journal of Marital and Family Therapy, 31,* 217–234. doi:10.1111/j.1752-0606.2005. tb01556.x

Bogaert, A. F., & Sadava, S. (2002). Adult attachment and sexual behavior. *Personal Relationships, 9,* 191–204. doi:10.1111/1475-6811.00012

Brown, E. (2001). *Patterns of Infidelity and their treatment.* Ann Arbor, MI: Edwards Brothers.

Carson, J. W., Carson, K. M., Gil, K. M., & Baucom, D. H. (2004). Mindfulness-based relationship enhancement. *Behavior Therapy, 35,* 471–494. doi:10.1016/S0005-7894(04)80028-5

Cluff Schade, L., & Sandberg, J. G. (2012). Healing the attachment injury of marital infidelity using emotionally focused couples therapy: A case illustration. *The American Journal of Family Therapy, 40,* 434–444. doi:10.1080/01926187.2011.631374

Fraley, R. C., Waller, N. G., & Brennan, K. A. (2000). An item-response theory analysis of self-report measures of adult attachment. *Journal of Personality and Social Psychology, 78,* 350–365.

Girard, A., Connor, J., & Woolley, S. (2018). An exploratory study of the role of infidelity typologies in predicting attachment anxiety and avoidance. *Journal of Marital and Family Therapy.* doi:10.1111/jmft.12371

Glass, S. P. (2003). *Not "just friends": Protect your relationship from infidelity and heal the trauma of betrayal.* New York, NY: Simon & Schuster, Inc.

Gordon, K. C., Baucom, D. H., & Snyder, D. K. (2004). An integrative intervention for promoting recovery from extramarital affairs. *Journal of Marital and Family Therapy, 30,* 1–12. doi:10.1111/j.1752-0606.2004.tb01235.x

Gordon, K. C., Khaddouma, A. M., Baucom, D. H., & Snyder, D. K. (2015). Couple therapy and the treatment of affairs. In A. Gurman, J. Lebow, & D. Snyder's (Eds.), *Clinical handbook of couple therapy* (5th ed., pp. 412–443). New York, NY: Guilford.

Gottman, J. M. (2011). *The science of trust: Emotional attunement for couples.* New York, NY: W. W. Norton & Company, Inc.

Halchuk, R. E., Makinen, J. A., & Johnson, S. M. (2010). Resolving attachment injuries in couples using emotionally focused therapy: A three-year follow-up. *Journal of Couple & Relationship Therapy, 9,* 31–47. doi:10.1080/15332690903473069

Harris, S. M., & Hall, E. L. (2020). Therapy with individuals and couples as they decide to continue or end the relationship. In K. S. Wampler & A. J. Blow (Eds.), *The handbook of systemic family therapy: Systemic family therapy with couples (3).* Hoboken, NJ: Wiley.

Hertlein, K. M. (2012). Digital dwelling: Technology in couple and family relationships. *Family Relations, 61*(3), 374–387. doi:10.1111/j.1741-3729.2012.00702.x

Hertlein, K. M., & Blumer, M. L. C. (2013). *The couple and family technology framework: Intimate relationships in a digital age.* New York, NY: Routledge.

Hertlein, K. M., & Brown, K. (2018). Challenges of forgiveness in psychotherapy. *Journal of Family Psychotherapy, 29*(2), 87–105.

Hertlein, K. M., Dulley, C., Cloud, R., Leon, D., & Chang, J. (2017). Does absence of evidence mean evidence of absence? Managing the issue of partner surveillance in infidelity treatment. *Sexual and Relationship Therapy, 32*(3-4), 323–333. doi:10.1080/14681994. 2017.1397952

Hertlein, K. M., & Webster, M. (2008). Technology, relationships, and problems: A research synthesis. *Journal of Marital and Family Therapy, 34,* 445–460. doi:10.1111/ j.1752-0606.2008.00087.x

John, K. N., Allen, E. S., & Coop Gordon, K. (2015). The relationship between mindfulness and forgiveness of infidelity. *Mindfulness, 6,* 1462–1471. doi:10.1007/s12671-015-0427-2

Johnson, S. M. (2005). Broken bonds: An emotionally focused approach to infidelity. *Journal of Couple & Relationship Therapy, 4,* 17–29. doi:10.1300/J398v04n02_03

Johnson, S. M., Hunsley, J., Greenberg, L. S., & Schindler, D. (1999). The effects of emotionally focused marital therapy: A meta-analysis. *Clinical Psychology: Science and Practice, 6,* 67–79. doi:10.1093/clipsy.6.1.67

Johnson, S. M., Makinen, J. A., & Millikin, J. W. (2001). Attachment injuries in couple relationships: A new perspective on impasses in couples therapy. *Journal of Marital and Family Therapy, 27,* 145–156. doi:10.1111/j.1752-0606.2001.tb01152.x

Lusterman, D. (1998). *Infidelity: A survival guide.* Oakland, CA: New Harbinger Publications, Inc.

Makinen, J. A., & Johnson, S. M. (2006). Resolving attachment injuries in couples using emotionally focused therapy: Steps toward forgiveness and reconciliation. *Journal of Consulting and Clinical Psychology, 74,* 1055–1064. doi:10.1037/0022-006X.74.6.1055

Negash, S., Carlson, S. H., & Linder, J. N. (2018). Emotionally focused therapy and eye movement desensitization and reprocessing: An integrated treatment to heal the trauma of infidelity. *Couple and Family Psychology: Research and Practice, 7,* 143–157. doi:10.1037/cfp0000107

Perel, E. (2006). *Mating in captivity: Reconciling the erotic + the domestic.* New York, NY: HarperCollins Publishers.

Perel, E. (2017). *The state of affairs: Rethinking infidelity.* New York, NY: HarperCollins Publishers.

Pittman, F. (1989). *Private lies: Infidelity and the betrayal of intimacy.* New York, NY: W. W. Norton & Company, Inc.

Raj, P., Elizabeth, C. S., & Padmakumari, P. (2016). Mental health through forgiveness: Exploring the roots and benefits. *Cogent Psychology, 3*(1), 1153817. doi:10.1080/23311908.2016.1153817

Snyder, D. K., Baucom, D. H., & Gordon, K. C. (2007). *Getting past the affair: A program to help you cope, heal and move on—Together or apart.* New York, NY: The Guilford Press.

Stith, S. M., Spencer, C. M., & Mittal, M. (2020). Couple violence: In-depth assessment and systemic interventions. In K. S. Wampler & A. J. Blow (Eds.), *The handbook of systemic family therapy: Systemic family therapy with couples* (3). Hoboken, NJ: Wiley.

Timm, T. M., & Blow, A. J. (2018). Healing the relational wounds from infidelity. In D. Flemons & S. Green (Eds.), *Quickies: The handbook of brief sex therapy* (2nd ed.). New York, NY: W.W. Norton & Company.

Toussaint, L., Worthington, E., & Williams, D. R. (2015). *Forgiveness and health: Scientific evidence and theories relating forgiveness to better health.* New York, NY: Springer.

Vossler, A. (2016). Internet infidelity 10 years on: A critical review of the literature. *The Family Journal, 24*(4), 359–366. doi:10.1177/1066480716663191

Weeks, G., Gambescia, N., & Jenkins, R. (2003). *Treating infidelity: Therapeutic dilemmas and effective strategies* (1st ed.). New York, NY: W. W. Norton & Company.

Whisman, M. A., & Snyder, D. K. (2007). Sexual infidelity in a national survey of American women: Differences in prevalence and correlates as a function of method of assessment. *Journal of Family Psychology, 21*(2), 147–154. doi:10.1037/0893-3200.21.2.147

World Health Organization. (2018). *International statistical classification of diseases and related health problems* (11th Rev.). Retrieved from https://icd.who.int/browse11/l-m/en

16

Integrating Couple Therapy into Work with Sexual Dysfunctions

Katherine Hertlein, Tina M. Timm, and Carissa D'Aniello

Sex therapy is a challenging modality of treatment. It requires that a therapist can appropriately assess sexual problems, understand the reciprocal influence of couple dynamics on those sexual issues, and use this information in determining how to triage treatment. Conducting sex therapy without considering the couple dynamics involved can, at best, keep the couple in the same place, or, at worst, result in the couple experiencing more distress. This can be devastating for a couple as therapy is typically their last resort (Bulow, 2009; Hertlein, Weeks, & Gambescia, 2015).

Couple therapists and sex therapists alike have found that sexual problems reflect and exacerbate relationship problems (Johnson & Zuccarini, 2010). Therapists often help couples address sexual problems and relationship problems in concert with one another. Sexual problems can result in increased frustration and discord in couple relationships, and therefore, couples may be prompted to enter couple therapy. Couples tend to be reluctant to come to therapy about their couple issues, let alone sex. Common issues that bring couples into therapy include communication issues, finances, decision making, and issues with emotional intimacy (Miller, Yorgason, Sandberg, & White, 2003), with sexual issues listed as only one of the 10 reasons listed for coming to therapy. It is likely, however, that sexual difficulties interface with some of the other presenting problems on the list. For example, power issues are tied to sexual behavior, both explicitly and implicitly (Bargh & Raymond, 1995). These power dynamics in a couple's relationship may play out in several ways in a couple's sex life, including the inability to orgasm, presence of hypoactive desire, etc.

Unfortunately, many of those who practice sex therapy are not well trained in couple therapy and vice versa (Hertlein et al., 2015). This is both a consequence of the lack of integration in the field of these two entities theoretically (Wiederman, 1998), as well as reflective of the divide in professional allegiances of practitioners. Couples are best suited to achieve sexual wellness when couple therapy is integrated into sex therapy (Schnarch, 1991). Therapists need the basics of assessment and treatment of

The Handbook of Systemic Family Therapy: Volume 3, First Edition.
Edited by Karen S. Wampler and Adrian J. Blow.
© 2020 John Wiley & Sons Ltd. Published 2020 by John Wiley & Sons Ltd.

couples' issues to ameliorate some of the issues that might prevent movement toward accomplishing sex therapy goals. Though it is important to assess each partner's cognitive and behavioral patterns related to sexual functioning, therapists working with couples need to examine how each person's behavior intersects with his/her partner and how both partners create and contribute to the development and maintenance of relational and sexual dynamics.

Factors That Contribute to Sexual Dysfunction

There are a few general factors that contribute to sexual wellness: biology, psychological issues of the individual, and systemic issues. Physiologically, there are countless conditions and situations can contribute to the development and maintenance of sexual problems. These include but are not limited to medications, neurotransmitters, heart conditions, musculoskeletal problems, nerve damage, physiological trauma, and hormonal imbalances (Abrams, 2017; Binik & Hall, 2014; Lipshultz, Pastuszak, Goldstein, Giraldi, & Perelman, 2016; Nagaraj, Pai, Rao, & Goyal, 2009; Segraves, 1989; Tsai, Yeh, & Hwang, 2011). While it is out of the scope of this chapter to discuss each of these contributions in detail, therapists who do not consider the biology as part of a couple's sexual wellness may potentially not be able to address the issue presented.

Individual psychological factors that contribute to sexual problems include the presence of pathology. Common conditions that can negatively impact a couple's sex life include depression, anxiety, personality disorders, and other mood disorders. Unfortunately, trauma can also be an individual experience that would contribute negatively to the development of sexual problems. For example, it is common for people who experience sexual abuse to experience high levels of anxiety when they encounter sexual situations. In the case of depression, anxiety, and mood disorders, it may be that the depression itself is contributing to the sexual problem, as well as any medications taken to manage the depression or anxiety.

For the couple, relational factors may be contributing to and/or maintaining the sexual problem (Schnarch, 1991). These relational factors contributing to sex problems include (but are not limited to) an inability to regulate emotional and physical intimacy, incompatibility, power struggles, perceived neglect, and the presence of fears, potentially leading to sabotaging efforts to address the sexual problem. Finally, by acknowledging the individual contributions of each to the couple's problems, therapists can better integrate couple work into sexual dysfunction treatment and move toward sustaining sexual wellness.

The purpose of this chapter is to reaffirm the central role couples work plays in the treatment of sexual issues and concerns. It begins with a review of previous models that have incorporated couple and sex therapy, identifies the barriers preventing therapists from integrating the two, and provides some practical strategies for how to remove those barriers in order to effectively conduct sex therapy in a systemic manner. We also discuss how couple therapy and sex therapy are critical components in the concept of sexual wellness and how a therapist can work effectively to augment sexual wellness in the couple. The focus of this chapter is limited to special cases of sexual problems in individuals in a committed relationship.

Sexual Health and Wellness

Sexual wellness and diversity

Because of its multidimensional nature, sexual wellness in couples is of paramount importance to a couple's relationship. Sexual wellness is often described as the absence of disease (Tetley, Lee, Nazroo, & Hinchliff, 2018). This is inherently problematic as one-third of older adults do indicate a sexual problem, usually rooted in physiology. This implies that an older adult with biological issues impairing their sexual functioning can never return to a state of sexual wellness (Syme, Cohn, Stoffregen, Kaempfe, & Schippers, 2018). In addition, many older adults are not distressed by the biological issues (Pascoal, De Santa Bárbara Narciso, & Pereira, 2014; Santos-Iglesias, Byers, & Moglia, 2016).

In Western culture, sexual wellness is defined as "understanding the human body, choosing the type and size of one's family, and experiencing satisfaction (alone or with consenting others), while maintaining autonomy, minimizing exposure to disease, and preserving safety" (SAMHSA, 2015). As a primary area in overall wellness, it plays a key role in sexual satisfaction, mental health, extraversion, emotional stability, and expectations of positive outcomes (Daugherty et al., 2016). For adults, sexual wellness has many facets including positive sexual well-being, high sexual self-esteem, positive attitudes toward sex, and sexual satisfaction (Santos-Iglesias et al., 2016; Træen et al., 2017).

What does not seem to be adding to the argument of sexual wellness is the media's portrayal of sex in pathological ways. The Western cultural norm of discouraging open conversations about sex is perpetuated in movies and on television alongside a constant stream of sexual images, topics, and advertisements regarding sex trafficking, rape, etc., communicating a lack of wholeness in understanding sexuality in context, thus making sex and relationships a commodity more than anything else (Iantaffi, 2016).

Attitudes and beliefs about sexual wellness

In fact, one's beliefs and attitudes about sex globally influence the presence of dysfunction. Women (particularly lesbian women) are more likely to view sexual desire as a sin; men who are more religious, are conservative, and have more erroneous beliefs about their partners' sexual satisfaction are more likely to exhibit sexual dysfunction (Peixoto & Nobre, 2014). In addition, gay men with sexual dysfunctions tended to believe that sex is an abuse of men's power (Peixoto & Nobre, 2014).

Another key area tied to sexual wellness is that of sexually addictive/compulsive behavior. Sexually addictive behavior may be characterized by instances when one's sexual behavior comes in conflict with one's commitments, values, and/or self-control, results in negative consequences, and lacks personal accountability (Herring, 2017). It may also activate pleasure centers in the brain consistent with other behavioral addictions (Redcay & Simonetti, 2018; Starcevic, 2016). Like the other sexual dysfunctions, the etiology of sex addiction is a complex weaving of varied experiences, conditions (both physiological and psychological), and environmental antecedents (Hertlein et al., 2015).

Factors compromising sexual wellness

Given the complex nature of sexual wellness, therapists may hold values and beliefs about sexual wellness that may impact the therapeutic process. Therapists may assume (incorrectly) that if clients experience a sexual problem, they would disclose it to the therapist (Julien, Thom, & Kline, 2010). Research consistently shows that clients may not disclose a sexual problem to the therapist due to fear, embarrassment, guilt, or shame (Haboubi & Lincoln, 2003; Strada, Vegni, & Lamiani, 2016). Therapists may also hold concerns about directly asking clients about sexual problems. For example, therapists may hold the concern that discussing sexual functioning may cause embarrassment to their clients (Ussher et al., 2013). Further, therapists may not initiate conversations about sexuality during couple therapy due to time constraints, client expectation about therapeutic tasks, and lack of confidence in addressing sexual issues (Julien et al., 2010).

In addition to the therapist's beliefs and feelings about sexual functioning, the client couple may hold beliefs that make it difficult to address sexuality in the context of couple therapy. Couples have limited or no awareness of how the couple dynamics affect sexual functioning. Further, couples may refuse to acknowledge the connection between couple dynamics and sexual functioning. In this situation, where the client and therapist take on opposing viewpoints, or positions, the therapist and client may each try to sell the other on their position. This is the principle that Minuchin discussed in structural therapy—the couple says "here is who were are" and then the therapist tries to tell them who they are (S. Minuchin, IFTA in Orlando).

Power and control are often at the heart of couple relationships. Couples often engage in daily negotiations related to who will influence who and who will accommodate or acquiesce to the other's will. Power is relational (Knudson-Martin, 2013) and manifests in the context of relationships. For example, power struggles are characterized by each partner trying to influence the other to no avail (Fishbane, 2011). Power struggles can have negative effects on partners' feelings of attachment, closeness, and intimacy with their partners. Alternatively, when couples experience distress, it may be because both partners are organized around the interests of the more powerful partner (Knudson-Martin, 2013; Knudson-Martin & Huenergardt, 2010). One partner may chronically caretake, or accommodate to the other partner regularly, such that this pattern becomes germane to the relationship and is no longer recognized as problematic. Studies find that power imbalances carry negative consequences in couple relationships. Specifically, male and female partners may experience depression, anxiety, invalidation, limited emotional attunement, and vulnerability (Knudson-Martin, 2013).

Research shows that both men and women do better in equal relationships (Steil, 1997). Therapists must be aware of how power manifests as part of couple therapy. Often, therapists proceed with therapy as if partners have equal power (Knudson-Martin, 2013; Leslie & Southard, 2009; Lyness & Lyness, 2007; Williams & Knudson-Martin, 2012). Though society has evolved to idealize more egalitarian relationship models, there has been little guidance on how to achieve such relationships (Coontz, 2005; Gerson, 2010; Knudson-Martin, 2013; Mahoney & Knudson-Martin, 2009). Therapists may be reluctant to bring up issues of power, as it can be a deeply personal and value-laden issue that may be uncomfortable for therapists to discuss.

Researchers and theorists have suggested that power issues in couple relationships may manifest in sexual issues (Brenzsnyak & Whisman, 2004). Low sexual desire has been conceptualized as an attempt to equalize the power dynamics in the relationship and gain control (Hardman & Gardner, 1986; Stone Fish, Fish, & Sprenkle, 1984). Brenzsnyak and Whisman (2004) found main effects for marital power as a predictor of sexual desire. They found that higher congruence between husbands' desired and perceived balance of decision-making power was correlated with higher sexual desire. Egalitarian relationships were also associated with higher levels of sexual desire for both husbands and wives (Brenzsnyak & Whisman, 2004).

When addressing power issues in couple relationships, therapists should consider the societal context of the relationship and consider what types of power structures might be in place. For example, gender, culture, and societal expectations are all parts of the relationship context that may impact the way that relational power manifests. Knudson-Martin (2013) suggests a model of equality in relationships characterized by shared relational responsibility, mutual vulnerability, mutual attunement, and mutual influence. Shared relational responsibility occurs when both partners are sensitive and accountable for the effects of their actions on the other. Both partners take an active interest and responsibility in the things that are necessary to maintain the relationship. Mutual vulnerability refers to a spirit of openness, curiosity, and self-honesty in the relationship. Each partner experiences the other as flexible and adaptive, permitting space for acceptance. Mutual attunement refers to each partner's awareness and interest in the needs of the other person. Mutual influence is being able to make an impression on and impact the other person's thoughts, feelings, and actions. Knudson-Martin (2013) asserts that relational change happens when the partner in the more powerful position takes a more relational orientation and focuses on the needs of the relationship (Fishbane, 2011; Huenergardt & Knudson-Martin, 2009; Silverstein, Bass, Tuttle, Knudson-Martin, & Huenergardt, 2006; Williams & Knudson-Martin, 2012). Therapists who are aware of power issues can help to facilitate the process of both partners taking a relationally oriented stance, rather than a power position.

Process and Content of Assessment in Couples

We approach working with sexual issues in couple therapy through an integrated couple therapy where attention is spent on multiple supporting systems, including physiological, emotional, and relational concerns. Assessment of the couple dynamics in sex therapy work is a comprehensive, continuous process that occurs at the beginning and is maintained throughout the course of therapy. It is a necessary process for establishing diagnoses and directing further questions to assess and improve a couple's sexual wellness. The first part of assessment is designed to obtain basic information on the relationship, the health histories of each person, and information about the sexual problem. Because discussing the sexual problem can cause shame and embarrassment, the therapist needs to proceed with these questions in a sensitive manner. Based on the information received, the therapist can ask about other areas of sexual functioning, such as foreplay, sex preferences, etc. The therapist needs to rule out any biological considerations that would underlie the sexual problem (Manara, 1991).

Sexual issues may reflect problems and concerns at varied levels in couples, and couple problems and sex problems reciprocally maintain and exacerbate each other (Schnarch, 1991). We believe sexual problems might mask couple problems or unconsciously be maintained by the couple to avoid intimacy. One key assessment is determining whether the sexual difficulty is the result of a primary or a secondary dysfunction. To determine this, consider the etiology of a sexual problem, issue, or concern. Primary sexual dysfunctions are the first problem to emerge. The etiology may be physiological, may be psychological, or may contain elements of both. Secondary sexual problems follow the first, are often a consequence of a couple's attempts to repair the first, and also are often psychological in nature. For example, one client reported nerve damage after a surgery that left her unable to feel her perineum and labia. At intake, she reported that sex with her husband was turning into a therapy session, because she was forcing herself to have sex to try and see if she was going to feel something. When she was unable to feel, she ended up in tears, and her husband took on the role of consoling her and listening to her pain about the situation. She stated she was beginning to have a negative association with sex because of the outcome of these interactions. In this example, the primary sexual dysfunction is the consequence of the nerve damage. The secondary dysfunction was an aversion to sex. In many cases, the secondary sexual dysfunction emerges as a classical conditioning pairing of the body's physiological state (most often anxiety) with a benign stimulus (in this case, sexual activity/behavior). The prevalence of the development of secondary sexual dysfunctions seems to be about the same for men and women (Çelik et al., 2013). For these reasons, prior to beginning the work on sexual problems, the therapist must first resolve the couple issues.

Process of assessment

Integrating couple therapy into work with sexual dysfunctions begins with the assessment phase. We tend to structure these sessions as a mix between individual and conjoint sessions, as individual sessions can allow for information to come out without judgment and couple sessions can be used to clarify sessions (Russell, 1990). In the first session, couples are seen together. We recommend that the first session be 1.5–2 hr long to account for the issues that will arise. The second and third sessions are individual sessions—one for each partner. In the individual session, the therapist needs to have a clear secrets policy outlined and communicated to clients. Ideally, the therapist will have discussed this secrets policy in the previous session with both clients are present; the secrets policy is developed by the therapist and limits the circumstances in which secrets are going to be held.

In our practice, we tell clients that when a secret is going to affect the outcome of treatment, that secret has to come out. For example, if a client in the individual sessions chooses to disclose marijuana usage, that may not be enough to warrant disclosing this information to the other partner because it likely will not affect the outcome of treatment. If one of the members of the relationship, however, discloses they are having an affair, such information will affect the outcome of treatment and the therapist will work with the individual to have that information communicated. For example, Martha[1] came into therapy and stated that she and her husband were having sexual problems. In the interview with the two of them together, neither of them noted any issues with her husband's erection. Yet in the individual sessions, she stated that he does not become a fully erect and she suspects this is the result of undiagnosed diabetes. Martha stated that she did not want to make him angry by telling him what she noticed. Another client, Louise, reported she could not stand the smell of her husband Paul's genital area and that this was preventing her from having sex with him. In each of these cases, such issues were disclosed in the individual sessions—critical information that shapes the course of therapy that would not have been reported if the therapist was not solely structured as couples work.

After the individual sessions (fourth session), the therapist meets with the couple and reviews the treatment plan. The treatment plan has five areas: individual psychology, dyadic issues, individual biological issues, psychological issues, and sociocultural issues. These areas will be the focus of treatment with the clients and therapist negotiated the priority in which they will be addressed. It is critically important that the therapist balance the treatment plan fight indicating both partners on it to nearly an equal degree. One partner would see that they were named all over the treatment plan, it would communicate that it was their problem dominantly and that is not a message that is helpful to the couple.

Content of assessment

Empirically, it is well established that the expression of sexuality in a relational context and sexual well-being is the result of a complex interplay between psychological, emotional, and physiological well-being (Carvalho & Nobre, 2011). For example, predictors of sexual desire in men include relationship adjustment and cognitive factors such as restrictive attitudes around sex, concern about the quality of their erection, the presence of erotic thoughts, shame, and sadness (Carvalho & Nobre, 2011; Nobre & Pinto-Gouveia, 2006a, 2006b, 2008, 2009; Peixoto & Nobre, 2017; Quinta Gomes & Nobre, 2012). In fact, emotional intimacy has been demonstrated in at least one study to be the strongest predictor of sexual satisfaction in both men and women (Pascoal, Narciso, & Pereira, 2013). At the same time, the factors contributing to sexual dysfunction in men still tend to overemphasize biology rather than belief systems, emotions, and relational issues (Carvalho & Nobre, 2011). Each of these areas is important content needing to be assessed.

A host of literature points to the complex etiology of physiology and psychology in the treatment of sexual dysfunctions and problems (see Hertlein et al. (2015) for a review). A couple's sexual relationship may, in part, be understood as being composed of holons (Zumaya, Bridges, & Rubio, 1999), or facets in a couple's relationship, including gender, eroticism, interpersonal bonding, and reproduction. For example, the nature of sexual dysfunction, such as arousal disorders, in those living with multiple sclerosis varies based on gender (Çelik et al., 2013), as does the expression of sexual dysfunction in those diagnosed with major depressive disorder (Isaac et al., 2012). Consideration of different facets of a couple's relationship has underwritten the constructivist sex therapy approach described by Zumaya et al. (1999) in the attachment and understanding of meaning and sexual response and behavior.

Area 1: Establishing the biological contribution

One area that needs to be assessed before anything else is whether there is any biological contribution to the presenting problem and to what degree the biological contribution is impacting sexual wellness. As mentioned earlier, there are number of conditions biologically that can contribute to sexual symptoms. In the case of 72-year-old Adam, he noticed he had lost the ability to maintain an erection. Part of the assessment involved setting a meeting with Adam's wife to ensure that there were no relationship difficulties that might be contributing to the sexual dysfunction. The relationship between Adam and his wife was quite strong, and he did not reveal pathology individually that would contribute to the sexual dysfunction he was experiencing. A review of the medications that Adam had been taking after a heart attack revealed that those medications might be the most likely cause of his dysfunction. Therefore, psychotherapy turned to helping the couple deal with the medication and talking to the heart doctor about the problem.

Area 2: Assessing individual psychological contributions

Psychosocial variables play an important role in the development and maintenance of sexual problems. *Patient variables* contributing to the sexual problem include depression, anxiety, idiosyncratic sexual patterns, and unrealistic expectations (Althof & Rosen, 2010). Depression, for example, can be one area where sexuality is compromised because of the individuals and ability to be able to make changes. Another contribution psychologically might be one's sense of esteem. For example, Jenny had always struggled with her body image. She did not feel comfortable changing in front of her husband or feel comfortable with her body in any capacity. As a consequence, she refused to have sex with her partner. In this case, her individual issues with regard to her own body image or primary factor contributing to the sexual problem.

Another psychosocial contributing area is the experience of trauma (McCarthy & Breez, 2010). This includes soliciting a trauma history and ascertaining how the traumas that occurred impacted the client's sexual self-esteem. For example, Joel and Maggie came to therapy set to divorce. In the context of taking their respective histories, Joel disclosed a history of giving his mother oral sex in his childhood. Joel reported this, however, not as being traumatic, but as being the point at which he was becoming trained to be a good lover. From an individual perspective, there was not only trauma but also some pretty severe cognitive distortions surrounding this sexual behavior. This distortion led to Joel's high value of sex placed on the relationship (above and beyond emotional commitment and intimacy building). His wife did not hold the same value regarding sex and the incompatibility sexually was a major reason why Marge wanted a divorce.

Partner variables are another set of psychosocial contributions (Althof & Rosen, 2010). These variables include a partner's individual lack of interest in sex, illness in the other partner (mental health or physical health), medication, biological and hormonal changes, etc. There are also *sexual variables* at play that must be considered in the assessment. Specifically, therapists need to assess incompatibility in terms of interest, activities, and frequency (Althof & Rosen, 2010). Finally, *contextual variables* that need to be addressed include cultural, developmental, and societal stressors such as acculturation, employment, finances, children concerns, parents, and others (Althof & Rosen, 2010).

Area 3: Identifying the couple dynamic contributions

The therapist works to more broadly assess the couple's relationship and context in addition to their role in sustaining the presenting problem. To determine the couple contribution to the relationship, the therapist needs to ask specific questions about how the couple's dynamics assisted in the development/maintenance of the sexual problem. The therapist should assess risk factors such as anger, resentment, fears (particularly of intimacy), conflict management styles, and power struggles (Gambescia & Weeks, 2015). For example, some couples who do not feel desire note that if they withhold sex from their partner, they are in control (Weeks & Gambescia, 2002). The therapist should inquire about the impact of the sexual problem on each of the partners. The easiest way to ask this is to say: "What impact has this problem had on your relationship?" (Weeks, Gambescia, & Hertlein, 2016). Specific areas of inquiry to assess the impact of the sexual problem on the couple include the following:

- Relationship history with one another and overall relationship satisfaction
- Relationship history prior to meeting one another and assess whether the sexual problem had ever manifested in those relationships
- View of sex (i.e., is sex spontaneous, fun, etc.) prior to the sexual problem and after the sexual problem
- The impact of the sexual problem on the couple's communication
- Overall sexual satisfaction and if this has changed as a result of the problem
- Sexual compatibility
- Other outward-reaching effects of the sexual problem

Further, the non-identified partner may also have a sexual problem, developed either in response to the problem held by the other partner, from something else in the relationship, or a combination. The therapist needs to be mindful of keeping a systemic view in asking questions about the development of sexual problems in the relationship.

Part of understanding the impact of the sexual wellness issue on a couple's life is gaining an understanding through obtaining a comprehensive history—both relational and sexual. The therapist gathers information about the specific nature of the sexual problem, the time of onset, the couple's own explanation and ideas about its occurrence, their specific attitudes toward sexuality, and the like. Further, the therapist should consider the couple's ages, family constellation, culture, occupation, health status, stress levels, mental health, substance abuse, and relationship history when conceptualizing treatment. The therapist should also inquire about life cycle events experienced by the couple, including normative, on-time events, or non-normative off-time events (McGoldrick, Carter, & Garcia-Preto, 2016). We advocate that the therapist adopt a "who, what where, and when" perspective in history gathering. Specific areas include assessing the initial attraction to each other, circumstances that surrounded their relationship development, and specific qualities they appreciate about their partner. These historical conversations naturally lend themselves to conversations that explore each person's family of origin, attitudes about couple relationships, and early experiences with sexuality (along with an assessment as to whether any of those experiences were forced areas). In addition, therapists can assess how each partner understood and witnessed intimacy, early sexual experiences, and the messages gained from their past experiences. Finally, therapists should be mindful to assess for trauma within the current relationship as well as outside of it.

Couple communication is an integral aspect of sex therapy and couple therapy. How couples communicate and discuss their relationship has a profound impact on how they experience their relationship (Weeks et al., 2016). Communication therapy is a type of couple therapy that focuses specifically on teaching couple communication skills and ways to cooperate and accommodate to one another (Everaerd & Dekker, 1981). This type of therapy aims to influence couple sexual relationships by enhancing a couple's ability to talk openly about their perceptions of the romantic relationship and sexual relationship. Communication therapy indirectly influences the couple sexual relationship by improving the overall relationship. A study by Everaerd and Dekker (1981) found that sex therapy and communication therapy are effective methods of treating sexual disorders. Communication therapy was found to be highly effective in improving female sexual satisfaction and relationship satisfaction (Everaerd & Dekker, 1981).

Both Manara (1991) and Everaerd and Dekker (1981) also attend to the role of communication in effective sex therapy. Manara's (1991) work highlights three levels of intervention aimed at improving communication. Level one is designed to address conflictual communication including contradictory messages and the expression of conflict in the relationship. It includes videotaping the interaction and showing it to the couple so they have a sense of how their dynamic looks. They are also asked to pay attention to relational patterns regarding power and aggression. The second level includes addressing other issues in the couple's relationship and their sexual skills. The third level helps the couple to integrate the skills learned in levels one and two and to apply the information to the couple and sexual relationship.

In European American cultures, there is a greater emphasis on companionship in marriage. In these relationships, couples also need to address emotional intimacy within sex therapy treatment (Hertlein et al., 2015; Russell, 1990). Research has shown that sexual problems are often the result of frustration and conflicts in romantic relationships. Intimacy is characterized as caring, emotional closeness via affection, communication, respect, satisfaction, and commitment (Moret, Glaser, Page, & Bargeron, 1998). Eight areas of intimacy have been identified (Waring, Tillman, Frelick, Russell, & Weisz, 1980): compatibility across a wide range of elements, affective expressions, affection and love, commitment, communication about sexual needs and desires, mutual pleasuring sexual behaviors, and trust. Intimacy is an important facet of understanding a couple's overall health and pathology, and sexual behavior is one manifestation of a couple's level of intimacy (Russell, 1990). Intimacy is a critical component of sexual satisfaction and overall relationship satisfaction (Yoo, Bartle-Haring, Day, & Gangamma, 2013). Intimacy and sexuality are intricately connected. Sexual functioning is one way that intimacy is expressed in couple relationships and must be addressed directly when couples report concerns in this area (Russell, 1990). Moret and colleagues (1998) found a correlation between sexual satisfaction and intimacy and that female partners reported higher ratings of intimacy and sexual satisfaction than male partners.

Another key piece of couple treatment is an assessment of a couple's attachment style. Adults who have developed a secure attachment style demonstrate low levels of anxiety and avoidance of close relationships and feel comfortable showing love and accepting love (Brassard, Péloquin, Dupuy, Wright, & Shaver, 2012). In contrast, adults who have developed a preoccupied attachment style experience high anxiety, but yet do not avoid intimacy, while a dismissive style of attachment is characterized by high intimacy avoidance. Those with a fearful attachment style experience high levels of both anxiety and avoidance. It stands to reason that attachment styles may be associated with sexual functioning (Brassard et al., 2012; Johnson & Zuccarini, 2010). Specifically, a secure attachment style has been found to facilitate relaxed and confident engagement in sex (Mikulincer & Shaver, 2007). Partners with anxious or avoidant attachment styles have been found to approach sex with higher levels of anxiety and therefore experience lower levels of intimacy and sexual pleasure (Johnson & Zuccarini, 2010). Anxiously attached individuals, for example, tend to rely on physical displays of sexual affection and are concerned about their sexual performance (Birnbaum, 2007; Davis, Shaver, & Vernon, 2004; Schachner & Shaver, 2004).

The Process of Integrating Couples Work in Sex Therapy

Obtaining investment

Couples needs to buy into the treatment process. They need to be advised of the rationale for arranging the treatment process in the way that makes sense to them. One way to discuss the rationale for the treatment sequence would be to present to them the treatment plan. This might include a discussion of sexual meaning and sexual scripts and how these may manifest in the presenting sexual concern (Atwood & Dershowitz, 1992; Derby, Peleg-Sagy, & Doron, 2016). Timm (2009) suggests that therapists in training may wish to get comfortable with talking about sex, to become more familiar with human sexuality, and to monitor their own sense of self in this process, and it may bring up some of their own experiences.

Timing is a critical part of treatment. Couples coming to sex therapy have frequently tried many home remedies and attendance in therapy is their last resort. The consequences of mistreatment and poor timing can be devastating for a couple. Therapists need to balance the sexual issue as a presenting problem with the knowledge that the couple dynamics are critical in the solution.

Developing a biopsychosocial treatment plan

Once the type of dysfunction is assessed, the therapist can begin building the stages of a treatment plan. The treatment plan may include triaging treatment and often involves treating the secondary dysfunction before the primary dysfunction. In the treatment plan, a biopsychosocial assessment with a focus on interactional and intrapsychic factors is preferred (Hertlein et al., 2015). Two presentations are rare: the presentation of only one sexual dysfunction and the presentation of a sexual dysfunction without a relational issue in accompaniment. At the same time, however, couples may not be aware that more than one dysfunction exists nor are they aware of the relational underpinnings contributing to the problem. With each of these pieces, therapists need to identify how to triage treatment, in consultation with the couple. In general, we recommend that the therapist first treat the presenting problems as opposed to other issues that warrant attention. This can be difficult for therapists to discern, as a couple may be aware of a sexual problem as a presenting problem, but be unaware of the underlying relational problems that underlie this issue. Because there may be issues that are associated with the clinical problem, it is important that the therapist treat those comorbid issues. For example, since depression is a major contributor to sexual dysfunction, the therapist needs to better manage the depression in order to achieve sexual wellness. The same is true for couple issues: if a comorbid couple issue is contributing to the sexual problem, the therapist needs to treat the couple issue first prior to starting more traditional and behavioral sex therapy methods. The therapist needs to do the couples work first or couples will not be able to successfully manage the sexual issue portion of treatment, and they will come to see therapy as hopeless.

Designing interventions

Another key part of the process is the warning to "go slow." The therapist needs to let the clients know that, due to the complex interweaving of sexual and couple issues, therapy will take time (Ridley, 2015). The therapist should never try to push a client into sexual changes and should monitor progress to ensure that the couple is making progress but is not overwhelmed. This is sometimes accomplished through telling the couple that this pacing is too fast and to warn them against making changes too quickly.

Another key part of treatment is being able to adapt this framework to commonly used theories in couple and family therapy. For example, if the therapist is using emotionally focused couple therapy (EFT), the therapist can track the sexual interaction cycles as a way to initially understand the couple's problematic dynamic. This might reveal the couple issues that are contributing to the sexual problem as well as identifying the secondary emotions that are manifesting in each stage. The therapist can then stay with their primary framework, but can still incorporate this framework to move toward greater sexual wellness. Another example would be application of these strategies within integrative behavioral couple therapy (IBCT). For example, the homework that is critical to the success of sex therapy can be incorporated into the behavioral component; the cognitions and acceptance, however, are addressed within the individual and dyadic foci prior to moving to the behavioral components specific to sex therapy In addition, the therapist may wish to give homework assignments related to the individual and couple work prior to moving ahead with the sex therapy work as a way to build hope and create a different, more positive expectancy set.

Couples often present with more than one sexual problem (see the section above on primary vs. secondary issues). Because the Diagnostic and Statistical Manual of Mental Disorders, 5th ed. (*DSM-5*) does not have a structure to indicate the reciprocal influence of one symptom on another, therapists need to triage treatment in a way to build hope rather than creating more hopelessness—in other words, intervening around the relationship issues first before asking for changes to the sexual behaviors. For example, Keith and Claire sought therapy due to Keith's communication problems. In the course of assessment, Keith acknowledged having some level of erectile dysfunction (ED). Keith stated that his ED was bothering him, and he felt that it mitigated his ability to feel sexual desire because he "knew" that he was going to fail if he were to engage in a sexual encounter with Claire. Claire, however, stated that she viewed sex as a burden or chore and was somewhat relieved that Keith had stopped making advances toward her. In this case, Keith seemed to be picking up that Claire was not interested in sex, thus subconsciously contributing to the development of ED. In other words, Keith developed ED as a way to distance from his perception of Claire's rejection of him. The ED, in turn, further contributed to the breakdown of the couple relationship more generally.

Interventions in sex therapy often involve both members of the couple and take place both in the therapy room and as homework. Some of these interventions may fall within the realm of self-help and can be effective provided they maintain the format described by the frame (Lankveld, 2009). Key elements necessary in the self-intervention process include "a relational frame of reference in which sexual problems are diagnosed and treated" (p. 147), establishing communication between partners regarding their sexual wishes, fears, and interactions, banning intercourse, and implementing sensate focus activities. Specific interventions include bibliotherapy, video therapy for the teaching of principles or skills such as those that teach sensate focus, computer-assisted sex therapy (involving a human therapist where the treatment is facilitated through the computer or a computer who is in the role of the human therapist), or a computerized sex expert program (Lankveld, 2009).

Because there is such a plethora of couple work in sex therapy, the interventions for sex therapy can transverse the scope of both couples work and specific sexual techniques. For example, in working with one heterosexual couple in their mid-40s, where the female partner presented with hypoactive sexual desire disorder, the female client was unwilling to make any changes in the relationship because of her discomfort with sex. Our intervention was to create two types of relational contracts—the one that they were living out and the one they said they wanted. In the session where we presented the relationship contract they were living, including low level complaints about sex with no real desire to change and an agreement for her to keep her low self-esteem. The male partner ripped up the contract; the female partner however tried to edit some of the sentence structure and said she thought that the agreement was appropriate. Therefore, treatment revolved around generating a new relationship contract before the work of sex therapy could begin.

One intervention called "SWEET" (Sexual Wellness Enhancement and Enrichment Training) has a dedicated focus on the biology of a client. This focus is not specifically because of the biology of the sexual response, but instead focuses on occurrences physiologically prior to the sexual response and how can we reduce the intensity or prevent a maladaptive response before it turns into a secondary sexual dysfunction (Baker & Absenger, 2013). Another approach is to use EFT in couples where there are differences in sexual compatibility (Gehring, 2003; Girard & Woolley, 2016). Finally, there are specific considerations in designing interventions that differ based on the presenting problems. For example, if the presenting problem is a female with low sexual desire or arousal, interventions might also be focused on her voice in the relationship, level of power, an expanded definition of sex, and conditions for sexual responsiveness. For men with impaired desire or arousal, there may also be some specific conversations about socialization (McCarthy & Farr, 2012; McCarthy & Thestrup, 2008; McCarthy & Wald, 2015).

Assigning homework

Homework is a critical part of the sex therapy treatment but is often met with resistance from the couple's end. Homework is a logical follow-up from what happens in session, typically a structured activity, and is designed to have a therapeutic impact. One of the first assignments often given is something related to sensate focus. It is likely that the couple will not comply with this assignment, as attempts to connect physically will exacerbate the potential couple dynamics underlying the problems. Homework should be designed so that each partner receives something from it—emotional, sensual, affectional, or sexual. All assignments should attend to both emotions and behavior (Charlton & Brigel, 1997). This might mean emotions and behaviors related to the sexual problems, the couple issues, or both. Weeks et al. (2016) outline several specific suggestions in assigning homework with a focus on systemic issues. They include assigning homework that is specific and understandable to the couple, clarifying misperceptions about the homework assignments, developing a contingency plan for homework completion, developing a network of support for the couple (including how the therapist can support), and identifying ways to manage perceived resistance and lack of compliance in homework completion.

Addressing sabotage and fears

Frequently, there are unconscious factors in the couple's relationship that may sabotage sex therapy. Couples' therapists understand that as one partner improves, the other partner exhibits pathology to return the couple back to homeostasis. In therapy, this looks like non-completion of homework, missing sessions, or other behaviors that are sabotaging of the process. Therapists need to address this head on with clients. One way to accomplish this is through addressing and normalizing the fears that emerge in therapy. A second way to do this is through conducting a negative consequence of change session where the couple discuss what would be challenging about changing and how the therapist and couple would know when some of these fears would be interfering with treatment. A third way is to frame assignments as "win-win." In other words, if the couple is successful in completing the assigning, what they get individually is more positive than the fear of change. The therapist must monitor anxiety when discussing topics and giving homework. The couple is asked about their level of anxiety regarding the homework and the assignment is modified until both partners agree the anxiety is low enough to allow them to complete the assignment (Weeks et al., 2016).

Attending to diversity

Sex therapy is fundamentally a therapy about competing value systems between each member of the relationship. This may mean incompatibility in frequency of sex or the desire to perform certain activities. Here the therapist has to be well aware of the couple's background, value systems, and who they are outside of the bedroom but have little insight into other aspects of one's life. In therapy with same-sex couples, the therapist should also address the experience the couple has had regarding oppression, the stages of sexual identity within the relationship, and the meaning of sexual orientation in relationships. The therapist needs to ensure that they are supportive and validating of the relationships and incorporate strengths of each partner into the relationship (Bradford, 2004). Considerations for polyamorous couples include a clear understanding of the boundaries in the relationship (McCoy, Stinson, Ross, & Hjelmstad, 2015). Without a conversation of those boundaries and agreements within those boundaries, the relationship will feel unsafe and therapy will fail.

There is also a need for sex therapists to understand the context for the couple relationship more broadly. Therapists need to have a full understanding of how religion, culture, and larger external systems are impacting the couple's belief system, their relationship agreement, and their arrangement and must be able to work within that frame (Rosenbaum, De Paauw, Aloni, & Heruti, 2013). With Chinese couples, for example, the therapist needs to work within a frame that is attentive and respectful of gender role issues, communication rules, and other elements that affect the couple relationship (So & Cheung, 2005).

Contraindications

Like any type of treatment, there are circumstances when integrating couple work in sex therapy may not be suitable. For instance, if the therapist comes to some information that conveys that the issue the client is having is rooted in a specific biological issue (i.e., nerve damage), there may be little efficacy when applying a partner approach (Bergeron, Meana, Biinik, & Khalife, 2010). Finally, the presence of interpersonal violence as well as the presence of severe psychopathology in one of the partners (i.e., narcissist–borderline, antisocial personality, etc.) may not permit for a level of safety in the room to be able to effectively conduct this work. Therapists need to be diligent about separating the symptom from the system and understanding that is contributing to the problems, as for so many who are severely mentally ill, there also tend to be some significant systemic problems (Maurice & Yule, 2010).

Areas for Further Training

In many sex therapy programs such as the certification outlined by the American Association of Sexuality Educators, Counselors, and Therapists (AASECT) and internationally (such as Argentine Society of Human Sexuality), the focus tends to be on individual issues. In contrast, in couple and family therapy programs, there is confusion as to what the Commission on Accreditation for Marriage and Family Therapy Education (COAMFTE) requires in terms of sex therapy training, with many agreeing that the COAMFTE does not specify any requirements (Zamboni & Zaid, 2017). In addition, couple and family therapist trainers may not have expertise or enough knowledge to provide appropriate sex therapy training (Zamboni & Zaid, 2017). The limiting of sex therapy and human sexuality training in couple and family therapy programs and the reverse in sexuality programs dilutes both training experiences (Schnarch, 2008).

Sexual issues at times activate our value and belief systems. It is for this reason that attention to the self-of-the-therapist is critical. This might involve the clinician doing some work on their own personal sexual genogram, creating a sexual experience timeline, or even attending a seminar on sexual attitudes (Sexual Attitude Reassessment [SAR]) (Timm, 2009). Couple therapists and sex therapists can get better training through well-developed course curricula that involve both couple work and sex work. In addition, participation in interprofessional teams may help develop an appreciation for the complexity of sexual behavior, interactions, and how each interact with one another in creating a couple's sexual wellness.

Resources

The AASECT outlines several areas for further training. They identify core knowledge areas focused on a comprehensive understanding of what affects sexual behavior, including family of origin, intimacy, and other psychological areas. For more information, visit https://www.aasect.org/aasect-certification

Research and Future Directions

We agree with the conceptualization offered by Binik and Meana (2009) who identified sex therapy as a subspecialty of couple therapy or an approach whose techniques are all under the larger umbrella of couple therapy. One of the contemporary areas of research in the field of sex therapy is that of sexual minorities in sexual wellness. There is recently a thrust in the literature regarding the concepts of invisibility management sexual minorities, the multiple marginalization experienced by those who identify with in the sexual minority spectrum, and in particular bisexuality invisibility management. While the proposed framework in this chapter would still apply to those populations, research has to follow along and demonstrate that the strategies will support these populations in ways that are sensitive to their unique needs. One way to accomplish this aim is to empirically test the proposed frameworks presented in this chapter. Testing the outcome of this and other proposed frameworks would serve to empirically validate this treatment modality, furthering the push toward evidence-based treatment.

Note

1   All vignettes in this chapter are inspired by actual cases but are composites rather than exact descriptions. Though the dynamics described are close to the original situations, the details of the cases have been altered significantly to protect confidentiality and meet ethical guidelines.

References

Abrams, M. (2017). *Sexuality and its disorders: Development, cases, and treatment.* New York, NY: Sage.

Althof, S., & Rosen, R. C. (2010). Combining medical and psychological interventions for the treatment of erectile dysfunction. In S. Levine, C. Risen, & S. E. Althof's (Eds.), *Handbook of clinical sexuality for mental health professionals* (pp. 251–266). New York, NY: Routledge.

Atwood, J. D., & Dershowitz, S. (1992). Constructing a sex and marital therapy frame: Ways to help couples deconstruct sexual problems. *Journal of Sex & Marital Therapy, 18*(3), 196. doi:10.1080/00926239208403407

Baker, A., & Absenger, W. (2013). Sexual wellness enhancement and enrichment training (SWEET): A hypothetical group model for addressing sexual health and wellbeing. *Sexual and Relationship Therapy, 28*(1–2), 48–62. doi:10.1080/14681994.2013.770142

Bargh, J. A., & Raymond, P. (1995). The naive misuse of power: Nonconscious sources of sexual harassment. *Journal of Social Issues, 51*(1), 85–96. doi:10.1111/j.1540-4560.1995.tb01310.x

Bergeron, S., Meana, M., Biinik, Y. M., & Khalife, S. (2010). Painful sex. In S. Levine, C. Risen, & S. E. Althof's (Eds.), *Handbook of clinical sexuality for mental health professionals* (pp. 193–214). New York, NY: Routledge.

Binik, Y., & Hall, K. (2014). *Principles and practice of sex therapy* (5th ed.). New York, NY: Guilford.

Binik, Y., & Meana, M. (2009). The future of sex therapy: Specialization or marginalization? *Archives of Sexual Behavior, 38*(6), 1016–1027. doi:10.1007/s10508-009-9475-9

Birnbaum, G. (2007). Attachment orientations, sexual functioning, and relationship satisfaction in a community sample of women. *Journal of Social and Personal Relationships, 24*(1), 21–35.

Bradford, M. (2004). Bisexual issues in same-sex couple therapy. *Journal of Couple & Relationship Therapy, 3*(2-3), 43–52. doi:10.1300/J398v03n02_05

Brassard, A., Péloquin, K., Dupuy, E., Wright, J., & Shaver, P. R. (2012). Romantic attachment insecurity predicts sexual dissatisfaction in couples seeking marital therapy. *Journal of Sex & Marital Therapy, 38*(3), 245–262. doi:10.1080/0092623X.2011.606881

Brenzsnyak, M., & Whisman, M. A. (2004). Sexual desire and relationship functioning: The effects of marital satisfaction and power. *Journal of Sex & Marital Therapy, 30*, 199–217. doi:10.1080/00926230490262393

Bulow, S. (2009). Integrating sex and couple therapy: A multifaceted case history. *Family Process, 48*(3), 379–389. doi:10.1111/j.1545-5300.2009.01289.x

Carvalho, J., & Nobre, P. (2011). Predictors of men's sexual desire: The role of psychological, cognitive-emotional, relational, and medical factors. *Journal of Sex Research, 48*(2–3), 254–262. doi:10.1080/00224491003605475

Çelik, D. B., Poyraz, E. C., Bingöl, A., İdiman, E., Özakbaş, S., & Kaya, D. (2013). Sexual dysfunction in multiple sclerosis: Gender differences. *Journal of the Neurological Sciences, 324*(1-2), 17–20. doi:10.1016/j.jns.2012.08.019

Charlton, R. S., & Brigel, F. W. (1997). Treatment of arousal and orgasmic disorders. In R. S. Charlton (Ed.), *Treating sexual disorders* (pp. 237–280). San Francisco, CA: Jossey-Bass.

Coontz, S. (2005). *Marriage, a history: From obedience to intimacy or how love conquered marriage*. New York, NY: Viking.

Daugherty, T. K., Julian, H. M., Lynch, N. M., Chen, S. J., Whipple, T. L., & Ginsburg, A. F. (2016). Beyond the absence of disease or infirmity: The case for sexual wellness. *College Student Journal, 50*(3), 404–408.

Davis, D., Shaver, P. R., & Vernon, M. L. (2004). Attachment style and subjective motivations for sex. *Personality and Social Psychology Bulletin, 30*(8), 1076–1090. doi:10.1177/0146167204264794

Derby, D. S., Peleg-Sagy, T., & Doron, G. (2016). Schema therapy in sex therapy: A theoretical conceptualization. *Journal of Sex & Marital Therapy, 42*(7), 648–658. doi:10.1080/0092623X.2015.1113586

Everaerd, W., & Dekker, J. (1981). A comparison of sex therapy and communication therapy: Couples complaining of orgasmic dysfunction. *Journal of Sex & Marital Therapy, 7*(4), 278–289. doi:10.1080/00926238108405429

Fishbane, M. D. (2011). Facilitating relational empowerment in couple therapy. *Family Process, 50*(3), 337–352. doi:10.1111/j.1545-5300.2011.01364.x

Gambescia, N., & Weeks, G. R. (2015). Systemic treatment of erectile disorder. In K. Hertlein, G. Weeks, & N. Gambescia (Eds.), *Systemic sex therapy* (2nd ed.). New York, NY: Routledge.

Gehring, D. (2003). Couple therapy for low sexual desire: A systemic approach. *Journal of Sex & Marital Therapy, 29*(1), 25–38. doi:10.1080/713847099

Gerson, K. (2010). *The unfinished revolution: How a new generation is reshaping family, work, and gender in America.* New York, NY: Oxford University Press.

Girard, A., & Woolley, S. R. (2016). Using emotionally focused therapy to treat sexual desire discrepancy in couples. *Journal of Sex & Marital Therapy.* doi:10.1080/00926 23X.2016.1263703

Haboubi, N. H., & Lincoln, N. (2003). Views of health professionals on discussing sexual issues with patients. *Disability & Rehabilitation, 25*, 291–296. doi:10.1080/ 096382802100003118

Hardman, R. K., & Gardner, D. J. (1986). Sexual anorexia: A look at inhibited sexual desire. *Journal of Sex Education & Therapy, 12*, 55–59.

Herring, B. (2017). A framework for categorizing chronically problematic sexual behavior. *Sexual Addiction & Compulsivity, 24*(4), 242–247. doi:10.1080/10720162.2017.1394947

Hertlein, K. M., Weeks, G. R., & Gambescia, N. (Eds.) (2015). *Systemic sex therapy* (2nd ed.). New York, NY: Routledge.

Huenergardt, D., & Knudson-Martin, C. (2009). Gender and power as a fulcrum for clinical change. In C. Knudson-Martin & A. Mahoney (Eds.), *Couples, gender, and power: Creating change in intimate relationships* (pp. 337–361). New York, NY: Springer.

Iantaffi, A. (2016). Seeking sexual wellness in an unwell culture. *Sexual and Relationship Therapy, 31*(2), 121–122. doi:10.1080/14681994.2016.1168251

Isaac, L., Chen, C., Yeh, L., Lee, H., Chen, S., … Kuang, Y. (2012). P-495—Gender difference in antidepressant-related sexual dysfunction in patients with major depressive disorder (MDD). *European Psychiatry, 27*, 1–1. doi:10.1016/S0924-9338(12)74662-X

Johnson, S., & Zuccarini, D. (2010). Integrating sex and attachment in emotionally focused couple therapy. *Journal of Marital and Family Therapy, 36*(4), 431–445. doi:10.1111/ j.1752-0606.2009.00155.x

Julien, J., Thom, B., & Kline, N. (2010). Identification of barriers to sexual health assessment in oncology nursing practice. *Oncology Nursing Forum, 37*(3), E186–E190.

Knudson-Martin, C. (2013). Why power matters: Creating a foundation of mutual support in couple relationships. *Family Process, 52*(1), 5–18. doi:10.1111/famp.12011

Knudson-Martin, C., & Huenergardt, D. (2010). A socio-emotional approach to couple therapy: Linking social context and couple interaction. *Family Process, 49*(3), 369–384. doi:10.1111/j.1545-5300.2010.01328.x

Lankveld, J. (2009). Self-help therapies for sexual dysfunction. *Journal of Sex Research, 46*(2–3), 143–155.

Leslie, L. A., & Southard, A. L. (2009). Thirty years of feminist family therapy: Moving into the mainstream. In S. A. Lloyd, A. L. Few, & K. R. Allen (Eds.), *Handbook of feminist family studies* (pp. 328–339). Los Angeles, CA: Sage Publications.

Lipshultz, L., Pastuszak, A., Goldstein, A., Giraldi, A., & Perelman, M. (2016). *Management of sexual dysfunction in men and women: An interdisciplinary approach.* New York, NY: Springer.

Lyness, A. M., & Lyness, K. P. (2007). Feminist issues in couple therapy. *Journal of Couple and Relationship Therapy, 6*, 181–195. doi:10.1300/j398v06n01_15

Mahoney, A. R., & Knudson-Martin, C. (2009). The social context of gendered power. In C. Knudson-Martin & A. Mahoney (Eds.), *Couples, gender, and power: Creating change in intimate relationships* (pp. 17–29). New York, NY: Springer Publishing Company.

Manara, F. (1991). Sex therapy for couples: An Italian perspective. *The Journal of Sex Research,* *28*(1), 157–162. doi:10.1080/00224499109551601

Maurice, W. L., & Yule, M. (2010). Sex and chronic and severe mental illness. In S. Levine, C. Risen, & S. E. Althof's (Eds.), *Handbook of clinical sexuality for mental health professionals* (pp. 469–482). New York, NY: Routledge.

McCarthy, B., & Breez, A. (2010). Confronting sexual trauma and enhancing adult sexuality. In S. Levine, C. Risen, & S. E. Althof's (Eds.), *Handbook of clinical sexuality for mental health professionals* (pp. 285–310). New York, NY: Routledge.

McCarthy, B., & Farr, E. (2012). Strategies and techniques to maintain sexual desire. *Journal of Contemporary Psychotherapy, 42*(4), 227–233. doi:10.1007/s10879-012-9207-7

McCarthy, B., & Thestrup, M. (2008). Integrating sex therapy interventions with couple therapy. *Journal of Contemporary Psychotherapy, 38*(3), 139–149. doi:10.1007/s10879-008-9083-3

McCarthy, B., & Wald, L. M. (2015). Strategies and techniques to directly address sexual desire problems. *Journal of Family Psychotherapy, 26*(4), 286–298. doi:10.1080/0897535 3.2015.1097282

McCoy, M. A., Stinson, M. A., Ross, D. B., & Hjelmstad, L. R. (2015). Who's in our clients' bed? A case illustration of sex therapy with a polyamorous couple. *Journal of Sex & Marital Therapy, 41*(2), 134–144. doi:10.1080/0092623X.2013.864366

McGoldrick, M., Carter, E. A., & Garcia-Preto, N. (2016). *The expanding family life cycle: Individual, family, and social perspectives.* New York, NY: Pearson.

Mikulincer, M., & Shaver, P. (2007). A behavioral systems perspective on psychodynamics of attachment and sexuality. In D. Diamond, S. Blatt, & J. Lichtenburg (Eds.), *Attachment and sexuality* (pp. 51–78). New York, NY: Analytic Press.

Miller, R. B., Yorgason, J. B., Sandberg, J. G., & White, M. B. (2003). Problems that couples bring to therapy: A view across the family life cycle. *American Journal of Family Therapy, 31*(5), 395–407.

Moret, L. B., Glaser, B. A., Page, R. C., & Bargeron, E. F. (1998). Intimacy and sexual satisfaction in unmarried couple relationships: A pilot study. *The Family Journal, 6*(1), 33–39. doi:10.1177/1066480798061006

Nagaraj, A. K., Pai, N. B., Rao, T. S. S., & Goyal, N. (2009). Biology of sexual dysfunction. *Online Journal of Health & Allied Sciences, 8*(1), 1–7.

Nobre, P., & Pinto-Gouveia, J. (2006a). Dysfunctional sexual beliefs as vulnerability factors for sexual dysfunction. *Journal of Sex Research, 43*(1), 68–75. doi:10.1080/00224490609552300

Nobre, P., & Pinto-Gouveia, J. (2006b). Emotions during sexual activity: Differences between sexually functional and dysfunctional men and women. *Archives of Sexual Behavior, 35*(4), 491–499. doi:10.1007/s10508-006-9047-1

Nobre, P., & Pinto-Gouveia, J. (2008). Differences in automatic thoughts presented during sexual activity between sexually functional and dysfunctional men and women. *Cognitive Therapy and Research, 32*(1), 37–49. doi:10.1007/s10608-007-9165-7

Nobre, P., & Pinto-Gouveia, J. (2009). Cognitive schemas associated with negative sexual events: A comparison of men and women with and without sexual dysfunction. *Archives of Sexual Behavior, 38*(5), 842–851. doi:10.1007/s10508-008-9450-x

Pascoal, P., De Santa Bárbara Narciso, I., & Pereira, N. (2014). What is sexual satisfaction? Thematic analysis of lay people's definitions. *Journal of Sex Research, 51*(1), 1–9.

Pascoal, P., Narciso, I., & Pereira, N. (2013). Emotional intimacy is the best predictor of sexual satisfaction of men and women with sexual arousal problems. *International Journal of Impotence Research, 25*(2), 51–55. doi:10.1038/ijir.2012.38

Peixoto, M., & Nobre, P. (2014). Dysfunctional sexual beliefs: A comparative study of heterosexual men and women, gay men, and lesbian women with and without sexual problems. *The Journal of Sexual Medicine, 11*(11), 2690–2700. doi:10.1111/jsm.12666

Peixoto, M., & Nobre, P. (2017). Incompetence schemas and sexual functioning in heterosexual and lesbian women: The mediator role of automatic thoughts and affective states during sexual activity. *Cognitive Therapy and Research, 41*(2), 304–312. doi:10.1007/s10608-016-9811-z

Quinta Gomes, A., & Nobre, L. (2012). Early maladaptive schemas and sexual dysfunction in men. *Archives of Sexual Behavior, 41*(1), 311–320. doi:10.1007/s10508-011-9853-y

Redcay, A., & Simonetti, C. (2018). Criteria for love and relationship addiction: Distinguishing love addiction from other substance and behavioral addictions. *Sexual Addiction & Compulsivity, 5*(1), 1–16. doi:10.1080/10720162.2017.1403984

Ridley, J. (2015). What every sex therapist needs to know. In K. M. Hertlein, G. R. Weeks, & N. Gambescia (Eds.), *Systemic sex therapy* (2nd ed., pp. 316). New York, NY: Routledge.

Rosenbaum, T. Y., De Paauw, E., Aloni, R., & Heruti, R. J. (2013). The ultra-orthodox Jewish couple in Israel: An interdisciplinary sex therapy case study. *Journal of Sex & Marital Therapy, 39*(5), 428–435. doi:10.1080/0092623X.2011.644653

Russell, L. (1990). Sex and couple therapy: A method of treatment to enhance physical and emotional intimacy. *Journal of Sex & Marital Therapy, 16*(2), 111–120. doi:10.1080/00926239008405257

SAMHSA (2015). *The eight dimensions of wellness.* Retrieved from https://www.samhsa.gov/wellness-initiative/eight-dimensions-wellness

Santos-Iglesias, P., Byers, E., & Moglia, R. (2016). Sexual well-being of older men and women. *The Canadian Journal of Human Sexuality, 25*(2), 86–98.

Schachner, D. A., & Shaver, P. R. (2004). Attachment dimensions and sexual motives. *Personal Relationships, 11*(2), 179–195. doi:10.1111/j.1475-6811.2004.00077.x

Schnarch, D. (2008). Sex therapy vs. couple therapy: A distinction without a difference? *Sexologies, 17*, S37–S37. doi:10.1016/S1158-1360(08)72613-6

Schnarch, D. M. (1991). *Constructing the sexual crucible: An integration of sexual and marital therapy.* New York, NY: W. W. Norton.

Segraves, R. (1989). Effects of psychotropic drugs on human erection and ejaculation. *Archives of General Psychiatry, 46*(3), 275–284.

Silverstein, R., Bass, L. B., Tuttle, A., Knudson-Martin, C., & Huenergardt, D. (2006). What does it mean to be relational? A framework for assessment and practice. *Family Process, 45*, 391–405. doi:10.1111/j.1545-5300.2006.00178.x

So, H., & Cheung, F. M. (2005). Review of Chinese sex attitudes & applicability of sex therapy for Chinese couples with sexual dysfunction. *Journal of Sex Research, 42*(2), 93–101. doi:10.1080/00224490509552262

Starcevic, V. (2016). Behavioural addictions: A challenge for psychopathology and psychiatric nosology. *Australian & New Zealand Journal of Psychiatry, 50*(8), 721–725.

Steil, J. (1997). *Marital equality: Its relationship to the well-being of husbands and wives.* Newbury Park, CA: Sage Publications.

Stone Fish, L. S., Fish, R. C., & Sprenkle, D. H. (1984). Treating inhibited sexual desire: A marital therapy approach. *American Journal of Family Therapy, 12*, 3–12.

Strada, I., Vegni, E., & Lamiani, G. (2016). Talking with patients about sex: Results of an interprofessional simulation-based training for clinicians. *Internal and Emergency Medicine, 11*(6), 859–866. doi:10.1007/s11739-016-1468-9

Syme, M., Cohn, T., Stoffregen, S., Kaempfe, H., & Schippers, D. (2018). "At My Age … ": Defining sexual wellness in mid- and later life. *The Journal of Sex Research*, 1–11.

Tetley, J., Lee, D., Nazroo, J., & Hinchliff, S. (2018). Let's talk about sex—What do older men and women say about their sexual relations and sexual activities? A qualitative analysis of ELSA Wave 6 data. *Ageing and Society, 38*(3), 497–521.

Timm, T. M. (2009). "Do I really have to talk about sex?" Encouraging beginning therapists to integrate sexuality into couple therapy. *Journal of Couple & Relationship Therapy, 8*(1), 15–33. doi:10.1080/15332690802626692

Træen, B., Carvalheira, A., Kvalem, I., Štulhofer, A., Janssen, E., Graham, C., … Enzlin, P. (2017). Sexuality in Older Adults (65)—An overview of the recent literature, Part 2: Body image and sexual satisfaction. *International Journal of Sexual Health, 29*(1), 11–21.

Tsai, T., Yeh, C., & Hwang, T. (2011). Female sexual dysfunction: Physiology, epidemiology, classification, evaluation and treatment. *Urological Science, 22*(1), 7–13.

Ussher, J. M., Perz, J., Gilbert, E., Wong, W. K., Mason, C., Hobbs, K., & Kirsten, L. (2013). Talking about sex after cancer: A discourse analytic study of health care professional accounts of sexual communication with patients. *Psychology and Health, 13*(1), 1370–1390. doi:10.1080/08870446.2013.811242

Waring, E. P., Tillman, M., Frelick, L., Russell, L., & Weisz, G. (1980). Concepts of intimacy in the general population. *The Journal of Nervous and Mental Disease, 168*(8), 471–474. doi:10.1097/00005053-198008000-00004

Weeks, G., & Gambescia, N. (2002). *Hypoactive sexual desire: Integrating couple and sex therapy*. New York, NY: W. W. Norton.

Weeks, G. W., Gambescia, N., & Hertlein, K. M. (2016). *A clinician's guide to systemic sex therapy* (2nd ed.). New York, NY: Routledge.

Wiederman, M. (1998). The state of theory in sex therapy. *Journal of Sex Research, 35*(1), 88–99.

Williams, K., & Knudson-Martin, C. (2012). Do therapists address gender and power in infidelity? A feminist analysis of the treatment literature. *Journal of Marital and Family Therapy, 39*(3), 271–284. doi:10.1111/j.1752-0606.2012.00303.x

Yoo, H., Bartle-Haring, S., Day, R. D., & Gangamma, R. (2013). Couple communication, emotional and sexual intimacy, and relationship satisfaction. *Journal of Sex & Marital Therapy, 40*(4), 275–293. doi:10.1080/0092623x.2012.751072

Zamboni, B., & Zaid, S. (2017). Human sexuality education in marriage and family therapy graduate programs. *Journal of Marital and Family Therapy, 43*(4), 605–616. doi:10.1111/jmft.12214

Zumaya, M., Bridges, S. K., & Rubio, E. (1999). A constructivist approach to sex therapy with couples. *Journal of Constructivist Psychology, 12*(3), 185–201. doi:10.1080/107205399266064

17

Couples and Infertility

Karina M. Shreffler, Kami L. Gallus,
Brennan Peterson, and Arthur L. Greil

Although an increasing proportion of couples in the United States and other industrialized nations are deciding to not to have children, parenthood remains a desired
and anticipated role for the vast majority of men and women (Debest & Mazuy,
2014; Holton, Fisher, & Rowe, 2011; Martinez, Daniels, & Chandra, 2012). Most
adults assume they can become parents when they are ready (Shreffler, Greil, &
McQuillan, 2017). Once they begin trying to have a baby, however, many couples
may find their expectations and plans disrupted by infertility (Loftus & Andriot,
2012). Infertility can be a highly distressing experience for some couples. This experience may include anxiety, challenges to identity, feelings of loss of control, a strong
sense of stigmatization, feelings of social isolation, a sense of being in "limbo," and
strain on romantic and social relationships (see Greil, Slauson-Blevins, and McQuillan
(2010)) for a review). Treatment can be a lengthy, expensive, and frustrating process,
and many couples report barriers such as cost of treatment, location of clinics, and
social factors such as racial/ethnic and/or sexual minority status (Bell, 2016; Greil,
1991). Decision making about infertility treatment (e.g., whether to pursue treatment, which type of treatment to pursue, how much time and money to spend on
pursuing treatment, etc.) and the experiences, stress, and risks associated with infertility treatments have been identified as additional stressors for couples experiencing
infertility (Shreffler et al., 2017). Many couples experiencing infertility opt for non-
medical alternatives to treatment (e.g., choosing alternatives such as adoption, fostering, or remaining childless).

Despite the fact that infertility is common and often has adverse consequences
for well-being, the impact of infertility on the couple relationship can be easily
overlooked because it "results in the loss of something that has never been" (Domar
& Seibel, 1997, p. 30). An estimated 15–20% of couples seeking medical treatment for fertility-related issues report experiencing emotional distress at levels
warranting couple therapy (Boivin, Scanlan, & Walker, 1999). As the systemic conceptualization of fertility has developed, infertility has increasingly been recognized as an emotional, physical, and financial burden that impacts both members
of a couple. Therefore, due to the high prevalence of infertility and its possible

The Handbook of Systemic Family Therapy: Volume 3, First Edition.
Edited by Karen S. Wampler and Adrian J. Blow.
© 2020 John Wiley & Sons Ltd. Published 2020 by John Wiley & Sons Ltd.

implications for individual and couple well-being, it is essential that systemic therapists understand the issues and challenges infertile couples face in order to better serve them. There are many aspects of the infertility experience where therapists can intervene to help couples as they cope with this unexpected barrier to having children. In this chapter, we describe infertility and its consequences for individual and couple well-being, provide a summary of systemic approaches to assessment and treatment, and conclude with a discussion of future directions for research and practice.

Couples and the Infertility Experience

Defining infertility

From a medical perspective, infertility is defined as the inability to achieve a clinical pregnancy after one year of regular, unprotected sexual intercourse (Zegers-Hochschild et al., 2017). Using this 12-month timeframe, the current prevalence of female infertility ranges from 3.5 to 16.7% in more developed nations and 6.9–9.3% in less developed nations, with an overall median prevalence of 9% (Boivin, Bunting, Collins, & Nygren, 2007). The prevalence of male infertility is less studied globally, but an estimate of infertility among US men aged 15–44 also revealed 9.4% were currently infertile in 2006–2010 (Chandra, Copen, & Stephen, 2013). The likelihood of experiencing at least a year of infertility during one's reproductive years, however, is much higher, at about 44% for women in the United States (Johnson, McQuillan, Greil, & Shreffler, 2014). A biomedical cause for infertility can be ascertained in about 80% of all cases. Of the cases of infertility that are explainable, approximately one-third of cases involve female factors only, one-third male factors only, and one-third due to a combination of male and female factors (Greil, Schmidt, & Peterson, 2014). Female infertility factors include conditions related to (a) ovulation, (b) the cervix or uterus, (c) the fallopian tubes, and/or (d) endometriosis, a condition in which the uterine lining migrates outside the uterine cavity. Male infertility is most commonly associated with low sperm count, poor sperm motility, and poor sperm mobility.

Not all infertile individuals are childless; individuals can be classified as infertile using the standard medical definition even if they have children. Healthcare providers classify women as having "primary infertility" if they have never had a pregnancy and as having "secondary infertility" if they have previously been pregnant (American Society for Reproductive Medicine [ASRM], 2008). Secondary infertility was about twice as common as primary infertility until recently, when primary infertility rates increased due to childbearing postponement (Chandra et al., 2013). The median age of first birth for women is almost 27 years (Martin, Hamilton, Osterman, Driscoll, & Drake, 2018)—an age at which female fertility has already begun to decline (Dunson, Colombo, & Baird, 2002). Moreover, more women are waiting until their 30s and 40s to have their first child, ages higher than ever before (Mathews & Hamilton, 2016). These recent changes in childbearing patterns have resulted in increased rates of involuntary childlessness and smaller families than many people desire (Schmidt, Sobotka, Bentzen, & Andersen, 2012).

Limitations in research   Data on the experience of infertility has typically come from small clinic-based samples or other nonrepresentative samples (Greil et al., 2010). This dependence on clinic samples of women and couples seeking treatment means that we know much less about infertile individuals who have not sought treatment, a group that constitutes about half of the infertile population (Greil & McQuillan, 2004). For example, women of color and of lower socioeconomic status (SES) are more likely than White women and higher SES women to be infertile, but they are less likely to receive treatment (Bell, 2014; Chandra et al., 2013; Chandra, Copen, & Stephen, 2014). Some women may be absent from research on treatment seeking because they do not view infertility as a major problem in their lives (Wilson, 2014), and still other women may not seek treatment due to religious convictions (Czarnecki, 2015). Men are just as likely as women to be infertile, but they are less likely to seek treatment or to be the subject of research (Barnes, 2014).

Experiencing infertility

Because infertility can interfere with the attainment of a desired social role (i.e., parenthood), it is not surprising that it can contribute to psychological distress and to challenges for couple relationships. Theoretical framing of the infertility experience for individuals and couples often draws on identity theory. Due to the centrality of the parenthood identity for both men and women (Becker, 2000; Greil, 1991; Greil et al., 2014; Sandelowski, 1993), infertility can be perceived as a threat to identity (Greil, 1991; McCarthy, 2008; Olshansky, 1987). Qualitative studies (e.g., Becker, 2000; Inhorn, 2015; Wirtberg, Moller, Hogström, Tronstad, & Lalos, 2007) often describe infertility as a devastating experience, associated with feelings of failure, defectiveness, and reduced competence, especially for women. Individuals may feel socially isolated because of the sense that they cannot avoid constant reminders of their infertility, such as having close family members or friends become pregnant, seeing child-related commercials on television, or encountering babies in the supermarket. In addition, infertile couples sometimes feel that the people they generally rely on most for social support (e.g., friends and family) do not understand what they are going through.

Quantitative studies do not always support the impression that clinic-based qualitative research presents of the infertile as an extremely distressed group, though they do tend to find that people with infertility report more symptoms of distress than those without infertility (Holter, Anderheim, Bergh, & Moller, 2006; Jordan & Ferguson, 2006). Although many women and men with infertility report adverse emotional consequences of the infertility experience, most do not meet criteria for clinically significant psychopathology (Thorn, 2009). This suggests that it is not that individuals with infertility are fundamentally different from others in terms of their psychological functioning, but rather that the experience of infertility is a source of psychological distress (Greil, McQuillan, & Sanchez, 2016).

Sociodemographic characteristics including race/ethnicity, income, sexuality, geographic location, and family structure as well as medical institutions and reproductive technologies (Becker, 2000; Inhorn, 2015) all shape the experience of infertility. Those experiencing primary infertility, those who value parenthood more highly, and those with lower social support report higher levels of distress (Greil, Shreffler, Schmidt, & McQuillan, 2011). Distress associated with infertility does not appear to vary by race/ethnicity (Greil et al., 2016), but feelings of not being seen as deserving of treatment may heighten the distress of marginalized groups (Ceballo, Graham, & Hart, 2015). Distress levels for mothers with adopted or biological children who have ever been infertile do not differ significantly from those found among the fertile. There is some evidence of long-term negative consequences of infertility for psychological well-being among the involuntary childless (Jacob, McQuillan, & Greil, 2007; McQuillan, Greil, White, & Jacob, 2003; Schwerdtfeger & Shreffler, 2009).

Gender differences Although both women and men report distress during the experience of infertility, findings suggest some gender differences in the experiences or consequences of infertility. Whereas women may feel more stigma and feelings of failure about infertility, men may experience it more as a challenge to virility (Clarke, Martin-Matthews, & Matthews, 2006). Literature reviews of infertility research (e.g., Eugster & Vingerhoets, 1999; Greil et al., 2010; Henning, Strauss, & Strauss, 2002) tend to support the claim that women experience more infertility-related stress than men, though men also suffer from infertility. Some studies suggest that women experience fertility problems as a direct blow to identity, whereas men experience them indirectly through the effect that they have on their partners (Greil, 1991; Greil et al., 2018; Martins, Peterson, Almeida, Mesquita-Guimarães, & Costa, 2014; Péloquin, Brassard, Arpin, Sabourin, & Wright, 2018). Andrews, Abbey, and Halman (1992) reported that there was a substantive difference between infertility and other problems among women, whereas men were affected by infertility in much the same way as they were affected by other problems.

Couple dynamics Medical practitioners tend to consider the couple as infertile, regardless of whether the physiological problem causing infertility is in one partner or both, yet not all individuals seek medical help to get pregnant with a partner (i.e., in a couple context) (Johnson & Johnson, 2009). Moreover, in more than a third of infertile couples, only one partner has recognized a fertility problem (nearly always the female partner) (McQuillan, Greil, Colaner, Tiemeyer, & Shreffler, 2018). However, trying for a pregnancy is usually a decision made by both partners in a couple; thus usually partners communicate if they have trouble achieving a pregnancy. Therefore, infertility may have psychological consequences for both partners as well as implications for the couple relationship (Johnson & Johnson, 2009; Martins et al., 2014; Peterson, Pirritano, & Christensen, & Schmidt, L., 2008). In the couple context, the attitudes, resources, and experiences of each partner will necessarily be relevant for the dyadic other. Stressful situations or events that affect both partners of a couple—either directly or indirectly through spillover from one partner to the other— have been referred to as "dyadic stressors" (Karney, Story, & Bradbury, 2005; Randall & Bodenmann, 2009). Infertility has been noted as a key example of a dyadic stressor (Berghuis & Stanton, 2002).

While most studies of infertility and psychological distress treat the individual as the unit of analysis, recently there have been more studies treating the couple as the unit of analysis and applying statistical techniques suitable for dyadic analysis. Many of these studies have focused on the coping strategies used by partners in infertile couples and have found that coping strategies used by one partner are associated with psychological distress experienced by the other partner (Berghuis & Stanton, 2002; Kim, Shin, & Yun, 2018; Martins et al., 2014; Peterson et al., 2008; Peterson,

Pirritano, Block, & Schmidt, 2011). Benyamini, Gozlan, and Kokia (2009) found that partners often differ in their perceptions of controllability of the fertility problem and that women reported the highest levels of distress when they perceived low controllability while their partners perceived high controllability. Moreover, perception of consequences has additive effects for both partners. Péloquin and colleagues (2018) discovered that when one partner exhibits self-blame, the other partner experiences elevated levels of depressive symptoms. Similarly, infertile men who reported a lack of emotional support from their partners were more than twice as likely to report severe depressive symptoms as infertile men who reported always receiving emotional support from their partners (Lund, Sejbæk, Christensen, & Schmidt, 2009). But Chachamovich et al. (2010) note that there is little congruence between assessment of one's partner's quality of life and the partner's own assessment, casting some doubt on how shared the experience of infertility actually is.

Relationship quality Research examining the ways in which couples respond to dyadic stressors—often called "dyadic coping" (Bodenmann, Pihet, & Kayser, 2006)—frequently use relationship satisfaction as the focal outcome (Bodenmann, Meuwly, & Kayser, 2011; Faulkner, Davey, & Davey, 2005; Randall & Bodenmann, 2009). Research findings on the consequences of infertility for couple relationships are contradictory (Greil et al., 2010; Verhaak et al., 2007). Whereas some prior studies describe the deleterious effects of infertility on relationships (Glover, McLellan, & Weaver, 2009; Ozkan, Orhan, Aktas, & Coskuner, 2016), other research suggests that infertility can lead to stronger couple relationships (Peterson et al., 2011; Wagner, Wrzus, Neyer, & Lang, 2015). Characteristics of the couple relationship dynamics may play a role, as partners who communicate and provide support to one another are better able to endure stressors of infertility treatment (Ying, Wu, & Loke, 2015). Greil (1991) also found that when partners perceive infertility as a shared problem, they are likely to describe the experience as bringing them closer together. Characteristics of the infertility episode may also affect relationship satisfaction; a longer duration of infertility, for example, is associated with a steeper decline in marital satisfaction (Wang et al., 2007).

Sexual aspects of the couple relationship can also be challenged in the context of infertility. Among the infertile trying to become pregnant, sex can become more "mechanical" or a chore rather than pleasure or intimacy (Piva, Lo Monte, Graziano, & Marci, 2014). Pressure to have sex, or sexual coercion, is not uncommon; a sample of 105 couples seeking infertility treatment found that 12% of women and 37% of men reported being verbally pressured into having sexual intercourse for the purposes of conception; among men, this sexual coercion was associated with more psychological distress and lower relationship quality (Peterson & Buday, 2018). Temporary sexual disorders associated with infertility diagnosis or treatment are common among couples experiencing infertility, with women affected more often than men (Wischmann, 2010).

Responding to infertility

Medical approaches to infertility treatment Many people who experience infertility, especially women, are strongly committed to pursuing medical treatment (Greil et al., 2014; Sandelowski, 1993). Diagnostic testing for infertility typically includes semen analysis, ovulation testing, hysterosalpingography (visualization of the fallopian tubes), hormone testing, and laparoscopy (visualization of the pelvic area). Treatments for infertility include ovulation induction, insemination with semen of husband/partner or donor semen, and assisted reproductive technology (ART), such as in vitro fertilization (IVF) (Zegers-Hochschild et al., 2017). Ovulation drug therapy is the most common type of infertility treatment for women (86%), followed by artificial insemination (30%) and surgery to correct blockages in the fallopian tubes (20%) (Kessler, Craig, Plosker, Reed, & Quin, 2013). IVF is less common, with 12.5% receiving this treatment. While most infertility treatments are invasive, IVF procedures are especially invasive. They are also time consuming and often prohibitively expensive where these procedures are not covered by health insurance. In the United States, treatment rates are higher in the 15 states with mandated insurance coverage for infertility treatments, particularly among older, more educated women (Bitler & Schmidt, 2012).

As with all medical treatments, there are risks associated with infertility treatment. Ovarian hyperstimulation syndrome and multiple gestation pregnancies are much more common after infertility treatment and are associated with greater risk for maternal complications and adverse infant birth outcomes including low birth weight, preterm delivery, and infant mortality. Risks for adverse birth outcomes are not solely due to multiple gestation pregnancies, however. Singleton births following ART are also associated with higher incidence of adverse birth outcomes (Macaluso et al., 2010).

Complications of infertility treatment   Because there are numerous contemporary medical technologies for infertility, few couples are told that they may never be parents (Greil, 1991; Van den Broeck et al., 2009), which can make it difficult for couples to decide when to terminate treatment (Klock, 2015). Yet there is wide variation in rates of live births following infertility treatment, most likely due to differences in couple characteristics, clinic characteristics, and cultural and policy contexts. Examining pooled data from a large number of published birth rates, Collins and Van Steirteghem (2004) reported a success rate of 37% for treatments that did not involve ART. The estimated rate of a live birth after one round of IVF is less than 25% in the United States (Centers for Disease Control, 2017). Of course, couples who are able to attempt various types of treatments over a period of time will increase their chances of having a live birth. A study of couples from a fertility clinic in Denmark—a country with a public, tax-financed healthcare system where couples have access to ART and other types of infertility treatment at no cost—found that 75% of women under 35 reported a live birth within 5 years of beginning infertility treatment (Pinborg, Hougaard, Nyboe Andersen, Molbo, & Schmidt, 2009). Among those who were 35 or older when treatment was initiated, however, only 52% reported a live birth. Since virtually all studies of treatment outcomes utilize data from specialized fertility clinics, we have very little idea what the live birth rates are for infertile individuals who do not receive treatment; however, the majority of women who experience infertility do not remain childless (Abma & Martinez, 2006).

Treatment for infertility is linked to distress over and above that caused by infertility itself (Greil, Lowry, McQuillan, & Shreffler, 2011). People undergoing treatment often report feeling they have little control over the treatment process (Redshaw, Hockley, & Davidson, 2007) and that they are intimidated by the language and technical aspects of infertility treatment (Becker, Castrillo, Jackson, & Nachtigall, 2005). Infertile couples may have difficulty accepting unresolved infertility following treatment that does not lead to a birth (Wirtberg et al., 2007) and describe the treatment process as a "roller coaster" of alternating hope and disappointment (Greil, 1991).

Disparities in and barriers to infertility treatment Only about half of infertile couples pursue infertility treatment globally, and only about half of those couples receive care (Boivin et al., 2007). While some of these couples may not desire treatment, many couples encounter barriers to treatment (Adashi & Dean, 2016). Treatment for infertility varies significantly by race and ethnicity (Chandra et al., 2014), SES (Bell, 2014), and country of origin (Boivin et al., 2007; Bunting, Tsibulsky, & Boivin, 2012). Reasons for lower rates of receipt of medical treatment include lack of economic resources, lack of encouragement for treatment from friends and family, a heightened level of ethical concern about fertility treatments, distrust of medical institutions, misinformation about fertility and/or treatments, allocations of healthcare resources, and country-specific healthcare regulations (Bell, 2016; Boivin et al., 2007; Bunting et al., 2012, Greil, McQuillan, Shreffler, Johnson, & Slauson-Blevins, 2013). Treatments can be quite expensive; Katz et al. (2011) found that median per-person costs ranged from $1,182 for medications only to $38,015 for IVF-donor egg groups; "successful" outcomes (e.g., IVF treatments resulting in a live birth) were even more costly, at $61,377. Sexual minority status and being un-partnered can also obstruct access to treatment (Ethics Committee of the ASRM, 2009). Perceiving infertility as a stigmatized condition (Bunting & Boivin, 2007) and ethical concerns about treatment, especially ART (Czarnecki, 2015) can be an additional barrier to seeking treatment (Bunting & Boivin, 2007). Ethical issues surrounding ART include concerns about selective reduction of embryos to reduce pregnancy risks, the separation of sexual intercourse from procreation, and concerns about whether a child that is not genetically related to one is really one's own (Shreffler, Johnson, & Scheuble, 2010). Ethical concerns toward ART, however, have been declining over time, and they have been declining fastest for those who initially had the greatest concerns (e.g., women who reported racial/ethnic minority group status and those who were more religious) (Greil et al., 2017).

Alternatives to medical approaches Of course, medical treatment is not the only option available to infertile individuals and couples. There are many actions couples can take in response to infertility besides medical treatment, including adoption or fostering, prayer, counseling, joining a support group, and seeking various forms of complementary and alternative medicine; most people experiencing infertility explore multiple options at the same time (Greil, Johnson, Lowry, McQuillan, & Slauson-Blevins, 2019). Considering adoption is one of the more common non-medical response options to infertility, though only half of those who consider adoption take concrete steps toward pursuing this option (Park & Wonch Hill, 2014). The expense of adoption and concerns about the difficult application and intake process can be barriers for adoption, and many couples view adoption as an option to be considered only after undergoing expensive treatments to conceive a biological child (Slauson-Blevins & Park, 2016). Fostering is another option some couples may want to consider. Information about adoption and fostering options may be useful for couples who desire to parent but do not pursue treatment or those for whom treatment is unsuccessful.

Life after infertility treatment It is important to recognize that achieving pregnancy will not automatically dissipate the emotional strain of the infertility experience. Pregnancy can be a particularly stressful time for women who have lost confidence in their bodies' abilities (Eugster & Vingerhoets, 1999). Once infertile women have children, they may have lower self-evaluations of themselves as mothers and may take longer to embrace the motherhood identity compared with those who have not experienced infertility (Gibson, Ungerer, Tennant, & Saunders, 2000). Letherby (1999) found that women who had given birth through ART reported feelings of anxiety and guilt and an obligation to be perfect mothers. On the other hand, Hjelmstedt, Widström, Wramsby, and Collins (2004) reported that, six months' postpartum, people who had a live birth after infertility treatment felt they had left infertility behind them. Women in this study said infertility led them to have stronger feelings for children, to have greater tolerance for the difficulties of parenting, and to be more grateful. Men felt infertility had made them emotionally closer to their children than they would otherwise have been. Researchers have not found evidence of problematic maternal behavior, marital problems, or psychological problems for couples following resolved infertility (Eugster & Vingerhoets, 1999; Golombok, 2015; Repokari et al., 2007).

Yet, more research is needed on the long-term psychological effects of infertility treatment for couples and their children (Van Voorhis, 2006). As noted above, there is evidence that the long-term negative consequences of infertility exist primarily among those who do not go on to give birth later (Jacob et al., 2007; McQuillan et al., 2003; Schwerdtfeger & Shreffler, 2009). A study of women who adopted, used ART, or pursued surrogacy (van den Akker, 2004) found that mothers reported a higher quality of life than non-mothers, regardless of the means by which they became parents. Wirtberg et al. (2007) found that women who had undergone tubal surgery that did not help them have a live birth still had vivid memories of their time as infertility patients even after 20 years. Nearly all reported long-term effects on their sexual lives and relationships. In addition, as their peers began to have grandchildren, many felt as if they were experiencing an echo of the distress of infertility.

Applying Systemic Models and Approaches in Treatment of Couples with Infertility

Historically, the main role of mental health professionals in infertility clinics has been to carry out screening of fertility clinic patients before treatment and to provide general support for patients in crisis. Over the past decade, the specialized practice of "infertility counseling" (Peterson et al., 2012) has grown more widespread, sophisticated, and systemic (Boivin & Gameiro, 2015). Today, infertility counseling encompasses a wide variety of services delivered by mental health and medical professionals and includes both the provision of implications counseling and therapeutic counseling for couples (Covington, 2015). Implications counseling is a mandatory element of fertility treatment that occurs before treatment begins and focuses on assisting couples in decision making, clarification of treatment options, and third-party arrangements (donor insemination, egg donation, or surrogacy). Therapeutic counseling refers to more traditional systemic couple therapy and interventions aimed at helping couples cope with the psychosocial challenges of infertility. Experts in the field recommend that couple therapy be included as a standard component of infertility treatment that is made available to all couples, even if such services are never used (Boivin et al., 1999; Cousineau & Domar, 2007; Peterson, Gold, & Feingold, 2007). Specifically, experts recommend that couple therapy be available at the beginning and at the end of specific medical treatments, times that are especially important as couples are faced with varying treatment options as well as potentially coping with significant loss.

Systemic therapists trained in traditional models of couple's therapy, such as emotion-focused and cognitive-behavioral approaches, can play a key role in helping couples facing infertility and other reproductive health issues. Despite research highlighting the relational impact of fertility issues on the couple relationship, there is a dearth of research or best practice guidelines to assist therapists in effectively working with infertile couples. Transcending traditional systemic therapy models, current research and clinical knowledge suggest the following guidelines for effective systemic assessment and intervention.

Fertility-focused assessment

A comprehensive assessment is the foundation for effective systemic intervention, and therapists who are unaware of how infertility impacts couples will lack the ability to effectively choose interventions that will best serve a couple's needs. Thus, systemic therapists must have a basic knowledge of how infertility impacts couples before conducting fertility-focused assessments. Therapists who lack such knowledge may be more at risk for marginalizing a couple's experiences as couples find themselves educating their therapists about basic fertility treatments and emotional challenges during the beginning sessions (Peterson et al., 2007). To gain a comprehensive understanding of how infertility is impacting a couple's personal, social, and relational stress levels, systemic therapists can use the combination of formal assessment measures with a detailed conjoint psychosocial interview (see Table 17.1).

Individual self-report There are a variety of formal assessment measures that can be used to determine the impact of an infertility diagnosis on both members of the couple. The Fertility Problem Inventory (FPI) Newton, Sherrard, & Glavac, 1999), a 46-item questionnaire, provides the clinician with a global stress score and stress indicators across five key domains for both men and women: social infertility stress, sexual infertility stress, relationship infertility stress, need for parenthood, and beliefs about living a child-free lifestyle. The FPI is particularly useful in noting which areas should be a focus of treatment by informing counselors of the domains that are causing the most significant stress for each member of the couple. It is also useful in showing clinicians if couples experience these domains of stress similarly or differently as this will likely inform how couples cope with infertility stress, as well how they may make future treatment decisions (Peterson et al., 2012; Peterson, Newton, & Rosen, 2003).

Systemic therapists can also have couples complete the 36-item FertiQol, the first validated instrument to reliably measure the impact of fertility problems and its treatment on quality of life for men and women (Boivin, Takefman, & Braverman, 2011).

Table 17.1   Components of couples' psychosocial fertility assessment.

Purpose of visit

Relationship history
- Length of relationship
- Children from current or past relationships
  - If yes, conceived naturally or from fertility treatment
- Length of time trying to start a family

Fertility history
- Length of infertility diagnosis
- Type of infertility (male factor/female factor/combined/unexplained)
- Fertility treatments
  - Medications/surgeries
  - Intrauterine insemination (IUI) cycles (if yes, how many)
  - In vitro fertilization (IVF) treatments (if yes, how many)
- Treatment results
  - Failed treatment, miscarriage, stillbirth, live birth
- Consideration of third-party reproduction and other family building options
  - Egg donation, sperm donation, surrogacy, adoption

Impact of infertility and treatment
- Individual and relational impact of fertility problem
- Individual and relational impact of treatment stress (managing medications, doctor visits, egg retrieval, 2-week waiting period)
- Communication about infertility (talked about too little, too much, agreement among couple)
- Coping patterns in dealing with infertility stress (gender differences)
- Impact of infertility on the sexual relationship
- Marital benefit (ways the relationship has been strengthened by the infertility experience)
- Ways of handling the stresses of treatment failure (if applicable)
- Potential concerns about future treatments impacting relationship

Family history
- History of infertility in family
- Quality of relationships with parents and siblings
- Family reaction to infertility—pressure to have children

Employment factors
- Employer stressor or support—employer flexibility to accommodate fertility treatments
- Concerns about work disruption and loss of income

Social support/social networks
- Friendship networks providing support or stress
- Close friends or family having children—couple reactions
- Impact of sharing infertility-related information with family and friends

Cultural/religious factors
- Cultural or religious factors that provide support
- Cultural or religious factors that add stress or strain

Type of counseling needed
- Therapeutic counseling
- Implications/decision-making counseling

Goals for counseling
- Relational and individual

Note. Reprinted with permission from Covington (2015). Copyright by Cambridge University Press.

FertiQoL can be easily accessed and scored online (http://www.fertistat.com/ fertiqol) and is currently available in over 30 different languages. Participants are assessed across four core domains: emotional, mind/body, relational, and social. If the couple is undergoing medical procedures, two additional domains are assessed: treatment environment and treatment tolerability. Scores are presented to clients and clinicians in easy-to-understand bar charts and scoring guidelines normed against other infertile men and women who have completed the survey. Therapists can use scores to identify targets of intervention to improve quality of life and help couples regain satisfaction in key life domains.

Screen IVF is a measure used to help identify patients at risk for emotional distress and pretreatment dropout prior to undergoing fertility treatment (Verhaak, Lintsen, Evers, & Braat, 2010). Screen IVF measures anxiety (state and trait), depression, fertility-related cognitions, and social support. At-risk patients can be identified using recommended cutoff scores (Ockhuijsen, van Smeden, van den Hoogen, & Boivin, 2017). Therapists can use the results from this assessment to identify couples who may be at risk for the stresses of treatment as well as to help couples avoid potential pitfalls that may worsen anxiety and depressive symptoms.

Clinicians can use general measures of relationship satisfaction and adjustment to provide a more complete picture of the overall health of the relationship. Measures such as the Couple Satisfaction Index (CSI-16; Funk & Rogge, 2007), Adapted Marital Decision-making Scale (MDMS) (Beach & Tesser, 1993), and Communication Patterns Questionnaire (CPQ) (Heavey, Larson, Zumtobel, & Christensen, 1996) can be completed by couples to inform clinicians about their overall relational health and patterns.

Conjoint psychosocial interview   A conjoint psychosocial interview can help clinicians assess the systemic and interactional nature of the couple's response to infertility. Table 17.1 presents an in-depth summary of the key components of this interview and can guide counselors through the variety of fertility-related challenges couples commonly navigate. The purpose of the interview is to obtain a comprehensive picture of the relationship and fertility history. Therapists should gather information regarding the relationship health and patterns prior to and during the infertility journey, as well as to assess their therapeutic goals and future fertility plans.

The length of an infertility diagnosis, number and types of treatments received, results of fertility treatments, and overall impact of infertility on both the individuals and the couple is a vital starting point for the clinician. Family histories, employment factors, and social support networks are also vital to understanding the larger systemic influences that impact couples. Culture/religious factors can either provide support or add stress and strain to a couple's infertility journey. For example, in Israel, because parenthood is deemed by many as essential for acceptance into the broader social structure, an infertility diagnosis can be an inescapable source of pain and discomfort, resulting in isolation and decreased self-esteem (Remennick, 2000). Clinicians must be aware of these larger systemic factors that impact couples experiencing infertility. Discovering the contexts of these systemic influences can be accomplished by asking focused yet sensitive questions regarding the impact of infertility on the couples' family, friendship, and broader social networks.

Fertility-focused systemic interventions

Couples experiencing infertility or other reproductive loss may present to therapy for a variety of reasons and are commonly suffering from a variety of symptoms associated with depression, anxiety, persistent complex bereavement, relationship distress, and/ or posttraumatic stress (Cousineau & Domar, 2007). There are a variety of areas systemic therapists can target when working with couples impacted by infertility. Fertility-focused interventions often include helping the couple to manage the stresses and demands of fertility treatment, improve couple communication patterns, alter problematic coping patterns that cause negative relational outcomes, reduce sexual distress, and prepare for the possibility of failed treatment cycles. Interventions are also critical in helping couples understand the aforementioned social, cultural, and religious factors that contextualize the infertility experience, cope with feelings of grief and loss associated with the inability to conceive, set appropriate boundaries related to sharing infertility-related information with others, and facilitate decision making regarding ending treatment and other family building options such as adoption, third-party reproduction, or child-free living (Peterson, 2015).

Although the best systemic approach for couples facing infertility has not been determined, many of the interpersonal dynamics and consequences are similar to other areas that are well known in the field of couple therapy. Systemic treatment approaches that draw from theories of grief/loss and crisis/trauma as well as evidence-based models such as cognitive-behavioral (e.g., cognitive restructuring), emotionally focused (e.g., enhancing emotional bonds), and narrative (e.g., externalization) approaches to working with couples are likely useful. Resources such as Covington's (2015) comprehensive guide to fertility counseling provide information and insights into the specific challenges and issues couples face when impacted by infertility. The specific objectives of couple therapy and the interventions used should be determined by the thorough assessment of the specific needs of the couple, the timing of treatment, and the couple's level of distress.

Low distressed couples   Less distressed couples may require brief therapy models such as behavioral couple therapy (Shadish & Baldwin, 2005) that emphasize psychoeducation, cognitive restructuring, communication skills training, problem solving and decision making, and emotional expressiveness training. A key issue for many couples is learning new skills that increase each partner's capacity to regulate emotions under difficult circumstances and convey emotions accurately. Systemic therapists can also play a key role in helping couples make decisions regarding specific fertility-related treatments. Therapists working with infertile couples may find it helpful to become knowledgeable about medical procedures and the treatment process so that clients feel their therapists have an informed understanding of what they are going through and can help them sort out the ethical, religious, and social dimensions of medical treatment versus other responses to infertility. Because these decisions will have lifelong implications, systemic therapists should use their expertise to help couples consider and understand the future consequences of such decisions, particularly as they pertain to the couples' marital and family relationships.

There are social justice considerations as well. Just because fewer people of color tend to seek medical help for infertility does not mean that the desire for a child is not there. Therapists can help couples work through feelings of not being welcome in certain treatment settings (Bell, 2014) and encourage them to advocate for themselves. Therapists should also consider that medical practitioners often assume that medical treatment is the best option for everyone and can help empower clients to make choices that they feel are right for themselves. Infertile couples will differ widely from one another in constraints on access to care, emotional needs of each partner, and ethical and religious values. Therapists can help inform couples about the many options in response to infertility and help them find accurate information about what is involved in the array of responses (e.g., fostering, adopting, IVF, surrogacy, choosing to remain childless), including age limits and costs. It is important to guide without directing because income, race/ethnicity, religiosity, ethics, education, wealth, relationship quality, and health all shape people's perspectives on infertility as well as their options for response. Furthermore, couples may be surprised by the value of nonmedical responses to infertility (e.g., fostering or adopting; using online support groups, with or without a live birth).

Therapists working with couples in the process of getting medical help for infertility can help by encouraging realistic expectations concerning the odds of a live birth, acknowledging the stresses associated with treatment processes, preparing couples for the transition to parenthood, and providing evidence that people who become parents through nonstandard routes become capable parents. For couples interested in third-party reproduction, therapists can guide clients through the exploration of options with which they might not be familiar, such as sperm donation, egg donation, and surrogacy. Helping people understand the physiology of pregnancy and the extra challenges of conception after age 35 could help some individuals and couples to find an alternative approach to parenthood or to lower expectations for a live birth.

Moderately distressed couples For more moderately distressed couples, systemic approaches such as emotionally focused therapy that provide a comprehensive treatment plan may prove beneficial (Wood, Crane, Schaalje, & Law, 2005). Systemic therapists can use their expertise in couple therapy to reduce couples' stress and increase partners' abilities to jointly cope with the challenge. Therapists who focus on the emotional well-being of infertile couples have several responsibilities, such as helping them to understand that emotional distress and strain on the couple relationship is common, helping them take emotional limits into account when making decisions about infertility treatments, helping them to communicate better as a couple about issues surrounding infertility, and helping them to cope with potentially traumatic experiences of pregnancy loss and with treatments that do not result in a live birth (Norre & Wischmann, 2011). Systemic therapists working with these couples can facilitate the management of infertility as a couple by assisting partners in identifying differences in motivation for having children, reactions to infertility, and differing coping styles, as well as through assisting couples in developing better conflict resolution skills.

High distressed couples Longer-term grief therapy (Worden, 2018) and trauma-focused models for couple therapy (Johnson, 2002; Monson, Monson, & Fredman, 2012) can be used when psychological stressors and symptoms are more severe or after a failed fertility treatment cycle when stress is greatest. Infertility and reproductive loss, along with postpartum depression, have been conceptualized as reproductive traumas that attack both the physical and emotional sense of self and present multiple, complicated losses impacting important relationships and often leading to a sense of isolation (Jaffe & Diamond, 2011). For many couples, infertility not only represents the loss of a dreamed-of or expected child but also the loss of health, financial security, and sexual intimacy. Interventions focused on supporting the grief and trauma-recovery processes both individually and within the couple contexts are critical for successful adjustment. Narrative approaches (Combs & Freedman, 2016) that support the couple in recognizing, validating, externalizing, and rewriting their reproductive story (Jaffe & Diamond, 2011) may also be helpful in assisting couples with developing a deeper understanding of their experiences and new ways of thinking that enables couples to integrate the reproductive trauma of infertility into their broader relational context.

Systemic therapists working with infertile couples should also be aware of adjuncts to couple therapy or complementary resources available to individuals and/or couples through the local community or technology. These resources may include support groups, online forums, fertility-focused apps, yoga, massage, mindfulness training, and self-compassion exercises. For example, FertiCalm (http://www.ferticalmapp.com) is designed to assist couples experiencing infertility and provides out of session coping tools for individuals and couples. FertiCalm contains over 500 coping options for clients to use when feeling distressed by infertility-specific life situations and includes a mixture of cognitive-behavioral techniques (such as restructuring negative infertility-related thoughts) and mindfulness techniques to promote resilience through this difficult life challenge. Education-based mindfulness centers such as UCLA's Mindful Awareness Research Center (www.marc.ucla.edu) offer valuable information and free guided meditations that can help couples accept thoughts, difficult emotions, and cultivate loving kindness toward others and themselves. Self-compassion resources offered by Dr. Kristin Neff (https://self-compassion.org) can provide helpful tools to help couples undermine the negative impact of self-criticism and blame, which can often accompany an infertility diagnosis.

Future Directions for Research, Education, and Clinical Practice

Over the past decade, there has been a marked increase in scholarly publications on the psychosocial consequences of infertility for individuals and couples. Recently, scholars have called for more longitudinal research to examine long-term consequences of infertility and more research that includes both partners of couples who experience infertility to better understand dyadic coping. For example, recent research highlights the negative impact that infertility can have on relationship satisfaction—particularly among women (Greil et al., 2018). Yet longitudinal data that measures both partners' relationship quality over time can highlight how much and for how long an infertility episode impacts relationship quality. Does relationship quality "bounce back" to pre-infertility episode levels relatively quickly? The implications of infertility for couples' sexual relationships over time are also unclear; do the medicalization, scheduling, and possible coercion of sexual intercourse during the infertility episode have long reaching effects for couples' sexual satisfaction?

Situating the experience of infertility within couples' broader reproductive careers is another virtually untapped area of research that is critically needed; there is a contingent and connected nature of past, present, and future reproductive experiences, attitudes, and behaviors (Johnson, Greil, Shreffler, & McQuillan, 2018). Couples' responses to infertility will be better understood when considering the broader reproductive context, such as childbearing desires, the timing of the infertility episode (e.g., primary vs. secondary), number or length of infertility episode, and other adverse events such as pregnancy losses (Shreffler, Greil, & McQuillan, 2011). We argue that in addition, more emphasis is needed on the application of these research findings, including research on the effectiveness of clinical assessments and interventions—particularly among systemic therapists who work with couples experiencing infertility or at risk of experiencing infertility. Clinical trials of empirically supported couple therapy approaches with infertile couples are needed to begin answering questions regarding best practices for working with couples experiencing variable levels of distress associated with infertility.

As research expands our understanding of infertility, psychoeducational materials and programming are needed that focus on enhancing general social awareness regarding infertility rates and individual and relational consequences. More couples are delaying childbearing until their mid-30s, and they tend to be more optimistic about their ability to conceive than statistics indicate they should be (Reproductive Medicine Associates of New Jersey, 2015). There also is a lack of reproductive knowledge in the general population that could help couples when they try to conceive, including lack of awareness about the most fertile time of the month, overestimating chances of pregnancy during ovulation, and uncertainty about factors that might increase risk of infertility (Bunting & Boivin, 2008). Therefore, an important role that both medical professionals and systemic therapists can share is providing psychoeducation regarding fertility and encouraging couples to discuss a plan for whether and when to have children and to specifically consider the importance of biological parenthood. If it is a strongly desired life goal, the risks of postponing childbearing should be considered against the benefits, particularly among couples who desire a larger family size. Discussions about infertility treatment considerations may also be relevant. Although many people are aware that treatments for infertility exist, they may not know how expensive they can be (Katz et al., 2011), and they tend to overestimate treatment success rates (Peterson et al., 2012). Further, as highlighted earlier, treatment adds to the stress that those experiencing infertility often feel. Awareness about treatment-related stress and strategies for coping may be helpful for couples who decide to pursue treatment.

Given the continuation of childbearing postponement to ever increasing ages, which is in turn associated with the recent increases in primary infertility and infertility treatment seeking, the issue of infertility is likely to become increasingly prevalent in couple therapy. We suggest that traditionally trained systemic therapists should seek additional education about infertility, medical treatments, and alternatives to treatment in order to most effectively work with couples navigating the decision-making process and unique relational burdens associated with infertility. Additionally, systemic therapy training programs must move from solely providing students with training in general couple therapy approaches to begin providing training in evidenced-based systemic models for specific presenting problems, like infertility, that are impacting a growing number of couples.

References

Abma, J. C., & Martinez, G. M. (2006). Childlessness among older women in the United States: Trends and profiles. *Journal of Marriage and Family, 68*(4), 1045–1056. https://doi.org/10.1111/j.1741-3737.2006.00312.x

Adashi, E., & Dean, L. A. (2016). Access to and use of infertility services in the United States: Framing the challenges. *Fertility and Sterility, 105,* 1113–1118. doi:10.1016/j.fertnstert.2016.01.017

American Society for Reproductive Medicine.(2008). Definitions of infertility and recurrent pregnancy loss. *Fertility and Sterility, 90,* S60. doi:10.1016/j.fertnstert.2012.09.023

Andrews, F. M., Abbey, A., & Halman, L. J. (1992). Is infertility problem stress different? The dynamics of stress in fertile and infertile couples. *Fertility and Sterility, 57,* 1247–1253. https://doi.org/10.1016/S0015-0282(16)55082-1

Barnes, L. W. (2014). *Conceiving masculinity: Male infertility, medicine, and identity.* Philadelphia, PA: Temple University Press.

Beach, S. R., & Tesser, A. (1993). Decision making power and marital satisfaction: A self-evaluation maintenance perspective. *Journal of Social and Clinical Psychology, 12*(4), 471–494. https://doi.org/10.1521/jscp.1993.12.4.471

Becker, G. (2000). *The elusive embryo: How women and men approach new reproductive technologies.* Berkeley, CA: University of California Press.

Becker, G., Castrillo, M., Jackson, R., & Nachtigall, R. D. (2005). Infertility among low-income Latinos. *Fertility and Sterility, 85,* 882–887. https://doi.org/10.1016/j.fertnstert.2005.09.052

Bell, A. V. (2014). *Misconception: Social class and infertility in America.* New Brunswick, NJ: Rutgers University Press.

Bell, A. V. (2016). The margins of medicalization: Diversity and context through the case of infertility. *Social Science & Medicine, 156,* 39–46. https://doi.org/10.1016/j.socscimed.2016.03.005

Benyamini, Y., Gozlan, M., & Kokia, E. (2009). Women's and men's perceptions of infertility and their associations with psychological adjustment: A dyadic approach. *British Journal of Health Psychology, 14,* 1–16. https://doi.org/10.1348/135910708X279288

Berghuis, J. P., & Stanton, A. L. (2002). Adjustment to a dyadic stressor: A longitudinal study of coping and depressive symptoms in infertile couples over an insemination attempt. *Psychological Bulletin, 70,* 433–438. doi:10.1037//0022-006X.70.2.433

Bitler, M. P., & Schmidt, L. (2012). Utilization of infertility treatments: The effects of insurance mandates. *Demography, 49,* 125–149. doi:10.1007/s13524-011-0078-4

Bodenmann, G., Meuwly, N., & Kayser, K. (2011). Two conceptions of dyadic coping and their potential for predicting relationship quality and individual wellbeing. *European Psychologist, 16,* 255–266. https://doi.org/10.1027/1016-9040/a000068

Bodenmann, G., Pihet, S., & Kayser, K. (2006). The relationship between dyadic coping and marital quality: A 2-year longitudinal study. *Journal of Family Psychology, 20,* 485–493. doi:10.1037/0893-3200.20.3.485

Boivin, J., Bunting, L., Collins, J. A., & Nygren, K. G. (2007). International estimates of infertility prevalence and treatment-seeking: potential need and demand for infertility medical care. *Human Reproduction, 22*(6), 1506–1512.

Boivin, J., & Gameiro, S. (2015). Evolution of psychology and counseling in infertility. *Fertility and Sterility, 104*(2), 251–259. https://doi.org/10.1016/j.fertnstert.2015.05.035

Boivin, J., Scanlan, L., & Walker, S. M. (1999). Why are infertile couples not using psychosocial counseling? *Human Reproduction, 14*(5), 1384–1391. https://doi.org/10.1093/humrep/14.5.1384

Boivin, J., Takefman, J., & Braverman, A. (2011). The fertility quality of life (FertiQol) tool: Development and general psychometric properties. *Fertility and Sterility, 96*(2), 409–415. https://doi.org/10.1093/humrep/der171

Bunting, L., & Boivin, J. (2007). Decision-making about seeking medical advice in an internet sample of women trying to get pregnant. *Human Reproduction, 22,* 1662–1668. doi:10.1093/humrep/dem057

Bunting, L., & Boivin, J. (2008). Knowledge about infertility risk factors, fertility myths and illusory benefits of healthy habits in young people. *Human Reproduction, 23,* 1858–1864. doi:10.1093/humrep/den168

Bunting, L., Tsibulsky, I., & Boivin, J. (2012). Fertility knowledge and beliefs about fertility treatment: Findings from the International Fertility Decision-making Study. *Human Reproduction, 28*(2), 385–397.

Ceballo, R., Graham, E. T., & Hart, J. (2015). Silent and infertile: An intersectional analysis of the experiences of socioeconomically diverse African American women with infertility. *Psychology of Women Quarterly, 39*(4), 497–511. https://doi.org/10.1177/0361684315581169

Centers for Disease Control.(2017). *2015 assisted reproductive technology fertility clinic success rates report.* Atlanta, GA: US Department of Health and Human Services.

Chachamovich, J. R., Chachamovich, E., Ezer, H., Fleck, M. P., Knauth, D. R., & Passos, E. P. (2010). Agreement on perceptions of quality of life in couples dealing with infertility. *Journal of Obstetric, Gynecologic, & Neonatal Nursing, 39,* 557–565. https://doi.org/10.1111/j.1552-6909.2010.01168.x

Chandra, A., Copen, C. E., & Stephen, E. H. (2013). *Infertility and impaired fecundity in the United States, 1982–2010: Data from the National Survey of Family Growth (National Health Statistics Reports 67).* Hyattsville, MD: National Center for Health Statistics.

Chandra, A., Copen, C. E., & Stephen E. H. (2014). *Infertility service use in the United States: Data from the National Survey of Family Growth, 1982–2010 (National Health Statistics Reports, 73).* Hyattsville, MD: National Center for Health Statistics.

Clarke, L. H., Martin-Matthews, A., & Matthews, R. (2006). The continuity and discontinuity of the embodied self in infertility. *The Canadian Review of Sociology and Anthropology* [La Revue Canadienne de Sociologie et d'Anthropologie], *43,* 95–113. https://doi.org/10.1111/j.1755-618X.2006.tb00856.x

Collins, J. A., & Van Steirteghem, A. (2004). Overall prognosis with current treatment of infertility. *Human Reproduction Update, 10,* 309–316. doi:10.1093/humupd/dmh029

Combs, G., & Freedman, J. (2016). Narrative therapy's relational understanding of identity. *Family Process, 55*(2), 211–224. doi:10.1111/famp.12216

Cousineau, T. M., & Domar, A. D. (2007). Psychological impact of infertility. *Best Practice & Research Clinical Obstetrics & Gynaecology, 21*(2), 293–308. doi:10.1016/j.bpobgyn.2006.12.003

Covington, S. N. (Ed.) (2015). *Fertility counseling: Clinical guide and case studies.* Cambridge, UK: Cambridge University Press.

Czarnecki, D. (2015). Moral women, immoral technologies: How devout women negotiate gender, religion, and assisted reproductive technologies. *Gender & Society, 29*(5), 716–742. https://doi.org/10.1177/0891243215591504

Debest, C., & Mazuy, M. (2014). Childlessness: A life choice that goes against the norm. *Population & Societies, 508,* 1–4.

Domar, A. D., & Seibel, M. M. (1997). Emotional aspects of infertility. In M. M. Seibel (Ed.), *Infertility: A Comprehensive Text* (pp. 29–44). Stamford, CT: Appleton & Lange.

Dunson, D. B., Colombo, B., & Baird, D. D. (2002). Changes with age in the level and duration of fertility in the menstrual cycle. *Human Reproduction, 17*(5), 1399–1403. https://doi.org/10.1093/humrep/17.5.1399

Ethics Committee of the American Society for Reproductive Medicine.(2009). Access to fertility treatment by gays, lesbians, and unmarried persons. *Fertility and Sterility, 92*(4), 1190–1193.

Eugster, A., & Vingerhoets, A. J. J. M. (1999). Psychological aspects of in vitro fertilization: A review. *Social Science & Medicine, 48*(5), 575–589. http://dx.doi.org/10.1016/S0277-9536(98)00386-4

Faulkner, R. A., Davey, M., & Davey, M. (2005). Gender-related predictors of change in marital satisfaction and marital conflict. *American Journal of Family Therapy, 33,* 61–83. http://dx.doi.org/10.1080/01926180590889211

Funk, J. L., & Rogge, R. D. (2007). Testing the ruler with item response theory: Increasing precision of measurement for relationship satisfaction with the Couples Satisfaction Index. *Journal of Family Psychology, 21*(4), 572. doi:10.1037/0893-3200.21.4.572

Gibson, F. L., Ungerer, J. A., Tennant, C. C., & Saunders, D. M. (2000). Parental adjustment and attitudes to parenting after in vitro fertilization. *Fertility and Sterility, 73,* 565–574. https://doi.org/10.1016/S0015-0282(99)00583-X

Glover, L., McLellan, A., & Weaver, S. M. (2009). What does having a fertility problem mean to couples? *Journal of Reproductive and Infant Psychology, 27,* 401–418. doi:10.1080/02646830903190896

Golombok, S. (2015). *Modern families: Parents and children in new family forms.* Cambridge, UK: Cambridge University Press.

Greil, A. L. (1991). *Not yet pregnant: Infertile couples in contemporary America.* New Brunswick, NJ: Rutgers University Press.

Greil, A. L., Johnson, K. M., Lowry, M. H., McQuillan, J., & Slauson-Blevins, K. S. (2019). Degrees of medicalization: The case of infertility health-seeking. *The Sociological Quarterly,* 1–19. doi:10.1080/00380253.2019.1625731

Greil, A. L., Lowry, M., McQuillan, J., & Shreffler, K. M. (2011). Infertility treatment and fertility-specific distress: A longitudinal analysis of a population-based sample of U.S. women. *Social Science & Medicine, 73,* 87–94. doi:10.1016/j.socscimed.2011.04.023

Greil, A. L., & McQuillan, J. (2004). Help-seeking patterns among subfecund women. *The Journal of Reproductive and Infant Psychology, 22,* 305–319. doi:10.1080/02646830412331298332

Greil, A. L., McQuillan, J., & Sanchez, D. (2016). Does fertility-specific distress vary by race among a probability sample of women in the United States? *Journal of Health Psychology, 21,* 183–192. doi:10.1177/1359105314524970

Greil, A. L., McQuillan, J., Shreffler, K. M., Johnson, K. M., & Slauson-Blevins, K. (2013). The importance of social cues for medical helpseeking: The example of infertility. *Sociological Inquiry, 8,* 209–237. doi:10.1111/soin.12000

Greil, A. L., Schmidt, L., & Peterson, B. (2014). Understanding and treating the psychosocial consequences of infertility. In A. Wenzel (Ed.), *The Oxford handbook of perinatal psychology* (pp. 524–547). Oxford, UK: Oxford University Press.

Greil, A. L., Shreffler, K. M., Schmidt, L., & McQuillan, J. (2011). Variation in distress among women with infertility: Evidence from a population-based sample. *Human Reproduction, 26*(8), 2101–2112. doi:10/1093/humrep/der148

Greil, A. L., Slauson-Blevins, K., & McQuillan, J. (2010). The experience of infertility: A review of recent literature. *Sociology of Health & Illness, 32,* 140–162. doi:10.1111/j.1467-9566.2009.01213.x

Greil, A. L., Slauson-Blevins, K., McQuillan, J., Lowry, M. H., Burch, A. R., & Shreffler, K. M. (2018). Relationship satisfaction among infertile couples: Implications of gender and self-identification. *Journal of Family Issues, 39*(5), 1304–1325. doi:10.1177/0192513X17699027}

Greil, A. L., Slauson-Blevins, K. S., Shreffler, K. M., Johnson, K. M., Lowry, M. H., Burch, A. R., & McQuillan, J. (2017). Decline in ethical concerns about reproductive technologies among a representative sample of US women. *Public Understanding of Science, 26*(7), 789–805. doi:10.11777/0963662515625402

Heavey, C. L., Larson, B. M., Zumtobel, D. C., & Christensen, A. (1996). The Communication Patterns Questionnaire: The reliability and validity of a constructive communication subscale. *Journal of Marriage and the Family, 3,* 796–800. http://dx.doi.org/10.2307/353737

Henning, K., Strauss, B., & Strauss, B. (2002). *Psychological and psychosomatic aspects of involuntary childlessness: State of research at the end of the 1990's.* Ashland, OH: Hogrefe & Huber Publishers.

Hjelmstedt, A., Widström, A. M., Wramsby, H., & Collins, A. (2004). Emotional adaptation following successful in vitro fertilization. *Fertility and Sterility, 81,* 1254–1264. doi:10.1016/j.fertnstert.2003.09.061

Holter, H., Anderheim, L., Bergh, C., & Moller, A. (2006). First IVF treatment—Short-term impact on psychological well-being and the marital relationship. *Human Reproduction, 21,* 3295–3302. doi:10.1093/humrep/del288

Holton, S., Fisher, J., & Rowe, H. (2011). To have or not to have? Australian women's child-bearing desires, expectations and outcomes. *Journal of Population Research, 28*(4), 353–379.

Inhorn, M. C. (2015). *Cosmopolitan conceptions: IVF sojourns in global Dubai.* Durham, NC: Duke University Press.

Jacob, M. C., McQuillan, J., & Greil, A. L. (2007). Psychological distress by type of fertility barrier. *Human Reproduction, 22,* 885–894. doi:10.1093/humrep/del452

Jaffe, J., & Diamond, M. O. (2011). *Reproductive trauma: Psychotherapy with infertility and pregnancy loss clients.* Washington, DC: American Psychological Association.

Johnson, K. M., Greil, A. L., Shreffler, K. M., & McQuillan, J. (2018). Fertility and infertility: Toward an integrative research agenda. *Population Research and Policy Review,* 1–26. doi:10.1007/s11113-018-9476-2

Johnson, K. M., & Johnson, D. R. (2009). Partnered decisions? U.S. couples and medical help-seeking for infertility. *Family Relations, 58,* 431–444. doi:10.1111/j.1741-3729.2009.00564.x

Johnson, K. M., McQuillan, J., Greil, A. L., & Shreffler, K. M. (2014). Towards a more inclusive framework for understanding fertility barriers. In M. Nash (Ed.), *Reframing reproduction* (pp. 23–38). London, UK: Palgrave Macmillan.

Johnson, S. M. (2002). *Emotionally focused couple therapy with trauma survivors: Strengthening attachment bonds.* New York, NY: Guilford Press.

Jordan, C. B., & Ferguson, R. J. (2006). Infertility-related concerns in two family practice sites. *Families, Systems and Health, 24*(1), 28–32. doi:10.1037/1091-7527.24.1.28

Karney, B. R., Story, L. B., & Bradbury, T. N. (2005). Marriages in context: Interactions between chronic and acute stress among newlyweds. In T. A. Revenson, K. Kayser, & G. Bodenmann (Eds.), *Couples, coping, and stress: Emerging perspectives on dyadic coping* (pp. 13–32). Washington, DC: American Psychological Association.

Katz, P., Showstack, J., Smith, J. F., Nachtigall, R. D., Millstein, S. G., Wing, H., … Adler, N. (2011). Costs of infertility treatment: Results from an 18-month prospective cohort study. *Fertility and Sterility, 95,* 915–921. doi:10.1016/j.fertnstert.2010.11.026

Kessler, L. M., Craig, B. M., Plosker, S. M., Reed, D. R., & Quin, G. P. (2013). Infertility evaluation and treatment among women in the United States. *Fertility and Sterility, 100,* 1025–1032. doi:10.1016/j.fertnstert.2013.05.040

Kim, J. H., Shin, H. S., & Yun, E. K. (2018). A dyadic approach to infertility stress, marital adjustment, and depression on quality of life in infertile couples. *Journal of Holistic Nursing, 36*(1), 6–14. doi:0898010116675987

Klock, S. C. (2015). When treatment appears futile: The role of the mental health professional and end-of-treatment counseling. *Fertility & Sterility, 104,* 267–270. doi:10.1016/j.fertnstert.2015.05.008

Letherby, G. (1999). Other than mother and mothers as others: The experience of mother-hood and non-motherhood in relation to "infertility" and "involuntary childlessness". *Women's Studies International Forum, 22,* 359–372. doi:10.1016/S0277-5395(99)00028-X

Loftus, J., & Andriot, A. L. (2012). "That's what makes a woman": Infertility and coping with a failed life course transition. *Sociological Spectrum, 32,* 226–243. doi:10.1080/02732173.2012.663711

Lund, R., Sejbæk, C. S., Christensen, U., & Schmidt, L. (2009). The impact of social relations on the incidence of severe depressive symptoms among infertile women and men. *Human Reproduction, 24,* 2810–2820. doi:10.1093/humrep/dep257

Macaluso, M., Wright-Schnapp, T. J., Chandra, A., Johnson, R., Satterwhite, C. L., Pulver, A., … Pollack, L. A. (2010). A public health focus on infertility prevention, detection, and management. *Fertility and Sterility, 93*, e1–e16. doi:10.1016/j.fertnstert.2008.09.046

Martin, J. A., Hamilton, B. E., Osterman, M. J. K., Driscoll, A. K., & Drake, P. (2018). *Births: Final data for 2016* (National Vital Statistics Reports, 67(1)). Hyattsville, MD: National Center for Health Statistics.

Martinez, G., Daniels, K., & Chandra, A. (2012). *National health statistics reports* (pp. 15–44). Hyattsville, MD: *National Center for Health Statistics.*

Martins, M. V., Peterson, B. D., Almeida, V., Mesquita-Guimarães, J., & Costa, M. E. (2014). Dyadic dynamics of perceived social support in couples facing infertility. *Human Reproduction, 29*, 83–89. doi:10.1093/humrep/det403

Mathews, T. J., & Hamilton, B. E. (2016). Mean age of mothers is on the rise: United States, 2000-2014. *NCHS Data Brief*, (232), 1–8. Retrieved from https://www.cdc.gov/nchs/data/databriefs/db232.pdf

McCarthy, M. P. (2008). Women's lived experience of infertility after unsuccessful medical intervention. *The Journal of Midwifery and Women's Health, 53*, 319–324.

McQuillan, J., Greil, A. L., Colaner, C., Tiemeyer, S., & Shreffler, K. M. (2018). *Does it matter who perceives a problem? Gender, perceptions of fertility problems, and depressive symptoms.* Paper presented at the 2018 European Population Council meeting in Brussels, Belgium.

McQuillan, J., Greil, A. L., White, L., & Jacob, M. C. (2003). Frustrated fertility: Infertility and psychological distress among women. *Journal of Marriage & Family, 65*, 1007–1018. https://doi.org/10.1111/j.1741-3737.2003.01007.x

Monson, C. M., Monson, C. M., & Fredman, S. J. (2012). *Cognitive-behavioral conjoint therapy for PTSD.* New York, NY: Guilford Press.

Newton, C. R., Sherrard, W., & Glavac, I. (1999). The Fertility Problem Inventory: Measuring perceived infertility-related stress. *Fertility and Sterility, 72*(1), 54–62. doi:10.1016/S0015-0282(99)00164-8

Norre, J., & Wischmann, T. (2011). The position of the fertility counsellor in a fertility team: A critical appraisal. *Human Fertility, 14*, 154–159. doi:10.3109/14647273.2011.580824

Ockhuijsen, H. D., van Smeden, M., van den Hoogen, A., & Boivin, J. (2017). Validation study of the SCREENIVF: An instrument to screen women or men on risk for emotional maladjustment before the start of a fertility treatment. *Fertility and Sterility, 107*(6), 1370–1379. doi:10.1016/j.fertnstert.2017.04.008

Olshansky, E. F. (1987). Identity of self as infertile: An example of theory-generating research. *Advances in Nursing Science, 9*, 54–63.

Ozkan, B., Orhan, E., Aktas, N., & Coskuner, E. R. (2016). Sexual dysfunction and depression among Turkish women with infertile husbands: The invisible part of the iceberg. *International Urology and Nephrology, 48*, 31–36. doi:10.1016/j.urology.2015.03.005

Park, N. K., & Wonch Hill, P. (2014). Is adoption an option? The role of importance of motherhood and fertility help-seeking in considering adoption. *Journal of Family Issues, 35*, 601–626. doi:10.1177/0192513X13493277

Péloquin, K., Brassard, A., Arpin, V., Sabourin, S., & Wright, J. (2018). Whose fault is it? Blame predicting psychological adjustment and couple satisfaction in couples seeking fertility treatment. *Journal of Psychosomatic Obstetrics & Gynecology, 39*, 64–72. doi:10.1080/0167482X.2017.1289369

Peterson, B. (2015). Fertility counseling for couples. In S. N. Covington (Ed.), *Fertility counseling: Clinical guide and case studies* (pp. 60–73). Cambridge, UK: Cambridge University Press.

Peterson, B., Boivin, J., Norré, J., Smith, C., Thorn, P., & Wischmann, T. (2012). An introduction to infertility counseling: A guide for mental health and medical professionals. *Journal of Assisted Reproduction and Genetics, 29*(3), 243–248. doi:10.1007/s10815-011-9701-y

Peterson, B. D., Gold, L., & Feingold, T. (2007). The experience and influence of Infertility: Considerations for couple counselors. *The Family Journal, 15*(3), 251–257. https://doi.org/10.1177/1066480707301365

Peterson, B. D., Newton, C. R., & Rosen, K. H. (2003). Examining congruence between partners' perceived infertility-related stress and its relationship to marital adjustment and depression in infertile couples. *Family Process, 42*, 59–70. doi:10.1111/j.1545-5300.2003.00059.x

Peterson, B. D., Pirritano, M., Block, J. M., & Schmidt, L. (2011). Marital benefit and coping strategies in men and women undergoing unsuccessful fertility treatments over a 5-year period. *Fertility and Sterility, 95*(5), 1759–1763. doi:10.1016/j.fertnstert.2011.01.125

Peterson, B. D., Pirritano, M., Christensen, U., & Schmidt, L. (2008). The impact of partner coping in couples experiencing infertility. *Human Reproduction, 23*, 1128–1137. doi:10.1093/humrep/den067

Peterson, Z. D., & Buday, S. K. (2018). Sexual coercion in couples with infertility: Prevalence, gender differences, and associations with psychological outcomes. *Sexual and Relationship Therapy*, 1–16. doi:10.1080/14681994.2018.1435863

Pinborg, A., Hougaard, C. O., Nyboe Andersen, A., Molbo, D., & Schmidt, L. (2009). Prospective longitudinal cohort study on cumulative 5-year delivery and adoption rates among 1338 couples initiating infertility treatment. *Human Reproduction, 24*(4), 991–999. doi:10.1093/humrep/den463

Piva, I., Lo Monte, G., Graziano, A., & Marci, R. (2014). A literature review on the relationship between infertility and sexual dysfunction: Does fun end with baby making? *The European Journal of Contraception and Reproductive Health Care, 19*, 231–237. doi:10.3109/13625187.2014.919379

Randall, A. K., & Bodenmann, G. (2009). The role of stress on close relationships and marital satisfaction. *Clinical Psychology Review, 29*, 105–115. doi:10.1016/j.cpr.2008.10.004

Redshaw, M., Hockley, C., & Davidson, L. L. (2007). A qualitative study of the experience of treatment for infertility among women who successfully became pregnant. *Human Reproduction, 22*, 295–304. doi:10.1093/humrep/del344

Remennick, L. (2000). Childless in the land of imperative motherhood: Stigma and coping among infertile Israeli women. *Sex Roles, 43*, 821–841.

Repokari, L., Punamäki, R. L., Unkila-Kallio, L., Vilska, S., Poikkeus, P., Sinkkonen, J., … Tulppala, M. (2007). Infertility treatment and marital relationships: A 1-year prospective study among successfully treated ART couples and their controls. *Human Reproduction, 22*(5), 1481–1491. doi:10.1093/humrep/dem013

Reproductive Medicine Associates of New Jersey [RMANJ].(2015). *Infertility in America: 2015 survey and report*. Basking Ridge, NJ: Reproductive Medicine Associates. Retrieved from http://www.rmanj.com/2015/04/infertility-in-america-2015-survey-report

Sandelowski, M. (1993). *With child in mind: Studies of the personal encounter with infertility*. Philadelphia, PA: University of Pennsylvania Press.

Schmidt, L., Sobotka, T., Bentzen, J. G., & Andersen, A. N. (2012). Demographic and medical consequences of the postponement of parenthood. *Human Reproduction Update, 18*, 29–43. doi:10.1093/humupd/dmr040

Schwerdtfeger, K. L., & Shreffler, K. M. (2009). Trauma of pregnancy loss and infertility for mothers and involuntarily childless women in the contemporary United States. *Journal of Loss and Trauma, 14*, 211–227. doi:10.1080/15325020802537468

Shadish, W. R., & Baldwin, S. A. (2005). Effects of behavioral marital therapy: A meta-analysis of randomized controlled trials. *Journal of Consulting and Clinical Psychology, 73*(1), 6. http://dx.doi.org/10.1037/0022-006X.73.1.6

Shreffler, K. M., Greil, A. L., & McQuillan, J. (2011). Pregnancy loss and distress among U.S. women. *Family Relations, 60*(3), 342–355.

Shreffler, K. M., Greil, A. L., & McQuillan, J. (2017). Responding to infertility: Lessons from a growing body of research and suggested guidelines for practice. *Translational Family Science: Family Relations, 66*(4), 644–658. doi:10.1111/fare.12281

Shreffler, K. M., Johnson, D. R., & Scheuble, L. K. (2010). Ethical problems with infertility treatments: Attitudes and explanations. *The Social Science Journal, 47*, 731–746. doi:10.1016/j.soscij.2010.07.012

Slauson-Blevins, K. S., & Park, N. K. (2016). Deciding not to adopt: The role of normative family ideologies in adoption consideration. *Adoption Quarterly, 19*, 237–260. doi:10.10 80/10926755.2015.1121185

Thorn, P. (2009). Understanding infertility: Psychological and social considerations from a counselling perspective. *International Journal of Fertility and Sterility, 3*(2), 48–51. Retrieved from http://www.ijfs.ir/journal/article/abstract/2362

van den Akker, O. (2004). Coping, quality of life and psychological symptoms in three groups of sub-fertile women. *Patient Education and Counseling, 57*, 183–189. doi:10.1016/j.pec.2004.05.012

Van den Broeck, U., Holvoet, L., Enzlin, P., Bakelants, E., Demyttenaere, K., & D'Hooghe, T. (2009). Reasons for dropout in infertility treatment. *Gynecologic and Obstetric Investigation, 68*, 58–64. doi:10.1159/000214839

Van Voorhis, B. J. (2006). Outcomes from assisted reproductive technology. *Obstetrics and Gynecology, 107*, 183–200. doi:10.1097/01.AOG.0000194207.06554.5b

Verhaak, C. M., Lintsen, A. M. E., Evers, A. W. M., & Braat, D. D. M. (2010). Who is at risk of emotional problems and how do you know? Screening of women going for IVF treatment. *Human Reproduction, 25*(5), 1234–1240. doi:10.1093/humrep/deq054

Verhaak, C. M., Smeenk, J. M. J., Evers, A. W. M., Kremer, J. A. M., Kraaimaat, F. W., & Braat, D. D. M. (2007). Women's emotional adjustment to IVF: A systematic review of 25 years of research. *Human Reproduction Update, 13*, 27–36. doi:10.1093/humupd/dml040

Wagner, J., Wrzus, C., Neyer, F. J., & Lang, F. R. (2015). Social network characteristics of early midlife voluntarily and involuntarily childless couples. *Journal of Family Issues, 36*, 87–110. doi:10.1177/0192513X13490931

Wang, K., Li, J., Zhang, J. X., Zhang, L., Yu, J., & Jiang, P. (2007). Psychological characteristics and marital quality of infertile women registered for in vitro fertilization-intracytoplasmic sperm injection in China. *Fertility and Sterility, 87*, 792–798. doi:10.1016/j.fertnstert.2006.07.1534

Wilson, K. J. (2014). *Not trying: Infertility, childlessness, and ambivalence.* Nashville, TN: Vanderbilt University Press.

Wirtberg, I., Moller, A., Hogström, L., Tronstad, S. E., & Lalos, A. (2007). Life 20 years after unsuccessful infertility treatment. *Human Reproduction, 22*, 598–604. doi:10.1093/humrep/del401

Wischmann, T. H. (2010). Couples' sexual dysfunctions: Sexual disorders in infertile couples. *The Journal of Sexual Medicine, 7*(5), 1868–1876. doi:10.1111/j.1743-6109.2010.01717

Wood, N. D., Crane, D. R., Schaalje, G. B., & Law, D. D. (2005). What works for whom: A meta-analytic review of marital and couples therapy in reference to marital distress. *The American Journal of Family Therapy, 33*(4), 273–287. doi:10.1080/01926180590962147

Worden, J. W. (2018). *Grief counseling and grief therapy: A handbook for the mental health practitioner.* New York, NY: Springer.

Ying, L.-Y., Wu, L. H., & Loke, A. Y. (2015). The experience of Chinese couples undergoing In Vitro fertilization treatment: Perception of the treatment process and partner support. *PLoS ONE, 10*(10), e0139691. https://doi.org/10.1371/journal.pone.0139691

Zegers-Hochschild, F., Adamson, G. D., Dyer, S., Racowsky, C., de Mouzon, J., … van der Poel, S. (2017). The international glossary on infertility and fertility care. *Human Reproduction, 32*, 1786–1801. doi:10.1093/humrep/dex234

18

Grief and Loss Effects in the Couple Relationship

Ileana Ungureanu and Cadmona A. Hall

Grief and loss are universal human experiences. Death is fundamentally a part of life, and according to Shakespeare, "we were born to die." Grief is a worldwide issue for all people, yet too often it is poorly acknowledged and goes unaddressed. Even in family therapy, the subject of death, grief, and bereavement continues to be seen as taboo (Boss, 2007; Walsh & McGoldrick, 2004). In the United States, critics have suggested that the lack of consideration of grief is because US culture is present and future oriented, making it a death-denying and grief-avoiding culture (Walsh & McGoldrick, 2004). In spite of this avoidance, research indicates that the death of a loved one is rated as one of life's top stressors (Spurgeon, Jackson, & Beach, 2001), and grief is a normal and appropriate response to loss. Walsh and McGoldrick (2004) believe that coming to terms with a loss is the most difficult task a family must confront. Yet, if family members fail to come to terms with loss, difficulties can result (Gilbert, 1997; Neimeyer, 2006; Oliver, 1999). Ester Gelcer (1983) presented the perspective that individual family members' difficulties in confronting death and grief can have harmful implications for the whole family and arrest its growth. She argued that because of this, family therapy should be the treatment of choice following a death in the family. This chapter will review the current bereavement literature, describe the impact of loss on the couple relationship, provide a framework for understanding dimensions of culture, and discuss clinical implications.

Key definitions and types of loss

Too often, therapists as well as clients do not have the language to describe grief experiences. As a result, we provide important definitions in the hopes and that these shared definitions will help in facilitating a healing dialogue. Human beings are faced with loss across the life cycle. Losses occur for various reasons, some death related and some not. When loss occurs, there is a separation and deprivation from a person,

The Handbook of Systemic Family Therapy: Volume 3, First Edition.
Edited by Karen S. Wampler and Adrian J. Blow.
© 2020 John Wiley & Sons Ltd. Published 2020 by John Wiley & Sons Ltd.

object, experience, status, or relationship (Corr, Corr, & Doka, 2018). Bereavement refers to the state of being bereaved, with the root word meaning to be robbed, despoiled, or deprived (Oxford English Dictionary, 2018). Therefore the bereaved are people who have experienced the loss of something valued (Corr et al., 2018).

Understanding grief   Grief describes all the responses we have when we experience a loss (Corr et al., 2018). According to Worden (2008), reactions to grief include emotions (sadness, fear, anger, relief, helplessness, yearning, guilt, numbness), physical sensations in the body (such as throat tightening, stomach pain, tension in the back and shoulders, lack of energy, and or restlessness), thoughts (confusion, disbelief, spiritual or paranormal experiences, meaning-making, dreams, and behaviors), and social withdrawal (avoidance, sleep disturbance, appetite changes, loss of interest in previously enjoyed activities). Grief is a normal reaction to loss and change. The term mourning is most often used to describe what people do with their grief in two spheres, the personal and the public. Mourning refers to the internal process of coping as well as the shared expressions of grief along with seeking social support (Corr et al., 2018). It is an outward expression of the internal experience.

Couples are impacted by various types of grief across their lifespan. It is important for family therapists to recognize the unique challenges present with each type of loss and how each can impact the couple relationship. While clients may not present with such distinct boundaries between their grief experiences, it is helpful for therapists to recognize some of the unique characteristics and how these dynamics impact the couples functioning. Couples often present in therapy with ideas and emotional experiences and often lack the language and framework to describe their experience. While some of the concepts have overlapping ideas, this information is a helpful way of conceptualizing the loss for the therapist and beginning to frame things for clients.

Ambiguous loss   Ambiguous loss refers to loss that remains unclear often due to lack of information and uncertainty (Boss, 2007). The inability to make sense of the loss is not the result of a disorder or pathological thinking. When the bereaved are prevented from accessing specific information about the death (such as how, where, when, or why), it ruptures the meaning of loss, so people may be frozen in both coping and grieving. Two types of ambiguous loss faced by couples address physical and psychological absence.

PHYSICAL ABSENCE WITH PSYCHOLOGICAL PRESENCE   This type of ambiguous loss occurs when a loved one is physically missing, that is, their status as dead or alive is unclear due to circumstances such as when someone is kidnapped, deserted, abandoned, lost at sea, 9/11 body never recovered in the twin towers, and similar losses (Boss & Yeats, 2014). An example of this type of ambiguous loss faced by couples was present in 2014, when 276 girls were kidnapped from their school in the town of Chibok in Borno State, Nigeria (Gaffey, 2017). While some of the young girls were released or escaped, over 100 have yet to be reunited with their parents. Couples are left dealing with the loss of their daughters without knowing if they are alive or dead. These parents have no way of finding out, and they are left questioning, searching, yearning, and grieving without resolution. They must contend with the question of holding hope while actively missing their daughter in the present. Do you acknowledge a birthday? Do you set a place for dinner? How do you answer the question of how many children you have?

PSYCHOLOGICAL ABSENCE WITH PHYSICAL PRESENCE   Families dealing with these types of losses have their loved one physically present, but they are not there in the same way as these losses are due to afflictions such as Alzheimer's disease, traumatic brain injury (TBI), dementia, addiction, or chronic severe mental illness (Boss, 2007, 2009). Couples may experience this type of loss while caring for a loved one, and these situations are stressful, for example, many middle-aged couples experience the stress of caring for children while simultaneously caring for an aging parent who is going through changes related to aging. An aging parent that has experienced a severe stroke may be physically healthy and present but no longer have the same mental acuity they once had. Couples often struggle with the emotions of grief when there has been no death, and there are no socially sanctioned spaces to process the non-death losses.

How couples deal with ambiguous loss is predicated on their tolerance and ability to sit with ambiguity in their lives. It is imperative to remember that this process of moving through ambiguous loss is a relational experience in which ideas about information and "truth" are co-constructed within systemic interactions influenced by power and access (Boss, 2009).

Disenfranchised grief   Grief that is disenfranchised does not fit into socially acceptable norms (Robson & Walter, 2013) due to a lack of social recognition, a dismissal of grieving style, or being socially unsupported and disallowed (Doka, 2002). The loss is not valued and the bereaved are not supported through mourning and participation in rituals (Bordere, 2017). Disenfranchised grief comes about in cases where there is no socially sanctioned right or permission to grieve. This may be due to the nature of the relationship, the type of loss, or the perception that grief is possible. Disenfranchised grief is directly linked to cultural and societal norms and expectations that govern the rules of how we live and relate to others. There are three specific ways in which grief can be disenfranchised: through devaluation, type of loss, or the griever is not permitted to grieve (Doka, 1999).

DEVALUATION   One way disenfranchised grief occurs is when the relationship itself is deemed unacceptable or is devalued in some way (Doka, 1999, 2002). For example, therapists may see this occur in couples in polyamorous relationships. Polyamory is the practice of simultaneously engaging in more than one significant intimate romantic/ sexual relationship with the full knowledge and consent of all parties (Klesse, 2018). While polyamory is practiced across the globe, there are many cultures that stigmatize those involved. Due to moral, ethical, legal, and/or spiritual reasons, couples may not be forthright about other members of their relationship, and when a partner dies, they may not have the ability to name and grieve a shared loss due to public perceptions. Another example of this type of disenfranchised loss occurs in families where there has been remarriage. A spouse may not feel they have permission to grieve a death of a stepchild whom they may no longer have contact with. The current partner may not even be made aware of the loss and does not understand their partner's mood or behavior and has no knowledge that their support would be helpful.

TYPE OF LOSS   Another type of disenfranchised grief is directly related to the nature or type of loss experienced. This type of grief occurs when the significance of the loss is not recognized by the society (Doka, 2002). Perinatal death such as an ectopic pregnancy, miscarriage, stillbirth, and other types of infant death are often treated as less significant than other types of death losses (Lang et al., 2011). Women express feeling isolated in their grief, distant from their partners, and unsure of how their significant other is processing their own feelings (Wing, Burge-Callaway, Rose Clance, & Armistead, 2001). Partners express not knowing how sooth or help, being unsure if they have the space to grieve because their partner experienced the physical impact of the loss. Most cultures have few if any rituals of support and guidelines for mourning for couples who have experienced this type of loss.

A non-death example that greatly impacts couples is physical losses due to medical reasons, such as the loss of limbs and other body parts. Often the goal of medical intervention is to focus on solving a problem and moving on; therefore, with these types of losses, most people are encouraged to develop new strategies and solutions while denying the need to acknowledge the loss in some way. The people who adopt a positive demeanor are validated and praised publicly while no mention is given to whether their "success" is also tied to their ability to acknowledge and process loss. In this system spouses and partners are mostly viewed as agents of support; they are rarely acknowledged for having their own emotional experience related to the loss and the relational impact it has on their lives. This denies both members of the couple from having an authentic and congruent relationship with themselves and each other.

LACK OF PERMISSION   The third way grief may be disenfranchised is when the griever is seen as unentitled to grief because they are not recognized as being capable of the cognitive and emotional experience of grief. The elderly, young children, and people with developmental disabilities are often impacted by this category of disenfranchised grief. They are seen by others as fragile, unaware, incapable of understanding dying and death, or their participation in rituals of mourning are seen as inappropriate (Doka, 1999). Parents often present to therapy with the concern that participation in therapy is too overwhelming for their children. The anxiety about this dilemma increases regarding grief and loss because most adults have not learned helpful and appropriate ways of talking to children about dying and death.

Stigmatized grief A stigma is a mark of disgrace associated with a circumstance, quality, or person, and the grief experienced is complicated by shame, disgrace, humiliation, and blame related to the loss (Doka, 2002). An important difference between stigmatized and disenfranchised grief is that with stigmatized grief the death is acknowledged and seen as a legitimate loss; however, there is a societal stain that creates dissonance for the griever (Doka, 2002). Examples of stigmatized grief include deaths due to suicide, addiction, or other seemingly preventable circumstances and non-death losses such as deportation, incarceration, or removal of children from the home due to abuse or neglect.

For example, of all cancer research being conducted, lung cancer receives the lowest financial support due to the social stigma of smoking (Lebow, Chambers, Christensen, & Johnson, 2012). Blame may be placed on the smoker for engaging in the behavior, leaving little room for their own experience of grief when they are diagnosed with a life-threatening illness. HIV/AIDS is another example. As the public's knowledge of how to prevent the transmission for HIV and AIDS has grown, there has been increased stigma and blame for having the disease because it is seen as preventable. This stigma can lead those diagnosed with the disease to not grieve as they may be filled with shame about their diagnosis. Another complex example occurs when a woman has an abortion. Too often, the response to this decision is callous because of the belief that if she made this choice, she has no right to be sad, angry, hurt, or disappointed about the pregnancy termination. Research demonstrates that even when women believe they made the right decision, for many, there is still a period of mourning what was lost (Williams, 2000). However, most societies provide little space for her right to grieve and almost no space for the grief response of a partner.

Complicated grief (prolonged grief disorder)   This concept is used to differentiate between normal grieving that usually requires limited or no clinical intervention and diagnosis and an acute grief response. Complicated grief is characterized as grief expression accompanied by symptoms that do not improve, but it is intense, chronic, unrelenting, and debilitating in its severity and impairs functioning in important domains (Shear, Reynolds, Simon, & Zisook, 2016). Complicated grief is said to affect 2–3% of the worldwide population, with a prevalence rate of 10–20% after the death of partner with an even higher potential after the death of a child (Shear, 2015). Therapists may encounter a couple who present for therapy as having communication and intimacy problems and, after a proper assessment, learn that they lost their daughter 4 years ago. While one member of the couple may have integrated the loss and developed healthy and helpful coping, the other may be frozen in the numbness of the grief. This partner has not been able to actively parent the remaining children, nor be an active partner. They may have been referred to therapy because they sought help for sleep problems from their medical provider. They may describe themselves as depressed, quick to sadness and anger, believing that the death of their child is no longer a factor because of the years that have passed. However, it is clear that this spouse has not processed the death of his/her child nor developed a way to reinvest back into his/her life.

Anticipatory grief   Anticipatory grief refers to grief responses that occur prior to a death, typically occur when an impending loss is known and the bereaved grieve the non-death losses that occur prior to the death (Overton & Cottone, 2016). This encompasses the mourning, coping, and planning as one comes to an understanding of one's own impending mortality and that of loved ones who grieve before the death has occurred. This is often accompanied by the accumulation of losses that occur prior to dying, such as loss of identity, functioning, and future expectations. The amassing of losses over time may become too overwhelming to manage, along with the knowledge that the only way the crescendo ends is with the death. Symptoms of anticipatory grief may be disguised as depression, anxiety, or stress. Therapists may encounter a client who is unable to participate in end-of-life decision making with their partner who is in the process of dying. They may present to others as competent and put together but be unable to talk with their loved one about their impending death. This may be a client who believes they have to appear strong for their children but is grieving in isolation as they await this life-changing event.

Suffocated grief   Suffocated grief occurs when a person is denied opportunities to express grief in a functional way and they as a result "suffocate" or silence their grief (Bordere, 2017). It also includes "penalties assessed for grief and mourning expressions that are devalued and misinterpreted or misdiagnosed" (Bordere, 2017, p. 37).

This often occurs when the expression of grief is seen as dysfunctional, inappropriate, pathological, and rejected. Suffocated grief is often a response to a lack of acknowledgment and support at the societal level. It becomes a coping strategy in the face of marginalization. The bereaved may use various strategies to quiet, muffle, and deny the normal and natural grief responses. Women and men who are survivors of sexual violence often experience suffocated grief where societal values sanction violence and create a context of shame and blame for survivors that impact the ability to disclose and seek appropriate support (Bordere, 2017). Another example is the sociocultural impact of racism in the lives of Black men. Due to racism, Black men are often viewed as hostile, angry, or aggressive when they express pain as opposed to being seen as vulnerable, traumatized, and grieving. Often their race-based expressions of mourning, such as methods of dress, tattoos of remembrance, poetry in the form of rap music, and or graffiti artwork are shamed, silenced, and judged.

Chronic sorrow   Chronic sorrow refers to episodic and pervasive grief due to losses that are living, ongoing, usually disenfranchised, and often ambiguous. This type of grief is unable to be resolved and is often difficult to integrate (Kelly & Kropf, 1995) such as with severe chronic or life-threatening diseases, developmental disabilities, physical disabilities, and severe mental health diagnoses. Chronic sorrow is a way of understanding the continuous and persistent grief related to an ongoing loss (Kelly & Kropf, 1995). Many therapists confuse this response with dysthymia or depression. Chronic sorrow is a grief response to loss that does not end.

One way to understand chronic sorrow is to think about a couple where one member has suffered a TBI. While the couple system may have adapted to the injury, each member of the couple may experience the waves of chronic sorrow. There may be a low level consistent feeling of sadness at what was lost and how the present and the future will forever be different. The person who experienced the injury may be aware that they are unable to function the way they used to and experience sadness about the way the system has to accommodate the change. The partner may also experience chronic sorrow as they grieve what once was and the expectations they had for their partner and themselves. People experiencing chronic sorrow have the ability to feel happy or content, making others confused when the sorrow shows itself again. Therapists must help the couple recognize that it might never truly go away because the loss is ever present and the TBI will not be healed. This is an ongoing wound, but there are ways of addressing the sorrow so that it is not the only experience present in their lives.

Social Myths About Bereavement

There are several myths that impact expectations and the process of bereavement. Many family therapists are unaware of the ways that they themselves, as well as the clients, have been impacted by these false narratives. The impact that these myths have is that these ideas leave the bereaved vulnerable to judgment or social sanctions and they may not receive the support and care from loved ones because they are unaware of the realistic expectations of bereavement. It is our job as family therapists to debunk these myths and provide helpful and accurate information.

According to Corr et al. (2018), the myths are grouped around the following ideas:

1 Minimization of the loss, suggesting that the loss was not as impactful or the person was not as unique or special. A powerful example is the comments parents may receive after the death of an infant—invalidating comments such as "you're healthy, and you can have other children." Another example is a comment that because an elder lived a long life, the death should be easier to bear.

2 Praise for stoicism and restraint of emotion in public, which tells the griever that their emotions are too difficult for others to handle. It may encourage shame and guilt when the individual is unable to suppress his/her emotions any longer.

3 Encouragement to move on and refrain from burdening others with grief. Typical comments from family and friends include "why are you still feeling this way, it's been 6 months since…." In addition to being a criticism, this type of response also communicates that it would be wrong to share their grief with that person.

Therapists mistakenly assume that distress is an inevitable sign that clients are grieving, often overlooking other powerful signs of grief (Stroebe, Van Den Bout, & Schut, 1994). This often coincides with the belief that clients must emotionally work through grief in order to resolve their feelings. The development of the dual process model (Stroebe & Schut, 2015) of grief provides therapists with a helpful framework for assisting clients with processing the emotional aspects as well as addressing the necessary tasks of moving forward (Rubin, Malkinson, & Witztum, 2012; Stroebe & Schut, 1999; Worden, 2008).

Overview of Bereavement Treatment Models

Despite the presence of individual-oriented approaches, there is a paucity of bereavement treatment models and research that address relational aspects in grief and bereavement. Field, Gao, and Paderna (2005) brought up a conceptualization of grief and bereavement from an attachment theory perspective that involves more of a relational perspective as it refers to the bonds between the deceased and the surviving person. This approach combines the intrapsychic approach and the relational aspects of a continued bond between the deceased and the person still living, looking at grief processes in the context of an ongoing, changed relationship that preserves qualities of intense affect. Several models of grieving are task oriented and focus more on the *how to* of the process (Rando, 1983; Rubin, 1981; Walsh & McGoldrick, 2004; Worden, 1991). Walsh and McGoldrick's (2004) task-oriented model of family bereavement is an adaptation of Worden's tasks through family systems lenses and it will be discussed below.

Meaning reconstruction model

Neimeyer, Burke, McKay, and van Dyke Stringer (2010) developed the meaning reconstruction model that is a constructivist perspective on grief. Founded on the idea that at the core of human existence is the way we make meaning of core assumptions about life, this model proposes that losses challenge these core life assumptions and that these will have to change in order for the loss to be integrated in the natural flow of life. The authors consider that "an individual's identity is essentially a narrative achievement, as our sense of self is established through the stories that we construct about ourselves and share with others" (Neimeyer et al., 2010, p. 75). When our sense of self is challenged by a loss that brings about questions of meaning of life and death, safety and benevolence of this world, and a sense of loss of control over life situations (Janoff-Bulman, 1992), we need to be able to make meaning differently in order to functionally adjust to the new context with which we are left. Neimeyer (2006) proposes that after a loss we can either *assimilate* or *accommodate* our assumptions through a process and meaning reconstruction. For example, a bereaved person may determine to *assimilate* their shattered assumptions about the safety of this world after a violent death of a loved one by incorporating them into previously held religious beliefs about the continuation of life after death. On the other hand, they may choose to *accommodate* to the loss by deepening and restructuring their beliefs and narratives on the purpose of life. From Neimeyer's (2006) perspective, people who can successfully reprocess their meaning-making are more likely to have a normative grief, while those that fail to either assimilate or accommodate new meanings will be more prone to experience complicated grief.

Examples of constructivist strategies in addressing grief from this perspective include narrative retelling, therapeutic writing, or evocative visualization (Neimeyer, 2006; Neimeyer et al., 2010). According to Neimeyer et al. (2010), "such retelling—specifically focusing on the hardest parts of the experience and 'staying with' them until the associated images and meanings can be held with less anguish—plays a pivotal part in demonstrably efficacious treatments for complicated grief" (p. 80).

Dual processing model

In their dual processing model (DPM), Stroebe and Schut's (1999) conceptualize grief and bereavement as being essentially coping mechanisms and consider loss-orientation and restoration-orientation processes as stressors that bereaved people will have to address by oscillating through confronting or avoiding them. Under the influence of loss-oriented factors, people take care of emotions, memories, and rituals that are related to it, while responding to restoration factors, they continue to live their lives without the deceased.

In a functional grieving process, mourners oscillate between confronting and avoiding these stressors. This process of oscillation is the central point of the DPM (Stroebe & Schut, 1999), and it makes this model distinctive from other grief models that focus more on confronting the loss than on the back and forth between confrontation and avoidance. According to the authors, bereaved people oscillate daily thorough reprocessing of sadness, intrusive memories with the deceased or related to the actual death and avoiding through a *restoration* process when the couple attends to life changes, new roles, and being involved in new activities.

Attachment-based approaches

Field et al. (2005) suggest an attachment-based perspective on the continuing bond (CB) with the deceased as central to the grieving process. Building on concepts from Bowlby (1980), the authors argue that what distinguishes between an adaptive and a maladaptive bereavement is the type of CB developed by the person involved in the process. An adaptive process resembles a secure bond and is moderated by attachment styles as well as culture and religion. For example, according to Field and Sundin (2001), for bereaved parents, a very important predictor between normative and complicated grief is the quality and strength of the attachment bond before the loss as well as the attachment styles of the couple, where more insecurely attached individuals will likely develop a more problematic CB with the deceased in the aftermath of the loss. For partners that had a secure bond inside their couple relationship as well as a secure bond with their child before the event, the likelihood of an adaptive bereavement and a secure CB after death is higher than in couple with low marital satisfaction and maybe a more insecure bond with the child.

The 6 Rs of grieving

Several models of grieving are task oriented and focus more on the *how to* of the process (Rando, 1983; Rubin, 1981; Walsh & McGoldrick, 2004; Worden, 1991). Rando (1983, Rando, 1986) developed the 6 Rs of grieving. She proposes that uncomplicated grief goes through six activities: recognize the loss, react, remember and re-experience, relinquish attachment and assumptions, readjust, and reinvest in the new world. These stages are chronological and need to be accomplished for the bereaved to be successful in transitioning to a new life. From a more relational perspective, Rubin (1981) suggests that grief follows a two-track model. Track 1 is a personal functioning one that refers to how an individual adjusts emotionally, cognitively, and behaviorally to the loss, how they are, or they are not able to continue fulfilling life tasks, to maintain their self-worth, to contribute well to their family life. Track 2 is the relationship track and refers to the relationship to the deceased and all the memories and behaviors associated with it. Furthermore, Rubin et al. (2009) developed a tool for measuring where the individual is in these two tracks that can be used as a marker for therapeutic planning in grief therapy.

Tasks of mourning: Individual

Worden's (1991, 2018) four tasks of mourning are as follows: "to accept the reality of the loss, to process the pain of grief, to adjust to a world without the deceased, and to find a way remember the deceased while continuing one's life journey" (Worden, 2018, p. 41). Worden (2018) conceptualizes grief as a cognitive process that requires confronting the loss and a meaning-making process that is used to adjust to the new context and continue with life. He highlights that while these tasks are not necessarily chronological in nature, there must be a certain order of processing. For example, one cannot process a pain that is not acknowledged first, and without the processing of pain, it would be difficult to adjust to a world where the loved one is missing. Worden (2008) also addresses multiple mediators that contribute to different facets of grief work. The relationship with the deceased, his/her role in the family, developmental and historical aspects of the person and the relationship, how the person died, personality variables in the mourner, and concurrent losses and stressors, all contribute to a successful and normative grief process. For example, in the case of a couple who lost a child, the age of the child, if they died a sudden or more expected death due to illness, if the loss happened after one of the parents suffered another significant loss, will all contribute to the success of the tasks of mourning and if they are accomplished or failed.

Family adaptational tasks

Adapting Worden's tasks of mourning to the family system, Walsh and McGoldrick (2004) offer the following tasks for the bereaved family: "shared acknowledgement of the reality of death, shared experience of the loss, reorganization of the family system, and reinvestment in other relationships and life pursuits" (Walsh & McGoldrick, 2004, p. 9). Their tasks are focused on "shared" experiences and processing of grief, as well as restructuring of family roles and attributes in the aftermath of loss, taking into consideration the family life cycle and communication styles in the family. For example, in a family with two young children when one of the partners dies, the remaining partner will be at least temporarily exclusively in charge with the parenting role, including providing financially, and emotionally, they will have to manage their own emotions as well as those of the children and according to the developmental stage to have an active role in modulating the children's behaviors and emotions. Other important aspects in Walsh and McGoldrick's (2004) conceptualization of loss are related to the transgenerational patterns and the legacies of loss. The way that a family adjusts and works through grief is many times influenced by a transgenerational transmission of rules and behaviors, unnamed loyalties, and family scripts. Among these scripts, gender roles play a very important role. Gender roles are impacted by both societal expectation and family rules. In the example given above, there are different tasks to be accomplished predicated by the gender of the parent who died based on both previous roles in the family and expectations from family of origin and/or society.

Couple Dynamics After Loss

The literature that addresses specifically the impact of grief on the couple relationship is scarce, and few authors and researchers looked at the couple dynamics from a dyadic perspective rather than individual aspects within the couple relationship (Essakow & Miller, 2013; Gilbert, 1989, 1997; Parker & Dunn, 2011, Schwab, 1990, 1992). Based on the assumption that grief and bereavement is mainly a cognitive process of creating a different meaning about the loss (Neimeyer, 2006; Worden, 2008), the majority of the studies look at cognitive processing and communication styles in the couple at the roots of successful grieving and couple satisfaction (Essakow & Miller, 2013; Gilbert, 1989, 1997; Hooghe, Neimeyer, & Rober, 2011; Oliver, 1999). Only a few conceptualize the impact of grief on couple dynamics and explore the impact of emotional transactions as relevant to couple satisfaction (e.g., Hooghe, Neimeyer, & Rober, 2012; Ungureanu & Sandberg, 2010). Other authors looked specifically at dynamics in sexual relationship and sexual satisfaction especially after the loss of a child (Hagemeister & Rosenblat, 1997; Schwab, 1992).

Being out of sync

Gilbert (1989, 1997) describes the incongruency in grieving, or how "being out of sync" can create problems in the couple relationship. In her studies, the "incongruent grieving" seems to be related to perceptions about what appropriate grieving looks like, what are the behaviors related to it, competition in grieving, and speed in resolution of mourning. She summarizes that "the picture of these negative interactions is one in which marital partners are unable to agree on the image of what they have lost, how they should respond, and what should be expected of each other. Partners are overburdened by the pressures placed on them. Because they are unable to agree on the appropriate means of responding to the death, the personal needs of one or both partners remain unmet" (Gilbert, 1989, p. 616).

She concludes that these processes impact the overall couple satisfaction. Kariv and Heiman (2005) bring a similar perspective. During bereavement, there are several potentially difficult issues that may impact couples' ability to grieve together. One of the more challenging phenomena is a process called incongruent grief, or when members of the couple experience of each other's grief as different from their own or and they are "out of sync."

Communication

Being out of sync can occur for several reasons. One of them is a breakdown in communication in the couple relationship. Avoidance of discussion of the death or misunderstanding is often associated with marital distress. Kariv and Heiman (2005) identify several such styles of communication. A task-oriented style is problem focused. It involves taking action to change the situation and reduce the amount of stress it evokes. Individuals attempt to manage their grief, problem-solve, and intellectualize. An emotion-oriented style is characterized by efforts directed at altering emotional responses to stressors. It also includes attempts to reframe the problem in such a way that it no longer evokes a negative emotional response and elicits less stress. Some individuals tend to reach out to others for social support and seek to process emotion. Couples with an avoidant-oriented style tend to avoid the situation, or denying its existence. It also includes the use of indirect efforts to adjust to stressors by distancing oneself, evading the problem, or distraction. All these styles can be affected in processing grief, even in couples with a previously successful communication.

Sexual mismatch

Sexual mismatch is another aspect that contributes to out-of-sync grieving (Gilbert, 1989, 1997) manifested in low intimacy or divergent needs, as well as different needs for sexual activity that are thought to contribute to a low sense of intimacy between partners. In a couple, one partner may have a need for more sexual closeness and the other may see the heightened desire as a sign of not grieving enough, thus contributing to distance in the relationship. Lower levels of intimacy and support from one's partner are associated with greater incidence, intensity, and duration of grief symptoms for both men and women.

Other issues

Differences in decisions related to daily life and the family have an impact on grieving in the couple. One salient example of this is when one partner wants to keep things the same as before the loss and the other seeks change. Another example can be the manner in which each member of the couple copes with stress, how likely are they to reach out for support or seek solitude in a way that meets both of their needs. Partners that cope with stress differently, one of them preferring to withdraw and the other needing more engagement than usual, are more likely to experience distress in their relationship, as neither of them will find comfort in the other at a time when they need it the most.

Belief in continuing focus on deceased

According to Gilbert (1997), another aspect of being out of sync is in the belief in continuing relationships (memories, keepsakes, what the other would have wanted, dreams, signals/signs from beyond) and how couples make sense of continuing relationships with the deceased. In some cultures, CB are expected, pervasive, and important. For example, in traditional Japanese ancestor rituals, contact on a daily basis is normal. There are words that clarify between "this world" and "that world" and the belief that the dead can move freely between the two.

Being-in-sync effects

However, Gilbert (1997) explains that being "in sync" in grieving comes with its own challenges. According to Gilbert, when grieving is synchronous, both partners can be overwhelmed by grief at the same time, and they cannot reach toward each other to give or receive comfort. This dynamic can also create distance in the relationship if partners are not able to support each other in their grieving. Some of the proposed positive couple coping strategies are intellectual intimacy (information exchange), expressing emotions, listening to each other, positive reframing of loss, sharing the loss through the ability to develop a shared view of it, flexibility in relationship, and awareness sensitivity to each other's needs (Gilbert, 1989, 1997), and these cannot be easily accessed if both partners are simultaneously grieving.

Communication in grief

Following Neimeyer's narrative approach of meaning reconstruction, Hooghe, Neimeyer, and Rober (2011) propose an analysis of communication styles and subsequently meaning-making in the grieving process. They approach grief communication as being a 3 "D" process: dialectical, dialogic, and dynamic (Hooghe et al., 2011). The authors are more nuanced and explain that "rather than approaching grief communication as a necessary condition for all grieving couples at all times, we propose to consider the contextual factors, ambivalences, and relational tensions at a specific moment in the grieving process of the individuals and relationships involved" (p. 917). They argue that contextual and cultural factors may play a role in sharing or not sharing grief content among family members, that communication is not only verbal, and that meaningful interactions can still happen without words.

Behavioral interactions that facilitate couple grieving

In their phenomenological study (Essakow & Miller, 2013), mutual understanding of different grieving styles was an aspect reported by resilient couples, who adaptively cope with grief. Making space for emotional expression for each partner as well as the need to distance one's self from time to time was considered very important. Three behavioral interactions were deemed very important by parents who lost children. First, the couples needed to be able to *look away* from the other and have the space to distance from each other and turn more inward in their mourning, while having the acceptance and patience of the other. Second, there were times when they both needed to distance themselves from the pain and focus more on the future of their relationship together. They needed to be able to *look at each other* and have a sense of togetherness. The third factor found by the researchers to contribute to successful grieving was an ability to reintegrate and reorganize the relationship. "Moving forward was seen as an important need in healing. Moving *forward with one another* was a major source of comfort and protection" (p. 306).

Emotional aspects of grieving

In one of the few articles that focus on emotional processing in couples that lost a child, Ungureanu and Sandberg (2010) propose that losing a child can be conceptualized as an attachment injury in certain couples (Johnson, 2002, 2004). When one partner realizes that he/she cannot rely on the other as a source of comfort for a highly stressful situation and that the other person is not accessible or responsive, it can affect the overall health of the relationship. The authors argue that "there is often a tearing apart and turning away among couples facing this devastating loss. A chasm may quickly begin to develop between partners as the shock wears off and the mourning begins. Often the pain and sorrow prevent both partners from reaching out to give or receive the closeness, support, and understanding each needs in this time of grief" (Ungureanu & Sandberg, 2010, p. 315).

An emotionally focused approach and attachment emphasis in understanding couple dynamics may be very beneficial given the need to express deep emotion (sorrow, grief, pain, guilt/shame) that seems almost overpowering while at the same time fostering a present, accepting, and nurturing response in one's partner.

In their qualitative in-depth study of a couple grieving with unexpected loss of a child, Hooghe et al. (2012) indirectly address the issue of emotional processing. Their findings support Stroebe and Schut's (1999) DPM and assert that an oscillation between closeness and distancing is healthy and contributes to couple satisfaction. What is not necessarily emphasized in this article is the core of what the couple is describing when they used the image of "cycling around an emotional core of sadness" (Hooghe, Neimeyer, & Rober, 2012). In other words, the authors looked at the aspect of "cycling around" but not necessarily at the "emotional core of sadness" that the couple was highlighting. More research needs to focus on the "core" of the grief experience that is emotional in nature rather than cognitive and behavioral processing.

Clinical Implications for Couples' Interventions

To support bereaved couples, therapists must be prepared to intervene in ways that facilitate understanding and healing. Basic skills such as validation and reassurance that grief is a normal reaction to loss. Couples need therapists who can provide psychoeducation that debunks grief myths and that provides basic grief-related information. Therapists must create a safe space for couples to express the vulnerability of grief and the fears that are common experiences. Goals for therapy include helping the couple process and understand what has happened and make meaning of the loss, facilitate the couple's ability to access and express thoughts and emotions in a healthy way, assist couples to develop ways to honor and remember the person who died, and support the couple in reinvesting in life and the future. Moreover, based on the literature reviewed, there are several aspects that need to be included in the treatment of a grieved couple.

Exploring emotional aspects related to grief

Processing emotions during couple sessions and being able to witness the intensity of sadness, anger, or other emotions can be very powerful in recreating a sense of togetherness for couples (Johnson, 2002). Addressing emotions always starts with creating a sense of safety in the couple that is necessary to address intense emotions such as sadness or anger. Safety is created in the therapeutic relationship through validation, empathic conjecture, and evocative responses that serve as modeling for the couple (Johnson, 2004). It can also contribute to create a sense of shared meaning about loss (Walsh & McGoldrick, 2004). While concentrating on communication and meaning-making, several of the authors reviewed and mentioned emotional processing (Essakow & Miller, 2013; Gilbert, 1989, 1992; Hooghe et al., 2012; Kariy & Heiman, 2005). We propose that emotionally focused couple therapy (EFCT) (Johnson, 2002) may be a well-suited approach to address emotional aspects related to grief works in couples. EFCT is an approach to couples' therapy based on adult attachment theories that helps couples gain a deeper understanding into their emotional processes, restructure key emotional responses, and foster the development of a safe and secure bond (Johnson, 2008).

Shared meaning-making

As evidenced by authors and researchers such as Neimeyer (2006), Neimeyer et al. (2010), and Gilbert (2002), reconstruction of meaning is a very important task in mourning. We agree with Walsh and McGoldrick (2004) that making meaning together in a shared process is a powerful way to approach grief work with a systemic lens and that this is particularly important for couples. It will contribute to a sense of togetherness and sharing of the burden for the couple, which has the potential to maintain and increase relational satisfaction. Couples' therapists can help partners create a shared meaning by helping them create shared rituals for grieving, participating together in events that celebrate their child's life, being involved in advocacy around different death circumstances such as suicide prevention or cancer research funding, and working together on restructuring roles within the family structure (Walsh & McGoldrick, 2004).

Oscillation between confronting and avoiding
grief processes (Stroebe & Schut)

We propose that couple therapists working with bereaved couples should be well aware of the dance of getting close and distancing from individual grief processes as well as an isomorph dance that happens relationally between partners. Couple therapists should be aware and flexible enough to create the space for this "within-between" dance of confronting and withdrawing that is necessary for healthy mourning.

Self-of-the-Therapist (S-o-T) Aspects in Working with Grief

Grief is a normal response to loss and all clients are faced with issues of loss during the course of their lifetime. Yet many family therapists struggle to address issues of loss in their personal and professional lives. Despite the critical need for quality bereavement support for families, many family therapists feel unequipped to work effectively with this population. It is imperative that family therapists are able to facilitate positive bereavement outcomes in the lives of families coping with grief. One of the best ways for therapists to develop sensitivity to bereavement is to engage in a process of deep self-of-the-therapist (S-o-T) exploration. This is a focused and specific exploration of attitudes, beliefs, values, and behaviors connected to loss.

Tending to S-o-T work allows the therapist to hone the most important tool they bring into the therapy room: themselves. Just like clients, most therapists fail to engage in this type of self-examination due to the desire to avoid thinking about grief and loss until forced to face the reality of death. Many therapists see little value in exploring a topic that has too often been described as "morbid." Reframing the process as giving necessary attention to a normal and natural part of the life cycle invites therapists to access aspects of their full authentic self.

Baldwin (2013) suggests four key principles of self-examination that therapists should utilize and when applied to grief and loss provide a helpful guide. The first principle is therapeutic transparency, allowing clients to view the therapist's humanity, removing the cloak of expert along with the false images of the professional. Secondly, the principle of authenticity is important and is defined as being fully present in relationship to one's self. The third principle, self-awareness, is the practice of consistent reflexivity including ongoing examination of one's beliefs, biases, and assumptions. Lastly, the principle of congruence refers to the close relationship between beliefs, feelings, communication, and behavior (Satir, 1988).

Before working with the bereaved, it is important for therapists to consider their own beliefs about dying, death, and bereavement. What happens when you think about your own death? What decisions and preparations have you made in regard to your own death? What are the covert and overt rules for care of the dying? What do you believe happens after death? Where do your beliefs come from? What does it mean to express them? What are your secret ideas about the right and wrong way to grieve? Where did these ideas come from? How do your dimensions of culture inform your beliefs about loss? Which values about dying, death, and bereavement have been informed from family of origin? How have your beliefs remained the same or changed? Where do you have the freedom to express grief and loss and when, where, and in what ways do you feel constrained?

We encourage therapists to take time to journal their thoughts and feelings as well as discuss them in supervision and in their own therapy. This is an opportune place to explore previously unacknowledged biases and the ways these beliefs have informed the therapy process. In addition to discovering the answers to these questions, therapists may find that they have new questions about themselves. Therapists should be curious about the relationship they have with their attitudes and beliefs and how much they inform their actual behavior. Therapists should then consider how the answers to the questions above directly impact their clinical work.

Dimensions of Culture and Its Impact on Bereavement

While it may be valuable to review the rituals and traditions of cultural groups across the globe, an extensive review is beyond the scope of this chapter. However, previous authors have summarized typical bereavement rituals for several cultural groups (Rubin et al., 2012; Walsh & McGoldrick, 2004). We find that it can be more helpful to explore the process of working with the bereaved in a socially just and culturally conscious manner, meaning the therapist is aware of dynamics of power and privilege as they work with clients taking into account the impact of various dimensions of culture in their lives (Molaison, Bordere, & Fowler, 2011). While grief and bereavement are known as universal experiences, they are informed by the dynamics of the culture in which we live (Rubin et al., 2012). Exploration of various traditions can be sought out during the therapy and assessment process. How one makes sense of loss is predicated on various dimensions of culture such as religion/spirituality, gender, sexual orientation, race/ethnicity class, and so forth. Therapists should explore dynamics of privilege and oppression related to dimensions of culture and how these impact the couples' grief. What follows are some considerations for therapists when working with grieving couples.

Religion and spirituality

When a loved one dies, it usually raises questions within the dimension of religion and spirituality. Religion includes beliefs, principles, rules, attendance, affiliation, intrinsic/extrinsic motivation, organized rituals, and patterns of behavior (Wortmann & Park, 2008). Spirituality is about understanding meaning, worldview, guidelines for living, purpose, and the elements that drive human understanding and relatedness (Helmeke & Bischoff, 2002). Spirituality is a universal experience that is not predicated on religious affiliation, although the two may go hand in hand. Spirituality is linked to how we make sense of who we are and our meaning in the world, including moral standards, ethics, and philosophy (Aponte, 2002). It is critical to explore spirituality and meaning-making with all clients regardless of religious affiliation.

Bereavement generally raises questions that people seek to answer through a spiritual lens. When a loved one dies, it is normal for there to be spiritual questions and answers sought. When a couple comes to therapy after experiencing a loss, a culturally competent therapist will ask about the death story, as well as ask the clients what they believe happens after death. The answers to these types of questions often have a spiritual connection. If this is an area that is causing a distress, the therapist can assess in what ways there may be a problem and begin to develop a plan to intervene.

There are many couples who practice different faith traditions. While this may not have been a problem in their relationship, it can pose a stressor at the time of a death. Whose traditions will take priority? How will they decide how to navigate their beliefs? What rituals feel necessary and is there room for compromise without compromising beliefs? Does the couple have specific religious beliefs that guide the grieving process? What are these tenets, and how will the couple choose when, where, and how to follow them? Are these religious tenets congruent with their spiritual beliefs and personal relationship to meaning-making? Is the couple able to discuss the rituals and practices they would like to engage in? Helmeke and Bischoff (2002) suggest therapists assess for how spirituality is impacting the current problem and explore the ways in which it may pose a solution to current dilemmas as well as the ways in which it may create barriers.

Gender

Gender norms and expectations are often covertly dictating appropriate grief expression with women being expected to be intuitive grievers (tears, sorrow, guilt, etc.) and men being often socialized to be instrumental (stoic, avoid emotional expression, isolate when grieving). Martin and Doka (2011) suggest shifting away from relying on gendered constructions of grief to a spectrum that suggests individuals fall on a continuum between intuitive (emotional responses and sharing of grief with others) and instrumental (cognitive understanding of the experience and focus on behaviors and activity). A culturally conscientious therapist will challenge a prescribed gendered idea of grieving and invite the clients to identify with a dominant style while normalizing the range. This allows the therapists to assist the client with exploring the ways that their socialization has affected their ability to access parts of themselves and both their cognitive and emotional responses to loss. This is particularly important for couples who may judge their partners' style of grieving and need reassurance that there is a way to support each other.

Sexual orientation

Lesbian and gay partners often still face discrimination that negatively impacts the grieving process. They too are impacted by societal gendered expectations as well as dealing with external hostility, violence, and lack of support and safe places to grieve. Partners and children may be excluded from rituals of mourning and isolated from social support. Therapists must critically examine their own ideas and biases of heteronormativity. Using appropriate and inclusive terminology, recognizing the fluidity of sexual identity, and challenging internalized homophobia are examples of how therapists can better support LGBTQ couples (Ashton, 2016; Goldman & Livoti, 2011).

LGBTQ couples often have to deliberately cultivate communities of support (Nealy, 2008). It is critical that therapists inquire about the support systems and ways they function that are helpful and in what ways they might stifle. Therapists should ask about how publicly they have shared their relationship and how decisions have been made. It is not uncommon for couples to be "out" to many friends and yet not have come out to extended family. In this case the therapy is an opportunity for the client to decide what would be best during the grief process. Is it possible that their early decision not to include others in this aspect of their life still makes sense? If so, then how might they choose to be mindful of physical and emotional safety, recognizing that each individual knows best?

Ethnicity and race

Ethnicity refers to a shared group identity based on common dynamics that may include shared history, language, customs, beliefs, traditions, and practices. Ethnic traditions and rituals are a fundamental part of meaning-making. They help create opportunities for external expressions of mourning. How race and ethnicity are experienced varies based on context; however people of color experience oppression due to racism, colorism, and colonization. Hardy and Laszloffy (1999) state that racially sensitive therapists are aware of the reality of race and anticipate the impact of privilege and oppression on the lives of clients. Family therapists should ask about racial and ethnic traditions that are important to the clients as well as those that may be expected of them by others. Couples may not share the same race or ethnicity, and if they do, their experience of this aspect of their culture may be different. Having an overt conversation about how race and ethnicity impact their grieving opens space for them to explore how they navigate this in their lives.

Socioeconomic status

Socioeconomic status refers to the ways in which the clients make sense of their lives in regard to values, beliefs, and behaviors regarding class, income, education, employment status, and the like. Class status dictates the bereaved's ability to access the desired resources to mourn. For some individuals, death and the rituals that accompany it are the last ways of demonstrating their love for the deceased, and there is an expectation that loved ones will contribute as much money as possible to display love. For others, there is an expectation of modesty and moderation because the deceased cannot appreciate the experience. While there is no wrong way to mourn, not being able to participate in the rituals due to financial circumstances can lead to immense guilt, shame, and humiliation. For couples living in poverty, it is quite possible that class also impacted the death, not just the experience of grief. Does the couple have the ability to bury their child where and how they would like? In what ways does the death of a partner change the current financial status of the remaining partner?

Culturally conscientious practice

According to Rubin et al. (2012), in order to plan culturally appropriate assessment and intervention, therapists must (a) recognize the specific cultural rituals relevant to the culture, (b) explore the beliefs about what happens after death, and (c) evaluate what the culture sanctions as appropriate and non-appropriate emotional expression of the loss in the specific culture.

The following are questions therapists can ask to begin to develop a culturally conscientious practice: What are the cultural rituals for coping with people who are

dying? How is the deceased person's body tended to? How are the final arrangements for the body handled? Are certain types of death less acceptable than others?
Are certain types of death especially hard to make sense of? What are the processes
for honoring the death? What are the couple's beliefs about what happens after
death? What do each member of the couple believe are normal expressions of grief
and how was this learned? What does the couple consider to be the roles of each
member in handling the death? How does one demonstrate the acceptance of the
loss? What does healing look like?

Freud wrote to his friend that lost a daughter: "The loss of a child is a trial from
which the adult never recovers because he finds that part of himself which he projected in his descendent is amputated. The death of a child seems against the nature;
when mourning the loss of an offspring the parent realizes that the natural order of
the generations has been reversed. This mourning involves a pain that escapes both
words and thoughts. Even the language does not have a name for those who lost a
child. It has terms for those who lost the adults they loved (orphan, widow, widower),
but there is no word to name the parents that have lost their child or the child that
has lost a sibling" (Freud as quoted by Ricoeur & Gentet, 1996, p. 260). The death
of a child takes a toll on the parents and on their relationship. Fortunately, as we
argued in this chapter, there are modalities in understanding this type of grief and
working with parents that can help salvage and improve relationships by supporting
them through healthier grieving, despite the pain of all that could have been and will
never happen.

References

Aponte, H. (2002). Spirituality: The Heart of Therapy. *Journal of Family Psychotherapy*,
   13(1/2), 13–27.

Ashton, D. (2016). Lessons learned in queer affirming supervision. In K. V. Hardy & T. Bobes
   (Eds.), *Culturally sensitive supervision and training: Diverse perspectives and practical
   applications* (pp. 50–57). New York, NY: Routledge.

Baldwin, M. (2013). *The use of self in therapy*. New York, NY: Routledge.

Bordere, T. (2017). Disenfranchisement and ambiguity in the face of loss: The suffocated grief
   of sexual assault survivors. *Family Relations, 66*(1), 29–45.

Boss, P. (2007). Ambiguous loss theory: Challenges for scholars and practitioners. *Family
   Relations, 56*(2), 105–111.

Boss, P. (2009). *Ambiguous loss: Learning to live with unresolved grief*. Cambridge, UK: Harvard
   University Press.

Boss, P., & Yeats, J. R. (2014). Ambiguous loss: A complicated type of grief when loved ones
   disappear. *Bereavement Care, 33*(2), 63–69.

Bowlby, J. (1980). *Attachment and loss* (Vol. *III*). New York, NY: Basic Books, Inc.

Corr, C. A., Corr, D. M., & Doka, K. J. (2018). *Death & dying, life & living*. Belmont, CA:
   Cengage Learning.

Dictionary, O. E. (2018). *bereaved n. 1. OED Online*. Oxford, UK: Oxford University Press.

Doka, K. J. (1999). Disenfranchised grief. *Bereavement Care, 18*(3), 37–39.

Doka, K. J. (2002). How we die: Stigmatized death and disenfranchised grief. In K. J. Doka
   (Ed.), *Disenfranchised grief: New directions, challenges, and strategies for practice* (pp. 323–
   336). Champaign, IL: Research Press.

Essakow, K. L., & Miller, M. M. (2013). Piecing together the shattered heirloom: Parents' experiences of relationship resilience after the violent death of a child. *The American Journal of Family Therapy, 41,* 299–310.

Field, N. P., Gao, B., & Paderna, L. (2005). Continuing bonds in bereavement: An attachment theory based perspective. *Death Studies, 29*(4), 277–299.

Field, N. P., & Sundin, E. C. (2001). Attachment style in adjustment to conjugal bereavement. *Journal of Social and Personal Relationships, 18*(3), 347–361.

Gaffey, C. (2017, May). Bring back our girls: A brief history of what we know about the missing Chibok women. *Newsweek.* https://www.newsweek.com/chibok-girls-boko-haram-583584

Gelcer, E. (1983). Mourning is a family affair. *Family Process, 22*(4), 501–516.

Gilbert, K. R. (1989). Interactive grief and coping in the marital dyad. *Death Studies, 13,* 625–646.

Gilbert, K. R. (1992). Religion as a resource for bereaved parents. *Journal of Religion and Health, 31,* 19–30.

Gilbert, K. R. (1997). Couple coping with the death of a child. In C. R. Figley (Ed.), *Death and trauma: The traumatology of grieving* (pp. 101–121). New York, NY: Routledge.

Gilbert, K. R (2002). Taking a narrative approach to grief therapy: Finding meaning in stories. *Death Studies, 26*(3), 223–239.

Goldman, L., & Livoti, V. (2011). Grief in GLBT populations: Focus on gay and lesbian youth. In R. A. Neimeyer, D. L. Harris, H. R. Winokuer, & G. F. Thornton (Eds.), *Grief and bereavement in contemporary society: Bridging research and practice* (pp. 249–259). New York, NY: Routledge.

Hagemeister, A. K., & Rosenblat, P. C. (1997). Grief and the sexual relationship of couples who have experienced a child's death. *Death Studies, 21,* 231–252.

Hardy, K., & Laszloffy, T. (1999). The dynamics of a pro-racist ideology: Implications for family therapy. In M. McGoldrick & K. V. Hardy (Eds.), *Re-visioning family therapy: Race, culture, and gender in clinical practice* (pp. 118–168). New York, NY: The Guilford Press.

Helmeke, K. B., & Bischoff, G. H. (2002). Recognizing and raising spiritual and religious issues in therapy: Guidelines for the timid. *Journal of Family Psychotherapy, 13*(1-2), 195–214.

Hooghe, A., Neimeyer, R. A., & Rober, P. (2011). The complexity of couple communication in bereavement: An illustrative case study. *Death Studies, 35,* 905–924.

Hooghe, A., Neimeyer, R. A., & Rober, P. (2012). "Cycling around an emotional core of sadness": Emotion regulation in a couple after the loss of a child. *Qualitative Health Research, 22*(9), 1220–1231.

Janoff-Bulman, R. (1992). *Shattered assumptions.* New York, NY: Free Press.

Johnson, S. M. (2002). *Emotionally focused couple therapy with trauma survivors: Strengthening attachment bonds.* New York, NY: The Guilford Press.

Johnson, S. M. (2004). *The practice of emotionally focused couple therapy: Creating connection.* New York, NY: Routledge.

Johnson, S. M. (2008). *Emotionally focused couple therapy with trauma survivors.* New York, NY: The Guilford Press.

Kariv, D., & Heiman, T. (2005). Task-oriented versus emotion-oriented coping strategies: The case of college students. *College Student Journal, 39*(1), 72–85.

Kelly, T. B., & Kropf, N. P. (1995). Stigmatized and perpetual parents: Older parents caring for adult children with life-long disabilities. *Journal of Gerontological Social Work, 24*(1-2), 3–16.

Klesse, C. (2018). Theorizing multi-partner relationships and sexualities—Recent work on non-monogamy and polyamory. *Sexualities, 21*(7), 1109–1124.

Lang, A., Fleiszer, A. R., Duhamel, F., Sword, W., Gilbert, K. R., & Corsini-Munt, S. (2011). Perinatal loss and parental grief: The challenge of ambiguity and disenfranchised grief. *OMEGA-Journal of Death and Dying, 63*(2), 183–196.

Lebow, J., Chambers, A., Christensen, A., & Johnson, S. (2012). Research on the treatment of couple distress. *Journal of Marital and Family Therapy, 38*, 145–168.

Martin, T. L., & Doka, K. J. (2011). The influence of gender and socialization on grieving styles. In R. A. Neimeyer, D. L. Harris, H. R. Winokuer, & G. F. Thornton (Eds.), *Grief and Bereavement in Contemporary Society: Bridging research and practice* (pp. 69–77). New York, NY: Routledge.

Molaison, V., Bordere, T., & Fowler, K. (2011). "The Remedy Is Not Working": Seeking socially just & culturally conscientious practices in bereavement. In R. A. Neimeyer, D. L. Harris, H. R. Winokuer, & G. F. Thornton (Eds.), *Grief and Bereavement in Contemporary Society: Bridging research and practice.* New York, NY: Routledge.

Nealy, E. (2008). Working with LGBT families. In M. McGoldrick & K. Hardy (Eds.), *Revisioning family therapy: Race, culture and gender in clinical practice.* New York, NY: The Guilford Press.

Neimeyer, R. A. (2006). Complicated grief and the reconstruction of meaning: Conceptual and empirical contributions to a cognitive-constructivist model. *Clinical Psychology: Science and Practice, 13*(2), 141–145.

Neimeyer, R. A., Burke, L. A., McKay, M. M., & van Dyke Stringer, J. G. (2010). Grief therapy and the reconstruction of meaning: From therapy to practice. *Journal of Contemporary Psychotherapy, 40*(2), 73–83.

Oliver, L. E. (1999). Effects of a child death on marital relationship: A review. *Omega, 39*, 197–227.

Overton, B. L., & Cottone, R. R. (2016). Anticipatory grief: a family systems approach. *The Family Journal, 24*(4), 430–432.

Parker, B. S., & Dunn, K. S. (2011). The continued lived experience of an unexpected death of a child. *Omega, 63*(3), 221–233.

Rando, T. A. (1983). An investigation of grief and adaptation in parents whose children have died from cancer. *Journal of Pediatric Psychology, 8*, 3–20.

Rando, T. A. (1986). *Parental loss of a child.* Champaign, IL: Research Press Company.

Ricoeur, J., & Gentet, J.C.I. (1996, June–July). *Fratrie et cancer. A propos de quelques observations. Neuropsychiatrie de l'enfance et de l'adolescence 44,* (pp. 258–267).

Robson, P., & Walter, T. (2013). Hierarchies of loss: A critique of disenfranchised grief. *OMEGA-Journal of Death and Dying, 66*(2), 97–119.

Rubin, S. S. (1981). The two-track model of bereavement: Overview, retrospect, and prospect. *Death Studies, 23*(8), 681–714.

Rubin, S. S., Malkinson, R., & Witztum, E. (2012). *Working with the bereaved: Multiple lenses on loss and mourning.* Washington, DC: Taylor & Francis.

Rubin, S. S., Nadav, O. B., Malkinson, R., Koren, D., Goffer-Shnarch, M., & Michaeli, E. (2009). The two-track model of bereavement questionnaire (TTBQ): Development and validation of a relational measure. *Death Studies, 33*(4), 305–333.

Satir.(1988). *The new people making.* Mountain View, CA: Science & Behavior Books.

Schwab, R. (1990). Paternal and maternal coping with death of a child. *Death Studies, 14*, 407–422.

Schwab, R. (1992). Effects of a child's death on the marital relationship: A preliminary study. *Death Studies, 16*, 141–157.

Shear, M. K. (2015). Complicated grief. *New England Journal of Medicine, 372*(2), 153–160.

Shear, M. K., Reynolds, C. F., Simon, N. M., & Zisook, S. (2016). *Complicated grief in adults: Epidemiology, clinical features, assessment, and diagnosis.* Waltham, MA: Uptodate.

Spurgeon, A., Jackson, C. A., & Beach, J. R. (2001). The Life Events Inventory: Re-scaling based on an occupational sample. *Occupational Medicine, 51*(4), 287–293.

Stroebe, M., & Schut, H. (1999). The dual processing model of coping with bereavement: Rationale and description. *Death Studies, 23*(3), 197–224.

Stroebe, M., & Schut, H. (2015). Family matters in bereavement: Toward an integrative intra-interpersonal coping model. *Perspectives on Psychological Science, 10*(6), 873–879.

Stroebe, M., Van Den Bout, J., & Schut, H. (1994). Myths and misconceptions about bereavement: The opening of a debate. *Journal of Death and Dying, 29*(3), 187–203.

Ungureanu, I., & Sandberg, J. G. (2010). "Broken together": Spirituality and religion as coping strategies for couples dealing with the death of a child: A literature review with clinical implication. *Contemporary Family Therapy, 32*, 302–319.

Walsh, F., & McGoldrick, M. (2004). *Living beyond loss: Death in the family.* New York, NY: W.W. Norton.

Williams, G. B. (2000). Grief after elective abortion: Exploring nursing interventions for another kind of perinatal loss. *AWHONN Lifelines, 4*(2), 37–40.

Wing, D. G., Burge-Callaway, K., Rose Clance, P., & Armistead, L. (2001). Understanding gender differences in bereavement following the death of an infant: Implications of or treatment. *Psychotherapy: Theory, Research, Practice, Training, 38*(1), 60.

Worden, J. W. (1991). *Grief counseling and grief therapy: A handbook for the mental health practitioner* (2nd ed.). New York, NY: Springer.

Worden, J. W. (2008). *Grief counseling and grief therapy: A handbook for the mental health practitioner* (4th ed.). New York, NY: Springer.

Worden, J. W. (2018). *Grief counseling and grief therapy: A handbook for the mental health practitioner* (5th ed.). New York, NY: Springer.

Wortmann, J. H., & Park, C. L. (2008). Religion and spirituality in adjustment following bereavement: An integrative review. *Death Studies, 32*(8), 703–736.

19

Couples in Later Life
The Process of Becoming
Jennifer J. Lambert-Shute, Hoa N. Nguyen,
and Christine A. Fruhauf

Later life provides opportunities for couples to further develop and nurture their relationships. Sandberg (2013) argued for the concept of *becoming*, which embodies a rethinking and reimagining of old age as a time of ongoing possibilities rather than a destination. This view provides scholars a lens for understanding how marriage and other committed relationships change over time to meet the different stressors or challenges in life (Cohen, Geron, & Farchi, 2010). In this chapter, we review current literature on aging couples in the areas of marital satisfaction, depression, diverse couple formations and living arrangements, and older adult's use of mental health services. We then discuss an affirmative approach to working with aging couples, which encompasses joining, assessment, sexuality and intimacy, early-stage dementia, health, finances, and retirement. Finally, we offer resources to support aging couplehood and recommendations for clinical practice and future research. Due to the limited amount of literature on aging in systemic family therapy (Lambert-Shute & Fruhauf, 2011), we are also informed in this review by the disciplines of gerontology, psychology, social work, and family studies.

The Landscape of Aging Couples

In the United States, the current life expectancy at birth is 81.2 years old for females and 76.3 years old for males (Center for Disease Control, 2017). Adults aged 65 and older comprise 14% of the US population and are projected to increase by 20% by 2050 (Ortman, Velkoff, & Hogan, 2014). These shifts in demographics are mostly due to the 70 million baby boomers born between 1946 and 1964. A large number of baby boomer adults choose to marry, and, as a result, therapists will see aging couples in their practices at greater rates. In addition, aging couples attending therapy will

The Handbook of Systemic Family Therapy: Volume 3, First Edition.
Edited by Karen S. Wampler and Adrian J. Blow.
© 2020 John Wiley & Sons Ltd. Published 2020 by John Wiley & Sons Ltd.

more likely be in their 70s, 80s, and 90s and more racially and ethnically diverse (Ortman et al., 2014) than ever before.

Race and marital status

There are vast differences in the distribution of marital status by race, with Asian men and women aged 65 and older having the highest rate of marriage, followed by White, Hispanic, and Black men and women (West, Cole, Goodkind, & He, 2014). Across racial groups, the majority of older men have marital partners, while the majority of older women do not (Connidis, 2010). For instance, 54.1% of Black men aged 65 and older reported being married in comparison with 23.3% of Black women (West et al., 2014). Additionally, Raley, Sweeney, and Wondra (2015) reported that Black women marry later in life and are less likely to marry in comparison with White and Hispanic women. Remarriage was also more common for White men and women. These racial gaps emerged in the 1960s and have been prevalent since (Raley et al., 2015). Thus, the qualitative experiences and social integration of older adults are shaped by the intersection of race and gender (Calasanti & Kiecolt, 2007; Connidis, 2010). In addition, the percentage of interracial or interethnic marriages between 2012 and 2016 increased from 7.4 to 10.2%, indicating that the landscape of marriage will continue to change in future cohorts (US Census Bureau, 2018).

Other factors such as socioeconomic disadvantages and lack of support play a role in the growing racial and ethnic divide that characterizes marriage patterns in the United States (Raley et al., 2015). However, it is also well documented that racial/ethnic disparities impact older adults' health well into later life (Warner & Brown, 2011). One compelling finding in Yao and Robert's (2008) study showed that even after controlling for socioeconomic context, African American older adults have a 71% greater likelihood of mortality than Caucasian older adults. Therefore, mortality and health are determinants that help us understand the varied marital distribution across racial divides. This highlights the importance of recognizing the complex interconnection of social locations and multiple layers of social inequalities.

LGBTQ couple relationships

The use of marital status as a primary determinant for investigating all couple relationships excludes other meaningful forms of intimate partnerships that have historically occurred in underrepresented groups (Kimmel, Hinrichs, & Fisher, 2015). Specifically, lesbian, gay, bisexual, transgender, and queer (LGBTQ) couples are often overlooked, as it may be difficult to accurately assess these numbers when conducting census studies (O'Connell & Feliz, 2011). For instance, many individuals may not report their sexual orientation or gender identity due to discriminatory attitudes and policies. As attitudes toward sexual and gender identity individuals shift and with the legalization of same-sex marriage, this population may be more willing to self-identify and thus be counted (Kimmel et al., 2015).

Fredriksen-Goldsen, Kim, Bryan, Shiu, and Emlet (2017) found that legally married LGBT adults aged 50 and older reported higher quality of life, social support, and financial capital than those who are unmarried, partnered, or single. In regard to aging LGBT couples, the common issue of housing in later life is compounded with discrimination, involuntary outing, threats, neglect, assault, and lack of access to resources that would be available for heterosexual and cisgender individuals (Addis, Davies, Greene, MacBride-Stewart, & Shepherd, 2009). Given these concerns, LGBT couples have fewer options and, thus, need to hide their status to live in elderly housing and communities.

Intersectionality

While scholarship on the individual aging experiences of sexual, gender, and racial/ethnic minorities is gaining a foothold, research on couples within these groups is largely invisible. Several explanations may underlie this gap in the literature, such as the limited use of research methods that intentionally target couples from marginalized and minority populations (Moreno-John et al., 2004). Since very little literature is found on the intersection between aging couples and race, class, gender identity, religion, etc., much of what we discuss in the literature is not representative of these diverse populations.

Literature on Aging Couple Relationships

Marital satisfaction

It is essential to understand older couples' marital satisfaction, as distress and conflict in couples' relationships contribute to physical health problems, such as cardiovascular, endocrine, immune, neurosensory, and other physiological systems (Kiecolt-Glaser & Newton, 2001; Robles, Slatcher, Trombello, & McGinn, 2014). Physical health concerns impact marital quality for older couples and vice versa. Overall, older couples tend to report lower incidences of conflict and higher marital satisfaction than couples at any other life stage (Henry, Berg, Smith, & Florsheim, 2007). In fact, older adults express lower negative affect and display greater affection during conflict than their younger counterparts (Carstensen, Gottman, & Levenson, 1995). This could be due to the fact that older adults use more strategies during conflicts to mediate the effects of the altercation, such as focusing on how to solve the problem rather than "win" the argument (Birditt & Fingerman, 2005).

To better understand these findings, researchers have used socioemotional selectivity theory (SST) to guide their work; this theory suggests that older couples are cognizant of the remaining time left, which influences how they relate to each other (Carstensen, Fung, & Charles, 2003). Given this outlook, older couples tend to reduce negative aspects in their experiences and focus on positive aspects in their lives, including those in their marriage (Smith et al., 2009). Birditt, Fingerman, and Almeida (2005) suggested that older couples experience conflict just as often as other couples, even though they reported less distress during disagreements. In Smith et al.'s (2009) study, they found that "older and more satisfied couples discount their spouse's negative actions, rather than as indicative of objective differences during marital interactions" (p. 16). Thus, older couples tend to encounter conflict similarly to couples in different life stages, but their perceptions of these interactions captures the positive rather than the observed negative behaviors.

Additionally, partners' perceptions of their spouses' supportive behaviors are significantly associated with relationship satisfaction (Landis, Peter-Wright, Martin, & Bodenmann, 2013). Gender also plays a vital role in shaping spouses' perception of marital satisfaction. McCoy, Rauer, and Sabey (2017) found that the husband's affectivity, positivity, and emotional attunement influence his partner's current and future satisfaction. One important consideration in this area of research is that the findings on older couple's' marital satisfaction are influenced by an inherent selection bias, given that maritally-satisfied couples tend to stay married longer (Carstensen et al., 1995). These results reflect not only age-related differences but length of marriage as well (Smith et al., 2009). Furthermore, older couples have a greater length of time together and, thus, additional opportunities to relate more effectively than couples in other life stages (Peter-Wright & Martin, 2011).

Depression and its impact on the marital relationship

Depression has been reported as one of the most common mental health disorders for the aging population (National Alliance on Mental Illness, 2009). However, older adults have reported lower levels of depression and better mental health overall, despite experiencing loss of cognitive and physical function (Thomas et al., 2016). In fact, rates of major depression were lower among older adults when compared with younger adults (Hasin, Goodwin, Stinson, & Grant, 2005). Researchers postulate that rates of depression in older adults often are underreported as these symptoms are masked by physical health concerns, including chronic pain, grief, heart problems, and even dementia (Allan, Valkanova, & Ebmeier, 2014). Due to this phenomenon, depression is a challenge experienced by older people (World Health Organization, 2017).

Only a few studies have sought to understand the connection between depression and relationships in the elderly, despite the strong connection found between relationship quality and depression in general (Monin et al., 2016). For example, Tower and Kasl (1995) conducted a secondary analysis with interview data of 317 older married couples. They found that husbands' and wives' depressive symptoms influenced those of their partner, even when controlling for race, education, financial strain, chronic health conditions, functional ability, and cognitive impairment. This finding was supported by Whisman and Uebelacker (2009).

In a qualitative study, Sandberg, Miller, and Harper (2002) found that marital conflict and confrontation are more often present in older depressed couples than older nondepressed couples. These couples are characterized by hostile patterns of communication including criticism and outbursts of anger. In regard to problem solving, Sandberg et al. (2002) found that depressed couples are more likely to withdraw from their spouse than to engage when a problem arose. Another key finding from this study supports past research, which highlights social support as a buffer to depression. Lastly, Sandberg et al. (2002) found that positive experiences in couple therapy are especially helpful for couples when one partner perceives their depression as being related to marital discord. Therefore, for these couples, it is essential to address the couple relationship when working with older adults who are diagnosed with depression.

Diverse couple formations and living arrangements

Childless aging couples Childless—not having biological/adopted children—couples are becoming increasingly common (Agree & Hughes, 2012). For example, a total of 30.8% of women aged 30–34 were childless in 2016, an increase of 4% in just 10 years (US Census Bureau, 2017). Childlessness is treated as voluntary, where an individual/couple chooses to live a childfree life, or involuntary, due to infertility (Connidis & McMullin, 1996); no matter the reason, remaining childless is a process, rather than a single decision in a couple's relationship (DeOllos & Kapinus, 2002). Certainly, couples may become childless due to the death of a child. Additionally, aging couples that are estranged from their adult children because of prison, addiction, immigration, illness, or other reasons may "feel" childless in the sense of having limited access to their children and that source of potential support.

The impact of childlessness on aging couples may influence a number of contextual factors and life transitions. First, childless couples are typically better educated, spend more time in the labor force, and are financially secure (DeOllos & Kapinus, 2002). Second, older childless couples oftentimes rely extensively on each other (rather than children) for support, have strong marital ties, and report higher life satisfaction (DeOllos & Kapinus, 2002). Yet, the death of a spouse may put the widow(er) at risk for isolation, though these aging couples may nurture stronger ties with extended family (e.g., siblings, nieces, nephews) and other social networks across the life course (Wenger, Dykstra, Melkas, & Knipscheer, 2007). Third, older childless women are more likely to live alone, enter into residential care, and need assistance with activities from formal care providers (DeOllos & Kapinus, 2002). Finally, childless older adults reported advantages, which include fewer worries with adult children, greater finances, and more freedom, as well as disadvantages, including lacking companionship or support/care, feeling lonely, and wondering if there was a missed experience during life (Connidis & McMullin, 1999). Regardless of the experience of aging couples, childlessness is increasing, and the increase provides greater opportunity to further investigate the influence childlessness has across the life course.

Second couplehood Second couplehood is a term associated with adults who enter a new intimate relationship in old age (Koren, 2015). The literature on second couplehood focuses on three main forms (Koren, 2015): remarriage, cohabitation, and living apart together. Second couplehood as a phenomenon has been growing for quite some time as evidenced by the number of older adults aged 55–64 remarrying. The number of adults remarrying in this age group has risen from 55% in 1960 to 67% in 2013 (Pew, 2014). While the number of US adults cohabiting has risen across all age groups, adults 50 and older grew by 75%, a growth rate faster than any group (Pew, 2017). In 2009, researchers Strohm, Seltzer, Cochran, and Mays (2009) estimated "one third of individuals we would classify as 'single' by conventional measures of union status are actually in LAT [living apart together] relationships" (p. 13).

REMARRIAGE   In a decade review of the scholarship on remarriage, Sweeney (2010) found that remarriage in later life received little attention, and only a limited number of researchers investigated remarriage beyond young or middle age. The research on older adults and remarriage has generally focused on gender differences. For instance, Carr (2004) found that men have an advantage due to the larger numbers of women available and that widows tend to express less interest than widowers in remarrying. Also, women most often reported not desiring a new partnership due to concerns about caretaking (Davidson, 2001). However, Carr (2004) suggested that remarriage will continue to grow given that baby boomers will likely shift the landscape of remarriage in comparison with other older adult cohorts. Reasons for this shift included changes in sexual attitudes (Thornton & Young-DeMarco, 2001) and innovations in medicine and technology, such as Internet dating and Facebook (Davis & Fingerman, 2015).

COHABITATION   While marriage has many benefits, a larger number of older adults are choosing not to remarry and are deciding to cohabitate instead (Vespa, 2012). Brown and Wright (2015) surveyed older adults in 2012 and found that 46% hold favorable attitudes for couples living together without intending to marry. McWilliams and Barrett (2014) noted that most older adults who cohabitate have been previously married and do not desire to be remarried, which is particularly true for women. Thus, cohabitation can offer support, companionship, and sharing of household labor (de Jong Gierveld, 2004) without the legal and financial entanglements of marriage. Wright and Brown (2017) found in their study that cohabiting women are less lonely than women without a partner but similar in levels of loneliness to dating or married women. However, men who cohabit feel less lonely than men who are daters or unpartnered (Wright & Brown, 2017). Thus, for unmarried men, sharing a residence seems to be a fundamental factor, while this is less salient for women. This difference could be attributed to gender, given that women tend to carry most of the household labor in the relationship (Lachance-Grzela & Bouchard, 2010). Additionally, they tend to be delegated the role of caregiver (Hirschfeld & Wikler, 2003), which has been found to be highly stressful (Pinquart & Sörensen, 2011). Due to these concerns, women are more likely to choose other partnership arrangements that allow for intimacy without necessarily involving marriage or cohabitation (Talbott, 1998).

LIVING APART TOGETHER   Living apart together relationships are a relatively new form of committed relationship for older adults in the United States (Benson & Coleman, 2016). However, Karlsson and Borell (2002) suggested that these relationships do occur in the United States, yet the lack of terminology to describe these types of relationships may have rendered them invisible. For example, aging couples have had to rely on youth cultural terminology such as "going steady" (Bulcroft & O'Connor, 1986). The term living apart together is used to denote a "long-term relationships that do not involve cohabitation" (Karlsson & Borell, 2002, p. 13). Older adults, as do individuals across the lifespan, choose these types of partnerships because they provide many of the same benefits of marriage and cohabitation, such as companionship, while also protecting their autonomy (Upton-Davis, 2012).

One of the few studies about living apart together couples produced in the United States was conducted by Benson and Coleman (2016). The findings from this study support previous research, which revealed living apart together as a legitimate arrangement instead of a stepping stone to marriage or cohabitation. The participants felt highly committed toward one another, yet did not desire "until death do us part" (Benson & Coleman, 2016, p. 808). Overall, the values of autonomy and choice are determining factors in having this type of relationship style. Furthermore, older adults take into account the approval or disapproval of adult children when considering living apart together relationships. For example, fear of their children's disapproval may discourage disclosure of their living apart together partnerships. In other circumstances, adult children can be more supportive of living apart together relationships as they allow for financial independence. Additionally, Benson and Coleman's (2016) results highlighted that the decision to live apart together is heavily influenced by gender. Both men and women wanted to protect themselves from commitments of marriage and cohabitation, but for different reasons. Women abstained due to caregiving demands and fear of inequitable labor, while men due to safeguarding their time spent with social groups or in leisure activities. The authors noted that financial reasons may be more important for older adults in the United States than in other countries due to our welfare system (Benson & Coleman, 2016).

Aging in place   Approximately 96.4% of older adults aged 65 and over live in households rather than assisted-living facilities, with 43.3% of them living with a spouse and 13.3% living with their spouse and other relatives in their own home (West et al., 2014). Even at ages 75–84, only 12.6% live in group quarters, that is, nursing home and assisted-living facilities (West et al., 2014). Older adults prefer to "age in place" as opposed to live in long-term care settings; however, it is known that when older adults have declines in physical or cognitive functioning, they need more assistance with instrumental activities of daily living (shopping, cleaning, etc.). Despite the likelihood that an increased number of older adults will utilize assisted-living facilities than previous generations, little is known about married couples in such living communities (Kemp, 2008).

Couples typically relocate from their private home to an assisted-living facility due to a health decline of at least one spouse (Reinardy & Kane, 2003) or no longer being able to manage their own home (Kemp, 2008). Gladstone (1995) found that spouses benefit from being together when living in a long-term care facility. Yet, couples may also have to cope with and navigate having less privacy (Neugebauer-Visano, 1995), and, for many older Americans, the financial costs of assisted-living facilities are a burden (Kemp, 2008) or may not be an option at all. Facility choice is important to life satisfaction (Morgan, Eckert, Piggee, & Frankowski, 2006) and may be challenging as facilities may better meet the needs of one spouse (i.e., the spouse that needs more care) than the other (Kemp, 2008). Secondly, when couples move into an assisted-living facility, issues of independence versus dependence, friendship formation, and engagement with activities within the facility need to be negotiated (Ball et al., 2000).

Older Adults' Attitudes and Use of Mental Health Services

According to the US Department of Health and Human Services (2001), less than 3% of older adults utilize mental health services even though 20% of adults aged 55 and over experience a mental disorder. Researchers have wondered if older generations are less likely to use mental health services because of their attitudes toward psychological illness and treatment (Karel, Gatz, & Smyer, 2012). Elder, Clipp, Brown, Martin, and Friedman (2009) reported that cohorts of older adults that grew up in the first half of the twentieth century tended to value self-reliance more than cohorts from later generations. However, Robb, Haley, Becker, Polivka, and Chwa (2003) found little empirical data supporting the assumption that older adults exhibit negative attitudes toward mental health services. In fact, older adults have reported generally positive attitudes toward seeking treatment (Conner et al., 2010). Additionally, older adults hold similarly positive attitudes regarding mental health services when compared with younger age groups (Segal, Coolidge, Mincic, & O'riley, 2005). More recently a study by SAMHSA (, 2014) found that adults aged 50 and older use services at about the same rate (15.4%) as adults aged 26–49 (15.3%) and slightly more services (11.9%) than adults aged 18–25. These may reflect the differing perspectives of the baby boomer cohorts (Knight & Lee, 2008). Therefore, the underuse of mental health services may be related to not only attitudes surround mental health conditions but also under-identification by healthcare professionals (WHO, 2017).

In addition to generational influences, race and ethnicity may play a role in older adults' perception and experience of therapy. For instance, Hispanic and Asian Pacific Islander older adults were more likely to report "concerns about not feeling comfortable talking to a professional as a reason for not seeking treatment" (Sorkin, Murphy, Nguyen, & Biegler, 2016, p. 2141), in comparison with their non-Hispanic White counterparts. African American older adults also reported a sense of mistrust in the effectiveness of mental health treatment (Conner et al., 2010). Thus, Sorkin et al. (2016) suggested therapists should strive to convey a sense of respect for their clients' worldviews, especially when working with older adults of color.

Our Approach to Working with Aging Couples

In our work, we advocate for a systemic framework that attends to the relational aspects of aging couples. We believe the process of aging takes place within the context of the couple relationship, where one partner's experience of aging inevitably shapes the other's experience (Becvar, Canfield, & Becvar, 1997). When possible, therapists should include all partners in treatment. However, even if only one partner is in the therapy room, the therapist should consider how the couple relationship impacts the issues being discussed. In addition, we recognize that couple systems are embedded within larger systems. Thus, at certain points in treatment, therapists may need to invite grown children, medical and mental health professionals, clergy, or other community members to be involved during the therapy process. Therapy can take place in many different environments and may need to adjust to the client's context. For example, therapy may be conducted in a client's home, a hospital room, or an assisted-living facility.

We also believe that utility of a model or intervention can only be decided relative to each unique client system (Becvar, 2005). Thus, we will not be presenting specific treatment models; rather, we advocate a framework of *affirmative old age*. This perspective "seeks to underline the facticity of the ageing body…" (Sandberg, 2013, p. 18) and also takes into account how power informs our privileging of youth, marking aging bodies as a difference that must be eradicated. Further, discourses on aging tend to emphasize a biological perspective, which may overfocus on the deficiencies of the human body as it ages. On the other hand, solely focusing on social context overemphasizes "successful" aging, which encourages us to overcome our aging bodies through youth-oriented narratives such as activity, productivity, and autonomy (Larner, 2000; Rozanova, 2010). This establishes and maintains a binary view of aging as either decline or success. Holding an either/or perspective pathologizes aging bodies, with youth as a measurement of success (Sandberg, 2013). Thus, an affirmative old age stance expands beyond the binary view of aging, integrating an affirming, both/and stance that embraces the complexities of older couples' lived experiences and the possibility of *becoming*.

Joining with older clients

More of an attitude than a technique, Minuchin and Fishman (1981) defined joining as the "glue that holds the therapeutic system together" (p. 32). Beyond offering support to the family, joining is when clients feel heard and understood by the therapist and recognize that "the therapist is working with and for them" (p. 32). Joining, which is often an ongoing process rather than an isolated or time-confined event, allows the therapist to enter the system.

Having an affirming, non-pathologizing frame is one method of joining with older couples. An affirming stance involves embodying compassion and acceptance toward the clients' positions. Flemons (2002) differentiates between compassion and pity. While pity distances and keeps us separate from our clients, compassion "plunges us inside our clients' experiences, providing the means for full-bodied, empathic entry into their pain. It allows us to imaginatively feel ourselves as them" (p. 47). Further, therapists can take a one-down stance and utilize curiosity to understand client experiences. Anderson (2009) suggests approaching clients from a learning position by:

> trying to respond to what the client is saying (not what the therapist thinks they should be saying)… making room for and giving the client the choice to tell their story in their own manner and at their own pace… [and] pausing and allowing silences for listening and reflecting spaces. (p. 10)

Approaching from a place of genuine curiosity and compassion allows therapists to join the client system.

In addition, therapists need to consider generational differences and cohort effects that contextualize the experiences of older clients (Knight, 2009). For example, a therapist may consider the level of formality in which they address an older client and their physical appearance when conducting therapy with clients from a different generation. Knight (2009) suggested that developmental maturation may influence older adult clients' pace of speech (i.e., slowing down, pausing), language use (i.e., colloquial speech), complexity of emotional expression, and the depth of life knowledge they can access.

Finally, therapists can build hope and expectancy by engaging in clients' wisdom and life experiences. Hibel and Polanco (2010) suggested intentional listening to attune to ideas, strengths, and resources that might go unnoticed. When therapists listen in this way, they can capture the faint indications of clients' hopes rather than capturing explanations of blame (Hibel & Polanco, 2010). Therefore, intentional listening elevates the voice and insight of our older clients. Given older adult couples' rich history and ability to survive difficulties, therapists should elicit the clients' past successes and lessons learned to highlight their expertise. Thus, listening in this way provides opportunities for clients to generate their own solutions and learn from their past successes (Berg & De Jong, 1996). As clients recognize their strengths and wisdom, they develop trust in their therapist, themselves, and the therapy process (Miller, Duncan, & Hubble, 1997).

Assessment

A few assessments examining aging adults have been modified and used with older couples. Haynes et al. (1992) developed the Marital Satisfaction Questionnaire for Older Persons (MSQFOP), which consists of 24 items that assess later life marital satisfaction. Also, Lauer and Lauer (1986) modified the Dyadic Adjustment Scale (Spanier, 1976) with additional questions to measure commitment in aging couple relationships. According to Miller, Hemesath, and Nelson (1997), researchers have applied several diagnostic aids and assessment tools when studying older couples. These assessments include the Locke–Wallace Marital Adjustment Test, Kansas Marital Satisfaction Scale, and Personal Assessment of Intimacy in Relationships. However, these assessments have not been modified or tested specifically with an aging population.

Formal methods of assessment fail to address significant life events that older couples face (Miller, Hemesath, & Nelson, 1997). Due to this gap in the literature, other types of tools could be used to informally assess the couple, such as genograms and life review. DeMaria, Weeks, and Twist (2017) have written on using focused genograms for intergenerational assessment of individuals, couples, and families, which allows the therapist to obtain information about family relationships across multiple generations. According to Erlanger (1990), therapists can use genograms with older adults to understand the problem in context, connect to past events, and highlight the continuity of experiences beyond the lifespan of the individual. Additionally, for aging couples, genograms can be used to assess crucial milestones in previous generations and how they have influenced the couple relationship over time (Swainson & Tasker, 2005). DeMaria et al. (2017) provided examples of genograms to assess how gender roles, race, sexuality, and other cultural aspects influence the couple relationship. Therapists can investigate gender roles in older couples by asking the following questions while conducting a genogram: (a) Given the generation you were born in, how have those views of gender influenced the gender roles you both have chosen in this relationship? (b) How have your parents' and grandparents' views regarding gender affected your relationship? and (c) How have your views regarding gender affected the relationships with your children and grandchildren?

Life review is a systematic process of intentional reminiscing on previous experiences and communicating this with another person (Bohlmeijer, Kramer, Smit, Onrust, & van Marwijk, 2009). Haber (2006) suggested that life review can be an evaluative process, allowing therapists to "examine how their [clients'] memories contribute to the meaning of their life…" (p. 154). Life review helps clients recall strands of memories from start to finish on a particular theme. An example of a couple theme would be recalling memories from the first meeting of their partner to their present-day relationship. Other themes include major turning points, work, experiences with aging and loss, etc. (Haber, 2006). Life review can be used by therapists to assess couples' life history in a more detailed and descriptive way than formal assessments.

These forms of assessment will require more time and multiple therapy sessions for the therapist to fully unpack and capture the rich history of older couples. We suggest that therapists conduct the genogram and life review with older couples conjointly, rather than separately, to foster a reciprocal process in which family relationships are enriched by sharing their history. Furthermore, these assessments can be used to facilitate the goals of therapy by recognizing intergenerational patterns of interaction, expanding from an individual focus to a relational view of the problem, and identifying meaningful moments in the lives of older adult couples.

Sexuality and intimacy

As life expectancy increases, the possibility of an engaged sexual life at an older age will likely grow in the relationships of partnered adults (DeLamater & Koepsel, 2015). Although the frequency of sex generally declines with age and length of a relationship, it remains an important component for most older couples (DeLamater, Hyde, & Fong, 2008). In fact, Heiman et al. (2011) conducted a cross-cultural study with couples from the United States, Germany, Japan, Spain, and Brazil and found that couples are sexually active after 60 years of age and into later adulthood. Additionally, 85% of older men and 61% of women consider sexual expression to be an important indicator of a good life (Fisher, 2010).

In a landmark study of 3005 US adults 57–85 years of age, Lindau et al. (2007) analyzed data collected from the National Social Life, Health, and Aging Project. They found that 83.7% of men and 61.6% of women aged 57–64 report having sex with a partner in the previous 12 months. Of this group, 67.5% of men and 62.6% of women indicate that they had sex two to three times per month. However, these rates steadily decrease over the years, with women having lower rates than men. Despite the decrease in frequency of intercourse, 44% of older couples reported improved satisfaction, sexually, physically, and emotionally. This finding was also supported by DeLamater and Karraker (2009) who proposed that the quality of sex may improve with age, countering assumptions that decline in frequency equates satisfaction.

The biology of sexuality   Health changes associated with age can affect sexual functioning in older adults (Waite, Laumann, Das, & Schumm, 2009). Men's sexual difficulties, in particular, are associated with physical health and aging (Laumann et al., 2005). An AARP survey of midlife and older adults found that erectile dysfunction increased as men age (Fisher, 2010). Results revealed 61% of men aged 45–49 reported that they are "always able to get and keep an erection good enough for sexual intercourse," which steadily decreases to 59% at ages 50–59, 45% at ages 60–69, and 20% at age 70+ (Fisher, 2010, p. 13). For older women, menopause has been suggested as a cause for low sexual functioning (Avis, Stellato, Crawford, Johannes, & Longcope, 2000) as it is often associated with urogenital atrophy (e.g., vaginal itching, soreness, dryness, pain during sex, etc.) (Taylor & Gosney, 2011). However, others found that women reported no change in sexual functioning (Koch, Mansfield, Thurau, & Carey, 2005). More recently, Ussher, Perz, and Parton's (2015) findings showed that sexual difficulties after menopause are more associated with psychosocial factors. Therapists should neither maximize nor discount the biological aspect when working with sexuality in later life. Thus, therapists need to collaborate with physicians to conduct a thorough medical assessment to learn about physical conditions that could be connected to the older couples' experience of their sexuality.

Sexuality as a lived experience for older adults   Sexual behavior in older couples is also influenced by relationship factors such as sexual satisfaction, relationship satisfaction, communication, and relationship duration (DeLamater & Karraker, 2009). These factors mutually reinforce one another; for example, better communication facilitates a more satisfying sex life, which in turn improves relationship satisfaction, and thus increases the duration of the relationship. Additionally, other factors such as sexual attitudes, cultural values, and gender scripts can impact couples' sexual behavior (Murray, 2018). Sexuality is a social construct shaped by our cultural values (Lodge & Umberson, 2012). For example, in Lodge and Umberson's (2012) study, Mary, a participant aged 60, revealed:

> In Scranton we weren't together an awful lot and that's where [sex] got to be scarce. He didn't seem to mind as much as I did and I think that bothered me quite a bit. I just couldn't see why. Everything I had grown up with was that the men were going to be a lot more [sexual] and that isn't the way it really is, I have discovered. (p. 10)

As shown in Mary's experience, older couples navigate these sexual scripts, confounded by gender, when negotiating aging-related changes in their relationship. These cultural discourses regarding sexuality reduce sex to the body and physicality (Tiefer, 2004). If we limit our view of sex to mechanistic, bodily functions, sex becomes "a fragmented collection of parts that pop in and out at different points in the performance sequence" (Tiefer, 2004, p. 53). This performance-driven perspective supports the idea of gendered, penetrative intercourse as natural and ideal, while all else is failure (Kleinplatz, 2013). Additionally, this way of thinking renders invisible the diverse spectrum of sexuality and reinforces heteronormative, cisnormative assumptions.

Tiefer (2004) expanded sex to a fuller experience, in which pleasure is discovered in varied experiences, such as feeling silk on your skin, tasting chocolate, listening to a sonata, hearing a good joke, embracing a memory, sharing a conversation, or watching a sunset (p. 210). Sexual pleasure transcends the genitals, and as Ackerman (1994) inquired, "What is erotic? The acrobatic play of the imagination. The sea of memories in which we bathe. The way we caress and worship things with our eyes...What is erotic is our passion of the liveliness of life" (p. 256). Thus, when working with couples in regard to sexuality, one must be aware of the cultural scripts of each partner and how they shape: "What is sex?" "What sex should and should not look like?" "Who is allowed to initiate?" As we know, one's sexual cultural script, which constructs the meaning of sex, sexuality, and intimacy, is informed by larger systems, such as gender, race, class, and gender identity. Therefore, therapists have the opportunity to question the dominant narratives of sexuality, which can foster intimate engagement for older adults that neither negates their aging bodies nor mirrors unrealistic societal expectations.

CULTIVATING NEW POSSIBILITIES By understanding sexual pleasure and the erotic as lived experiences, we can delve into the unknown territory of sex within the context of age and maturity. The unknown territory refers to what older couples may have missed or not yet noticed before in their current sexual and intimate relationships. To facilitate such discovery, therapists must first expand what is known by helping their clients explore new possibilities of thinking about and experiencing their sexuality. Possible questions to ask clients include the following: (a) What is your first memory of sexuality? (b) Who taught you about sexuality? (c) What did you hear growing up about sexuality from friends, school, family, church, etc.? (d) What ideas about sexuality did you feel like you had to let go of as you aged? (e) What do you think sexuality has to look like now? (f) For you, what are the differences and similarities between sexuality and intimacy? (g) What are you embarrassed or ashamed about when it comes to sexuality? (h) What do you think your partner may be missing about your sexuality? In this dialogue, the therapist should be intentional in bringing forth possible meanings that widen the scope of their lived sexual experience, remembering that the erotic happens in, as well as beyond, the bedroom.

PRACTICING THE UNKNOWN AND UNTRIED As clients open space for other meanings, therapists can engage in collaborative conversations about what is pleasurable and delightful for the couple. Therapists then invite clients to take action and start practicing the unknown and untried. To ensure that practicing is not aimed toward performance or perfection, therapists can help clients adopt the *beginner's mind*. This is a position of observing and noticing in the present moment as it occurs (Gehart & McCollum, 2008). Clients can notice with the same intentions they would have while viewing a painting. Instead of judging the painting as beautiful or ugly, they merely describe the texture, colors, lines, and how they feel as they observe the picture. When they accept the moment as a teacher, older adults can begin to wonder, explore, and play together. This cultivates opportunities for understanding, learning, and relearning. In venturing through this process, clients may move from practicing to questioning the known and expanding more possibilities and then to more practicing.

Working with early-stage dementia and memory loss

Most research and interventions for dementia have focused on either the patient or the caregiver (Moon & Adams, 2013; Whitlatch, Judge, Zarit, & Femia, 2006). Creating techniques or programs that address one person's needs and neglect the other, in essence, only solves one part of the problem. Thus, illness is not a process that happens as an isolated monad, but rather occurs in relationship (Beach & Inui, 2005). Past literature assumed that people with dementia were permanently lost to their condition and nothing could be done to support or preserve their individual identity (Ray, 2016). Kitwood (1997) has questioned the notion that a person with memory loss or dementia is a nonperson or has somehow lost their "personhood." Therefore, the current accepted practice of working with a person with dementia is to use a person-centered approach. Ray (2016) outlined the following framework to assist practitioners in working with person with dementia:

Recognizing each person as a unique individual with their own strengths, resources, and capabilities

1 Challenging the tendencies to homogenise individual experience into the dementia experience
2 Contextualises the experience of dementia within a whole life course—the life lived as well as a person's present and their future
3 Supports the recognition of potential, as well as actual strengths and resources
4 Encourages consideration of life course inequalities which influence the resources a person may be able to draw upon
5 Highlights the importance of relationship and reciprocity (p. 221)

To engage everyone's participation, we advocate for working with a person-centered approach when one partner has dementia. The therapist can encourage and support the person with dementia by being careful not to use infantilizing language and deficit labels to describe them, exclude either partner from the therapy room, or have a conversation that is beyond the person with dementia's ability to process or understand (Kitwood, 1997). In the early stages, people with dementia are still able to participate and desire to do so (Hirschman, Joyce, James, Xie, & Karlawish, 2005). In Moon and Adams' (2013) review, dyadic interventions in early-stage dementia were shown to improve the couple relationship, decrease caregiver depression and anxiety, and enhance the cognitive function, knowledge, and coping skills of the person with dementia.

Couplehood in memory loss   Clinicians can support and encourage ideas of couplehood in therapy when one partner has dementia. For instance, therapists might use normalizing to assist each partner in understanding how the symptoms and behaviors associated with memory loss or dementia are part of the normal trajectory of the disease, rather than assume the partner with dementia is intentionally forgetting in order to cause harm. Another technique therapists can utilize is externalizing to facilitate an alliance between the couple against "forgetfulness." Externalizing helps clients personify the problem by separating the problem from the person (White & Epston, 1990). This allows clients to engage differently with the "problem" so that they can discover ways to decrease the stress and strain the problem has brought into their lives. For instance, in working with a couple frustrated by one partner's forgetfulness, the therapist can inquire the following: (a) How has forgetfulness created arguments between you and your partner? (b) How has forgetfulness gotten each of you to act against your better judgment? (c) How does forgetfulness keep you from noticing your partner's efforts to connect? These strategies aid the couple in making sense of the struggles they encounter while also facilitating connection.

Couples Life Story Approach   The Couples Life Story Approach, developed for working with dementia from a couples-oriented framework (Ingersoll-Dayton, Spencer, Campbell, Kurokowa, & Ito, 2016). This approach is similar to life review; however, the focus of this approach is to work conjointly and invite all partners to participate in a meaningful task to notice strengths within the couple (Scherrer, Ingersoll-Dayton, & Spencer, 2014). In the Couples Life Story Approach, as outlined by Ingersoll-Dayton et al. (2016), the practitioner and the couple meet over a 5-week period to complete the Couple's Life Story and their Life Story Book. Each week, the couple reviews a time period in their life from early, middle, and more recent years. During each of these time periods, the clinician assists the couple in highlighting their strengths, important events, and people and records the stories to provide feedback to the couple and reflect on what each partner heard, noticed, and stated. For example, the therapist may inquire about the couple's spiritual or religious beliefs that have been a resource in their relationship (Marterella & Brock, 2008). This brings forth the strengths of each person, as well as the couple, to support them. These are also included in the Life Story Book, along with pictures/letters/cards, which help the couple capture their experience. Finally, in the last session, they read the Life Story Book together, and the clinician discusses what they have learned about themselves as a couple and how they can continue to add to their book. Also, the clinician will encourage the couple to revisit the book during times of challenge to remind themselves of who they are as a couple, what they have accomplished together, and what strengths they can draw on to face this current difficulty.

The influences of health on couple relationships

Today, spousal or family care is a normative experience for individuals in long-term marriages or aging families (Brody, 1985; Family Caregiver Alliance, 2018). Spouses (usually the wife in heterosexual marriages, as women live longer than men) are first in line to assume caregiving responsibilities. In general, spouses often experience greater rates of stress and strain compared with other types of caregiving relationships (Pinquart & Sörensen, 2011), and, in particular, wives express more burden than husbands (Simonelli et al., 2008).

When adults are caring for a spouse with Alzheimer's disease (AD) or related dementias, caregiver stress and strain are compounded. Caregivers of spouses with AD often experience higher rates of depression and increased rates of loneliness when compared with non-caregiving peers their age (Beeson, 2003). Further, spouses often discuss challenges to their marital relationship, particularly when communicating with a spouse who has AD (Wright, 1993). For example, non-caregiving couples were more interactive and expressed more support for each other during mealtime and when planning a future event (Gallagher-Thompson, Dal Canto, Jacob, & Thompson, 2001). Although a large proportion of the literature addresses the negative outcomes of caregiving, spousal caregivers have reported rewards related to their caregiver role. Marital bonds may actually increase for some couples as a result of this relationship (Weishaus & Field, 1988).

Perhaps what is most interesting about older couples' relationships in the context of chronic disease is how they support each other. Nearly 100% of wives and husbands reported that they initiated health-promoting spousal support in the previous month, and nearly 100% of spouses reported receiving such support (Franks, Wendorf, Gonzalez, & Ketterer, 2004). For instance, Roberto, Gold, and Yorgason (2004) conducted research with older couples where wives had osteoporosis and found that almost all of the couples said they were in supportive marriages. Additionally, Yorgason, Piercy, and Piercy (2007) found that couples with hearing loss learn to communicate nonverbally with each other when one partner has hearing loss. This reflects couples' ability not only to serve as a resource during illness but also to be considered collaborators in regard to cognitive functioning as partners serve to enhance cognitive performance (Bookwala, 2012) and everyday problem-solving tasks (Cheng & Strough, 2004). Finally, among couples where a spouse experiences prostate cancer, both individuals reported more coping effectiveness on days they perceive their spouse to be more collaborative in their care (Berg et al., 2008). We wonder if the partners' levels of cooperation are influenced by how well/sick they feel on those particular days.

A framework for thinking about health and older couples   Therapists may encounter older adult clients in which one partner may have to provide care to the other. Often, at least one partner has been diagnosed with a heart condition, arthritis, diabetes, or cancer. In these instances, couples may come to therapy reporting disagreements about the amount and type of care, issues around loss of physical functioning, and feelings of disconnection from their partner. When working with older couples around health and caregiving, we suggest focusing on the dynamic and reciprocal interplay between the couple and how it impacts their ability to cope together (Berg et al., 2008). Rather than dealing with health changes and illnesses in silos, a couple's mutual support for one another and the relationship is a potential source for intervening. In dyadic coping, couples confront their stressors and illnesses from a "we" stance, which can be particularly useful when experiencing a sense of loss for self and other. Weingarten (2013) described this sense of self-loss and other loss as the painful experience of losing who they are as individuals and partners and the value they bring to the couplehood.

For the couple, the disease becomes "an unwelcome interloper" (Boss & Couden, 2002, p. 1354) that brings suffering to their relationship. The therapist can generate conversations that become "a container for the intense sorrow that these couples bear" (Weingarten, 2013, p. 94). For aging couples with health issues, partners may be aware of their loved one's struggle but not know what to do, or they may want to empower their partner without having an authentic awareness of how they are suffering. It is important to guide these conversations in ways that shift the partner's position of witnessing from a place of *disempowered unawareness* to *empowered awareness* (Weingarten, 2010).

Disempowered unawareness occurs when partners find it challenging to acknowledge and validate these difficult emotions because of their own fears. Thus, partners may suggest "quick fixes" to alleviate the sorrow by focusing on the positive areas, such as having grandchildren or still being able to take a walk in the park. While these are not inherently problematic ideas, the way in which they occur can leave the partner with health issues feeling dismissed and disconnected. Therapists can assist their clients in adopting an *empowered awareness* by listening to their partners' suffering without trying to fix or change their experiences. O'Hanlon (2018) suggested the idea of validating and giving clients permission to feel however they feel, which can free them from the shame or guilt of not wanting to go to the doctor, take medications, or continue to fight. For example, the therapist may ask the partner who is ill: (a) How have the changes in your body affected your sense of who you are and your relationship with your partner? (b) What has it been like to try not to give up? (c)

What do you miss most about not being well? (d) Can you tell me more about what it is like to be so tired? Next, the clinician asks the witnessing partner to self-reflect on the following questions: (a) Are there questions I should be asking but I am not? (b) Are there areas of mixed feelings or uncertainties I have about my partner's illness that I have not expressed? (c) How can I encourage my partner to express what they need? (McNamee, 2009). This can also facilitate modeling about how to hear and empower their partner.

Forming collaborative healthcare teams   As couples age and enter the medical community, family members, such as grown children, grandchildren, and extended family, are likely to become more involved in part of the decision making around their medical care and treatment. When at least one partner falls ill, the family is the "first circle of health specialists to respond" and becomes their "context of care" (McDaniel, Campbell, & Seaburn, 1995, p. 287). Thus, the couple system expands and is influenced by the larger family system as well as the healthcare environment. In recent years, medical family therapy has grown as a practice that utilizes collaborative health teams and embodies an integrative, holistic approach (Hodgson, Lamson, Mendenhall, & Crane, 2014). This is vastly different from the "split biopsychosocial approach" that focuses on either the organic disease or the emotions and relationships (Doherty, Baird, & Becker, 1987). Doherty and Baird (1983) argued that centering on just the patient and physician creates an "illusion of the dyad" by discounting how the couple and family impact health, disease, and the patient's response to the physician. McDaniel et al. (1995) argued that "the family and patient must be respected as partners in care rather than treated as objects of care" (p. 287). Thus, the collaborative family healthcare team expands beyond the patient and medical provider. When thinking about who to include in the healthcare team, clinicians should consider the patient's context, which also involves relevant aspects of diversity. For example, in same-sex or polyamorous couples, significant partners may not be seen as legitimate (i.e., not legally married) and, therefore, oftentimes excluded from the patient's treatment process. Therapists can then ask, "Is there anyone who needs to be on the team, but is not currently present?" This allows therapists to ask the questions that others will not bring up due to the effect of powerful social, economic, and political institutions (Markowitz, 1997).

   McDaniel et al. (1995) highlighted the need for common goals within the healthcare team. Oftentimes, the voice of the medical professional is louder than the voices and views of the patient and/or family, out of concern and fear for the patient's well-being. Thus, a key component of creating common goals is to facilitate a collaborative environment where all voices are valued equally. This is critical when working with clients whose voices are often left in the margins, leading to a sense of mistrust in the medical system. As we know, this often characterizes the experiences of racial and ethnic minorities, particularly those in the Black and Latino communities. These historical experiences inevitably shape how families and professionals may hold different and competing ideas about treatment. Therapists can then seek moments to repair the relationship of mistrust in the medical system by inviting dialogue about the deeper concerns and worries of all team members involved and encouraging understanding and empathy for all points of view.

For instance, a Hispanic family finds themselves in opposition with each other and the medical doctor's recommendations for treatment. From the medical team's perspective, the mother's wish to continue working contributes to the deterioration of her health, and her partner also agrees that working may be necessary but encourages her to slow down. On the other hand, their grown children are demanding for their mother to quit altogether and only focus on self-care. In these instances, the therapist serves as a choreographer in helping the patient and family, as well as the medical professionals, navigate their different ideas about what is best. The therapist could adopt a multi-directed partiality stance, which requires the therapist to support and value each and every person's perspective (Böszörményi-Nagy & Krasner, 1986). We advocate for the family and medical professionals to articulate their understandings and meanings of the illness and associated symptoms (Wright & Bell, 2009). Therapists can facilitate this process by using reflexive questioning, which helps individuals reflect on the meaning constructed from their perspective, behavior, and value systems (Tomm, 1987). For example, therapists could ask each person: (a) What is your understanding of mom's diagnosis? (b) What symptoms worry you the most? (c) What needs to happen to help mom and the family through this illness? (d) Can each of you share your past experiences with doctors and hospitals, and how it might affect the way you relate to medical professionals (e.g., questioning or not questioning, doing your own research, getting second opinions)? (e) Sometimes families of color experience discrimination in hospitals or with doctors; has this also happened, and how does this affect your current experience with our healthcare team? (f) How do you know when the treatment needs to be changed in order for mom to have a satisfying life? These questions can encourage the healthcare team to consider other ways of thinking and acting.

Additionally, family members may be at different points on the continuum of denial to acceptance about the medical diagnosis (McDaniel et al., 1995). One example that illustrates this dynamic is when the oldest son denies his parent's medical condition and advocates for homeopathic treatments while dad pushes for surgery and increased medication. Other siblings may oscillate along the denial/acceptance continuum. This creates strain between husband and wife, as they are trying to manage the conflict between their grown children. These differences among the siblings and parents may inform the ways in which each member responds to the other. Oftentimes when individuals hold opposing views, a monologue, rather than a dialogue, ensues. Gergen, McNamee, and Barrett (2001) suggest the use of transformative dialogue to engage family members in understanding each person's position. A transformative dialogue is a "form of interchange that succeeds in transforming a relationship between those committed to otherwise separate and antagonistic realities…" (Gergen et al., 2001, p. 698). We suggest asking the following questions to shift family members from opponents to allies.

Therapists can ask: (a) What happens for you [son] when you hear dad tell mom she has to have surgery? (b) What are you [son] concerned will happen if mom consents to surgery? (c) What might be some of your [husband] concerns about your wife having surgery? (d) When listening to your husband's and son's views, what fits for you [mom] about what your husband has said and what your son has said? (e) What do you [mom] think both of them have missed that you believe is important? These questions are essential to increase the family members' empathy for each other's place along the continuum and to recognize that these positions are not static, but rather evolving. This allows the therapist to invite the family members' strengths and capacities to the forefront, which moves families from passive recipients of care to active contributors.

Finances in later life

Financial issues are an important component in relationship satisfaction (Dakin & Wampler, 2008; Dean, Carroll, & Yang, 2007). In fact, financial stressors have been found to be associated with marital satisfaction and stability (Kerkmann, Lee, Lown, & Allgood, 2000). For instance, financially-satisfied couples tend to report higher levels of marital satisfaction; however, this correlation decreases when the number of financial stressors increases (Archuleta, Britt, Tonn, & Grable, 2011). Dakin and Wampler (2008) found that low-income couples face additional economic challenges, such as not being able to procure full-time employment and education. While economic hardships play a role in couple's financial and marital satisfaction, money management and how couples work together when handling financial problems are also important to their relationship satisfaction (Bradbury, Fincham, & Beach, 2000).

Financial concerns have risen given the recent recession (Boveda & Metz, 2016), the increased instability of the global market (Stiglitz, 2010), and decreases in social security (Vernon, 2013). Additionally, Riffkin (2014) reported that the actual age of retirement has increased from 59 to 62. Even if one can afford to retire, many do not, given the changes in social security benefits, which require one to be 65 to receive full benefits. Consequently, many older adults have decided to remain in the workforce (Ensinger, 2010), and may continue to do so as age requirements keep extending, and workers born after 1960 will have to wait until age 67 (Social Security Administration, n.d.). Overall, older adults are concerned about whether or not they will have enough retirement income assets to last them over the years, a trend that began even before the housing market recession. Specifically, in 2002, 54% worried they would not have enough money to retire, and this grew to 66% in 2017 (Pew, 2012).

Money and the couple relationship Shapiro (2007) suggests that couples' relationships, emotions, and conflict around money are situated within one's life experiences, historical context, family of origin, social class, race, gender, and culture. Therapists can assist the couple in recognizing how their ideas about money influence their interactional patterns (e.g., under- and overfunctioning, keeping secrets). While these experiences are informed by family of origin, they are also inevitably connected to issues of social class. For instance, couples from financially disadvantaged families may internalize cultural discourses that blame and shame individuals, such as "pull oneself up by the bootstraps," "poverty as caused by religious sin or karma," "poor people are lazy," and "wealth comes from our individual effort." Generational differences will determine particular stereotypes linked to each social class identity. These prejudices affect the individual's family of origin and thus have been unknowingly transferred to the couple. Therapists need to explore how these institutional inequalities inform the individual's and couple's relationships to work, money, spending, saving, and financial planning.

Shapiro (2007) recommends using a family financial questionnaire during therapy, which examines each partner's emotions and past experiences with money. For example, (a) How was money discussed in your family? (b) Was money used as a reward, punishment, a tool to get what you need, to add pleasure to life, as an end in itself, and/or as a status symbol? (c) Which of your parents' or grandparents' beliefs about money/work did you keep, and which ones did you reject? (d) What messages from society or other people shape how you think about money? (e) How are your attitudes, feelings, and experiences around money different than or similar to your partner's? In addition, when working with older couples, therapists can explore how money affects their relationship by asking: (a) What have you learned, together, about how to talk about finances over the years? (b) How has your approach and conversations about money changed over time? (c) What works and what does not work for your relationship? (d) How have your financial concerns changed or stayed the same? (e) What financial decisions are imminent for you as a couple, for example, working, retirement, insurance, social security benefits, health concerns, or healthcare? Using this framework, money can serve as a vehicle for understanding the couple dynamics as well as an entrance for intervention.

Financial planning in aging couples   Kim, Gale, Goetz, and Bermúdez (2011) created an intervention for working with couples and financial issues. In this approach, marriage and family therapists collaborate with a financial planner in assisting couples to reduce their financial stress, increase their ability to manage their finances, and improve their couple and family stability (Kim et al., 2011). This intervention was tested on a small sample of couples and found that clients who were hesitant to seek mental health services were more willing to engage in financial planning sessions paired with couple therapy (Kim et al., 2011, p. 237). Given the benefits of combining financial and relational therapy, the use of this intervention can encourage older couples to enter the therapy door, as they tend to be less likely to seek therapeutic services for their relationships.

Retirement

Retirement is becoming understood more as an extended, ongoing process, rather than an abrupt phase or a distinct point (Sterns & McQuown, 2015). Pleau and Shauman (2013) noted that retirees may move in and out of retirement in response to financial demands or changing personal or family needs. Whitaker and Bokemeier's (2018) research revealed that children, the health of spouse, and spousal participation in retirement planning all significantly impact the timing of retirement; thus, the retirement decision-making process is a family issue. Further, Moen, Huang, Plassmann, and Dentinger (2006) suggested that spouses often influence each other's decisions and plans for retiring. For example, they may want to enjoy more leisure time together or feel pressured by the already retired partner. Other scholars have suggested that retirement may not be the "golden years," as some wives are bothered by their husbands' intrusion into their domain (Bushfield, Fitzpatrick, & Vinick, 2008), while other partners are negatively impacted by the increased time together (Kulik, 2001). Rauer and Jensen (2016) discussed potential moderators between retirement and marital quality, including voluntary vs. forced retirement (Wickrama, O'Neal, & Lorenz, 2013), couple's marital history (Zissimopoulos, Karney, & Rauer, 2015), and health declines (Higginbottom, Barling, & Kelloway, 1993). In addition, Rauer and Jensen (2016) suggested that couples may experience enhanced marital quality if their spouse retires from a stressful job; conversely, if the partner's job was rewarding, this may add stress to the couple's relationship and adjustment during retirement.

Smith and Moen (1998) investigated the patterns of joint (or synchronized) retirement and its impact on older couple relationships. Generally, joint retirement has been linked to retirement satisfaction (Smith & Moen, 2004) and marital quality (Moen, Kim, & Hofmeister, 2001). However, Davey and Szinovacz (2004) suggested that postretirement marital quality mirrors preretirement marital quality. Therefore, retirement stress was mitigated by the resources and ability of the couple to negotiate the stress and challenges associated with this phase. Moen et al. (2001) found that couples who were retired for two or more years experienced higher marital quality than recent retirees, indicating that with time, couples adjust to this transition. Additionally, Dew and Yorgason (2010) tested three groups of couples in later life: those who were already retired, those in the midst of retirement, and those who continued working. They found that economic stress was not associated with marital conflict for couples who have been retired for a longer period of time, suggesting that financial concerns lessened throughout the transition.

One aspect of retirement is the renegotiation of roles and rules in the marital relationship (Barnes & Parry, 2004). Specifically, household tasks are often renegotiated around transitions such as having children, launching children, changes in health, and retirement. Szinovacz (2000) investigated how timing and gender of the partner shifted household responsibilities for the couple. In this study, both retired husbands and wives spent more time participating in household work postretirement and contributed to each other's chores in their domain. Yet, when husbands retired first, they increased involvement in traditionally considered "women's work," and this continued until wives retired, at which point wives resumed the chores belonging to their gendered domain (Szinovacz, 2000). However, when wives retired first, they increased their participation in the other's domain and did so even past their partner's retirement. These changes and adaptations in household labor were contingent on spouses' gender roles and power structures (Thompson & Walker, 1989).

Family conflict around retirement Oftentimes couples' retirement concerns are situated within the family system. For example, an older couple is seeking therapy for family conflict around decisions regarding whether to retire or continue working and, concerns about asking their youngest son to move out. The couple describes arguments involving the oldest daughter, who believes her younger brother is a financial and emotional burden on her parents. She is demanding that her brother move out, get a job, and start contributing to the care of their parents. The brother believes it is more important for him to stay in the household to take care of his parents than to get a job. The wife/mother sides with the son, as she wants help taking care of her husband and the house, while the husband/father feels that his son is taking advantage of his wife's kindness and should therefore "man up" and get a job.

One way of thinking about this scenario is to understand how the established patterns of the family only allow them to behave within a limited range of possibilities (Minuchin & Fishman, 1981). The family's certainty of the problem maintains the same pattern of interaction (Minuchin, Reiter, & Borda, 2014). Minuchin and Fishman (1981) suggest challenging the family's reality to pursue alternative ways of organizing the system. For instance, therapists can challenge the family's perception through the use of visual representations, such as drawings, to capture how they perceive their relationships at a given moment. This idea is based on the technique of sculpting (Satir & Baldwin, 1983). Therapists guide the couple in depicting each family member during one of their family arguments. In this example, the mom draws herself standing in between her husband and son, with each of them pulling on one of her arms, and she draws the daughter yelling on the sidelines. Dad draws oldest daughter next to him, in support of his position, while he points his finger at son and protects mom with his other arm. Next, the therapist asks questions, such as the following: (a) If you were to retire, how would each of your pictures change and stay the same? (b) In looking at each other's picture, what are other ways in which you could position yourself that might be helpful for your partner? (c) What would you add to your partner's picture that they cannot see? By asking these questions, the therapist encourages each person to think about their role and placement in the system and how they might contribute to the conflict and stalemates that occur in these moments.

Resources for aging couples

The Older American's Act (OAA), a federal agency tasked to advocate for the needs of older adults and their caregivers, was passed and signed into law in 1965. Many programs and services to support the aging population are also available through federal, state, and local governmental initiatives (Wacker & Roberto, 2014). Although such programs exist, these services are often difficult to locate (Kane & Kane, 2005). Therefore, therapists may need to serve as a bridge between clients and these programs to assist aging couples and their families. For example, the National Family Caregiver Support Program (NFCSP) was implemented by the OAA in 2000 to mitigate the associated risks for caregivers. Therapists can inform clients of federal programs, such as the NFCSP, as well as respite care and support groups.

Respite care   Individuals can access respite programs, which provide a temporary, short-term (hours or days), supervisory personal/nursing care break from their duties as a spousal caregiver or custodial grandparent (Roberto & Qualls, 2003). Respite programs allow caregivers to utilize services in their own home, at adult day centers, or in nursing homes. Oftentimes, caregivers seek the support of respite programs during a time of crisis or when they are overburdened by caregiving stress and strain. While these provide short-term relief, they may not have a lasting positive effect on individuals' well-being (Roberto & Qualls, 2003).

Support groups   Both educational and process-orientated support groups have been found useful among family caregivers and custodial grandparents. Educational groups usually offer a presentation or lecture from a professional, while process-orientated support groups allow attendees the time to check in about immediate concerns (Roberto & Qualls, 2003). Overall, support groups can provide caregivers helpful advice and space to deal with feelings of guilt. However, it is important to recognize that support groups are not helpful for everyone, and some individuals believe that attending support groups encourages wallowing in self-pity and, therefore, choose not to participate (Wright, 1993).

Clinical Recommendations and Future Research

We recommend future practitioners and researchers think about aging from an affirming stance to facilitate a perspective that neither negates aging bodies nor mirrors unrealistic and dominant youth-driven narratives. Therefore, scholars and practitioners need to examine their own assumptions and biases regarding aging issues and older couples (Ivey, Wieling, & Harris, 2000). We must ask ourselves: (a) What myths might I hold about aging couples? (b) What am I assuming about these particular clients because of their age or life cycle stage? (c) What messages from family, society, and culture have I accepted as facts about older adults and couples? Recognizing our participation in the outcome of therapy and research, we suggest engaging in an ongoing inner dialogue about how our perceptions influence our work.

Additionally, future researchers need to address how intersectionality shapes the experiences of aging couples, particularly in the areas of race, ethnicity, and social class. Further, scholars can investigate contemporary couple relationships, such as childless couples and dating in later life. Scholars can also address how family conflict affects the older adult couples. Finally, in the age of growing technology, researchers should continue to study how these advancements can assist with interpersonal connections, health, support, and resources for the aging population.

References

Ackerman, D. (1994). *A natural history of love*. New York, NY: Random House.

Addis, S., Davies, M., Greene, G., MacBride-Stewart, S., & Shepherd, M. (2009). The health, social care and housing needs of lesbian, gay, bisexual and transgender older people: A review of the literature. *Health & Social Care in the Community, 17*(6), 647–658.

Agree, E. M., & Hughes, M. E. (2012). Demographic trends and later life families in the 21st century. In R. Blieszner & V. H. Bedford (Eds.), *Handbook of families and aging* (2nd ed., pp. 9–33). Santa Barbara, CA: Praeger.

Allan, C. E., Valkanova, V., & Ebmeier, K. P. (2014). Depression in older people is underdiagnosed. *The Practitioner, 258*, 19–22.

Anderson, H. (2009). Collaborative practice: Relationships and conversations that make a difference. In J. H. Bray & M. Stanton (Eds.), *The Wiley-Blackwell handbook of family psychology* (pp. 300–313). Hoboken, NJ: John Wiley & Sons.

Archuleta, K. L., Britt, S. L., Tonn, T. J., & Grable, J. E. (2011). Financial satisfaction and financial stressors in marital satisfaction. *Psychological Reports, 108*(2), 563–576.

Avis, N., Stellato, R., Crawford, S., Johannes, C., & Longcope, C. (2000). Is there an association between menopause status and sexual functioning? *Menopause, 7*(5), 297–309.

Ball, M. B., Whittington, F. J., Perkins, M. M., Patterson, V. L., Hollingsworth, C., King, S. V., & Combs, B. L. (2000). Quality of life in assisted living facilities: Viewpoints of residents. *Journal of Applied Gerontology, 19*, 304–325.

Barnes, H., & Parry, J. (2004). Renegotiating identity and relationships: Men and women's adjustments to retirement. *Ageing & Society, 24*(2), 213–233.

Beach, M. C., & Inui, T. (2005). Relationship-centered care: A constructive reframing. *Journal of General Internal Medicine, 21*(S1), S3–S8.

Becvar, D. S. (2005). Families in later life: Issues, challenges, and therapeutic responses. In J. L. Lebow (Ed.), *Handbook of clinical family therapy* (pp. 591–609). Hoboken, NJ: John Wiley & Sons.

Becvar, R. J., Canfield, B. S., & Becvar, D. S. (1997). *Group work: Cybernetic, constructivist, and social constructionist perspectives.* Denver, CO: Love Publishing Company.

Beeson, R. A. (2003). Loneliness and depression in spousal caregivers of those with Alzheimer's disease versus non-caregiving spouses. *Archives of Psychiatric Nursing, 17*(3), 135–143.

Benson, J. J., & Coleman, M. (2016). Older adults developing a preference for living apart together. *Journal of Marriage and Family, 78*(3), 797–812.

Berg, I. K., & De Jong, P. (1996). Solution-building conversations: Co-constructing a sense of competence with clients. *Families in Society: The Journal of Contemporary Human Services, 77*(6), 376–391.

Berg, C. A., Wiebe, D. J., Butner, J., Bloor, L., Bradstreet, C., Upchurch, R., ... Patton, G. (2008). Collaborative coping and daily mood in couples dealing with prostate cancer. *Psychology and Aging, 23*(3), 505–516.

Birditt, K. S., Fingerman, K., & Almeida, D. (2005). Age differences in exposure and reactions to interpersonal tensions: A daily diary study. *Psychology and Aging, 20*(2), 330–340.

Birditt, K. S., & Fingerman, K. L. (2005). Do we get better at picking our battles? Age group differences in descriptions of behavioral reactions to interpersonal tensions. *The Journals of Gerontology Series B: Psychological Sciences and Social Sciences, 60*(3), 121–128.

Bohlmeijer, E., Kramer, J., Smit, F., Onrust, S., & Marwjik, H. V. (2009). The effects of integrative reminiscence on depressive symptomatology and mastery of older adults. *Community Mental Health Journal, 45*(6), 476–484.

Bookwala, J. (2012). Marriage and other partnered relationships in middle and late adulthood. In R. Blieszner & V. H. Bedford (Eds.), *Handbook of families and aging* (pp. 91–123). Santa Barbara, CA: Praeger.

Boss, P., & Couden, B. A. (2002). Ambiguous loss from chronic physical illness: Clinical interventions with individuals, couples, and families. *Journal of Clinical Psychology, 58*(11), 1351–1360.

Böszörményi-Nagy, I., & Krasner, B. (1986). *Between give and take: A clinical guide to contextual therapy.* New York, NY: Brunner-Routledge.

Boveda, I., & Metz, A. J. (2016). Predicting end-of-career transitions for baby boomers nearing retirement age. *The Career Development Quarterly, 64*(2), 153–168.

Bradbury, T. N., Fincham, F. D., & Beach, S. R. (2000). Research on the nature and determinants of marital satisfaction: A decade in review. *Journal of Marriage and Family, 62*(4), 964–980.

Brody, E. (1985). Parent care as a normative family stress. *The Gerontologist, 25*, 19–29.

Brown, S. L., & Wright, M. R. (2015). Older adults' attitudes toward cohabitation: Two decades of change. *Journals of Gerontology Series B: Psychological Sciences and Social Sciences, 71*(4), 755–764.

Bulcroft, R. A., & O'Connor, M. (1986). The importance of dating relationships on quality of life for older persons. *Family Relations, 35*(3), 397–401. doi:10.2307/584367

Bushfield, S. Y., Fitzpatrick, T. R., & Vinick, B. H. (2008). Perceptions of "impingement" and marital satisfaction among wives of retired husbands. *Journal of Women & Aging, 20*(3–4), 199–213.

Calasanti, T., & Kiecolt, K. J. (2007). Diversity among late-life couples. *Generations, 31*(3), 10–17.

Carr, D. (2004). The desire to date and remarry among older widows and widowers. *Journal of Marriage and Family, 66*(4), 1051–1068.

Carstensen, L. L., Fung, H. H., & Charles, S. T. (2003). Socioemotional selectivity theory and the regulation of emotion in the second half of life. *Motivation and Emotion, 27*(2), 103–123. doi:10.1023/A:1024569803230

Carstensen, L. L., Gottman, J. M., & Levenson, R. W. (1995). Emotional behavior in long-term marriage. *Psychology and Aging, 10*, 140–149.

Center for Disease Control and Prevention. (2017). *Deaths: Final data for 2015*. Retrieved from https://www.cdc.gov/nchs/data/nvsr/nvsr66/nvsr66_06.pdf

Cheng, S., & Strough, J. (2004). A comparison of collaborative and individual everyday problem solving in younger and older adults. *The International Journal of Aging and Human Development, 58*(3), 167–195.

Cohen, O., Geron, Y., & Farchi, A. (2010). A typology of marital quality of enduring marriages in Israel. *Journal of Family Issues, 31*(6), 727–747.

Conner, K. O., Copeland, V. C., Grote, N. K., Koeske, G., Rosen, D., Reynolds, C. F., & Brown, C. (2010). Mental health treatment seeking among older adults with depression: The impact of stigma and race. *The American Journal of Geriatric Psychiatry, 18*(6), 531–543.

Connidis, I. A. (2010). *Family ties and aging* (2nd ed.). Thousand Oaks, CA: Pine Forge Press.

Connidis, I. A., & McMullin, J. A. (1996). Reasons for and perceptions of childlessness among older persons: Exploring the impact of marital status and gender. *Journal of Aging Studies, 10*(3), 205–222.

Connidis, I. A., & McMullin, J. A. (1999). Permanent childlessness: Perceived advantages and disadvantages among older persons. *Canadian Journal of Aging, 18*(4), 447–465.

Dakin, J., & Wampler, R. (2008). Money doesn't buy happiness, but it helps: Marital satisfaction, psychological distress, and demographic differences between low-and middle-income clinic couples. *The American Journal of Family Therapy, 36*(4), 300–311.

Davey, A., & Szinovacz, M. E. (2004). Dimensions of marital quality and retirement. *Journal of Family Issues, 25*, 431–464.

Davidson, K. (2001). Late life widowhood, selfishness, and new partnership choices: A gendered perspective. *Ageing and Society, 21*(3), 297–317.

Davis, E. M., & Fingerman, K. L. (2015). Digital dating: Online profile content of older and younger adults. *Journals of Gerontology Series B: Psychological Sciences and Social Sciences, 71*(6), 959–967.

de Jong Gierveld, J. (2004). Remarriage, unmarried cohabitation, living apart together: Partner relationships following bereavement or divorce. *Journal of Marriage and Family, 66*(1), 236–243. doi:10.1111/j.0022-2445.2004.00015.x

Dean, L. R., Carroll, J. S., & Yang, C. (2007). Materialism, perceived financial problems, and marital satisfaction. *Family and Consumer Sciences Research Journal, 35*(3), 260–281.

DeLamater, J., Hyde, J. S., & Fong, M. C. (2008). Sexual satisfaction in the seventh decade of life. *Journal of Sex and Marital Therapy, 35*(5), 439–454.

DeLamater, J., & Karraker, A. B. (2009). Sexual functioning in older adults. *Geriatric Disorders, 11*(1), 6–11.

DeLamater, J., & Koepsel, E. (2015). Relationships and sexual expression in later life: A biopsychosocial perspective. *Sexual & Relationship Therapy, 30*(1), 37–59. doi:10.1080/14681 994.2014.939506

DeMaria, R., Weeks, G., & Twist, M. C. (2017). *Focused genograms: Intergenerational assessment of individuals, couples, and families* (2nd ed.). New York, NY: Routledge.

DeOllos, I. Y., & Kapinus, C. A. (2002). Aging childless individuals and couples: Suggestions for new directions in research. *Sociology Inquiry, 72*(1), 72–80.

Dew, J., & Yorgason, J. (2010). Economic pressure and marital conflict in retirement-aged couples. *Journal of Family Issues, 31*(2), 164–188.

Doherty, W. J., & Baird, M. A. (1983). *Family therapy and family medicine: Toward the primary care of families*. New York, NY: Guilford Press.

Doherty, W. J., Baird, M. A., & Becker, L. A. (1987). Family medicine and the biopsychosocial model: The road toward integration. *Marriage & Family Review, 10*(3-4), 51–69.

Elder, G. H., Clipp, E. C., Brown, J. S., Martin, L. R., & Friedman, H. S. (2009). The lifelong mortality risks of World War II experiences. *Research on Aging, 31*(4), 391–412. doi:10.1177/0164027509333447

Ensinger, D. (2010). *More Americans putting off retirement*. Retrieved July 16, 2018, from http://economoyincrisis.org/content/more-americans-putting-off-retirement

Erlanger, M. (1990). Using the genogram with the older client. *Journal of Mental Health Counseling, 12*(3), 321–331.

Family Caregiver Alliance. (2018). *Caregiver statistics: Demographics.* Retrieved from https://www.caregiver.org/caregiver-statistics-demographics

Fisher, L. (2010). *Sex, romance and relationships: AARP survey of midlife and older adults.* Retrieved from https://assets.aarp.org/rgcenter/general/srr_09.pdf

Flemons, D. (2002). *Of one mind: The logic of hypnosis, the practice of therapy.* New York, NY: W. W. Norton.

Franks, M. M., Wendorf, C. A., Gonzalez, R., & Ketterer, M. (2004). Aid and influence: Health-promoting exchanges of older married partners. *Journal of Social and Personal Relationships, 21*(4), 431–445.

Fredriksen-Goldsen, K. I., Kim, H. J., Bryan, A. E., Shiu, C., & Emlet, C. A. (2017). The cascading effects of marginalization and pathways of resilience in attaining good health among LGBT older adults. *The Gerontologist, 57*(suppl_1), S72–S83.

Gallagher-Thompson, D., Dal Canto, P. G., Jacob, T., & Thompson, L. W. (2001). A comparison of marital interaction patterns between couples in which the husband does or does not have Alzheimer's disease. *The Journals of Gerontology Series B: Psychological Sciences and Social Sciences, 56*(3), S140–S150.

Gehart, D., & McCollum, E. E. (2008). Inviting therapeutic presence: A mindfulness-based approach. In S. F. Hick & T. Bien (Eds.), *Mindfulness and the therapeutic relationship* (pp. 176–194). New York, NY: Guilford.

Gergen, K. J., McNamee, S., & Barrett, F. J. (2001). Toward transformative dialogue. *International Journal of Public Administration, 24*(7-8), 679–707.

Gladstone, J. (1995). The marital perceptions of elderly persons living or having a spouse living in a long-term care institution in Canada. *The Gerontologist, 35*, 52–60.

Haber, D. (2006). Life review: Implementation, theory, research, and therapy. *International Journal of Aging & Human Development, 63*(2), 153–171.

Hasin, D. S., Goodwin, R. D., Stinson, F. S., & Grant, B. F. (2005). Epidemiology of major depressive disorder: Results from the National Epidemiologic Survey on Alcoholism and Related Conditions. *Archives of General Psychiatry, 62*(10), 1097–1106.

Haynes, S. N., Floyd, F. J., Lemsky, C., Rogers, E., Winemiller, D., Heilman, N., … Cardone, L. (1992). The marital satisfaction questionnaire for older persons. *Psychological Assessment, 4*(4), 473–482. doi:10.1037/1040-3590.4.4.473

Heiman, J., Long, J., Smith, S., Fisher, W., Sand, S., & Rosen, R. (2011). Sexual satisfaction and relationship happiness in midlife and older couples in five countries. *Archives of Sexual Behavior, 40*, 741–753.

Henry, N. M., Berg, C. A., Smith, T. W., & Florsheim, P. (2007). Positive and negative characteristics of marital interaction and their association with marital satisfaction in middle-aged and older couples. *Psychology and Aging, 22*(3), 428–441. doi:10.1037/0882-7974.22.3.428

Hibel, J., & Polanco, M. (2010). Tuning the ear: Listening in narrative therapy. *Journal of Systemic Therapies, 29*(1), 51–66.

Higginbottom, S. F., Barling, J., & Kelloway, E. K. (1993). Linking retirement experiences and marital satisfaction: A mediational model. *Psychology and Aging, 8*(4), 508.

Hirschfeld, M., & Wikler, D. (2003). An ethics perspective on family caregiving worldwide: Justice and society's obligations. *Generations, 27*(4), 56–60.

Hirschman, K. B., Joyce, C. M., James, B. D., Xie, S. X., & Karlawish, J. H. (2005). Do Alzheimer's disease patients want to participate in a treatment decision, and would their caregivers let them? *The Gerontologist, 45*(3), 381–388.

Hodgson, J., Lamson, A., Mendenhall, T., & Crane, D. R. (2014). *Medical family therapy.* New York, NY: Springer.

Ingersoll-Dayton, B., Spencer, B., Campbell, R., Kurokowa, Y., & Ito, M. (2016). Creating a duet: The couples life story approach in the United States and Japan. *Dementia, 15*(4), 481–493.

Ivey, D. C., Wieling, E., & Harris, S. M. (2000). Save the young—The elderly have lived their lives: Ageism in marriage and family therapy. *Family Process, 39*(2), 163–175.

Kane, R. L., & Kane, R. A. (2005). Long term care. In M. L. Johnson (Ed.), *The Cambridge handbook of age and ageing*. Cambridge, UK: Cambridge University Press.

Karel, M. J., Gatz, M., & Smyer, M. A. (2012). Aging and mental health in the decade ahead: What psychologists need to know. *American Psychologist, 67*, 184–198. doi:10.1037/a0025393

Karlsson, S. G., & Borell, K. (2002). Intimacy and autonomy, gender and ageing: Living apart together. *Ageing International, 27*(4), 11–26.

Kemp, C. L. (2008). Negotiating transitions in later life: Married couples in assisted living. *Journal of Applied Gerontology, 27*, 231–251. doi:10.1177/0733464807311656

Kerkmann, B. C., Lee, T. R., Lown, J. M., & Allgood, S. M. (2000). Financial management, financial problems and marital satisfaction among recently married university students. *Journal of Financial Counseling and Planning, 11*(2), 55.

Kiecolt-Glaser, J. K., & Newton, T. L. (2001). Marriage and health: His and hers. *Psychological Bulletin, 127*(4), 472–503. doi:10.1037/0033-2909.127.4.472

Kim, J. H., Gale, J., Goetz, J., & Bermúdez, J. M. (2011). Relational financial therapy: An innovative and collaborative treatment approach. *Contemporary Family Therapy, 33*(3), 229–241.

Kimmel, D. C., Hinrichs, K. M., & Fisher, L. D. (2015). Understanding lesbian, gay, bisexual, and transgender older adults. In P. A. Lichtenberg, B. T. Mast, B. D. Carpenter, J. Loebach Wetherell, P. A. Lichtenberg, B. T. Mast, et al. (Eds.), *APA and book of clinical geropsychology, Vol. 1:History and status of the field and perspectives on aging* (pp. 459–472). Washington, DC: American Psychological Association. doi:10.1037/14458-019

Kitwood, T. M. (1997). *Dementia reconsidered: The person comes first*. Berkshire, UK: Open University Press.

Kleinplatz, P. J. (2013). *New directions in sex therapy: Innovations and alternatives*. New York, NY: Routledge.

Knight, B.G. (2009). *Psychotherapy and older adults resource guide*. Retrieved February 8, 2018, from http://www.apa.org/pi/aging/resources/guides/psychotherapy.aspx

Knight, B. G., & Lee, L. O. (2008). Contextual adult lifespan theory for adapting psychotherapy. In K. Laidlaw & B. Knight (Eds.), *Handbook of emotional disorders in later life: Assessment and treatment* (pp. 59–88). New York, NY: Oxford University Press.

Koch, P. B., Mansfield, P. K., Thurau, D., & Carey, M. (2005). "Feeling frumpy": The relationship between body image and sexual response changes in midlife women. *Journal of Sex Research, 42*(3), 215–223.

Koren, C. (2015). The intertwining of second couplehood and old age. *Ageing & Society, 35*(9), 1864–1888. doi:10.1017/S0144686X14000294

Kulik, L. (2001). The impact of men's and women's retirement on marital relations: A comparative analysis. *Journal of Women & Aging, 13*(2), 21–37.

Lachance-Grzela, M., & Bouchard, G. (2010). Why do women do the lion's share of housework? A decade of research. *Sex Roles, 63*(11-12), 767–780.

Lambert-Shute, J., & Fruhauf, C. A. (2011). Aging issues: Unanswered questions in marital and family therapy literature. *Journal of Marital and Family Therapy, 37*(1), 27–36.

Landis, M., Peter-Wright, M., Martin, M., & Bodenmann, G. (2013). Dyadic coping and marital satisfaction of older spouses in long-term marriage. *The Journal of Gerontopsychology and Geriatric Psychiatry, 26*(1), 39–47.

Larner, W. (2000). Neo-liberalism: Policy, ideology, governmentality. *Studies in Political Economy, 63*(1), 5–25.

Lauer, R. H., & Lauer, J. C. (1986). Factors in long-term marriages. *Journal of Family Issues, 7*(4), 382–390.

Laumann, E. O., Nicolosi, A., Glasser, D. B., Paik, A., Gingell, C., Moreira, E., & Wang, T. (2005). Sexual problems among women and men aged 40-80 y: Prevalence and correlates identified in the Global Study of Sexual Attitudes and Behaviors. *International Journal of Impotence Research, 17*(1), 39–57.

Lindau, S. T., Schumm, L. P., Laumann, E. O., Levinson, W., O'Muircheartaigh, C. A., & Waite, L. J. (2007). A study of sexuality and health among older adults in the United States. *The New England Journal of Medicine, 357*(8), 762–774.

Lodge, A. C., & Umberson, D. (2012). All shook up: Sexuality of mid- to later life married couples. *Journal of Marriage & Family, 74*(3), 428–443. doi:10.1111/j.1741-3737. 2012.00969.x

Markowitz, L. (1997). The cultural context of intimacy: Helping couples face issues of race, class, sexual orientation and culture in the consulting room. *Family Therapy Networker, 21*, 50–61.

Marterella, M. K., & Brock, L. J. (2008). Religion and spirituality as a resource in marital and family therapy. *Journal of Family Psychotherapy, 19*(4), 330–344.

McCoy, A., Rauer, A., & Sabey, A. (2017). The meta marriage: Links between older couples' relationship narratives and marital satisfaction. *Family Process, 56*(4), 900–914. doi:10.1111/famp.12217

McDaniel, S. H., Campbell, T. L., & Seaburn, D. B. (1995). Principles for collaboration between health and mental health providers in primary care. *Family Systems Medicine, 13*(3-4), 283.

McNamee, S. (2009). Postmodern psychotherapeutic ethics: Relational responsibility in practice. *Human Systems: The Journal of Therapy, Consultation & Training, 20*(1), 57–71.

McWilliams, S., & Barrett, A. E. (2014). Online dating in middle and later life: Gendered expectations and experiences. *Journal of Family Issues, 35*(3), 411–436. doi:10.1177/019 2513X12468437

Miller, R. B., Hemesath, D., & Nelson, B. (1997). Marriage in middle and later life. In T. D. Hargrave & S. M. Hanna (Eds.), *The aging family* (pp. 178–198). New York, NY: Brunner/Mazel.

Miller, S. D., Duncan, B. L., & Hubble, M. A. (1997). Escape from Babel: Toward a unifying language for psychotherapy practice. *Adolescence, 32*(125), 247.

Minuchin, S., & Fishman, H. C. (1981). *Family therapy techniques.* Cambridge, MA: Harvard University Press.

Minuchin, S., Reiter, M. D., & Borda, C. (2014). *The craft of family therapy: Challenging certainties.* New York, NY: Routledge.

Moen, P., Huang, Q., Plassmann, V., & Dentinger, E. (2006). Deciding the future: Do dual-earner couples plan together for retirement? *American Behavioral Scientist, 49*(10), 1422–1443. doi:10.1177/0002764206286563

Moen, P., Kim, J. E., & Hofmeister, H. (2001). Couples' work/retirement transitions, gender, and marital quality. *Social Psychology Quarterly, 64*, 55–71.

Monin, J., Doyle, M., Levy, B., Schulz, R., Fried, T., & Kershaw, T. (2016). Spousal associations between frailty and depressive symptoms: Longitudinal findings from the cardiovascular health study. *Journal of the American Geriatrics Society, 64*(4), 824–830.

Moon, H., & Adams, K. B. (2013). The effectiveness of dyadic interventions for people with dementia and their caregivers. *Dementia, 12*(6), 821–839.

Moreno-John, G., Gachie, A., Fleming, C. M., Napoles-Springer, A., Mutran, E., Manson, S. M., & Pérez-Stable, E. J. (2004). Ethnic minority older adults participating in clinical research. *Journal of Aging and Health, 16*(5_suppl), 93S–123S.

Morgan, L. A., Eckert, K., Piggee, T., & Frankowski, A. C. (2006). Two lives in transition: Agency and context for assisted living residents. *Journal of Aging Studies, 20*(2), 123–132.

Murray, S. (2018). Heterosexual men's sexual desire: Supported by, or deviating from, traditional masculinity norms and sexual scripts? *Sex Roles, 78*(1/2), 130–141. doi:10.1007/s11199-017-0766-7

National Alliance on Mental Illness. (2009). *Depression in older persons*. Retrieved July 16, 2018, from https://www.ncoa.org/wp-content/uploads/Depression_Older_Persons_ FactSheet_2009.pdf

Neugebauer-Visano, R. (1995). Seniors and sexuality? Confronting cultural contradictions. In R. Neugebauer-Visano (Ed.), *Seniors and sexuality: Experiencing intimacy in later life* (pp. 17–34). Toronto, ON: Canadian Scholars' Press.

O'Connell, M., & Feliz, S. (2011). *Same-sex couple household statistics from the 2010 census. Social, economic and housing statistics division* (working paper 2011–2026).

O'Hanlon, B. (2018). Come again? From possibility therapy to sex therapy. In D. Flemons & S. Green (Eds.), *Quickies: The handbook of brief sex therapy* (pp. 1–14). New York, NY: W. W. Norton.

Ortman, J. M., Velkoff, V. A., & Hogan, H. (2014). *An aging nation: The older population in the United States* (pp. 25–1140). United States Census Bureau, Economics and Statistics Administration, US Department of Commerce.

Peter-Wright, M., & Martin, M. (2011). When 2 is better than 1 + 1: Older spouses' individual and dyadic problem solving. *European Psychologist, 16*, 288–294.

Pew Research Center. (2012). *More Americans worry about financing retirement*. Retrieved April 12, 2018, from http://www.pewsocialtrends.org/2012/10/22/more-americans-worry-about-financing-retirement/

Pew Research Center. (2014). *Chapter 2: The demographics of remarriage*. Retrieved April 25, 2018, from http://www.pewsocialtrends.org/2014/11/14/chapter-2-the-demographics-of-remarriage/

Pew Research Center. (2017). *Number of U.S. adults cohabiting with a partner continues to rise, especially among those 50 and older*. Retrieved April 25, 2018, from http://www.pewresearch.org/fact-tank/2017/04/06/number-of-u-s-adults-cohabiting-with-a-partner-continues-to-rise-especially-among-those-50-and-older/

Pinquart, M., & Sörensen, S. (2011). Spouses, adult children, and children-in-law as caregivers of older adults: A meta-analytic comparison. *Psychology and Aging, 26*(1), 1–14.

Pleau, R., & Shauman, K. (2013). Trends and correlates of post-retirement employment, 1977–2009. *Human Relations, 66*(1), 113–141.

Raley, R. K., Sweeney, M. M., & Wondra, D. (2015). The growing racial and ethnic divide in US marriage patterns. *The Future of Children, 25*(2), 89–109.

Rauer, A., & Jensen, J. F. (2016). These happy golden years? The role of retirement in marital quality. In J. Bookwala (Ed.), *Couple relationships in the middle and late years: Their nature, complexity, and role in health and illness* (pp. 157–176). Washington, DC: American Psychological Association.

Ray, M. (2016). Person-centered care and dementia. In C. A. Chew-Graham & M. Ray (Eds.), *Mental health and older people: A guide for primary care practitioners* (pp. 219–228). New York, NY: Springer.

Reinardy, J. R., & Kane, R. A. (2003). Anatomy of a choice: Deciding on assisted living or nursing home care in Oregon. *Journal of Applied Gerontology, 22*(1), 152–174.

Riffkin, R. (2014). *Average U.S. retirement age rises to 62*. Retrieved July 16, 2018, from https://news.gallup.com/poll/168707/average-retirement-age-rises.aspx

Robb, C., Haley, W. E., Becker, M. A., Polivka, L. A., & Chwa, H. J. (2003). Attitudes towards mental health care in younger and older adults: Similarities and differences. *Aging & Mental Health, 7*(2), 142–152.

Roberto, K. A., Gold, D. T., & Yorgason, J. B. (2004). The influence of osteoporosis on the marital relationship of older couples. *Journal of Applied Gerontology, 23*(4), 443–456. doi:10.1177/0733464804270856

Roberto, K. A., & Qualls, S. H. (2003). Intervention strategies for grandparents raising grandchildren: Lessons learned from the caregiving literature. In B. Hayslip, Jr. & J. H. Patrick (Eds.), *Working with custodial grandparents* (pp. 13–26). New York, NY: Springer.

Robles, T. F., Slatcher, R. B., Trombello, J. M., & McGinn, M. M. (2014). Marital quality and health: A meta-analytic review. *Psychological Bulletin, 140*(1), 1–80.

Rozanova, J. (2010). Discourse of successful aging in The Globe & Mail: Insights from critical gerontology. *Journal of Aging Studies, 24*(4), 213–222.

Sandberg, J. G., Miller, R. B., & Harper, J. M. (2002). A qualitative study of marital process and depression in older couples. *Family Relations, 51*(3), 256–264.

Sandberg, L. (2013). Affirmative old age-the ageing body and feminist theories on difference. *International Journal of Ageing and Later Life, 8*(1), 11–40.

Satir, V., & Baldwin, M. (1983). *Satir step by step: A guide to creating change in families.* Palo Alto, CA: Science and Behavior Books.

Scherrer, K., Ingersoll-Dayton, B., & Spencer, B. (2014). Constructing couples' stories: Narrative practice insights from a dyadic dementia intervention. *Clinical Social Work Journal, 42*(1), 90–100. doi:10.1007/s10615-013-0440-7

Segal, D. L., Coolidge, F. L., Mincic, M. S., & O'riley, A. (2005). Beliefs about mental illness and willingness to seek help: A cross-sectional study. *Aging & Mental Health, 9*(4), 363–367.

Shapiro, M. (2007). Money: A therapeutic tool for couples therapy. *Family Process, 46*(3), 279–291.

Simonelli, C., Tripodi, F., Rossi, R., Fabrizi, A., Lembo, D., Cosmi, V., & Pierleoni, L. (2008). The influence of caregiver burden on sexual intimacy and marital satisfaction in couples with an Alzheimer spouse. *International Journal of Clinical Practice, 62*(1), 47–52.

Smith, D. B., & Moen, P. (1998). Spousal influence on retirement: His, her, and their perceptions. *Journal of Marriage and the Family, 60,* 734–744.

Smith, D. B., & Moen, P. (2004). Retirement satisfaction for retirees and their spouses: Do gender and the retirement decision-making process matter? *Journal of Family Issues, 25,* 262–285.

Smith, T. W., Berg, C. A., Florsheim, P., Uchino, B. N., Pearce, G., Hawkins, M., ... Olsen-Cerny, C. (2009). Conflict and collaboration in middle-aged and older couples: I. Age differences in agency and communion during marital interaction. *Psychology and Aging, 24*(2), 259–273. doi:10.1037/a0015609

Social Security Administration. (n.d.). *Full retirement age: If you were born between 1943 and 1954.* Retrieved July 16, 2018, from https://www.socialsecurity.gov/planners/retire.1943.html

Sorkin, D. H., Murphy, M., Nguyen, H., & Biegler, K. A. (2016). Barriers to mental health care for an ethnically and racially diverse sample of older adults. *Journal of the American Geriatrics Society, 64*(10), 2138–2143.

Spanier, G. B. (1976). Measuring dyadic adjustment: New scales for assessing the quality of marriage and similar dyads. *Journal of Marriage and the Family, 38*(1), 15–28. doi:10.2307/350547

Sterns, H. L., & McQuown, C. K. (2015). Retirement redefined. In P. A. Lichtenberg, B. T. Mast, B. D. Carpenter, & J. Loebach Wetherell (Eds.), *APA handbook of clinical geropsychology, Vol. 2: Assessment, treatment, and issues of later life* (pp. 601–616). Washington, DC: American Psychological Association. doi:10.1037/14459-023

Stiglitz, J. E. (2010). *Freefall: America, free markets, and the sinking of the world economy.* Chicago, IL: W.W. Norton.

Strohm, C. Q., Seltzer, J. A., Cochran, S. D., & Mays, V. M. (2009). "Living apart together" relationships in the United States. *Demographic Research, 21,* 177–214.

Substance Abuse and Mental Health Services Administration. (2014). *Receipt of services for behavioral health problems: Results from the 2014 national survey on drug use and health.* Retrieved July 16, 2018, from https://www.samhsa.gov/data/sites/default/files/NSDUH-DR-FRR3-2014/NSDUH-DR-FRR3-2014/NSDUH-DR-FRR3-2014.pdf

Swainson, M., & Tasker, F. (2005). Genograms redrawn: Lesbian couples define their families. *Journal of GLBT Family Studies, 1*(2), 3–27.

Sweeney, M. M. (2010). Remarriage and stepfamilies: Strategic sites for family scholarship in the 21st century. *Journal of Marriage and Family, 72*(3), 667–684.

Szinovacz, M. E. (2000). Changes in housework after retirement: A panel analysis. *Journal of Marriage and the Family, 62*, 78–92.

Talbott, M. M. (1998). Older widows' attitudes towards men and remarriage. *Journal of Aging Studies, 12*(4), 429–449. doi:10.1016/S0890-4065(98)90028-7

Taylor, A., & Gosney, M. A. (2011). Sexuality in older age: Essential considerations for healthcare professionals. *Age and Ageing, 40*(5), 538–543.

Thomas, M. L., Kaufmann, C. N., Palmer, B. W., Depp, C. A., Martin, A. S., Glorioso, D. K., … Jeste, D. V. (2016). Paradoxical trend for improvement in mental health with aging: A community-based study of 1,546 adults aged 21–100 years. *The Journal of Clinical Psychiatry, 77*(8), e1019.

Thompson, L., & Walker, A. J. (1989). Gender in families: Women and men in marriage, work, and parenthood. *Journal of Marriage and the Family*, 845–871.

Thornton, A., & Young-DeMarco, L. (2001). Four decades of trends in attitudes toward family issues in the United States: The 1960s through 1990s. *Journal of Marriage and Family, 63*(4), 1009–1037.

Tiefer, L. (2004). *Sex is not a natural act and other essays* (2nd ed.). Boulder, CO: Westview Press.

Tomm, K. (1987). Interventive interviewing: Part II. Reflexive questioning as a means to enable self-healing. *Family Process, 26*(2), 167–183.

Tower, R. B., & Kasl, S. V. (1995). Depressive symptoms across older spouses and the moderating effect of marital closeness. *Psychology and Aging, 10*(4), 625–638.

US Department of Health and Human Services: Administration on Aging. (2001). *Older adults and mental health: Issues and opportunities.* Retrieved July 16, 2018, from https://www.public-health.uiowa.edu/icmha/training/documents/Older-Adults-and-Mental-Health-2001.pdf

United States Census Bureau. (2017). *Childlessness rises for women in their early 30s.* Retrieved from https://www.census.gov/newsroom/blogs/random-samplings/2017/05/childlessness_rises.html

United States Census Bureau. (2018). *Race, ethnicity and marriage in the United States.* Retrieved from https://www.census.gov/library/stories/2018/07/interracial-marriages.html

Upton-Davis, K. (2012). Living apart together relationships (LAT): Severing intimacy from obligation. *Gender Issues, 29*(1-4), 25–38.

Ussher, J. M., Perz, J., & Parton, C. (2015). Sex and the menopausal woman: A critical review and analysis. *Feminism and Psychology, 25*(4), 449–468. doi:10.1177/0959353515579735

Vernon, S. (2013). *Will social security run out of money?* Retrieved July 16, 2018, from https://www.cbsnews.com/news/will-social-security-run-out-of-money/

Vespa, J. (2012). Union formation in later life: Economic determinants of cohabitation and remarriage among older adults. *Demography, 49*(3), 1103–1125. doi:10.1007/s13524-012-0102-3

Wacker, R. R., & Roberto, K. A. (2014). *Community resources for older adults: Programs and services in an era of change* (4th ed.). Thousand Oaks, CA: Sage.

Waite, L. J., Laumann, E. O., Das, A., & Schumm, L. P. (2009). Sexuality: Measures of partnerships, practices, attitudes, and problems in the National Social Life, Health, and Aging Study. *Journals of Gerontology Series B: Psychological Sciences and Social Sciences, 64*(suppl_1), i56–i66.

Warner, D. F., & Brown, T. H. (2011). Understanding how race/ethnicity and gender define age-trajectories of disability: An intersectionality approach. *Social Science & Medicine, 72*(8), 1236–1248.

Weingarten, K. (2010). Reasonable hope: Construct, clinical applications, and supports. *Family Process, 49*(1), 5–25.

Weingarten, K. (2013). The "cruel radiance of what is": Helping couples live with chronic illness. *Family Process, 52*(1), 83–101.

Weishaus, S., & Field, D. (1988). A half century of marriage: Continuity or change? *Journal of Marriage and the Family*, 763–774.

Wenger, G. C., Dykstra, P. A., Melkas, T., & Knipscheer, K. C. (2007). Social embeddedness and late-life parenthood: Community activity, close ties, and support networks. *Journal of Family Issues, 28*(11), 1419–1456.

West, L. A., Cole, S., Goodkind, D., & He, W. (2014). *65+ in the United States*. Washington, DC: US Government Printing Office. Retrieved from https://www.commongroundhealth. org/Media/Default/documents/Senior%20Health/2010%20Census%20 Report_%2065-lowest_Part1.pdf

Whisman, M. A., & Uebelacker, L. A. (2009). Prospective associations between marital discord and depressive symptoms in middle-aged and older adults. *Psychology and Aging, 24*(1), 184–189. doi:10.1037/a0014759

Whitaker, E. A., & Bokemeier, J. L. (2018). Spousal, family and gender effects on expected retirement age for married pre-retirees. *Journal of Family and Economic Issues, 9*(1), 1–15.

White, M., & Epston, D. (1990). *Narrative means to therapeutic ends*. New York, NY: W. W. Norton.

Whitlatch, C. J., Judge, K., Zarit, S. H., & Femia, E. (2006). Dyadic intervention for family caregivers and care receivers in early-stage dementia. *The Gerontologist, 46*(5), 688–694.

Wickrama, K. A. S., O'Neal, C. W., & Lorenz, F. O. (2013). Marital functioning from middle to later years: A life course–stress process framework. *Journal of Family Theory & Review, 5*(1), 15–34.

World Health Organization. (2017). *Mental health of older adults*. Retrieved July 16, 2018, from http://www.who.int/news-room/fact-sheets/detail/mental-health-of-older-adults

Wright, L. K. (1993). *Alzheimer's disease and marriage*. Newbery Park, CA: Sage.

Wright, L. M., & Bell, J. M. (2009). *Beliefs and illness: A model for healing*. Calgary, AB: 4th Floor Press.

Wright, M. R., & Brown, S. L. (2017). Psychological well-being among older adults: The role of partnership status. *Journal of Marriage and Family, 79*(3), 833–849.

Yao, L., & Robert, S. A. (2008). The contributions of race, individual socioeconomic status, and neighborhood socioeconomic context on the self-rated health trajectories and mortality of older adults. *Research on Aging, 30*(2), 251–273.

Yorgason, J. B., Piercy, F. P., & Piercy, S. K. (2007). Acquired hearing impairment in older couple relationships: An exploration of couple resilience processes. *Journal of Aging Studies, 21*(3), 215–228.

Zissimopoulos, J. M., Karney, B. R., & Rauer, A. J. (2015). Marriage and economic well-being at older ages. *Review of Economics of the Household, 13*(1), 1–35.

20

Clinical Work with Unpartnered Individuals Seeking a Long-Term Intimate Relationship

Jeffrey B. Jackson and Nicole Sabatini Gutierrez

Research indicates that rates of singlehood and loneliness have steadily increased over the last several decades (Cacioppo & Patrick, 2008; US Census Bureau, 2017a). Although there are multiple pathways to adult singlehood, they can typically be characterized as one of the following primary pathways: *design* (unpartnered by choice), *delay* (not yet having been in a desired committed long-term couple relationship), *divorce* (unpartnered by separation or divorce), and *death* (widowed; Landgraf, 1990). The percentage of American adults who are unmarried has increased from 31% in the 1950s to 45% today, and of these, 14% are widowed, 23% are divorced, and 63% have not yet ever married (US Census Bureau, 2017a). Slightly more unmarried American adults are women (53%), with the ratio being approximately 9 unmarried American adult men for every 10 unmarried American adult women (US Census Bureau, 2017a). Relatedly, the percent of American adults who live alone has increased from 17% in 1970 to 27% in the latest census (US Census Bureau, 2017b).

Whereas the percentage of unmarried American adults who are divorced or widowed has remained relatively stable over the last three decades, the percentage of married American adults has decreased, and the percentage of unmarried American adults who have never married has increased over the same period of time. Although a part of this trend is explained by increased rates of cohabitation, even after taking cohabitation into account, rates of singlehood are still on the rise (Jackson, 2018). In fact, 42% of American adults do not live with a partner or a spouse (Fry, 2017). Not only are rates of singlehood increasing, but given that the average age at first marriage has also steadily increased from 21.5 in the 1950s to 28.5 in 2017 (US Census Bureau, 2017b), people are increasingly single longer. Some research suggests that similar trends are happening globally with regard to increased rates of singlehood (Santos, Varnum, & Grossmann, 2017), including Africa (Shapiro & Gebreselassie, 2014), Asia (Jones & Yeung, 2014), Europe (Bellani, Esping-Andersen, & Nedoluzhko, 2017; Fokkema & Liefbroer, 2008), and Latin and South America (Laplante, Castro-Martín, Cortina, & Martín-García, 2015).

The Handbook of Systemic Family Therapy: Volume 3, First Edition.
Edited by Karen S. Wampler and Adrian J. Blow.
© 2020 John Wiley & Sons Ltd. Published 2020 by John Wiley & Sons Ltd.

Possible explanations for the increase in singlehood include societal shifts toward valuing independence, self-fulfillment, and personal growth; societal shifts in the institution of marriage with an emphasis on companionship, individualism, and consumerism; increased expectations from partners; limited or poor partner choices; delayed adulthood; career development; education priorities; and economic conditions (Cherlin, 2004; Cox, 2006; Doherty, 2000; Lee & Payne, 2010; Lewis, 1994; Prabhakar, 2011; Vespa, 2017). It is important to emphasize that being single does not necessarily equate to being alone (e.g., children, roommates, family, friends) nor does it equate to feeling lonely or distressed (Cacioppo & Patrick, 2008; DePaulo & Morris, 2005).

Whereas singlehood is more and more common and lasting longer, the majority of Americans (53–58%) indicate they aspire to marry someday, with about one-third (27–32%) reporting they are unsure if they want to marry and about one-seventh (13–14%) reporting that they definitely do not want to marry (Parker & Stepler, 2017; Wang & Parker, 2014); even though these statistics are based on desire to marry instead of desire to be in a committed intimate relationship, it follows that there are many people who are single and wish they were coupled. Because people who are single yet desire to be coupled may experience distress, some of these people may seek therapy specifically for distress related to relationship status, and others may seek therapy for other issues and relationship status may or may not become an area of clinical focus.

Why address singlehood in a volume on couple therapy? Relational therapists are particularly qualified to work with clients who experience singlehood distress because people who are distressed about being unpartnered may intentionally seek out relational therapists for help understanding why they are single, if there is something wrong with their ability to engage in and navigate romantic relationships (e.g., process breakups, identify reasons behind patterns of failed relationships, evaluate readiness to date again), if there is something about them that makes them less desirable to potential partners, why they are attracted to the types of people who tend to not make for the type of relationship they want, and whether they should move forward with a current romantic relationship (Jackson, 2018; Lewis, 1994; Lewis & Moon, 1997). In this chapter, we provide a brief overview of the singlehood literature, frameworks for conceptualizing singlehood, and considerations for the treatment of singlehood.

Language

It is important for therapists to use terminology that is sensitive, inclusionary, accurate, descriptive, and concise to refer to groups of people who are often labeled and marginalized. For example, people who are unmarried and are widowed, people who are unmarried and have partners, and people who are unmarried and have children may not self-identify as being *single* (US Census Bureau, 2018). When discussing people who are single, the relevant terminology tends to endorse a deficit perspective: *never married* (lacking marriage), *divorced* (lacking marriage and the former spouse), and widowed (lacking marriage and the deceased spouse). Even attempts at less deficit terminology such as *always single* (Lewis, 1994) as an alternative to *never married* might connote that a person who has been single will always remain single. The term *married* also carries bias, as some people in committed intimate relationships may not choose marry, and only until recently, as a result of the marriage equality movement, can same-sex partners choose to marry in the United States.

Person-first language (e.g., *women who are single* instead of *single women*) can be helpful in affirming that personhood precedes an aspect of a person's life. In the absence of accepted affirming terms, we use the terms *single, singlehood,* and *unpartnered* in this chapter to refer to people who are not in committed romantic relationships. We recommend that therapists pay attention to how clients talk about singlehood, ask clients how they would like the therapist to talk about their singlehood, and assist clients in identifying preferred language that is more empowering and more accurately describes their lived experiences.

Relevant Literature

Reasons for desiring committed romantic relationships

Internal and external motivations for partnering provide some context as to why adults are likely to desire being in a committed intimate relationship. Internal and external motivations for partnering also explain why adults experiencing prolonged singlehood may experience pain, sadness, and loneliness because they desire to be partnered but are not presently partnered.

Internal motivations   According to attachment theory, one of the primary internal motivations for seeking out committed romantic relationships is adults typically desire forming committed romantic relationships with other adults, which is discussed more fully in the section in this chapter on attachment theory for conceptualizing singlehood. There are also time-sensitive motivators such as expectations around desired age for committed intimate relationships and having children (Berliner, Jacob, & Schwartzberg, 2011). Even though there can be variation, the longer adults continue in singlehood beyond their desired age for committed couplehood, the more likely they are to experience distress regarding singlehood (Jackson, 2018). For example, a person hoping to couple in their early 30s will likely not experience much distress about being single in their early 20s. As they approach their early 30s, if they are not in a committed intimate relationship, they will likely experience some level of distress about their relationship status. As they pass their expected age for coupling, the distress will likely increase, especially if most of their peer group is coupled. This trend typically continues until people reach an age in which they no longer have an expectation of partnering (Jackson, 2018). In terms of time sensitivity of having children, the more obvious internal pressure is having biological children among women. However, adults, regardless of assigned sex or gender identification, who desire having children are similarly likely to have expectations around the timing of having children. The more time that elapses without committed partnering beyond the expected timeframe for having children, the more internal pressure they may feel to partner. Social external pressures against intentional single parenting also increase the amount of internal motivation around partnering within a certain timeframe. Finally, economic stability, religious reasons, a rite of passage to advance to next stage of life, and avoiding family-of-origin problems can serve as other internal motivators for partnering (Aldous & Ganey, 1999; Berliner et al., 2011).

External motivations Coupling, especially marriage, is in line with social norms that can be a powerful external motivator for wanting and seeking committed intimate relationships (DePaulo & Morris, 2005). Concerns and pressures from family members and friends to couple and have children (if the person does not already have children) are common external motivations for partnering (Lee & Payne, 2010). These external motivations for seeking committed intimate relationships are discussed more fully in the section in this chapter on feminist theory for conceptualizing singlehood.

Social support in the age of technology

There is considerable research demonstrating that individuals with strong social support tend to have better long-term physical health outcomes. Social support is thought to be a protective factor in terms of stress: those who have supportive others in their lives are better able to handle life stressors and tend to engage in more health-promoting behaviors, which in turn improves cardiovascular, neuroendocrine, and immune system functioning and mitigates the deleterious effects that stress can have on overall physical health (Uchino, Uno, & Holt-Lunstad, 1999).

Americans may be less socially connected than in prior generations as the result of changes in marriage rates, household sizes, and rates of procreation (Holt-Lunstad, 2017). These generational shifts can have serious consequences for Americans' overall health, particularly during older adulthood, as those with less social connection are more likely to experience early death and mental health challenges such as depression, cognitive decline, and dementia later in life. The literature on social support often focuses on cohabitating romantic relationships, largely neglecting other relevant relationships that can contribute to the same (or at least a similar) sense of connectedness and belonging (i.e., sibling relationships, friendships, etc.). Compared with adults who are not single, adults who are single may have larger social support networks and be in more frequent contact with supportive family and friends (Sarkisian & Gerstel, 2016), which seems to benefit those who have not previously partnered more than adults who are divorced or widowed (Pinquart, 2003).

Although adults who are single are more likely to have more social relationships and social contact with family and friends, they are also more likely to experience higher levels of loneliness, mental health problems, and physical health problems than adults who are partnered (Bernardon, Babb, Hakim-Larson, & Gragg, 2011). Social support from a romantic partner has been found to serve as a protective factor against mental health issues and physical health issues (Feder, Heatherington, Mojtabai, & Eaton, 2018; Gore, 2014). Conversely, adults who are single may be at increased risk for higher levels of stress and mental health issues compared with adults who are partnered (Kiecolt-Glaser & Newton, 2001; Miller, Hollist, Olsen, & Law, 2013; Robles, Slatcher, Trombello, & McGinn, 2013). With regard to mental health issues, regardless of whether they are single by choice or by circumstance, adults who are single are at risk for higher levels of insomnia, anxiety, depression, neuroticism, and other psychiatric symptoms and disorders, as well as lower levels of self-esteem, sexual satisfaction, and overall psychological functioning (Adamczyk, 2017; Barrett, 2000; Carlson, 2012; Lehnart, Neyer, & Eccles, 2010; Schachner, Shaver, & Gillath, 2008).

DePaulo and Morris (2005) stress the importance of expanding the idea of social connection beyond just that of romantic relationships. Further, they invite researchers and clinicians to differentiate individuals who desire romantic connection from those who do not. Perceptions of loneliness and social isolation (and the symptoms that may result) are likely to be different among individuals who intentionally remain single compared with their counterparts who actively desire a romantic relationship. The mental health symptoms associated with being single may be more severe in those adults who desire a romantic relationship than those who are intentionally single. In order to help mitigate the effects of loneliness and singlehood on the mental health of these individuals, they can seek to increase their social support outside of romantic relationships. Individuals who lack a sense of belongingness and do not have meaningful connections with others are more likely to experience suicide ideation or attempt suicide, particularly in those who use substances to cope with psychological distress (You, Van Orden, & Conner, 2011).

There is conflicting information in the literature about whether the prevalence of social media engagement exacerbates or diminishes loneliness and isolation in American adults (Holt-Lunstad, 2017). Some studies have shown that the use of social media has decreased loneliness and isolation in older adults (Chen & Schulz, 2016), whereas other research has shown that the more people use technology and social media, the less direct communication they have with family members, the smaller their social circle is, and they report more depressive symptoms and loneliness (Kraut et al., 1998). Advancements in technology and the ever-increasing popularity of dating apps also have both advantages and disadvantages for adults who are single and seeking long-term partnerships, as over a third of contemporary marriages are the result of Internet dating (Wiederhold, 2015).

Advantages of Internet dating include access to a wider range of potential partners and the ability to screen or filter potential mates based upon characteristics or traits that would not be desirable. Disadvantages, particularly for those who are single and desire a monogamous romantic relationship, include increased objectification of and by potential partners, decreased willingness of partners to commit (possibly related to having more choices), and delayed in-person interaction. If in-person interactions are delayed or even nonexistent with potential partners met through dating apps, how might this impact experiences of loneliness or social isolation? How well (or poorly) might individuals get their needs for connection and emotional intimacy met?

Theoretical Conceptualizations of Singlehood

In this section, we explore singlehood from the following theoretical frameworks: attachment theory, feminist theory, and ambiguous loss theory. Attachment theory provides an explanation for why adults seek intimate relationships, feminist theory provides an explanation for why some adults do not seek intimate relationships and a contextualization for singlehood with regard to socialization and power, and ambiguous loss theory provides a framework for understanding singlehood as the unclear loss of an anticipated partner and other related aspirations such as marriage or parenthood.

Attachment conceptualization of singlehood

Attachment theory provides a framework for understanding why most adults desire to be in an enduring and committed romantic relationship and why the absence of such relationships can be distressing. Attachment theory posits that emotionally intimate relationships give life meaning. The central tenet of attachment theory is that human beings have an innate need for interconnectedness and enduring affectional bonds (Ainsworth, 1989; Bowlby, 1973):

> Intimate attachments to other human beings are the hub around which a person's life revolves.... From these intimate attachments a person draws his strength and enjoyment of life and, through what he contributes, he gives strength and enjoyment to others. (Bowlby, 1980, p. 442)

The desire to form adult romantic attachment bonds is well supported in the research literature (Schachner et al., 2008). The pathway from childhood to adulthood is marked by transitioning from caregivers such as parents functioning as the primary attachment figures to romantic partners functioning as the primary attachment figures in the context of a committed and lasting relationship (Weiss, 1987). The concept of adult attachment with a romantic attachment figure coincides with Erikson's psychosocial stages of development that suggest *intimacy* versus *isolation* is the primary task of young adulthood. Human beings have specific innate yearnings for meaningful adult romantic attachment bonds that further growth and development (Ainsworth, 1991; Fraley & Davis, 1997; Waters, Merrick, Treboux, Crowell, & Albersheim, 2000). Human beings experience an innate yearning for meaningful adult romantic attachment bonds that provide reassurance during times of distress and enhance psychological functioning (Bowlby, 1988).

In particular, adults with anxious attachment styles, especially women, experience lower levels of relationship satisfaction possibly because of the intense need for intimacy, fear of abandonment, and emotional instability that characterizes anxious attachment style (Collins & Read, 1990; Simpson, 1990). Furthermore, adults with avoidant attachment styles, especially men, tend to rate their relationships more negatively and indicate lower levels of commitment, which may be due to the higher levels of independence, and the discomfort with intimacy, closeness, and trust that characterizes avoidant attachment style (Kirkpatrick & Davis, 1994). Adults consistently rated avoidant attachment styles as the least desirable in a partner (Chappell & Davis, 1998; Latty-Mann & Davis, 1996; Pietromonaco & Carnelley, 1994). It is important to note that the literature on attachment styles does not always attend to the effects of gender socialization when reporting gender-based statistics.

Because human beings are hardwired for meaningful social interaction (Cacioppo & Patrick, 2008), isolation—particularly emotional isolation—and loss can be traumatizing (Johnson, 2003). The discrepancy between desiring meaningful romantic attachment bonds and the absence of such bonds has been associated with loneliness and emotional distress (De Jong Gierveld, van Tilburg, & Dykstra, 2006; Shaver & Hazan, 1987). In fact, adults who are single report higher levels of anxiety, depression, and sexual dissatisfaction (Schachner et al., 2008). Bowlby described the protective nature of adult attachment relationships as follows:

The urgent desire for comfort and support in adversity is not regarded as childish, as dependency theory implies. Instead the capacity to make emotional bonds with other individuals, sometimes in the care seeking role and sometimes in the caregiving one, is regarded as a principal feature of effective personality functioning and mental health. (Bowlby, 1988, p. 121)

In accordance with attachment theory, adults with a secure attachment style have characteristics and skills that help them develop closeness and connectedness in intimate relationships such as self-esteem, confidence, emotion regulation, emotional expressivity, and positive emotionality (Collins & Read, 1990; Davila, Karney, & Bradbury, 1999). In addition, their intimate relationships tend to be based on commitment, trust, interdependence, and reciprocal support (Shaver & Mikulincer, 2006). People with secure attachment styles tend to have healthy internal working models—moderately stable beliefs about self, other, and relationships based on early attachment experiences that organize perceptions and shape behavior in relationships (Howe, Brandon, Hinings & Schofield, 1999). Adults who are securely attached seek reciprocal relationships that provide a *secure base* and *safe haven* through *goal-corrected partnerships* (e.g., a partner who has the ability to infer their goals and needs and then engage in attuned behaviors that convey compromise, empathy, flexibility, and understanding, which, in turn, strengthen the attachment bond; Bowlby, 1988; Hanson & Spratt, 2000).

In contrast, adults with insecure attachment styles tend to have maladaptive coping strategies such as emotional reactivity, relational withdrawal, and self-blame that appear to put them at increased risk for distress (e.g., anxiety, depression; Feeney, 2008). Specifically, adults with an avoidant attachment style tend to be uncomfortable with relationship intimacy, trust, communication, and dependence (Hazan & Shaver, 1987). Furthermore, adults with an anxious attachment style are more likely to have characteristics that make establishing healthy and lasting relationships difficult, such as poor self-esteem, an overwhelming drive for intimacy that disrupts relational functioning, and emotion dysregulation during conflict and distress (Campbell, Simpson, Boldry, & Kashy, 2005). Finally, Although difficult family-of-origin experiences during childhood, such as attachment injuries caused by abuse, might make interpersonal closeness complicated, attachment style does not appear to be significantly associated with singlehood (Schachner et al., 2008).

Feminist conceptualization of singlehood

The feminist conceptualization of singlehood differs from other perspectives in that it does not view the experience of being single as evidence of some deficiency or injury (DePaulo & Morris, 2005, 2006). It is paramount to differentiate between loneliness and intentional singlehood. Those who have made a conscious choice to remain single may experience loneliness from time to time, but no more so than anyone in a romantic relationship might experience loneliness during times of relationship conflict or when individuals may simply feel disconnected or distant from their partner. The loneliness that is experienced in these contexts is temporary: it is not a statement about the person's overall sense of being in the world. From the feminist perspective, even those individuals who do experience distress or grief related to their single relationship status and desire to be in a committed romantic relationship should not be viewed as lacking something (a romantic relationship). Their distress is conceptualized as being related to internalized rigid gendered discourses that pathologize singlehood in such a way that their view of self as competent and worthy is compromised without being linked to a partner (DePaulo & Morris, 2005, 2006; McKeown, 2015; Seccombe & Ishii-Kuntz, 1994).

In order to understand singlehood from the feminist lens, one must deconstruct the social messages about intimate partnerships—messages that tend to be very heteronormative and limiting (DePaulo & Morris, 2005). Monogamous long-term relationships and marriage are so privileged in Western society that singlehood is often misrepresented as a deficiency in a person's ability to create intimate connection (Koeing, Zimmerman, Haddock, & Banning, 2010). In contrast to this viewpoint, single people reportedly have more friends and more regular intimate contact with both friends and family members and participate more actively in their local communities than people who are in romantic partnerships (DePaulo, 2018). There is a widely perpetuated perception (and related judgment) that adults who are single are more alone and therefore lonelier than those in committed relationships, and other cultural discourses imply that adulthood is only truly reached through marriage and procreation. These negative biases about singlehood, termed *singlism*, may have a larger impact on the mental health and well-being of adults who are single than actually being single (DePaulo & Morris, 2005, 2006). Furthermore, in our field that is focused on family relationships, relationship status is often not a part of our conversations when we talk about diversity, privilege, and marginalization, indicating that *singlism* exists in our field.

Because adults who are single live in a marriage-oriented society (DePaulo & Morris, 2005; Seccombe & Ishii-Kuntz, 1994), they may feel external pressures to be in committed romantic relationships (Anderson, Stewart, & Dimidjian, 1994). Family and friends often pathologize adults who are single by trying to identify one or more fundamental shortcomings in their personality, mental health, intelligence, and physical attractiveness that might explain why they are single, divorced, or separated (DePaulo & Morris, 2006; Lewis & Moon, 1997; Reynolds, 2002). Adults who are single may, in turn, internalize these explanations for their singlehood (Lewis, 1994; e.g., "You are too picky" becoming "I must be too picky"). In addition to *stigmatizing* singlehood, people often *glamorize* child-free singlehood (e.g., "You are so lucky you are single because you can do whatever you want whenever you want"), which can feel invalidating by adults whose singlehood is undesired (Lewis & Moon, 1997).

Adulthood is most often discussed in terms of coupling and procreating both anecdotally in the dominant culture and in family life stage research. For example, in the literature on the family life cycle, adults are identified as recently coupled, parenting young children through adolescence, and launching adolescents into adulthood, neglecting those adults who are single and do not have children, are single and do have children, and are coupled but do not have children (Erickson, 1998). People who are single and do not have children may be particularly stigmatized as not yet being adult (or remaining stuck in adolescence), as the processes of coupling and having children seem to denote adulthood for many. As with any repeated exposure to microaggressions, people who remain single (either by choice or by chance) may be so adversely affected by the stigma that they internalize these pathological discourses to be statements about the validity or value that their lives hold.

Ambiguous loss conceptualization of singlehood

Long-term singlehood among adults who wish they were in an intimate partnership can lead to an ambiguous loss of an indefinitely missing anticipated partner (Jackson, 2018; Lewis, 1994; Sharp & Ganong, 2007). An ambiguous loss most commonly occurs when someone we love is there but not there (Dahl & Boss, 2020, vol. 4). Unlike a loss such as a death that is clear with rituals like a funeral, burial, and cemetery visits on anniversaries that acknowledge the death, an ambiguous loss is a loss that is not clear-cut. No rituals exist for acknowledging the invisible loss of being single, and even if there were, it would not be clear when to engage in them, which can result in *disenfranchised grief*:

> Grief that results when a person experiences a significant loss and the resultant grief is not openly acknowledged, socially validated, or publicly mourned. In short, although the individual is experiencing a grief reaction, there is no social recognition that the person has a right to grieve or a claim for social sympathy or support. (Doka, 2008, p. 224)

Because a loss like death is concrete, we can grieve it and, over time, heal and move forward; a loss that is ambiguous typically lacks the type of information about it that makes it clear to the point that we do not know if and when the experience of loss may resolve or become more substantial. Although we might experience loss, we do not necessarily see it as a loss because it does not fit the loss framework to which we are accustomed. The absence of information about the person who is indefinitely missing creates uncertainty about how to manage the situation. When somebody dies, it is clear that they are gone, which allows us to find ways to manage the loss; when we are not sure if someone is gone, then it is harder to manage.

There are two types of ambiguous loss. The first type occurs when the person is physically there but not psychologically there. For instance, a loved one who has dementia is physically alive, but the person is not psychologically present in the same way as before: there could be times when the person is more lucid and times when the person is more psychologically inaccessible (Boss, Caron, Horbal, & Mortimer, 1990). We lack clear information about what will happen in the future around the level of dementia, so it is difficult to know if we should mourn because the person is not physically gone and psychologically present to varying degrees. Other common examples include chronic mental illness such as schizophrenia, addictions, traumatic brain injuries, extramarital affairs, mixed sexual orientation marriages, marriage to one's job, and birth of a child with severe developmental disabilities.

By contrast, the second type occurs when the person is psychologically there but not physically there. For instance, parents of children who are kidnapped frequently experience ambivalence about *holding on* to hope that their child is still alive somewhere and *moving on* so they can grieve the loss. As long as parents hope their child is still out there, they cannot truly mourn the loss of their child. Parents often feel torn because they do not want to give up hope that their child is still out there, but as long as they hold on to hope, they tend to remain in a state of perpetual grief due to the lack of clear information about the loss (Boss, 2006). Infertility can also be an ambiguous loss in which the loss is the child or the children that prospective parents anticipated having that not yet physically materialized that exist psychologically in prospective parents' minds. The ambivalence about holding on to the hope of having children or moving on and accepting the permanent absence of children tends to occur because the prospective parents may not know if and when they might get pregnant. With age, a tipping point of acceptance may occur, but leading up to that, the possibilities of the unknown make potential pregnancy unclear and perpetuate the ambivalence and what Boss terms *frozen grief*: a specific type of ongoing unresolved grief that occurs due to the absence of information regarding if and when the ambiguous loss will end (Boss, 2004). Additional examples of ambiguous losses in which the person is psychologically present but physically absent include missing-in-action war casualties, natural disasters, deportation, divorce, stillborn children, adoption, foster care, and prolonged singlehood.

The ambiguous loss of prolonged singlehood is similar to the ambiguous loss of infertility in that the loss is of a person who was expected to materialize but has not materialized and may or may not materialize at some point in the near or distant future. This indefinitely missing anticipated partner exists psychologically but not physically with no clarity about if and when they will materialize. Therefore, the ambiguous loss of prolonged singlehood is the loss of a non-materialized relationship with the type of person with whom a person would like to be partnered who exists psychologically but does come along physically. Not knowing whether or not they will remain single or not can be very challenging for people who are single. Part of what makes the ambiguous loss of singlehood particularly ambiguous is that the loss is related to the absence of someone who was never clearly in the picture.

The primary reaction to ambiguous loss is ambivalence, and the most common cause is not knowing whether to *hold on* or *move on*. Hoping that the indefinitely missing anticipated partner will eventually materialize prevents true grieving from taking place, perpetuating grieving because the grieving process cannot move forward. On the other hand, completely accepting the permanent loss of the non-materialized indefinitely missing anticipated partner and resigning oneself to permanent singlehood allows for some closure, grieving, and healing. However, the inherent desire for attachment with another adult in the context of a committed intimate relationship tends to make complete acceptance of permanent singlehood difficult, and as long as there is some holding on to hope, the loss will remain ambiguous.

Adults who are single may experience ambivalence about celebrating family-centric holidays and related rituals because they may make the loss feel even more present. Holidays are generally enjoyable rituals for celebration, togetherness, and connection; however, adults who are single and wish to be partnered may experience ambivalence because holidays that should be enjoyable are painful reminders of singlehood. Furthermore, adults who are single often face questions like "Are you dating anyone right now?" "How's your love life?" and "Any prospects?" at holiday gatherings. Consequently, holidays may be times of loneliness and longing for belonging for adults who are single and wish to be partnered.

Adults who are single often experience ambivalence about settling or continued singlehood. The indefinitely missing anticipated partner that exists psychologically can sometimes actually perpetuate singlehood if expectations cause viable partners to be overlooked. Adults who are single may question whether they should settle with a partner who falls short of expectations or hold out for someone to come along who is more in line with the psychological indefinitely missing anticipated partner. Adults who are single who want to have children or additional children may also experience the ambiguous loss of non-materialized children.

The nuances of singlehood vary from person to person, as do the ways in which singlehood ambiguous loss is experienced, if experienced at all. However, there are commonalities based on whether a person has not yet been in a long-term committed intimate relationship (e.g., cohabitation, marriage) or has been in a long-term committed intimate relationship and has returned to being single (e.g., separated, divorced, widowed).

Not previously married Adults who have not previously married make up almost two-thirds of adults who are single in the United States (US Census Bureau, 2017a). There can be a wide variety of relationship experiences among adults who have not yet ever married: they may or may not have previously been in one or more committed romantic relationships (e.g., exclusively dating, engaged, living together), may or may not currently be in in another type of committed romantic relationship, and may or may not have children. In terms of developmental timing, people who are single when societal and cultural norms indicate one should be single will typically not experience singlehood ambiguous loss; by contrast, people who are single when societal and cultural norms indicate one should be permanently partnered are more likely to experience singlehood ambiguous loss of an indefinitely missing anticipated partner, especially if most of their peer group is partnered. Adults who have not previously married and experience prolonged singlehood are probably more likely to experience singlehood ambiguous loss of an indefinitely missing anticipated partner than people who are separated, divorced, or widowed because they have yet to have permanently partnered. See Jackson (2018) for more information on the ambiguous loss of singlehood among people who have not previously married.

Separated People who are separated but not divorced may experience ambivalence from several ambiguities. Approximately 2% of adult Americans are separated (US Census Bureau, 2017a). People who are separated commonly face ambivalence about whether to permanently end the relationship (e.g., divorce) or get back together (e.g., a part of them does not want to give up on their marriage, feel like a failure, feel guilt, be criticized by others, be single again; another part of them feels exhausted, hurt, lonely, and hopeless that things will get better). They may also experience ambivalence about their relationship status as they are neither completely coupled nor completely single.

In addition, people who are separated might experience ambivalence due to their partner likely being perceived as psychologically absent (e.g., the person I'm separated from is no longer the same person I originally fell in love with), as well as sometimes physically absent but sometimes physically present, especially if there are shared children. Therefore, adults who are separated may potentially experience multiple psychological and physical losses, such as the loss of the once more caring and responsive—and possibly idealized—partner, and in some situations (particularly shared children) the varying physical presence of the spouse because of the separation (sometimes physically present, sometimes physically absent).

People who are separated may also experience *re-partnering ambivalence* in which they wonder if they would be able to find someone better if they were to permanently end the relationship (e.g., divorce). Unclear information about the future creates ambivalence: if they knew whether or not their current partner would return to being more like they were earlier in the relationship or if they knew whether or not they would end up with someone better, there would be less ambivalence about separation.

The fear of being single again (Lewis, 1994) can further complicate their ambivalence about getting back together or permanently ending the relationship. Reconciling ambivalent feelings about so many ambiguities can prove challenging and sometimes overwhelming.

Divorced   Given that approximately 50% of all marriages in the United States end in divorce (US Census Bureau, 2008), it is not surprising that a quarter of adults who are single are divorced (US Census Bureau, 2017a). Similarly to people who are separated but not divorced, people who are divorced often experience multiple ambiguities, including experiencing both types of ambiguous loss simultaneously, a phenomenon that has been documented for other types of ambiguous loss (e.g., Boss, 2006; Roper & Jackson, 2007). The likelihood of experiencing both types of ambiguous loss simultaneously is substantially higher for people who have children with their ex-spouse because of ongoing interactions to co-parent the children. For instance, a straight man who is divorced, is single, and has joint custody of his children with his ex-wife may experience his ex-wife as sometimes physically present but psychologically absent (e.g., when he interacts with his ex-wife to pick up and drop off the children he experiences her very differently than he did when they fell in love: harsh, critical, condescending, and resentful) and sometimes psychologically present and physically absent (e.g., when he is home alone, he misses the way his ex-wife used to be with him: warm, kind, loving, and affectionate).

Consider the clinical case of a woman who sought therapy for protracted grief from her divorce. Because her ex-husband was so cold, distant, and hurtful toward the end of the marriage, she felt weak when she mourned his absence (e.g., "Why should I feel so sad when he was so mean to me? My divorce was a good thing as it set me free from the pain"). When the client realized the end of her marriage was an ambiguous loss (i.e., the physical absence of her ex-husband and psychological presence of both the ex-husband she loved and the ex-husband she hated), she was able to process her ambivalence about her marriage and grieve the loss of the husband and the parts of the relationship that she loved.

Similarly to adults who are separated, adults who are divorced and single may also experience *remarriage ambivalence* about entering into another long-term committed intimate partnerships (e.g., "What if I get married again and that relationship goes the same way that my last one did?"). Of note, adults who are single and have children may seek to have both their parental and their romantic attachment needs met through their children, which may unintentionally lead to parentification.

Widowed   People who are widowed may be the most invisible singlehood subgroup. American women are more likely to be widowed and single than American men: 9.2% of adult American women are widowed and single, while only 2.7% of adult American men are widowed and single (US Census Bureau, 2017a). People who are widowed may also experience *remarriage ambivalence* about hoping to remarry or coping with perpetual singlehood, loss, and loneliness (e.g., "Should I try to remarry or should I remain single?"). The hardwiring for romantic attachment can lead people who are widowed to yearn for a new partner, and, at the same time, they might not want to betray or replace their deceased spouse (e.g., "Should I remain single and cling to my memories of my deceased spouse for comfort and connection or try to remarry?" "Could I ever find someone who I would love as much as I loved my deceased spouse and who would love me as much as my deceased spouse loved me?"). The perception of the death as an on-time normative event (i.e., occurs when it is expected) or an off-time normative event (i.e., occurs before or after it is expected) may account for some variation in the intensity of the loss and in the intensity of the ambivalence about remarriage. An on-time loss of a spouse may result in less ambivalence because single-hood at that life stage is more expected; conversely, an off-time loss of a spouse may create more ambivalence about remarriage. For instance, people who are older and widowed might experience less ambivalence about remarrying because they view sin-glehood more as a short-term stage preceding their own deaths compared with peo-ple who are younger and widowed and may have other complicating considerations such as children or extended family. People who are widowed who did not have posi-tive or satisfying relationships with their deceased spouse may experience *remarriage ambivalence* similarly to someone who is divorced.

Although death is typically not associated with ambiguous loss, the death of a spouse may result in an ambiguous loss in which the deceased spouse is physically absent and psychologically present. The lack of clear information about whether death is finite or whether life and romantic relationship continue in some way after death can result in ambivalence about the future of the relationship with a deceased spouse, creating the potential for ambiguity about the loss. Ambivalence about whether or not people will be reunited with their spouses in an afterlife can lead to ambivalence about mourning the loss and moving on with life or hoping that the relationship will continue postmortem (e.g., "I'm not sure what I believe about what happens after this life. I both hope that I will see my deceased spouse again and fear that I will never see my deceased spouse again."). This *afterlife ambivalence* (e.g., "Should I hope to be reunited with my former spouse or grieve the permanent loss of my former spouse?") can lead to situations of frozen grief that can be further complicated if the person who is widowed has mixed feelings toward the deceased spouse. Strong spir-itual or religious convictions in an afterlife or convictions that death is finite can unfreeze the grief by reducing ambivalence about reunification. Although such con-victions might not make loss created by the death any less painful (e.g., loneliness and sadness related to the deceased spouse), they can make the loss less ambiguous and, therefore, easier to manage.

Treatment Approaches

The academic literature on clinical treatments for adults who are struggling with sin-glehood is limited to the following approaches: (a) feminist (Lewis, 1994; Lewis & Moon, 1997), (b) psychodynamic (Bickerton, 1983; Lieberman, 1991; Rucker, 1993), (c) social constructionist (Reynolds, 2002), and (d) multicontextual life cycle (Schwartzberg, Berliner, & Jacob, 1995), none of which address singlehood from an ambiguous loss treatment framework. Furthermore, with the exception of the multi-contextual life cycle approach (Schwartzberg et al., 1995), the other approaches are specific to working with adult single women. We propose that any systemic therapy approach can be used to treat clients experiencing relational distress related to single-hood, regardless of gender identity. We also suggest that clients be assessed for single-hood ambiguous loss and that adaptations be made to the systemic therapy approach selected in cases of singlehood ambiguous loss to address the ambiguous loss (Jackson, 2018). We conclude this chapter by providing suggestions for clinicians working with clients who are single and wish they were not and examples of how different systemic theories can be adapted to better address the needs of these clients.

Major goals of treatment

In clinical work with adults who are single, therapists should assess for potential intrapsychic and interpersonal difficulties that may be related to the presenting problem or to singlehood without assuming that such difficulties exist or explain client singlehood (Lewis, 1994). It is important to determine if there are issues that might be contributing to singlehood, as making them a focus of treatment will likely be beneficial for clients; at the same time, it is also important to avoid pathologizing clients and inadvertently reinforcing self-blaming narratives they may have about why they are single. Thus, clinicians should avoid normalizing problematic intrapsychic and interpersonal functioning, as well as avoid problematizing normal intrapsychic and interpersonal functioning (Miller, Rathus, & Linehan, 2006).

Therapists working with clients who desire to be in romantic relationships should approach treatment from a social justice perspective that takes into consideration different intersecting factors of diversity, such as ethnicity, race, socioeconomic status, level of education, sexual orientation, gender identification, culture, spirituality, and age. Therapists should be realistic about any challenges that clients may face in regard to their social location. For example, a client who is LGBTQ and, for safety reasons, is not out to everyone in their family or community may have more challenges in terms of finding a viable romantic relationship while also experiencing pressure from these social groups to conform to heteronormative relational ideals.

When determining goals for therapy, therapists should assess for any dissonance regarding differences between clients' personal beliefs about romantic relationships, the dominant discourses, and the beliefs held by their family, culture, and religion of origin. How a client is affected by different gendered discourses regarding singlehood is also important to consider. For example, a person's gender and age may significantly influence the way that others view and discuss their singlehood. There are many derogatory terms for women who remain single after a certain age (e.g., spinster, cougar) that imply that these women have not chosen to be single, whereas men who remain single are typically perceived to be so by choice (DePaulo & Morris, 2006). Likewise, clients who are from different highly religious cultures that view marriage as the ultimate venue to demonstrate faithfulness and piety may receive messages from people in their family or community about their "marriageability"—the older they get, the less desirable they will be for potential spouses (particularly if they have been sexually active).

Stigmatization around singlehood may be more distressing for some clients than others. Deconstructing the influence that different sociocultural factors may have had on the development of deficit-based perceptions about clients' singlehood is essential to determine exactly where clients would like to create change in their own lives. Would helping clients to shift their perceptions about their relationship status be sufficient for decreasing distress, or are there underlying relational issues that need to be addressed in order for clients to be able to develop meaningful relationships in which they can create connection and get their needs met more effectively?

It is also important for therapists to check their own biases and beliefs about singlehood and romantic relationships—has the client expressed distress regarding their relationship status, or has the therapist made assumptions about the clients' grief over their relationship status? Clients' singlehood should become the focus of therapy only if the client wishes to address it. Likewise, clients who do want to address their singlehood should also be asked what their ultimate relational goal is: do they desire a monogamous relationship, or would a polyamorous or consensual non-monogamous relationship better fit their beliefs about relationships and their relational needs?

If clients do report distress regarding their singlehood and want to address their singlehood in therapy, there are different factors to attend to, irrespective of the theoretical model chosen. Primary tasks of therapy might include helping clients (a) pinpoint how singlehood has created discrepancies between how they expected their lives to turn out and how their lives have turned out thus far and (b) explore how they might change their expectations and perceptions of reality in ways that would work better for them. Reducing the discrepancy between expectations and perceptions of reality reduces distress. Perception is everything; even though clients might not be able to change the circumstances surrounding their singlehood, they can change their perceptions of their singlehood. Focusing on the advantages of single life can prove helpful. Commonly reported singlehood advantages include independence and freedom (e.g., relational, occupational, financial, geographical, temporal, leisure; Cox, 2006; Lewis, 1994).

Additionally, therapy should help clients to navigate certain transitional processes (e.g., differentiation of self, individuation in a way that is congruent with their culture, making peace with their relationships with their caregivers, and negotiating other standard transitional life stage issues). Often clients' ability to complete a task such as individuating from their family of origin is hindered by their perception that in order to do so, they must first find a long-term partner or spouse. Exploring beliefs about transitional life stage issues can help clients accomplish (or at least begin) those tasks and increase their ability to establish and maintain emotional intimacy in various relationships (not just romantic). Additionally, this work can help clients identify and address sexual feelings and needs in a way that is culturally appropriate for them (Lewis, 1994). For example, clients whose spiritual or cultural beliefs are against exploring their sexuality with a partner with whom they are not in a long-term monogamous relationship may benefit from discussions in therapy that help identify ways to explore their sexuality that are more congruent with their value system while they remain unpartnered. The therapist working with these clients must inherently create space for them to confront the dialectic of moving forward in their lives while simultaneously hoping for a romantic relationship (or marriage). Because adults who are single often feel disempowered and immobilized by their singlehood, it can be therapeutic and empowering when they are more focused on the types of choices over which they have more control. Though they are single and desire not to be, they can work on improving the quality of their existing relationships in order to increase connection and emotional intimacy while also remaining hopeful for the future.

Ambiguous loss

Detailed treatment recommendations for working with clients who are single from an ambiguous loss framework (Jackson, 2018) are briefly summarized here. Even the most resilient people can become immobilized by ambiguity and by ambivalence. Many people who experience singlehood ambiguous loss attempt to deal with it through seeking closure by settling or giving up on having a long-term committed intimate relationship completely; however, this can be difficult to achieve due to attachment needs. Furthermore, the very nature of an ambiguous loss makes it difficult to eliminate. Consequently, the objective of treatment is to not eliminate the ambiguous loss or have closure around it; instead we want to help clients become more resilient and reduce the type of distress and anxiety that they feel about the ambiguous loss by helping them learn how to live with it and accept that that loss cannot be changed; what they can change are their perceptions around the ambiguous loss in an effort to more effectively manage the ambiguity of the loss (Boss, 2006).

The approach for managing ambiguous loss integrates interventions from multiple theoretical orientations in the service of increasing clients' abilities to effectively manage the ambiguous loss. The specific objectives for helping clients cope with any type of ambiguous loss are normalizing ambivalence (helping clients realize singlehood can be an ambiguous loss), tempering mastery (balancing the desire to control things by accepting what cannot be changed and making intentional and reasonable efforts to change what can), finding meaning (making sense of the ambiguous loss including how it gives life additional meaning), reconstructing identity (developing rich and multidimensional ways of seeing oneself that include various roles), revising attachment (learning to live with ambivalence regarding the situation of ambiguous loss), and discovering hope (figuring out which old and new hopes to hold on to and which old hopes to give up on; Boss, 2006).

One of the key interventions for facilitating progress toward many of the clinical treatment objectives for ambiguous loss is dialectical thinking (the ability to simultaneously hold seemingly contradictory beliefs). Dialectical thinking promotes balance between acceptance ("I am doing the best that I can give my current situation and the skills that I currently have to manage it") and change ("I need to learn, grow, and manage my current situation better"; Linehan, 2015). Dialectical thinking helps clients think about being single in more complex ways that will allow them to better tolerate the distress caused by the ambiguity of singlehood and decrease emotional suffering. Replacing *either/or thinking* with dialectical *both/and thinking* can help them think about being single more complexly, such as thinking about the person they want to be with as being both psychologically present and physically absent— present in their mind and absent from their lives. Moving from oversimplified and one-sided thoughts like "I hate being single" to a dialectical thought like "I enjoy certain aspects of being single and I struggle with certain aspects of being single" can help clients better manage the ambiguous loss of singlehood.

Case Examples[1]

In this section, we will provide case examples using an integration of treatment framework for singlehood ambiguous loss (Jackson, 2018) and different widely used systemic theoretical approaches. Case examples include a client who had not yet experienced a romantic relationship, a client who had been in multiple short-term relationships, and a client who had a traumatic relationship history. It is important to note that although the presenting concern that brought each of these clients to therapy was different, all of these clients shared a strong desire for a romantic relationship and experienced significant pain related to the ambiguous loss of not being partnered in the way that they wanted to be.

Not previously partnered or married

Sometimes clients come to therapy specifically to address their singlehood. These clients most often view their singlehood from a pathologized perspective, filtered through the dominant discourses that privilege those in committed relationships and imply that those who have not yet partnered have not hit some developmental milestone or experienced some important rite of passage related to the coupling process. Such was the case with Isabella, a 27-year-old Mexican American heterosexual woman. Isabella sought therapy with a couple and family therapist because she wanted to answer the question that so many well-intentioned yet critical people in her life continuously asked her: *Why had she never been in a long-term committed relationship?* For Isabella, her ambiguous loss was compounded by the fact that not only had she not previously been married, but she had not yet had the experience of any long-term romantic partnership.

Prior to therapy, in an attempt to answer this question for herself, Isabella had internalized Western ideals about attractiveness and thinness and believed that she had not been in a romantic relationship yet because she was not perceived to be attractive by conventional beauty standards held by the cisgender heterosexual men that she wanted to date. A narrative therapy approach, which maintains that reality is socially constructed through language and people experience distress when harmful discourses subjugate their lived experiences (White & Epston, 1990), was particularly salient for a client like Isabella. The focus of therapy was to enact Isabella's preferred narrative about her singlehood by altering the problem-saturated story that said that she was somehow less than or inadequate because she had not yet been in a romantic relationship.

In the initial stage of therapy, Isabella worked on deconstructing the culturally based meaning-making systems that informed the problem-saturated narrative (White & Epston, 1990) about her singlehood. She identified cultural beliefs in her family of origin that contributed to her internalization of feelings of inadequacy and unattractiveness: people in her family often made comments to her about not ever having had a boyfriend, and her career accomplishments were often overshadowed by things like the engagement announcements, weddings, and pregnancies of her sisters and female cousins. Her weight was always a topic of discussion growing up, and even after she moved out of the home, the conversation often returned to dieting suggestions and exercise plans whenever she visited her parents and siblings.

In the middle phase of therapy, Isabella was able to externalize (White & Epston, 1990) the problems of "inadequacy" and "loneliness" and began to identify a preferred narrative: she was not a single woman who was unable to find a partner, rather she was an empowered woman who chose to focus on her education and career in order to create a rich life for herself and would like to incorporate a romantic relationship into that life. She was able to identify many unique outcomes (alternatives to the problem-saturated story; White & Epston, 1990) in which she experienced deep connection, vulnerability, and emotional intimacy with friends and extended family members. She began to engage in conversations with other peers and colleagues who had similar experiences and surrounded herself with narratives that promoted body positivity. She identified a discrepancy between what she viewed as beauty in others and the beauty standards to which she held herself. She acknowledged multiple ways in which she was able to give and receive love in her relationships. When she had established a less deficit-based perspective on her singlehood, she was able to hold space for the ambiguous loss she experienced around not yet having experienced reciprocal romantic love, as she had identified many examples of unrequited love in which the object of her affection did not return her feelings. She unpacked the meaning that she had made about such experiences and recognized that she had held on to the belief that these men were not interested in her because she was not thin or pretty enough and saw these experiences as confirmation of that problem-saturated narrative.

In the final stage of therapy, Isabella began enacting her preferred narrative in her daily life (White & Epston, 1990). She was much more aware of times when men expressed attraction toward her and was able to see that there were many examples of her desirability that confirmed her preferred narrative. Prior to termination of therapy, Isabella invited her sisters and her mother into therapy wherein they witnessed her read a letter to her teenage self about body image and being single. When they heard about Isabella's grief, loneliness, and internalized shame and inadequacy, they expressed sadness; when they heard about Isabella's newfound empowerment, they shared their own experiences of gendered discourses that contributed to painful perceptions about themselves. Isabella reported that she was able to be more vulnerable with her family after that experience and she felt more supported by them as she began dating. Isabella was able to grieve the ambiguous loss of the idealized relationship that she had not yet had while also acknowledging the value of the deeply meaningful friendships and family relationships she had cultivated over the years. The grief process was ongoing, and acknowledging that her grief was valid helped her to be simultaneously hopeful for the romantic connection that she desired.

Frequent short-term relationships

Some clients who eventually express grief and ambiguous loss about their singlehood come into therapy for other reasons. Sometimes these reasons are peripherally related to their experience of singlehood, and sometimes they are not. Sally, a 34-year-old Caucasian lesbian woman, initially came to therapy to address trauma related to a sexual assault she experienced in her early twenties that had become activated when she experienced a trauma trigger during sex with a partner. After several months in therapy, it became apparent that, in addition to the single-incident trauma of her assault, Sally had also experienced complex trauma related to her sexual orientation and her coming out process with her parents. Furthermore, because Sally was an only child, her parents were hyperfocused on her partnering and potential procreation.

Though Sally's parents appeared to be supportive of her sexual orientation on the surface, there were actually countless examples of microaggressions committed by her parents over the years: they were constantly trying to set her up with their friends' sons and other men they knew professionally, and they made jokes about her not expressing her gender identity in stereotypically feminine ways. The incongruence in the way that Sally's parents directly and indirectly communicated with her led to much confusion and internal conflict. Sally's self-esteem and identity as a lesbian woman were affected as a result. She often dated women who she identified as "bisexual but hetero-romantic," meaning that they were sexually attracted to her, but romantically preferred to be in relationships with men. She believed that being lesbian meant that she had fewer options for potential partners than her straight friends. Satir's human validation process approach (Satir & Baldwin, 1983) was used to help Sally address some of the relational challenges and complex trauma she experienced.

At the start of therapy, Sally was in so much emotional distress related to her single-incident and complex trauma and the losses associated with the frequent termination of short-term relationships that she had been self-harming. She described her grief as never ending: she felt like each breakup compounded the loss of the previous one, and the emotional pain of not ever having her emotional needs met was so unbearable that she sought escape through the physical pain of cutting. The initial stage of therapy with Sally focused on crisis intervention to address her self-injurious behavior, decrease the shame and guilt associated with it, and develop safer coping mechanisms. After safety was established, the focus of therapy shifted to uncovering different survival stances that Sally and her parents took in order to maintain the status quo of the family dynamics. Sally was a *placater* (disregarding her own feelings or value in order to appease her parents and prevent them from experiencing any discomfort), while her mother was a *blamer* (very domineering; Sally and her father were at fault for any disruption in the family homeostasis), and her father was the *superreasonable* one (lacking emotional expression, overly logical, and linear in negotiation of family conflict; Satir & Baldwin, 1983). Sally's placatory role was replicated in her romantic relationships: she often minimized her own feelings and needs for commitment and intimacy because she feared that vocalizing her desires would push her partners away and ultimately lead to her disappointment and rejection. Sally tended to seek out partners who were noncommittal and often fit the blamer profile as well. If she could rationalize that her relationships did not last because her partners preferred long-term relationships with men, then that was less painful by her way of thinking than being directly rejected. Sally's underlying feelings of pain and experiences of subjugation in a very heteronormative (if not homophobic) environment were expressed and validated in therapy. Her experience as a lesbian woman in a family system that was not very LGBTQ informed was acknowledged.

In the middle stage of therapy, Sally's communication style in romantic relationships was unpacked further. Sally believed that if she communicated her needs to her partners, she would ultimately force them to admit that they did not see a future with her. Sally identified that her placatory role extended to the point of sacrificing herself in order to keep all others around her more comfortable. She would avoid holding hands with her partners or showing affection toward them at all in public in an effort to protect them from homophobic responses from others and to protect those "others" from the discomfort she believed they would feel if they saw two women who were romantically linked. In this middle stage of therapy, Sally's character strengths and positive attributes were highlighted to support her self-esteem and differentiation of self. Sally began to generalize the newfound emotional intimacy, vulnerability, and authenticity that she was able to engage in through the therapeutic relationship to other relationships with her friends and family members. Sally addressed the oppressive and painful microaggressions she experienced and sought support from others in the LGBTQ community. The dialectic of ambiguous loss presented differently for Sally than it had for Isabella. For Sally, the dialectic was desiring intimacy while at the same time being terrified of rejection and abandonment. The work for Sally was acknowledging that in order to obtain the thing she desired (long-term intimacy and commitment), she would have to open herself up to the possibility of loss if the relationship did not work out.

In the final stage of therapy, Sally identified the qualities she was looking for in a partner and began dating again. She acknowledged in the "getting to know one another" process with potential partners that she was looking for a long-term commitment and wanted to start a family. Instead of cutting when she felt the pain of intense and ongoing loss, she practiced communicating her thoughts, feelings, needs, and desires with potential partners and other close platonic relationships. Vulnerability was still challenging for her, and she still feared that people would ultimately decide to leave her if she became too "needy," but she was able to be transparent about these fears when they arose.

Traumatic relationship history

Sometimes clients come to therapy because they recognize that they keep perpetuating dysfunctional relationship patterns that they would like to interrupt. Kal, a 38-year-old, third-generation Korean American heterosexual male, sought therapy because he wanted to understand why he repeatedly entered into relationships with emotionally abusive partners. Kal's family genogram (McGoldrick, Gerson, & Petry, 2008) revealed intergenerational patterns of trauma, loss, and substance abuse. He was the youngest surviving child with an older brother and two older sisters. Prior to coming to therapy, he knew little about his grandparents' immigration stories, but had an awareness that they experienced deep losses when they separated from their family in Korea. Kal's mother experienced several pregnancy losses and had lost another son at just 10 weeks old when Kal was three. Kal reported that his mother "never recovered" from that loss and was very emotionally neglectful of him. His mother would use alcohol to numb her pain, a pattern that Kal had adopted. Differences in acculturation between generations (his grandparents', parents', and his own generation) also contributed to disconnect in his family. They had a pattern of conflict avoidance, which Kal described as fostering a very passive–aggressive environment that made him "always feel on edge."

Kal reported that, as the youngest child, he felt as though no one ever took him seriously and he was always living in the shadows of his older brother and his younger brother who died. This pattern of having to continuously prove himself played out in his romantic relationships as well. Kal had a history of long-term romantic partnerships that lasted several years, but were filled with emotional and sometimes physical abuse. Kal had always wanted a family of his own and had begun to give up hope of ever having one when he came into therapy: he was very much grieving this loss. He was coping with his grief by working extremely long hours during the week and binge drinking throughout the weekend to the point where he would pass out. Bowen's intergenerational family therapy model (Kerr & Bowen, 1988) was the treatment approach that was used.

The initial stage of therapy focused on crisis intervention centered on identifying coping mechanisms for Kal's grief other than drinking or working himself to the point of exhaustion. After Kal was able to decrease high-risk behaviors and establish an important level of safety, his work focused on gathering more information about his family, his position in the family, and their cultural contexts (Kerr & Bowen, 1988). Kal's grandparents were deceased at the time of therapy, but he attempted to get more information from his parents about their parents' immigration stories. Kal identified patterns in his parents' relationships with their parents that mirrored his relationship with them. Although his family was from a collectivistic culture, Kal's family lacked cohesiveness and closeness. Emotional cutoff was more common than differentiation of its members. Kal's mother was the only of her siblings to still have contact with either of their parents at the time of their deaths. Similarly, Kal's father was not very close with either of his siblings, and Kal did not grow up having close relationships with his cousins. Kal reported that his relationship with his mother was complicated and he felt a strong obligation to take care of her as she aged. Her drinking had worsened over the years, and as a result, his sisters and brother had significantly withdrawn from their relationships with her and their father. Kal's siblings said that he was the "most sensitive" of all of them, and so he was implicitly elected to be his parents' caretaker. He often found himself triangulated into their relationship and had to smooth things over between them as somewhat of a go-between or translator when they were upset with one another (Kerr & Bowen, 1988). Kal began to see that he was primed to be the emotional caretaker of his romantic partners given his position in his family of origin. He had also begun to rely on alcohol to cope with emotional pain, as he had never been able to get his emotional needs met by his parents or partners.

In the middle stage of therapy, the emotional processes of his family of origin were evaluated at a deeper level. Kal was able to address the ambiguous losses of not yet becoming a husband or a father himself as he desired, as well as the loss of the younger brother that he never got to know, and the relationship with his mother that he may have had if she were not so overcome with her own grief and alcoholism. Kal recognized that in his romantic relationships, he had misinterpreted familiarity to mean safety and comfort. He tended to choose partners who were either emotionally withdrawn and neglectful like his mother or emotionally expressive but very demanding and verbally abusive like his father. As Kal began to detriangulate (Kerr & Bowen, 1988) himself from his parents' relationship and his mother's alcoholism, he noticed that he also felt more empowered to advocate for himself in his professional life and in his friendships. He strengthened his social support system through engagement in his spiritual community and participation in a 12-step program.

The final stage of therapy with Kal focused on reducing the anxiety that he experienced in his relationships (in his family of origin and romantic partnerships) and fostering his differentiation of self (Kerr & Bowen, 1988) in a way that was appropriate and realistic in given his collectivistic cultural values. This allowed Kal to reengage with his parents while not absorbing their anxiety or abuse. This process of developing a sense of agency and autonomy allowed Kal to better advocate for his needs in romantic relationships.

Conclusion

Individuals who seek intimate partnerships are likely to be coping with a myriad of emotional and relational challenges and therapists who practice systemic therapy are uniquely qualified to work with such clients. When treating clients who are unpartnered, it is essential to assess for the level of distress they feel about their relationship status and determine if they are intentionally single or actively desire a romantic relationship. Whatever systemic approach to therapy is used to address the relational issues associated with clients' singlehood, we suggest that clinicians approach clients through the lens of ambiguous loss that attends to the grief that clients experience around the indefinitely missing anticipated partner. A thorough assessment of any co-occurring issues associated with loneliness such as depression, anxiety, self-harm, substance abuse, and suicide ideation should be conducted. Social support systems should be expanded in order to decrease the deleterious effects of any social isolation or loneliness. Additionally, the meaning that clients have created around their single-hood should be unpacked in order to challenge any negative or pathologizing dis-courses that may be detrimental to their overall sense of self-efficacy.

Note

1   We have protected the confidentiality of the clients described in all three case examples by using fictitious names, omitting identifying information, and limiting specific descriptions.

References

Adamczyk, K. (2017). Voluntary and involuntary singlehood and young adults' mental health: An investigation of mediating role of romantic loneliness. *Current Psychology, 36,* 888–904. doi:10.1007/s12144-016-9478-3

Ainsworth, M. (1989). Attachments beyond infancy. *American Psychologist, 44,* 709–716.

Ainsworth, M. D. S. (1991). Attachments and other affectional bonds across the life cycle. In C. M. Parkes, J. Stevenson-Hinde, & P. Marris (Eds.), *Attachment across the life cycle* (pp. 33–51). New York, NY: Routledge.

Aldous, J., & Ganey, R. F. (1999). Family life and the pursuit of happiness: The influence of gender and race. *Journal of Family Issues, 20,* 155–180.

Anderson, C., Stewart, S., & Dimidjian, S. (1994). *Flying solo: Single women in midlife.* New York, NY: Norton.

Barrett, A. E. (2000). Marital trajectories and mental health. *Journal of Health and Social Behavior, 41*(4), 451–464.

Bellani, D., Esping-Andersen, G., & Nedoluzhko, L. (2017). Never partnered: A multilevel analysis of lifelong singlehood. *Demographic Research, 37,* 53–100. doi:10.4054/DemRes.2017.37.4

Berliner, K., Jacob, D., & Schwartzberg, N. (2011). Single adults and the life cycle. In M. McGoldrick, B. Carter, & N. A. G. Preto (Eds.), *The expanded family life cycle: Individual, family, and social perspectives* (4th ed., pp. 163–175). Boston, MA: Allyn & Bacon.

Bernardon, S., Babb, K. A., Hakim-Larson, J., & Gragg, M. (2011). Loneliness, attachment, and the perception and use of social support in university students. *Canadian Journal of Behavioural Science, 43*(1), 40–51. doi:10.1037/a0021199

Bickerton, T. (1983). Women alone. In S. Cartledge & J. Ryan (Eds.), *Sex and love: New thoughts on old contradictions* (pp. 157–166). London, UK: Women's Press.

Boss, P. (2004). Ambiguous loss. In F. Walsh & M. McGoldrick (Eds.), *Living beyond loss* (2nd ed., pp. 237–246). New York, NY: Norton.

Boss, P. (2006). *Loss, trauma, and resilience.* London, UK: Norton.

Boss, P., Caron, W., Horbal, J., & Mortimer, J. (1990). Predictors of depression in caregivers of dementia patients: Boundary ambiguity and mastery. *Family Process, 29,* 245–254.

Bowlby, J. (1973). *Attachment and loss, Vol. 2: Separation: Anxiety and anger.* New York, NY: Basic Books.

Bowlby, J. (1980). *Attachment and loss, Vol. 3: Loss, sadness, and depression.* New York, NY: Basic Books.

Bowlby, J. (1988). *A secure base: Parent-child attachment and healthy human development.* New York, NY: Basic Books.

Cacioppo, J. T., & Patrick, W. (2008). *Loneliness: Human nature and the need for social connection.* New York, NY: Norton.

Campbell, L., Simpson, J. A., Boldry, J., & Kashy, D. A. (2005). Perceptions of conflict and support in romantic relationships: The role of attachment anxiety. *Journal of Personality and Social Psychology, 88,* 510–531. doi:10.1037/0022-3514.88.3.510

Carlson, D. L. (2012). Deviations from desired age at marriage: Mental health differences across marital status. *Journal of Marriage and Family, 74,* 743–758. doi:10.1111/j.1741-3737.2012.00995.x

Chappell, K. D., & Davis, K. E. (1998). Attachment, partner choice, and perception of romantic partners: An experimental test of the attachment-security hypothesis. *Personal Relationships, 5*(3), 327–342.

Chen, Y.-R. R., & Schulz, P. J. (2016). The effect of information communication technology interventions on reducing social isolation in the elderly: A systematic review. *Journal of Medical Internet Research, 18*(1). doi:10.2196/jmir.4596

Cherlin, A. J. (2004). The deinstitutionalization of American marriage. *Journal of Marriage and Family, 66*(4), 848–861.

Collins, N. L., & Read, S. J. (1990). Adult attachment, working models, and relationship quality in dating couples. *Journal of Personality and Social Psychology, 58,* 644–663. doi:10.1037/0022-3514.58.4.644

Cox, F. D. (2006). *Human intimacy: Marriage, the family, and its meaning* (10th ed.). Belmont, CA: Thompson/Wadsworth.

Dahl, C. M., & Boss, P. (2020). Ambiguous loss: Theory-based guidelines for therapy with individuals, families, and communities. In K. S. Wampler, M. Rastogi, & R. Singh (Eds.), *The handbook of systemic family therapy: Systemic family therapy and global health issues (4).* Hoboken, NJ: Wiley.

Davila, J., Karney, B. R., & Bradbury, T. N. (1999). Attachment change processes in the early years of marriage. *Journal of Personality and Social Psychology, 76,* 783–802. doi:10.1037/0022-3514.76.5.783

De Jong Gierveld, J., van Tilburg, T., & Dykstra, P. A. (2006). Loneliness and social isolation. In A. L. Vangelisti & D. Perlman (Eds.), *The Cambridge handbook of personal relationships* (pp. 485–499). Cambridge, UK: Cambridge University Press.

DePaulo, B. M. (2018). As the number of single people grows, so does the significance of families of choice [Family Focus: Fictive Kin]. *National Council on Family Relations Report Magazine, 63*(4), F14–F15.

DePaulo, B. M., & Morris, W. L. (2005). Singles in society and in science. *Psychological Inquiry, 16,* 57–83. doi:10.1080/1047840X.2005.9682918

DePaulo, B. M., & Morris, W. L. (2006). The unrecognized stereotyping and discrimination against singles. *Current Directions in Psychological Science, 15,* 251–254. doi:10.1111/j.1467-8721.2006.00446.x

Doherty, W. J. (2000). Consumer marriage and modern covenant marriage. *Marriage and Families, 3*(1), 16–22. Retrieved from https://scholarsarchive.byu.edu/cgi/viewcontent.cgi?article=1020&context=marriageandfamilies

Doka, K. J. (2008). Disenfranchised grief in historical and cultural perspective. In M. S. Stroebe, R. O. Hansson, H. Schut, & W. Stroebe (Eds.), *Handbook of bereavement research and practice: Advances in theory and intervention* (pp. 223–240). Washington, DC: American Psychological Association. doi:10.1037/14498-011

Erickson, M. J. (1998). Re-visioning the family life cycle theory and paradigm in marriage and family therapy. *American Journal of Family Therapy, 26*(4), 341–355.

Feder, K. A., Heatherington, L., Mojtabai, R., & Eaton, W. W. (2018). Perceived marital support and incident mental illness: Evidence from the National Comorbidity Survey. *Journal of Marital and Family Therapy*. Advance online publication. doi:10.1111/jmft.12343

Feeney, J. A. (2008). Adult romantic attachment: Developments in the study of couple relationships. In J. Cassidy & P. R. Shaver (Eds.), *Handbook of attachment: Theory, research, and clinical applications* (2nd ed., pp. 456–481). New York, NY: Guilford.

Fokkema, T., & Liefbroer, A. C. (2008). Trends in living arrangements in Europe: Convergence or divergence? *Demographic Research, 19*(36), 1351–1418. doi:10.4054/DemRes.2008.19.36

Fraley, R. C., & Davis, K. E. (1997). Attachment formation and transfer in young adults' close friendships and romantic relationships. *Personal Relationships, 4,* 131–144. doi:10.1111/j.1475-6811.1997.tb00135.x

Fry, R. (2017). *The share of Americans living without a partner has increased, especially among young adults.* Retrieved from http://www.pewresearch.org/fact-tank/2017/10/11/the-share-of-americans-living-without-a-partner-has-increased-especially-among-young-adults

Gore, J. S. (2014). The influence of close others in daily goal pursuit. *Journal of Social and Personal Relationships, 31*(1), 71–92. doi:10.1177/0265407513486976

Hanson, R. F., & Spratt, E. G. (2000). Reactive attachment disorder: What we know about the disorder and implications for treatment. *Child Maltreatment, 5*(2), 137–145.

Hazan, C., & Shaver, P. (1987). Romantic love conceptualized as an attachment process. *Journal of Personality and Social Psychology, 52,* 511–524.

Holt-Lunstad, J. (2017). The potential public health relevance of social isolation and loneliness: Prevalence, epidemiology, and risk factors. *Public Policy & Aging Report, 27*(4), 127–130. doi:10.1093/ppar/prx030

Howe, D., Brandon, M., Hinings, D., & Schofield, G. (1999). *Attachment theory, child maltreatment and family support: A practice and assessment model.* Houndmills, UK: Macmillan.

Jackson, J. B. (2018). The ambiguous loss of singlehood: Conceptualizing and treating singlehood ambiguous loss among never-married adults. *Contemporary Family Therapy, 40*(2), 210–222. doi:10.1007/s10591-018-9455-0

Johnson, S. M. (2003). Introduction to attachment: A therapist's guide to primary relationships and their renewal. In S. M. Johnson & V. E. Whiffen (Eds.), *Attachment processes in couple and family therapy* (pp. 3–17). New York, NY: Guilford Press.

Jones, G. W., & Yeung, W. J. J. (2014). Marriage in Asia. *Journal of Family Issues, 35*(12), 1567–1583. doi:10.1177/0192513X14538029

Kerr, M., & Bowen, M. (1988). *Family evaluation.* New York, NY: Norton.

Kiecolt-Glaser, J. K., & Newton, T. L. (2001). Marriage and health: His and hers. *Psychological Bulletin, 127,* 472–503. doi:10.1037/0033-2909.127.4.472

Kirkpatrick, L. A., & Davis, K. E. (1994). Attachment style, gender, and relationship stability: A longitudinal analysis. *Journal of Personality and Social Psychology, 66*(3), 502–512.

Koeing, J., Zimmerman, T. S., Haddock, S. A., & Banning, J. H. (2010). Portrayals of single women in the self-help literature. *Journal of Feminist Family Therapy, 22*(4), 253–274. doi:10.1080/08952833.2010.525963

Kraut, R., Patterson, M., Lundmark, V., Kiesler, S., Mukophadhyay, T., & Scherlis, W. (1998). Internet paradox: A social technology that reduces social involvement and psychological well-being? *American Psychologist, 53*(9), 1017–1031. doi:10.1037/0003-066X.53.9.1017

Landgraf, J. R. (1990). *Singling: A new way to live the single life.* Louisville, KY: Westminster.

Laplante, B., Castro-Martín, T., Cortina, C., & Martín-García, T. (2015). Childbearing within marriage and consensual union in Latin America, 1980–2010. *Population and Development Review, 41*(1), 85–108.

Latty-Mann, H., & Davis, K. E. (1996). Attachment theory and partner choice: Preference and actuality. *Journal of Social and Personal Relationships, 13*(1), 5–23.

Lee, G. R., & Payne, K. K. (2010). Changing marriage patterns since 1970: What's going on, and why? *Journal of Comparative Family Studies, 41,* 537–555.

Lehnart, J., Neyer, F. J., & Eccles, J. (2010). Long-term effects of social investment: The case of partnering in young adulthood. *Journal of Personality, 78*(2), 639–670. doi:10.1111/j.1467-6494.2010.00629.x

Lewis, K. G. (1994). *Single* heterosexual women through the life cycle. In M. P. Mirkin (Ed.), *Women in context: Toward a feminist reconstruction of psychotherapy* (pp. 170–187). New York, NY: Guilford Press.

Lewis, K. G., & Moon, S. (1997). Always single and single again women: A qualitative study. *Journal of Marital and Family Therapy, 23,* 115–134. doi:10.1111/j.1752-0606.1997.tb00238.x

Lieberman, J. S. (1991). Issues in the psychoanalytic treatment of single females over thirty. *Psychoanalytic Review, 78,* 177–198.

Linehan, M. M. (2015). *DBT skills training manual* (2nd ed.). New York, NY: Guildford.

McGoldrick, M., Gerson, R., & Petry, S. (2008). *Genograms: Assessment and intervention* (3rd ed.). New York, NY: Norton.

McKeown, J. K. L. (2015). I will not be wearing heels tonight: A feminist exploration of singlehood, dating, and leisure. *Journal of Leisure Research, 47*(4), 485–500.

Miller, A. L., Rathus, J. H., & Linehan, M. M. (2006). *Dialectical behavior therapy with suicidal adolescents.* New York, NY: Guilford Press.

Miller, R. B., Hollist, C. S., Olsen, J., & Law, D. (2013). Marital quality and health over 20 years: A growth curve analysis. *Journal of Marriage and Family, 75,* 667–680. doi:10.1111/jomf.12025

Parker, K., & Stepler, R. (2017). *As U.S. marriage rate hovers at 50%, education gap in marital status widens.* Retrieved from http://www.pewresearch.org/fact-tank/2017/09/14/as-u-s-marriage-rate-hovers-at-50-education-gap-in-marital-status-widens

Pietromonaco, P. R., & Carnelley, K. B. (1994). Gender and working models of attachment: Consequences for perceptions of self and romantic relationships. *Personal Relationships, 1*(1), 63–82.

Pinquart, M. (2003). Loneliness in married, widowed, divorced, and never-married older adults. *Journal of Social and Personal Relationships, 20*(1), 31–53.

Prabhakar, B. (2011). Causes for remaining single: A comparative study. *Journal of Psychosocial Research, 6*(2), 203–210.

Reynolds, J. (2002). Constructing the single woman in therapy. *Journal of Critical Psychology, Counselling and Psychotherapy, 2,* 20–31.

Robles, T. F., Slatcher, R. B., Trombello, J. M., & McGinn, M. M. (2013). Marital quality and health: A meta-analytic review. *Psychological Bulletin, 140,* 140–187. doi:10.1037/a0031859

Roper, S. O., & Jackson, J. B. (2007). The ambiguities of out-of-home care: Children with severe or profound disabilities. *Family Relations, 56,* 147–161.

Rucker, N. (1993). Cupid's misses: Relational vicissitudes in the analyses of single women. *Psychoanalytic Psychology, 20,* 377–391. doi:10.1037/h0079468

Santos, H. C., Varnum, M. E., & Grossmann, I. (2017). Global increases in individualism. *Psychological Science, 28*(9), 1228–1239. doi:10.1177/0956797617700622

Sarkisian, N., & Gerstel, N. (2016). Does singlehood isolate or integrate? Examining the link between marital status and ties to kin, friends, and neighbors. *Journal of Social and Personal Relationships, 33*(3), 361–384.

Satir, V., & Baldwin, M. (1983). *Satir's step by step: A guide to creating change in families.* Palo Alto, CA: Science and Behavior Books.

Schachner, D. A., Shaver, P. R., & Gillath, O. (2008). Attachment style and long-term singlehood. *Personal Relationships, 15*(4), 479–491. doi:10.1111/j.1475-6811.2008.00211.x

Schwartzberg, N., Berliner, K., & Jacob, D. (1995). *Single in a married world: A life cycle framework for working with the unmarried adult.* New York, NY: Norton.

Seccombe, K., & Ishii-Kuntz, M. (1994). Gender and social relationships among the never-married. *Sex Roles, 30*(7/8), 585–603.

Shapiro, D., & Gebreselassie, T. (2014). Marriage in sub-Saharan Africa: Trends, determinants, and consequences. *Population Research and Policy Review, 33*(2), 229–255. doi:10.1007/s11113-013-9287-4

Sharp, E. A., & Ganong, L. (2007). Living in the gray: Women's experiences of missing the marital transition. *Journal of Marriage and Family, 69*, 831–844. doi:10.1111/j.1741-3737.2007.00408.x

Shaver, P. R., & Hazan, C. (1987). Being lonely, falling in love: Perspectives from attachment theory. *Journal of Social Behavior and Personality, 2*(2), 105–124.

Shaver, P. R., & Mikulincer, M. (2006). Attachment theory, individual psychodynamics, and relationship functioning. In A. L. Vangelisti & D. Perlman (Eds.), *The Cambridge handbook of personal relationships* (pp. 251–271). New York, NY: Cambridge University Press.

Simpson, J. A. (1990). Influence of attachment styles on romantic relationships. *Journal of Personality and Social Psychology, 59*(5), 971–980.

Uchino, B. N., Uno, D., & Holt-Lunstad, J. (1999). Social support, physiological processes, and health. *Current Directions in Psychological Science, 8*(5), 145–148.

US Census Bureau. (2008). *Marriage and divorce rates by country.* Retrieved from http://www.census.gov/compendia/statab/tables/09s1292.xls

US Census Bureau. (2017a). *Historical marital status tables.* Retrieved from https://www.census.gov/data/tables/time-series/demo/families/marital.html

US Census Bureau. (2017b). *America's families and living arrangements: 2017.* Retrieved from https://www.census.gov/data/tables/2017/demo/families/cps-2017.html

US Census Bureau. (2018). *Unmarried and single Americans week.* Retrieved from https://www.census.gov/newsroom/stories/2018/unmarried-single-americans-week.html

Vespa, J. (2017). *The changing economics and demographics of young adulthood: 1975-2016. Current Population Reports.* Washington, DC: US Census Bureau.

Wang, W., & Parker, K. (2014). *Record share of Americans have never married.* Retrieved from http://www.pewsocialtrends.org/2014/09/24/record-share-of-americans-have-never-married

Waters, E., Merrick, S., Treboux, D., Crowell, J., & Albersheim, L. (2000). Attachment security in infancy and early adulthood: A twenty-year longitudinal study. *Child Development, 71*(3), 684–689.

Weiss, R. S. (1987). Reflections on the present state of loneliness research. *Journal of Social Behavior and Personality, 2*(2), 1–16.

White, M., & Epston, D. (1990). *Narrative means to therapeutic ends.* New York, NY: Norton.

Wiederhold, B. K. (2015). Twenty years of online dating: Current psychology and future prospects. *Cyberpsychology, Behavior and Social Networking, 18*(12), 695–696.

You, S., Van Orden, K. A., & Conner, K. R. (2011). Social connections and suicidal thoughts and behavior. *Psychology of Addictive Behaviors, 25*(1), 180–184.

Part V
Future Directions

21

Couple Therapy
Therapist Development, Innovations in Treatment, and Needed Research
Benjamin E. Caldwell

The practice of couple therapy has leapt forward in the past 30 years. Multiple models now carry the banner of empirically supported treatments (Carr, 2020, vol. 1; Johnson, 2002b; Lebow, Chambers, Christensen, & Johnson, 2012). Neurological research reinforces the physiological benefits of our work to restore couple relationships (Johnson, Moser, Beckes, Smith, Dalgleish, Halchuk, et al., 2013). New methods of service delivery to couples via technology are already available, and more are close at hand.

At the same time, uncomfortable questions about couple therapy and the development of couple therapists persist, many of them foundational. When couples sometimes are satisfied with therapy that ends in dissolution of the relationship, how do we define treatment success? As a corollary to that question, how can we define an effective therapist? Does the model of treatment really matter in couple therapy, given research in individual therapy suggesting that models have little to no influence on therapeutic outcome? Do therapists who provide emotionally focused couple therapy, Gottman method therapy, or integrative behavioral couple therapy (IBCT) demonstrably improve outcomes through the extensive certification programs now offered for each model—and if so, are those benefits seen only within that model? Within these or any other models, can couple therapy be effectively provided online?

Put more simply: What does it mean to be good at couple therapy? And how do we help new couple therapists get there?

In short, couple therapy works (Lebow et al., 2012; Shadish & Baldwin, 2003). Therapy can help many couples in distress. However, we do not yet fully understand *why* couple therapy works, when it does, and for whom it is best suited. And as will be reviewed here, there are outstanding questions about what exactly it means—and how impactful it is in the long term—when we say couple therapy has "worked."

In this largely forward-looking chapter, I will briefly review recent progress in the world of couple therapy, in the context of calls to action from prior reviews of the

The Handbook of Systemic Family Therapy: Volume 3, First Edition.
Edited by Karen S. Wampler and Adrian J. Blow.
© 2020 John Wiley & Sons Ltd. Published 2020 by John Wiley & Sons Ltd.

couple therapy literature. Then I will discuss the current process of training couple therapists and some outstanding questions about the kinds of training that matter most. I will examine current and near-future innovations in treatment, including new technologies that aim to make couple therapy more accessible and effective. Finally, drawing on my own professional experiences, I will talk about the research needed to support the next generation of advancements in couple therapy.

Recent Progress

To understand where we are in relation to where we have been, it is worth a review of other authors' perspectives on the status of couple therapy. Here, we start at the turn of the century and make our way forward.

In a decade review of the literature, Johnson and Lebow (2000) declared the 1990s to be the "coming of age" of couple therapy. The relationship science supporting the concepts of major couple therapy models had advanced significantly in that time, and the effectiveness of couple therapy had been repeatedly demonstrated, both in terms of improving relationships themselves and in terms of reducing symptoms of mental disorders. The authors offered a number of calls to action for future research, including the following:

- The identification of key change moments in therapy
- The development of "core outcome batteries" to standardize the measurement of couple therapy outcomes
- Greater attention to treatment dropouts
- More specific definitions of couple problems and associated treatments

A short time later, Johnson (2002b) expanded on her perspective of rapid advancement in couple therapy research, declaring that "a revolution is occurring in the field of couples therapy" (p. 378). That revolution, Johnson wrote, was driven by the integration of theory, research, and practice. It would be complete when the three could create a coherent whole, with each seamlessly impacting and inspiring the others.

In their own review of the couple therapy literature, Snyder, Castellani, and Whisman (2006) reached similar conclusions, encouraging researchers to:

- Focus on small-scale studies (in part due to funding difficulties)
- Seek out specific individual, relationship, and therapy factors that contributed to treatment failures
- Examine integrative approaches, including identifying any factors that might influence the selection, sequence, or pace of specific components of these approaches
- Examine intermediate and long-term effects of couple interventions
- Address generalizability of research findings across populations and relationship types (i.e., cohabiting and same-sex couples)
- Examine cost-effectiveness of couple treatments
- Research couple therapy change processes in addition to change outcomes
- Incorporate research on emotion regulation
- Address research design issues to better identify mediators and moderators of treatment success

A number of studies have sought to address these specific calls. As just a few examples, the key change event of softening has been specifically examined in emotionally focused therapy (EFT) (Dalgleish, Johnson, Burgess Moser, Tasca, & Wiebe, 2015); generalizability of existing models to same-sex couples has been an area of great research interest (Heiden-Rootes, Addison, & Pettinelli, 2020, vol. 3); cost-effectiveness has been reviewed, with an eye toward promoting insurance reimbursement (Caldwell, Bischoff, Derrig-Palumbo, & Liebert, 2017); and multiple studies have examined specific change processes and interventions in addition to outcomes (e.g., Gottman & Tabares, 2018; Woolley, Wampler, & Davis, 2012). Each of these represents a meaningful advance in our knowledge about how to heal couple relationships.

In 2012, Johnson joined Lebow, Chambers, and Christensen to again take stock of the couple therapy landscape. Notably, a meaningful amount of their work involved summaries of research specific to Johnson's and Christensen's models (EFT and IBCT, respectively), each of which showed compelling evidence of effectiveness. Other models had not made meaningful progress in demonstrating effectiveness during the time period of their review. While the authors did not offer explicit calls to action for future researchers, they did note that despite the extant research on common factors, the "buyer should beware" of approaches other than EFT and IBCT (p. 159).

To be sure, tremendous progress has been made in our knowledge of how to effectively treat couples in distress. There is strong and increasing support for the use of specific treatment models, better understanding of what it is that happens within these models that makes them successful, and better understanding of how applications to specific populations can be successful.

However, those foundational questions—What does it mean to be good at couple therapy? And how do we help new couple therapists get there?—remain largely unanswered, casting doubt on our understanding of those more advanced findings. For example, most couples improve in EFT and IBCT (Lebow et al., 2012). But in the studies Lebow et al. reviewed, did the researchers' definitions of improvement match what the couples themselves sought? While we hope—and indeed, generally presume—that what a model seeks to achieve is the same as what a couple seeks to achieve, there is reason to consider that this may not be the case for all couples. To define a specific therapy process, or a larger therapeutic model, as successful requires a clear understanding of what "success" actually means.

Defining Positive Outcomes

What makes couple therapy successful? Measurement of couple relationships has traditionally focused on three variables: *satisfaction*, or each partner's positive emotional experience of the relationship; *stability*, or the likelihood of the couple remaining together; and *adjustment*, or the cognitive and behavioral adaptations couples make to accommodate the presence of the other. While these variables positively correlate (it makes sense that a happy couple would be more likely to stay together), they capture meaningfully different concepts. After all, some unhappy couples are quite stable, out of religious belief, commitment to their children, or other reasons.

Measurement of the impact of couple *therapy* may expand beyond those three couple variables. For example, couple therapy has been measured based on its impact on a multitude of physical and mental health factors (for reviews related to physical and mental health respectively, see Snyder & Halford, 2012, and Baucom, Whisman, & Paprocki, 2012). One reason to measure couple therapy outcomes in this way is to avoid some of the thornier questions of measurement and even morality that can come with the three couple variables: most of us would agree that the absence of health problems is good. Whether a relationship that is stable but not satisfying represents a positive therapeutic outcome is much more debatable, an issue to which we will return later in this chapter.

Further complicating the task of defining positive therapeutic outcomes, some therapists (and, to be sure, some couples) would define the ending of the couple's relationship as a positive outcome of therapy. The therapy process may bring the couple clarity on what they want in their relationship and whether that can be achieved with their current partner. Researchers have struggled to take this into account in studies. One clinical response to this dilemma, discernment counseling, has emerged as a specific protocol for helping ambivalent or mixed-commitment couples make the difficult decision to remain in or leave a relationship (Doherty & Harris, 2017; Harris & Hall, 2020, vol. 3). If every breakup is considered a treatment failure, then we as a field could risk being seen as imposing our own values about relationship commitment onto the couples with whom we work. Not every couple would share those values. And if a breakup can still be considered a treatment success, then what is the appropriate metric for evaluating couple therapy and couple therapists?

Suppose Therapist A sees 10 couples, and those couples are likely to leave therapy broken up but ultimately satisfied with that decision and with the therapist who helped them to reach this decision. Therapist B sees 10 similar couples, and those couples report some improvement during therapy but are generally still struggling—and in their relationships—at follow-up. Which one is the more effective therapist?

The question as to whether a breakup equals a failure, and ongoing couplehood equals a success, is a thorny question that rapidly becomes moral in nature. It is, however, a question worth asking. Indeed, it is necessary to ask if we are to meaningfully evaluate students and supervisees on their work with couples, and it is appropriate to ask when considering the merits of research studies. While it is appropriate from an ethical perspective to defer to each couple's definition of success in treatment, this cannot forestall the important work of keeping therapists accountable for their outcomes. To do so requires making active choices as to which outcomes are most valued.

Professional Development

Assuming that we could meaningfully define what makes an effective couple therapist, the next foundational question arises: How are effective couple therapists made? The training processes widely used today exist largely out of tradition and commercial interests. There has been remarkably little scientific inquiry into the kinds and amounts of training that most benefit couple therapists or even make them minimally competent.

Graduate education

In marriage and family therapy graduate programs accredited by the Commission on Accreditation for Marriage and Family Therapy Education, students must learn a variety of approaches to couple therapy (COAMFTE, 2017). While these programs may spend a semester or more focused on couple therapy, the focus on each *specific* couple therapy approach can remain limited. It is unlikely that any program student graduates with competency in any one model of couple therapy, never mind an evidence-based model. This is particularly true when training in couple therapy is also expected to include specific training on intimate partner violence, sexuality, and other couple-related topics. In other licensed mental health professions, specific training in couple therapy is generally not required at all, despite the fact that couple therapy is usually within the scope of practice of all licensed psychotherapists.

Certifications

There are now a number of certification programs available in specific models, including emotionally focused therapy and Gottman therapy (Gottman Institute, 2018; International Centre for Excellence in Emotionally Focused Therapy, 2018). These certification processes typically provide a combination of lecture-style teaching, small group discussion, individual supervision, and submitting session tapes to be reviewed and graded on model fidelity. It is an extensive, and expensive, process.

Scales have been developed to measure a therapist's model fidelity (e.g., Denton, Johnson, & Burleson, 2009), and these can be used to ensure that the therapist is practicing the model in its correct form. However, there is little research in couple therapy to date that correlates certification in one of these approaches with improved treatment outcomes, especially in community settings. We also know little about if those who obtain a certification actually then go on to practice the model with fidelity over the course of time. While participants generally report positive effects from these trainings (e.g., Montagno, Svatovic, & Levenson, 2011 found that participants in a four-day EFT externship reported perceiving greater competence, in addition to experiencing personal growth as a result of the training), what little research exists that is on them is notably not comparative in nature. As a result, we currently have little knowledge of whether any particular type, focus, or amount of couple therapy training is generally superior to any other.

Less extensive and expensive are the wide variety of specific continuing education (CE) courses available surrounding couple work. Many of these courses cover specific couple *issues*, such as infidelity, in a way that is not specific to any therapy model. Other courses are designed to facilitate therapist development within a specific model. Indeed, model certification processes generally begin with courses that award CE credits (Gottman Institute, 2018; International Centre for Excellence in Emotionally Focused Therapy, 2018). In either case, while therapists generally like CE and believe that the courses make them more competent (Neimeyer, Taylor, & Cox, 2012), there is scant evidence linking CE courses in any area of psychotherapy with measurable changes in therapist effectiveness.

This begs the question: Do our existing processes for training couple therapists actually produce more effective couple therapists? There is surprisingly little research to support the notion that *any* of the ways therapists are taught to work with couples—an overview of couple therapy models in graduate education, CE focused on specific couple issues, or model-specific certification for those who seek it—actually improves a couple therapist's treatment outcomes.

Couple therapist characteristics

More general research in psychotherapy is suggesting that differences in therapeutic models themselves account for very little of the variability in treatment outcome (Wampold & Imel, 2015). And common factors theorists have made a compelling case, specific to couple therapy, that effective couple therapy models do largely the same things (Davis, Lebow, & Sprenkle, 2012; Sprenkle & Blow, 2004). They have also made the case that the therapist delivering the treatment is a core component of the effectiveness of the treatment (Blow, Sprenkle, & Davis, 2007; Wampold & Imel, 2015). Research on individual psychotherapy shows that, unsurprisingly, some therapists are more effective than others (Wampold & Imel, 2015). While *credible models* of therapy show little difference in therapeutic outcomes in head-to-head studies, there are meaningful outcome differences between individual therapists (Okiishi et al., 2006; Wampold & Imel, 2015). It stands to reason, then, that teaching models of couple therapy and specific interventions may be less important than fostering those specific characteristics and behaviors in therapists that correlate with stronger couple therapy outcomes.

Deliberate practice (Rousmaniere, 2016), outcome measurement (Miller & Hubble, 2011), and a workplace culture of accountability (Goldberg, Babins-Wagner et al., 2016; Miller & Hubble, 2011) have all emerged as key mechanisms for facilitating continued improvement in individual psychotherapy. However, there is little research, so far, to tell us how these mechanisms might impact outcomes in couple therapy. In individual work, the relationship between client and therapist is critical to outcomes (Wampold & Imel, 2015). In couple work, the therapist has to manage the therapeutic relationship between each client as well as the couple as a whole. We do not yet know the degree to which couple therapy outcomes are driven by therapist personality and presence, as they seem to be for individual therapy, versus being driven by the effective execution of technique. A component analysis of EFT showed that therapist alliance accounted for 22% of the variability in treatment outcome (Johnson & Talitman, 1997)—meaningfully greater than what previous studies of psychotherapy in general have attributed to the therapeutic alliance, which typically is around 10%.

Fife, Whiting, Bradford, and Davis (2014) proposed the "therapeutic pyramid" as a way of integrating technique, therapeutic alliance, and therapist way of being. They focused on how this model can be applied in therapist training, with therapist way of being as the foundational component. Under this thinking, a therapist's way of being allows for the development of a meaningful therapeutic alliance. Then that alliance allows for the therapist to effectively execute techniques, which would surely fall flat if the therapist had not first built a good relationship with the clients. What is notable in this conceptualization is the degree to which current therapist training (including specific training in couple therapy) focuses on technique, rather than the more foundational elements necessary for those techniques to work. Training in couple therapy may discuss some elements of therapist way of being but tends to emphasize ways of *doing*.

Even proponents of specific couple therapy models have placed some emphasis on therapist traits in the process of therapist development. Zeytinoglu-Saydam and Niño (2019) proposed the use of person-of-the-therapist training in EFT supervision, while Montagno, Svatovic, and Levenson (2011) found that self-compassion and emotional processing improved for therapists who had taken an EFT training.

Accountability has become a driving force in individual psychotherapy, with increasing calls for therapists and counselors to measure their outcomes (e.g., Blow & Karam, 2017) and at least some tentative discussion about using that outcome data to determine which therapists to keep and which to let go (Imel, Sheng, Baldwin, & Atkins, 2015). While there are meaningful concerns about using outcome data in this manner, they must be weighed against the ethical implications of allowing therapists who achieve poor outcomes to continue working with clients.

Innovations in Treatment

The first two questions can be boiled down to "How do we define good couple therapy?" and "How do we build effective couple therapists?" It is on those key foundations that any specific therapeutic tasks are built. With or without that foundation, however, every therapist entering into a therapeutic relationship with a couple needs an answer to the question, "What am I supposed to do here?" There has been rapid growth in the research base supporting EFT and IBCT, two models that provide answers to that question. Furthermore, researchers are advancing more specific couple therapy assessments, customizations, and delivery mechanisms. In some cases, these innovations raise interesting and necessary questions about the very nature of our work.

Assessment

While the defining success in couple therapy may be complicated, we have collectively grown much stronger when it comes to defining and measuring the specific changes in individual and relational well-being that can worsen as a result of relationship dysfunction and improve as a result of couple therapy. Assessment of couples and their relationships has advanced with the development of new self-report measurement tools, including some that effectively assess key variables for same-sex couples. For more information on current self-report measures for couples, see Balderrama-Durbin, Snyder, Heyman, and Haynes (2020, vol. 3).

In an effort to bring greater objectivity and precision to the study of couple interactions, the Specific Affect Coding System (SPAFF) (Coan & Gottman, 2007) was developed. The SPAFF allows researchers to code even subtle facial movements. It is because of SPAFF coding, for example, that Gottman was able to assess the impact of facial expressions of contempt on one's spouse and ultimately determine that contempt was the most damaging of Gottman's "four horsemen" (Lisitsa, 2013). Use of the SPAFF has been expanded to other interpersonal interactions, including family relationships and group therapy (Coan & Gottman, 2007).

Customization of treatment

Couple therapy is a complex undertaking. Couples bring to their relationships their own histories, personalities, communication and attachment styles, and social and cultural contexts. Furthermore, the couple system is continually influenced by the social stressors and supports they experience. For a therapist to positively impact a couple's relationship in a lasting way requires the therapist to utilize a mechanism of change that is at once precise enough to be influenced through a relatively short-term therapy process and yet also powerful enough to exert meaningful influence in spite of outside factors and stressors that could lead couples back to more familiar, if less functional, ways of being. In this light, the main effects found for couple therapy are a remarkable achievement.

At the same time, systemic therapists will recognize that even positive changes in a relationship can produce unintended consequences. Studies of premarital education and of couple therapy have shown that increases in women's positive communication predicted greater *dis*satisfaction in their relationships at follow-up (Baucom, Sevier, Eldridge, Doss, & Christensen, 2011; Schilling, Baucom, Burnett, Allen, & Ragland, 2003). Schilling et al. suggested that this may have resulted from the women mistakenly thinking that their therapists had instructed them to interact positively *instead of* talking about their problems. In any case, the effect disappeared in the Baucom et al. study once the authors controlled for withdrawal.

Given this complexity, couple therapists often engage in a difficult balancing act: they seek to maintain model fidelity while also adapting to the unique circumstances and challenges posed by each new case. Some models allow for more customization than others without violating the tenets of the model; Gottman (1999), for example, suggests a modular approach to intervention where clinicians can pick and choose what interventions might be appropriate and in what order. Toward the other end of the spectrum, EFT consists of a sequence of nine steps, though Johnson (2004) is quick to caution therapists that there is more flexibility within the approach than a strict stepwise model might suggest.

Even when there is flexibility in intervention, current models each tend to suggest that couple problems flow from a narrow range of relational dysfunctions. EFT has attachment injuries and negative interaction cycles; Gottman has unsolvable problems; IBCT has polarization. When a therapist from any of these models encounters a couple whose struggle does not appear to fit that mold, the therapist may be in the awkward position of choosing between model fidelity and reasonable treatment.

The hypothesis that couple therapy could become more effective if treatment were better tailored to the specific traits and needs of each couple stands to reason. Several couple therapy theorists are pushing the field in this direction.

Event-specific treatments Historically, specific couple problems have been understood by couple therapists as the manifestations of similar underlying processes. Couple therapists have been taught to focus their attention on those processes to help couples heal. Recently, there has been renewed interest in treatments that focus on specific couple events and challenge the assumption that problems are merely content while the therapy should focus on process.

DISCERNMENT COUNSELING Discernment counseling (Harris & Hall, 2020, vol. 3) fills a long-standing gap in the couple therapy literature, as well as in day-to-day practice: What to do with couples who have reached ambivalence about their relationships? Other models at least implicitly assume that the couple entering therapy wants to stay together and that the therapist's job is to help them find a way to do so. But many couples come to therapy at least in part to determine *whether* they should stay together. This brief model helps couples make that choice. If they choose to renew their commitment to one another and work on their problems, then they may progress to a more typical couple therapy treatment model.

BRINGING BABY HOME Bringing Baby Home (e.g., Shapiro et al., 2011) is a couple intervention model designed specifically for a couple's transition to being parents. The birth of a couple's first child can be quite stressful for a marriage, particularly if the pregnancy was not planned (Lawrence, Rothman, Cobb, Rothman, & Bradbury, 2008). Bringing Baby Home is based on the Gottmans' work and focuses on normalizing and easing the strain of the transition.

Applications of existing models EFT has been specifically applied to couples where one partner identifies as transgender (Chapman & Caldwell, 2012), couples with trauma (Johnson, 2002a), couples experiencing infertility (Soltani, Shairi, Roshan, & Rahimi, 2014), and couples where one partner has end-stage cancer. While IBCT researchers have focused more on process research than on applications to specific populations, IBCT has been applied to infidelity (Atkins, Eldridge, Baucom, & Christensen, 2005). In each instance, the authors propose or test specific application methods while also suggesting that no fundamental changes are needed to the underlying model in order for it to be effective with these particular populations.

Medication-assisted couple therapy In 2016, the US Drug Enforcement Agency approved new research in MDMA-assisted psychotherapy for post-traumatic stress disorder (PTSD) in couples. In the study group, one partner from each couple had been diagnosed with PTSD, and the other partner did not carry a PTSD diagnosis but did experience meaningful distress. The study seeks to develop a protocol for combining methylenedioxy-methamphetamine (MDMA) with cognitive-behavioral conjoint therapy (Monson & Fredman, 2012), a model similar to IBCT.

This study is innovative in many ways, one of which being its codification of medication into the treatment protocol. It has long been known, for example, that depression and relationship distress co-occur in a large number of individuals initially presenting for treatment of either problem (Beach, 2014). Further, the interaction between those two clinical issues presents a clear opportunity for a coordinated treatment protocol, where effective resolution for both issues is more likely if treatment is organized around the issue that developed first. However, there remains no treatment manual that expressly integrates medication into the treatment of couple distress. This is strong evidence of the amount of ground yet to cover to truly integrate the treatment of mental and emotional health concerns with the treatment of physical ailments.

Delivery mechanisms

Consumers who want their couple therapy packaged a particular way can now, in all likelihood, get it that way. In addition to traditional office visits, couple therapy is now offered in retreat formats, online, and via smartphone apps (e.g., Talkspace, 2018).

And of course, self-help books and couple education programs (Carlson, Daire, & Hipp, 2020, vol. 3) continue to proliferate.

Notably, there has been very little research to date on couple therapy performed in any environment other than a traditional, weekly office visit. One finding of the American Association for Marriage and Family Therapy (AAMFT) workgroup on best practices in the online practice of couple and family therapy was that, given this lack of research, couple therapy performed via technology would best be described to clients as experimental in nature (Caldwell et al., 2017).

Innovations in service delivery should be supported insofar as they show the potential for effectiveness and advance either the therapy itself or the clients' ability to access couple therapy when needed. There is nothing inherently magical about 50- to 90-minute session lengths in a therapist's office. Some of these delivery mechanisms suggest a need to reconsider what exactly qualifies as "therapy" and requires a trained, licensed human to deliver.

Application-based therapy   Couples can receive a service described as relationship counseling or therapy through a variety of smartphone applications (apps). There is some variability in the degree to which these apps make use of trained, licensed, or certified therapists. There is also variability in the degree to which these apps engage couples in a process that therapists themselves might describe as couple therapy. As one example, the app Lasting advertises itself as "Marriage counseling made simple" (The Knot Worldwide, 2018). However, the app provides couples with "accessible 5-minute sessions" that involve readings, quizzes, and exercises, but no interaction with an actual therapist. On the other hand, the app Talkspace offers couples the opportunity to connect, through their app, with a licensed or registered therapist via messaging (Talkspace, 2018). There is clearly a market for these services, though they are untested in terms of effectiveness.

Needed research

Many of the calls to action reviewed at the beginning of this chapter have been meaningfully pursued. Others have gone unanswered. In particular, the repeated calls from multiple authors to look more closely at treatment failures have been met with little apparent interest. This is troubling, considering that (a) examining failures represents a meaningful avenue for improving existing treatments and (b) dropout rates, while generally low, have exceeded one-third of couples who begin treatment in some studies (Byrne, Carr, & Clark, 2004).

Research funding is an ongoing concern. While research on couple education received meaningful support in the early 2000s as part of US government efforts to better understand and assist "fragile families," the results of this research were middling at best (e.g., Wood, Moore, Clarkwest, Killewald, & Monahan, 2012). Today, despite efforts to integrate mental healthcare and medical care in service delivery, research appears to be growing further segmented. The National Institutes of Mental Health in 2013 announced that they would be deprioritizing *DSM-5* diagnosis in their research and giving preference to mental health markers that can be measured through medical testing (Insel, 2013). While it may be easy to see this as a setback for couple therapy, it also represents an opportunity to highlight and expand upon research findings that already show couple therapy's dramatic impact on a wide variety of measurable physiological disorders (Snyder & Halford, 2012).

As has been evident throughout this chapter, advances in couple therapy have led us to a wealth of new and interesting questions about how to best help relationships in distress. Seeking answers to these questions, even when they are methodologically difficult or politically touchy, will make the work of couple therapy and the development of effective couple therapists more powerful and efficient.

Future Directions: A Personal Perspective

When examining the current status of couple therapy, my perspective is informed by my own context. I completed a doctorate in marriage and family therapy, in the process examining MFTs' attitudes and beliefs toward marriage (Caldwell & Woolley, 2008a, 2008b). I found that MFTs were no more positive about marriage than the general population, with those attitudes generally declining over time. Furthermore, MFTs actually knew much *less* about marriage and its impact than a sample of marriage educators taken more than 20 years before (Larson, 1988). This opened my eyes to a reality of couple therapy that rarely is discussed in research: I concluded that a great deal of couple therapists' work seems to be based in intuition and belief, rather than what might be objectively described as knowledge. This raised meaningful questions about the kind of training necessary for couple therapists to be effective. Does knowledge of the divorce rate, or of the impact of remarriage on families, make one a more effective couple therapist? While it stands to reason that personal attitudes and beliefs would have *some* impact on clinical work—someone who believes strongly in the benefits of marriage might work harder to help a couple stay married, compared with a therapist who does not share that belief—it is far less clear whether this leads to measurable differences in outcome.

After I completed my doctorate, I spent more than a decade serving as core faculty for a private university with master's and doctoral programs in MFT. I have now taught couple therapy coursework for multiple universities. While I can confidently say that I have fulfilled the expectations of those courses, I am far less confident that I helped to develop effective couple therapists. Simply put, there is no evidence that couple therapy training, as it currently exists at the graduate level, improves couple therapy outcomes. For all of the specific research findings now available in the world of couple therapy and even therapist education, this is a frighteningly absent foundation.

I have also specialized in couple therapy in my clinical work. I have worked as a therapist and supervisor in both agency and private practice contexts. I have trained in, and used, EFT in my work. I have also, like most therapists, deviated from the model when I felt it appropriate. The research on model adherence leaves me wondering whether such deviations are good ideas. I tend to trust my own clinical judgment, but that very construction—that my knowledge of a specific case outweighs the more general directives of a model—may be part of why couple therapists in practice do not achieve the level of treatment success seen in controlled studies (Halford, Pepping, & Petch, 2016).

Ultimately, my interest is in what I can do better as a couple therapist. Like most couple therapists, I have experienced this work as more of a calling than a career.

I want to take every opportunity I can to have as much positive impact as I can on as many couples as I can. My questions for the profession are simply broader expressions of the questions I have for myself: How can I maintain accountability for my work while also respecting each specific couple's values and needs about whether they stay together? How can I reach diverse audiences, including those who may be skeptical of therapy in general and couple therapy specifically, with treatments that are tailored to their needs? How can I identify those couples who, despite wanting to continue in their relationships, are at greatest risk of divorce or dissolution? How can I bring the benefits of couple therapy to couples who cannot or will not go to a therapist's office? And in my work as an educator, how can I teach and train couple therapists in ways that most influence their effectiveness?

Even here, I fall into a trap inherent to this work: I find myself trying to answer moral questions scientifically. Consider the essence of the questions above:

- How can I define good couple therapy?
- How can I get better as a couple therapist?
- How can I help other couple therapists be better?

Most of the research on couple therapy speaks in terms of correlation, with its underlying values allowed to serve as presumptions in the background. This is at once entirely understandable, as well as a deep crack in the foundation of our work. For example, the 5-year follow-up studies on IBCT described above looked at marital status years after treatment had ended. Nowhere do these articles state that keeping couples together is inherently good. Still, the selection of variables for measurement is, in itself, a choice that reflects specific values. While the authors cared about stability enough to measure it, they cared less about other outcomes, such as physical health.

To be clear, I in no way intend to criticize these or any authors for their choices of variables. Rather, my aim is to make clear the unanswered (and too often unasked) question of what it means to be effective (i.e., to be good) as a couple therapist. *Reducing divorce* is a worthwhile goal on a broad societal level and also one that is inappropriate for some specific couples. The same goes for *improving marital happiness*. While most of us would surely agree that *reducing relationship violence* is worthwhile, we would also likely split on whether the dissolution of a relationship that both partners want to remain in is a good means of achieving that end. The morality of these questions may further change based on specific elements of the couple's life, such as whether they have children. Indeed, some therapists might prefer a goal of *providing a family structure where children thrive* above any of the others mentioned here.

There is little reason to doubt that couple therapists generally share similar ideals: we want to assist couples in achieving happy, stable relationships that are free from violence and, if the couple has children, provide a safe and nurturing environment for those children. But the "dirty work" of defining values becomes necessary when a couple appears unable, at least in the short term, to achieve more than one of those aims (indeed, if any). Which do we give preference to over the others? Could we comfortably defer to a client's preferences, particularly if their values did not line up with our own?

Advances in the field of couple therapy will be inherently constrained until we can answer such value-based questions more clearly. To be sure, we do not all need to agree on these questions. But researchers and model developers must be more explicit about the goals they are trying to achieve and the reasons those particular goals were selected. Doing so may demonstrate that our work was far more effective than we knew: imagine if a study specific to therapy "failures," along the lines of what Snyder, Castellani, and Whisman (2006) specifically suggested, revealed that most of them ultimately broke up *and credited what they learned in therapy for helping with that decision.* The proportion of couples we could rightly say were helped by the therapy would rise.

We must be willing to ask difficult, politically sensitive questions about our work. Below are several questions that I believe we must be willing to ask, organized into three categories: therapist development, treatment of couple distress, and research standards.

Therapist development

Blow (2017), speaking about therapists broadly, noted three questions about therapist training that were in need of research-based answers: (a) Can the characteristics associated with high-performing therapists be taught to lower-performing therapists? (b) What needs to happen such that we can put greater effort into the study of effective therapists, rather than effective therapies? (c) How can we best track outcomes to improve therapist effectiveness and accountability? These questions are specifically applicable to couple therapy, even if their examination faces added layers of difficulty or complexity.

What training matters?   As the profession's title suggests, marriage and family therapy has traditionally placed strong emphasis on relationships within a family, including couple relationships. Does this emphasis equate to better success in treatment? More specifically, given that in couple therapy graduate training it is common to gear programs toward licensure as a marriage and family therapist, but are these MFT profession trained clinicians more effective in couple work when compared to psychologists, clinical social workers, or counselors? The other professions are typically not given specific training in couple therapy in their graduate programs, unless they take elective coursework—another important variable, but does this matter in terms of therapy outcomes? Intuitively, it would seem that the answer should be yes, but we do not have this evidence to support this claim. Even though this is the case, does one's profession matter in terms of outcomes? Considering the above discussion of the weaknesses in CE research, do model certifications, for example, present any real value or assurance when it comes to therapy outcomes?

Does the treatment model matter?   Snyder, Castellani, and Whisman (2006) encouraged couple therapy trainers to ensure that new couple therapists are "trained to conceptualize and practice integratively across diverse theoretical orientations" (p. 338). While there is a meaningful argument in support of this idea, it remains untested. Integrative clinicians may indeed be more successful than those who more strictly adhere to a model, but they also may not. And it is worth noting that the certification processes within models tend to encourage therapists toward model fidelity, suggesting a meaningful disagreement with more integrative practice.

Are those events, traits, or processes that produce effective individual therapists the same as those that produce effective couple therapists? It would be worth knowing whether the benefits of improving therapist way of being, and focusing on a therapist's ability to effectively build alliance with clients, translate across *all* constellations of therapy, including couple work. This question remains unanswered.

Do couple therapists get better with experience? The largest study to date of therapist experience and its impact on outcomes found that, for the average therapist, outcomes actually *declined* a bit each year (Goldberg, Rousmaniere et al., 2016). But this was a study of individual, rather than couple, therapy. Similar studies have not yet appeared for outcomes of couple therapists over time. It is possible that the complex and sometimes more conflictual nature of couple therapy lends itself well to the impact of experience. It is also possible that couple therapists fall into the same patterns as individual therapists.

Is it possible to remediate an ineffective couple therapist? If so, how? It is as true for couple therapists as it is for individual therapists: some couple therapists are simply not as effective as others. Regularly removing underperforming therapists from a clinic is likely to improve the overall effectiveness of that clinic, even if replacement therapists are drawn at random from the therapist population (Imel et al., 2015). Most educators and supervisors, however, would prefer not to (or may not legally be able to) simply cast away those therapists who are struggling in their couple work. Blow's (2017) question is appropriately pointed and may even have a different answer in the couple therapy world than it would in therapy writ large: Can the characteristics associated with high-performing *couple* therapists be taught to lower-performing couple therapists? Perhaps even more pointedly, at what point should we cut our losses, so to speak, on a specific couple therapist in training or under supervision? And how do training programs go about this legally and without high stress for all involved? Even those therapists who perform poorly relative to others may still be achieving positive results with a proportion of their couples, so this too raises difficult ethical questions about when a couple therapist is good enough.

What supervision practices improve effectiveness in couple therapy? There are some guidelines about what couple therapy supervision should entail, but these guidelines are typically based on theory and common practices and not on research. In other words, there is a lot of *writing* on couple therapy supervision, but surprisingly little actual *research* especially on how supervision might be related to improved outcomes. Indeed, while journal articles on couple therapy supervision raise important points about culture and other factors in the therapy room (e.g., Estrada, 2008), I found no studies that linked couple therapy outcomes to any supervision-related factors.

Treatment of couple distress

For as much as the field has advanced in the overall treatment of couple distress, there remain areas where we see little progress. Here, I will discuss three examples: the treatment of violent couples, the long-term prevention of divorce, and impacts on health.

Violent couples   The treatment of violent couples, discussed at greater length by Stith, Spencer, and Mittal (Chapter 5, Volume 3), is still largely dictated by the Duluth model (Pence & Paymar, 1993). The model conceptualizes and treats intimate partner violence in a manner that does not align with current understanding of most instances of relationship violence (Dutton & Corvo, 2007). Despite a fair amount of research demonstrating couple therapy to be an effective intervention that does not raise risk of future violence when couples are carefully assessed at intake (for a review, see Karakurt, Whiting, Van Esch, Bolen, & Calabrese, 2016), the conjoint treatment of violent couples is often prohibited by provider policy or even by applicable legal standards. Violent couples instead receive treatment in gender-segregated groups, often based on the Duluth model's conceptualization of IPV as a misogynistic exercise of power and control. This remains common despite research clearly indicating that most couple violence does not fit that mold.

Given high dropout and recidivism rates, Dutton and Corvo convincingly describe the Duluth-dominated current standard of treatment for IPV as "a data-impervious paradigm and a failed strategy" (Dutton & Corvo, 2007, p. 658; for a counterargument, see Paymar & Barnes, n.d.). Researchers here would do well to examine not only those processes that actually serve to repair and prevent relationship violence but also a more difficult one: Why do policy makers and treatment providers appear to demonstrate relatively little interest in moving away from a treatment that has not shown strong effectiveness and toward one with better evidence of effectiveness? Offering descriptions of agencies or policy-making bodies that have moved to allow multiple forms of treatment for couple violence, alongside the results they achieved by doing so, would be a useful first step.

Prevention of divorce   We still know very little about the long-term prevention of divorce through couple therapy. Johnson (2002b) identified this as a meaningful concern, yet in the years that have followed, few longitudinal studies have appeared for the leading couple therapy models. A 5-year follow-up on IBCT showed that one specific change in communication—wives' positivity—correlated with later relationship stability (Baucom et al., 2011). This study also found some unexpected relationships, including the fact that among couples who remained married at 5-year follow-up, their positivity was more likely to have *decreased* relative to couples who had separated. A separate 5-year follow-up specific to couples who had experienced infidelity (Marin, Christensen, & Atkins, 2014) found that, among those where the infidelity was revealed, many were able to maintain the gains they achieved in treatment. Among couples where the infidelity had been kept secret during therapy, divorce was common. No differences were found between infidelity couples who had received traditional behavioral couple therapy and IBCT, though the small sample size may be a factor.

While the research is certainly strong in supporting short-term impacts of couple therapy, its long-term impact remains unclear: Does couple therapy actually *prevent* relationship decline and breakup, or merely *delay* it? The distinction is significant. As described above, some research at least lends credence to the notion that couple therapy's impact is more lasting in nature. In addition to those studies, EFT has been shown to impact relationship-specific attachment orientation (Burgess Moser et al., 2015), which is considered to be a more lasting quality than a more immediate variable like relationship satisfaction. But the logical conclusion we may draw from these findings—that couple therapy actually *prevents* divorce, rather than delaying it—remains untested. The longest of these studies have extended 5 years beyond the conclusion of therapy, which is undoubtedly a long time to expect any healthcare intervention to remain impactful. At the same time, these studies are showing specific impacts that do not always match the predictions or intentions of therapy (e.g., Baucom et al., 2011), suggesting that additional longitudinal studies would be valuable.

Returning to the difficult and value-based questions of what makes therapy effective, longitudinal questions should continue to pursue knowledge beyond whether couples simply remain together over time. How do those couples who remain together after couple therapy remain impacted by the therapy process? And as discussed above, what treatment "failures"—meaning dropouts, relationship dissolutions, or couples who did not show short-term improvement—might actually be characterized in the long term as successes?

Impacts on health   Kiecolt-Glaser and colleagues at Ohio State have been successfully utilizing measures of biological markers to track the impacts that couples have on one another, both in immediate interactions and in overall longer-term health. Notably, she has found two paths through which distressed couple relationships appear to negatively impact overall health: distressed sleep and "metabolic alterations that promote obesity and its comorbidities" (Kiecolt-Glaser & Wilson, 2017, p. 421). While this research does not focus on therapy per se, its relevance to therapy is unmistakable. First, it confirms and reinforces the notion that relationships impact health. It is easy to wonder how many patients have been put on sleep medications or diet plans when they may have benefited more from relationship counseling. Second, Kiecolt-Glaser's work has examined short-term shifts in biological markers, directly demonstrating how negative interactions with one's partner impact the body's systems. For example, expressions of anger are linked with slow wound healing (Gouin, Kiecolt-Glaser, Malarkey, & Glaser, 2008). Transformative moments in therapy would logically appear to have the potential to promote physical healing.

Here, as in the Beach (2014) work noted above, and Gottman's work surrounding couple interactions and illness (Gottman, Levenson, & Woodin, 2001), the powerful links between relationship functioning and physical health markers show a potentially fruitful avenue for couple therapy researchers to demonstrate the systemic impact of our work. Indeed, further work in this area could make great strides in supporting couple therapy generally and its insurance reimbursement specifically. However, these links seem to be treated as little more than trivia, even among couple therapists. We must ask in greater detail, how can the impacts of couple therapy be more intentionally harnessed to improve physical health? And how can our knowledge of the links between physical and relational health be leveraged to better integrate couple therapy into routine health care?

Research standards

We do not all need to agree on the proper conceptualization of couple factors or couple treatments in order for our concepts to be useful. However, problems in research methodology in couple therapy regularly muddy the waters on matters so basic as what exactly is being studied. It is challenging enough that we lack a consistently useful definition of success in treatment; when researchers' own definitions of success do not match the measurements they use, this only further confuses the issue.

As a simple example, the Dyadic Adjustment Scale (DAS) (Spanier, 1976) is an adjustment scale (as its name suggests) with a satisfaction subscale. While there is ample debate to be had about the specific utility and measurement properties of the DAS (see Eddy, Heyman, & Weiss, 1991), the correlation between adjustment and satisfaction makes it sensible that satisfaction would be a subscale. The two concepts would indeed partially overlap on a Venn diagram. However, studies of couple satisfaction routinely use scores on the DAS—an *adjustment* measure—as their operational definition of *satisfaction* (e.g., Christensen, Atkins, Baucom, & Yi, 2010). This makes the interpretation of such studies' findings confusing at best and misleading at worst.

Modern, robust measures like the Couples Satisfaction Index (CSI) (Funk & Rogge, 2007) may partially address this concern. However, it ultimately is on us as researchers to clarify what we are attempting to measure and use instruments consistent with that concept. Far too many studies of couple therapy and couple functioning currently rely on concepts defined in ways that are unclear or inconsistent with the tools used to measure them. Researchers, educators, and clinicians alike must be able to better explain why specific outcome variables are chosen above others as defining success in treatment.

Conclusion

My hope in this chapter has been to provide something of a philosophical counter-weight to the useful specificity and practicality afforded in the other chapters of this volume and point out that any field only "advances" insofar as it knows where it is going and why it wants to get there. There is no doubt that we are more effective than ever at improving couples' satisfaction and stability, at least in the short term. Indeed, for a great deal of research, that is, as much of a destination as is needed to pursue meaningful advancement.

But it is also possible that our current paradigm of model-based intervention in an ostensibly value-free context has taken us about as far as it can. The next true innovation in couple therapy may be a significant shift in paradigm for couple therapy and research. Both individually and collectively we reach our goals more effectively once we clearly define them and understand our motivations for achieving them.

References

Atkins, D. C., Eldridge, K., Baucom, D. H., & Christensen, A. (2005). Infidelity and behavioral couple therapy: Optimism in the face of betrayal. *Journal of Consulting and Clinical Psychology, 73*(1), 144–150.

Balderrama-Durbin, C. M., Snyder, D. K., Heyman, R. E., & Haynes, S. N. (2020). Systemic and culturally-sensitive assessment of couple distress. In K. S. Wampler & A. J. Blow (Eds.), *The handbook of systemic family therapy: Systemic Family Therapy with Couples (3)*. Hoboken, NJ: Wiley.

Baucom, D. H., Whisman, M. A., & Paprocki, C. (2012). Couple-based interventions for psychopathology. *Journal of Family Therapy*, *34*(3), 250–270. doi:10.1111/j.1467-6427. 2012.00600.x

Baucom, K. J. W., Sevier, M., Eldridge, K. A., Doss, B. D., & Christensen, A. (2011). Observed communication in couples 2 years after integrative and traditional behavioral couple therapy: Outcome and link with 5-year follow-up. *Journal of Consulting and Clinical Psychology*, *79*(5), 565–576.

Beach, S. R. H. (2014). The couple and family discord model of depression: Updates and future directions. In C. R. Agnew & S. C. South (Eds.), *Interpersonal relationships and health: Social and clinical psychological mechanisms* (pp. 133–155). New York, NY: Oxford University Press.

Blow, A., Sprenkle, D., & Davis, S. (2007). Is who delivers the treatment more important than the treatment Itself? The role of the therapist in common factors. *Journal of Marital and Family Therapy*, *33*(3), 298–317.

Blow, A. J. (2017). The therapist's role in effective therapy: Three key priorities for research. *Administration and Policy in Mental Health and Mental Health Services Research*, *44*(5), 729–731. doi:10.1007/s10488-017-0804-3

Blow, A. J., & Karam, E. A. (2017). The therapist's role in effective marriage and family therapy practice: The case for evidence based therapists. *Administration and Policy in Mental Health and Mental Health Services Research*, *44*(5), 716–723. doi:10.1007/ s10488-016-0768-8

Burgess-Moser, M., Johnson, S. M., Dalgleish, T. L., Lafontaine, M.-. F., Wiebe, S. A., & Tasca, G. A. (2015). Changes in relationship-specific attachment in emotionally focused couple therapy. *Journal of Marital and Family Therapy*, *42*(2), 231–245. doi:10.1111/ jmft.12139

Byrne, M., Carr, A., & Clark, M. (2004). The efficacy of behavioral couples therapy and emotionally focused therapy for couple distress. *Contemporary Family Therapy*, *26*(4), 361–387.

Caldwell, B. E., Bischoff, R. J., Derrig-Palumbo, K. A., & Liebert, J. D. (2017). *Best practices in the online practice of couple and family therapy*. Alexandria, VA: AAMFT.

Caldwell, B. E., & Woolley, S. R. (2008a). Marital therapists' endorsement of myths about marriage. *American Journal of Family Therapy*, *36*(5), 367–387.

Caldwell, B. E., & Woolley, S. R. (2008b). Marriage and family therapists' attitudes toward marriage. *Journal of Couple & Relationship Therapy*, *7*(4), 321–336. doi:10.1080/ 15332690802368386

Carlson, R. G., Daire, A. P., & Hipp, C. J. (2020). Early prevention of couple distress: Education and enrichment programs and premarital counseling. In K. S. Wampler & A. J. Blow (Eds.), *The handbook of systemic family therapy: Systemic Family Therapy with Couples (3)*. Hoboken, NJ: Wiley.

Carr, A. (2020). Evidence for the efficacy and effectiveness of systemic family therapy. In K. S. Wampler, R. B. Miller, & R. B. Seedall (Eds.), *The handbook of systemic family therapy: The profession of systemic family therapy (1)*. Hoboken, NJ: Wiley.

Chapman, D. M., & Caldwell, B. E. (2012). Attachment injury resolution in couples when one partner is trans-identified. *Journal of Systemic Therapies*, *31*(2), 36–53.

Christensen, A., Atkins, D. C., Baucom, B., & Yi, J. (2010). Marital status and satisfaction five years following a randomized clinical trial comparing traditional versus integrative behavioral couple therapy. *Journal of Consulting and Clinical Psychology*, *78*(2), 225–235. doi:10.1037/a0018132

Coan, J. A., & Gottman, J. M. (2007). The specific affect coding system (SPAFF). In J. A. Coan & J. J. B. Allen (Eds.), *Series in affective science. Handbook of emotion elicitation and assessment* (pp. 267–285). New York, NY: Oxford University Press.

Commission on Accreditation for Marriage and Family Therapy Education (2017). *Accreditation standards*. Alexandria, VA: Author.

Dalgleish, T. L., Johnson, S. M., Burgess Moser, M., Tasca, G. A., & Wiebe, S. A. (2015). Predicting key change events in emotionally focused couple therapy. *Journal of Marital and Family Therapy, 41*, 260–275. doi:10.1111/jmft.12101

Davis, S. D., Lebow, J. L., & Sprenkle, D. H. (2012). Common factors of change in couple therapy. *Behavior Therapy, 43*(1), 36–48. doi:10.1016/j.beth.2011.01.009

Denton, W. H., Johnson, S. M., & Burleson, B. R. (2009). Emotion focused therapy-therapist Fidelity scale (EFT-TFS): Conceptual development and content validity. *Journal of Couple & Relationship Therapy, 8*(3), 226–246. doi:10.1080/15332690903048820

Doherty, W. J., & Harris, S. M. (2017). *Helping couples on the brink of divorce: Discernment counseling for troubled relationships.* Washington, DC: American Psychological Association.

Dutton, D. G., & Corvo, K. (2007). The Duluth model: A data-impervious design and a failed strategy. *Aggression and Violent Behavior, 12*(6), 658–667. doi:10.1016/j.avb.2007.03.002

Eddy, J. M., Heyman, R. E., & Weiss, R. L. (1991). An empirical evaluation of the dyadic adjustment scale: Exploring the differences between marital "satisfaction" and "adjustment.". *Behavioral Assessment, 13*, 199–220.

Estrada, D. (2008). Supervision of cross-cultural couples therapy: Giving voice to the code of silence in the supervision and therapy room. *Journal of Family Psychotherapy, 16*, 17–30.

Fife, S. T., Whiting, J. B., Bradford, K., & Davis, S. (2014). The therapeutic pyramid: A common factors synthesis of techniques, alliance, and way of being. *Journal of Marital and Family Therapy, 40*, 20–33. doi:10.1111/jmft.12041

Funk, J. L., & Rogge, R. D. (2007). Testing the ruler with item response theory: Increasing precision of measurement for relationship satisfaction with the Couples Satisfaction Index. *Journal of Family Psychology, 21*, 572–583.

Goldberg, S. B., Babins-Wagner, R., Rousmaniere, T., Berzins, S., Hoyt, W. T., Whipple, J. L., … Wampold, B. E. (2016). Creating a climate for therapist improvement: A case study of an agency focused on outcomes and deliberate practice. *Psychotherapy, 53*(3), 367–375. doi:10.1037/pst0000060

Goldberg, S. B., Rousmaniere, T., Miller, S. D., Whipple, J., Nielsen, S. L., Hoyt, W. T., & Wampold, B. E. (2016). Do psychotherapists improve with time and experience? A longitudinal analysis of outcomes in a clinical setting. *Journal of Counseling Psychology, 63*(1), 1–11. doi:10.1037/cou0000131

Gottman Institute. (2018, August 1). *Certification track.* Retrieved form https://www.gottman.com/professionals/training/certification

Gottman, J. M. (1999). *The marriage clinic: A scientifically based marital therapy.* New York, NY: Norton.

Gottman, J. M., Levenson, R., & Woodin, E. (2001). Facial expressions during marital conflict. *Journal of Family Communication, 1*(1), 37–57.

Gottman, J. M., & Tabares, A. (2018). The effects of briefly interrupting marital conflict. *Journal of Marital and Family Therapy, 44*, 61–72. doi:10.1111/jmft.12243

Gouin, J. P., Kiecolt-Glaser, J. K., Malarkey, W. B., & Glaser, R. (2008). The influence of anger expression on wound healing. *Brain, Behavior, and Immunity, 22*(5), 699–708. doi:10.1016/j.bbi.2007.10.013

Halford, W. K., Pepping, C. A., & Petch, J. (2016). The gap between couple therapy research efficacy and practice effectiveness. *Journal of Marital and Family Therapy, 42*(1), 32–44. doi:10.1111/jmft.12120

Harris, S. M., & Hall, E. L. (2020). Therapy with individuals and couples as they decide to continue or end the relationship. In K. S. Wampler & A. J. Blow (Eds.), *The handbook of systemic family therapy: Systemic family therapy with couples (3).* Hoboken, NJ: Wiley.

Heiden-Rootes, K. M., Addison, S., & Pettinelli, J. D. (2020). Working with LGBT couples. In K. S. Wampler & A. J. Blow (Eds.), *The handbook of systemic family therapy: Systemic Family Therapy with Couples (3).* Hoboken, NJ: Wiley.

Imel, Z. E., Sheng, E., Baldwin, S. A., & Atkins, D. C. (2015). Removing very low-performing therapists: A simulation of performance-based retention in psychotherapy. *Psychotherapy, 52*(3), 329–336. doi:10.1037/pst0000023

Insel, T. (2013). *Transforming diagnosis*. Retrieved form https://www.nimh.nih.gov/about/directors/thomas-insel/blog/2013/transforming-diagnosis.shtml

International Centre for Excellence in Emotionally Focused Therapy. (2018, August 1). *Road to certification*. Retrieved form https://iceeft.com/road-to-certification

Johnson, S., Moser, M., Beckes, L., Smith, A., Dalgleish, T., Halchuk, R., et al. (2013). Soothing the threatened brain: Leveraging contact comfort with emotionally focused therapy. *Plos One, 8*(11), e79314. doi:10.1371/journal.pone.0079314

Johnson, S. M. (2004). *The practice of emotionally focused couple therapy: Creating connection* (2nd Ed.). New York: Brunner/Routledge.

Johnson, S. M. (2002a). *Emotionally focused couple therapy with trauma survivors: Healing attachment bonds*. New York, NY: Guilford.

Johnson, S. M. (2002b). Marital problems. In D. H. Sprenkle (Ed.), *Effectiveness research in marriage and family therapy* (pp. 163–190). Alexandria, VA: American Association for Marriage and Family Therapy.

Johnson, S. M., & Lebow, J. (2000). The "coming of age" of couple therapy: A decade review. *Journal of Marital and Couple Therapy, 26*(1), 23–38.

Johnson, S. M., & Talitman, E. (1997). Predictors of success in emotionally focused marital therapy. *Journal of Marital and Family Therapy, 23*(2), 135–152. doi:10.1111/j.1752-0606.1997.tb00239.x

Karakurt, G., Whiting, K., Van Esch, C., Bolen, S., & Calabrese, J. (2016). Couple therapy for intimate partner violence: A systematic review and meta-analysis. *Journal of Marital and Family Therapy, 42*(4), 567–583. doi:10.1111/jmft.12178

Kiecolt-Glaser, J. K., & Wilson, S. J. (2017). Lovesick: How couples' relationships influence health. *Annual Review of Clinical Psychology, 13*(1), 421–443. doi:10.1146/annurev-clinpsy-032816-045111

Larson, J. H. (1988). The marriage quiz: College students' beliefs in selected myths about marriage. *Family Relations, 37*, 3–11.

Lawrence, E., Rothman, A. D., Cobb, R. J., Rothman, M. T., & Bradbury, T. N. (2008). Marital satisfaction across the transition to parenthood. *Journal of Family Psychology, 22*(1), 41–50.

Lebow, J. L., Chambers, A. L., Christensen, A., & Johnson, S. M. (2012). Research on the treatment of couple distress. *Journal of Marital and Family Therapy, 38*(1), 145–168.

Lisitsa, E. (2013 May 13). *The four horsemen: Contempt*. The Gottman Institute. Retrieved from https://www.gottman.com/blog/the-four-horsemen-contempt/

Marin, R. A., Christensen, A., & Atkins, D. C. (2014). Infidelity and Behavioral couple therapy: Relationship outcomes over 5 years following therapy. *Couple and Family Psychology: Research and Practice, 3*(1), 1–12.

Miller, S. D., & Hubble, M. (2011). The road to mastery. *Psychotherapy Networker, 35*, 22–60.

Monson, C. M., & Fredman, S. J. (2012). *Cognitive-behavioral conjoint therapy for PTSD: Harnessing the healing power of relationships*. New York, NY: Guilford.

Montagno, M., Svatovic, M., & Levenson, H. (2011). Short-term and long-term effects of training in emotionally focused couple therapy: Professional and personal aspects. *Journal of Marital and Family Therapy, 37*(4), 380–392. doi:10.1111/j.1752-0606.2011.00250.x

Neimeyer, G. J., Taylor, J. M., & Cox, D. R. (2012). On hope and possibility: Does continuing professional development contribute to ongoing professional competence? *Professional Psychology: Research and Practice, 43*(5), 476–486. doi:10.1037/a0029613

Okiishi, J. C., Lambert, M. J., Eggett, D., Nielsen, L., Dayton, D. D., & Vermeersch, D. A. (2006). An analysis of therapist treatment effects: Toward providing feedback to individual therapists on their clients' psychotherapy outcome. *Journal of Clinical Psychology*, 62(9), 1157–1172.

Paymar, M., & Barnes, G. (n.d.). *Countering confusion about the Duluth model*. Retrieved form https://www.theduluthmodel.org/wp-content/uploads/2017/03/Countering Confusion.pdf

Pence, E., & Paymar, M. (1993). *Education groups for men who batter: The Duluth model*. New York, NY: Springer.

Rousmaniere, T. (2016). *Deliberate practice for psychotherapists: A guide to improving clinical effectiveness*. New York, NY: Routledge.

Schilling, E. A., Baucom, D. H., Burnett, C. K., Allen, E. S., & Ragland, L. (2003). Altering the course of marriage: The effect of PREP communication skills acquisition on couples' risk of becoming maritally distressed. *Journal of Family Psychology*, 17(1), 41–53.

Shadish, W. R., & Baldwin, S. A. (2003). Meta-analysis of MFT interventions. *Journal of Marital and Family Therapy*, 29(4), 547–570.

Shapiro, A. F., Nahm, E. Y., Gottman, J. M., & Content, K. (2011). Bringing baby home together: Examining the impact of a couple-focused intervention on the dynamics within family play. *American Journal of Orthopsychiatry*, 81(3), 337–350. doi:10.1111/j.1939-0025.2011.01102.x

Snyder, D. K., Castellani, A. M., & Whisman, M. A. (2006). Current status and future directions in couple therapy. *Annual Review of Psychology*, 57, 317–344.

Snyder, D. K., & Halford, W. K. (2012). Evidence-based couple therapy. *Journal of Family Therapy*, 34(3), 229–249. doi:10.1111/j.1467-6427.2012.00599.x

Soltani, M., Shairi, M. R., Roshan, R., & Rahimi, C. (2014). The impact of emotionally focused therapy on emotional distress in infertile couples. *International Journal of Fertility and Sterility*, 7(4), 337–344.

Spanier, G. B. (1976). Measuring dyadic adjustment: New scales for assessing the quality of marriage and similar dyads. *Journal of Marriage and the Family*, 38(1), 15–28.

Sprenkle, D., & Blow, A. (2004). Common factors and our sacred models. *Journal of Marital and Family Therapy*, 30(2), 113–129.

Talkspace (2018). *Online couples therapy*. Retrieved from https://www.talkspace.com/online-therapy/couples-therapy/

The Knot Worldwide. (2018). *Get lasting*. Retrieved from https://www.getlasting.com/

Wampold, B. E., & Imel, Z. E. (2015). *The great psychotherapy debate: The evidence for what makes psychotherapy work*. New York, NY: Routledge.

Wood, R. G., Moore, Q., Clarkwest, A., Killewald, A., & Monahan, S. (2012). *The Long-Term Effects of Building Strong Families: A Relationship Skills Education Program for Unmarried Parents*. OPRE Report # 2012-28A. Washington, DC: Office of Planning, Research and Evaluation, Administration for Children and Families, US Department of Health and Human Services (OPRE).

Woolley, S. R., Wampler, K. S., & Davis, S. D. (2012). Enactments in couple therapy: Identifying therapist interventions associated with positive change. *Journal of Family Therapy*, 34(3), 284–305. doi:10.1111/j.1467-6427.2011.00577.x

Zeytinoglu-Saydam, S., & Nino, A. (2019). A tool for connection: Using the person-of-the-therapist training (POTT) model in emotionally focused couple therapy supervision. *Journal of Marital and Family Therapy*, 45(2), 233–243. doi:10.1111/jmft.12349

22

Improving Couple Interventions for Underserved Populations

Shruti Singh Poulsen

According to the Substance Abuse and Mental Health Services Administration (SAMHSA, 2017), "underserved populations" may also be referred to as "hidden" and "hard-to-reach" populations. Therefore, it is helpful to have a rigorous definition of what is meant by these terms and the implications for systemic couple therapy intervention, research, and policy formation. SAMHSA delineated five groups as "hard-to-reach" "priority populations." These groups are lesbian, gay, bisexual, transgender, and questioning (LGBTQ), veterans and military families, Hispanic and Latinx people, American Indians and Alaska Natives, and people with disabilities. People of color globally as well as in the United States are underserved and receive inadequate quality of mental healthcare and experience challenges to accessing mental health services (Greene & Blitz, 2011). Globally in predominantly White European countries or in Australia and New Zealand, people of color, for example, people of African and Middle Eastern descent, or Indigenous peoples, experience a lack in mental health services. And while globally there is limited data on the definition of "underserved" client populations, people of color, client populations in rural areas, those experiencing poverty, those living with conditions such as HIV/AIDS, and people who identify as LGBTQ are often hidden client populations with limited or no adequate mental health services (Barnett et al., 2018; Kim & Cardemil, 2011; Sodi et al., 2010).

African Americans and people of color

Many ethnic and racial minorities in the United States and globally (particularly Indigenous people of color, that is, Black and mixed-race South Africans, Australian Aboriginal and Torres Strait people, and the Maori people of New Zealand, to name a few) are underserved in terms of mental health services. In the United States, a key demographic client population that is historically underserved is African Americans

The Handbook of Systemic Family Therapy: Volume 3, First Edition.
Edited by Karen S. Wampler and Adrian J. Blow.
© 2020 John Wiley & Sons Ltd. Published 2020 by John Wiley & Sons Ltd.

(Davey & Watson, 2008). African Americans experience challenges receiving mental healthcare, and when it is available to them, it is frequently of poor quality. This is also the experience of people of color and Indigenous peoples globally (Sodi et al., 2010). The history of slavery and racism, colonization, and imperialism globally, and their continued negative implications in contemporary United States and global societies, is a considerable impediment to developing trust between underserved client populations and the mental health service delivery system (Roberts et al., 2014). African Americans, especially in rural areas, will often first turn to community and family resources when mental health needs arise. The next line of treatment then often tends to be medical health professionals and services, before lastly turning to mental health treatment providers (Davey & Watson, 2008). Davey and Watson's review on more effectively engaging client populations concurs with Brackertz's (2007) description of the characteristics of underserved populations that are critical for mental health treatment providers to grasp to better reach and serve these population's mental health needs. Demographics can impact engagement in mental health services; for example, in African American communities, the elderly and younger populations are less likely to access mental healthcare, and women are more likely to turn to mental health treatment than men. According to Davey and Watson, attitudinal characteristics and belief systems, that is, religious or other cultural beliefs, are a source of support and strength in managing mental health concerns but may also contribute to the stigmatization of seeking outside help for these concerns. African Americans may choose to rely on their own personal and community-based resources before turning to external professional mental health treatment sources including couple and family therapy modalities. This is in part due to suspicion of these systems; negative mental health services experiences that contribute to experiencing help as ineffectual and ultimately harmful; implicit and explicit experiences with systemic racism; and the stigma associated with mental health problems (Davey & Watson, 2008). These challenges are also similar to those that people of color and Indigenous peoples encounter in the global context (Sodi et al., 2010).

Nuances to definitions of "hard-to-reach" and underserved

Globally and within the United States, categories and particular identities may be useful in identifying and targeting underserved populations for possible mental health interventions. The terminology and categorization, however, is limited and limiting to a systemic and contextually sensitive understanding of how to meet the needs of these populations (Barnett et al., 2018; Brackertz, 2007; Davey & Watson, 2008; Nutt, 2007).

Rigid categorizations into specific groups limit the nuances of within-group diversity and assume homogeneity of each group (Brackertz, 2007). The author highlights additional non-stigmatizing ways in identifying populations that have challenges accessing and utilizing available community resources. These characteristics of "underserved" or "hard-to-reach" populations can include aspects of demographics, culture, behavior and attitudes, and structure. Demographics include variables such as age, gender, income, employment, education, location (e.g., rural), and populations that are under- or overrepresented in a particular demographic region. Cultural characteristics can include ethnicity or cultural background and lack of knowledge and information about mental health resources and services.

Behavioral and attitudinal characteristics can encompass lack of time, level of mistrust or trust of outside entities, and different priorities. Structural characteristics can include location of services, attitudes and competence level of outside entities' staff, challenges in procedures, difficulty accessing services, and red tape (Brackertz, 2007). Using a more nuanced approach to identifying the "underserved" or "hard-to-reach" is congruent with the systemic lens that honors contextual considerations and provides a much more holistic picture of the populations systemic family therapists aim to serve. Therefore, in addition to recognizing that people of color (African Americans, immigrants, people of color living in predominantly European White countries, for example, people of Middle Eastern or African descent), or other marginalized client populations such as LGBTQ, may be at risk of not being able to access and receive appropriate mental health services given their racial or sexual identity, they may also be at risk because of additional variables such as their age, their income level, where they live in a particular community, the lack of information about services, and the lack of service professionals who are appropriately trained and skilled to work in culturally responsive ways with diverse client populations. In understanding who are underserved clients, it is important that mental health providers have an integrative approach to understanding clients' multiple identities and contextual characteristics and experiences, which is attuned to the intersectionality of these identities and experiences (Barnett et al., 2018; Davey & Watson, 2008; Nutt, 2007).

In addition to the categories of underserved, "hard-to-reach" client populations that SAMHSA delineates, these clients also include those from disadvantaged communities who face poverty, low educational attainment, lack of health insurance, severity of mental health issues, and medical health concerns (Jones et al., 2014; Kim & Cardemil, 2011), and these individuals are also disproportionately impacted by inadequate mental health services.

Barriers to mental health services and treatment

Underserved client populations frequently report barriers to treatment including the cost of treatment along with insurance issues and difficulties gaining access to mental health services (Kim & Cardemil, 2011). Relational therapies such as couple therapy can be challenging to access due to many practitioners offering their services in private practice settings that are based on self-paying clients rather than third-party payors such as insurance companies. Becoming part of insurance panels or certified to provide mental healthcare covered by public resources such as Medicaid and Medicare can often feel like a cumbersome, time- and energy-consuming venture, with limited financial return for private practice clinicians. Funding sources such as Medicaid and Medicare often pay less for mental health services, a situation contributing to mental health service providers' lack of incentive to pursue such funding options in their practices. Additionally, in other countries, private insurance for mental health issues and treatment may not exist unless services are provided by a medical professional such as a psychiatrist. Private practitioners' fees in many countries including the United States may be out of reach for the majority of clients coming from a disadvantaged context, which then in turn contributes to these client populations being underserved. According to Jones et al., the majority of mental health needs of underserved clients tend to be partially addressed through medical health facilities and clients'

primary care resources as avenues for some mental healthcare and as a source for referrals and continuing mental health treatment (2014).

Shifts in demographics and impact on systemic interventions

Practitioners of systemic therapies, both foundational and postmodern, are increasingly paying attention to the changing demographics in the United States as well as
globally and are taking on the challenge of reaching client populations who have
historically been "hard to reach" or had difficulty accessing couple and family therapy (Lebow, 2017). Couple and family therapy, and therapy and counseling in general, has long been viewed as accessible and desirable to primarily White, middle- to
upper-middle-class urban populations (Gehart, 2013). However, with increasing
recognition of multiculturalism, cultural responsiveness, and social justice in counseling and therapy, practitioners and scholars are looking at ways to improve systemic
interventions so that they are attentive to the needs of underserved populations and
more inclusive in their reach and impact. An important aspect to becoming more
inclusive and expanding the impact of systemic therapies is the attention to hard-to-
reach, underserved client populations globally as well as in the United States (Mocan-
Aydin, 2000).

Systemic couple therapy

Couple therapy is widely accepted in the United States as a treatment of choice for
relationship and marital problems (Johnson & Lebow, 2000). In the past two decades, there has been an increasing knowledge and research base highlighting the
efficacy of couple therapy models and the specific and unique skills required to function effectively as a couple therapist (Roberts et al., 2014). However, as Johnson
and Lebow point out, much of this knowledge is based on interventions with White,
middle-class couples whose values around concepts such as closeness and intimacy
in a relationship are based on North American norms and cultural beliefs (Gurman,
Lebow, & Snyder, 2015; Johnson & Lebow, 2000). While couple therapy in the
West, and in particular North America, has progressed from being the solution of
"last resort" for troubled couple relationships, with more and more couples turning
to couple therapy for improving and building on the already existing stability in
their relationship, it remains a modality that is not often accessible to or utilized by
underserved populations for a variety of reasons, both in the United States and
globally. Across the world, in places such as China, Taiwan, Turkey, and India, and
some European countries, couple therapy continues to be the mental health modality of "last resort" with couples typically seeking therapy only in extreme cases such
as with infidelity or to deal with the divorce process (Arduman, 2013). Johnson and
Lebow (2000) report that the feminist lens and perspective have brought attention
in the couple therapy context to variables such as power, privilege, diversity in family forms, and gender. However, attunement to the needs of underserved populations impacted by these variables within the couple therapy context, and whether
they can access couple therapy interventions, has been less prevalent in the field of
systemic therapies. The purpose of this current chapter is to describe ways in which
systemic couple therapy interventions might be improved to make them more accessible to underserved populations in the United States and globally, given that these

populations are often also described as "hard to reach" when it comes to mental health service delivery and usage.

Overview of Systemic Couple and Relational Therapy Interventions

Systemic couple therapists have a rich and unique mental health perspective and theoretical orientation to draw from in determining how best to work with clients from diverse backgrounds. Systemic therapies, foundational and contemporary, are based on key core concepts (attunement to boundaries, relational processes, here-and-now perspective, focus on process rather than content, etc.) (Gehart, 2013) that are particularly well suited in working with clients from diverse backgrounds and experiences and who may be "difficult to reach" or engage in the process of therapy.

Foundational systemic couple therapy

Foundational family and couple therapy models such as Bowenian, experiential, structural, and strategic provide strong systemic understanding of family and relational functioning and pragmatic and applicable concepts, skills, and techniques in working therapeutically with a variety of relational systems such as couples (Gehart, 2013; Nutt, 2007). A critique of foundational systemic models is that given the historical and social context within which these models were developed, where traditional ways of defining family and couple structures was the norm, they have limited application and utility in many current contemporary social contexts. Another critique of foundational systemic models is that they were developed in a historical context where attunement to diversity and cross-cultural responsiveness and issues of power and privilege were virtually nonexistent. While foundational therapy models were developed by primarily male White theorists and scholars and were focused on the mental health needs of primarily White, middle-class North American client populations, they are still relevant to the practice of couple therapy in the contemporary mental health context. For example, Bowenian therapy concepts and techniques (Gehart, 2013) such as differentiation, intergenerational patterns, reducing reactivity, and the use of the multigenerational genogram for a deeper, more nuanced understanding of family-of-origin experiences, patterns, context, and meaning can be useful in working with clients from diverse backgrounds. Particularly for clients where extended family relationships, multigenerational communities, and welfare are privileged, couple therapy that emphasizes multi- and intergenerational relationships and understanding may be an avenue to focus on couple-level issues and concerns while honoring clients' cultural values.

Experiential family and couple therapy concepts such as connection, safe and secure relationships, experiencing self and others differently in the moment, and open and direct communication have great applicability as well. A key component of experiential therapy is the creation of a safe therapeutic environment and the role of the therapist as a trusted facilitator of therapeutic processes (Gehart, 2013). The Satir method of experiential therapy has a long history globally in Turkey, for example, where training in clinical services using Satir's method is widely recognized among mental health professionals (Arduman, 2013). Emotionally focused therapy's (EFT) basis in experiential and systemic concepts and interventions such as workshops for couples based on Susan Johnson's book *Hold Me Tight* (Johnson, 2008) have been particularly accessible and useful for underserved client populations globally in places such as Turkey, Taiwan, China, South Africa, and Singapore. Given that clients from underserved and hard-to-reach populations may have a mistrust of outside institutions and systems, couple therapy models with an experiential and attachment-based focus on creating trust, safety, and connection could be an important part of engaging clients positively in the couple therapy process (Johnson, 2007). In a study focusing on couples from the United States and Canada, researchers concluded that the group workshop format for the "Hold Me Tight" intervention may work well for couples who might typically avoid seeking outside help for their relationship (Kennedy et al., 2018).

Contemporary and postmodern systemic couple therapy

Systemic therapy concepts (Gehart, 2013; Nutt, 2007) such as family roles and rules, boundaries, hierarchy, organization, and communication patterns offer ways of working with diverse populations that can also honor diverse meanings and lived realities. If these concepts are defined in flexible, open ways that allow for clients to understand themselves from their own experience and meaning, therapy and couple therapy can feel like a more inclusive and accepting process for clients. For example, if therapists adhere to more traditional definitions of concepts such as family structure or boundaries and what constitutes health and good functioning (i.e., Western conceptualizations), diverse and hard-to-reach clients may have trouble relating and trusting the therapeutic process and the facilitators of that process (Carson, Jain, & Ramirez, 2009).

While foundational family and couple therapy models provide a useful systemic basis for couple therapy in the contemporary mental health context, postmodern systemic models are also well suited to working with diverse and hard-to-reach client populations (Combs & Freedman, 2012). Foundational and postmodern systemic therapies incorporate key systemic concepts (intergenerational relationships and patterns, understanding roles and rules of the system, honoring and hearing multiple realities and perspectives, a relational/holistic/contextual lens, a focus on process rather than content, on the here-and-now, in-the-moment interactions and experiences, and on intra- and interpsychic processes) that can be invaluable when working with diverse client populations and those clients that are "hard to reach." With a focus on making space for deconstructing personal and systemic narratives and meanings, the impact of dominant and potentially oppressive language and meaning, and for empowering clients in their own change process, postmodern models, in particular, have much to offer in accessing and engaging underserved client populations (Combs & Freedman, 2012; Gehart, 2013). Systemic therapies that privilege the clients' narratives, experiences, and meanings provide a valuable space for clients who are impacted day in and day out with systemic, problem-saturated, and oppressive messages and narratives. These messages and narratives are taken for granted and yet can negatively impact clients' functioning and relationships. Systemic couple therapy that can be used to make the invisible visible can thus begin to create less problem-saturated stories while also making visible the oppression of larger systemic problem narratives such as racism, classism, ageism, sexism, and so forth (Combs & Freedman, 2012). Postmodern models honor the perspective that there can be multiple realities and meanings within systems that can be valid and that the therapeutic discourse should have space to understand and process these realities.

Contemporary and empirically based systemic couple therapy

Currently in the mental health field, empirically based therapy models have come to the forefront especially in the delivery of couple therapy. Models such as EFT (Johnson, 2004), Gottman's couple therapy methods (Gottman, 1999), and integrative behavioral couple therapy (IBCT) (Christensen & Jacobson, 1998) have gained traction in various mental health settings globally and in the United States, which provide services to diverse populations. While each of these models privileges a particular mechanism of change, for example, emotional regulation and change as in the case of EFT or behavioral change in the case of Gottman's method, they are all models that are integrative in that they draw from both foundational and postmodern systemic theories and concepts. Thus, these empirically based models can offer flexible ways of working with diverse client couples but would need to be adapted to specific contexts. A critique of current empirically based couple therapy models is that much of the research is still based on client populations that are predominantly white, middle class, and heterosexual and with very specific mental health issues (e.g., mood disorders in intimate partner relationships) (Lebow et al., 2012); however, there is an increasing body of research on the use of these models with diverse couple clients, such as same-sex couples, interracial relationships, lower socioeconomic status clients, and other diverse, potentially underserved couple client populations. IBCT has been effectively used with veterans in the United States and is the couple therapy model of choice in the veteran mental health service delivery system (Erbes et al., 2008). Globally in countries such as Taiwan, Singapore, China, and Turkey, EFT is increasingly being embraced in a variety of mental health service delivery settings with clinicians from community mental health systems, psychiatry and psychology, and social work systems seeking out EFT training and supervision to promote the use of EFT with couples internationally (Arduman, 2013). EFT is a couple therapy modality that privileges the experiences of connection, a safe haven, and secure bonding within relationships. According to Karakurt and Keiley (2009, p. 13), "a basic need for human beings is having a sense of belonging to historical continuity and identity." Cultural sensitivity and awareness in couple therapists are important aspects of being able to reach out to underserved client populations, providing a much needed opportunity and space for a sense of belonging and connectedness to larger support systems. As has been demonstrated in US and Canadian context, the EFT-based "Hold Me Tight" workshop intervention (Johnson, 2008) provides couples, who may be less willing to seek out traditional one-on-one couple therapy, a group workshop format that feels less stigmatizing and is cost-effective and does not require the lengthier commitment of couple therapy (Kennedy et al., 2018). While this research has been primarily with US and Canadian couples, it may also be helpful in understanding how program and interventions such as "Hold Me Tight" workshops could be useful in reaching underserved couple client populations globally and in the United States. Underserved client populations may find it challenging to commit for lengthy couple therapy in the traditional format, may find this format financially cumbersome, and may be somewhat wary of accessing couple therapy in the one-on-one setting because of the stigma attached to seeking out mental health services. Therefore, group interventions such as "Hold Me Tight" provide a unique, nonthreatening, and valuable resource for underserved, hard-to-reach couple clients (Kennedy et al., 2018).

Underserved Populations and Accessing Systemic Couple Treatment

Utilizing Brackertz's (2007) nuanced definition of who constitutes an "underserved" or "hard-to-reach" population may be a useful way in which to begin to understand the challenges of providing couple therapy interventions to these populations. As Brackertz points out, defining who are the underserved needs to be more complex than just identifying distinct categorizations of groups of people—taking into account additional variables such as demographics, culture, behavior and attitudinal issues, and structural issues of diverse groups. These variables interact and intersect with each other as well, thus providing a more complex and complete picture of underserved couple clients. While it is widely acknowledged that therapy itself is value-laden and is a cultural context that can be quite distinct from many laypeople's experiences, values, and belief systems, couple therapy in particular is a therapy modality and context that can be challenging for potential clients to consider. When considering access to and the use of couple therapy interventions versus other individual and family therapy modalities, clinicians may need to acknowledge these potential challenges in providing couple interventions to underserved and hard-to-reach populations.

Demographic variables

Demographic variables such as age, gender, income, employment, education, location (e.g., rural), and population numbers can have an impact on how, when, whether, and where underserved clients might choose or not to access couple therapy. Rural client populations in sparsely populated communities may have difficulty accessing good couple therapy due to the lack of qualified clinicians close by. Smaller communities may also engender a sense of support for couples among their social support networks and religious communities, with troubled couples turning to these resources rather than considering more formal approaches such as couple therapy. Conversely, smaller communities may also lead couples to feel they do not have the privacy or anonymity within their communities to pursue outside support options due to perceived stigmatization and criticism from others in their community. Globally, especially in countries outside of Europe, couple therapy may still be an emerging mental health modality, thus limiting couples' knowledge and information about such resources. In countries such as China, Taiwan, India, Turkey, Middle East, and Eastern Europe, mental health services often focus on individual needs and are administered typically by psychiatry and psychology professionals and clinicians (Kaslow, 2000; Mocan-Aydin, 2000). In India, familiarity with and availability of mental health services in general is more commonly found in the large urban areas such as Chennai, Delhi, Mumbai, and Bangalore (Carson et al., 2009). Family and other systemic mental health needs are often met through social work avenues rather than systemic therapies and therapists.

Age and gender: Intrapersonal characteristics

Age and gender of clients also impact openness to couple therapy. Clients who identify as female tend to be the partner in heterosexual relationships most likely to take active steps to initiate couple therapy during times of relationship stress. The male partner may reluctantly agree to go along with his partner, but often female partners continue with pursuing therapy in some form with or without their partner. Younger client populations, and those living in urban areas, tend to be more familiar and amenable to the possibilities of couple therapy than older generations. Additionally, level of formal postsecondary education can also be an indicator of openness to couple therapy as a relationship support and intervention. Clients' exposure to the idea and concept of couple therapy through mainstream media or social media and within their own age cohorts, education, and vocational contexts can have a significant impact on their openness to pursue such a support.

Cultural variables

Cultural characteristics can include difficulty accessing services, ethnicity or cultural background, and lack of knowledge and information about resources and services. These characteristics also interact and intersect with demographic characteristics, adding to the complexity of clients' identity, experience, and understanding of couple therapy. Clients' ethnic or cultural backgrounds can have an impact on their understanding and openness to couple therapy, with some cultures and ethnicities being more open to and familiar with this resource (Paniagua, 1996). The lack of knowledge and information about diverse mental health modalities and gaining access to them can be particularly challenging to recent immigrants as they adapt and settle in their host country. Globally, services for couple therapy may be limited to urban areas and may be limited to client populations with adequate financial resources, as well as familiarity and openness to more Western sensibilities in considering couple therapy as a mental health option (Arduman, 2013; Carson et al., 2009).

Behaviors and attitudes

Behavioral and attitudinal characteristics can encompass lack of time, level of mistrust or trust of outside entities, and different ties (Brackertz, 2007). These characteristics are also influenced by demographics and cultural variables. Lack of financial resources and lower socioeconomic status can impact behaviors and attitudes by putting constraints on the time, energy, and resources that are needed for day-to-day survival; prioritizing the mental and emotional needs of the couple relationship may not be at the forefront for these clients (Carson et al., 2009). Additionally, underserved and hard-to-reach client populations may be culturally and ethnically different from most couple therapists and have also had past negative experiences with mental health providers. Thus, attitudes toward couple therapy and therapists may be underscored by mistrust and skepticism about the ability of therapists to truly understand the concerns of clients and provide them with the services they desire. Underserved client populations might turn more readily and with more trust to within-community resources and support such as religious and community leaders, family members, and close friends. In the global context, in countries such as China, Taiwan, India, and

Turkey, and even more Western-oriented countries such as Australia with Indigenous populations of people of color, there is systemic suspicion and mistrust of therapy as a primarily Western concept. Others view therapists as not being trained in the "hard" sciences of medicine, and this may impact whether clients would access couple therapy as a resource for relational and mental health problems (Arduman, 2013; Carson et al., 2009; Mocan-Aydin, 2000).

Structural challenges

Structural characteristics that may present challenges to providing couple therapy to underserved clients can include location of services, attitudes and competence level of agency staff, challenges in procedures, and red tape (Brackertz, 2007). Underserved client populations may justifiably have difficulties accessing couple therapy services when these services are primarily available in communities with which they may be quite unfamiliar and may feel unsafe to potential clients. Large universities in the United States often have clinical training labs and clinics that offer low-cost mental health services including couple therapy to the community beyond the university. However, an oft-mentioned concern in accessing these types of services is the "town-and-gown" divide potential clients experience: that they live and function in the less rarefied environment of the town or city, while the university and its services function in an "ivory tower" context with little understanding of the realities of life for people outside that context. Underserved population clients may be less likely to trust and believe that mental health providers and couple therapists have the knowledge, expertise, and competence to work with people who are diverse in various ways. Other concerns that may be a deterrent for underserved client populations include dealing with institutions and systems that are bound by unfamiliar processes, procedures, and functioning that may be perceived as bureaucracy and unnecessary red tape required to obtain desired services (Arduman, 2013). An example of this type of challenge in the global context is the author's experience as a visiting scholar in Turkey where she provided assistance in the development of a new couple and family graduate program and training clinic. In developing clinic and client forms and paperwork for the new training clinic, the author was told by her Turkish colleagues that if forms such as the consent and disclosure forms were modeled after what is required in the United States, that is, lengthy, full of details about licensure and legal and ethical issues, and so forth. Turkish clients would balk at signing such extensive paperwork and view it as unnecessary red tape and bureaucracy. This would reduce the likelihood of these clients pursuing mental health services such as couple therapy.

Additional considerations and intersectionality

Additional considerations that intersect with client demographics, cultural variables, behavioral and attitudinal issues, and structural issues are beliefs and meanings about intimate relationships, couple relationships, bonds, attachment, familial relationships, and different family structures and organization. Cross-culturally, different ethnic and cultural groups may privilege a variety of familial relationships such as the adult child and parent bond as primary, or the parents and child/children relationships that may present a philosophical challenge for couple therapists who are trained to prioritize the intimate adult partners' relationship in the therapy process (Arduman, 2013;

Gabb & Singh, 2015; Tamura & Lau, 1992). Clients from cultures that prioritize the extended family system and communal bonds and welfare in relationships may be less amenable to the concept of focusing on the intimate partner relationship primarily in the mental health setting (Carson et al., 2009).

When determining therapy modalities to utilize with diverse, underserved populations, it is important for clinicians to be skilled at assessing and understanding their clients' experiences, identities, level of acculturation, and level of connection with their cultural contexts and communities (Sperry, 2010). Sperry highlights a strategy for assessing the needs of clients for culturally sensitive therapy and then using the modalities that are most consistent with clients' beliefs, values, and understanding of self and their systems. The strategy includes understanding clients' beliefs about the source of their concern or problem, their expectations for treatment, and their family dynamics and influences. For example, in India, mental health treatment may not be as well received or accepted as other medical health concerns and treatment (Carson et al., 2009). There may also be additional hindrances to utilizing mental health services such as the stigma and shame associated with needing these services, the belief that mental health treatment is primarily for severe disorders, suspicion of mental health service providers, and views that mental health problems are a result of Westernization and imposition of Western values (Carson et al., 2009).

While it is beyond the scope of this chapter to address exhaustively the variability and complexity of diversity represented within underserved client populations, it is helpful to note that therapies such as couple therapy, when utilized from a holistic systemic lens with attunement and responsiveness to clients' contexts, meanings, and lived experiences, have the potential to benefit a wide range of couple clients. As Sperry (2010) points out, an important consideration of using couple therapy modalities so that they are culturally sensitive and responsive is that clinicians are skilled at assessing their clients' lived cultural and identity experiences and selecting intervention modalities that are congruent with clients' values, beliefs, and sense of self. Couple therapy modalities currently in use draw from a rich bank of foundational systemic theoretical perspectives, as well as progressive postmodern and empirically based theories and models. Foundational, postmodern, and empirically based systemic couple and family therapy models have much to offer diverse, underserved populations when used in ways that are flexible, adaptable, integrative, and culturally responsive/sensitive.

Challenges in engaging and retaining couple clients

Potential couple clients may go underserved and continue to be hard to reach because of lack of knowledge of marital and intimate partner relationship distress and when and how to seek appropriate treatment. Couple clients may view couple therapy as unnecessary or may have trouble being aware of and identifying relationship distress and risk factors (Morrill et al., 2011). Adding to demographic and cultural variables, lack of knowledge and misperceptions about the need for couple therapy also negatively impact access to couple therapy for underserved populations.

In a review of the research on empirically based couple treatments such as EFT and IBCT, the authors conclude that while couple therapy can be quite effective, marital and couple distress is difficult to treat (Lebow et al., 2012). Some of the reasons for this are that engaging and retaining clients can be challenging, couples who need therapy often do not seek it out or stay in the process long enough to experience the benefits, and the benefits gained in therapy may not be long lasting. The cost and often the time commitment necessary for typical systemic couple therapy in the private practice setting can be challenging. Additionally, a focus on culture needs to be included in continuing research on empirically based couple treatments (Lebow et al., 2012).

A key element to increased acceptance and use of couple therapy globally appears to be the changing demographics of family and couple systems in countries outside of North America (Kaslow, 2000). While the value and belief in the benefits of extended family systems remain consistent, the day-to-day practice of living in extended families is changing in countries such as India due to changes in the job market requiring young couples and families to migrate to locations away from their larger family systems. Increased mobility and transience for populations in countries such as India is increasingly an issue in order to meet the needs of dynamic and changing economic systems (Carson et al., 2009). These changes have led to philosophical and cultural shifts in the primacy and priority of some familial relationships, such as the importance of extended family relationships as emotional and physical support systems. The couple system structure is undergoing more of an emphasis and burden to provide for the emotional and physical needs of individuals within these systems. Thus, there has been a shift in the awareness and acceptance that the couple system may require outside intervention such as couple therapy even in cultural, international contexts, where therapy in general has often in the past been met with suspicion and stigmatization. One might argue that globalization, and thus Westernization, is leading to the promotion of Western values and ideals regarding intimate partner relationships and therefore to the demise of indigenous cultural practices, beliefs, and values (Carson et al., 2009; Mocan-Aydin, 2000). However, the changing economic realities for families and couples across the globe are also opening space for a better understanding on the delivery of couple therapy in diverse cultural contexts and to client populations that have historically been underserved and hard to reach. This opportunity for increased understanding of utilizing couple therapy models cross-culturally provides great opportunity for clinicians in the United States to improve their skills and better adapt these models to working with the increasing diversity of client populations in the North American context as well.

Adapting Couple Therapy Interventions: Integration

Systemic theories—foundational, postmodern, and empirically based—offer couple therapists a plethora of useful, flexible concepts, techniques, and skills from which to draw in working with underserved, hard-to-reach, and diverse clients. Systemic therapies are particularly useful as they provide a lens that is more meaning based, that is, flexible, and that is validating and empowering of diverse cultural realities and experiences (Combs & Freedman, 2012; Gehart, 2013). Increasingly integrative approaches to systemic and couple therapy also acknowledge the need to move away from a "one-size-fits-all" approach to therapy in order to evolve and adapt to the changing needs of diverse client populations (Blow, Sprenkle, & Davis, 2007). The common factors approach is one such way to structure an integrative way of delivering culturally responsive couple therapy services (D'Aniello, Nguyen, & Piercy, 2016). With its focus on client factors, therapist factors, the therapeutic alliance, and the role of expectancy in the therapy process, a common factors approach offers a way to draw from multiple theories and models to meet the specific needs of different clients. A common factors lens allows clinicians to effectively assess and draw from different therapy models concepts and techniques that promote an in-depth understanding of clients' experiences, contexts, and lived experiences that are a good fit for the therapist and their own skill and competence level, engender a strong and productive therapeutic alliance, and promote in clients a sense of hopefulness, possibility, and positive outcomes (Blow et al., 2007; Davis, Lebow, & Sprenkle, 2012; Sprenkle & Blow, 2004).

The common factors approach in training professionals and lay mental health service providers allows practitioners to utilize a wider array of models in ways that are theoretically sound, are culturally sensitive, and meet the needs of diverse client populations. This is a useful approach in other countries as well, such as India and China (Roberts et al., 2014). Systemic and integrative ways of working with couples cut across models and focus on using what is shown to work in therapy; this includes understanding patterns of communication and behavioral interactional patterns, building strong alliances with not only the clients in therapy but also their extended systems, supporting and motivating clients, dealing with interpersonal conflicts, and highlighting strengths and resources (Roberts et al., 2014).

Utilizing community-based service delivery systems

Community mental health service delivery practices can provide insight into connecting with underserved couple client populations, both in the United States and globally. Utilizing interventionists without formal mental health treatment training, but who are part of the communities they serve, is one recommended way to provide services to underserved client populations (Barnett et al., 2018). Couple therapists willing to engage informal support systems within the communities they serve may be more successful in making their services accessible to and utilized by underserved client populations. Additionally, couple therapists should consider increasing their knowledge and use of empirically based treatments, providing a much needed resource to communities that historically have been underserved in accessing cutting-edge, research-based interventions (La Roche & Christopher, 2008). Given some of the licensing constraints that impact billing issues in the United States, the use of community interventionists without formal training might limit the opportunities to use them in collaborations for couple therapy. However, couple therapists can also provide valuable training and supervision opportunities and consultative services to such community-based interventionists to collaborate and provide couple therapy interventions in underserved communities (Barnett et al., 2018).

Systemic couple therapy and cultural sensitivity

Couple therapy interventions, with their systemic, contextual lens, may be an ideal avenue to engage parts of the larger client system, by first accessing the intimate partner and parental subsystem. One of the common factors unique to relational therapy is the ability and opportunity to engage both members of the couple in therapy, build alliances with each partner, and include in treatment the expanded relational systems that are connected to the couple. Of course, couple therapists must be willing to and skilled in engaging the expanded system, optimizing the clients' ability to utilize both the resources that couple therapy provides and the resources that are part of the clients' expanded systems. In my own work in the United States with Asian Indian couples, having an understanding of the impact and influence of larger systems on the intimate relationship including in-laws (particularly the female partner's mother-in-law) has been critical in providing culturally responsive couple therapy. While Western perspectives privilege the intimate partner dyad and the couple's romantic relationship and connection, in many Indian couple relationships, the familial relationships and connections are privileged. In particular, even after marriage, the continued emotional connection between mother and the male partner in a heterosexual couple relationship is something that cannot be ignored in the privileging of the couple relationship. The emotional health of the couple relationship, and therefore the female partner as well, can be highly contingent on including other parts of the family system such as in-laws (Nath & Craig, 1999). Positive and inclusive experiences that support integrating other parts of the client's systems in couple therapy may promote trust in mental health service providers and institutions and thus lead to increased access of these services.

Cultural sensitivity as part of systemic work

D'Aniello, Nguyen, and Piercy (D'Aniello et al., 2016) also present a novel and useful conceptualization of a common factor that can be unique to relational therapies—that of cultural sensitivity. The authors argue that cultural sensitivity should be part of all therapy models, couple therapy included, regardless of modality. They also suggest that cultural sensitivity as a common factor in relational therapy is a characteristic of the therapist, rather than specific to a particular model. This is a useful way to conceptualize the importance and utility of cultural sensitivity in working with underserved populations. Rather than try to identify which model works with which specific client population, the authors suggest that when cultural sensitivity is viewed as a feature of the therapist rather than the model, then any model can be implemented with cultural sensitivity (D'Aniello et al., 2016).

Innovative and cutting-edge models of couple therapy such as socio-emotional relational therapy (SERT) are examples of the type of culturally sensitive and responsive mental health work that is gaining traction in the United States, particularly in accessing and treating diverse client couples (Chenfeng et al., 2017). The use of SERT in working with diverse couples includes attunement to the contextual aspects of emotional experiences within relationships and in interaction with different systems. The model also allows clinicians to attend to power and privilege and their impact in their clients' relationships and systems as well as between clinicians and clients (Chenfeng et al., 2017). The cultural humility endorsed by a model such as SERT provides an important way to reach out to diverse client populations, an approach that is less threatening and non-pathologizing.

Cultural factors and impact on accessing systemic couple therapy

Couple therapy may feel more threatening than other forms of relational therapy for client populations that are underserved and hard to reach. All therapy is value-laden and may feel stigmatizing or based on misinformed assumptions about client groups (La Roche & Christopher, 2008). Couple therapy may particularly trigger negative responses in some clients given their fears that they might be stereotyped and oppressed even further if they expose their most vulnerable aspects of their intimate partner relationships to outside scrutiny. This may be particularly challenging for the male partner in heterosexual relationships in places such as India (Carson et al., 2009). The experience of their intimate partner relationship being under a microscope may feel too close and generate some anxiety in clients. The value of "saving face" can be quite critical in cultural contexts outside of the West, such as India and China; therefore, seeking help from an outside party would be considered risky and shame-inducing not just for the couple system but for the entire family system (Roberts et al., 2014). Some clients may be more open to family therapy or therapy that focuses on their role as parents as this provides some distance and differentiation between their sense of self and the focus of the therapy interventions (Carson et al., 2009). For clients of some cultural groups, couple therapy may also feel self-centered when cultural values privilege other types of relationship connections within the family system (Paniagua, 1996). Many religious traditions in India sanction marriage as a religious and sacred responsibility, focusing on the greater welfare of families, rather than only the husband–wife dyad (Dupree et al., 2013). Gender roles that privilege the authority of the male partner, the influence and importance of the extended family system on the marital system, the continued prevalence of arranged marriages over the euphemistically termed "love marriage," and conflicts in Indian married relationships rarely focusing only on the marital dyad are all variables that have the potential to impact when, whether, and how Indian couples make choices about couple therapy treatment (Dupree et al., 2013).

In countries such as China and India, the parent–child relationship is often privileged over the intimate partner relationship (Roberts et al., 2014). Therefore, it is important for clinicians coming from other cultural contexts to be able to recognize that the primacy of the couple relationship may be a Western concept that does not always feel supportive or relevant to couples in other countries. For couple therapy to succeed in appealing to and being useful for underserved client populations, it needs to take an approach that is fully systemic in that it can focus on and support every level of system, from the micro to the macro (Nath & Craig, 1999).

Future Directions

The contributions and future potential of systemic therapies such as couple therapy remain positive and promising, especially in considering their utility in reaching diverse, underserved client populations. Whether in considering couple therapy research, or clinical practice, or training and supervision, there are several important questions to be addressed, especially for improving couple therapy services to underserved populations not just in the United States, but globally as well. Roberts et al. (2014, p. 568) highlight these questions in their paper on family therapy challenges and innovations around the world:

> How do the political aspects of mental health infrastructures and higher education affect training and the delivery of services? Who has access to systems training? At what age/ developmental stage? What keeps others away? What status/power do family therapists have? How will these dynamics shape the future of family therapy in different countries, and around the world?

These are important and useful questions that should be considered in moving the field of couple and systemic therapies forward.

Research on culturally responsive systemic couple therapy

Future directions for continued improvement to the field include adding to the understanding of how best to provide services to these populations through advancing and supporting research. Research in couple therapy can be advanced by increasing understanding of the characteristics and experiences of underserved client populations, the impediments these communities may experience in obtaining important resources, and the reasons that couple therapy has historically and traditionally had difficulty moving past its challenge of being pigeonholed as a mental health service primarily for White, middle-class Euro-American clients. Outcome research examining various systemic couple therapy models and their utility with diverse client populations in the United States and globally is also needed (La Roche & Christopher, 2008). Dissemination and implementation research has been recommended as an effective approach to advancing the connection between research and application of much needed quality interventions particularly to disadvantaged and underserved client populations (Withers et al., 2016). While it is beyond the scope of this chapter to fully describe dissemination and implementation research practices and implications, some key aspects of this type of research are useful for couple and family therapists to consider. According to Withers et al., this type of research is critical in bridging the researcher–practitioner divide and to bringing research findings to everyday practice. This is particularly important when considering public mental health practice and well-being for underserved client populations. Dissemination and implementation research in MFT has the potential to increase and improve systemic interventions in diverse mental health service settings such as social service agencies and community mental health locations, providing valuable resources to underserved client populations in those settings (Withers et al., 2016).

Implications for clinical practice of systemic couple therapy

Future directions for clinical practice could include practitioners finding ways to expand their couple therapy practices by extending outreach and psychoeducation services to diverse clients in their larger communities (Carson et al., 2009; Greene & Blitz, 2011). Practitioners may want to consider ways in which they can collaborate with community systems such as religious institutions, cultural organizations, volunteer organizations, community mental health agencies, and nontraditional healers and support systems to engage clients from underserved populations in couple therapy. Clinicians may also want to consider providing pro bono couple therapy services and psychoeducational workshops and talks in community settings (Zimmerman & Haddock, 2001) in the effort to promote and increase awareness of and acceptance of couple therapy as an important mental health treatment modality. In countries such as India, couples may be more amenable to engaging first in support groups or parenting workshops, which can then be an avenue for further engagement in couple therapy (Carson et al., 2009). The more couple therapists actively engage with their communities and the larger systems around their practice, the more opportunities there are for underserved client populations to become familiar with services such as couple therapy. Additionally, community engagement and service are ways to address the social justice aspects of meeting the needs of underserved and hard-to-reach client populations (Zimmerman & Haddock, 2001). Putting a human face of compassion, openness, and respectful curiosity to the practice of couple therapy may be useful in reducing the potential threat and stigma this type of mental health service might elicit in hard-to-reach client populations.

The future of systemic couple therapy training and supervision

Supervision and training must include developing trainees' level of comfort in talking about diversity, differences, and biases and must include opportunities to challenge one's personal and professional development to become culturally sensitive and responsive (D'Aniello et al., 2016). Many couple and family therapy trainees in graduate programs in the United States have opportunities to complete their clinical training in community mental health settings. This type of engagement at the graduate level can be encouraged and supported by therapy training programs, providing trainees opportunities to learn about and practice in settings that provide mental health services to diverse and underserved clients (Zimmerman & Haddock, 2001). Recruiting, training, and mentoring of couple therapists from racial and cultural minority populations are much needed in the mental health field (Davey & Watson, 2008). The need for a better match between the demographic, cultural, and racial characteristics of underserved client populations and the couple therapists who can serve them is critical when considering future directions in education, training, and supervision. Post-master's education and continuing education are a requirement of the majority of state licensure boards as a condition for license renewal and maintenance. The choices practicing and licensed clinicians make to accomplish their continuing education requirements can be supported to include becoming more knowledgeable and skilled in serving hard-to-reach, diverse client populations. Clinicians can also become better educated and trained in empirically based couple therapy modalities and make these a part of their practice and collaboration efforts. Cross-cultural competence and responsiveness and increasing multicultural sensitivity (Lee, 2012) and the ability to work with diverse client populations can be a priority of couple and family therapy masters and post-degree programs, thus enhancing the field's relevance and survival as a go-to mental health treatment modality that is clearly responsive to the demographic shifts in the United States and globally.

An additional concern regarding the quality in cross-cultural competence for trainees is that while students and graduates of therapy and counseling programs are able to articulate and intellectualize the understanding of cross-cultural values and beliefs (e.g., awareness of the importance of other systems such as the extended family to the couple relationship), scholars such as Nutt (2007, p. 162) wonder about:

> the depth of their understanding and their ability to deal with the complexities, loyalties, and emotions of a communal society ... wonder if their understanding is truly experiential and integrated, not merely intellectual. By this, I mean do they truly "get it," that is, get it in the sense of when, for example, we are learning a new language we transition from translating in our minds to thinking in the new language.

This is an important distinction when considering the challenge of training culturally competent and responsive couple therapists, whether they are trying to reach underserved clients in the United States or internationally. The challenge is exposing students, trainees, and supervisees to learning experiences that allow them to really integrate the knowledge in a way that is deep and meaningful and not from some sort of rote learning and memorization process.

Globally, there are opportunities for couple therapy scholars, clinicians, supervisors, and trainers to engage and promote this systemic treatment modality. Systemic scholars obtaining their education in the United States are increasingly returning to their countries of origin to introduce new couple and family therapy programs and develop the next generation of couple and family therapists internationally. Training and certification programs in Canada and the United States focusing on empirically based couple treatment modalities such as emotionally focused couple therapy, Gottman's couple therapy methods, and IBCT are increasingly being offered at the international level in places such as Southeast Asia, Turkey, and Europe. While couple and family therapy has had a long history in parts of Europe such as Great Britain and Italy, newer European republics such as the Czech Republic are in their infancy in terms of bringing the practice of couple therapy and other systemic modalities to clinical, research, and training contexts (Skorunka & Hajna, 2013). Internationally, there is a hunger, passion, and drive for mental health treatment modalities and training that are systemic and empirically based and that challenge the traditional mental health delivery systems of psychiatry and medicine (Arduman, 2013; Kaslow, 2000). Research, mental health services, supervision, and training in broader theoretical perspectives such as systemic, attachment based, and experiential in global settings where cognitive-behavioral modalities or medically based modalities tend to be more in use are needed to advance the outreach and access of systemic couple therapy to underserved and hard-to-reach client populations (Carson et al., 2009). Well-trained, systemically oriented, and culturally sensitive and responsive couple therapists who have clinical experience working with underserved client populations, and also understand the challenges and needs of underserved couple client populations in the United States and globally, may also be able to better advocate and promote the benefits of systemic couple therapy to a wider, more diverse client population. As advocates and promoters of the field of couple of family and couple therapy, newly and well-trained clinicians are well positioned to engage in outreach and client recruitment efforts in much needed areas of the United States and globally.

Technology advances and the impact on training and practice

The advances in technology are allowing for multiple creative ways for the practice, science, and art of couple therapy to be disseminated worldwide, meeting the education, training, supervision, and certification needs of couple therapists in places outside of North America. The use of inexpensive technologies such as Skype can allow new and seasoned clinicians, supervisors, and trainers to communicate internationally. Work groups, supervision groups, peer supervision, and innovative ways to provide training opportunities could be provided via such technologies (Roberts et al., 2014). Additionally, the AAMFT Code of Ethics endorses and provides ethical guidelines to the use of technology platforms such as phone and the Internet (Standard IV, 2015).

In concert with the AAMFT Code of Ethics, the 2014 standards for approved supervisor training and mentoring also provide support for utilizing technology platforms for training, supervision, and mentoring of new clinicians and supervisor candidates. New technologies are also pushing the boundaries of what can be achieved in mental health service delivery to areas such as rural communities and client populations that have historically lacked convenient access to interventions such as couple therapy. This is a promising time for the advancement of the couple therapy field and an opportunity for these treatment practices to be more accessible and benefit underserved client populations in the United States and globally.

References

AAMFT. (2014). *Approved Supervisor Designation: Standards Handbook*. Alexandria, VA: AAMFT. Retrieved from https://www.aamft.org/Legal_Ethics/Code_of_Ethics.aspx

AAMFT Code of Ethics. (2015). *American Association for Marriage & Family Therapy*. Alexandria, VA: AAMFT. Retrieved from https://www.aamft.org/Legal_Ethics/Code_of_Ethics.aspx

Arduman, A. (2013). A perspective on evolving family therapy in Turkey. *Contemporary Family Therapy 35*: 364–375. doi:10.1007/s10591-013-9268-0.

Barnett, M.L., Gonzalez, A., Miranda, J. et al. (2018). Mobilizing community health workers to address mental health disparities for underserved populations: A systematic review. *Administration and Policy in Mental Health 45*: 195–211. doi:10.1007/s10488-017-0815-0.

Blow, A.J., Sprenkle, D.H., and Davis, S.D. (2007). Is who delivers the treatment more important than the treatment itself? The role of the therapist in common factors. *Journal of Marital and Family Therapy 33*: 298–317. doi:10.1111/j.1752-0606.2007.00029.x.

Brackertz, N. (2007). *ISR Working Paper: Who is hard to reach and why? SISRQ/EL 06.07*. Retrieved from http://library.bsl.org.au/jspui/bitstream/1/875/1/Whois_htr.pdf

Carson, D.K., Jain, S., and Ramirez, S. (2009). Counseling and family therapy in India: Evolving professions in a rapidly developing nation. *International Journal for the Advancement of Counselling 31*: 45–56. doi:10.1007/s10447-008-9067-8.

Chenfeng, J., Kim, L., Wu, Y., and Knudson-Martin, C. (2017). Addressing culture, gender, and power with Asian American couples: Application of socio-emotional relationship therapy. *Family Process 56* (3): 558–573. doi:10.1111/famp.12251.

Christensen, A. and Jacobson, N.S. (1998). *Acceptance and change in couple therapy: Therapist's guide to transforming relationships*. New York, NY: W. W. Norton Company.

Combs, G. and Freedman, J. (2012). Narrative, poststructuralism, and social justice: Current practices in narrative therapy. *The Counseling Psychologist 40* (7): 1033–1060. doi:10.1177/0011000012460662.

D'Aniello, C., Nguyen, H.N., and Piercy, F.P. (2016). Cultural sensitivity as an MFT common factor. *The American Journal of Family Therapy 44* (5): 234–244. doi:10.1080/01926187.2016.1223565.

Davey, M.P. and Watson, M.F. (2008). Engaging African Americans in therapy: Integrating a public policy and family therapy perspective. *Contemporary Family Therapy 30*: 31–47. doi:10.1007/s10591-007-9053-z.

Davis, S.D., Lebow, J.L., and Sprenkle, D.H. (2012). Common factors of change in couple therapy. *Behavior Therapy 43* (1): 36–48. doi:10.1016/j.beth.2011.01.009.

Dupree, W.J., Bhakta, K.A., Patel, P.S., and Dupree, D.G. (2013). Developing culturally competent marriage and family therapists: Guidelines for working with Asian Indian American couples. *The American Journal of Family Therapy 41*: 311–329. doi:10.1080/01926187. 2012.698213.

Erbes, C.R., Polusny, M.A., MacDermid, S., and Compton, J.S. (2008). Couple therapy with veterans and their partners. *Journal of Clinical Psychology 64* (8): 972–983. doi:10.1002/ jclp.20521.

Gabb, J. and Singh, R. (2015). The uses of emotion maps in research and clinical practice with families and couples: Methodological innovation and critical inquiry. *Family Process 54* (1): 185–197. doi:10.1111/famp.12096.

Gehart, D.R. (2013). *Mastering competencies in family therapy: A practical approach to theory and clinical case documentation*, 2e. Boston, MA: Cengage Learning.

Gottman, J.M. (1999). *The marriage clinic: A scientifically based marital therapy*. New York, NY: W. W. Norton & Company.

Greene, M.P. and Blitz, L.V. (2011). The elephant is not pink: Talking about white, black, and brown to achieve excellence in clinical practice. *Clinical Social Work 40*: 203–212. doi:10.1007/s10615-011-0357-y.

Gurman, A.S., Lebow, J.L., and Snyder, D.K. (2015). *Clinical handbook of couple therapy*, 5e. New York, NY: Guilford Press.

Johnson, S.M. (2004). *The practice of emotionally focused couple therapy: Creating connection*, 2e. New York, NY: Taylor & Francis Routledge.

Johnson, S.M. (2007). The contribution of emotionally focused couples therapy. *Journal of Contemporary Psychotherapy 37*: 47–52. doi:10.1007/s10879-006-9034-9.

Johnson, S.M. (2008). *Hold me tight: Seven conversations for a lifetime of love*. New York, NY: Little, Brown & Co.

Johnson, S.M. and Lebow, J. (2000). The "coming of age" of couple therapy: A decade in review. *Journal of Marital and Family Therapy 26* (1): 23–38. doi:10.1111/j.1752-0606.2000. tb00273.x.

Jones, E., Lebrun-Harris, L.A., Sripipatana, A., and Ngo-Metzger, Q. (2014). Access to mental health services among patients at health centers and factors associated with unmet needs. *Journal of Health Care for the Poor and Underserved 25*: 425–436. doi:10.1353/ hpu.2014.0056.

Karakurt, G. and Keiley, M. (2009). Integration of a cultural lens with emotionally focused therapy. *Journal of Couple & Relationship Therapy 8* (1): 4–14. doi:10.1080/ 15332690802626684.

Kaslow, F.W. (2000). History of family therapy. *Journal of Family Psychotherapy 11* (4): 1–35. doi:10.1300/J085v11n04_01.

Kennedy, N., Johnson, S.M., Wiebe, S.A. et al. (2018). Conversations for connection: An outcome assessment of the *Hold me Tight Relationship Education* program, and recommendations for improving future research methodology in relationship education. *Journal of Marital & Family Therapy*: 1–16. doi:10.1111/jmft.12356.

Kim, S. and Cardemil, E. (2011). Effective psychotherapy with low-income clients: The importance of attending to social class. *Journal of Contemporary Psychotherapy 42*: 27–35. doi:10.1007/s10879-011-9194-0.

La Roche, M. and Christopher, M.S. (2008). Culture and empirically supported treatments: On the road to a collision? *Culture & Psychology 14* (3): 333–356. doi:10.1177/13540 67X08092637.

Lebow, J. (2017). Editorial: The expanding world of couple and family therapy. *Family Process 56*: 281–284. doi:10.1111/famp.12295.

Lebow, J., Chambers, A.L., Christensen, A., and Johnson, S.M. (2012). Research on the treatment of couple distress. *Journal of Marital and Family Therapy 38* (1): 145–168. doi:10.1111/j.1752-0606.2011.00249.x.

Lee, E. (2012). A working model of cross-cultural clinical practice (CCCP). *Clinical Social Work Journal 40*: 23–26. doi:10.1007/s10615-011-0360-3.

Mocan-Aydin, G. (2000). Western models of counseling and psychotherapy within Turkey: Crossing cultural boundaries. *The Counseling Psychologist 28* (2): 281–298. doi:10.1177/0011000000282007.

Morrill, M.I., Eubanks-Fleming, C.J., Harp, A.H. et al. (2011). The marriage checkup: Increasing access to marital health care. *Family Process 50* (4): 471–485. doi:10.1111/j.1545-5300.2011.01372.x.

Nath, R. and Craig, J. (1999). Practising family therapy in India: How many people are there in a marital therapy. *Journal of Family Therapy 21*: 390–406. doi:10.1111/1467-6427.00127.

Nutt, R.L. (2007). Society of counseling psychology, division 17 of the American Psychological Association, implications of globalization for training in counseling psychology: Presidential address. *The Counseling Psychologist 35* (1): 157–171. doi:10.1177/0011000006294671.

Paniagua, F.A. (1996). Cross-cultural guidelines in family therapy practice. *The Family Journal: Counseling and Therapy for Couples and Families 4* (2): 127–138. doi:10.1177/1066480796042005.

Roberts, J., Abu-Baker, K., Fern-Andez, C.D. et al. (2014). Up close: Family therapy challenges and innovations around the world. *Family Process 53* (3): 544–576. doi:10.1111/famp.12093.

Skorunka, D. and Hajna, D. (2013). Family therapy in the heart of Europe. *Contemporary Family Therapy 35*: 212–222. doi:10.1007/s10591-013-9242-x.

Sodi, S., Esere, M.O., Gichinga, E.M., and Hove, P. (2010). Marriage and counselling in African communities: Challenges and counselling approaches. *Journal of Psychology in Africa 20* (2): 335–340. doi:10.1080/14330237.2010.10820383.

Sperry, L. (2010). Culture, personality, health, and family dynamics: Cultural competence in the selection of culturally sensitive treatments. *The Family Journal: Counseling and Therapy for Couples and Families 18* (3): 316–320. doi:10.1177/1066480710372129.

Sprenkle, D. and Blow, A.J. (2004). Common factors and our sacred models. *Journal of Marital and Family Therapy 30*: 113–129. doi:10.1111/j.1752-0606.2004.tb01228.x.

Substance Abuse and Mental Health Services Administration. (2017). *Shining a light on "Hidden" and "Hard-to-Reach" populations*. Retrieved from https://www.samhsa.gov/capt/sites/default/files/resources/increasing-cultural-competence-reduce-behavioral-hd.pdf

Tamura, T. and Lau, A. (1992). Connectedness Versus Separateness: Applicability of Family Therapy to Japanese Families. *Family Process 31* (4): 319–340. doi:10.1111/j.1545-5300.1992.00319.x.

Withers, M.C., Reynolds, J.E., Reed, K., and Holtrop, K. (2016). Dissemination and implementation research in marriage and family therapy: An introduction and call to the field. *Journal of Marital and Family Therapy 43* (2): 183–197. doi:10.1111/jmft.12196.

Zimmerman, T.S. and Haddock, S.A. (2001). The weave of gender and culture in the tapestry of a family therapy training program. *Journal of Feminist Family Therapy 12* (2–3): 1–31. doi:10.1300/J086v12n02_01.

23

Public Policy and Systemic Family Therapy for Couples

William J. Doherty

Of all the systems that systemic family therapy engages, the public policy arena may be the most invisible in everyday practice, the least emphasized in training—and the one with the most far-reaching implications for the field. Because people do not become therapists because they are policy enthusiasts, they are inclined to entrust this domain to their organizational leaders. This chapter makes a case for the vital significance of public policy for the ability of systemic family therapists to do their clinical work—and for their ability to make unique contributions to society, government, and culture.

I will deal with four areas: (a) a brief history of state and federal policies that have regulated the profession and made it a legitimate form of therapy practice, (b) government policies that have mandated reimbursement for systemic family therapists and stimulated private insurers to do the same, (c) the ongoing challenge of institutionalizing "relationship therapy" as a reimbursable treatment domain, and (d) the profession's untapped potential for contributing in societal and policy areas. The chapter can be read as a companion piece to Doherty (2020, vol. 1), on the sociocultural origins and development of systemic family therapy. The focus will be on US public policy, particularly as it relates to couple therapy, although there is much to be learned from global policy work on how to support families in an increasingly complex world (United Nations, 2015). The chapter can also be read as a companion piece with Hodgson and Lamson (2020, vol. 1) who offer detailed guidelines for how therapists can become involved in public policy and with Cowan and Cowan (2020, vol. 2) who describe ways for researchers in the field to engage with public policy priorities and with government officials.

Becoming a Profession

New forms of professional practice arise not just because professionals have innovative ideas (i.e., the standard insider account), but when they are seen as responding to important societal needs of the day (Sullivan, 2015). In the case of systemic family

---

The Handbook of Systemic Family Therapy: Volume 3, First Edition.
Edited by Karen S. Wampler and Adrian J. Blow.
© 2020 John Wiley & Sons Ltd. Published 2020 by John Wiley & Sons Ltd.

therapy, that context was growing concerns for the durability of marriages during the Great Depression and the post-World War II era and worries about the ability of families to raise well-adjusted children during the Cold War era (Elder, 2018; May, 2017).

Two branches of systemic family therapy emerged separately under the umbrellas of "marriage counseling" and "family therapy." Many early practitioners of the former were outside of the mental health field (gynecologists were the most prominent early group, along with social workers, pastoral counselors, and social scientists who did not consider themselves mental health practitioners) (Dowbiggin, 2014; Nichols, 1992). Leaders in this slowly emerging field in the 1930s–1950s avoided conflict with psychiatrists, who were the only group licensed to practice psychotherapy, by framing their work in terms of counseling for here-and-now relationship adjustment problems rather than in-depth psychotherapy in the dominant Freudian tradition (Nichols, 1992).

As the 1960s approached, there was a loosening of the medical monopoly on psychotherapy, with psychologists winning the right to practice psychotherapy outside of medical supervision. This opened the door for marriage counselors to present themselves to the public as treating both relationship dysfunction and the psychological issues connected to relationship dysfunction, not just life adjustment problems, albeit they still called themselves "counselors" as distinguished from psychotherapists.

Starting in the late 1950s, family therapy, which developed independently from marriage counseling, was founded by psychiatrists and other mental health professionals. Over the next two decades, marriage counselors and family therapists moved closer together, and the main professional and credentialing organization changed its name several times, from the American Association of Marriage Counselors to the American Association of Marriage and Family Therapists to the American Association for Marriage and Family Therapy (AAMFT) (Nichols, 1992).

The tremendous growth of the field in the 1970s, now with a trove of books, several academic journals, and new training programs, led its leaders to push for an independent profession. Thus emerged the distinction between the *practice* of systemic family therapy (which can be done by any licensed mental health professional) and the *profession* of marriage and family therapists (a title that can only be used in the United States by individuals credentialed to use that name based on specified academic coursework and supervised training). For new professions like marriage and family therapy, the process of winning public and legislative approval can be tortuous, involving opposition from existing professions that feel threatened and extensive lobbying efforts to convince public officials to create a new license and regulatory board. The first breakthrough, which showed what was possible, had come via licensing in California in 1963, then followed a difficult multi-decade effort into the twenty-first century when all states credentialed what were by then called marriage and family therapists. This effort was a central focus of the resources of AAMFT and its state divisions.

The distinction between the profession and the practice has been a divisive issue for systemic family therapy. When AAMFT decided to prioritize the profession, emphasizing the accrediting of stand-alone masters and doctoral programs in universities, many systemic family therapists from other mental health professions felt excluded. They had learned systemic family therapy largely outside of formal academic programs by taking a course or two in their social work or psychology graduate program and then learning through training institutes, workshops, and clinical supervision. To their dismay, these practitioners were no longer eligible to become clinical members of AAMFT. In reaction to AAMFT, the American Family Therapy Association (AFTA) was founded in 1978 by Murray Bowen and other family therapy leaders to promote the theory and practice of family therapy outside of the credentialing umbrella. After starting out in competition with (and even antagonism toward) AAMFT, AFTA leaders eventually went their own way with a smaller organization of more senior family therapists, eventually changing the name to the American Family Therapy Academy. Bowen later reconciled with AAMFT by doing a master founder interview at an AAMFT conference a few days before his death in 1990. (I remember it well because I was the interviewer.) But the distinction between profession and practice remains a challenging issue for the field, given that many practitioners of systemic family therapy do not identify with the profession of marriage and family therapy. Other countries have had their own varied experiences with the evolution of this new profession alongside more established mental health professions (Sim & Sim, 2020, vol. 1; Sim & Shamai, 2020, vol. 4).

Government Support for Reimbursement for Systemic Family Therapy

In addition to the importance of creating standards for ethical, competent practice, a principal reason for prioritizing government credentialing of marriage and family therapists was to ensure the economic viability of those who entered the field through marriage and family therapy academic programs as opposed to social work, counseling, psychology, and other mental health disciplines. Insurance coverage, which the public increasingly expected, depended on state licensure or certification. In the early decades of AAMFT, systemic family therapists charged fees for service, worked for agencies that covered their salaries, or were reimbursed as members of established professions. The first significant breakthrough for reimbursing AAMFT members (after a 1976 court battle) came from the federal CHAMPUS program for military members and their families (Nichols, 1992). This ruling allowed for direct reimbursement for those whose only professional identity was marriage and family therapy. Another important breakthrough came in 1978 when the US Department of Health, Education, and Welfare recognized accredited marriage and family therapy training programs. This meant that two major government bodies officially recognized the distinctive nature of the profession with a special body of knowledge and skills to contribute to the public good.

The 1980 publication of DSM III and the subsequent movement toward requiring mental health diagnosis to show that the treatment was "medically necessary" presented a major challenge for the field of systemic family therapy. AAMFT leaders believed it was crucial for the economic future of the profession to represent itself to government and insurers as a bona fide mental health profession whose members were able to diagnose and treat mental disorders. This stance was far from origins of the field in marriage counseling (treating relationship problems, not individual mental disorders) and in family therapy (whose pioneers were anti-diagnosis and focused attention away from the "identified patient"). On the other hand, AAMFT, whose lobbyists frequently encountered the stereotype among policy makers that marriage and family therapists were mere "marriage counselors," wanted to emphasize that systemic family therapy was actually a modality for treating mental health disorders. Indeed, research evidence was mounting that systemic family therapy was effective in treating a number of disorders (Carr, 2020, vol. 1; Sprenkle, 2002). But this strategic decision to pivot away from an emphasis on the treatment of relational problems and instead toward relationship interventions only to treat individual disorders would come to haunt the field thereafter, particularly affecting couple therapy, where the most common focus of treatment is the relationship and not an impaired individual (see discussion later in this chapter).

The combination of state credentialing and emphasizing systemic family therapy as a specialized mental health treatment modality was ultimately successful in forging an economic base for marriage and family therapists. Medicaid reimbursement plans, which are decided at the state level, began to reimburse marriage and family therapists, who argued that all state-credentialed mental health practitioners should be included on Medicaid panels. It became more difficult for private insurers to exclude MFTs, although they could and did use other means of limiting the number of therapists on their panels. And, when other professional groups mounted campaigns to exclude MFTs from diagnosing and conducting mental health treatment, AAMFT successfully used lobbyists and the courts to defeat those threats to the independence of the profession. By the second decade of the twenty-first century, the profession was institutionally established beyond what the pioneers could have imagined. Whether they would have liked all aspects of what the field had become is another question.

Public Policy Challenges for the Systemic Family Therapy

A major challenge for the profession is that Medicare, which arrived in the 1960s prior to the solidification of the profession, has not allowed for reimbursement for professionals whose only license is marriage and family therapy. Obtaining federal recognition for Medicare proved more difficult than state recognition for Medicaid, perhaps because state lobbying is easier than federal. The consequences are serious: in addition to depriving elderly individual and their families of the services of systemic family therapists, Medicare exclusion limits the access of systemic family therapists to an important population and to employment in integrative care medical settings, where managers are reluctant to hire therapists whose services cannot be reimbursed by Medicare (American Association for Marriage and Family Therapy [AAMFT], 2005).

A second important public policy challenge for the field is how to define itself in terms of its historical, paradigmatic emphasis on family relationships. As mentioned, Medicare and Medicaid (and most private insurers) reimburse only for medically necessary treatment, which in practice means that an individual must carry a mental health diagnosis and the therapist must designate a procedure code for treating that individual. Systemic family therapists seeing families have generally adapted by diagnosing an individual child or adolescent and using a family therapy procedure code. They justify reimbursement for additional sessions (beyond what the insurer initially allows) with reference to the functioning of the diagnosed family member, not to the functioning of the family itself.

Couple therapy has had more difficulty qualifying for reimbursement because its explicit focus has on repairing relationship problems instead of individual mental health problems. Neither government nor most private insurers regularly reimburse for couple therapy for distressed relationships. Systemic family therapists who do couple therapy have responded in two ways. Some ask clients to pay out of pocket for couple therapy, while others work around the insurance requirements by diagnosing one spouse/partner and using an individual psychotherapy treatment code—a practice that is approved by some insurers but not others. In my own experience, some insurance case managers engage in a "don't ask/don't tell" approach by indirectly encouraging that couple therapy be done via individual coding. A consequence is that couple therapy remains underground in the healthcare system, a largely undocumented treatment whose prevalence and costs are not known. It is hard to know how these compromises with the realities of the current healthcare system may have influenced the practice of systemic family therapy, although it is known that half or more of the clinical work conducted by systemic family therapists is individual psychotherapy (Doherty & Simmons, 1996; Rampage, 2014).

When systemic family therapists try to make the case for reimbursing couple therapy, the opposing argument from insurers is that this would open up excessive new costs—this despite widespread agreement that marital distress leads to mental health issues for spouses and other family members. To this point, Clawson, Davis, Miller and Webster (2017), in their article laying out the case for insurance reimbursement for couple therapy, summarize the evidence for the high costs of marital distress (both health and financial) already borne by insurance carriers and employers. They conclude that there are strong reasons, both economic and health related, for making couple therapy a mainstream, reimbursed form of treatment. They document how marital distress is a leading influencer of a range of medical, mental health, and job-related problems. And they argue that couple therapy can be viewed as affordable in the healthcare system through offsetting the costs of other, more expensive, medical care treatments and by offering preventive help before relationship problems lead to individual psychological problems that insurance must cover.

There is also an unspoken obstacle to covering relationship therapies: their lack of fit of the prevailing medical model and with the mainstream culture of American individualism. Although Americans value their marriages and families, mainstream American cultural and legal prisms focus on individual rights and freedoms (Bellah, Madsen, Sullivan, Swidler, & Tipton, 1986), with professional services therefore mainly oriented to individuals. Families come into the conventional picture as caregivers to say a child or elderly parent, but not as relational units themselves with their own needs for solidarity, mutual support, and ways to deal with differences. The research mechanisms of the federal health agencies dealing with health are focused almost exclusively on the health of individual persons, not on families or relationships per se. In other words, the health of families or couples is rarely the direct outcome to be promoted in a government-funded program of research or service. Rather, it is the well-being of individuals with health or other personal problems. Even the cogent case made by Clason, Davis, Miller, & Webster (2018) for Medicare reimbursement is based on the assumption that society (and funders) should care mainly about the consequences of untreated marital distress for individual health and for the costs of treating individuals.

There is an irony here. The only profession named for relationship (i.e., marriage and family) has come to justify its legitimacy in the healthcare system without affirming the importance of relationships for their own sake, aside from their role in individual health, as necessary for human flourishing and as a bedrock of human societies—and therefore as worthy of support and therapeutic intervention when their health and viability are threatened. We thus yield to the American culture of individualism and fail to assert the core value of the profession (Doherty, 1995, 2020, vol. 1).

Systemic Family Therapy and Public Policy Challenges and Controversies

In the earliest decades of the profession, programs at the annual meeting of the American Association of Marriage Counselors suggested that leaders were concerned with large public issues affecting marriage and family life (Nichols, 1992). Indeed, there was a sense that the world needed this new profession to cope with contemporary social problems. But the subsequent almost singular focus on creating a publicly recognized new profession—an understandable priority for many decades—steered the new profession away from conversations about major public policy issues related to family life. This is especially true of changes in marriage and marriage-related policies. Here I will refer both to formal public policy and to the public/cultural conversations that inform public policy, giving examples of missed opportunities that I argue we should learn from as we look at the future relevance of the field.

The public dimensions of divorce

First, we were invisible in the public dialog on no-fault divorce, which has reshaped the landscape of American marriage since the first law was passed in California in 1971 and then spread across the country over the next 30 years. Perhaps no public policy has affected so many marriages and families. To repeat a refrain, the only profession with the word "marriage" in its name did not engage this policy change in a visible way at the academic, clinical, or organizational level (as far I can determine). The family law community drove the no-fault divorce movement, and sociologists and child psychologists studied its mixed effects on families and children. But our field did not engage in the public conversation about the pluses and minuses of no-fault divorce and, nowadays, with the related controversy over issues such as presumption of shared parenting. The question can be asked, "What could systemic family therapists uniquely offer in this arena, beyond what other professions contribute?" Don't we have a unique, on the ground perspective on the family as a system and its health during and after a divorce?

As an example, I believe that the prevailing legal standard of the "best interests of the child" lacks a systemic perspective and therefore has encouraged the development of professional child advocates and competition between parents for who can better promote the child's well-being. A systemic/relational perspective has something to offer here, including how unresolved marital issues play out in divorce proceedings and create triangulation with professionals. My work with collaborative lawyers and courts has shown how the neat legal category of no-fault can create a fiction that powerful marital and family of origin dynamics are not playing out and creating damage that could be prevented with a systemically informed divorce system. Ambivalence about the divorce goes on well into the legal process for many couples, whereas most professionals assume that both partners are on board with getting divorced (Doherty, Willoughby, & Peterson, 2011).

Second, we did not join the cultural conversation about the dramatic rise in divorce in the United States. The divorce rate doubled from 1968 to 1980, a period during which the field of systemic family therapy was coalescing as a profession. We responded clinically by developing methods of divorce counseling (Lebow, 2015), but once again, there was little commentary from our field about the implications of an escalating divorce rate, which together with rising cohabitation and nonmarital birth rates transformed marriage and family life in the United States. As I discussed in Doherty (2020, vol. 1), part of the silence may have stemmed from the uncertainly in the field about the balance between personal fulfillment and commitment in marriage and family relationships.

We have also lacked a tradition of considering the public health aspects of high divorce and nonmarital birth rates for American families and for society. Our clinical emphasis has appropriately been on accepting every couple as they come to us—married, divorce, cohabiting, and so forth—but as a profession we also have missed our responsibility to engage the cultural and public health dimensions of the clinical issues that we work with. A particular divorce may be a healthy individual choice for a client, given the alternative of staying in a damaging marriage, but at a societal level, escalating rates of divorce (and nonmarital births) have brought a host of social and economic problems. A challenge for the field in the future is to embrace a both/and approach: to develop clinical tools to help every kind of family and to engage in the cultural and public health dimensions of large-scale shifts in how couples and families form, break up, and reconstitute.

The public dimensions of same sex marriage

Third, we were late to the public and legal conversation on same-sex marriage, which, along with divorce reform laws, has been the most important public policy issue concerning marriage in the past 60 years. On a broader level than just support or nonsupport for legalized same-sex marriage, systemic family therapists could have engaged this public issue in the kind of nuanced terms that stem from a systemic/relational perspective rather than only an individual rights perspective. The latter is that gay people have a right to the public benefits of marriage and to be treated with respect by systemic family therapists. True enough, but a systemic perspective also engages the important value of marital relationships for individuals, couples, families, and communities—marriage as a public good and source of human flourishing.

We still have a chance to make a difference on the gay marriage issue by applying systemic thinking. After the Supreme Court approved gay marriage, the US population has been involved in an extended conversation about the conflict between the right to commercial services of engaged gay couples and the rights of religious proprietors to decline services for gay weddings. If we simply weigh in on the basis of which side has the greater individual right—the couple or the business owner—we miss the opportunity to add a systemic/relational perspective that could engage both sides in reaching solutions together. I have had experience bringing people from these two sides together for meaningful conversation across their differences, where stereotypes were broken down and no one was devalued. The gatherings involved storytelling and listening for common values as well as points of difference. Participants become more human to each other as they look for ways we can have a society where gay people do not experience discrimination and wedding service providers do not feel they are compromising their religious beliefs. My point is that if systemic family therapists simply weigh in on the individualistic terms of contemporary cultural conflicts—which are usually framed in terms of competing personal rights—then we do not make a unique contribution in the public sphere.

The public dimensions of marriage formation

Finally, we have been missing on the structural and cultural barriers to forming and sustaining marriages and long-term committed relationships—issues such as poverty, discrimination, housing, healthcare, mass incarceration, education, and immigration policies. These are social determinants of stable, healthy marriages and long-term committed relationships (akin to the social determinants of health). As mentioned in Doherty (2020, vol. 1), a large social class divide has opened up in recent decades along social class lines between those with college education who are more likely to marry and stay married to raise children and the rest of the population, whose relationship journeys more often involve nonmarital births, multiple cohabitations and breakups, and marriages that end in divorce and further instability (Cherlin, 2010; Putnam, 2016).

This social class divide is showing up in clinical practice. In my personal observation, couple therapists nowadays tend to see middle-class couples who married before having children, while family therapists tend to see children and single parents whose prior couple unions dissolved before marriage or through divorce and who experience a churning through multiple complex family forms. Decades ago, many family therapists learned to do couple therapy in the second stage of family therapy, when the adolescent identified client was doing better and the marital issues emerged. Although I am aware of no studies to support my observation, it seems far less common nowadays for a family therapist to treat a family of a child or adolescent where the parents are in an intact first marriage. Although systemic family therapists do not have solutions for this growing class divide when it comes to family stability, I believe we have to more actively engage the cultural and public policy implications of this driver of social inequality.

Reasons we have not been involved

The question can be asked: "Why has the field of systemic family therapy been largely uninvolved in the public health conversation about families?" As mentioned, like many other professions, we have focused on important professional guild issues (especially licensure and reimbursement). Other factors are resource limitations in our professional organizations (time, money, staff) and the political and religious diversity of their members (an especially strong factor for AAMFT). In addition, systemic family therapists in academic positions earn their tenure and reputation more for clinical research than for writing about broader cultural and policy issues. Of course, there is a robust literature on social justice for marginalized groups in society, but that focus is not a substitute for a broader family public health and public policy perspective.

A final underlying factor may be the micro focus of all therapy fields. In our academic programs, there is little attention to family demographic changes such as the social class gap in marital stability or to issues such as how rapid technological changes are affecting families. Systemic family therapists are not trained to think of the family in sociological terms as a social institution influenced by social and economic trends; rather, we are trained to think of families as a set of interpersonal relationships.

This distinction is important. Social institutions come with bodies of law and social norms because they are seen as serving vital social goods (Giddens, 1984). Parenthood, for example, is not just a personal relationship between a parent and a child, but a social institution (you cannot decide one day to stop fulfilling your parenting responsibilities). When it comes to relationship therapy, the field moved away from using the social institution term "marriage" and substituted the term "couples" in order to be more inclusive of the range of relationships seen in therapy, particularly when gay couples could not legally marry. However, marriage in contemporary US society is more than one form of intimate relationship among others—both institutionally and culturally. That is why the controversy over gay marriage was so important, with advocates not wanting to settle for "civil unions" that would fall short of the legal protections (and obligations) and the cultural endorsement involved with marriage.

In my view, our blind spot about the social institution and public good aspects of marriage limits our ability to be persuasive players in public policy and in contemporary cultural conversations and controversies about marriage. If we cannot even say the word "marriage" in our literature and at our conferences, then how do we participate in cultural and public policy deliberations about marriage? As a start, I suggest that we start using "marriage and couple therapy" to refer to clinical practice with couples who have made a permanent and public commitment (this is a functional definition of marriage even if some couples do not make it legal) and couples who seek our services without a lifelong commitment. The distinction has clinical implications too, particularly when a divorce/breakup in on the table, because generally the stakes are higher and the emotions more intense when there has been a prior assumption of lifelong commitment. Our movement away from the term "marriage therapy" came out of an era when the institution of marriage was not available to all couples, a situation no longer the case. If we can become more comfortable with the "M word" (marriage), we will be able to better engage the public and cultural dimensions of the institution of marriage, such as the implications for social inequality of high marriage rates for college educated Americans and declining rates for other Americans.

Public Policy Recommendations for the Future

The field's engagement with public policy can be strengthened on two levels: professional advancement and wider public policy issues affecting families. The former directly relates to the self-interest of systemic family therapists. In addition to protecting state licensure from threats that would diminish the scope of practice of systemic family therapists, the most urgent priority is recognition by Medicare. Marriage and family therapists will be on the periphery of healthcare without Medicare reimbursement. We cannot expect AAMFT staff to make this happen without the direct engagement of members' time, energy, and money. Much more local education and pressure on members of Congress will be needed—the very strategies that won state licensure across the country. The formation and strengthening of alliances with professional counselors and other groups who are currently excluded from Medicare could be an effective strategy, just as it has been at the state level.

The second most important profession-related public policy area is the acceptance of couple therapy and other forms of direct relationship therapy (such as between adult family members in a world of family cutoffs) as worthy of reimbursement by government and private insurance systems. This may have to occur first in the government-sponsored programs of Medicaid or Medicare for other insurers to come on board. Although more cost-offset research is needed (Clawson et al., 2017), progress will also depend on finding legislators who will champion this change and expend time and political capital on it—that is the key to moving legislation forward. A breakthrough in one state and a careful evaluation of the fiscal impact could alleviate concerns that reimbursing for relationship therapy will break the budget.

Another key strategy for placing relational therapy into the healthcare system is being pursued mostly by family psychologists and psychiatrists working on the inclusion of relational diagnoses in the DSM diagnostic manual (Wamboldt, Kaslow, & Reiss, 2015). For example, Foran, Whisman, and Beach (2015) present a way to use more precise diagnosis of intimate partner violence relational problems to differentiate couples in the "clinical" range from those within the "normal" range of complaints. If therapy reimbursement is inevitably going to be tied to a diagnosis, then sophisticated relational diagnosis may be the point of entry into the system.

A third priority area is more direct federal funding for academic training in systemic family therapy along the lines of doctoral fellowships available to psychologists. A current example of success is the minority fellowship program through AAMFT, which has opened up federal support for specialized training and mentoring of doctoral students in accredited marriage and family therapy programs and does include an emphasis on public policy. Goodman, Morgan, Hodgson, and Caldwell (2018) provide guidelines for how to develop a public policy identity as a family therapist.

A fourth area is promoting federal research funding for couple therapy outcome studies, which would require an explicit funding priority on relationships per se, not just relationships as a context for individual functioning. A vigorous champion in the federal government might be needed for this to happen, as occurred in the 1960s when Senator Robert Kennedy pushed through legislation calling for military members and their families to have access to marriage and family counselors (Nichols, 1992). Of course it is also the responsibility of researchers in our field to come up with better research questions and enhanced ways to measure the impact of our interventions.

A fifth area is changing state laws that ban conjoint therapy when there has been interpersonal violence. This is an unnecessary limitation on practice of couple therapists who, if they follow the law, would refuse treatment for couples with a history of violence but where the current risk is low. The laws were passed prior to recent research showing that many of these couples can be treated successfully in couple therapy (McCollum & Stith, 2011).

Key Areas for Policy Work

In this chapter I have argued for the importance of engaging the national public policy discussion beyond the direct needs of the profession. At a minimum this could take the form of white papers published by groups of systemic family therapy thought leaders on their own or through AAMFT or AFTA. In other cases it could involve direct advocacy for policies that improve family well-being. Following are some areas ripe for policy work, followed by ideas for how systemic family therapists could make unique contributions to social change based on a systemic/relational lens:

- The effects of poverty on the ability of families to do their work of raising the next generation. A particularly powerful perspective of systemic family therapist would be that of how poverty (combined with the experience of racism by minority families) makes healthy couple and parent–child relationships exceedingly difficult both currently and for generations to come. We see this clearly in our practice. Unfortunately, the issue of poverty has declined as a focal point of public policy attention in recent decades; systemic family therapists could help put it back into focus from a multigenerational family perspective.
- The effects of immigration laws and policies on families. Here too the contributions of systemic family therapists could start from the challenges we see in our offices—the family dislocation, the absent parents, the fear of being seized and deported (even among documented immigrant families), and the desire to live normal, safe lives in a new land. The emphasis would be on calling out the legal and cultural burdens created for immigrant families, both those with legal documents and those without. A statement that went beyond into policy solutions would take a systemic perspective on the divisions in the country on this issue, offering something to both sides (including the fears of working class people about losing their jobs and communities to immigrants) while emphasizing the needs of immigrant and migrant families. It should be noted here (and in the other examples I have provided) that I am encouraging an approach that does not simply take a traditional one-sided approach (liberal versus conservative) but that shows an understanding of the lived experience of all stakeholders in public policy controversies—in other words, a systemic/relational approach that is not blind to power differences but that does not dismiss the concerns of groups who have traditionally had more status. This is pragmatic as well because political backlash from threatened groups can easily derail important policy initiatives.
- Support for policies that would increase the capacity of people to form and sustain lifelong intimate partnerships (which will usually take the form of marriage), especially when children are involved.

Illustrative policy ideas

What follows is a series of illustrative policy ideas that happen to be ones I have worked on as a systemic family therapist with an interest in public policy around marriage. There are many other possibilities.

Promoting premarital education   Promoting premarital education via waiving marriage license fees for couples who taken educational programs. I helped champion legislation in my state of Minnesota, and similar laws are in place in a number of other states. This kind of requirement puts the stamp of the state on the idea that it is good for couples to prepare for marriage and that there are effective tools to help them prepare. In practice, it encourages those who do premarital education to raise their standards to match the statute's requirements so that couples can get a rebate on their license fee.

Legislation   Legislation that would mandate "marriage impact analyses" of state and federal laws and policies: What are their direct and indirect effects on the ability of couples to form and sustain healthy marriages? An example is tax policy that discourages marriage by increasing tax rates for cohabiting couples who marry.

Mandatory education   Mandatory education for couples forming a stepfamily via marriage (in recognition of the high divorce rates for remarriages and the risks to children in stepfamilies). This could be done inexpensively online and follow the precedent in many states of court-mandated parent education after divorce. It would be the first population-level intervention on marriage in the country, that is, something that all couples in the remarriage/stepfamily category would be exposed to. Of course, careful evaluation would be required.

Judicial process   A judicial process in which courts screen for "divorce ambivalence" in couples filing for divorce and refer for services when deemed appropriate. This idea is based on research documenting the prevalence of ambivalence about proceeding with a divorce among spouses in the divorce process and an openness to referrals for reconciliation services (Doherty, Harris, & Didericksen, 2016). The largest county court system in Minnesota is using a research-validated tool to assess for divorce ambivalence among all divorcing couples with minor children. In my experience, local data gathering like this is usually necessary for government officials to consider implementing new policies; general research information from larger populations is not enough. Leaders need to see that the bigger picture fits their local people.

Seek state funding   Seeking state funding for working with couples on the brink of divorce who want to take another look at the possibilities for their marriage. In 2010 in Minnesota, we were able to convince the legislature to create a surcharge on the marriage license fee to provide ongoing fund the Minnesota Couples on the Brink Project with the mission of developing best practices for helping couples on the brink of divorce and training therapists, lawyers, clergy, and others to assist these couples. This project has provided a way to train couple therapists in discernment counseling for a particularly challenging group of couples, where one is leaning out of the marriage (and is reluctant to do couple therapy) and the other is leaning in and wants couple therapy (Doherty & Harris, 2016). Passing the law creating funding for this project happened in one legislative session but came after more than a decade of working with legislators on various bills and policies. Public policy influence comes out of relationships, something we know a thing or two about.

   This partial list of potential policy initiatives shows how this work does not have to be left to national organizational leaders. Local groups of systemic family therapists can decide on a policy to work on (preferably including at least one policy that is not guild related). A practical proposal would be that MFT graduate programs engage students and faculty working together (with students getting academic credit) on a specific policy for learning and for potential social impact. Just as in clinical work, public policy work requires practice and teamwork to develop competency (Trudeau et al., 2018).

We Can Contribute a Relational/Systemic Lens for Public Policy

At our best, systemic family therapists help couples and families get past either/or understandings of the conflicts and zero-sum options for solutions. We look for both/ and solutions. We credit everyone's perspective and introduce higher-order alternatives through reframing and accessing deeper needs and desires. Although everyone is accountable for their actions, we avoid suggesting that one family member is entirely wrong and another is entirely right. We are "multi-partial" (to adapt Boszorymenyi-Nagy's term "multilateral partiality"; Boszorymenyi-Nagy, 1986). I believe that we can contribute significantly to our society by using these skills when addressing divisive policy issues and in particular when we use a relational systems lens that transcends the liberal versus conservative divide.

Note that this approach is different from the social justice perspective, which is the most prominent "public" lens in our literature. That perspective focuses on advocating for victimized groups against oppressor groups and on dismantling structures of exploitation, marginalization, and colonization in therapy and society (e.g., McDowell, 2015). I acknowledge the powerful insights of the social justice perspective, including an understanding of historical and current systems of inequity where therapy can either perpetuate or challenge. However, I find the social justice model not pragmatically useful for policy work and for on-the-ground efforts to fostering positive social change, in part because it offers no tools for creating problem-solving partnerships between groups with traditional power and groups with less traditional power and in part because its discourse tends to be binary and polarizing, emphasizing a dichotomy of good versus evil.

In sum, the advantages of applying a systemic/relational approach to public issues are both conceptual, offering new perspectives on issues, and pragmatic—we will be taken more seriously by policy makers if we avoid taking one-sided views (usually politically liberal/progressive) on issues. Professional groups who take predictably partisans positions on policy issues tend to be less effective because they are not listened to by the side who disagrees with them and they are taken for granted by the side who counts them as reliably in their camp (Bogenschneider, 2014).

Bringing a systemic/relational perspective to public issues

I offer three illustrations from my own efforts to bring a systemic/relational perspective to challenging public issues, using The Families and Democracy model (Doherty, Mendenhall, & Berge, 2010). This approach uses systemic/relational and community organizing strategies for working across differences without asking anyone to embrace an ideological analysis of power and privilege before embarking on joint work to solve problems.

Police and Black Men Project   First is the Police and Black Men Project. In 2017, I began facilitating a group of police officers and Black community members, which met for two hours every other week to build relationships of trust out of which have emerged new approaches to the disconnect between police and Black men. We created a new narrative that transcends the either/or solutions of the traditional liberal narrative (the problem is police misconduct, so that is where the change has to come from) and the conservative narrative (the problem is crime in the Black community, so that where the change must come) into a narrative of shared partnership for safe communities. The interventions the group is working on are at three levels: face-to-face community conversations, involvement of community members in police training, and joint work to change the structural forces (such as lack of good housing) that make communities unsafe. The Police and Black Men Project's narrative does not shy away from the historical truths about the use of police by people in power to control the Black community and especially Black men. The solution is framed in terms of relational power, coming closer together to do what neither side can do alone, namely, create safe communities. I think of social change in this arena (and others) as requiring two steps: (a) serious challenge to the status quo, which has occurred through Black Lives Matter and related groups, and then (b) serious relationship work to forge partnerships for change. Systemic family therapists may be uniquely suited for the second kind of relational work.

Strategy to approach policy conflict   With changes on the US Supreme Court, abortion has returned to the front burner of political and public policy conflict in the United States. What can systemic family therapists contribute here? If we simply accept the traditional framing of pro-life or pro-choice, we will not contribute anything unique—we simply adopt the terms of an entrenched conflict, something we know from clinical experience does not lead to second-order change. Fortunately, we have a track record here via a 1992 statement crafted by a task force of senior systemic family therapists and adopted by the board of AAMFT (disclosure: I was the lead writer). The statement approached the abortion conflict as a systemic family therapist would approach a relationship conflict: crediting and challenging both the pro-life and pro-choice perspectives, offering an original perspective on abortion decisions as emerging in a relational field of stakeholders, and then offering policy recommendations knowing that, in this area, reasonable people of good will differ dramatically. This approach could serve as a model for how systemic family therapists can approach a number of public policies connected to deep cultural conflicts.

Better Angels   A final example is Better Angels (www.better-angels.org), a national citizens' initiative I helped to create in 2016 after the presidential election, which aims to reduce political polarization in the United States. As discussed in Doherty (2020, vol. 1), polarization and social fragmentation are quintessential cultural challenges of the early decades of the twenty-first century in the United States and internationally. In the United States, we are at risk of a civic divorce between conservatives and liberals. After the 2016 election I was invited by a liberal and a conservative to design a workshop experience that would help a group of Trump voters and Clinton voters in Ohio to understand each other beyond stereotypes and find common ground. Using tools developed by family therapists Laura and Dick Chasin (who founded an organization called Public Conversations in the 1980s to use family therapy principles with social conflicts such as abortion), as well as what I have learned in working with communities (Doherty et al., 2010), and with couples on the brink of divorce project (Doherty & Harris, 2016), I designed a set of workshops and trained several hundred therapists and other professionals to implement them in communities. These workshops are sponsored by the nonprofit Better Angels (the name is based on Lincoln's phrase in his first inaugural address) whose leadership is deliberately half conservative and half liberal.

The workshop design involves 14 people (seven "reds" who are conservatives and seven "blues" who are liberals) in structured exercises designed to maximize listening and minimize reactivity (Doherty, 2017)—akin to what we try to accomplish in the first session of couple therapy. Being a workshop moderator requires the neutrality (or multi-partiality) of a couple therapist along with skills in holding the group process so that people can hear one another. One key exercise involves stereotypes. Reds and blues go to separate rooms to generate the top five false negative stereotypes about their own side (what others think about them that is wrong or exaggerated). For each stereotype, the group is asked to first correct it (what is wrong about the stereotype and what is true instead?) and then to work to identify a kernel of truth about the stereotype. The results are then shared with the other group. Afterward, around the table with the whole group of 14 participants, two questions are posed: What did you learn (from listening to the other's report) about how the other side sees themselves, and did you see anything in common? This exercise helps both sides define themselves beyond stereotypes and invites self-reflection and sharing about their side's flaws and weaknesses. A systemic family therapist can readily see the parallel to couple therapy, which begins to take off when both spouses own their individual contributions to the problems in the relationship.

These three initiatives illustrate what is possible when systemic family therapists bring what we know about relationship systems into the public square. Note again that it involves transcending traditional liberal/conservative frames and does not use the traditional social justice approach that asks for a change in consciousness of oppression and privilege as the beginning of change. A systemic/relational approach involves bringing polarized groups into closer relationship to solve problems that neither group can solve alone—in this case, the problem of toxic political polarization. It invites everyone to be agents of democratic change.

Conclusion

Public policy shapes the environment of the people we work with, and it limits or enhances our ability to be helpful. We ignore it at our peril. One important role we can play is advocacy for the viability of the profession in the healthcare system, which includes making the case that relationship health is a central dimension of overall health and well-being at every level from the individual to society. Another important role is involvement in broader public policy and cultural developments affecting families and communities. We have something unique and precious to offer as systemic family therapists by applying what we know about relationship systems to the leading public issues of our time. Our professional ancestors, who aspired to change the world and not just create a better therapeutic mouse trap, would be proud if we choose to vigorously engage the wider world and its problems in our time.

References

American Association for Marriage and Family Therapy. (2005). *Medicare coverage of marriage and family therapists*. Retrieved from https://www.aamft.org/Advocacy/Medicare.aspx

Bellah, R. N., Madsen, R., Sullivan, W. M., Swidler, A., & Tipton, S. M. (1986). *Habits of the heart: Individualism and commitment in American life*. Berkley, CA: University of California Press.

Bogenschneider, K. (2014). *Family policy matters* (3rd ed.). New York, NY: Routledge.

Boszorymenyi-Nagy, I. (1986). *Between give and take: A clinical guide to contextual therapy*. New York, NY: Routledge.

Carr, A. (2020). Evidence for the efficacy and effectiveness of systemic family therapy. In K. S. Wampler, R. B. Miller, & R. B. Seedall (Eds.), *The Handbook of systemic family therapy: The profession of systemic family therapy (1)*. Hoboken, NJ: Wiley.

Cherlin, A. J. (2010). *The marriage go round: The state of marriages and families in the U.S. Today*. New York, NY: Vintage.

Clason, R. E., Davis, S. Y., Miller, R. B., & Webster, T. N. (2018). The case for insurance reimbursement for couple therapy. *Journal of Marital and Family Therapy, 44*, 512–526.

Clawson, R. E., Davis, S. Y., Miller, R. B., & Webster, T. N. (2017). The case for insurance reimbursement of couple therapy. *Journal of Marital and Family Therapy, 44*, 512–526.

Cowan, P. A., & Cowan, C. P. (2020). Breaking down silos with systemically-oriented preventative interventions: Implications for public policy. In K. S. Wampler & L. M. McWay (Eds.), *The handbook of systemic family therapy: Systemic family therapy with children and adolescents (2)*. Hoboken, NJ: Wiley.

Doherty, W. J. (1995). *Soul searching*. New York, NY: Basic Books.

Doherty, W. J. (2017). Is there hope for a divided America? Tales from the Better Angels bus tour. *Psychotherapy Networker, November/December*, 23–29, 54.

Doherty, W. J. (2020). The evolution and current status of systemic family therapy: A sociocultural analysis. In K. S. Wampler, R. B. Miller, & R. B. Seedall (Eds.), *The handbook of systemic family therapy: The profession of systemic family therapy (1)*. Hoboken, NJ: Wiley.

Doherty, W. J., & Harris, S. M. (2016). *Helping couples on the brink of divorce: Discernment counseling for troubled relationships*. Washington, DC: American Psychological Association.

Doherty, W. J., Harris, S. M., & Didericksen, K. W. (2016). A typology of attitudes toward proceeding with divorce among parents in the divorce process. *Journal of Divorce & Remarriage, 56*, 1–11.

Doherty, W. J., Mendenhall, T, J., & Berge, J. M. (2010). The families and democracy and citizen health care project. *Journal of Marital and Family Therapy, 36*, 389–402.

Doherty, W. J., & Simmons, D. S. (1996). Clinical practice patterns of marriage and family therapists: A national survey of therapists and their clients. *Journal of Marital and Family Therapy, 22*, 9–25.

Doherty, W. J., Willoughby, B. J., & Peterson, B. (2011). Interest in reconciliation among divorcing parents. *Family Court Review, 49*, 313–321.

Dowbiggin, I. (2014). *The search for domestic bliss: Marriage and family counseling in 20th-century America*. Lawrence, Kansas: University of Kansas Press.

Elder, G. H. (2018). *Children of the great depression*. 25th anniversary edition. New York, NY: Routledge.

Foran, H. M., Whisman, M. A., & Beach, S. R. H. (2015). Intimate partner relationship distress in the DSM-5. *Family Process, 54*(1), 48–63. doi:10.1111/famp.12122

Giddens, A. (1984). *The constitution of society: Outline of the theory of structuration*. Cambridge, MA: Polity Press.

Goodman, J., Morgan, A., Hodgson, J., & Caldwell, B. (2018). From private practice to academia: Integrating social and political advocacy into every MFT identity. *Journal of Marital and Family Therapy, 44*, 32–45. doi:10.1111/jmft.12298

Hodgson, J., & Lamson, A. L. (2020). The importance of policy and advocacy in systemic family therapy. In K. S. Wampler, R. B. Miller, & R. B. Seedall (Eds.), *The handbook of systemic family therapy: The profession of systemic family therapy (1)*. Hoboken, NJ: Wiley.

Lebow, J. (2015). Separation and divorce issues in couple therapy. In A. S. Gurman, J. L. Lebow, & D. K. Snyder (Eds.), *Clinical handbook of couple therapy* (5th ed., pp. 445–466). New York, NY: Guilford Press.

May, E. T. (2017). *Homeward bound: American families during the Cold War era*. New York, NY: Basic Books.

McCollum, E. E., & Stith, S. M. (2011). Conjoint couples treatment and intimate partner violence: Best practices. In J. L. Wetchler (Ed.), *Handbook of clinical issues in couple therapy* (2nd ed., pp. 115–128). New York, NY: Routledge.

McDowell, T. (2015). *Applying critical social theories to family therapy practice*. New York, NY: Springer.

Nichols, W. C. (1992). *The AAMFT: Fifty years of marital and family therapy*. Washington, DC: The American Association for Marriage and Family Therapy.

Putnam, R. D. (2016). *Our kids: The American dream in crisis*. New York, NY: Vintage.

Rampage, C. (2014). The role of the family institutes in promoting the practice of family therapy. *Family Process, 59*, 489–499.

Sim, T., & Shamai, M. (2020). Global perspectives: Taking family therapy forward into globally diverse contexts. In K. S. Wampler, M. Rastogi, & R. Singh (Eds.), *The handbook of systemic family therapy: Systemic family therapy and global health issues (4)*. Hoboken, NJ: Wiley.

Sim, T., & Sim, C. (2020). Global contexts for the profession of systemic family therapy. In K. S. Wampler, R. B. Miller, & R. B. Seedall (Eds.), *The handbook of systemic family therapy: The profession of systemic family therapy (1)*. Hoboken, NJ: Wiley.

Sprenkle, D. H. (2002). *Effectiveness research in marriage and family therapy*. Washington, DC: American Association for Marriage and Family Therapy.

Sullivan, W. M. (2015). *Work and integrity: The crisis and promise of professionalism in America*. New York, NY: Wiley.

Trudeau, S., Sudano, L., Reitz, R., Hodgson, J., Mendenhall, T., Williams-Reade, J., & Tyndall, L. (2018). *Core healthcare management and policy competencies for family therapists working in healthcare settings*. Retrieved from http://blog.aamft.org/2018/06/core-healthcare-management-and-policy-competencies-for-family-therapists-working-in-healthcare-setti.html

United Nations. (2015). *Family policy development: Achievements and challenges*. United Nations Expert Group Meeting. Retrieved from https://www.un.org/esa/socdev/family/docs/egm15/finalreport.pdf

Wamboldt, M., Kaslow, N., & Reiss, D. (2015). Description of relational processes: Recent changes in DSM-5 and proposals for ICD-11. *Family Process, 54*(1), 6–16. doi:10.1111/famp.12120

Index